Communication Technology Update and Fundamentals

13th Edition

Communication Technology Update and Fundamentals

13th Edition

Editors

August E. Grant

Jennifer H. Meadows

In association with Technology Futures, Inc.

Focal Press
Taylor & Francis Group

NEW YORK AND LONDON

Editors:

August E. Grant
Jennifer H. Meadows

Technology Futures, Inc.:

Production & Art Editor: Helen Mary V. Marek
Production Assistants: John Erik Vanston and Robert Grant

First published 2012
by Focal Press
225 Wyman Street, Waltham, MA 02451

Simultaneously published in the UK
by Focal Press
2 Park Square, Milton Park, Abingdon, Oxon OX14 4RN

Focal Press is an imprint of the Taylor & Francis Group, an informa business

Library of Congress Cataloging in Publication Data
A catalog record has been requested.

ISBN: 978-0-240-82456-7 (pbk)
ISBN: 978-0-240-82466-6 (ebk)

Companion website for Recent Developments: http://www.tfi.com/ctu

Printed and bound in the United States of America by Sheridan Books, Inc. (a Sheridan Group Company).

Table of Contents

Glossary and Updates can be found on the

Communication Technology Update and Fundamentals website

http://www.tfi.com/ctu/

Preface

In 1992, new communication technologies held as much interest as today, with entire courses devoted to studying these technologies, how and why they were adopted, and how they impacted society. But there was one big problem in teaching such a course—there was no textbook that covered all of these technologies. Individual books discussed television technologies, computers, and telephony, and instructors had to pick and choose chapters from these books and combine them with articles from journals and the popular press. It was a cumbersome process, but a necessary one. There was one other place that the latest information could be found—in the final papers written by students taking one of these classes. From those papers, an idea emerged—what if the final papers from one term could become the readings for the next term?

From that simple idea, the *Communication Technology Update* was born. In that first edition, published by Technology Futures, Inc. in 1992, the papers from two University of Texas classes—one graduate and one undergraduate—were combined with a few chapters written by faculty experts and edited into a short, 124-page book that provided an up-to-date picture of the status of new communication technologies. Five hundred copies were sold. A year later, the process was repeated, this time including more technologies, plus background information on each technology. When 2,500 copies were sold, Focal Press requested the rights to publish and distribute the book worldwide, and the rest, as they say, is history.

We've made a few changes in the last 20 years. After creating a new edition annually for the first six years, we built a website for updates and created new editions only every two years. In 1996, Jennifer Meadows joined the team as permanent co-editor, and authorship gradually shifted to faculty and industry experts on each technology. In 2008, we added four chapters of "fundamentals" to provide more context for the study of new communication technologies. The most important change, though, was in the Table of Contents. As new technologies emerged, they replaced more established technologies that were combined or dropped. In 1992, the Internet, social media, and IPTV were not envisioned; today, they impact most of the technologies discussed in this book.

In this edition, all-new chapters explore e-books and mobile commerce, chapters covering older technologies including telephony, cinema, and digital television have been completely rewritten, and every chapter has been revised to include the latest developments and statistics. What hasn't changed, though, is the original purpose of the book—to provide you with an up-to-date discussion of the most important communication technologies in mass media, computers, consumer electronics, and networking.

One thing shared by all of the contributors to this book is a passion for communication technology. In order to keep this book as current as possible we ask the authors to work under extremely tight deadlines. Authors begin working in January 2012 and most chapters were submitted in April 2012 with the final details added in May 2012. Individually, the chapters provide snapshots of the state of the field for individual technologies, but together they present a broad overview of the role that communication technologies play in our everyday lives. The efforts of these authors have produced a remarkable compilation, and we thank them for all for their hard work in preparing this volume.

Preface

As in the previous 12 editions, TFI's Helen Mary Marek played a pivotal role in production, moving all 24 chapters from draft to camera-ready. Helen Mary also provided on-demand graphics production, adding visual elements to help make the content more understandable. Almost everyone on the TFI team contributed to the process, including Larry Vanston and John Erik Vanston. Our editorial and marketing team at Focal Press, led by Lauren Mattos, ensured that production and promotion of the book were as smooth as ever.

On a personal note, we could not do what we do without the support of our families. Our better halves, Diane Grant and Floyd Meadows, provide the emotional support that make it possible for us to immerse ourselves in producing this book every two years. Bobby Grant played a critical role in helping to polish the final manuscript, and Jessica Grant and McGruber the cat provided just enough distraction to keep us grounded during the process of writing and editing.

Your search for insight into the technologies explored in this book can continue on the companion website for the *Communication Technology Update and Fundamentals:* www.tfi.com/ctu. The complete Glossary for the book is on the site, where it is much easier to find individual entries than in the paper version of the book. We have also moved the vast quantity of statistical data on each of the communication technologies that were formerly printed in Chapter 2 to the site. We've also placed two expanded chapters on the website to provide you with greater depth than we can in the paper version of the book. As always, we will periodically update the Web site to supplement the text with new information and links to a wide variety of information available over the Internet.

As a reader of this book, you are also part of the *Communication Technology Update* community. Each edition of this book has been improved over previous editions with the help and input from readers like you. You are invited to send us updates for the website, ideas for new topics, and other contributions that will inform all members of the community. You are invited to communicate directly with us via e-mail, snail mail, or voice.

Thank you for being part of the CTU community!

Augie Grant and Jennifer Meadows

May 10, 2012

Augie Grant
College of Mass Communications & Information Studies
University of South Carolina
Columbia, SC 29208
Phone: 803.777.4464
augie@sc.edu

Jennifer H. Meadows
Department of Communication Design
California State University, Chico
Chico, CA 95929-0504
Phone: 530.898.4775
jmeadows@csuchico.edu

Fundamentals

The Communication Technology Ecosystem

August E. Grant, Ph.D.*

Communication technologies are the nervous system of contemporary society, transmitting and distributing sensory and control information and interconnecting a myriad of interdependent units. These technologies are critical to commerce, essential to entertainment, and intertwined in our interpersonal relationships. Because these technologies are so vitally important, any change in communication technologies has the potential to impact virtually every area of society.

One of the hallmarks of the industrial revolution was the introduction of new communication technologies as mechanisms of control that played an important role in almost every area of the production and distribution of manufactured goods (Beniger, 1986). These communication technologies have evolved throughout the past two centuries at an increasingly rapid rate. This evolution shows no signs of slowing, so an understanding of this evolution is vital for any individual wishing to attain or retain a position in business, government, or education.

The economic and political challenges faced by the United States and other countries since the beginning of the new millennium clearly illustrate the central role these communication systems play in our society. Just as the prosperity of the 1990s was credited to advances in technology, the economic challenges that followed were linked as well to a major downturn in the technology sector. Today, communication technology is seen by many as a tool for making more efficient use of energy sources.

Communication technologies play as big a part in our private lives as they do in commerce and control in society. Geographic distances are no longer barriers to relationships thanks to the bridging power of communication technologies. We can also be entertained and informed in ways that were unimaginable a century ago thanks to these technologies—and they continue to evolve and change before our eyes.

This text provides a snapshot of the state of technologies in our society. The individual chapter authors have compiled facts and figures from hundreds of sources to provide the latest information on more than two dozen communication technologies. Each discussion explains the roots and evolution, recent developments, and current status of the technology as of mid-2012. In discussing each technology, we will address them from a systematic perspective, looking at a range of factors beyond hardware.

The goal is to help you analyze technologies and be better able to predict which ones will succeed and which ones will fail. That task is harder to achieve than it sounds. Let's look at Google for an example of how unpredictable technology is.

* J. Rion McKissick Professor of Journalism, College of Mass Communications and Information Studies, University of South Carolina (Columbia, South Carolina).

The Google Tale

As this book goes to press in mid-2012, Google is the most valuable media company in the world in terms of market capitalization (the total value of all shares of stock held in the company). To understand how Google attained that lofty position, we have to go back to the late 1990s, when commercial applications of the Internet were taking off. There was no question in the minds of engineers and futurists that the Internet was going to revolutionize the delivery of information, entertainment, and commerce. The big question was how it was going to happen.

Those who saw the Internet as a medium for information distribution knew that advertiser support would be critical to its long-term financial success. They knew that they could always find a small group willing to pay for content, but the majority of people preferred free content. To become a mass medium similar to television, newspapers, and magazines, an Internet advertising industry was needed.

At that time, most Internet advertising was banner ads, horizontal display ads that stretched across most of the screen to attract attention, but took up very little space on the screen. The problem was that most people at that time accessed the Internet using slow, dial-up connections, so advertisers were limited in what they could include in these banners to about a dozen words of text and simple graphics. The dream among advertisers was to be able to use rich media, including full-motion video, audio, animation, and every other trick that makes television advertising so successful.

When broadband Internet access started to spread, advertisers were quick to add rich media to their banners, as well as create other types of ads using graphics, video, and sound. These ads were a little more effective, but many Internet users did not like the intrusive nature of rich media messages.

At about the same time, two Stanford students, Sergey Brin and Larry Page, had developed a new type of search engine, Google, that ranked results on the basis of how often content was referred to or linked from other sites, allowing their computer algorithms to create more robust and relevant search results (in most cases) than having a staff of people indexing Web content. What they needed was a way to pay for the costs of the servers and other technology.

According to Vise & Malseed (2006), their budget did not allow Google to create and distribute rich media ads. They could do text ads, but they decided to do them differently from other Internet advertising, using computer algorithms to place these small text ads on the search results that were most likely to give the advertisers results. With a credit card, anyone could use this "AdWords" service, specifying the search terms they thought should display their ads, writing the brief ads (less than 100 characters total—just over a dozen words), and even specifying how much they were willing to pay every time someone clicked on their ad. Even more revolutionary, the Google founders decided that no one should have to pay for an ad unless a user clicked on it.

For advertisers, it was as close to a no-lose proposition as they could find. Advertisers did not have to pay unless a person was interested enough to click on the ad. They could set a budget that Google computers could follow, and Google provided a control panel for advertisers that gave a set of measures that was a dream for anyone trying to make a campaign more effective. These measures indicated not only overall effectiveness of the ad, but also the effectiveness of each message, each keyword, and every part of every campaign.

The result was remarkable. Google's share of the search market was not that much greater than the companies that had held the number one position earlier, but Google was making money—lots of money—from these little text ads. Wall Street investors noticed, and, once Google went public, investors bid up the stock price, spurred by increases in revenues and a very large profit margin. Today, Google is involved in a number of other ventures designed to aggregate and deliver content ranging from text to full-motion video, but its little text ads are still the primary revenue generator.

In retrospect, it was easy to see why Google was such a success. Their little text ads were effective because of context—they always appeared where they would be the most effective. They were not intrusive, so people did not mind the ads on Google pages, and later on other pages that Google served ads to through its "content network." And advertisers had a degree of control, feedback, and accountability that no advertising medium had ever offered before (Grant & Wilkinson, 2007).

So what lessons should we learn from the Google story? Advertisers have their own set of lessons, but there are a separate set of lessons for those wishing to understand new media. First, no matter how insightful, no one is ever able to predict whether a technology will succeed or fail. Second, success can be due as much to luck as to careful, deliberate planning and investment. Third, simplicity matters—there are few advertising messages as simple as the little text ads you see when doing a Google search.

The Google tale provides an example of the utility of studying individual companies and industries, so the focus throughout this book is on individual technologies. These individual snapshots, however, comprise a larger mosaic representing the communication networks that bind individuals together and enable them to function as a society. No single technology can be understood without understanding the competing and complementary technologies and the larger social environment within which these technologies exist. As discussed in the following section, all of these factors (and others) have been considered in preparing each chapter through application of the "technology ecosystem." Following this discussion, an overview of the remainder of the book is presented.

The Communication Technology Ecosystem

The most obvious aspect of communication technology is the hardware—the physical equipment related to the technology. The hardware is the most tangible part of a technology system, and new technologies typically spring from developments in hardware. However, understanding communication technology requires more than just studying the hardware. One of the characteristics of today's digital technologies is that most are based upon computer technology, requiring instructions and algorithms more commonly known as "software."

In addition to understanding the hardware and software of the technology, it is just as important to understand the content communicated through the technology system. Some consider the content as another type of software. Regardless of the terminology used, it is critical to understand that digital technologies require a set of instructions (the software) as well as the equipment and content.

The hardware, software, and content must also be studied within a larger context. Rogers' (1986) definition of "communication technology" includes some of these contextual factors, defining it as "the hardware equipment, organizational structures, and social values by which individuals collect, process, and exchange information with other individuals" (p. 2). An even broader range of factors is suggested by Ball-Rokeach (1985) in her media system dependency theory, which suggests that communication media can be understood by analyzing dependency relations within and across levels of analysis, including the individual, organizational, and system levels. Within the system level, Ball-Rokeach identifies three systems for analysis: the media system, the political system, and the economic system.

These two approaches have been synthesized into the "Technology Ecosystem" illustrated in Figure 1.1. The core of the technology ecosystem consists of the hardware, software, and content (as previously defined). Surrounding this core is the organizational infrastructure: the group of organizations involved in the production and distribution of the technology. The next level moving outwards is the system level, including the political, economic, and media systems, as well as other groups of individuals or organizations serving a common set of functions in society. Finally, the individual users of the technology cut across all of the other areas, providing a focus for understanding each one. The basic premise of the technology ecosystem is that all areas of the ecosystem interact and must be examined in order to understand a technology.

(The technology ecosystem is an elaboration of the "umbrella perspective" (Grant, 2010) that was explicated in earlier editions of this text in order to illustrate the elements that need to be studied in order to understand communication technologies.)

Adding another layer of complexity to each of the areas of the technology ecosystem is also helpful. In order to identify the impact that each individual characteristic of a technology has, the factors within each area of the ecosystem may be identified as "enabling," "limiting," "motivating," and "inhibiting," depending upon the role they play in the technology's diffusion.

Enabling factors are those that make an application possible. For example, the fact that the coaxial cable used to deliver traditional cable television can carry dozens of channels is an enabling factor at the hardware level. Similarly, the decision of policy makers to allocate a portion of the spectrum for cellular telephony is an enabling factor at the system level (political system). One starting point to use in examining any technology is to make a list of the underlying factors from each area of the technology ecosystem that make the technology possible in the first place.

Limiting factors are the opposite of enabling factors; they are those factors that create barriers to the adoption or impacts of a technology. A great example is related to the cable television illustration above. Although coaxial cable increased the number of television programs that could be delivered to a home, most analog coaxial networks cannot transmit more than 100 channels of programming. To the viewer, 100 channels may seem to be more than is needed, but to the programmer of a new cable television channel unable to get space on a filled-up cable system, this hardware factor represents a definite limitation. Similarly, the fact that the policy makers discussed above initially permitted only two companies to offer cellular telephone service in each market was a system-level limitation on that technology. Again, it is useful to apply the technology ecosystem to create a list of factors that limit the adoption, use, or impacts of any specific communication technology.

Figure 1.1
The Communication Technology Ecosystem

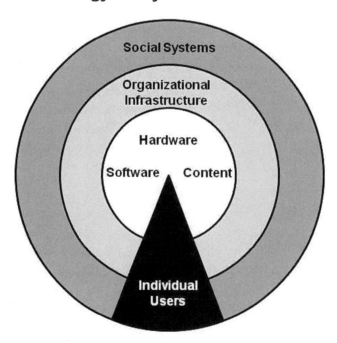

Source: A. E. Grant

Motivating factors are a little more complicated. They are those factors that provide a reason for the adoption of a technology. Technologies are not adopted just because they exist. Rather, individuals, organizations, and social systems must have a reason to take advantage of a technology. The desire of local telephone companies for increased profits, combined with the fact that growth in providing local telephone service is limited, is an organizational factor motivating the telcos to enter the markets for new communication technologies. Individual users desiring information more quickly can be motivated to adopt electronic information technologies. If a technology does not have sufficient motivating factors for its use, it cannot be a success.

Inhibiting factors are the opposite of motivating ones, providing a disincentive for adoption or use of a communication technology. An example of an inhibiting factor at the content level might be a new electronic information technology that has the capability to update information more quickly than existing technologies, but provides only "old" content that consumers have already received from other sources. One of the most important inhibiting factors for most new technologies is the cost to individual users. Each potential user must decide whether the cost is worth the service, considering his or her budget and the number of competing technologies. Competition from other technologies is one of the biggest barriers any new (or existing) technology faces. Any factor that works against the success of a technology can be considered an inhibiting factor. As you might guess, there are usually more inhibiting factors for most technologies than motivating ones. And if the motivating factors are more numerous and stronger than the inhibiting factors, it is an easy bet that a technology will be a success.

All four factors—enabling, limiting, motivating, and inhibiting—can be identified at the system, organizational, content, and individual user levels. However, hardware and software can only be enabling or limiting; by themselves, hardware and software do not provide any motivating factors. The motivating factors must always come from the messages transmitted or one of the other areas of the ecosystem.

The final dimension of the technology ecosystem relates to the environment within which communication technologies are introduced and operate. These factors can be termed "external" factors, while ones relating to the technology itself are "internal" factors. In order to understand a communication technology or be able to predict the manner in which a technology will diffuse, both internal and external factors must be studied and compared.

Each communication technology discussed in this book has been analyzed using the technology ecosystem to ensure that all relevant factors have been included in the discussions. As you will see, in most cases, organizational and system-level factors (especially political factors) are more important in the development and adoption of communication technologies than the hardware itself. For example, political forces have, to date, prevented the establishment of a single world standard for high-definition television (HDTV) production and transmission. As individual standards are selected in countries and regions, the standard selected is as likely to be the product of political and economic factors as of technical attributes of the system.

Organizational factors can have similar powerful effects. For example, as discussed in Chapter 4, the entry of a single company, IBM, into the personal computer business in the early 1980s resulted in fundamental changes in the entire industry, dictating standards and anointing an operating system (MS-DOS) as a market leader. Finally, the individuals who adopt (or choose not to adopt) a technology, along with their motivations and the manner in which they use the technology, have profound impacts on the development and success of a technology following its initial introduction.

Perhaps the best indication of the relative importance of organizational and system-level factors is the number of changes individual authors made to the chapters in this book between the time of the initial chapter submission in March 2012 and production of the final, camera-ready text in May 2012. Very little new information was added regarding hardware, but numerous changes were made due to developments at the organizational and system levels.

To facilitate your understanding of all of the elements related to the technologies explored, each chapter in this book has been written from the perspective of the technology ecosystem. The individual writers have endeavored to update developments in each area to the extent possible in the brief summaries provided. Obviously, not every technology experienced developments in each area of the ecosystem, so each report is limited to areas in which relatively recent developments have taken place.

So Why Study New Technologies?

One constant in the study of media is that new technologies seem to get more attention than traditional, established technologies. There are many reasons for the attention. New technologies are more dynamic and evolve more quickly, with greater potential to cause change in other parts of the media system. Perhaps the reason for our attention is the natural attraction that humans have to motion, a characteristic inherited from our most distant ancestors.

There are a number of other reasons for studying new technologies. Perhaps you want to make a lot of money off a new technology—and there is a lot of money to be made (and lost!) on new technologies. If you are planning a career in the media, you may simply be interested in knowing how the media are changing and evolving, and how those changes will affect your career.

Or you might want to learn lessons from the failure of new communication technologies so you can avoid failure in your own career, investments, etc. Simply put, the majority of new technologies introduced do not succeed in the market. Some fail because the technology itself was not attracttive to consumers (such as the 1980s' attempt to provide AM stereo radio). Some fail because they were far ahead of the market, such as Qube, the

first interactive cable television system, introduced in the 1970s. Others failed because of bad timing or aggressive marketing from competitors that succeeded despite inferior technology.

The final reason we offer for studying new communication technologies is to identify patterns of adoption, effects, economic opportunity, and competition so that we can be prepared to understand, use, and/or compete with the next generation of new media. Virtually every new technology discussed in this book is going to be one of those "traditional, established technologies" in just a few short years, but there will always be another generation of new media to challenge the status quo.

Overview of Book

The key to getting the most out of this book is therefore to pay as much attention as possible to the reasons that some technologies succeed and others fail. To that end, this book provides you with a number of tools you can apply to virtually any new technology that comes along. These tools are explored in the first five chapters, which we refer to as the *Communication Technology Fundamentals*. You might be tempted to skip over these to get to the "fun facts" about the individual technologies that are making an impact today, but you will be much better equipped to learn lessons from these technologies if you are armed with these tools.

The first of these is the "technology ecosystem" discussed before that broadens attention from the technology itself to the users, organizations, and system surrounding that technology. To that end, each of the technologies explored in this book provides details about all of the elements of the ecosystem.

Of course, studying the history of each technology can help you find patterns and apply them to different technologies, times, and places. In addition to including a brief history of each technology, the following chapter, A History of Communication Technologies, provides a broad overview of most of the technologies discussed later in the book, allowing a comparison along a number of dimensions: the year each was first introduced, growth rate, number of current users, etc. This chapter anchors the book to highlight commonalties in the evolution of individual technologies, as well as presents the "big picture" before we delve into the details. By focusing on the number of users over time, this chapter also provides the most useful basis of comparison across technologies.

Another useful tool in identifying patterns across technologies is the application of theories related to new communication technologies. By definition, theories are general statements that identify the underlying mechanisms for adoption and effects of these new technologies. Chapter 3 provides an overview of a wide range of these theories and provides a set of analytic perspectives that you can apply to both the technologies in this book and any new technologies that follow.

The structure of communication industries is then addressed in Chapter 4. The complexity of organizational relationships, along with the need to differentiate between the companies that make the technologies and those that sell the technologies, are explored in this chapter. The most important force at the system level of the ecosystem, regulation, is then introduced in Chapter 5.

These introductory chapters provide a structure and a set of analytic tools that define the study of communication technologies in all forms. Following this introduction, the book then addresses the individual technologies.

The technologies discussed in this book are organized into three sections: electronic mass media, computers and consumer electronics, and networking technologies. These three are not necessarily exclusive; for example, Internet video technologies could be classified as either an electronic mass medium or a computer technology. The ultimate decision regarding where to put each technology was made by determining which set of current technologies most closely resembled the technology from the user's perspective. Thus, Internet video was classified with electronic mass media. This process also locates the discussion of a cable television technology—cable modems—in the Broadband and Home Networks chapter in the Networking Technology section.

Each chapter is followed by a brief bibliography. These reference lists represent a broad overview of literally hundreds of books and articles that provide details about these technologies. It is hoped that the reader will not only use these references, but will examine the list of source material to determine the best places to find newer information since the publication of this *Update*.

Each chapter in this book includes a section discussing sustainability issues that relate to the technologies discussed in that chapter. These sections explore a range of sustainability factors ranging from energy consumption and savings to the environmental impact from manufacturing and disposing of these technologies. These sustainability discussions provide you with insight that can help you understand the impact of communication technologies on the environment, as well as helping you discover ways of minimizing your own environmental impact.

Most of the technologies discussed in this book are continually evolving. As this book was completed, many technological developments were announced but not released, corporate mergers were under discussion, and regulations had been proposed but not passed. Our goal is for the chapters in this book to establish a basic understanding of the structure, functions, and background for each technology, and for the supplementary Internet home page to provide brief synopses of the latest developments for each technology. (The address for the home page is http://www.tfi.com/ctu.)

The final chapter returns to the "big picture" presented in this book, attempting to place these discussions in a larger context, noting commonalties among the technologies and trends over time. Any text such as this one can never be fully comprehensive, but ideally this text will provide you with a broad overview of the current developments in communication technology.

Bibliography

Ball-Rokeach, S. J. (1985). The origins of media system dependency: A sociological perspective. *Communication Research, 12* (4), 485-510.

Beniger, J. (1986). *The control revolution.* Cambridge, MA: Harvard University Press.

Grant, A. E. (2010). Introduction to communication technologies. In A. E. Grant & J. H. Meadows (Eds.) *Communication Technology Update and Fundamentals (12ᵗʰ ed).* Boston: Focal Press.

Grant, A. E. & Wilkinson, J. S. (2007, February). Lessons for communication technologies from Web advertising. Paper presented to the Mid-Winter Conference of the Association of Educators in Journalism and Mass Communication, Reno.

Rogers, E. M. (1986). *Communication technology: The new media in society.* New York: Free Press.

Vise, D. & Malseed, M. (2006). *The Google story: Inside the hottest business, media, and technology success of our time.* New York: Delta.

A History of Communication Technology

Dan Brown, Ph.D.*

The history of communication technologies can be examined from many perspectives. Each chapter in this book provides a brief history and a current update of the technology discussed in that chapter, but providing a "big picture" overview is important in studying the growth of respective technologies. This chapter focuses on early developments and brief updates in various communications media. The discussion is organized into categories that cover eras of print media, electronic media, and digital media.

The most useful perspective permits comparisons among technologies across time: numerical statistics of adoption and use of these technologies. To that end, this chapter follows patterns adopted in previous summaries of trends in U.S. communications media (Brown & Bryant, 1989; Brown, 1996, 1998, 2000, 2002, 2004, 2006, 2008, 2010). Nonmonetary units are favored as more meaningful tools for assessing diffusion of media innovations, although dollar expenditures appear as supplementary measures. A notable exception is the de facto standard of measuring motion picture acceptance in the market: box office receipts.

Government sources are preferred. Although they are frequently based on private reports, they provide some consistency. However, many government reports in recent years offered inconsistent units of measurement and discontinued annual market updates. Readers should use caution in interpreting data for individual years and instead emphasize the trends over several years. One limitation of this government data is the lag time before statistics are reported, with the most recent data being a year or more old. The companion website for this book (www.tfi.com/ctu) reports more detailed statistics than could be printed in this chapter.

Figure 2.1 illustrates the introduction of various media types and the increase in the pace of introduction of new media technologies. This rapid increase in development is the logical consequence of the relative degree of permeation of technology in recent years versus the lack of technological sophistication of earlier eras. This figure and this chapter exclude several media that the marketplace abandoned, such as quadraphonic sound, 3-D television, CB radios, 8-track audiotapes, and 8mm film cameras. Other media that receive mention have already and may yet suffer this fate. For example, long-playing vinyl audio recordings, audiocassettes, and compact discs seem doomed in the face of rapid adoption of newer forms of digital audio recordings. This chapter traces trends that reveal

---

* Associate Dean of Arts & Sciences, East Tennessee State University (Johnson City, Tennessee).

clues about what has happened and what may happen in the use of respective media forms.

To illustrate the growth rates and specific statistics regarding each technology, a large set of tables and figures have been placed on the companion website for this book at www.tfi.com/ctu. Your understanding of each technology will be aided by referring to the website as you read each section.

The Print Era

Printing began in China thousands of years before Johann Gutenberg developed the movable type printing press in 1455 in Germany. Gutenberg's press triggered a revolution that began an industry that remained stable for another 600 years (Rawlinson, 2011).

Printing in the United States grew from a one-issue newspaper in 1690 to become the largest print industry in the world (U.S. Department of Commerce/International Trade Association, 2000). This enterprise includes publishers of newspapers, periodicals, books, directories, greeting cards, and other print media.

Newspapers

Publick Occurrences, Both Foreign and Domestick was the first newspaper produced in North America, appearing in 1690 (Lee, 1917). Table 2.1 and Figure 2.2 from the companion website for this book (www.tfi.com/ctu) show that U.S. newspaper firms and newspaper circulation had extremely slow growth until the 1800s. Early growth suffered from relatively low literacy rates and the lack of discretionary cash among the bulk of the population. The progress of the industrial revolution brought money for workers and improved mechanized printing processes. Lower newspaper prices and the practice of deriving revenue from advertisers encouraged significant growth beginning in the 1830s. Newspapers made the transition from the realm of the educated and wealthy elite to a mass medium serving a wider range of people from this period through the Civil War era (Huntzicker, 1999).

The Mexican and Civil Wars stimulated public demand for news by the middle 1800s, and modern journalism practices, such as assigning reporters to cover specific stories and topics, began to emerge. Circulation wars among big city newspapers in the 1880s featured sensational writing about outrageous stories. Both the number of newspaper firms and newspaper circulation began to soar. Although the number of firms would level off in the 20th century, circulation continued to rise.

The number of morning newspapers more than doubled after 1950, despite a 16% drop in the number of daily newspapers over that period. Overall newspaper circulation remained higher at the start of the new millennium than in 1950, although it inched downward throughout the 1990s. Although circulation actually increased in many developing nations, both U.S. newspaper circulation and the number of U.S. newspaper firms are today lower than the respective figures posted in the early 1990s. Many newspapers that operated for decades are now defunct, and many others offer only online electronic versions.

Periodicals

"The first colonial magazines appeared in Philadelphia in 1741, about 50 years after the first newspapers" (Campbell, 2002, p. 310). Few Americans could read in that era, and periodicals were costly to produce and circulate. Magazines were often subsidized and distributed by special interest groups, such as churches (Huntzicker, 1999). The Saturday Evening Post, the longest running magazine in U.S. history, began in 1821 and became the first magazine to both target women as an audience and to be distributed to a national audience. By 1850, nearly 600 magazines were operating.

By early in the 20th century, national magazines became popular with advertisers who wanted to reach wide audiences. No other medium offered such opportunity. However, by the middle of the century, the many successful national magazines began dying in face of advertiser preferences for the new medium of television and the increasing costs of periodical distribution. Magazines turned to smaller niche audiences that were more effective at reaching these audiences. Table 2.2, Figure 2.3, and Figure 2.4 on the companion website (www.tfi.com/ctu) show the number of American periodical titles by year, revealing that the number of new periodical titles nearly doubled from 1958 to 1960.

Single copy magazine sales were mired in a long period of decline in 2009 when circulation fell by 17.2%. However, subscription circulation fell by only 5.9%. In 2010, the Audit Bureau of Circulation reported that, among the 522 magazine titles monitored by the Bureau, the number of magazine titles in the United States fell by 8.7% (Agnese, 2011).

In 2010, 20,707 consumer magazines were published in North America, reaching a paid circulation of $8.8 billion. Subscriptions accounted for $6.2 billion (71%) of that circulation. During that year, 193 new North American magazines began publishing, but 176 magazines closed. Many print magazines were also available in digital form, and many had eliminated print circulation in favor of digital publishing. In 2009, 81 North American magazines moved online, but the number in 2010 dropped to 28 (Agnese, 2011).

Books

Stephen Daye printed the first book in colonial America, The Bay Psalm Book, in 1640 (Campbell, 2002). Books remained relatively expensive and rare until after the printing process benefited from the industrial revolution. Linotype machines developed in the 1880s allowed for mechanical typesetting. After World War II, the popularity of paperback books helped the industry expand. The current U.S. book publishing industry includes 87,000 publishers, most of which are small businesses. Many of these literally operate as "mom-and-pop desktop operations" (Peters & Donald, 2007, p. 11).

Table 2.3 and Figures 2.4 and 2.5 from the companion website (www.tfi.com/ctu) show new book titles published by year from the late 1800s through 2008. These data show a remarkable, but potentially deceptive, increase in the number of new book titles published annually, beginning in

1997. The U.S. Bureau of the Census reports furnished data based on material from R. R. Bowker, which changed its reporting methods beginning with the 1998 report. Ink and Grabois (2000) explained the increase as resulting from the change in the method of counting titles "that results in a more accurate portrayal of the current state of American book publishing" (p. 508). The older counting process included only books included by the Library of Congress Cataloging in Publication program. This program included publishing by the largest American publishing companies, but omitted such books as "inexpensive editions, annuals, and much of the output of small presses and self publishers" (Ink & Grabois, 2000, p. 509). Ink and Grabois observed that the U.S. ISBN (International Standard Book Number) Agency assigned more than 10,000 new ISBN publisher prefixes annually.

The most startling development in book publishing in more than a century is clearly the success of electronic or e-books. Books have long been available for reading via computers, but dedicated e-book readers have transformed the reading experience by bringing many readers into the digital era. By the end of 2009, 3.7 million Americans were reading e-books. In 2010, the readership grew to more than 10.3 million, an increase of 178%, and surveys reported by the Book Industry Study Group (BISG) reported that 20% of respondents had stopped buying printed books in favor of e-books within a year. By July 2010, Amazon reported that sales of e-books surpassed that of print hardcover sales for the first time, with "143 e-books sold for every 100 print hardcover books" (Dillon, 2011, p. 5). From mid-December 2011 through January 2012, the proportion of Americans owning both e-book readers and tablet computers nearly doubled from 10% to 19%, with 29% owning at least one of the devices (Rainie, 2012).

Figure 2.1
Communication Technology Timeline

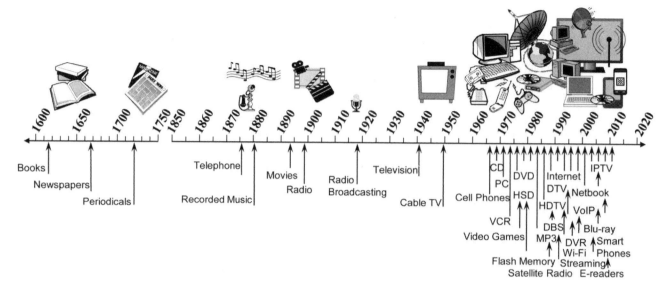

Source: Technology Futures, Inc.

The Electronic Era

The telegraph transitioned from the print era to a new period by introducing a means of sending messages far more rapidly than was previously possible. Soon, Americans and people around the world enjoyed a world enhanced by such electronic media as wired telephones, motion pictures, audio recording, radio, television, cable television, and satellite television.

Telephone

With the telephone, Alexander Graham Bell became the first to transmit speech electronically in 1876. By June 30, 1877, 230 telephones were in use, and the number rose to 1,300 by the end of August, mostly to avoid the need for a skilled interpreter of telegraph messages. The first switching office onnected three company offices in Boston beginning on May 17, 1877, reflecting a focus on business rather than residential use during the telephone's early decades. Hotels became early adopters of telephones as they sought to reduce the costs of employing human messengers, and New York's 100 largest hotels had 21,000 telephones by 1909. After 1894, non-business telephone use became ordinary, in part because business use lowered the cost of telephone service. By 1902, 2,315,000 telephones were in service in the United States (Aronson, 1977). Table 2.4 and Figure 2.6 on the companion website (www.tfi.com/ctu) document the growth to near ubiquity of telephones in U.S. households and the expanding presence of wireless telephones.

Wireless telephones. Guglielmo Marconi sent the first wireless data messages in 1895. The growing popularity of telephony led many to experiment with Marconi's radio technology as another means for interpersonal communication. By the 1920s, Detroit police cars had mobile radiophones for voice communication (ITU, 1999). The Bell system offered radio telephone service in 1946 in St. Louis, the first of 25 cities to receive the service. Bell engineers divided reception areas into cells in 1947, but cellular telephones that switched effectively among cells as callers moved did not arrive until the 1970s. The first call on a portable, handheld cell phone occurred in 1973. However, in 1981, only 24 people in New York City could use their mobile phones at the same time, and only 700 customers could have active contracts. To increase the number of people who could receive service, the Federal Communications Commission (FCC) began offering cellular telephone system licenses by lottery in June 1982 (Murray, 2001). Other countries, such as Japan in 1979 and Saudi Arabia in 1982, operated cellular systems earlier than the United States (ITU, 1999).

The U.S. Congress promoted a more advanced group of mobile communication services in 1993 by creating a classification of commercial mobile services that became known as Commercial Mobile Radio Service. This classification allowed for consistent regulatory oversight of these technologies and encouraged commercial competition among providers (FCC, 2005). By the end of 1996, about 44 million Americans subscribed to wireless telephone services (U.S. Bureau of the Census, 2008).

The new century saw an explosion of the use of wireless telephones. New developments included expansion of how the devices were used. Phones morphed into multi-purpose devices that enabled users to send text messages, access the Internet, play games, and perform a variety of tasks, in addition to making voice calls. Watching video by mobile phone became more widespread in 2010, averaging 4 hours and 20 minutes monthly, up by 20% from 2009. Such viewing occurred among 28.5 million subscribers in 2010, up by 41% from 2009 (Amobi, 2011a). By May 2011, among Americans age 13 and older, almost 234 million were using mobile devices, and smartphone penetration had grown significantly, to 76.8 million users (comScore Inc. as cited by Amobi, 2011b, p. 12).

Motion Pictures

In the 1890s, George Eastman improved on work by and patents purchased from Hannibal Goodwin in 1889 to produce workable motion picture film. The Lumière brothers projected moving pictures in a Paris café in 1895, hosting 2,500 people nightly at their movies. William Dickson, an assistant to Thomas Edison, developed the kinetograph, an early motion picture camera, and the kinetoscope, a motion picture viewing system. A New York movie house opened in 1894, offering moviegoers several coin-fed kinetoscopes. Edison's Vitascope, which expanded the length of films over

those shown via kinetoscopes and allowed larger audiences to simultaneously see the moving images, appeared in public for the first time in 1896. In France in that same year, Georges Méliès started the first motion picture theater. Short movies became part of public entertainment in a variety of American venues by 1900 (Campbell, 2002), and average weekly movie attendance reached 40 million people by 1922.

Average weekly motion picture theater attendance, as shown in Table 2.5 and Figure 2.7 on the companion website (www.tfi.com/ctu), increased annually from the earliest available census reports on the subject in 1922 until 1930. After falling dramatically during the Great Depression, attendance regained growth in 1934 and continued until 1937. Slight declines in the prewar years were followed by a period of strength and stability throughout the World War II years. After the end of the war, average weekly attendance reached its greatest heights: 90 million attendees weekly from 1946 through 1949. After the introduction of television, weekly attendance would never again reach these levels.

Although a brief period of leveling off occurred in the late 1950s and early 1960s, average weekly attendance continued to plummet until a small recovery began in 1972. This recovery signaled a period of relative stability that lasted into the 1990s. Through the last decade of the century, average weekly attendance enjoyed small but steady gains.

Box office revenues, which declined generally for 20 years after the beginning of television, began a recovery in the late 1960s, then began to skyrocket in the 1970s. The explosion continued until after the turn of the new century. However, much of the increase in revenues came from increases in ticket prices and inflation, rather than from increased popularity of films with audiences, and total motion picture revenue from box office receipts declined during recent years, as studios realized revenues from television and videocassettes (U.S. Department of Commerce/International Trade Association, 2000).

As shown in Table 2.5 on the companion website (www.tfi.com/ctu), American movie fans spent an average of 12 hours per person per year from

13

1993 through 1997 going to theaters. That average stabilized through the first decade of the 21st century (U.S. Bureau of the Census, 2010), despite the growing popularity of watching movies at home with new digital tools. In 2011, movie rental companies were thriving, with *Netflix* boasting 25 million subscribers and *Redbox* having 32,000 rental kiosks in the United States (Amobi, 2011b).

The record-breaking success of *Avatar* as a 3-D motion picture triggered a spate of followers who tried to revive the technology that was a brief hit in the 1950s. *Avatar* earned more than $761 million at American box offices and nearly $2.8 billion worldwide.

In the United States, nearly 8,000 of 39,500 theater screens were set up for 3-D at the end of 2010, half of them having been installed in that year. The ticket prices for 3-D films ran 20-30% higher than that of 2-D films, and 3-D films comprised 20% of the new films released. Nevertheless, American audiences preferred subsequent 2-D films to 3-D competitors, although 3-D response remained strong outside the United States, where 61% of the world's 22,000 3-D screens were installed. Another factor in the lack of success of 3-D in America might have been the trend toward viewing movies at home, often with digital playback. In 2010, home video purchases and rentals reached $18.8 billion in North America, compared with only $10.6 billion spent at theaters (Amobi, 2011b).

China offers an example of the globalization of the film industry. Film box office revenues in China increased by 35% in the six years ending in 2010. Total box office earnings in that year reached the equivalent of $10.6 billion, even though China allowed only 20 foreign film releases each year (Amobi, 2011b).

Audio Recording

Thomas Edison expanded on experiments from the 1850s by Leon Scott de Martinville to produce a talking machine or phonograph in 1877 that played back sound recordings from etchings in tin foil. Edison later replaced the foil with wax. In the 1880s, Emile Berliner created the first flat records from metal and shellac designed to play on his gramophone, providing mass production of recordings. The early standard recordings played at 78 revolutions per minute (rpm). After shellac became a scarce commodity because of World War II, records were manufactured from polyvinyl plastic. In 1948, CBS Records produced the long-playing record that turned at 33-1/3 rpm, extending the playing time from three to four minutes to 10 minutes. *RCA* countered in 1949 with 45 rpm records that were incompatible with machines that played other formats. After a five-year war of formats, record players were manufactured that would play recordings at all of the speeds (Campbell, 2002).

The Germans used plastic magnetic tape for sound recording during World War II. After the Americans confiscated some of the tapes, the technology was improved and became a boon for Western audio editing and multiple track recordings that played on bulky reel-to-reel machines. By the 1960s, the reels were encased in cassettes, which would prove to be deadly competition in the 1970s for single song records playing at 45 rpm and long-playing albums playing at 33-1/3 rpm. At first, the tape cassettes were popular in 8-track players. As technology improved, high sound quality was obtainable on tape of smaller width, and 8-tracks gave way to smaller audiocassettes. Thomas Stockholm began recording sound digitally in the 1970s, and the introduction of compact disc (CD) recordings in 1983 decimated the sales performance of earlier analog media types (Campbell, 2002). Table 2.6 and` 2.6A and Figures 2.8 and 2.8A on the companion website (www.tfi.com/ctu) show that total unit sales of recorded music generally increased from the early 1970s through 2008. Although vinyl recordings are hanging on, cassettes vanished after 2000, and CD units sold began a downturn in 2001.

The 21st century saw an explosion in new digital delivery systems for music. Digital audio players, which began in earnest in 1998 (Beaumont, 2008) hit a new gear of growth with the 2001 introduction of the *Apple iPod*, which increased the storage capacity and became responsible for about 19% of music sales within its first decade. Apple's online iTunes store followed in 2003 and became the world's largest music seller (Amobi, 2009).

Radio

Guglielmo Marconi's wireless messages in 1895 on his father's estate led to his establishing a British company to profit from ship-to-ship and ship-to-shore messaging. He formed a U.S. subsidiary in 1899 that would become the American Marconi Company. Reginald A. Fessenden and Lee De Forest independently transmitted voice by means of wireless radio in 1906, and a radio broadcast from the stage of a performance by Enrico Caruso occurred in 1910. Various U.S. companies and Marconi's British company owned important patents that were necessary to the development of the infant industry, so the U.S. firms formed the Radio Corporation of America (*RCA*) to buy out the patent rights from Marconi.

The debate still rages over the question of who became the first broadcaster among *KDKA* in Pittsburgh, *WHA* in Madison (Wisconsin), *WWJ* in Detroit, and *KQW* in San Jose (California). In 1919, Dr. Frank Conrad of *Westinghouse* broadcast music from his phonograph in his garage in East Pittsburgh. *Westinghouse's KDKA* in Pittsburgh announced the presidential election returns over the airwaves on November 2, 1920. By January 1, 1922, the Secretary of Commerce had issued 30 broadcast licenses, and the number of licensees swelled to 556 by early 1923. By 1924, *RCA* owned a station in New York, and *Westinghouse* expanded to Chicago, Philadelphia, and Boston. In 1922, *AT&T* withdrew from *RCA* and started *WEAF* in New York, the first radio station supported by commercials. In 1923, *AT&T* linked *WEAF* with *WNAC* in Boston by the company's telephone lines for a simultaneous program. This began the first network, which grew to 26 stations by 1925. *RCA* linked its stations with telegraph lines, which failed to match the voice quality of the transmissions of *AT&T*. However, *AT&T* wanted out of the new business and sold WEAF in 1926 to the *National Broadcasting Company*, a subsidiary of *RCA* (White, 1971).

The 1930 penetration of radio sets in American households reached 40%, then approximately doubled over the next 10 years, passing 90% by 1947 (Brown, 2006). Table 2.7 and Figure 2.9 on the companion website (www.tfi.com/ctu) show the rapid rate of increase in the number of radio households from 1922 through the early 1980s, when the rate of increase declined. The increases resumed until 1993, when they began to level off.

Although thousands of radio stations were transmitting via the Internet by 2000, *Channel1031.com* became the first station to cease using FM and move exclusively to the Internet in September 2000 (Raphael, 2000). Many other stations were operating only on the Internet when questions about fees for commercial performers and royalties for music played on the Web arose. In 2002, the Librarian of Congress set royalty rates for Internet transmissions of sound recordings (U.S. Copyright Office, 2003). A federal court upheld the right of the *Copyright Office* to establish fees on streaming music over the Internet (*Bonneville v. Peters*, 2001).

In March 2001, the first two American digital audio satellites were launched, offering the promise of hundreds of satellite radio channels (Associated Press, 2001). Consumers were expected to pay about $9.95 per month for access to commercial-free programming that would be targeted to automobile receivers. The system included amplification from about 1,300 ground antennas. By the end of 2003, about 1.6 million satellite radio subscribers tuned to the two top providers, *XM* and *Sirius* (Schaeffler, 2004). These two players merged soon before the 2008 stock market crisis, during which the new company, *Sirius XM Radio* lost nearly all of its stock value. In 2011, the service was used by 20.5 million subscribers (Sirius XM Radio, 2011).

Television

Paul Nipkow invented a scanning disk device in the 1880s that provided the basis from which other inventions would develop into television. In 1927, Philo Farnsworth became the first to electronically transmit a picture over the air. Fittingly, he transmitted the image of a dollar sign. In 1930, he received a patent for the first electronic television, one of many patents for which *RCA* would be forced, after court challenges, to negotiate. By 1932, Vladimir Zworykin discovered a means of converting light rays into electronic signals that could be transmitted and reconstructed at a receiving device.

RCA offered the first public demonstration of television at the 1939 World's Fair.

The *FCC* designated 13 channels in 1941 for use in transmitting black-and-white television, and the commission issued almost 100 television station broadcasting licenses before placing a freeze on new licenses in 1948. The freeze offered time to settle technical issues, and it ran longer because of U.S. involvement in the Korean War (Campbell, 2002). As shown in Table 2.8 on the companion website (www.tfi.com/ctu), nearly 4,000 households had television sets by 1950, a 9% penetration rate that would escalate to 87% a decade later. Penetration has remained steady at about 98% since 1980. Figure 2.9 illustrates the meteoric rise in the number of households with television by year from 1946 through the turn of the century. In 2010, 288.5 million Americans had television, up by 0.8% from 2009, and average monthly time spent viewing reached 158 hours and 47 minutes, an increase of 0.2% from the previous year (Amobi, 2011a).

By the 1980s, Japanese high-definition television (HDTV) increased the potential resolution to more than 1,100 lines of data in a television picture. This increase enabled a much higher-quality image to be transmitted with less electromagnetic spectrum space per signal. In 1996, the *FCC* approved a digital television transmission standard and authorized broadcast television stations a second channel for a 10-year period to allow the transition to *HDTV*. As discussed in Chapter 6, that transition made all older analog television sets obsolete because they cannot process *HDTV* signals (Campbell, 2002).

The *FCC* (2002) initially set May 2002 as the deadline by which all U.S. commercial television broadcasters were required to be broadcasting digital television signals. Progress toward digital television broadcasting fell short of *FCC* requirements that all affiliates of the top four networks in the top 10 markets transmit digital signals by May 1, 1999.

Within the 10 largest television markets, all except one network affiliate had begun *HDTV* broadcasts by August 1, 2001. By that date, 83% of American television stations had received construction permits for *HDTV* facilities or a license to broadcast *HDTV* signals (FCC, 2002). *HDTV* penetration into the home marketplace would remain slow for the first few years of the 21st century, in part because of the high price of the television sets. By fall 2010, 60% of American television households had at least one *HDTV* set (Nielsen tech survey finds more HDTVs, VCRs, 2010), and 3.2 million (9%) televisions were connected to the Internet (Amobi, 2011b).

Although 3-D television sets were available in 2010, little sales success occurred. The sets were quite expensive, not much 3-D television content was available, and the required 3-D viewing glasses were inconvenient to wear (Amobi, 2011b).

During the fall 2011-12 television season, The Nielsen Company reported that the number of households with television in the United States dropped for the first time since the company began such monitoring in the 1970s. The decline to 114.7 million from 115.9 million television households represented a 2.2% decline, leaving the television penetration at 96.7%. Explanations for the reversal of the long-running trend included the economic recession, but the decline could represent a transition to digital access in which viewers were getting TV from devices other than television sets (Wallenstein, 2011).

Cable Television

Cable television began as a means to overcome poor reception for broadcast television signals. John Watson claimed to have developed a master antenna system in 1948, but his records were lost in a fire. Robert J. Tarlton of Lansford (Pennsylvania) and Ed Parsons of Astoria (Oregon) set up working systems in 1949 that used a single antenna to receive programming over the air and distribute it via coaxial cable to multiple users (Baldwin & McVoy, 1983). At first, the FCC chose not to regulate cable, but after the new medium appeared to offer a threat to broadcasters, cable became the focus of heavy government regulation. Under the Reagan administration, attitudes swung toward deregulation, and cable began to flourish. Table 2.9 and Figure 2.10 on the companion website (www.tfi.com/ctu) show the growth of cable systems and subscribers, with penetration remaining below

25% until 1981, but passing the 50% mark before the 1980s ended.

In the first decade of the 21st century, cable customers began receiving access to such options as digital video, video on demand, DVRs, HDTV, and telephone services. The success of digital cable led to the *FCC* decision to eliminate analog broadcast television as of February 17, 2009. However, in September 2007, the *FCC* unanimously required cable television operators to continue to provide carriage of local television stations that demand it in both analog and digital formats for three years after the conversion date. This action was designed to provide uninterrupted local station service to all cable television subscribers, protecting the 40 million (35%) U.S. households that remained analog-only (Amobi & Kolb, 2007).

Telephone service became widespread via cable during the early years of the 21st century. For years, some cable television operators offered circuit-switched telephone service, attracting 3.6 million subscribers by the end of 2004. Also by that time, the industry offered telephone services via voice over Internet protocol (*VoIP*) to 38% of cable households, attracting 600,000 subscribers. That number grew to 1.2 million by July 2005 (Amobi, 2005).

The growth of digital cable in the first decade of the new century also saw the growth of video-on-demand (VOD), offering cable television customers the ability to order programming for immediate viewing. VOD purchases increased by 21% over the previous year in 2010, generating revenue of $1.8 billion (Amobi, 2011b).

Cable penetration declined in the United States after 2000, as illustrated in Figure 2.10 on the companion website (www.tfi.com/ctu). However, estimated use of a combination of cable and satellite television increased steadily over the same period (U.S. Bureau of the Census, 2008).

Worldwide, pay television flourished in the new century, especially in the digital market. From 2009 to 2010, pay TV subscriptions increased from 648 million households to 704 million households. ABI Research estimated that 704 million pay TV subscribers would exist in 2011, about half of whom would be digital television subscribers, and an estimated 225 million households would subscribe to HDTV (HDTV subscribers, 2011).

Direct Broadcast Satellite and Other Cable TV Competitors

Satellite technology began in the 1940s, but HBO became the first service to use it for distributing entertainment content in 1976 when the company sent programming to its cable affiliates (Amobi & Kolb, 2007). Other networks soon followed this lead, and individual broadcast stations (*WTBS, WGN, WWOR,* and *WPIX*) used satellites in the 1970s to expand their audiences beyond their local markets by distributing their signals to cable operators around the United States.

Competitors for the cable industry include a variety of technologies. Annual *FCC* reports distinguish between home satellite dish (*HSD*) and direct broadcast satellite (*DBS*) systems. Both are included as *MVPDs*, which include cable television, wireless cable systems called multichannel multipoint distribution services (*MMDS*), and private cable systems called satellite master antenna television (*SMATV*). Table 2.10 and Figure 2.11 on the companion website for this book (www.tfi.com/ctu), show trends in home satellite dish, Direct Broadcast Satellite, MMDS, and SMATV subscribers.

Two satellite home viewing providers, *DISH* and *DirecTV*, dominated the market in the years up to 2009. Together in that year, they reached 32 million subscribers. Two new telecom players in the multichannel television market emerged in 2009: *Verizon* and *AT&T*, serving a total of 4.5 million households, raising the total number of non-cable, multichannel television subscribers to 36.5 million (Amobi & Kolb, 2010). During the next year, the veteran providers, *DISH* and *DirecTV*, reached a total of 33.6 million households, and the two telcom companies reached another 6.5 million subscribers. These figures compared with the 59.8 million cable television subscribers (60% of pay television market) in 2010 (Amobi, 2011a).

Home Video

Although VCRs became available to the public in the late 1970s, competing technical standards slowed the adoption of the new devices. After the longer taping capacity of the VHS format won greater public acceptance over the higher-quality images of the *Betamax*, the popularity of home recording and playback rapidly accelerated, as shown in Table 2.11 and Figure 2.12 on the companion website (www.tfi.com/ctu).

By 2004, rental spending for videotapes and DVDs reached $24.5 billion, far surpassing the $9.4 billion spent for tickets to motion pictures in that year. During 2005, DVD sales increased by 400% over the $4 billion figure for 2000 to $15.7 billion. However, the annual rate of growth reversed direction and slowed that year to 45% and again the following year to 2%. VHS sales amounted to less than $300 million in 2006 (Amobi & Donald, 2007).

Factors in the decline of VHS and DVD use included growth in cable and satellite video-on-demand services, growth of broadband video availability, digital downloading of content, and the transition to DVD *Blu-ray* format (Amobi, 2009). The competing new formats for playing high-definition content was similar to the one waged in the early years of VCR development between the *Betamax* and VHS formats. Similarly, in early DVD player development, companies touting competing standards settled a dispute by agreeing to share royalties with the creator of the winning format. Until early 2008, the competition between proponents of the HD-DVD and *Blu-ray* formats for playing high-definition DVD content remained unresolved, and some studios were planning to distribute motion pictures in both formats. *Blu-ray* seemed to emerge the victor in 2008 when large companies (e.g., *Time Warner*, *Wal-Mart*, *Netflix*) declared allegiance to that format. By July 2010, *Blu-ray* penetration reached 17% of American households (Gruenwedel, 2010), and 170 million *Blu-ray* discs shipped that year (Amobi, 2011b).

Digital video recorders (DVRs, also called personal video recorders, PVRs) debuted during 2000, and about 500,000 units were sold by the end of 2001 (FCC, 2002). The devices save video content on computer hard drives, allowing fast-forwarding, rewinding, and pausing of live television; retroactive recording of limited minutes of previously displayed live television; automatic recording of all first-run episodes; automatic recording logs; and superior quality to that of analog VCRs. Multiple tuner models allow viewers to watch one program, while recording others simultaneously.

DVR providers generate additional revenues by charging households monthly fees, and satellite DVR households tend to be less likely to drop their satellite subscriptions. Perhaps the most fundamental importance of DVRs is the ability of consumers to make their own programming decisions about when and what they watch. This flexibility threatens the revenue base of network television in several ways, including empowering viewers to skip standard commercials. Amobi (2005) cited potential advertiser responses, such as sponsorships and product placements within programming.

Reflecting the popularity of the Digital Video Recorder (DVR), time shifting was practiced in 2010 by 107.1 million American households (up 13.2% from 2009). Time shifted viewing increased by 12.2% in 2010 from 2009 to an average of 10 hours and 46 minutes monthly (Amobi, 2011a).

The Digital Era

The digital era represents a transition in modes of delivery of mediated content. Although the tools of using digital media may have changed, in many cases, the content remains remarkably stable. With other media, such as social media, the digital content fostered new modes of communicating. This section contains histories of the development of computers and the Internet. Segments of earlier discussions could be considered part of the digital era, such as audio recording, HDTV, films on DVD, etc., but discussions of those segments remain under earlier eras.

Computers

The history of computing traces its origins back thousands of years to such practices as using bones as counters (Hofstra University, 2000). Intel introduced the first microprocessor in 1971. The MITS Altair, with an 8080 processor and 256 bytes of RAM (random access memory), sold for $498 in 1975, introducing the desktop computer to individuals. In 1977, Radio Shack offered the TRS80 home computer, and the *Apple II* set a new standard for personal computing, selling for $1,298. Other companies began introducing personal computers, and, by 1978, 212,000 personal computers were shipped for sale.

Early business adoption of computers served primarily to assist practices such as accounting. When computers became small enough to sit on office desktops in the 1980s, word processing became a popular business use and fueled interest in home computers. With the growth of networking and the Internet in the 1990s, both businesses and consumers began buying computers in large numbers. Computer shipments around the world grew annually by more than 20% between 1991 and 1995 (Kessler, 2007b).

By 1997, the majority of American households with annual incomes greater than $50,000 owned a personal computer. At the time, those computers sold for about $2,000, exceeding the reach of lower income groups. By the late 1990s, prices dropped below $1,000 per system (Kessler, 2007b), and American households passed the 60% penetration mark in owning personal computers within a couple of years (U.S. Bureau of the Census, 2008).

Factors other than prices that fueled computer purchases include both software and hardware upgrades. For example, operating systems such as Windows Vista and Windows XP and major applications such as new word processors and video editors stimulated demand for systems with more processing power. Computer peripherals such as color monitors and compact disc drives that replaced floppy disc drives also motivated upgrades. A major upgrade period occurred in 1999 when consumers feared the millennium bug.

Table 2.12 and Figure 2.13 on the companion website (www.tfi.com/ctu) trace the rapid and steady rise in American computer shipments and home penetration. By 1998, 42.1% of American households owned personal computers (U.S. Bureau of

the Census, 2006). After the start of the 21st century, personal computer prices declined, and penetration increased from 63% in 2000 to 77% in 2008 (Forrester Research as cited in Kessler, 2011). Worldwide personal computer sales increased by 34% from 287 million in 2008 to 385 million in 2011 (IDC as cited Kessler, 2011).

Internet

The Internet began in the 1960s with ARPANET, or the Advanced Research Projects Agency (ARPA) network project, under the auspices of the U.S. Defense Department. The project intended to serve the military and researchers with multiple paths of linking computers together for sharing data in a system that would remain operational even when traditional communications might become unavailable. Early users, mostly university and research lab personnel, took advantage of electronic mail and posting information on computer bulletin boards. Usage increased dramatically in 1982 after the National Science Foundation supported high-speed linkage of multiple locations around the United States. After the collapse of the Soviet Union in the late 1980s, military users abandoned ARPANET, but private users continued to use it, and multimedia transmissions of audio and video became possible once this content could be digitized. More than 150,000 regional computer networks and 95 million computer servers hosted data for Internet users (Campbell, 2002).

Penetration and Usage

Tables 2.13 and 2.14 and 2.14 and 2.15 on the companion website (www.tfi.com/ctu) show trends in Internet usage in the United States. By 2008, 74 million (63%) American households had high-speed broadband access (Kessler, 2011). In 2009, the penetration increased to 70.9%, then to 75.3% in 2010 (More Americans, 2012). IDC reported that Internet users worldwide reached 1.5 billion in 2008 and forecast that the number would reach 2.3 billion in 2013, an annual growth rate of 9% (Kessler, 2011).

In 2010, the average amount of time per month spent connected to the Internet ranged from 22.3 hours for users of ages 12-17 to 39.3 hours for users of ages 45-54. Other age groups (18-24; 25-34; 35-44; 55-64; and 65+) all averaged between 32.2 and 37.4 monthly hours of Internet activity (Kessler, 2011).

During the first decade of the 21st century, the Internet became the primary reason that consumers purchased new computers (Kessler, 2007a). Cable modems and DSL telephone line connections increased among home users as the means for connecting to the Internet, as more than half of American households accessed the Net with high-speed broadband connections. Outside the United States, DSL has an edge over cable Internet access because of the much greater penetration of wired telephone lines relative to cable infrastructure (Bensinger, 2007).

YouTube, an online video viewing service, was created in 2005, and viewers watched 63 billion videos online that year (comScore as cited in Kessler, 2011). By 2010, 441 billion videos were seen online, representing an annual growth rate of 38% (Kessler, 2011).

In 2010, 142.4 million American households were viewing videos via the Internet, up by 4.8% from 2009. The average household viewing of this type occurred for 14 hours and 33 minutes monthly, an increase of 34.5% from the previous year (Amobi, 2011a). In July 2011, more than 180 million unique viewers of Internet video consumed an average of 1,107 minutes of online video (Kessler, 2011).

Commerce is among the popular uses of the Internet. In 1994, Internet content was hosted on about 10,000 web servers. By 2006, more than 100 million servers were operating. In 2008, 187 million websites were operating. That number increased to 234 million in 2009 and 255 million in 2010. 2011 was the sixth consecutive year in which growth in online commercial revenues occurred. Revenue in 2011 was 25% higher than in the previous year. "By any measure, the Internet has been one of the fastest growing commercial phenomena in history" (Kessler, 2011, p. 17).

Online access spurred the development of social networking services, particularly among teenagers and later among adults, too. Social networking also operates through a variety of online services that allow individuals to use mobile phones to send out reports of daily activities. Users obtain software for their phones from websites. This software allows messages and photographs to be sent to receivers who use phones or computers to access websites for reception (Stone & Richtel, 2007).

Facebook emerged as the most popular social networking service (Kessler, 2009). In February 2010, the service reported more than 400 million users, a number equivalent to the third most populous country in the world, larger than the United States. The number of users passed 500 million in July 2010 and 750 million by mid-2011. More than 250 million users accessed the service in 2011 with mobile devices. By late 2010, Facebook had become not only the largest social network in the world, but the third largest Internet company of any kind (Kessler, 2011).

Blogging and microblogging became popular in the early 21st century. *Twitter*, a microblogging service that takes advantage of the Internet, was created in 2006 by a group working at *Odeo, Inc.* (Sagolla, 2009). The group created *Twitter* while attempting to develop a technique of communicating short text messages by mobile phone. The messages, or *tweets*, consist of 140 characters. By March 2011, Twitter registered 175 million users, equivalent with the seventh most populous nation in the world (Kessler, 2011).

Synthesis

Older media, including both print and electronic types, have gone through transitions from their original forms into digital media. Many media that originated in digital form have enjoyed explosive growth during the digital age.

Horrigan (2005) noted that the rate of adoption of high-speed Internet use approximated that of other electronic technologies. He observed that 10% of the population used high-speed Internet access in just more than five years. Personal computers required four years, CD players needed 4.5 years, cell phones required eight years, VCRs took 10 years, and color televisions used 12 years to reach 10% penetration.

The *Apple iPad* tablet computer, introduced in April 2010, may be the most rapidly adopted new technology device in history. Within the same business quarter of the year of its introduction, the device was in 3.6% of American homes (Nielsen, VCRs, 2010). In 2010, consumers purchased nearly 15 million *iPads* (IDC as cited in Cathers, 2011). By the spring of 2011, 10% of American adult online participants (a group that included 75% of the American population and 80% of households) owned a tablet computer (Tablets take off, 2011). After the iPad2 was introduced in the second quarter of 2011, 9.2 million were purchased in that quarter (IDC as cited in Cathers, 2011). In slightly more than one year after the introduction of the *iPad*, consumers purchased nearly 25 million of them (Amobi, 2011b). This rapid acceptance illustrated, not merely the success of a product, but the high degree of commitment that consumers were willing to make to new digital equipment.

Early visions of the Internet (see Chapter 21) did not include the emphasis on entertainment and information to the general public that has emerged. The combination of this new medium with older media belongs to a phenomenon called *convergence*, referring to the merging of functions of old and new media. By 2002, the *FCC* (2002) reported that the most important type of convergence related to video content is the joining of Internet services. The report also noted that companies from many business areas were providing a variety of video, data, and other communications services.

Just as media began converging nearly a century ago when radios and record players merged in the same appliance, media in recent years have been converging at a much more rapid pace. As the popularity of print media forms generally declined throughout the 1990s, the popularity of the Internet grew rapidly, particularly with the increase in high-speed broadband connections, for which adoption rates achieved comparability with previous new communications media. Consumer flexibility through the use of digital media became the dominant media consumption theme during the first decade of the new century.

Bibliography

Agnese, J. (2011, October 20). Industry surveys: Publishing & advertising. In E. M. Bossong-Martines (Ed.), *Standard & Poor's industrysSurveys*, Vol. 2.

Amobi, T. N. (2005, December 8). Industry surveys: Broadcasting, cable, and satellite industry survey. In E. M. Bossong-Martines (Ed.), *Standard & Poor's industry surveys*, 173 (49), Section 2.

Amobi, T. N. (2009). Industry surveys: Movies and home entertainment. In E. M. Bossong-Martines (Ed.), *Standard & Poor's industry surveys*, 177 (38), Section 2.

Amobi, T. N. (2011a). Industry surveys: Broadcasting, cable, and satellite. In E. M. Bossong-Martines (Ed.), *Standard & Poor's industry surveys*, Vol. 1.

Amobi, T. N. (2011b). Industry surveys: Movies & entertainment. In E. M. Bossong-Martines (Ed.), *Standard & Poor's industry surveys*, Vol. 2.

Amobi, T. N. & Donald, W. H. (2007, September 20). Industry surveys: Movies and home entertainment. In E. M. Bossong-Martines (Ed.), *Standard & Poor's industry surveys*, 175 (38), Section 2.

Amobi, T. N. & Kolb, E. (2007, December 13). Industry surveys: Broadcasting, cable & satellite. In E. M. Bossong-Martines (Ed.), *Standard & Poor's industry surveys*, 175 (50), Section 1.

Amobi, T. N. & Kolb, E. (2010). Industry surveys: Broadcasting, cable & satellite. In E. M. Bossong-Martines (Ed.), *Standard & Poor's industry surveys*, Vol. 1.

Aronson, S. (1977). Bell's electrical toy: What's the use? The sociology of early telephone usage. In I. Pool (Ed.). *The social impact of the telephone*. Cambridge, MA: The MIT Press, 15-39.

Aspan, M. (2006, January 16). Recording that show? You won't escape Nielsen's notice. *New York Times*. Retrieved from http://www.nytimes.com/2006/01/16/business/media/16delay.html.

Associated Press. (2001, March 20). Audio satellite launched into orbit. *New York Times*. Retrieved from http://www.nytimes.com/aponline/national/AP-Satellite-Radio.html?ex=986113045& ei=1&en=7af33c7805ed8853.

Baldwin, T. & McVoy, D. (1983). *Cable communication*. Englewood Cliffs, NJ: Prentice-Hall.

Beaumont, C. (2008, May 10). Dancing to the digital tune as the MP3 turns 10. *The Daily Telegraph,* p. 19. Retrieved from LexisNexis Database.

Belson, K. (2006, November 14). With a dish, broadband goes rural. *New York Times.* Retrieved from http://www.nytimes.com/ 2006/11/14/technology/14satellite.html?em&ex=1163826000&en=24bff61f6033f7c5&ei=5087%0A.

Bensinger, A. (2007, August 2). Industry surveys: Communications equipment. In E. M. Bossong-Martines (Ed.), *Standard & Poor's industry surveys, 153* (31), Section 1.

Bonneville International Corp., et al. v. Marybeth Peters, as Register of Copyrights, et al. Civ. No. 01-0408, 153 F. Supp.2d 763 (E.D. Pa., August 1, 2001).

Brown, D. & Bryant, J. (1989). An annotated statistical abstract of communications media in the United States. In J. Salvaggio & J. Bryant (Eds.), *Media use in the information age: Emerging patterns of adoption and consumer use.* Hillsdale, NJ: Lawrence Erlbaum Associates, 259-302.

Brown, D. (1996). A statistical update of selected American communications media. In Grant, A. E. (Ed.), *Communication Technology Update* (5th ed.). Boston, MA: Focal Press, 327-355.

Brown, D. (1998). Trends in selected U. S. communications media. In Grant, A. E. & Meadows, J. H. (Eds.), Communication Technology Update (6th ed.). Boston, MA: Focal Press, 279-305.

Brown, D. (2000). Trends in selected U. S. communications media. In Grant, A. E. & Meadows, J. H. (Eds.), *Communication Technology Update* (7th ed.). Boston, MA: Focal Press, 299-324.

Brown, D. (2002). Communication technology timeline. In A. E. Grant & J. H. Meadows (Eds.), *Communication technology update* (8th ed.) Boston: Focal Press, 7-45.

Brown, D. (2004). Communication technology timeline. In A. E. Grant & J. H. Meadows (Eds.). *Communication technology update* (9th ed.). Boston: Focal Press, 7-46.

Brown, D. (2006). Communication technology timeline. In A. E. Grant & J. H. Meadows (Eds.), *Communication technology update* (10th ed.). Boston: Focal Press. 7-46.

Brown, D. (2008). Historical perspectives on communication technology. In E. Grant & J. H. Meadows (Eds.), *Communication technology update and fundamentals* (11th ed.). Boston: Focal Press. 11-42.

Brown, D. (2010). Historical perspectives on communication technology. In E. Grant & J. H. Meadows (Eds.), *Communication technology update and fundamentals* (12th ed.). Boston: Focal Press. 9-46.

Campbell, R. (2002). *Media & culture.* Boston, MA: Bedford/St. Martins.

Cathers, D. (2011). Industry surveys: Computers. In E. M. Bossong-Martines (Ed.), *Standard & Poor's industry surveys, Vol. 1.*

Dillon, D. (2011). E-books pose major challenge for publishers, libraries. In D. Bogart (Ed.), *Library and book trade almanac* (pp. 3-16). Medford, NJ: Information Today, Inc.

Federal Communications Commission. (2002, January 14). *In the matter of annual assessment of the status of competition in the market for the delivery of video programming* (eighth annual report). CS Docket No. 01-129. Washington, DC 20554.

Federal Communications Commission. (2005). *In the matter of Implementation of Section 6002(b) of the Omnibus Budget Reconciliation Act of 1993: Annual report and analysis of competitive market conditions with respect to commercial mobile services* (10th report). WT Docket No. 05-71. Washington, DC 20554.

Federal Communications Commission. (2010a, January 20). *In the Matter of Review of the Commission's Program Access Rules and Examination of Programming Tying Arrangements.* MB Docket No. 07-198. Washington, DC 20554.

Federal Communications Commission. (2010b, February). High-Speed Services for Internet Access: Status as of December 31, 2008. Washington, DC 20554.

Federal Communications Commission. (2011, October). Internet access services: Status as of December 31, 2010. Washington, DC 20554.

Grabois, A. (2005). Book title output and average prices: 2003 final and 2004 preliminary figures. In D. Bogart (Ed.), *The Bowker annual library and trade book almanac* (50th edition, pp. 521-525). Medford, NJ: Information Today.

Grabois, A. (2006). Book title output and average prices: 2004 final and 2005 preliminary figures. In D. Bogart (Ed.), *The Bowker annual library and trade book almanac* (51st edition, pp. 516-520). Medford, NJ: Information Today.

Gruenwedel, E. (2010). Report: Blu's household penetration reaches 17%. *Home Media Magazine, 32,* 40.

HDTV subscribers to total 225 million globally in 2011 (2011, March). *Broadcast Engineering* [Online Exclusive].

Hofstra University. (2000). *Chronology of computing history.* Retrieved from http://www.hofstra.edu/pdf/ CompHist_9812tla1.pdf.

Horrigan, J. B. (2005, September 24). *Broadband adoption at home in the United States: Growing but slowing.* Paper presented to the 33rd Annual Meeting of the Telecommunications Policy Research Conference. Retrieved from http://www.pewinternet.org/PPF/r/164/report_display.asp.

Huntzicker, W. (1999). *The popular press, 1833-1865*. Westport, CT: Greenwood Press.

Ink, G. & Grabois, A. (2000). *Book title output and average prices: 1998 final and 1999 preliminary figures*, 45th edition. D. Bogart (Ed.). New Providence, NJ: R. R. Bowker, 508-513.

International Telecommunications Union. (1999). *World telecommunications report 1999*. Geneva, Switzerland: Author.

Kessler, S. H. (2007a, September 20). Industry surveys: Computers: Consumer services & the Internet. In E. M. Bossong-Martines (Ed.), *Standard & Poor's industry surveys, 175* (38), Section 1.

Kessler, S. H. (2007b, August 26). Industry surveys: Computers: Hardware. In E M. Bossong-Martines (Ed.), *Standard & Poor's industry surveys, 175* (17), Section 2.

Kessler, S. H. (2009). Industry surveys: Consumer services and the Internet. In E. M. Bossong-Martines (Ed.), *Standard & Poor's industry surveys, 173* (49), Section 2.

Kessler, S. H. (2011). Industry surveys: Computers: Consumer services and the Internet. In E. M. Bossong-Martines (Ed.), *Standard & Poor's industry surveys, Vol. 1.*

Kissell, R. (2010, October 12). DVRs draw bigger auds. *Daily Variety* (309), 7.

Lee, J. (1917). *History of American journalism*. Boston: Houghton Mifflin.

More Americans cutting the cord, but paid TV still dominates. (2012, February). *PC Magazine Online*, 9.

Murray, J. (2001). *Wireless nation: The frenzied launch of the cellular revolution in America*. Cambridge, MA: Perseus Publishing.

Nielsen tech survey finds more HDTVs, VCRs. (2010, October 4). *Multichannel News*, 28.

OECD. (2007). *OECD broadband statistics to December 2006*. Retrieved from http://www.oecd.org/ document/7/0,2340,en_2649_34223_38446855_1_1_1_1,00.html.

Peters, J. & Donald, W. H. (2007). Industry surveys: Publishing. In E. M. Bossong-Martines (Ed.), *Standard & Poor's industry surveys*. 175 (36). Section 1.

Pfanner, E. (2009). Book sales in Europe are gaining in tough times. *New York Times*. Retrieved from http://www.nytimes.com/2009/03/16/business/worldbusiness/16books.html?ref=media.

Rainie, L. (2012, January 23). Tablet and e-book reader ownership nearly doubles over the holiday gift-giving period. *Pew Research Center's Internet & American Life Project*. Retrieved from http://pewinternet.org/Reports/2012/E-readers-and-tablets.aspx

Raphael, J. (2000, September 4). Radio station leaves earth and enters cyberspace. Trading the FM dial for a digital stream. *New York Times*. Retrieved from http://www.nytimes.com/library/tech/00/ 09/biztech/articles/04radio.html.

Rawlinson, N. (2011, April 28). Books vs ebooks. *Computer Act!ve*. Retrieved from General OneFile database.

Sagolla, D. (2009, January 30). 140 characters: How Twitter was born. Retrieved from http://www.140characters.com/2009/01/30/how-twitter-was-born/

Schaeffler, J. (2004, February 2). The real satellite radio boom begins. *Satellite News, 27* (5). Retrieved from Lexis-Nexis.

Sirius XM Radio Poised for Growth, Finally. (2011, May 10). *Newsmax*.

Stelter, B. (2010). Viacom and Hulu part ways. *New York Times*. Retrieved from http://www.nytimes.com/2010/03/03/ business/ media/03hulu.html?adxnnl=1&ref=technology&adxnnlx=1267625269-7LOKJ+wiTvnH0xceeIa5vg.

Stone, B. & Richtel, M. (2007, April 30). Social networking leaves the confines of the computer. *New York Times*. Retrieved from http://www.nytimes.com/2007/04/30/technology/30social.html?_r=1& ref=technology.

Tablets take off: usage is booming for search, social networking, and reading. Not so for TV and video viewing. (2011, September). *Adweek*, 5.

Television Bureau of Advertising. (2012). TV basics. Retrieved from http://www.tvb.org/trends/95487.

U.S. Bureau of the Census. (2006). *Statistical abstract of the United States: 2006* (125th Ed.). Washington, DC: U.S. Government Printing Office.

U.S. Bureau of the Census. (2008). *Statistical abstract of the United States: 2008* (127th Ed.). Washington, DC: U.S. Government Printing Office. Retrieved from http://www.census.gov/compendia/statab/.

U.S. Bureau of the Census. (2010). *Statistical abstract of the United States: 2008* (129th Ed.). Washington, DC: U.S. Government Printing Office. Retrieved from http://www.census.gov/compendia/statab/.

U.S. Copyright Office. (2003). *106th Annual report of the Register of Copyrights for the fiscal year ending September 30, 2003*. Washington, DC: Library of Congress.

U.S. Department of Commerce/International Trade Association. (2000). *U.S. industry and trade outlook 2000*. New York: McGraw-Hill.

Wallenstein, A. (2011, September 16). Tube squeeze: economy, tech spur drop in TV homes. *Daily Variety*, 3.

White, L. (1971). *The American radio*. New York: Arno Press.

Understanding Communication Technologies

Jennifer H. Meadows, Ph.D.*

Today, you can do dozens of things that your parents never dreamed of: surfing the Internet anytime and anywhere, watching crystal-clear sports on a large high definition television (HDTV) in your home, battling aliens on "distant worlds" alongside game players scattered around the globe, and "Googling" any subject you find interesting. This book was created to help you understand these technologies, but there is a set of tools that will not only help you understand them, but also understand the next generation of technologies.

All of the communication technologies explored in this book have a number of characteristics in common, including how their adoption spreads from a small group of highly interested consumers to the general public, what the effects of these technologies are upon the people who use them (and on society in general), and how these technologies affect each other.

For more than a century, researchers have studied adoption, effects, and other aspects of new technologies, identifying patterns that are common across dissimilar technologies, and proposing theories of technology adoption and effects. These theories have proven to be valuable to entrepreneurs seeking to develop new technologies, regulators who want to control those technologies, and everyone else who just wants to understand them. The utility of these theories is that they allow you to apply lessons from one technology to another or from old technologies to new technologies. The easiest way to understand the role played by the technologies explored in this book is to have a set of theories you can apply to virtually any technology you discuss. The purpose of this chapter is to give you those tools by introducing you to the theories.

The technology ecosystem discussed in Chapter 1 is a useful framework for studying communication technologies, but it is not a theory. This perspective is a good starting point to begin to understand communication technologies because it targets your attention at a number of different levels that might not be immediately obvious: hardware, software, content, organizational infrastructure, the social system, and, finally, the user. Understanding each of these levels is aided by knowing a number of theoretical perspectives that can help us understand the different sections of the ecosystem for these technologies. Indeed, there are a plethora of theories that can be used to study these technologies. Theoretical approaches are useful in understanding the origins of the information-based economy in which we now live, why some

* Professor, Department of Communication Design, California State University, Chico (Chico, California).

technologies take off while others fail, the impacts and effects of technologies, and the economics of the communication technology marketplace.

The Information Society and the Control Revolution

Our economy used to be based on tangible products such as coal, lumber, and steel. That has changed. Now, information is the basis of our economy. Information industries include education, research and development, creating informational goods such as computer software, banking, insurance, and even entertainment and news (Beniger, 1986). Information is different from other commodities like coffee and pork bellies, which are known as "private goods." Instead, information is a "public good" because it is intangible, lacks a physical presence, and can be sold as many times as demand allows without regard to consumption. For example, if 10 sweaters are sold, then 10 sweaters must be manufactured using raw materials. If 10 subscriptions to an online dating service are sold, there is no need to create new services: 10—or 10,000—subscriptions can be sold without additional raw materials.

This difference actually gets to the heart of a common misunderstanding about ownership of information that falls into a field known as "intellectual property rights." A common example is the purchase of a digital music download. A person may believe that because he or she purchased the music, that he or she can copy and distribute that music to others. Just because the information (the music) was purchased doesn't mean you own the song and performance (intellectual property).

Several theorists have studied the development of the information society, including its origin. Beniger (1986) argues that there was a control revolution: "A complex of rapid changes in the technological and economic arrangements by which information is collected, stored, processed, and communicated and through which formal or programmed decisions might affect social control" (p. 52). In other words, as society progressed, technologies were created to help control information.

For example, information was centralized by mass media. In addition, as more and more information is created and distributed, new technologies must be developed to control that information. For example, with the explosion of information available over the Internet, search engines were developed to help users find it.

Another important point is that information is power, and there is power in giving information away. Power can also be gained by withholding information. At different times in modern history, governments have blocked access to information or controlled information dissemination to maintain power.

Adoption

Why are some technologies adopted while others fail? This question is addressed by a number of theoretical approaches including the diffusion of innovations, social information processing theory, and critical mass theory.

Diffusion of Innovations

The diffusion of innovations, also referred to as diffusion theory, was developed by Everett Rogers (1962; 2003). This theory tries to explain how an innovation is communicated over time through different channels to members of a social system. There are four main aspects of this approach. First, there is the innovation. In the case of communication technologies, the innovation is some technology that is perceived as new. Rogers also defines characteristics of innovations: relative advantage, compatibility, complexity, trialability, and observability. So if someone is deciding to purchase a new mobile phone, characteristics would include the relative advantage over other mobile phones, whether or not the mobile phone is compatible with the existing needs of the user, how complex it is to use, whether or not the potential user can try it out, and whether or not the potential user can see others using the new mobile phone with successful results. Information about an innovation is communicated through different channels. Mass media is good for awareness knowledge. For example, each new iPhone has Web content, television commercials, and print advertising announcing its existence and its features. Interpersonal channels are also an important means of communication about innovations. These interactions generally involve subjective evaluations of the innovation. For example, a person might ask some friends how they like their new iPhones.

Rogers (2003) outlines the decision-making process a potential user goes through before adopting an innovation. This is a five-step process. The first step is knowledge. You find out there is a new mobile phone available and learn about its new features. The next step is persuasion—the formation of a positive attitude about the innovation. Maybe you like the new phone. The third step is when you decide to accept or reject the innovation. Yes, I will get the new mobile phone. Implementation is the fourth step. You use the innovation, in this case, the mobile phone. Finally, confirmation occurs when you decide that you made the correct decision. Yes, the mobile phone is what I thought it would be; my decision is reinforced.

Another stage that is discussed by Rogers (2003) and others is "reinvention," the process by which a person who adopts a technology begins to use it for purposes other than those intended by the original inventor. For example, mobile phones were initially designed for calling other people regardless of location, but users have found ways to use them for a wide variety of applications ranging from alarm clocks to personal calendars and more.

Have you ever noticed that some people are the first to have the new technology gadget, while others refuse to adopt a proven successful technology? Adopters can be categorized into different groups according to how soon or late they adopt an innovation. The first to adopt are the innovators. Innovators are special because they are willing to take a risk adopting something new that may fail. Next come the early adopters, the early majority, and then the late majority, followed by the last category, the laggards. In terms of percentages, innovators make up the first 2.5% percent of adopters, early adopters are the next 13.5%, early majority follows with 34%, late majority are the next 34%, and laggards are the last 16%. Adopters can also be

described in terms of ideal types. Innovators are venturesome. These are people who like to take risks and can deal with failure. Early adopters are respectable. They are valued opinion leaders in the community and role models for others. Early majority adopters are deliberate. They adopt just before the average person and are an important link between the innovators, early adopters, and everyone else. The late majority are skeptical. They are hesitant to adopt innovations and often adopt because they pressured. Laggards are the last to adopt and often are isolated with no opinion leadership. They are suspicious and resistant to change. Other factors that affect adoption include education, social status, social mobility, finances, and willingness to use credit (Rogers, 2003).

Adoption of an innovation does not usually occur all at once; it happens over time. This is called the rate of adoption. The rate of adoption generally follows an S-shaped "diffusion curve" where the X-axis is time and the Y-axis is percent of adopters. You can note the different adopter categories along the diffusion curve. Figure 3.1 shows a diffusion curve. See how the innovators are at the very beginning of the curve, and the laggards are at the end. The steepness of the curve depends on how quickly an innovation is adopted. For example, DVD has a steeper curve than VCR because DVD players were adopted at a faster rate than VCRs. Also, different types of decision processes lead to faster adoption. Voluntary adoption is slower than collective decisions, which, in turn, are slower than authority decisions. For example, a company may let its workers decide whether to use a new software package, the employees may agree collectively to use that software, or finally, the management may decide that everyone at the company is going to use the software. In most cases, voluntary adoption would take the longest, and a management dictate would result in the swiftest adoption.

Moore (2001) further explored diffusion of innovations and high-tech marketing in *Crossing the Chasm*. He noted there are gaps between the innovators and the early adopters, the early adopters and the early majority, and the early majority and late majority. For a technology's adoption to move from innovators to the early adopters the technology must show a major new benefit. Innovators are visionaries that take the risk of adopting something new such as 3-D televisions. Early adopters then must see the new benefit of 3-D televisions before adopting. The chasm between early adopters and early majority is the greatest of these gaps. Early adopters are still visionary and want to be change agents. They don't mind dealing with the troubles and glitches that come along with a new technology. Early adopters were likely to use a beta version of a new service like Google+. The early majority, on the other hand, are pragmatists and want to see some improvement in productivity—something tangible. Moving from serving the visionaries to serving the pragmatists is difficult; hence Moore's description of "crossing the chasm." This phenomenon could explain why Google+ hasn't moved beyond the early adopter stage. Finally, there is a smaller gap between the early majority and the late majority. Unlike the early majority, the late majority reacts to the technical demands on the users. The early majority is more comfortable working with technology. So, the early majority would be comfortable using social networking like Pinterest but the late majority is put off by the perceived technical demands. The technology must alleviate this concern before late majority adoption.

Figure 3.1
Innovation Adoption Rate

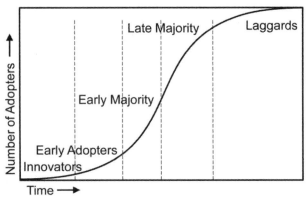

Source: Technology Futures, Inc.

Another perspective on adoption can be found in most marketing textbooks (e.g., Kottler & Keller, 2011), the product lifecycle. As illustrated in Figure 3.2, the product lifecycle extends the diffusion curve to include the maturity and decline of the technology. This perspective provides a more complete picture of a technology because it focuses our attention beyond the initial use of the technology to the time that the technology is in regular use, and ultimately, disappears from market. Considering the short lifespan of many communication technologies, it may be just as useful to study the entire lifespan of a technology rather than just the process of adoption.

Figure 3.2
Product Lifecycle

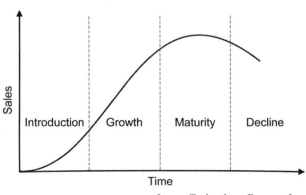

Source: Technology Futures, Inc.

Other Theories of Adoption

Other theorists have attempted to explain the process of adoption as well. Among the most notable perspectives in this regard are the Theory of Planned Behavior (TPB) and the Technology Acceptance Model (TAM). Both of these models emerged from the need to identify factors that can help predict future adoption of a new technology when there is no history of adoption or use of the technology.

The Theory of Planned Behavior (TPB) (Ajzen, 1991; Ajzen & Fishbein, 1980; Fishbein & Ajzen, 1975) presumes that a suitable predictor of future behavior is "behavioral intention," a cognitive rather than behavioral variable that represents an individual's plans for adopting (or not adopting!) an innovation. Behavioral intentions are, in turn, predicted by attitudes toward the innovation and the innovators.

The Technology Acceptance Model (Davis, 1986; Davis, Bagozzi & Warshaw, 1989) elaborates on TPB by adding factors that may predict attitudes toward an innovation and behavioral intentions, including perceived usefulness, perceived ease of use, and external variables. A substantial body of research has demonstrated the efficacy of these factors in predicting behavioral intentions (e.g., Mathieson, 1991; Jiang, Hsu & Klein, 2000; Chau & Hu, 2002; Park, Lee & Cheong, 2007), but much more research is needed regarding the link between behavioral intentions and actual adoption at a later point in time.

Another theory that expands upon Rogers' diffusion theory is presented in Chapter 4. Grant's pre-diffusion theory identifies organizational functions that must be served before any consumer adoption of the technology can take place.

Critical Mass Theory

Have you ever wondered who had the first e-mail address or the first telephone? Who did he communicate with? Interactive technologies such as telephony and e-mail become more and more useful as more people adopt these technologies. There have to be some innovators and early adopters who are willing to take the risk to try a new interactive technology. These users are the "critical mass," a small segment of the population that chooses to make big contributions to the public good (Markus, 1987). In general terms, any social process involving actions by individuals that benefit others is known as "collective action." In this case, the technologies become more useful if everyone in the system is using the technology, a goal known as universal access.

Ultimately universal access means that you can reach anyone through some communication technology. For example, in the United States, the landline phone system reaches almost everywhere, and everyone benefits from this technology, although a small segment of the population initially chose to adopt the telephone to get the ball rolling. There is a stage in the diffusion process that an interactive medium has to reach in order for adoption to take off. This is the "critical mass."

Another conceptualization of critical mass theory is the "tipping point" (Gladwell, 2002). Here is an example. The videophone never took off, in part, because it never reached critical mass. The videophone was not really any better than a regular phone unless the person you were calling also had a videophone. If there were not enough people you knew who had videophones, then you might not adopt it because it was not worth it. On the other hand, if most of your regular contacts had videophones, then that critical mass of users might drive you to adopt the videophone. Critical mass is an important aspect to consider for the adoption of any interactive technology.

Another good example is facsimile or fax technology. The first method of sending images over wires was invented in the '40s—the 1840s—by Alexander Bain, who proposed using a system of electrical pendulums to send images over wires (Robinson, 1986). Within a few decades, the technology was adapted by the newspaper industry to send photos over wires, but the technology was limited to a small number of news organizations. The development of technical standards in the 1960s brought the fax machine to corporate America, which generally ignored the technology because few businesses knew of another business that had a fax machine.

Adoption of the fax took place two machines at a time, with those two usually being purchased to communicate with each other, but rarely used to communicate with additional receivers. By the 1980s, enough businesses had fax machines that could communicate with each other that many businesses started buying fax machines one at a time. As soon as the "critical mass" point was reached, fax machine adoption increased to the point that it became referred to as the first technology adopted out of fear of embarrassment that someone would ask, "What's your fax number?" (Wathne & Leos, 1993). In less than two years, the fax machine became a business necessity.

Social Information Processing

Another way to look at how and why people choose to use or not use a technology is social information processing. This theory begins by critiquing rational choice models, which presume that people make adoption decisions and other evaluations of technologies based upon objective characteristics of the technology. In order to understand social information processing, you first have to look at a few rational choice models.

One model, social presence theory, categorizes communication media based on a continuum of how the medium "facilitates awareness of the other person and interpersonal relationships during the interaction (Fulk, et al., 1990, p. 118)." Communication is most efficient when the social presence level of the medium best matches the interpersonal relationship required for the task at hand. For example, a person would break up with another person face to face instead of using a text message. Another rational choice model is information richness theory. In this theory, media are also arranged on a continuum of richness in four areas: speed of feedback, types of channels employed, personalness of source, and richness of language carried (Fulk, et al., 1990). Face-to-face communications is the highest in social presence and information richness. In information richness theory, the communication medium chosen is related to message ambiguity. If the message is ambiguous, then a richer medium is chosen. In this case, teaching someone how to dance would be better with a DVD that illustrates the steps rather than just an audio CD that describes the steps.

Social information processing theory goes beyond the rational choice models because it states that perceptions of media are "in part, subjective and socially constructed." Although people may use objective standards in choosing communication media, use is also determined by subjective factors such as the attitudes of coworkers about the media and vicarious learning, or watching others' experiences. Social influence is strongest in ambiguous situations. For example, the less people know about a medium, then the more likely they are to rely on social information in deciding to use it (Fulk, et al., 1987).

Think about whether you prefer a Macintosh or a Windows-based computer. Although you can probably list objective differences between the two, many of the important factors in your choice are based upon subjective factors such as which one is owned by friends and coworkers, the perceived usefulness of the computer, and advice you receive from people who can help you set up and maintain your computer. In the end, these social factors probably play a much more important role in your decision than "objective" factors such as processor speed, memory capacity, etc.

Impacts and Effects

Do video games make players violent? Do users seek out social networking sites for social interactions? These are some of the questions that theories of impacts or effects try to answer. To begin, Rogers (1986) provides a useful typology of impacts. Impacts can be grouped into three dichotomies: desirable and undesirable, direct and indirect, and anticipated and unanticipated. Desirable impacts are the functional impacts of a technology. For example a desirable impact of e-commerce is the ability to purchase goods and services from your home. An undesirable impact is one that is dysfunctional, such as credit card fraud. Direct impacts are changes that happen in immediate response to a technology. A direct impact of wireless telephony is the ability to make calls while driving. An indirect impact is a byproduct of the direct impact. To illustrate, laws against driving and using a handheld wireless phone are an impact of the direct impact described above. Anticipated impacts are the intended impacts of a technology. An anticipated impact of text messaging is to communicate without audio. An unanticipated impact is an unintended impact, such as people sending text messages in a movie theater and annoying other patrons. Often, the desirable, direct, and anticipated impacts are the same and are considered first. Then, the undesirable, indirect, and unanticipated impacts are noted later.

Here is an example using e-mail. A desirable, anticipated, and direct impact of e-mail is to be able to quickly send a message to multiple people at the same time. An undesirable, indirect, and unanticipated impact of e-mail is spam—unwanted e-mail clogging the inboxes of millions of users.

Uses and Gratifications

Uses and gratifications research is a descriptive approach that gives insight into what people do with technology. This approach sees the users as actively seeking to use different media to fulfill different needs (Rubin, 2002). The perspective focuses on "(1) the social and psychological origins of (2) needs, which generate (3) expectations of (4) the mass media or other sources, which lead to (5) differential patterns of media exposure (or engagement in other activities), resulting in (6) needs gratifications and (7) other consequences, perhaps mostly unintended ones" (Katz, et al., 1974, p. 20).

Uses and gratification research surveys audiences about why they choose to use different types of media. For example, uses and gratifications of television studies have found that people watch television for information, relaxation, to pass time, by habit, excitement, and for social utility (Rubin, 2002). This approach is also useful for comparing the uses and gratifications between media, as illustrated by studies of the World Wide Web (WWW) and television gratifications that found that, although there are some similarities such as entertainment and to pass time, they are also very different on other variables such as companionship, where the Web was much lower than for television (Ferguson & Perse, 2000). Uses and gratifications studies have examined a multitude of communication technologies including mobile phones (Wei, 2006), radio (Towers, 1987), and satellite television (Etefa, 2005).

Media System Dependency Theory

Often confused with uses and gratifications, media system dependency theory is "an ecological theory that attempts to explore and explain the role of media in society by examining dependency relations within and across levels of analysis" (Grant, et al., 1991, p. 774). The key to this theory is the focus it provides on the dependency relationships that result from the interplay between resources and goals. The theory suggests that, in order to understand the role of a medium, you have to look at relationships at multiple levels of analysis, including the individual level—the audience, the organizational level, the media system level, and society in

general. These dependency relationships can by symmetrical or asymmetrical. For example, the dependency relationship between audiences and network television is asymmetrical because an individual audience member may depend more on network television to reach his or her goal than the television networks depend on that one audience member to reach their goals.

A typology of individual media dependency relations was developed by Ball-Rokeach & DeFleur (1976) to help understand the range of goals that individuals have when they use the media. There are six dimensions: social understanding, self-understanding, action orientation, interaction orientation, solitary play, and social play. Social understanding is learning about the world around you, while self-understanding is learning about yourself. Action orientation is learning about specific behaviors, while interaction orientation is about learning about specific behaviors involving other people. Solitary play is entertaining yourself alone, while social play is using media as a focus for social interaction. Research on individual media system dependency relationships has demonstrated that people have different dependency relationships with different media. For example, Meadows (1997) found that women had stronger social understanding dependencies for television than magazines, but stronger self-understanding dependencies for magazines than television.

In the early days of television shopping (when it was considered "new technology"), Grant, et al. (1991) applied media system dependency theory to the phenomenon. Their analysis explored two dimensions: how TV shopping changed organizational dependency relations within the television industry and how and why individual users watched television shopping programs. By applying a theory that addressed multiple levels of analysis, a greater understanding of the new technology was obtained than if a theory that focused on only one level had been applied.

Social Learning Theory/Social Cognitive Theory

Social learning theory focuses on how people learn by modeling others (Bandura, 2001). This observational learning occurs when watching another person model the behavior. It also happens with symbolic modeling, modeling that happens by watching the behavior modeled on a television or computer screen. So, a person can learn how to fry an egg by watching another person fry an egg in person or on a video.

Learning happens within a social context. People learn by watching others, but they may or may not perform the behavior. Learning happens, though, whether the behavior is imitated or not. Reinforcement and punishment play a role in whether or not the modeled behavior is performed. If the behavior is reinforced, then the learner is more likely to perform the behavior. For example, if a student is successful using online resources for a presentation, other students watching the presentation will be more likely to use online resources. On the other hand, if the action is punished, then the modeling is less likely to result in the behavior. To illustrate, if a character drives drunk and gets arrested on a television program, then that modeled behavior is less likely to be performed by viewers of that program.

Reinforcement and punishment is not that simple though. This is where cognition comes in—learners think about the consequences of performing that behavior. This is why a person may play Grand Theft Auto and steal cars in the videogame, but will not then go out and steal a car in real life. Self-regulation is an important factor. Self-efficacy is another important dimension: learners must believe that they can perform the behavior.

Social learning/cognitive theory, then, is a useful framework for examining not only the effects of communication media, but also the adoption of communication technologies (Bandura, 2001). The content that is consumed through communication technologies contains symbolic models of behavior that are both functional and dysfunctional. If viewers model the behavior in the content, then some form of observational learning is occurring. A lot of advertising works this way. A movie star uses a new shampoo and then is admired by others. This message models a positive reinforcement of using the shampoo. Cognitively, the viewer then thinks about the consequences of using the shampoo. Modeling can happen with live models and symbolic models. For example, a person can watch another playing Wii bowling, a videogame where the player has to manipulate the controller to mimic rolling the ball. Their avatar in the game also models the bowling action. The other player considers the consequences of this modeling. In addition, if the other person had not played with this gaming system, watching the other person play with the Wii and enjoy the experience will make it more likely that he or she will adopt the system. Therefore, social learning/cognitive theory can be used to facilitate the adoption of new technologies and to understand why some technologies are adopted and why some are adopted faster than others (Bandura, 2001).

Economic Theories

Thus far, the theories and perspectives discussed have dealt mainly with individual users and communication technologies. How do users decide to adopt a technology? What impacts will a technology have on a user? Theory, though, can also be applied to organizational infrastructure and the overall technology market. Here, two approaches will be addressed: the theory of the long tail that presents a new way of looking at digital content and how it is distributed and sold, and the principle of relative constancy that examines what happens to the marketplace when new media products are introduced.

The Theory of the Long Tail

Wired editor Chris Anderson developed the theory of the long tail. This theory begins with the realization that there are not any huge hit movies, television shows, and albums like there used to be. What counts as a hit TV show today, for example, would be a failed show just 15 years ago. One of the reasons for this is choice: 40 years ago viewers had a choice of only a few television channels.

Today, you could have hundreds of channels of video programming on cable or satellite and limitless amounts of video programming on the Internet. You have a lot more choice. New communication technologies are giving users access to niche content. There is more music, video, video games, news, etc. than ever before because the distribution is no longer limited to the traditional mass media of over-the-air broadcasting, newspapers, etc. The theory states that, "our culture and economy are increasingly shifting away from a focus on a relatively small number of 'hits' at the headend of the demand curve and toward a huge number of niches in the tail" (Anderson, n.d.). Figure 3.3 shows a traditional demand curve; most of the hits are at the head of the curve, but there is still demand as you go into the tail. There is a demand for niche content and there are opportunities for businesses that deliver content in the long tail.

Figure 3.3
The Long Tail

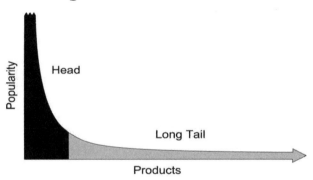

Source: Anderson (n.d.)

Both physical media and traditional retail have limitations. For example, there is only so much shelf space in the store. Therefore, the store, in order to maximize profit, is only going to stock the products most likely to sell. Digital content and distribution changes this. For example, Amazon and Netflix can have huge inventories of hard-to-find titles, as opposed to a bricks-and-mortar video rental store, which has to have duplicate inventories at each location. All digital services, such as the iTunes store, eliminate all physical media. You purchase and download the content digitally, and there is no need for a warehouse to store DVDs and CDs. Because of these efficiencies, these businesses

can better serve niche markets. Taken one at a time, these niche markets may not generate significant revenue but when they are aggregated, these markets are significant.

Anderson (2006) suggests rules for long tail businesses. Make everything available, lower the price, and help people find it. Traditional media are responding to these services. For example, Nintendo is making classic games available for download. Network television is putting up entire series of television programming on the Internet. The audience is changing, and expectations for content selection and availability are changing. The audience today, Anderson argues, wants what they want, when they want it, and how they want it.

The Principle of Relative Constancy

So now that people have all of this choice of content, delivery mode, etc., what happens to older media? Do people just keep adding new entertainment media, or do they adjust by dropping one form in favor of another? This question is at the core of the principle of relative constancy, which says that people spend a constant fraction of their disposable income on mass media over time. People do, however, alter their spending on mass media categories when new services/products are introduced (McCombs & Nolan, 1992). What this means is that, if a new media technology is introduced, in order for adoption to happen, the new technology has to be compelling enough for the adopter to give up something else. For example, a person who signs up for Netflix may spend less money on movie tickets. A satellite radio user will spend less money purchasing music downloads or CDs. So, when considering a new media technology, the relative advantage it has over existing service must be considered, along with other characteristics of the technology discussed earlier in this chapter. Remember, the money users spend on any new technology has to come from somewhere.

Conclusion

This chapter has provided a brief overview of several theoretical approaches to understanding communication technology. As you work through the book, consider theories of adoption, effects, and economics and how they can inform you about each technology and allow you to apply lessons from one technology to others. For more in-depth discussions of these theoretical approaches, check out the sources cited in the bibliography.

Bibliography

Ajzen, I. (1991). The theory of planned behavior. *Organizational Behavior and Human Decision Processes*, **50**, 179–211.

Ajzen, I. & Fishbein, M. (1980). *Understanding attitudes and predicting social behavior.* Englewood Cliffs, NJ: Prentice-Hall.

Anderson, C. (n.d.). *About me.* Retrieved from http://www.thelongtail.com/about.html.

Anderson, C. (2006). *The long tail: Why the future of business is selling less of more.* New York, NY: Hyperion.

Ball-Rokeach, S. & DeFleur, M. (1976). A dependency model of mass-media effects. *Communication Research, 3,* 1 3-21.

Bandura, A. (2001). Social cognitive theory of mass communication. *Media Psychology, 3,* 265-299.

Beniger, J. (1986). The information society: Technological and economic origins. In S. Ball-Rokeach & M. Cantor (Eds.). *Media, audience, and social structure.* Newbury Park, NJ: Sage, pp. 51-70.

Chau, P. Y. K. & Hu, P. J. (2002). Examining a model of information technology acceptance by individual professionals: An exploratory study. *Journal of Management Information Systems, 18*(4), 191–229.

Davis, F. D. (1986). *A technology acceptance model for empirically testing new end-user information systems: Theory and results.* Unpublished doctoral dissertation, Massachusetts Institute of Technology, Cambridge.

Davis, F. D., Bagozzi, R. P. & Warshaw, P. R. (1989). User acceptance of computer technology: A comparison of two theoretical models. *Management Science,* **35**(8), 982–1003.

Etefa, A. (2005). *Arabic satellite channels in the U.S.: Uses & gratifications.* Paper presented at the annual meeting of the International Communication Association, New York. Retrieved May 2, 2008 from http://www.allacademic.com/ meta/p14246_index.html.

Ferguson, D. & Perse, E. (2000, Spring). The World Wide Web as a functional alternative to television. *Journal of Broadcasting and Electronic Media.* 44 (2), 155-174.

Fishbein, M. & Ajzen, I. (1975). *Belief, attitude, intention and behavior: An introduction to theory and research.* Reading, MA: Addison-Wesley.

Fulk, J., Schmitz, J. & Steinfield, C. W. (1990). A social influence model of technology use. In J. Fulk & C. Steinfield (Eds.), *Organizations and communication technology.* Thousand Oaks, CA: Sage, pp. 117-140.

Fulk, J., Steinfield, C., Schmitz, J. & Power, J. (1987). A social information processing model of media use in organizations. *Communication Research, 14* (5), 529-552.

Gladwell, M. (2002). *The tipping point: How little things can make a big difference.* New York: Back Bay Books.

Grant, A., Guthrie, K. & Ball-Rokeach, S. (1991). Television shopping: A media system dependency perspective. *Communication Research, 18* (6), 773-798.

Jiang, J. J., Hsu, M. & Klein, G. (2000). E-commerce user behavior model: An empirical study. *Human Systems Management,* 19, 265–276.Mathieson, K. (1991). Predicting user intentions: Comparing the technology acceptance model with the theory of planned behavior. *Information Systems Research,* **2**, 173–191.

Katz, E., Blumler, J. & Gurevitch, M. (1974). Utilization of mass communication by the individual. In J. Blumler & E. Katz (Eds.). *The uses of mass communication: Current perspectives on gratifications research.* Beverly Hills: Sage.

Kottler, P. and Keller, K. L. (2011) *Marketing Management (14ᵗʰ ed.)* Englewood Cliffs, NJ: Prentice-Hall.

Markus, M. (1987, October). Toward a "critical mass" theory of interactive media. *Communication Research, 14* (5), 497-511.

McCombs, M. & Nolan, J. (1992, Summer). The relative constancy approach to consumer spending for media. *Journal of Media Economics,* 43-52.

Meadows, J. H. (1997, May). *Body image, women, and media: A media system dependency theory perspective.* Paper presented to the 1997 Mass Communication Division of the International Communication Association Annual Meeting, Montreal, Quebec, Canada.

Moore, G. (2001). *Crossing the Chasm.* New York: Harper Business.

Park, N., Lee, K. M. & Cheong, P. H. (2007). University instructors' acceptance of electronic courseware: An application of the technology acceptance model. *Journal of Computer-Mediated Communication*, **13**(1), Retrieved from http://jcmc.indiana.edu/vol13/issue1/park.html.

Robinson, L. (1986). *The facts on fax*. Dallas: Steve Davis Publishing.

Rogers, E. (1962). *Diffusion of Innovations*. New York: Free Press.

Rogers, E. (1986). *Communication technology: The new media in society*. New York: Free Press.

Rogers, E. (2003). *Diffusion of Innovations, 3rd Edition*. New York: Free Press.

Rubin, A. (2002). The uses-and-gratifications perspective of media effects. In J. Bryant & D. Zillmann (Eds.). *Media effects: Advances in theory and research*. Mahwah, NJ: Lawrence Earlbaum Associates, pp. 525-548.

Towers, W. (1987, May 18-21). *Replicating perceived helpfulness of radio news and some uses and gratifications*. Paper presented at the Annual Meeting of the Eastern Communication Association, Syracuse, New York.

Wathne, E. & Leos, C. R. (1993). Facsimile machines. In A. E. Grant & K. T. Wilkinson (Eds.). *Communication technology update: 1993-1994*. Austin: Technology Futures, Inc.

Wei, R. (2006). Staying connected while on the move. *New Media and Society, 8* (1), 53-72.

4

The *Structure* of the Communication Industries

August E. Grant, Ph.D.[*]

The first factor that many people consider when studying communication technologies is changes in the equipment and utility of the technology. But, as discussed in Chapter 1, it is equally important to study and understand all areas of the technology ecosystem. In editing the Communication Technology Update for the past 20 years, one factor stands out as having the greatest amount of change in the short term: the organizational infrastructure of the technology.

The continual flux in the organizational structure of communication industries makes this area the most dynamic area of technology to study. "New" technologies that make a major impact come along only a few times a decade. New products that make a major impact come along once or twice a year. Organizational shifts are constantly happening, making it almost impossible to know all of the players at any given time.

Even though the players are changing, the organizational structure of communication industries is relatively stable. The best way to understand the industry, given the rapid pace of acquisitions,

mergers, start-ups, and failures, is to understand its organizational functions. This chapter addresses the organizational structure and explores the functions of those industries, which will help you to understand the individual technologies discussed throughout this book.

In the process of using organizational functions to analyze specific technologies, do not forget to consider that these functions cross national as well as technological boundaries. Most hardware is designed in one country, manufactured in another, and sold around the globe. Although there are cultural and regulatory differences that are addressed in the individual technology chapters later in the book, the organizational functions discussed in this chapter are common internationally.

What's in a Name? The AT&T Story

A good illustration of the importance of understanding organizational functions comes from analyzing the history of AT&T, one of the biggest names in communication of all time. When you hear the name "AT&T," what do you think of? Your answer probably depends on how old you are and where you live. If you live in Florida, you may know AT&T as your local phone company. In New York, it is the name of one of the leading wireless

[*] J. Rion McKissick Professor of Journalism, College of Mass Communications and Information Studies, University of South Carolina (Columbia, South Carolina).

telephone companies. If you are older than 55, you might think of the company's old nick-name, "Ma Bell."

The Birth of AT&T

In the study of communication technology over the last century, no name is as prominent as AT&T. The company known today as AT&T is an awkward descendent of the company that once held a monopoly on long-distance telephone service and a near monopoly on local telephone service through the first four decades of the 20th century. The AT&T story is a story of visionaries, mergers, divestiture, and rebirth.

Alexander Graham Bell invented his version of the telephone in 1876, although historians note that he barely beat his competitors to the patent office. His invention soon became an important force in business communication, but diffusion of the telephone was inhibited by the fact that, within 20 years, thousands of entrepreneurs established competing companies to provide telephone service in major metropolitan areas. Initially, these telephone systems were not interconnected, making the choice of telephone company a difficult one, with some businesses needing two or more local phone providers to connect with their clients.

The visionary who solved the problem was Theodore Vail, who realized that the most important function was the interconnection of these telephone companies. As discussed in the following chapter, Vail led American Telephone & Telegraph to provide the needed interconnection, negotiating with the U.S. government to provide "universal service" under heavy regulation in return for the right to operate as a monopoly. Vail brought as many local telephone companies as he could into AT&T, which evolved under the eye of the federal government as a behemoth with three divisions:

- ✦ AT&T Long Lines—the company that had a virtual monopoly on long distance telephony in the United States.

- ✦ The Bell System—Local telephone companies providing service to 90% of U.S. subscribers.

- ✦ Western Electric—A manufacturing company that made equipment needed by the other two divisions, from telephones to switches. (Bell Labs was a part of Western Electric.)

As a monopoly that was generally regulated on a rate-of-return basis (making a fixed profit percentage), AT&T had little incentive—other than that provided by regulators—to hold down costs. The more the company spent, the more it had to charge to make its profit, which grew in proportion with expenses. As a result, the U.S. telephone industry became the envy of the world, known for "five nines" of reliability; that is, the telephone network was available 99.999% of the time. The company also spent millions every year on basic research, with its "Bell Labs" responsible for the invention of many of the most important technologies of the 20th century, including the transistor and the laser.

Divestiture

The monopoly suffered a series of challenges in the 1960s and 1970s that began to break AT&T's monopoly control. First, AT&T lost a suit brought by the "Hush-a-Phone" company, which made a plastic mouthpiece that fit over the AT&T telephone mouthpiece to make it easier to hear a call made in a noisy area (*Hush-a-phone v. AT&T*, 1955; *Hush-a-phone v. U.S.*, 1956). (The idea of a company having to win a lawsuit in order to sell such an innocent item might seem frivolous today, but this suit was the first major crack in AT&T's monopoly armor.) Soon, MCI successfully sued for the right to provide long-distance service between St. Louis and Chicago, allowing businesses to bypass AT&T's long lines (*Microwave Communications, Inc.*, 1969).

Since the 1920s, the Department of Justice (DOJ) had challenged aspects of AT&T's monopoly control, earning a series of consent decrees to limit AT&T's market power and constrain corporate behavior. By the 1970s, it was clear to the antitrust attorneys that AT&T's ownership of Western Electric inhibited innovation, and the DOJ attempted to force AT&T to divest itself of its manufacturing arm. In a surprising move, AT&T proposed a different divestiture, spinning off all of its local telephone companies into seven new "Baby Bells," keeping the now-competitive long distance service and manufacturing arms. The DOJ agreed, and a new AT&T was born (Dizard, 1989).

Cycles of Expansion & Contraction

After divestiture, the leaner, "new" AT&T attempted to compete in many markets with mixed success; AT&T long distance service remained a national leader, but few people bought the overpriced AT&T personal computers. In the meantime, the seven Baby Bells focused on serving their local markets, with most of them named after the region they served. Nynex served New York and states in the extreme northeast, Bell Atlantic served the mid-Atlantic states, BellSouth served the southeastern states, Ameritech served the Midwest, Southwestern Bell served the south central states, U S West served a set of western states, and Pacific Telesis served California and the far western states.

Over the next two decades, consolidation occurred among these Baby Bells. Nynex and Bell Atlantic merged to create Verizon. U S West was purchased by Qwest Communication and renamed after its new parent, which was, in turn, acquired by CenturyTel in 2010. As discussed below, Southwestern Bell was the most aggressive Baby Bell, ultimately reuniting more than half of the Baby Bells.

In the meantime, AT&T entered the 1990s with a repeating cycle of growth and decline. It acquired NCR Computers in 1991 and McCaw Communications (at that time the largest U.S. cellular telephone company) in 1993. Then, in 1995, it divested itself of its manufacturing arm (which became Lucent Technologies) and the computer company (which took the NCR name). It grew again in 1998 by acquiring TCI, the largest U.S. cable television company, renaming it AT&T Broadband, and then acquired another cable company, MediaOne. In 2001, it sold AT&T Broadband to Comcast, and it spun off its wireless interests into an independent company (AT&T Wireless), which was later acquired by Cingular (a wireless phone company co-owned by Baby Bells SBC and BellSouth) (AT&T, 2008).

The only parts of AT&T remaining were the long distance telephone network and the business services, resulting in a company that was a fraction the size of the AT&T behemoth that had a near monopoly on the telephone industry in the United States just two decades earlier.

Under the leadership of Edward Whitacre, Southwestern Bell became one of the most formidable players in the telecommunications industry. With a visionary style not seen in the telephone industry since the days of Theodore Vail, Whitacre led Southwestern Bell to acquire Baby Bells Pacific Telesis and Ameritech (and a handful of other, smaller telephone companies), renaming itself SBC. Ultimately, SBC merged with BellSouth and purchased what was left of AT&T, then renamed the company AT&T, an interesting case comparable to a child adopting its parent.

Today's AT&T is a dramatically different company with a dramatically different culture than its parent, but the company serves most of the same markets in a much more competitive environment. The lesson is that it is not enough to know the technologies or the company names; you also have to know the history of both in order to understand the role that company plays in the marketplace.

Functions within the Industries

The AT&T story is an extreme example of the complexity of communication industries. These industries are easier to understand by breaking their functions into categories that are common across most of the segments of these industries. Let's start by picking up the heart of the technology ecosystem introduced in Chapter 1, the hardware, software, and content. For this discussion, let's use the same definitions used in Chapter 1, with hardware referring to the physical equipment used, software referring to instructions used by the hardware to manipulate content, and content referring to the messages transmitted using these technologies. Some companies produce both hardware and software, ensuring compatibility between the equipment and programming, but few companies produce both equipment and content.

The next distinction has to be made between "production" and "distribution" of both equipment and content. As these names imply, companies involved in "production" engage in the manufacture of equipment or content, and companies involved in "distribution" are the intermediaries between production and consumers. It is a common practice for some companies to be involved in both production and distribution, but, as discussed below, a large number of companies choose to focus on one or the other.

These two dimensions interact, resulting in separate functions of equipment production, equipment distribution, content production, and content distribution. As discussed below, distribution can be further broken down into national and local distribution. The following section introduces each of these dimensions, which are applied in the subsequent section to help identify the role played by specific companies in communication industries.

One other note: These functions are hierarchical, with production coming before distribution in all cases. Let's say you are interested in creating a new type of telephone, perhaps a "high-definition telephone." You know that there is a market, and you want to be the person who sells it to consumers. But you cannot do so until someone first makes the device. Production always comes before distribution, but you cannot have successful production unless you also have distribution—hence the hierarchy in the model. Figure 4.1 illustrates the general pattern, using the U.S. television industry as an example.

Hardware Path

When you think of "hardware," you typically envision the equipment you handle to use a communication technology. But it is also important to note that there is a second type of hardware for most communication industries—the equipment used to make the messages. Although most consumers do not deal with this equipment, it plays a critical role in the system.

Production

Production hardware is usually more expensive and specialized than other types. Examples in the television industry include TV cameras, microphones, and editing equipment. A successful piece of production equipment might sell only a few hundred or a few thousand units, compared with tens of thousands to millions of units for consumer equipment. The profit margin on each piece of production equipment is usually much higher than on consumer equipment, making it a lucrative market for electronics manufacturing companies.

Consumer Hardware

Consumer hardware is the easiest to identify. It includes anything from a digital video recorder (DVR) to a mobile phone or DirecTV satellite dish. A common term used to identify consumer hardware in consumer electronics industries is "CPE," which stands for "customer premises equipment." An interesting side note is that many companies do not actually make their own products, but instead hire manufacturing facilities to make products they design, shipping them directly to distributors. For example, Microsoft does not manufacture the Xbox 360; Flextronics, Wistron, and Celestica do. As you consider communication technology hardware, consider the lesson from Chapter 1—people are not usually motivated to buy equipment because of the equipment itself, but because of the content it enables, from the pictures recorded on a camera to the conversations (voice and text!) on a wireless phone to the information and entertainment provided by a high-definition television (HDTV) receiver.

Figure 4.1
Structure of the Traditional Broadcast TV Industry

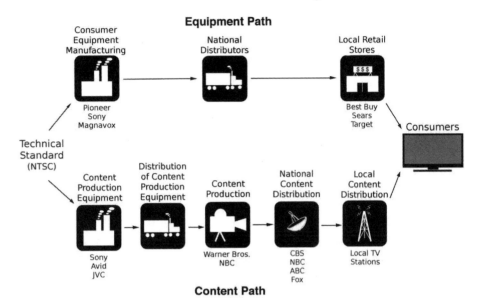

Source: R. Grant & G. Martin, 2012

Distribution

After a product is manufactured, it has to get to consumers. In the simplest case, the manufacturer sells directly to the consumer, perhaps through a company-owned store or a website. In most cases, however, a product will go through multiple organizations, most often with a wholesaler buying it from the manufacturer and selling it, with a mark-up, to a retail store, which also marks up the price before selling it to a consumer. The key point is that few manufacturers control their own distribution channels, instead relying on other companies to get their products to consumers.

Content Path: Production & Distribution

The process that media content goes through to get to consumers is a little more complicated than the process for hardware. The first step is the production of the content itself. Whether the product is movies, music, news, images, etc., some type of equipment must be manufactured and distributed to the individuals or companies who are going to create the content. (That hardware production and distribution goes through a similar process to the one discussed above.) The content must then be

created, duplicated, and distributed to consumers or other end users.

The distribution process for media content/ software follows the same pattern for hardware. Usually there will be multiple layers of distribution, a national wholesaler that sells the content to a local retailer, which in turn sells it to a consumer.

Disintermediation

Although many products go through multiple layers of distribution to get to consumers, information technologies have also been applied to reduce the complexity of distribution. The process of eliminating layers of distribution is called disintermediation (Kottler & Keller, 2005); examples abound of companies that use the Internet to get around traditional distribution systems to sell directly to consumers. Netflix is a great example. Traditionally, DVDs (digital videodiscs) of a movie would be sold by the studio to a national distributor, which would then deliver them to hundreds or thousands of individual movie rental stores, which would then rent or sell them to consumers. (Note: The largest video stores buy directly from the studio, handling both national and local distribution.) Netflix cuts one step out of the distribution process, directly bridging the link from the movie studio and the consumer. (As discussed below, iTunes serves the same function for the music industry, simplifying music distribution.) The result of getting rid of one "middleman" is greater profit for the companies involved, lower costs to the consumer, or both.

Illustrations: HDTV & HD Radio

The emergence of digital broadcasting provides two excellent illustrations of the complexity of the organizational structure of media industries. HDTV and its distant cousin HD radio have had a difficult time penetrating the market because of the need for so many organizational functions to be served before consumers can adopt the technology.

Let's start with the simpler one: HD radio. As illustrated in Figure 4.2, this technology allows existing radio stations to broadcast their current programming (albeit with much higher fidelity), so no changes are needed in the software production area of the model. The only change needed in the software path is that radio stations simply need to add a digital transmitter.

The complexity is related to the consumer hardware needed to receive HD radio signals. One set of companies needs to make the radios, another has to distribute the radios to retail stores and other distribution channels, and stores and distributors have to agree to sell them. The radio industry is therefore taking an active role in pushing diffusion of HD radios throughout the hardware path. In addition to airing thousands of radio commercials promoting HD radio, the industry is promoting distribution of HD radios in new cars (because so much radio listening is done in automobiles). As discussed in Chapter 10, adoption of HD radio has begun, but has been slow because listeners see little advantage in the new technology. However, if the number of receivers increases, broadcasters will have the incentive to begin broadcasting the additional channels available with HD. As with FM radio, programming and receiver sales have to *both* be in place before consumer adoption takes place. Also, as with FM, the technology may take decades to take off.

Figure 4.2
Structure of the HD Radio Industry

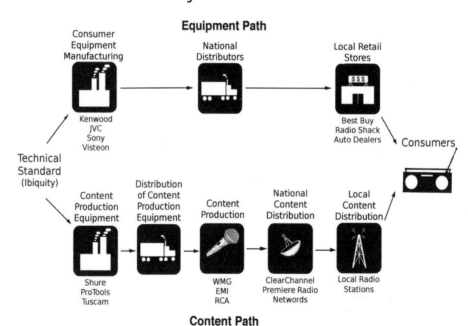

Source: R. Grant & G. Martin, 2012

Figure 4.3
Structure of the HDTV Industry

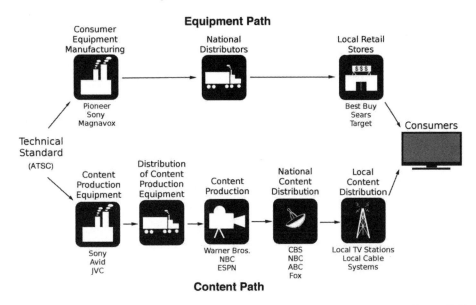

Source: R. Grant & G. Martin, 2012

The same structure is inherent in the adoption of HDTV, as illustrated in Figure 4.3. Before the first consumer adoption could take place, both programming and receivers (consumer hardware) had to be available. Because a high percentage of prime-time television programming was recorded on 35mm film at the time HDTV receivers first went on sale in the United States, that programming could easily be transmitted in high-definition, providing a nucleus of available programming. (On the other hand, local news and network programs shot on video required entirely new production and editing equipment before they could be distributed to consumers in high-definition.)

As discussed in Chapter 6, the big force behind the diffusion of HDTV and digital TV was a set of regulations issued by the Federal Communications Commission (FCC) that first required stations in the largest markets to begin broadcasting digital signals, then required that all television receivers include the capability to receive digital signals, and finally required that all full-power analog television broadcasting cease on June 12, 2009. In short, the FCC implemented mandates ensuring production and distribution of digital television, easing the path toward both digital TV and HDTV.

From Target to iTunes

One of the best examples of the importance of distribution comes from an analysis of the popular music industry. Traditionally, music was recorded on CDs and audiotapes and shipped to retail stores for sale directly to consumers. At one time, the top three U.S. retailers of music were Target, Walmart, and Best Buy.

Once digital music formats that could be distributed over the Internet were introduced in the late 1990s, dozens of start-up companies created online stores to sell music directly to consumers. The problem was that few of these stores offered the top-selling music. Record companies were leery of the lack of control they had over digital distribution, leaving most of these companies to offer a marginal assortment of music. The situation changed in 2003 when Apple introduced the iTunes store to provide content for its iPods, which had sold slowly since appearing on the market in 2001. Apple obtained contracts with major record companies that allowed them to provide most of the music that was in high demand. Initially, record companies resisted the iTunes distribution model that allowed a consumer to buy a single song for $0.99; they preferred that a person have to buy an entire album of music for $13 to $20 to get the one or two songs he or she wanted. Record company delays spurred consumers to create and use file-sharing services that allowed listeners to get the music for free—and the record companies ended up losing lots of money. Soon, the $0.99 iTunes model began to look very attractive to the record companies, and they trusted Apple's digital rights management system to protect their music.

Today, as discussed in Chapter 18, iTunes is the number one music retailer in the United States. The music is similar, but the distribution of music today is dramatically different from what it was when this decade began. The change took years of experimentation, and the successful business model that emerged required cooperation from dozens of separate companies serving different roles in the production and distribution process.

Two more points should be made regarding distribution. First, there is typically more profit potential and less risk in being a distributor than a creator (of either hardware or software) because the investment is less and distributors typically earn a percentage of the value of what they sell. Second, distribution channels can become very complicated when multiple layers of distribution are involved; the easiest way to unravel these layers is simply to "follow the money."

Importance of Distribution

As the above discussion indicates, distributors are just as important to new communication technologies as manufacturers and service providers. When studying these technologies, and the reasons for success or failure, the distribution process (including the economics of distribution) must be examined as thoroughly as the product itself.

Diffusion Threshold

Analysis of the elements in Figure 4.1 reveals an interesting dimension—there cannot be any consumer adoption of a new technology until all of the production and distribution functions are served, along both the hardware and software paths. This observation adds a new dimension to Rogers'

(2003) diffusion theory, discussed in the previous chapter. The point at which all functions are served has been identified as the "diffusion threshold," the point at which diffusion of the technology can begin (Grant, 1990).

It is easier for a technology to "take off" and begin diffusing if a single company provides a number of different functions, perhaps combining production and distribution, or providing both national and local distribution. The technical term for owning multiple functions in an industry is "vertical integration," and a vertically integrated company has a disproportionate degree of power and control in the marketplace. Vertical integration is easier said than done, however, because the "core competencies" needed for production and distribution are so different. A company that is great at manufacturing may not have the resources needed to sell the product to end consumers.

Let's consider the newest innovation in radio, HD radio, again (also discussed in Chapter 10). A company such as JVC or Pioneer might handle the first level of distribution, from the manufacturing plant to the retail store, but they do not own and operate their own stores—that is a very different business. They are certainly not involved in owning the radio stations that broadcast HD radio signals; that is another set of organizations.

In order for HD radio to become popular, one organization (or set of organizations) has to make the radios, another has to get those radios into stores, a third has to operate the stores, a fourth has to make HD radio transmitters and technical equipment for radio stations, and a fifth has to operate the radio stations. (Fortunately, the content is already available in the form of existing music or talk radio, or even more organizations would have to be involved in order for the first user to be able to listen to HD radio or see any value in buying an HD radio receiver.)

Most companies that would like to grow are more interested in applying their core competencies by buying up competitors and commanding a greater market share, a process known as "horizontal integration." For example, it makes more sense for a company that makes radio receivers to grow by making other electronics rather than by buying radio stations. Similarly, a company that already owns radio stations will probably choose to grow by buying more radio stations rather than by starting to make and sell radios.

The complexity of the structure of most communication industries prevents any one company from serving every needed role. Because so many organizations have to be involved in providing a new technology, many new technologies end up failing. The lesson is that understanding how a new communication technology makes it to market requires comparatively little understanding of the technology itself compared with the understanding needed of the industry in general.

A "Blue" Lesson

One of the best examples of the need to understand (and perhaps exploit) all of the paths illustrated in Figure 4.1 comes from the earliest days of the personal computer. When the PC was invented in the 1970s, most manufacturers used their own operating systems, so that programs and content could not easily be transferred from one type of computer to other types. Many of these manufacturers realized that they needed to find a standard operating system that would allow the same programs and content to be used on computers from different manufacturers, and they agreed on an operating system called CP/M.

Before CP/M could become a standard, however, IBM, the largest U.S. computer manufacturer—mainframe computers, that is—decided to enter the personal computer market. "Big Blue," as IBM was known (for its blue logo and its dominance in mainframe computers, typewriters, and other business equipment) determined that its core competency was making hardware, and they looked for a company to provide them an operating system that would work on their computers. They chose a then-little-known operating system known as MS-DOS, from a small start-up company called Microsoft.

IBM's open architecture allowed other companies to make compatible computers, and dozens of companies entered the market to compete with Big Blue. For a time, IBM dominated the personal

computer market, but, over time, competitors steadily made inroads on the market. (Ultimately, IBM sold its personal computer manufacturing business in 2006 to Lenovo, a Chinese company.) The one thing that most of these competitors had in common was that they used Microsoft's operating systems. Microsoft grew…and grew…and grew. (It is also interesting to note that, although Microsoft has dominated the market for software with its operating systems and productivity software such as *Office*, it has been a consistent failure in most areas of hardware manufacturing. Notable failures include Microsoft's routers and home networking hardware, keyboards and mice, and WebTV hardware. The only major success Microsoft has had in manufacturing hardware is with its Xbox video game system, discussed in Chapter 16.)

The lesson is that there is opportunity in all areas of production and distribution of communication technologies. All aspects of production and distribution must be studied in order to understand communication technologies. Companies have to know their own core competencies, but a company can often improve its ability to introduce a new technology by controlling more than one function in the adoption path.

What are the Industries?

We need to begin our study of communication technologies by defining the industries involved in providing communication-related services in one form or another. Broadly speaking, these can be divided into:

✦ *Mass media*, including books, newspapers, periodicals, movies, radio, and television.

✦ *Telecommunications*, including networking and all kinds of telephony (landlines, long distance, wireless, and voice over Internet protocol).

✦ *Computers*, including hardware (desktops, laptops, tablets, etc.) and software.

✦ *Consumer electronics*, including audio and video electronics, video games, and cameras.

✦ *Internet*, including enabling equipment, network providers, content providers, and services.

These industries are introduced in Chapter 2 and individual chapters. At one point, these industries were distinct, with companies focusing on one or two industries. The opportunity provided by digital media and convergence enables companies to operate in numerous industries, and many companies are looking for synergies across industries. Figure 4.4 lists examples of well-known companies in the communication industries, some of which work across many industries, and some of which are (as of this writing) focused on a single industry. Part of the fun in reading this chart is seeing how much has changed since the book was printed in mid-2012.

There is a risk in discussing specific organizations in a book such as this one; in the time between when the book is written and when it is published, there are certain to be changes in the organizational structure of the industries. For example, as this chapter was being written in early 2012, Yahoo! had announced plans to distribute its own "channels" of television programming over the Internet. By the time you read this, that venture may have expanded or been abandoned, or Yahoo! itself might be acquired by another company.

Fortunately, mergers and takeovers of that magnitude do not happen that often—only a couple a year! The major players are more likely to acquire other companies than to be acquired, so it is fairly safe (but not completely safe) to identify the major players and then analyze the industries in which they are doing business. As in the AT&T story earlier in this chapter, the specific businesses a company is in can change dramatically over the course of a few years.

Figure 4.4
Examples of Major Communication Company Industries, 2012

	TV/Film/Video Production	TV/Film/Video Distribution	Print	Telephone	Wireless	Internet
AT&T		●●		●●●	●●●	●●
Disney	●●●	●●●	●			●●
Gannett	●	●●●	●●●			
Google		●			●	●●●
News Corp.	●●●	●●●	●●●			●●
Sony	●●●	●				●
Time Warner, Inc.	●●●	●	●			●
Time Warner Cable		●●●		●●		●●
Verizon				●●●	●●●	●●
Viacom	●●●	●●●	●			●●
Yahoo!		●				●●●

The number of dots is proportional to the importance of this business to each company.

Source: Grant (2012)

Future Trends

The focus of this book is on changing technologies. It should be clear that some of the most important changes to track are changes in the organizational structure of media industries. The remainder of this chapter projects organizational trends to watch to help you predict the trajectory of existing and future technologies.

Disappearing Newspapers

For decades, newspapers were the dominant mass medium, commanding revenues, consumer attention, and significant political and economic power. As the second decade of the 21st century is beginning, however, newspaper publishers are reconsidering their core business. Some have even predicted the demise of the printed newspaper completely, forcing newspaper companies to plan for digital distribution of their news and advertisements.

Before starting the countdown clock, it is necessary to define what we mean by a "newspaper publisher." If a newspaper publisher is defined as an organization that communicates and obtains revenue by smearing ink on dead trees, then we can easily predict a steady decline in that business. If, however, a newspaper publisher is defined as an organization that gathers news and advertising messages, distributing them via a wide range of available media, then newspaper publishers should be quite healthy through the century.

The current problem is that there is no comparable revenue model for delivery of news and advertising through new media that approaches the revenues available from smearing ink on dead trees. It is a bad news/good news situation. The bad news is that traditional newspaper readership and revenues are both declining. Readership is suffering because of competition from the Web and other new media, with younger cohorts increasingly ignoring print in favor of other news sources. Advertising revenues are suffering for two reasons. The decline in readership and competition from new media are impacting revenues from display advertising. More significant is the loss in revenues from classified advertising, which at one point comprised up to one-third of newspaper revenues.

The good news is that newspapers remain profitable, at least on a cash flow basis, with gross margins of 10% to 20%. This profit margin is one that many industries would envy. But many newspaper companies borrowed extensively to expand their reach, with interest payments often exceeding these gross profits. Stockholders in newspaper publishers have been used to much higher profit margins, and the stock prices of newspaper companies have been punished for the decline in profits.

Some companies such as Belo reacted by divesting themselves of their newspapers in favor of TV and new media investments. Some newspaper publishers are using the opportunity to buy up other newspapers; consider McClatchy's 2006 purchase of the majority of Knight-Ridder's newspapers (McClatchy, 2008).

Gannett, on the hand, is taking the boldest, and potentially the riskiest, strategy by aggressively transforming both their newspaper and television newsrooms into "Information Centers," where the goal is to be platform agnostic, getting news out in any available medium as quickly as possible. According to former Gannett CEO Craig Dubow, the goal was to deliver the news and content anywhere the consumer is, and then solve the revenue question later (Gahran, 2006). Gannett's approach is a risky one, but it follows the model that has worked for new media in the past—the revenue always follows the audience, and the companies that are first to reach an audience through a new medium are disproportionately likely to profit from their investments.

Advertiser-Supported Media

For advertiser-supported media organizations, the primary concern is the impact of the Internet and other new media on revenues. As discussed above, some of the loss in revenues is due to loss of advertising dollars (including classified advertising), but that loss is not experienced equally by all advertiser-supported media.

The Internet is especially attractive to advertisers because online advertising systems have the most comprehensive reporting of any advertising medium. For example, an advertiser using the Google AdWords system discussed in Chapter 1 gets comprehensive reports on the effectiveness of every message—but "effectiveness" is defined by these advertisers as an immediate response such as a click-through. As Grant and Wilkinson (2007) discuss, not all advertising is this type of "call-to-action" advertising. There is another type of advertising that is equally important—image advertising, which does not demand immediate results, but rather works over time to build brand identity and increase the likelihood of a future purchase.

Any medium can carry any type of advertising, but image advertising is more common on television (especially national television) and magazines, and call-to-action advertising is more common in newspapers. As a result, newspapers, at least in the short term, are more likely to be impacted by the increase in Internet advertising. Interestingly, local advertising is more likely to be call-to-action advertising, but local advertisers have been slower than national advertisers to move to the Internet, most likely because of the global reach of the Internet. This paradox could be seen as an opportunity for an entrepreneur wishing to earn a million or two by exploiting a new advertising market (Wilkinson, Grant & Fisher, 2012).

The "Mobile Revolution"

Another important trend that can help you analyze media organizations is the shift toward mobile communication technologies. Companies that are positioned to produce and distribute content and technology that further enable the "mobile revolution" are likely to have increased prospects for growth.

Areas to watch include mobile Internet access (involving new hardware and software, provided by a mixture of existing and new organizations), mobile advertising, new applications of GPS technology, and a host of new applications designed to take advantage of Internet access available anytime, anywhere.

Consumers—Time Spent Using Media

Another piece of good news for media organizations in general is the fact that the amount of time consumers are spending with media is increasing, with much of that increase coming from simultaneous media use (Papper, et al., 2009). Advertiser-supported media thus have more "audience" to sell, and subscription-based media have more prospects for revenue. Furthermore, new technologies are increasingly targeting specific messages at specific consumers, increasing the efficiency of message delivery for advertisers and potentially reducing the clutter of irrelevant advertising for consumers. Already, advertising services such as Google's Double-Click and Google's AdWords provide ads that are targeted to a specific person or the specific content on a Web page, greatly increasing their effectiveness. Imagine a future where every commercial on TV that you see is targeted—and is interesting—to you! Technically, it is possible, but the lessons of previous technologies suggest that the road to customized advertising will be a meandering one.

Principle of Relative Constancy

On the other hand, the potential revenue from consumers is limited by the fact that consumers devote a limited proportion of their disposable income to media, the phenomenon discussed in Chapter 3 as the "Principle of Relative Constancy." The implication is that emerging companies and technologies have to wrest market share and revenue from established companies. To do that, they cannot be just as good as the incumbents. Rather, they have to be faster, smaller, less expensive, more versatile, or in some way better so that consumers will have the motivation to shift spending from existing media.

Conclusions

The structure of the media system may be the most dynamic area in the study of new communication technologies, with new industries and organizations constantly emerging and merging. In the following chapters, organizational developments are therefore given a significant amount of attention. Be warned, however; between the time these chapters are written and published, there is likely to be some change in the organizational structure of each technology discussed in this book.

To keep up with these developments, visit the *Communication Technology Update and Fundamentals* home page at www.tfi.com/ctu.

Bibliography

AT&T. (2008). *Milestones in AT&T history*. Retrieved from http://www.corp.att.com/history/ milestones.html.

Dizard, W. (1989). *The coming information age: An overview of technology, economics, and politics, 2nd ed*. New York: Longman.

Gahran, A. (2006). Gannett "Information Centers"—Good for daily journalism? *Poynter Online E-Media Tidbits*. Retrieved May 4, 2008 from http://www.poynter.org/dg.lts/id.31/aid.113411/column.htm.

Grant, A. E. (1990, April). The "pre-diffusion of HDTV: Organizational factors and the "diffusion threshold. Paper presented to the Annual Convention of the Broadcast Education Association, Atlanta.

Grant, A. E. & Wilkinson, J. S. (2007, February). Lessons for communication technologies from Web advertising. Paper presented to the Mid-Winter Conference of the Association of Educators in Journalism and Mass Communication, Reno.

Hush-A-Phone Corp. v. AT&T, et al. (1955). FCC Docket No. 9189. Decision and order (1955). 20 FCC 391.

Hush-A-Phone Corp. v. United States. (1956). 238 F. 2d 266 (D.C. Cir.). Decision and order on remand (1957). 22 FCC 112.

Kottler, P. & Keller, K. L. (2005). *Marketing management, 12th ed*. Englewood Cliffs, NJ: Prentice-Hall.

McClatchy. (2008). *About the McClatchy Company*. Retrieved from http://www.mcclatchy.com/100/story/ 179.html.

Microwave Communications, Inc. (1969). FCC Docket No. 16509. Decision, 18 FCC 2d 953.

Meyer, P. (2006). *The vanishing newspaper: Saving journalism in the information age*. Columbia, MO: University of Missouri Press.

Papper, R. E., Holmes, M. A. & Popovich, M. N. (2009). Middletown media studies II: Observing consumer interactions with media. In A. E. Grant & J. S. Wilkinson (Eds.) *Understanding media convergence: The state of the field*. New York: Oxford.

Rogers, E. M. (2003). *Diffusion of innovations, 5th ed*. New York: Free Press.

Wilkinson, J.S., Grant, A. E. & Fisher, D. J. (2012). *Principles of convergent journalism (2nd ed.)*. New York: Oxford University Press.

5

Communication Policy & Technology

Lon Berquist, M.A.[*]

Throughout its history, U.S. communication policy has been shaped by evolving communication technologies. As a new communication technology is introduced into society, it is often preceded by an idealized vision, or Blue Sky perspective, of how the technology will positively impact economic opportunities, democratic participation, and social inclusion. Due, in part, to this perspective, government policymakers traditionally look for policies and regulations that will foster the wide diffusion of the emerging technology. At the same time, however, U.S. policy typically displays a light regulatory touch, promoting a free-market approach that attempts to balance the economic interests of media and communication industries, the First Amendment, and the rights of citizens.

Indeed, much of the recent impetus for media deregulation was directly related to communication technologies as "technological plenty is forcing a widespread reconsideration of the role competition can play in broadcast regulation" (Fowler & Brenner, 1982, p. 209). From a theoretical perspective, some see new communication technologies as technologies of freedom where "freedom is fostered when the means of communication are dispersed, decentralized, and easily available" (Pool, 1983, p. 5). Others fear technologies favor government and private interests and become technologies of

control (Gandy, 1989). Still others argue that technologies are merely neutral in how they shape society. No matter the perspective, the purpose of policy and regulation is to allow society to shape the use of communication technologies to best serve the citizenry.

Background

The First Amendment is a particularly important component of U.S. communication policy, balancing freedom of the press with the free speech rights of citizens. The First Amendment was created at a time when the most sophisticated communication technology was the printing press. Over time, the notion of "press" has evolved with the introduction of new communication technologies. The First Amendment has evolved as well, with varying degrees of protection for the traditional press, broadcasting, cable television, and the Internet.

Communication policy is essentially the balancing of national interests and the interests of the communications industry (van Cuilenburg & McQuail, 2003). In the United States, communication policy is often shaped in reaction to the development of a new technology. As a result, policies vary according to the particular communication policy regime: press, common carrier, broadcasting, cable TV, and the Internet. Napoli (2001) characterizes this policy tendency as a "technologically particularistic" approach leading to distinct policy and regulatory structures for each new technology.

[*] Telecommunications and Information Policy Institute, University of Texas at Austin (Austin, Texas).

Thus, the result is differing First Amendment protections for the printed press, broadcasting, cable television, and the Internet (Pool, 1983).

In addition to distinct policy regimes based on technology, scholars have recognized differing types of regulation that impact programming, the industry market and economics, and the transmission and delivery of programming and information. These include content regulation, structural regulation, and technical regulation. Content regulation refers to the degree to which a particular industry enjoys First Amendment protection. For example, in the United States, the press is recognized as having the most First Amendment protection, and there certainly is no regulatory agency to oversee printing. Cable television has limited First Amendment protection, while broadcasting has the most limitations on its First Amendment rights. This regulation is apparent in the type of programming rules and regulations imposed by the Federal Communication Commission (FCC) on broadcast programming that is not imposed on cable television programming.

Structural regulation addresses market power within (horizontal integration) and across (vertical integration) media industries. Federal media policy has long established the need to promote diversity of programming by promoting diversity of ownership. The *Telecommunications Act of 1996* changed media ownership limits for the national and local market power of radio, television, and cable television industries; however, the FCC is given the authority to review and revise these rules. Structural regulation includes limitations or permissions to enter communication markets. For example, the *Telecommunications Act of 1996* opened up the video distribution and telephony markets by allowing telephone companies to provide cable television service and for cable television systems to offer telephone service (Parsons & Frieden, 1998).

Technical regulation needs prompted the initial development of U.S. communication regulation in the 1920s, as the fledgling radio industry suffered from signal interference while numerous stations transmitted without any government referee (Starr, 2004). Under FCC regulation, broadcast licensees are allowed to transmit at a certain power, or wattage, on a precise frequency within a particular market. Cable television systems and satellite transmission also follow some technical regulation to prevent signal interference.

Finally, in addition to technology-based policy regimes and regulation types, communication policy is guided by varying jurisdictional regulatory bodies. Given the global nature of satellites, both international (International Telecommunications Union) and national (FCC) regulatory commissions have a vested interest in satellite transmission. Regulation of U.S. broadcasting is exclusively the domain of the federal government through the FCC. The telephone industry is regulated primarily at the federal level through the FCC, but also with regulations imposed by state public utility commissions. Cable television, initially regulated through local municipal franchises, is regulated both at the federal level and the local municipal level (Parsons & Frieden, 1998). Increasingly, however, state governments are developing statewide cable television franchises, preempting local franchises (Eleff, 2006).

The Evolution of Communication Technologies

Telegraph

Although the evolution of technologies has influenced the policymaking process in the United States, many of the fundamental characteristics of U.S. communication policy were established early in the history of communication technology deployment, starting with the telegraph. There was much debate on how best to develop the telegraph. For many congressmen and industry observers, the telegraph was viewed as a natural extension of the Post Office, while others favored government ownership based on the successful European model as the only way to counter the power of a private monopoly (DuBoff, 1984). In a prelude to the implementation of universal service for the telephone (and the current discussion of a "digital divide"), Congress decreed that, "Where the rates are high and facilities poor, as in this country, the number of persons who use the telegraph freely, is limited. Where the rates are low and the facilities are great, as in Europe, the telegraph is extensively used by all classes for all kinds of business" (Lubrano, 1997, p. 102).

Despite the initial dominance of Western Union, there were over 50 separate telegraph companies operating in the United States in 1851. Interconnecting telegraph lines throughout the nation became a significant policy goal of federal, state, and local governments. No geographic area wanted to be disconnected from the telegraph network and its promise of enhanced communication and commerce. Eventually, in 1887, the *Interstate Commerce Act* was enacted, and the policy model of a regulated privately-owned communication system was initiated and formal federal regulation began. Early in the development of communication policy, the tradition of creating communications infrastructure through government aid to private profit-making entities was established (Winston, 1998).

Telephone

Similar to the development of the telegraph, the diffusion of the telephone was slowed by competing, unconnected companies serving their own interests. Although AT&T dominated most urban markets, many independent telephone operators and rural cooperatives provided service in smaller towns and rural areas. Since there was no interconnection among the various networks, some households and businesses were forced to have dual service in order to communicate (Starr, 2004). As telephone use spread in the early 1900s, states and municipalities began regulating and licensing operators as public utilities, although Congress authorized the Interstate Commerce Commission (ICC) to regulate interstate telephone service in 1910. Primarily an agency devoted to transportation issues, the ICC never became a major historical player in communication policy. However, two important phrases originated with the commission and the related *Transportation Act of 1920*. The term, common carrier, originally used to describe railroad transportation, was used to classify the

telegraph and eventually the telephone (Pool, 1983). Common carriage law required carriers to serve their customers without discrimination. The other notable phrase utilized in transportation regulation was a requirement to serve the "public interest, convenience, or necessity" (Napoli, 2001). This nebulous term was adopted in subsequent broadcast legislation, and continues to guide the FCC even today.

As telephone use increased, it became apparent that there was a need for greater interconnection among competing operators, or the development of some national unifying agreement. In 1907, AT&T President Theodore Vail promoted a policy with the slogan, "One system, one policy, universal service" (Starr, 2004, p. 207). There are conflicting accounts of Vail's motivations: whether it was a sincere call for a national network available to all, or merely a ploy to protect AT&T's growing power in the telephone industry (Napoli, 2001). Eventually, the national network envisioned by Vail became a reality, as AT&T was given the monopoly power, under strict regulatory control, to build and maintain local and long distance telephone service throughout the nation. Of course, this regulated monopoly was ended decades ago, but the concept of universal service as a significant component of communication policy remains today.

Broadcasting

While U.S. policymakers pursued an efficient national network for telephone operations, they developed radio broadcasting to primarily serve local markets. Before the federal government imposed regulatory control over radio broadcasting in 1927, the industry suffered from signal interference and an uncertain financial future. The *Federal Radio Act* imposed technical regulation on use of spectrum and power, allowing stations to develop a stable local presence. Despite First Amendment concerns about government regulation of radio, the scarcity of spectrum was considered an adequate rationale for licensing stations. In response to concerns about freedom of the press, the *Radio Act* prohibited censorship by the Radio Commission, but the stations understood that the power of the commission to license implied inherent censorship

(Pool, 1983). In 1934, Congress passed the *Communication Act of 1934*, combining regulation of telecommunications and broadcasting by instituting a new Federal Communications Commission.

The *Communication Act* essentially reiterated the regulatory thrust of the 1927 *Radio Act*, maintaining that broadcasters serve the public interest. This broad concept of "public interest" has stood as the guiding force in developing communication policy principles of competition, diversity, and localism (Napoli, 2001; Alexander & Brown, 2007). Rules and regulations established to serve the public interest for radio transferred to television when it entered the scene. Structural regulation limited ownership of stations, technical regulation required tight control of broadcast transmission, and indirect content regulation led to limitations on station broadcast of network programming and even fines for broadcast of indecent material (Pool, 1983). One of the most controversial content regulations was the vague Fairness Doctrine, established in 1949, that required broadcasters to present varying viewpoints on issues of public importance (Napoli, 2001). Despite broadcasters' challenges to FCC content regulation on First Amendment grounds, the courts defended the commission's Fairness Doctrine (*Red Lion Broadcasting v. FCC*, 1969) and its ability to limit network control over programming (*NBC v. United States*, 1943). In 1985, the FCC argued the Fairness Doctrine was no longer necessary given the increased media market competition, due in part to the emergence of new communication technologies (Napoli, 2001).

Historically, as technology advanced, the FCC sought ways to increase competition and diversity in broadcasting with AM radio, UHF television, low-power TV, low-power FM, and more recently, digital television.

Cable Television and Direct Broadcast Satellite

Since cable television began simply as a technology to retransmit distant broadcast signals to rural or remote locations, early systems sought permission or franchises from the local authorities to lay cable to reach homes. As cable grew, broadcasters became alarmed with companies making

revenue off their programming, and they lobbied against the new technology. Early on, copyrights became the major issue, as broadcasters complained that retransmission of their signals violated their copyrights. The courts sided with cable operators, but Congress passed compulsory license legislation that forced cable operators to pay royalty fees to broadcasters (Pool, 1983). Because cable television did not utilize the public airwaves, courts rebuffed the FCC's attempt to regulate cable.

In the 1980s, the number of cable systems exploded and the practice of franchising cable systems increasingly was criticized by the cable industry as cities demanded more concessions in return for granting rights-of-way access and exclusive multi-year franchises. The *Cable Communications Act of 1984* was passed to formalize the municipal franchising process while limiting some of their rate regulation authority. The act also authorized the FCC to evaluate cable competition within markets (Parsons & Frieden, 1998).

After that, cable rates increased dramatically. Congress reacted with the *Cable Television Consumer Protection and Competition Act of 1992*. With the 1992 Cable Act, rate regulation returned with the FCC given authority to regulate basic cable rates. To protect broadcasters and localism principles, the act included "must carry" and "retransmission consent" rules that allowed broadcasters to negotiate with cable systems for carriage (discussed in more detail in Chapter 7). Although challenged on First Amendment grounds, the courts eventually found that the FCC had a legitimate interest in protecting local broadcasters (*Turner Broadcasting v. FCC*, 1997).

To support the development of direct broadcast satellites (DBS), the 1992 act prohibited cable television programmers from withholding channels from DBS and other prospective competitors. As with cable television, DBS operators have been subject to must-carry and retransmission consent rules. The *1999 Satellite Home Viewers Improvement Act* (SHIVA) required and, more recently, the *Satellite Home Viewer Extension and Reauthorization Act* (SHVER) reconfirmed that DBS operators must carry all local broadcast signals within a local market if they choose to carry one (FCC, 2005). DBS operators challenged this in court, but as in *Turner Broadcasting v. FCC*, the courts upheld the FCC rule (Frieden, 2005).

Policies to promote the development of cable television and direct broadcast satellites have become important components of the desire to enhance media competition and video program diversity, while at the same time preserving localism principles within media markets.

Convergence and the Internet

The *Telecommunications Act of 1996* was a significant recognition of the impact of technological innovation and convergence occurring within the media and telecommunications industries. Because of that recognition, Congress discontinued many of the cross-ownership and service restrictions that had prevented telephone operators from offering video service and cable systems from providing telephone service (Parsons & Frieden, 1998). The primary purpose of the 1996 Act was to "promote competition and reduce regulation in order to secure lower prices and higher-quality service for American telecommunications consumers and encourage the rapid deployment of new telecommunications technologies" (*Telecommunications Act of 1996*). Competition was expected by opening up local markets to facilities-based competition and deregulating rates for cable television and telephone service to let the market work its magic. The 1996 Act also opened up competition in the local exchange telephone markets and loosened a range of media ownership restrictions.

In 1996, the Internet was a growing phenomenon, and some in Congress were concerned with the adult content available online. In response, along with passing the act, Congress passed the *Communication Decency Act* (CDA) to make it a felony to transmit obscene or indecent material to minors. The Supreme Court struck down the CDA on First Amendment grounds in *Reno v. ACLU* (Napoli, 2001). Congress continued to pursue a law protecting children from harmful material on the Internet with the *Child Online Protection Act* (COPA), passed in 1998; however, federal courts have found it, too, unconstitutional due to First Amendment concerns (McCullagh, 2007). It is noteworthy that the courts consider the Internet's First Amendment protection more similar to the press, rather than broadcasting or telecommunications (Warner, 2008).

Similarly, from a regulatory perspective, the Internet does not fall under any traditional regulatory regime such as telecommunications, broadcasting, or cable television. Instead, the Internet is considered an "information service" and therefore not subject to regulation (Oxman, 1999). There are, however, policies in place that indirectly impact the Internet. For example, section 706 of the *Telecommunications Act of 1996* requires the FCC to "encourage the deployment on a reasonable and timely basis of advanced telecommunications capability to all Americans," with advanced telecommunications essentially referring to broadband Internet connectivity (Grant & Berquist, 2000).

Recent Developments

Broadband

In response to a weakening U.S. economy, Congress passed the American Recovery and Reinvestment Act (ARRA) of 2009. Stimulus funds were appropriated for a wide range of infrastructure grants, including broadband, to foster economic development. Congress earmarked $7.2 billion to encourage broadband deployment, particularly in unserved and underserved regions of the country. The U.S. Department of Agriculture Rural Utility Service (RUS) was provided with $2.5 billion to award Broadband Initiatives Program (BIP) grants, while the National Telecommunications and Information Administration (NTIA) was funded with $4.7 billion to award Broadband Technology Opportunity Program (BTOP) grants. In addition, Congress appropriated funding for the Broadband Data Improvement Act, legislation that was approved during the Bush Administration in 2008 but lacked the necessary funding for implementation. Finally, as part of ARRA, Congress directed the FCC to develop a *National Broadband Plan* that addressed broadband deployment, adoption, affordability, and the use of broadband to advance healthcare, education, civic participation, energy, public safety, job creation, and investment.

While developing the comprehensive broadband plan, the FCC released its periodic broadband progress report, required under section 706 of the *Telecommunications Act of 1996*. Departing from the favorable projections in previous progress reports, the FCC recognized that "broadband deployment to *all* Americans is not reasonable and timely" (FCC, 2010c, p. 3). In addition, the Commission revised the dated broadband benchmark of 200 Kb/s by redefining broadband as having download speeds of 4.0Mb/s and upload speeds of 1.0 Mb/s. The broadband plan, entitled *Connecting America: National Broadband Plan*, was released in 2010 and prominently declared that "Broadband is the great infrastructure challenge of the early 21st century" (FCC, 2010a, p. 19). The plan offered a direction for government partnership with the private sector to innovate the broadband ecosystem and advance "consumer welfare, civic participation, public safety and homeland security, community development, healthcare delivery, energy independence and efficiency, education, employee training, private sector investment, entrepreneurial activity, job creation and economic growth, and other national purposes" (FCC, 2010a, p. xi).

In preparing the *National Broadband Plan*, the FCC commissioned a number of studies to determine the current state of broadband deployment in the United States. In analyzing U.S. broadband adoption, the FCC determined 65% of U.S. adults use broadband (Horrigan, 2010); however, researchers forecast that regions around the country, particularly rural areas, will continue to suffer from poor broadband service due to lack of service options or slow broadband speeds (Atkinson & Schultz, 2009). In examining foreign broadband markets and their success with broadband deployment and enhanced bandwidth capability, the Berkman Center for Internet and Society (2009) suggested U.S. policymakers should consider more aggressive policies, adopted throughout Asia and Europe, to foster competition among U.S. broadband service providers.

International comparisons of broadband deployment confirm that the U.S. continues to lag in access to broadband capability. Broadband data from the Organisation for Economic Co-operation and Development (OECD) report the United States ranked 15th among developed nations for fixed wireline broadband penetration (see Table 5.1). Other OECD studies show the United States ranked a lowly 17th for average advertised download speed (29.4 Mb/s), with top-ranked Japan offering significantly greater broadband speed (156 Mb/s), followed by Sweden (102.8 Mb/s), Portugal (83.4 Mb/s), Slovenia (79.9 Mb/s), and Korea (76.9 Mb/s) (OECD, 2011).

The *National Broadband Plan* highlights a number of strategies and goals to connect the 100 million Americans who do not have broadband at home. Among the strategies are plans to:

✦ Design policies to ensure robust competition.

✦ Ensure efficient allocation and use of government-owned and government-influenced assets.

✦ Reform current universal service mechanisms to support deployment of broadband.

✦ Reform laws, policies, standards, and incentives to maximize the benefits of broadband for government priorities, such as public education and health care.

The targeted goals of the plan through 2020 include 1) at least 100 million homes should have affordable access to download speeds of 100 Mb/s and upload speeds of 50 Mb/s, 2) the United States should lead the world in mobile innovation with the fastest and most extensive wireless network in the world, 3) every American should have affordable access to robust broadband service, and the means and skills to subscribe, 4) every American community should have affordable access to at least 1 Gb/s broadband service to schools, hospitals, and government buildings, 5) every first responder should have access to a nationwide, wireless, interoperable broadband public safety network, and 6) every American should be able to use broadband to track and manage their real-time energy consumption (FCC, 2010a).

The most far-reaching components of the plan include freeing 500 MHz of wireless spectrum, including existing television frequencies, for wireless broadband use, and reforming the current telephone Universal Service Fund to support broadband deployment.

Universal Service Reform

For a hundred years, universal service policies have served the United States well, resulting in significant telephone subscription rates throughout the country. But telephone service, an indispensable technology for 20th century business and citizen use, has been displaced by an even more essential technology in the 21st century--broadband Internet access. Just as the universal deployment of telephone infrastructure was critical to foster business and citizen communication in the early 1900s, broadband has become a crucial infrastructure for the nation's economic development and civic engagement. However, nearly a third of Americans have not adopted broadband, and broadband deployment gaps in rural areas remain significant (FCC, 2011b). In response to uneven broadband deployment and adoption, the FCC has shifted most of the billions of dollars currently subsidizing voice networks in the Universal Service Fund (USF) to supporting broadband deployment. Two major programs have been introduced to modernize universal service in the United States: The Connect America Fund, and the Mobility Fund.

The Connect America Fund will provide $4.5 billion annually over six years to fund broadband and high-quality voice in geographic areas throughout the U.S. where private investment in communication is limited or absent. The funding will be released to telecommunications carriers in phases, with Phase I releasing $300 million in 2012 to connect broadband to 400,000 homes, businesses, and institutions that currently lack access to broadband. The Mobility Fund will target wireless availability in unserved regions of the nation by ensuring all areas of the country achieve 3G service, with enhanced opportunities for 4G data and voice service in the future (Gilroy, 2011).

The Connect America Fund and the Mobility Fund maintain the long tradition of government support for communication development, as intended by Congress in 1934 when they created the FCC to make "available...to all the people of the United States...a rapid, efficient, Nation-wide, and world-wide wire and radio communication service with adequate facilities at reasonable charges" (FCC, 2011a, p. 4). Ultimately the Connect America Fund is expected to connect 18 million unserved Americans to broadband, with the hope of creating 500,000 jobs and generating $50 billion in economic growth (FCC, 2011b).

Spectrum Reallocation

Wireless spectrum, or the "invisible infrastructure," that allows wireless communications, is rapidly facing a deficit as demand for mobile data continues to grow (FCC, 2010b). Mobile wireless connections have increased 160% from 2008 to 2010, while the average data per line has increased 500% (Executive Office of the President, 2012). The increase in wireless data traffic is projected to grow by a factor of 20 by 2015. Globally, the United States ranks 7th in wireless broadband penetration (See Table 5.2); however, mobile broadband speeds are much greater in most Asian and European countries due to greater spectrum availability and wireless technology (Executive Office of the President, 2012). In response to the U.S. spectrum crunch, the *National Broadband Plan* calls for freeing 500 MHz of spectrum for wireless broadband. President Obama also established a National Wireless Initiative for federal agencies to support the FCC in making available the 500MHz of spectrum before 2020 for mobile and fixed wireless broadband (The White House, 2010).

The FCC has begun the steps to repurpose spectrum for wireless broadband service by making spectrum from the 2.3 GHz, Mobile Satellite Service, and TV bands available for mobile broadband service. The Commission will make additional spectrum available for unlicensed wireless broadband by leveraging unused portions of the TV bands, or "white space" that might offer unique solutions for innovative developers of broadband service. Congress has supported the effort with passage of the Middle Class Tax Relief and Job Creation Act of 2012, including provisions from the Jumpstarting Opportunity with Broadband Spectrum (JOBS) Act of 2011 (Moore, 2012).

The spectrum reallocation will be accomplished through the FCC's authority to conduct incentive auctions where existing license holders, such as broadcasters, will relinquish spectrum in exchange for proceeds that will be shared with the Federal government. The scarcity of spectrum has led to significant yields in previous auctions because of high demand. From 1994-2009 there were 79 auctions for wireless spectrum resulting in $52.6 billion dollars for the federal government. In 2009, the Digital Television migration allowed over 50 MHz to be sold in the FCC's 700 MHz auction for $20 billion (Sprung, 2010).

Network Neutrality

In 2005, then-AT&T CEO Edward Whitacre, Jr. created a stir when he suggested Google and Vonage should not expect to use his pipes for free (Yang, 2005). Internet purists insist the Internet should remain open and unfettered, as originally designed, and decried the notion that broadband providers might discriminate by the type and amount of data content streaming through their pipes. Users of Internet service are concerned that, as more services become available via the Web such as video streaming and voice over IP (VoIP), Internet service providers (ISPs) will become gatekeepers limiting content and access to information (Gilroy, 2008).

In 2007, the FCC received complaints accusing Comcast of delaying Web traffic on its cable modem service for the popular file sharing site BitTorrent (Kang, 2008). Because of the uproar among consumer groups, the FCC held hearings on the issue and ordered Comcast to end its discriminatory network management practices (FCC, 2008). Although Comcast complied with the order and discontinued interfering with peer-to-peer traffic like BitTorrent, it challenged the FCC's authority in court. In April 2010, the U.S. Court of Appeals for the D.C. Circuit determined that the FCC had failed to show it had the statutory authority to regulate an Internet service provider's network practices and

vacated the order (*Comcast v. FCC*, 2010). Because broadband service is an unregulated information service, the FCC argued it had the power to regulate under its broad "ancillary" authority highlighted in Title I of the Telecommunications Act. The court's rejection of the FCC argument disheartened network neutrality proponents who feared the court's decision would encourage broadband service providers to restrict network data traffic, undermining the traditional openness of the Internet.

In evaluating the court decision, the FCC revisited net neutrality and determined it could establish rules for an open Internet through a combination of regulatory authority. First, since broadband is considered an information service under Title I, the Commission is directed under Section 706 of the *Telecommunications Act of 1996* to take action if broadband capability is not deployed in a reasonable and timely fashion. Second, under Title II of the Telecommunications Act, the FCC has a role in protecting consumers who receive broadband over telecommunications services. Third, Title III of the Telecommunications Act provides the FCC with the authority to license spectrum used to provide wireless broadband services, and last, Title IV gives the FCC authority to promote competition in video services (Gilroy, 2011).

The FCC Open Internet Rule was adopted in November 2010 and established three basic rules to ensure Internet providers do not restrict innovation on the Internet. The rules require Internet service providers to disclose information about their network management practices and commercial terms to consumers and content providers to ensure *transparency*. Internet service providers are also subject to *no blocking* requirements of lawful content and applications. Finally, to prevent *unreasonable discrimination*, broadband Internet providers cannot unreasonably discriminate in transmitting lawful network traffic over a consumer's Internet service.

In January, 2011, both Verizon Communications and Metro PSC filed lawsuits challenging the FCC's Open Internet Rule, and some members of Congress feel the FCC has overstepped its authority, resulting in a number of Bills attempting to restrict the FCC's network neutrality efforts (Gilroy, 2012). In contrast, open access advocates, such as the Open Internet Coalition, and a number of high technology corporations applaud the FCC's network neutrality efforts (Hill, 2010).

Piracy, Privacy and Censorship

According to the U.S. Chamber of Commerce, movie studios, record labels, and publishers lose $135 billion a year in revenues due to piracy and counterfeiting (Kang, 2011). To protect U.S. business, Congress has attempted to pass legislation that will offer remedies to restrict piracy of intellectual property. 2011 was a year of intense Congressional activity and lobbying with the introduction of the Preventing Real Online Threats to Economic, Creative and Theft of Intellectual Property Act (PROTECT IP ACT) in the Senate; and the introduction of the Stop Online Piracy Act (SOPA) in the House. The PROTECT IP ACT, or PIPA, would allow the government to seek a court order against a foreign website suspected of piracy, along with connected U.S. based domain name servers, search engines, Internet advertisers, or financial transaction providers. SOPA has similar restrictions as PIPA, but includes more stringent criminal penalties for online streaming of copyrighted material (Yeh, 2012). The provisions in both proposed Bills also allow for Internet Service Providers to use filters to prevent users from accessing websites which potentially infringe on copyright.

Opponents of PIPA and SOPA argue they hinder free speech and expression, have the potential to intrude on individual privacy, and will limit the traditional openness of the Internet. Technology professionals also claimed provisions in PIPA and SOPA would interfere with network security protections. To protest the PIPA and SOPA legislative proposals, prominent websites such as Wikipedia, Reddit, and Boing Boing conducted a global "blackout" of their sites on January 18, 2012. The international publicity of the Internet blackout empowered advocates and legislators opposed to the legislation, and efforts to pass the anti-piracy Bills have been postponed for now.

Table 5.1
International Fixed Broadband Penetration

Country	Broadband Penetration*
Netherlands	38.5
Switzerland	38.3
Denmark	37.7
Korea	36.0
Norway	34.9
France	33.8
Iceland	33.6
United Kingdom	32.6
Germany	32.6
Sweden	31.9
Luxembourg	31.7
Belgium	31.6
Canada	31.2
Finland	28.9
United States	27.3

* Fixed Broadband access per 100 inhabitants

Source: OECD (2011)

Table 5.2
International Wireless Broadband Penetration

Country	Broadband Penetration*
Korea	99.3
Sweden	93.6
Japan	80.0
Finland	79.1
Norway	76.4
Denmark	73.6
United States	65.5
Australia	64.8
Portugal	64.7
Czech Republic	54.9
Luxembourg	54.6
New Zealand	54.3
Ireland	54.2
Iceland	54.1
Poland	50.9

* Wireless Broadband access per 100 inhabitants

Source: OECD (2011)

Factors to Watch

Congress will continue to explore legislation attacking piracy and protecting the intellectual property rights of U.S. corporations. Advocates of an open Internet will ensure Congress maintains a balance of preserving the free flow of information with any regulations of Internet content. Some observers suggest the U.S. would be better served by seeking greater international cooperation to protect copyrights, rather than strict domestic regulation, since the Internet is global in nature (Jackson, 2012).

As the Federal Communications Commission implements its Open Internet Rule, the U.S. Court of Appeals will again consider the proper role, and the limits of FCC authority for regulating broadband service. Since the FCC's *National Broadband Plan* was authorized by Congress, the final direction of any significant broadband policy will be guided by Congressional action. Still, the plan offers one of the most significant communication policy plans in the history of the FCC, and the interaction of Congress, the FCC, and the communications industry will ultimately determine its fate. Some in Congress have expressed concerns about recent FCC actions and are exploring the FCC policymaking process as evident in the introduction of the FCC Reform Act of 2012 (Feinberg, 2012).

In 2009, as the *National Broadband Plan* was being written, the FCC discovered that 65% of Americans had broadband in the home. By 2011, broadband adoption had no significant increase in adoption with the National Telecommunications and Information Administration reporting that 68% of Americans subscribed to broadband (Horrigan, 2012). However, when examining the emerging mobile and fixed wireless broadband market, and the expected increase in spectrum available for broadband, the future looks promising.

As communication policy is reshaped to accommodate new technologies, policymakers must continue to explore ways to serve the public interest. In the current policy and regulatory environment, the promotion of broadband to enhance economic development and enrich civic life is undoubtedly in the public interest (Varona, 2009). As broadband supplants the telephone as the desired ubiquitous service, Theodore Vail's 1907 slogan of "one system, one policy, universal service" has been replaced with policies that promote many competing systems, using a variety of technologies, with the goal of universal service.

Bibliography

Alexander, P. J. & Brown, K. (2007). Policy making and policy tradeoffs: Broadcast media regulation in the United States. In P. Seabright & J. von Hagen (Eds.). *The economic regulation of broadcasting markets: Evolving technology and the challenges for policy*. Cambridge: Cambridge University Press.

Atkinson, R.C. & Schultz, I.E. (2009). Broadband in America: Where it is and where it is going (according to broadband service providers). Retrieved from http://broadband.gov/docs/Broadband_in_America.pdf.

Berkman Center for Internet and Society. (2009). Next generation connectivity: A review of broadband Internet transitions and policy from around the world. Retrieved from http://www.fcc.gov/stage/pdf/Berkman_Center_Broadband_Study_13Oct09.pdf.

The Broadband Data Improvement Act of 2008, Pub. L. 110-385, 122 Stat. 4096 (2008). Retrieved from http://www.ntia.doc.gov/advisory/onlinesafety/BroadbandData_PublicLaw110-385.pdf.

Comcast v. FCC. No. 08-1291 (D.C. Cir., 2010). Retrieved from http://hraunfoss.fcc.gov/edocs_public/attachmatch/DOC-297356A1.pdf.

DuBoff, R. B. (1984). The rise of communications regulation: The telegraph industry, 1844-1880. *Journal of Communication, 34* (3), 52-66.

Eleff, B. (2006, November). *New state cable TV franchising laws*. Minnesota House of Representatives Research Department. Retrieved from http://www.house.leg.state.mn.us/hrd/pubs/cablelaw.pdf.

Executive Office of the President: Council of Economic Advisors (2012, Feb. 12). *The economic benefits of new spectrum for wireless broadband*. Retrieved from http://www.whitehouse.gov/sites/default/files/cea_spectrum_report_2-21-2012.pdf.

Federal Communications Commission. (2005, September 8). *Retransmission consent and exclusivity rules: Report to Congress pursuant to section 208 of the Satellite Home Viewer Extension and Reauthorization Act of 2004*. Retrieved from http://hraunfoss.fcc.gov/edocs_public/attachmatch/DOC-260936A1.pdf.

Federal Communications Commission. (2008, August 20). *Memorandum opinion and order* (FCC 08-183). Broadband Industry Practices. Retrieved from http://hraunfoss.fcc.gov/edocs_public/attachmatch/FCC-08-183A1.pdf.

Federal Communications Commission. (2010a). *Connecting America: National broadband plan.* Retrieved from http://hraunfoss.fcc.gov/edocs_public/attachmatch/DOC-296935A1.pdf.

Federal Communications Commission. (2010b). *Mobile broadband: The benefits of additional spectrum.* OBI Technical Report. Retrieved from http://transition.fcc.gov/Daily_Releases/Daily_Business/2010/db1021/DOC-302324A1.pdf.

Federal Communications Commission. (2010c). *Sixth broadband deployment report* (FCC 10-129). Retrieved from http://transition.fcc.gov/Daily_Releases/Daily_Business/2011/db0331/FCC-10-129A1.pdf

Federal Communications Commission. (2011a). *Bringing broadband to rural America: Update to report on rural broadband strategy.* Retrieved from http://transition.fcc.gov/Daily_Releases/Daily_Business/2011/db0622/DOC-307877A1.pdf.

Federal Communications Commission. (2011b). FCC releases 'Connect America Fund" order to help expand broadband, create jobs, benefit consumers. Press Release. Retrieved from http://hraunfoss.fcc.gov/edocs_public/attachmatch/DOC-311095A1.pdf

Feinberg, A. (2012, March 27). Walden, Stearns argue FCC process bill locks in reforms. *The Hill.* Retrieved from http://thehill.com/blogs/hillicon-valley/technology/218453-walden-stearns-argue-fcc-process-bill-locks-in-reforms.

Fowler, M. S. & Brenner, D. L. (1982). A marketplace approach to broadcast regulation. *University of Texas Law Review 60* (207), 207-257.

Frieden, R. (2005, April). *Analog and digital must-carry obligations of cable and satellite television operators in the United States.* Retrieved from http://ssrn.com/abstract=704585.

Gandy, O. H. (1989). The surveillance society: Information technology and bureaucratic control. *Journal of Communication, 39* (3), 61-76.

Gilroy, A. A. (2008, Sept. 16). Net neutrality: Background and issues. *CRS Reports to Congress.* CRS Report RS22444. Retrieved from http://www.fas.org/sgp/crs/misc/RS22444.pdf.

Gilroy, A.A. (2011, June 30). Universal service fund: Background and options for reform. *CRS Reports to Congress.* CRS Report RL33979. Retrieved from http://www.fas.org/sgp/crs/misc/RL33979.pdf.

Gilroy, A.A. (2012, Feb. 12). Access to broadband networks: The net neutrality debate. *CRS Reports to Congress.* CRS Report R40616. Retrieved from http://www.fas.org/sgp/crs/misc/R40616.pdf

Grant, A. E. & Berquist, L. (2000). Telecommunications infrastructure and the city: Adapting to the convergence of technology and policy. In J. O. Wheeler, Y, Aoyama & B. Wharf (Eds.). *Cities in the telecommunications age: The fracturing of geographies.* New York: Routledge.

Horrigan, J. (2010). *Broadband adoption and use in America* (OBI Working Paper No. 1). Retrieved from http://hraunfoss.fcc.gov/edocs_public/attachmatch/DOC-296442A1.pdf.

Horrigan, J. (2012). Little movement since 2009 & stakeholders can do more to spur adoption. TechNet. Retrieved from http://www.technet.org/wp-content/uploads/2012/03/TechNet-NBP-Broadband-Report-3-20-2012-FINAL1.pdf.

Hill, K. (2010, June 18). FCC forges ahead with '3rd way' to broadband regulation. *E-commerce Times.* Retrieved from http://www.ecommercetimes.com/story/70238.html.

Jackson, W. (2012, Feb.). It's time to shelve SOPA, PIPA bills as anti-piracy remedies. *Government Technology.* 11.

Kang, C. (2008, March 28). Net neutrality's quiet crusader. *Washington Post,* D01.

Kang, C. (2011, Nov. 15). Web giants at odds with chamber over piracy bill. *Washington Post.* Retrieved from http://www.washingtonpost.com/business/economy/web-giants-at-odds-with-chamber-of-commerce-over-piracy-bill/2011/11/15/gIQAkY5hPN_story.html

Lubrano, A. (1997). *The telegraph: How technology innovation caused social change.* New York: Garland Publishing.

McCullagh, D. (2007, March 22). Net porn ban faces another legal setback. *C/NET News.* Retrieved from http://www.news.com/Net-porn-ban-faces-another-legal-setback/2100-1030_3-6169621.html.

Moore, L.K. (2012, Jan. 5). Spectrum policy in the age of broadband: Issues for Congress. *CRS Reports to Congress.* CRS Report R40674. Retrieved from http://www.fas.org/sgp/crs/misc/R40674.pdf.

Napoli, P. M. (2001). *Foundations of communications policy: Principles and process in the regulation of electronic media.* Cresskill, NJ: Hampton Press.

National Broadcasting Co. v. United States, 319 U.S. 190 (1949).

National Telecommunications and Information Administration. (2011, November). *Exploring the digital nation: Computer and Internet use at home.* Retrieved from http://www.ntia.doc.gov/files/ntia/publications/exploring_the_digital_nation_computer_and_internet_use_at_home_11092011.pdf.

Organisation for Economic Co-operation and Development. (2011). *OECD broadband portal.* Retrieved from http://www.oecd.org/document/54/0,3746,en_2649_34225_38690102_1_1_1_1,00.html.

Oxman, J. (1999). *The FCC and the unregulation of the Internet*. OPP Working Paper No. 31. Retrieved from http://www.fcc.gov/Bureaus/OPP/working_papers/oppwp31.pdf.

Parsons, P. R. & Frieden, R. M. (1998). *The cable and satellite television industries*. Needham Heights, MA: Allyn & Bacon.

Poirier, J. (2010, April 5). FCC forms strategy to defend broadband powers. *Reuters.com*. Retrieved from http://www.reuters.com/article/idUSTRE6341CB20100405.

Pool, I. S. (1983). *Technologies of freedom*. Cambridge, MA: Harvard University Press.

Red Lion Broadcasting Co. v. Federal Communications Commission, 395 U.S. 367 (1969).

Sprung, K. (2010). Broadcast v. broadband? A survey of the reallocation of broadcast spectrum for wireless broadband. *Media, Law & Policy, 19* (2), 238-249.

Stanton, L. (2012). Action on PIPA, SOPA postponed in wake of protest; Both sides vow to continue work on online copyright bills. *Telecommunications Reports, 78* (3). 3-7.

Starr, P. (2004). *The creation of the media*. New York: Basic Books.

Telecommunications Act of 1996, Pub. L. No. 104-104, 110 Stat. 56 (1996). Retrieved from http://transition.fcc.gov/Reports/tcom1996.pdf.

The White House. (2010, June 28). *Presidential memorandum: Unleashing the wireless broadband revolution*. Retrieved from http://www.whitehouse.gov/the-press-office/presidential-memorandum-unleashing-wireless-broadband-revolution

Turner Broadcasting System, Inc. v. FCC, 512 U.S. 622 (1997).

van Cuilenburg, J. & McQuail, D. (2003). Media policy paradigm shifts: Toward a new communications policy paradigm. *European Journal of Communication, 18* (2), 181-207.

Varona, A.E. (2009). Toward a broadband public interest standard. *Administrative Law Review, 61* (1), 1-136.

Warner, W. B. (2008). Networking and broadcasting in crisis. In R. E. Rice (Ed.), *Media ownership research and regulation*. Creskill, NJ: Hampton Press.

Winston, B. (1998). *Media technology and society: A history from the telegraph to the Internet*. New York: Routledge.

Yang, C. (2005, December 26). At stake: The net as we know it. *Business Week*, 38-39.

Yeh, B.T. (2012, Jan. 12). Online copyright infringement and counterfeiting legislation in the 112th Congress. *CRS Reports to Congress*. CRS Report R42112. Retrieved from http://www.kelleydrye.com/email/PIPASOPAandtheOPENAct.pdf

Electronic Mass Media

6

Digital Television & Video

Peter B. Seel, Ph.D.*

Why Study Digital Television & Video?

✦ Television is one of the most ubiquitous communication technologies.

✦ Technological advances are creating new ways to produce, distribute and view television programs.

✦ Television is increasingly delivered on mobile devices, changing not only where people watch TV but also how programming must be produced.

Digital television in the United States has an evolving name—*Over-The-Top* television—with OTT TV as the obligatory acronym. It should more accurately be called over-the-top **video** as the term refers to non-broadcast, Internet-streamed video content viewed on a digital display, but the confusion reflects the blurring of the line between broadcast/cable/DBS-delivered television and online streamed content (Hansell, 2009). Over-The-Top indicates that there is an increasingly popular means of accessing television and video content that is independent of traditional over-the-air (OTA) television and multichannel video programming distributors (MVPDs, which includes satellite TV services, cable companies, and telco providers).

* Peter B. Seel is Associate Professor, Department of Journalism and Technical Communication, Colorado State University (Fort Collins, Colorado).

However, much of the content consists of television programs previously broadcast (or cablecast) accessed on websites such as Hulu.com, in addition to streamed movies and television series from providers such as Netflix and Blockbuster. There is some confusion between OTT-delivery of motion media content and proprietary IPTV programming such as U-verse provided by AT&T in the U.S. (See Chapter 8 for more information on IPTV). In addition, the term "Over-The-Top" is unique to the U.S.—in the United Kingdom it is called "Connected" television. To move past this confusion, we suggest the introduction of an all-encompassing term: **Internet-Delivered Television** or **IDTV**. The use of this meta-term would subsume all OTT, Connected, and IPTV streamed programming and create a clear demarcation between this mode of reception and broadcast-cable-DBS delivery.

For the first time in 12 years, the number of U.S. television households declined: between 2011 and 2012, household penetration fell from 98.9 to 97.1 percent, with 114.7 million TV homes in 2012 (Nielsen, 2011). The Nielsen Company offered several rationales for this first significant decline in 62 years of measuring the size of the U.S. television audience. One factor was the ongoing global recession that reduced consumers' incomes and their ability to purchase new digital sets. Nielsen researchers also hypothesized that Over-The-Top viewing on multiple displays may be a key factor in the drop in the number of television households, especially among younger viewers who have forsaken cable and DBS subscriptions in favor of "free" IDTV (Nielsen, 2011).

Americans between the ages of 12 and 34 are spending less time watching traditional television in favor of viewing programs streamed on computers and mobile phones (Stelter, 2012). This is a shift with multi-billion-dollar consequences for traditional broadcasters as advertising campaigns target younger viewers watching multimedia online.

Most flat-screen displays larger than 42 inches sold in the U.S. in 2012 and beyond will be "smart" televisions that can easily display these motion media sources and websites such as Facebook and Twitter. At the 2012 Consumer Electronics Show in Las Vegas, Korean manufacturer Samsung introduced "Smart Hub" displays in multiple sizes that offer Kinect-type gesture control, voice control, and face recognition in accessing a panoply of Internet-delivered and MVPD-provided content (Sharwood, 2012). Remote controls for these displays can easily toggle between broadcast/cable/DBS content and Internet-streamed videos (see Figure 6.1). Older digital televisions can be easily connected to the Internet with specialized boxes provided by Roku and Apple or via Blu-ray players and most high-end game consoles.

Figure 6.1
Samsung's "Smart Hub" interface screen for its digital television displays.

Source: Samsung

Digital television displays and high-definition video recording are increasingly common features in mobile phones used by five billion people of the world's population of seven billion. Digital video cameras have also become more powerful and less expensive. An example is the $110 Samsung HMX-

W200 (see Figure 6.3) which records video at 1080p and is shockproof and waterproof. Digital storage for these cameras has also decreased in price while simultaneously increasing in capacity—a 16 GB SDHC memory card is now available for $16, at one dollar per Gigabyte. However, the prevalence of HD-quality recording in mobile devices is affecting the market for low-end, stand-alone video recorders. In 2011, Flip camera manufacturer Cisco Systems announced they were ceasing production, and in 2012, the Eastman Kodak Company filed for bankruptcy and indicated that the company was exiting the market for digital cameras (Richmond, 2012). The popular Kodak Zi-8 pocket HD camcorder will be a victim of this decision. Mobile phone models such as Apple's iPhone 4S feature eight Megapixel cameras that can acquire high-definition 1080p video images. Similar features in future 4G and 5G models means that anyone with a mobile phone will be able to shoot HD-quality video.

The democratization of "television" production generated by the explosion in the number of devices that can record digital video has created a world where 60 hours of video are uploaded every minute on YouTube and over four billion videos are viewed there each day (YouTube Statistics, 2012). The online distribution of digital video and television programming is an increasingly disruptive force to established broadcasters and program producers. They have responded by making their content available online for free or via subscription as increasing numbers of viewers seek to "pull" digital television content on request rather than watch at times when it is "pushed" as broadcast programming. Television news programs routinely feature video shot by bystanders, such as the swarm of tornadoes that hit the U.S. Midwest in February 2012. The increasing ubiquity of digital video recording capability also bodes well for the global free expression and exchange of ideas via the Internet. The expanding "universe" of digital television and video is being driven by improvements in high-definition video cameras for professional production and the simultaneous inclusion of higher-quality video capture capability in mobile phones.

Figures 6.2 and 6.3
Two contemporary high-definition cameras

The $65,000 Sony F65 CineAlta camera is used to shoot motion pictures and high-end television programs with 4K image resolution (2160 X 4096 pixels).

The $110 pocket Samsung HMX-W200 camera captures 1080p HD-quality videos and is also shockproof and waterproof (back and front are shown).

Sources: Sony and Samsung

Another key trend is the on-going global conversion from analog to digital television (DTV) technology. The United States completed its national conversion to digital broadcasting in June 2009; Japan will complete its transition in 2012, along with most European nations, and China plans to do so by 2015. At the outset of high-definition television (HDTV) development in the 1980s, there was hope that one global television standard might emerge, easing the need to perform format conversions for international program distribution. There are now multiple competing DTV standards based on regional affiliations and national political orientation. In many respects, global television has reverted to a Babel of competing digital formats reminiscent of the advent of analog color television. However, DTV programming in the widescreen 16:9 aspect ratio is now a commonplace sight in all nations that have made the conversion.

The good news for consumers is that digital television displays have become commodity products with prices dropping rapidly each year. In the United States, a consumer can purchase a 37-inch LCD digital television for $300—falling below the $10 per diagonal inch benchmark that was crossed in 2010.

Background

The global conversion from analog to digital television technology is the most significant change in television broadcast standards since color images were added in the 1960s. Digital television combines higher-resolution image quality with improved multi-channel audio, and new "smart" models include the ability to seamlessly integrate Internet-delivered "television" programming into these displays. In the United States, the Federal Communications Commission (FCC, 1998) defines DTV as "any technology that uses digital techniques to provide advanced television services such as high definition TV (HDTV), multiple standard definition TV (SDTV) and other advanced features and services" (p. 7420). One key attribute of digital technology is "scalability"—the ability to produce audio-visual quality as good (or as bad) as the viewer desires (or will tolerate). The two most common digital display options are:

✦ HDTV (high-definition television, scalable)

✦ SDTV (standard-definition television, scalable)

High-definition television (HDTV) represents the highest image and sound quality that can be transmitted through the air. It is defined by the FCC in the United States as a system that provides image quality approaching that of 35 mm motion picture film, that has an image resolution of approximately twice that of analog television, and has a picture aspect ratio of 16:9 (FCC, 1990) (see Table 6.1). Broadcast formats are described with a number signifying the number of scanning lines and a letter indicating whether these lines are scanned in order (progressive) or with alternating odd and even lines (interlaced). Thus, 1080i refers to a format with 1080 lines of information and interlaced scanning. The two most common HDTV formats are 1080i and 720p. SDTV, or standard-definition television, is another type of digital television technology that can be transmitted along with, or instead of, HDTV. Digital SDTV transmissions offer lower resolution (480p or 480i) than HDTV, and they are available in both narrowscreen and widescreen formats. Using digital video compression technology, it is feasible for U.S. broadcasters to transmit up to five SDTV signals instead of one HDTV signal within the allocated 6 MHz digital channel.

The development of multichannel SDTV broadcasting, called "multicasting," is an approach that some U.S. broadcasters at national and local levels have adopted, especially the Public Broadcasting Service (PBS). Many PBS stations broadcast two child-oriented SDTV channels in the daytime along with educational channels geared toward adults. Most public and commercial networks reserve true HDTV programming for evening prime-time hours.

Digital television programming can be accessed via over-the-air (OTA) fixed and mobile transmissions, through cable/telco/satellite multichannel video program distributors, and through Internet-delivered IDTV sites. IDTV is a "pull" technology in that viewers seek out a certain program and watch it in a video stream or as a downloaded file. OTA broadcasting is a "push" technology that transmits a digital program to millions of viewers at once. IDTV, like other forms of digital television, is a scalable technology that can be viewed as lower quality, highly compressed content be accessed in HDTV quality on sites such as Vimeo.com. IDTV and its subset IPTV are the subject of Chapter 8 in this text and, as noted above, are a rapidly growing method of accessing digital television programming as more viewers seek to watch their favorite shows on demand.

In the 1970s and 1980s, Japanese researchers at NHK (Japan Broadcasting Corporation) developed two related analog HDTV systems: an analog "Hi-Vision" *production* standard with 1125 scanning lines and 60 fields (30 frames) per second; and an analog "MUSE" *transmission* system with an original bandwidth of 9 MHz designed for satellite distribution throughout Japan. The decade between 1986 and 1996 was a significant era in the diffusion of HDTV technology in Japan, Europe, and the United States. There were a number of key events during this period that shaped advanced television technology and related industrial policies:

In 1986, the Japanese Hi-Vision system was rejected as a world HDTV production standard by the CCIR, a subgroup of the International Telecommunication Union (ITU). By 1988, a European research and development consortium, EUREKA EU-95, had created a competing system known as HD-MAC that featured 1250 widescreen scanning lines and 50 fields (25 frames) displayed per second (Dupagne & Seel, 1998).

In 1987, the FCC in the United States created the Advisory Committee on Advanced Television Service (ACATS). This committee was charged with investigating the policies, standards, and regulations that would facilitate the introduction of advanced television (ATV) services in the United States (FCC, 1987).

U.S. testing of analog ATV systems by ACATS was about to begin in 1990 when the General Instrument Corporation announced that it had perfected a method of digitally transmitting a high-definition signal. Ultimately, the three competitors (AT&T/Zenith, General Instrument/MIT, and Philips/Thomson/Sarnoff) merged into a consortium known as the Grand Alliance and developed a single digital broadcast system for ACATS evaluation (Brinkley, 1997).

The FCC adopted a number of key decisions during the ATV testing process that defined a national transition process from analog NTSC to an advanced digital television broadcast system:

✦ In 1990, the Commission outlined a *simulcast* strategy for the transition to an ATV standard (FCC, 1990). This strategy required that U.S. broadcasters transmit *both* the new ATV signal and the existing NTSC signal concurrently for a period of time, at the end of which all NTSC transmitters would be turned off.

Table 6.1

U.S. Advanced Television Systems Committee (ATSC) DTV Formats

Format	Active Lines	Horizontal Pixels	Aspect Ratio	Picture Rate*
HDTV	1080 lines	1920 pixels/line	16:9	60i, 30p, 24p
HDTV	720 lines	1280 pixels/line	16:9	60p, 30p, 24p
SDTV	480 lines	704 pixels/line	16:9 or 4:3	60i, 60p, 30p, 24p
SDTV	480 lines	640 pixels/line	4:3	60i, 60p, 30p, 24p

*In the picture rate column, "i" indicates interlace scan in television *fields*/second with two fields required per frame and "p" is progressive scan in *frames*/second.

Source: ATSC

✦ The Grand Alliance system was successfully tested in the summer of 1995, and a U.S. digital television standard based on that technology was recommended to the FCC by the Advisory Committee (Advisory Committee on Advanced Television Service, 1995).

✦ In May 1996, the FCC proposed the adoption of the *ATSC Digital Television (DTV) Standard* that specified 18 digital transmission variations as outlined in Table 6.1 (FCC, 1996).

In April 1997, the FCC defined how the United States would make the transition to DTV broadcasting and set December 31, 2006 as the target date for the phase-out of NTSC broadcasting (FCC, 1997). In 2005, after it became clear that this deadline was unrealistic due to the slow consumer adoption of DTV sets, it was reset at February 17, 2009 for the cessation of analog full-power television broadcasting (*Deficit Reduction Act*, 2005).

However, as the February 17, 2009 analog shutdown deadline approached, it was apparent that millions of over-the-air households with analog televisions had not purchased the converter boxes needed to continue watching broadcast programs. This was despite a widely publicized national coupon program that made the boxes almost free to consumers. Cable and satellite customers were not affected as provisions were made for the digital conversion at the cable headend or with a satellite set-top box. Neither the newly inaugurated Obama administration nor members of Congress wanted to invite the wrath of millions of disenfranchised analog television viewers, so the shut-off deadline was moved by

an act of Congress 116 days to June 12, 2009 (*DTV Delay Act*, 2009). Despite years of on-air public service announcements about the digital conversion, many local television stations received irate calls on this date from OTA viewers who wondered why their TV signals had disappeared.

Recent Developments

There are two primary areas affecting the diffusion of digital television and video in the United States—an ongoing battle over the digital television spectrum between broadcasters, regulators, and mobile telecommunication providers—and the diffusion of new digital technologies such as mobile DTV, 3-D DTV, thin-screen displays such as OLED, and the advent of smart televisions. The spectrum battle is significant in the context of what is known as the *Negroponte Switch*, which describes the conversion of "broadcasting" from a predominantly over-the-air service to one that is now wired for many American households—and the simultaneous transition of telephony from a traditional wired service to a wireless one for an increasing number of users (Negroponte, 1995). The growth of wireless broadband services has placed increasing demands on the available radio spectrum—and broadcast television is a significant user of that spectrum. The advent of digital television in the United States made this conflict possible in that the assignment of new DTV channels demonstrated that spectrum assigned to television could be "repacked" at will without the adjacent-channel interference problems presented by analog transmission. The required separation between analog channels is much less of an issue with digital transmissions and DTV channels can be "packed" more tightly within the radio-frequency bands assigned to television. It appears that U.S. broadcasters are a victim of their own success in making more efficient digital use of the terrestrial television spectrum and that this success invited additional attempts at repacking it (Seel, 2011).

The DTV Spectrum Battle

At the 2011 National Association of Broadcasters (NAB) conference in Las Vegas, FCC Chairman Julius Genachowski gave a speech to an audience of U.S. broadcast executives who were decidedly unenthusiastic about his message (Seel, 2011). As part of the Obama administration's National Broadband Plan, the FCC proposed that U.S. television broadcast networks and their affiliate stations voluntarily surrender additional DTV broadcast spectrum for auction to wireless telecommunication providers. The interesting twist in this offer is that the federal government proposed to share a portion of the auction revenue with stations that would voluntarily surrender their spectrum. Chairman Genachowski told the NAB audience that the auction of 120 MHz of the 294 MHz television spectrum used by U.S. broadcasters had the potential to raise up to $30 billion, a guesstimate since the need for wireless spectrum varies widely between U.S. cities (Seel, 2011). Only over-the-air television viewers (who comprise about 15 percent of U.S. television households) would be disenfranchised by the plan (OTA TV Homes, 2011). The radio and television spectrum is a national resource and the government, through sharing the auction proceeds, would be paying broadcasters for what is essentially public property. Despite the proposed incentives, U.S. broadcasters were hostile to the proposed voluntary plan. Those who chose not to participate, but lost their spectrum in DTV repacking plan after the auction, would not share in the revenue. Thus the reaction to FCC Chairman Genachowski's speech in Las Vegas was thinly veiled hostility on the part of many broadcasters.

In a general session for conference attendees that followed the speech, NAB president Gordon Smith asked CBS Corporation president Leslie Moonves what he thought of the Chairman's voluntary plan.

To laughter and applause from the audience, Moonves stated, "As long as [the repacking process] is voluntary, that's fine. Because we're not going to volunteer" (Seel, 2011, p. 373). President Smith reiterated the NAB's adamant opposition to the FCC's auction plan stating, "It concerns us that the FCC could forcibly relocate a broadcaster, crowd channels closer together, reduce their coverage, destroy innovation for viewers, increase interference, or otherwise degrade their signal. This endangers our digital future, and violates President Obama's promise to prevent a world of digital haves and have-nots" and added that the NAB was "in full battle mode" on the DTV spectrum issue (Seel, 2011, p. 373). The NAB then proceeded to roll out a national public relations campaign in opposition to the auction plan and began lobbying members of Congress to defeat it.

Some context is necessary to understand why the federal government was seeking the return of digital spectrum that it had just allocated in the 2009 U.S. DTV switchover. As a key element of the transition, television spectrum between former channels 52-70 was auctioned off for $20 billion to telecommunication service providers, and the existing 1,500 broadcast stations were "repacked" into lower terrestrial broadcast frequencies (Seel & Dupagne, 2010). The substantial auction revenue was not overlooked by federal officials, and as the U.S. suffered massive budget deficits in the global recession of 2008-2010, they proposed auctioning more of the television spectrum as a way to increase revenue without raising taxes in a recession. The outcome of this legislative process is addressed in the Current Status section below.

Mobile Digital Television

The creation of a national mobile standard for digital television broadcasting in the United States was proposed by the industry consortium Open Mobile Video Coalition (OMVC) in 2007, and the ATSC (the same organization that codified the DTV standard in 1995) assumed a similar role for a mobile standard (Advanced Television Systems Committee, 2009). After two years of testing in the lab and in the field, the A/153 ATSC Mobile DTV Standard (mDTV) was approved on October 15, 2009 by a vote of the ATSC membership (O'Neal, 2009). The mDTV standard uses the same 8VSB modulation scheme as the DTV terrestrial broadcast standard, but incorporates decoding technology specifically added to improve mobile reception. Local television broadcasters in the U.S. can include these mobile signals along with their regular DTV transmissions.

Adoption of the new mDTV standard by U.S. broadcasters is accelerating, and manufacturers of mobile phones, laptops, netbooks, and small portable TV sets are incorporating mDTV receiver chips in them. Mobile DTV reception was tested between 2009 and 2011 in Washington, DC, Seattle, and Atlanta, (O'Neal, 2009). Tests of the technology by WRAL-TV in Raleigh, North Carolina, on the local bus system indicated that the transmission technology was robust and functioned effectively (see Figure 6.4). Local U.S. broadcasters are expected to embrace the technology as the $100,000 investment required to transmit an identical DTV signal is relatively small compared to the cost of the DTV conversion, and there is significant advertising revenue potential in reaching mobile television viewers.

As of April 2011, 70 U.S. affiliate stations in 23 markets were transmitting an mDTV signal (Merli, 2011). The Open Mobile Video Coalition, the ATSC, and the Mobile 500 Alliance sponsored an exhibit at the NAB show that included flash-drive-sized mDTV receivers for laptops and tablets, automobile backseat display screens (see Figure 6.5), and a glasses-free 3-D mDTV receiver developed by LG Electronics. By the time of the January 2012 CES show in Las Vegas, 120 stations in 46 markets were transmitting a mobile DTV signal—almost a doubling in diffusion in less than 10 months (Winslow, 2012). An Android smartphone developed by Samsung will be among mDTV-equipped consumer devices introduced in 2012. The Mobile Content Venture (a consortium of 12 major U.S. broadcast groups) announced a contract with wireless provider MetroPCS to deliver mDTV telecasts to their U.S. subscribers, the first company of its type to offer mobile television content to their customers. The advantage of enlisting a national wireless company for mDTV service is that their customer's phones provide a signal return path for offering broadcast interactive and video-on-demand services in the future (Winslow, 2012).

Figures 6.4 and 6.5
Mobile DTV

Riders on a city bus in Raleigh, North Carolina, view a mobile DTV telecast during their morning commute.

Photo: WRAL-TV

Open Mobile Video Coalition demonstrated mDTV displays in an automobile at the 2011 NAB exhibition.

Photo: P. Seel

3-D TV

There are two primary technologies that apply to 3-D digital television (3-D TV): *passive* anaglyphic and *active* electro-optical. Passive 3-D TV systems use polarized glasses similar to those used in movie theaters to deliver unique information to the viewer's right eye and left eye as the frames alternate on the television display. Active electro-optical systems developed by Panasonic, Sony, and other manufactures use special battery-powered glasses with liquid-crystal lenses that open and close 60 times a second in sync with the alternate left-eye and right-eye frames displayed on the screen (Seel, 2010). What is remarkable about these proprietary systems is that the display is cycling at 120 frames per second and maintaining perfect sync with the glasses. The downside to these systems is that the glasses are expensive (from $100-150 per pair, with 1-2 pairs included with each display) and require constant recharging. 3-D TV sales have been disappointing to manufacturers who were hoping that this new technology would boost profits in high-end 3-D models to compensate for the low margins on conventional HDTVs. In the first nine months of 2011, 2.4 million 3-D TV sets were shipped to North America—less than 8.5 percent of the 28.1 million HDTV displays sold in that period (Spangler, 2011). Consumers may be experiencing "sticker shock" when they see that, in addition to the premium prices for 3-D TV displays, they may need to spend $300 to $450 for an additional two or three pairs of active glasses (beyond the two that come with most 3-D TVs).

In response, LG and other manufacturers are selling *passive* 3-D TV displays that work with inexpensive polarized glasses. Passive-technology 3-D TV displays are less expensive than the active shutter type models and may entice more consumers to include—capability when they upgrade to a new DTV set. Expect to see more passive 3-D TV models in the future with lower-priced models of all sizes.

What can purchasers of these receivers expect in 3-D video and television? One primary type of 3-D content viewable on a home system will be motion pictures produced in 3-D and viewed from Blu-ray discs. There has been a significant increase in 3-D film production in the past five years, especially for animated films. Martin Scorsese's 3-D film *Hugo* grossed $124 million worldwide since its 2011 release and it won five Oscars® at the 2012 Academy Awards. It's a rare animated film that is not produced in 3-D for theatrical distribution. In 2011 these included *Rio*, *Thor*, *The Adventures of Tintin*, *Puss in Boots*, and *Arthur Christmas*. Even classic 2-D films are being reformatted for 3-D projection including *Lion King* in 2011 and *Titanic* in 2012.

Figures 6.6 and 6.7
3-D Television Camera

3ALITY videographer shoots a wheelchair basketball game in their outdoor exhibit area at the 2011 NAB show. The dual-camera rig used for high-definition 3-D TV sports coverage uses a half-silvered mirror in the matte box to split the right-eye and left-eye images.

NAB Show, Sony displayed a new twin-lens XD-CAM for 3-D TV field production that featured the key 3-D convergence control (the silver knob) on the left side of the lens for easy access by videographers.

Photos: P Seel

Consumer electronics companies have studied these box office returns and see a significant audience for 3-D home viewing of these films and other television programs. To drive the sales of 3-D TV sets, both Sony and Panasonic paid broadcasters to produce and telecast programs in 3-D in 2010 and 2011. Panasonic will sponsor NBC's 3-D TV coverage of the 2012 Olympic Games in London as an inducement for consumers to purchase 3-D televisions

(Spangler, 2012). This situation is similar to the roll-out of digital television programming when Mitsubishi subsidized CBS's first season of DTV programming in 1999 and Panasonic underwrote the DTV simulcast of *Monday Night Football* and the Super Bowl on ABC in 2000 (Seel & Dupagne, 2000).

Current Status

United States

Receiver Sales. Consumers are in a dominant position when buying a new television set. Prices are down, screen sizes are larger, and most new receivers are "smart" models with a host of features more typically found in a computer than in a traditional television. A top-of-the line 55-inch Sony "Bravia" model that sold for $6,000 in 2009 can be purchased for $2,600 in 2012. Even more dramatic price reductions have occurred in conventional LCD and plasma models as shown in Table 6.2. A typical 42-inch LCD model (with 720p resolution) that sold for an average price of $1,200 in 2007 could be purchased for $523 (with 1080p resolution) in 2011. Consumers are buying sets with improved quality at less than half the cost (compared to four years earlier). What is good news for consumers has not been greeted warmly by television manufacturers. Profits are down for both display manufacturers and retailers as HDTV sets have become a commodity item. Increases in manufacturing capacity combined with downward price pressures introduced by new manufacturers such as Vizio have reduced profit margins for many famed brands. In response, Sony is overhauling its television manufacturing operations, and an executive stated that the company was feeling a "grave sense of crisis as we have continued to post losses in TVs" (Martin, 2011).

HDTV Adoption and Viewing. U.S. DTV penetration in 2011 was estimated at 79 million television households (of 116 million total) or 68 percent, up from 38 percent in 2009 (Briel, 2012; Leitchman, 2009)—and one third of these households have more than four television sets (Gorman, 2012). As consumers retire their older analog televisions, their only choice at this point is to purchase a DTV model—so the percentage of TV homes with digital televisions will continue to climb toward 100 percent. The conversion is being propelled by the rapidly falling prices of DTV displays as shown in Table 6.2.

HDTV Adoption and Viewing. U.S. DTV penetration in 2011 was estimated at 79 million television households (of 116 million total) or 68 percent, up from 38 percent in 2009 (Briel, 2012; Leitchman, 2009)—and one third of these households have more than four television sets (Gorman, 2012). As consumers retire their older analog televisions, their only choice at this point is to purchase a DTV model—so the percentage of TV homes with digital televisions will continue to climb toward 100 percent. The conversion is being propelled by the rapidly falling prices of DTV displays as shown in Table 6.2.

DTV Spectrum. On February 17, 2012, the U.S. Congress passed the *Middle Class Tax Relief and Job Creation Act of 2012* (*Middle Class*, 2012), and it was quickly signed into law by President Barack Obama (Eggerton, 2012). The *Act* authorized the Federal Communication Commission to reclaim DTV spectrum assigned to television broadcasters and auction it off to the highest bidder (likely wireless broadband providers) over the coming decade. As noted earlier, broadcasters who voluntarily surrender some (or all) of their assigned spectrum will share in the auction revenue (Eggerton, 2012). If insufficient numbers of broadcasters surrender the 120 MHz of spectrum needed for the auction, the FCC could seek Congressional authority to seize it involuntarily. No one knows at this point how this battle will play out, but broadcasters are adamant that they won't surrender their spectrum without a legal battle, so this litigation could take years to resolve.

Table 6.2

Average Retail Prices of LCD, LCD-LED, Plasma, and 3-D displays, 2007-2011

Display Sizes (diagonal)	Average retail price in 2007	Average retail price in 2009	Average retail price in 2011
32-inch LCD TV	$745 (720p)	$424 (720p)	$300 (720p)
37-inch LCD TV	$963 (720p)	$596 (1080p)	$300 (1080p)
40-42 inch LCD TV	$1,200 (720p)	$709 (1080p)	$523 (1080p)
40-42 inch LCD-LED TV	n/a	n/a	$610 (1080p)
46-47 inch LCD TV	$2,300 (720p)	$1,293 (1080p)	$664 (1080p)
46-47 inch LCD-LED TV	n/a	n/a	$950 (1080p)
52-55 inch LCD TV	$3,000 (720p)	$1,575 (1080p)	$1050 (1080p)
52-55 inch LCD-LED TV	n/a	n/a	$1208 (1080p)
42-inch plasma TV	$900 (720p)	$600 (720p) / $800 (1080p)	$450 (720p) / $650 (1080p)
50-55 inch plasma TV	$1,555 (1080p)	$900 (720p) / $1,300 (1080p)	$700 (1080p)
50-55 inch 3-D plasma TV	n/a	n/a	$1,150 (1080p)
60-inch 3-D plasma TV	n/a	n/a	$2250 (1080p)
60-inch OLED TV (available in 2013)	n/a	n/a	$8,000 (estimated)

Sources: Personal retail surveys by the author for all data. LCD-LED and 3-D models were not widely available until 2010 and new large-screen OLED displays won't be available until 2013. n/a = set not available

Digital Television Technology

Display Types. Consumers have many technological options for digital television displays, and standard sets sold today include higher-resolution screens (1080p vs. 720p) and more interactive features. The dominant display technologies are:

✦ *Liquid Crystal Display (LCD) and LCD-LED models*—LCDs work by rapidly switching color crystals off and on. A variant technology is LED (light emitting diode) backlit LCDs that use this alternate light source instead of Cold Cathode Fluorescent (CCFL) backlighting. The use of LEDs for screen backlighting provides higher image contrast ratios with richer blacks and brighter highlights than CCFL models. Table 6.2 shows that LCD-LED models are typically 20-30 percent more expensive than conventional LCD displays as manufacturers seek to wring higher profits out of their more advanced LED models.

✦ *Organic Light Emitting Diode (OLED)* —The Sony Corporation introduced remarkably bright and sharp OLED televisions in 2008 that had a display depth of 3mm or about the thickness of three credit cards. The suggested retail price in Japan at that time for the ultra-thin 11-inch diagonal model was $2,200. The company decided in 2010 that the sets would be too expensive to manufacture and discontinued production (Uranaka, 2010). Korean manufacturers LG and Samsung have decided to stake their futures on OLED technology as a way to improve their profit margins. One of the most talked-about technologies at the 2012 Consumer Electronics Show was LG's 55-inch OLED display that dazzled observers with its colorful, high-definition images and its remarkable thinness—about that of a candy bar (see Figure 6.8). The set is estimated to cost approximately $8,000 when it goes on sale early in 2013 (Griggs, 2012). Consumers will likely see OLED technology used in their mobile device screens long before buying an expensive home display. Samsung and other manufacturers are already deploying AMOLED (active-matrix organic light-emitting diode) versions of these high-definition displays for their touchscreen phones.

✦ *Plasma displays*—Plasma gas is used in these sets as a medium in which tiny color elements are switched off and on in milliseconds. Compared with early LCD displays, plasma sets offered wider viewing angles, better color fidelity and brightness, and larger screen sizes, but these advantages have diminished over the past decade. Many manufacturers have stopped making plasma sets in favor of LCD-LED models, but Panasonic is the exception.

✦ *Digital Light Processing (DLP) projectors*—Developed by Texas Instruments, DLP technology utilizes hundreds of thousands of tiny micro-mirrors mounted on a 1-inch chip that can project a very bright and sharp color image. This technology is used in a three-chip system to project digital versions of "films" in movie theaters. For under $3,000, a consumer can create a digital home theater with a DLP projector, a movie screen, and a multichannel surround-sound system.

✦ *Indium Gallium Zinc Oxide (IGZO)*—Apple Inc. is developing a digital television set to be introduced in 2012, and given its reputation for innovation, many pundits have been making guesses as to its design (Crothers, 2012). It will certainly feature a very high-definition screen and experts have been studying the "Retina" displays on the iPhone 4S and the iPad for clues. Apple may decide to adapt the IGZO displays developed for the iPad by Sharp Electronics (Crothers, 2012). The new iPad has a screen resolution of 1,536 by 2,048 pixels or 3.1 million pixels, and the technology could be scaled to much larger displays as the iPad screen is only 9.7 inches measured diagonally.

Figure 6.8
OLED TV

LG Electronics exhibited ultra-thin, 55-inch OLED displays at the 2012 Consumer Electronics Show.

Source: LG Electronics.

Programming. All network and cable channel programming in the United States is now produced in widescreen HDTV. There are many legacy 4:3 productions still being telecast (and there will be for years to come given each network's extensive analog archives), but these are typically being shown on widescreen displays with pillarbox graphics at the left and right side of the screen. Most cable operators have provided space on their systems for additional HD-quality channels and eventually (10–15 years) will phase out the down-converted 4:3 channels for subscribers with older analog sets. This move will free up a great deal of bandwidth, now occupied by narrow-screen simulcasts of HDTV programs, on most cable systems. Satellite multichannel video program providers, such as DirecTV and DISH, are each competing to see how many HDTV channels they can provide, and each now offers more than 150 channels (Greczkowski, 2010).

Table 6.3
Global DTV Standards and Switch-Off Dates of Analog Terrestrial Television

Asia/Oceania	Year	Standard	Europe	Year	Standard	Americas	Year	Standard
Taiwan	2010	DVB-T	Netherlands	2006	DVB-T	United States	2009	ATSC
Japan	2012	ISDB-T	Sweden	2007	DVB-T	Canada	2011	ATSC
South Korea	2012	ATSC	Germany	2008	DVB-T	Mexico	2022p	ATSC
New Zealand	2012	DVB-T	Switzerland	2009	DVB-T	Panama	N.D.	DVB-T
Australia	2013	DVB-T	Spain	2010	DVB-T	Columbia	N.D.	DVB-T
Philippines	2015p	DVB-T	France	2011	DVB-T	Brazil	2016p	SBTVD
China	2015p	DMB-TH	United Kingdom	2012	DVB-T	Peru	N.D.	SBTVD

p = projected date. N.D. = No analog termination date set. The SBTVD standards used in Brazil and Peru are South American variants of the Japanese ISDB-T terrestrial DTV standard. DMB-TH is a unique DTV standard developed in China.

Sources: DigiTAG and TV Technology

The Global Digital Transition

The period from 2012 to 2015 will be a crucial one for the global conversion of analog to digital television transmission. France made the transition on November 29, 2011, and Japan will complete the switch on March 31, 2012 (due to a delay in three prefectures affected by the 2011 earthquake and tsunami). Between 2012 and 2013, Japan, South Korea, New Zealand, Australia, and the United Kingdom will all switch to digital-only broadcasting (see Table 6.3).

Japan

HDTV developer NHK moved its next-generation HDTV system called Super Hi-Vision (SHV) from the laboratory to the marketplace in 2011 (see Figure 6.9). SHV's technical characteristics include: a video format resolution of 7,680 (wide) × 4,320 (high) pixels, an aspect ratio of 16:9, a progressive scanning frequency of 60 frames, and a 22.2 multichannel audio system with a top layer of nine channels, a middle layer of 10 channels, a bottom layer of three channels, and two low-frequency effects channels (Shishikui, Fujita, & Kubota, 2009; Sugawara, 2008). SHV has 33 million pixels per frame—16 times that of HDTV. Beyond the pixel count, this advanced technology "produces three-dimensional spatial sound that augments the sense of reality and presence" (Shishikui et al., 2009, p. 1).

At the 2012 Consumer Electronics Show in Las Vegas in 2012, NHK exhibited an enormous 85-inch Super Hi-Vision display that drew large crowds straining to see the fine detail visible on the screen. (Figure 6.9).

Figure 6.9
Super Hi-Vision TV

In 2011, Sharp introduced an 85-inch LCD display featuring **Super Hi-Vision** images of cherry blossoms that are 16-times the resolution of HDTV. The SHV pixel count is 7,680 wide by 4,320 in height.

Source: Sharp Electronics

Europe

Most of the terrestrial broadcasters in the European Union will turn off their analog television transmitters in 2012. Using the Digital Video Broadcasting-Terrestrial (DVB-T) standard, European broadcasters have focused for many years on delivering lower-definition SDTV programs to provide more digital viewing options to their audiences. But by the mid-2000s, they realized the long-term inevitability of providing widescreen HDTV services, driven in part by the growing popularity of flat-panel displays and Blu-ray disc players in Europe (DigiTAG, 2007).

In 2008, the Digital Video Broadcasting (DVB) Project adopted the technical parameters for the second-generation terrestrial transmission system called DVB-T2. In addition to the United Kingdom, Finland launched DVB-T2 services in 2010, and other European countries are conducting DVB-T2 trials. The United Kingdom has avoided the trap of setting a DTV conversion date and then having to postpone it (as the U.S. did twice) by defining two key benchmarks: availability (of DTV coverage) and affordability (of receivers by consumer) (Starks, 2011). This process took over 14 years and yielded a sliding end-date timetable from 2008 to 2012, with the latter date defining the actual switchover and one that coincided with many European Union nations. To date, 47 nations have deployed or adopted DVD-T2 as a terrestrial digital television transmission standard, including most of the European Union and many nations in Eastern Europe, Africa, and South Asia. DVB-T2 utilizes an enhanced transmission compression scheme that is 30-50 percent more efficient (in data rate) than DVB-T and one that can be received by mobile devices. It was designed with Future Extension Frame (FEF) technology that will allow DVB-T2 to be "compatibly enhanced" in the future without making the standard obsolete (DVB Fact Sheet, 2012).

Factors to Watch

The global diffusion of DTV technology will evolve over the second decade of the 21st century. In the United States, the future inclusion of mDTV receivers and HD-quality video recording capability in most mobile phones will enhance this diffusion on a personal and familial level. On a global scale, the more developed nations of the world will phase out analog television transmissions as they transition to digital broadcasting. A significant number of nations will have completed the digital transition by 2015. In the process, digital television and video will influence what people watch, especially as smart televisions, tablet computers, and 4G phones will offer easy access to Internet-delivered content that is more interactive than traditional television.

These evolving trends will be key areas to watch between 2012 and 2015:

✦ *OTT TV*—As noted above, the number of younger television viewers seeking out alternative viewing options on the Internet is steadily increasing. Expect to see more mainstream television advertisers placing ads on popular Internet multimedia sites such as YouTube to reach this key demographic. MVPDs such as cable and satellite companies are concerned about this trend as it enables these viewers to "cut the cable" or "toss the dish," so these companies are seeking unique programming such as premium sports events (the Super Bowl and the NCAA Basketball Tournament) to hold on to their customer base.

✦ *Two-Screen Viewing*—This is an emerging trend where viewers watch television programs while accessing related content (via Tweets, texts, and related social media sites) on a mobile phone, tablet, laptop, or via picture-in-picture on their DTV. Note that Samsung's Smart Hub screen in Figure 6.1 facilitates this type of multitasking while watching television. Producers of all types of television programming are planning to reach out to dual-screen viewers with streams of texts and supplementary content while shows are on the air.

✦ *3-D TV* (but only if the price is right)—The initial high cost ($1,500 and up) of 3-D televisions that use electro-optical technology has limited its adoption by consumers who recently upgraded their analog sets to HDTV.

In addition, the limited number of 3-D television and film programs has been an inhibiting factor in consumer purchasing decisions. However, if television manufacturers include 3-D display capability in HDTV sets at a modest price premium, it may boost sales and encourage more television production in 3-D. This parity in pricing may not occur until 2015 or later. Future 3-D television technologies may not require the use of active or passive glasses, which is a key inhibiting factor in consumer adoption.

✦ *Mobile DTV*—Given the relatively modest investment of $100,000 needed by local stations in major cities to transmit mDTV, it is expected that this technology will become a service that most urban U.S. broadcasters will offer. The investment will be offset by increased revenue from advertising targeted to mobile DTV viewers. The dramatic uptake from 70 stations with mDTV service in April 2011 to 120 stations transmitting it in January of 2012 is indicative of its rapid adoption by larger market stations.

✦ *HD News*—Even though the DTV transition is now complete in the United States, many TV stations still need to upgrade their news operations to HD. According to Mark Siegel, president of the system integrator company Advanced Broadcast Solutions, a TV station in a top 25 market will have to invest between $3 and $5 million to upgrade all facilities from SD to HD (Kaufman, 2009). Many U.S. television stations have decided to make the switch to HD news production with lower cost digital camcorders such as the XDCAM. Some stations have even supplied all their employees with aim-and-shoot pocket HDTV cameras so that they might capture breaking news on the way to work or driving home.

✦ *ATSC 2.0 and 3.0*—The Advanced Television Systems Committee (ATSC) in the U.S. is investigating new technologies for over-the-air 3-D broadcasting, on-demand programming, and delivery of Internet content as part of the development of ATSC 2.0 standards that are compatible with the present DTV broadcast system. The group is also investigating the long-term creation of "next-generation" ATSC 3.0 DTV standards that would be incompatible with the present digital broadcast system in the U.S. and would require yet another DTV transition at some point in the distant future.

The blend of televisions and computers has arrived. Most large-screen televisions are now "smart" models capable of displaying multimedia content from multiple sources: broadcast, cablecast, DBS, and all Internet-delivered motion media. As the typical home screen has evolved toward larger (and smarter) models, it is also getting thinner. Consumers who recall trying to heft a very heavy 35-inch, glass-tube television onto a TV stand will appreciate the relative ease of moving a comparatively light, ultra-thin, 55-inch OLED model that they can mount on the wall of their home theatre. The image quality of new high-definition displays is startling and will improve further with the delivery of 4K and 8K super-HDTV models in the near future. Television, which has been called a "window on the world," will literally resemble a large window in the home for viewing live sports, IMAX-quality motion pictures in 2-D and 3-D, and any content that can be steamed over the Internet. On the other end of the viewing scale, mobile customers with 4G phones will have access to this same diverse content on their high-definition AMOLED screens, thanks to WiFi and mDTV technology. Human beings are inherently visual creatures and this is an exciting era for those who like to watch motion media programs of all types in high-definition at home and away.

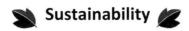

Sustainability

With the end of analog television broadcasting in the U.S. on June 12, 2009, approximately 200 million narrow-screen television sets were made obsolete. Many can be used for years with a digital converter box or hooked up to cable or satellite services. Most of these older sets have CRT screens with heavy glass tubes infused with lead to limit radiation exposure to viewers (e.g. children) sitting close to the set. The tubes have the potential to leach this lead into landfills if they are not disposed of properly. The circuit boards in older television sets, VCRs, DVD players, and computers contain toxic metals that also require proper disposal. For this reason many states and local landfills have prohibited the dumping of consumer electronics items and require their recycling or proper disposal. New York City and 11 states have passed laws to create television recycling programs and Illinois now requires television and computer manufacturers to pay for the recycling of their products (Koch, 2008). Some retailers such as Best Buy will recycle many electronic products for free, but they charge $10 to recycle televisions that are smaller than 32 inches diagonal (Best Buy, 2010). A useful Web site is *Earth911.com* that provides online information about the nearest approved disposal options for televisions, computers, and other home electronics.

Large-screen digital televisions are notorious energy hogs, especially large plasma displays. In response, California mandated state-wide energy efficiency standards in 2009 for all new HDTV sets, effective January 1, 2011. More stringent standards taking effect in 2013 are expected to reduce television-related power consumption by 50 percent in the state. Nationwide, television-related power usage has tripled in 10 years to 10 billion kilowatt hours each year, or 10 percent of residential energy consumption (Lifsher & Chang, 2009). Manufacturers are developing new DTV models that use less power, and the ideal set for energy–efficiency is a LCD model with LED backlighting (see chapter for detailed description) as these are bright displays with vivid colors and use less energy than conventional LCD sets. New OLED models use an ultra-thin display technology that will draw even less power than LCD-LED sets.

One common problem with electronic devices is that some draw power while supposedly switched off. This "vampire power" demand wastes energy while home users are asleep or when workers are away from their offices. Cable set-top boxes, digital video recorders, and computer monitors are typical culprits. One simple solution is to put multiple electronic items on a single power strip and use that switch to completely power them down when not in use. These simple energy conservation steps are not only good for the environment (fewer new power plants are needed), they will save consumers money each month on their utility bills.

Bibliography

Advanced Television Systems Committee. (2009, October 15). *A/153: ATSC mobile* DTV standard, parts 1-8. Washington, DC: Author.

Advisory Committee on Advanced Television Service. (1995). *Advisory Committee final report and recommendation.* Washington, DC: Author.

Balanced Budget Act of 1997. Pub. L. No. 105-33, § 3003, 111 Stat. 251, 265 (1997).

Best Buy. (2010). *Frequently asked questions for electronics recycling program.* Retrieved from, http://www.bestbuy.com/site/null/null/pcmcat174700050009.c?id=pcmcat174700050009.

Briel. R. (2012, January 13). Standard definition switch off looms. *Broadband TV News.* Retrieved from, http://www.broadbandtvnews.com/2012/01/13/standard-definition-switch-off-looms/.

Brinkley, J. (1997). *Defining vision: The battle for the future of television.* New York: Harcourt Brace & Company.

Crothers, B. (2012, January 22). Secrets to Apple's success. *CNET News.* Retrieved from, http://news.cnet.com/8301-13924_3-57363246-64/secrets-to-apple-success-displays/.

Deficit Reduction Act of 2005. Pub. L. No. 109-171, § 3001-§ 3013, 120 Stat. 4, 21 (2006).

DigiTAG. (2007). *HD on DTT: Key issues for broadcasters, regulators and viewers.* Geneva: Author. Retrieved from, http://www.digitag.org/HDTV_v01.pdf

DVB Fact Sheet. (2012). DVB Project Office. Retrieved from, http://www.dvb.org/technology/fact_sheets/DVB-T2_Factsheet.pdf.

DTV Delay Act of 2009. Pub. L. No. 111-4, 123 Stat. 112 (2009).

Dupagne, M., & Seel, P. B. (1998). *High-definition television: A global perspective.* Ames: Iowa State University Press.

Eggerton, J. (2012, February 27). Spectrum auctions: What now? *Broadcasting & Cable. 142,* 9. pp. 8, 9.

Federal Communications Commission. (1987). Formation of Advisory Committee on Advanced Television Service and Announcement of First Meeting, 52 Fed. Reg. 38523.

Federal Communications Commission. (1990). Advanced Television Systems and Their Impact Upon the Existing Television Broadcast Service (*First Report and Order*), 5 FCC Rcd. 5627.

Federal Communications Commission. (1996). Advanced Television Systems and Their Impact Upon the Existing Television Broadcast Service (*Fifth Further Notice of Proposed Rule Making*), 11 FCC Rcd. 6235.

Federal Communications Commission. (1997). Advanced Television Systems and Their Impact Upon the Existing Television Broadcast Service (*Fifth Report and Order*), 12 FCC Rcd. 12809.

Federal Communications Commission. (1998). Advanced Television Systems and Their Impact Upon the Existing Television Broadcast Service (Memorandum Opinion and Order on Reconsideration of the Sixth Report and Order), 13 FCC Rcd. 7418.

Gorman, B. (2012, January 6). 1 in 3 U.S. TV households own 4 or more TVs. TV By the Numbers. Retrieved from, http://tvbythenumbers.zap2it.com/2012/01/06/almost-1-in-3-us-tv-households-own-4-or-more-tvs/115607/.

Greczkowski, S. (2010, February 11). The new DISH HD is up for many. *Multichannel News*. Retrieved from, http://www.multichannel.com/blog/The_Satellite_Dish/30776-The_New_DISH_HD_Is_Up_For_Many.php.

Griggs, B. (2012, January 10). TVs in 2012 will get brighter, thinner, more social. CNN.com Retrieved from, http://www.cnn.com/2012/01/10/ tech/gaming-gadgets/tv-trends-ces/index.html.

Hansell, S. (2009, March 3). Time Warner goes over the top. *New York Times* (Bits blog). Retrieved from, http://bits.blogs.nytimes.com/2009/03/03/jeff-bewkes-goes-over-the-top/.

Hayes, R. M. (1989). 3-D movies: A history and filmography of stereoscopic cinema.

Jefferson, NC: McFarland & Company.

Kaufman, D. (2009, October 1). Stations moving HD news off back burner. TVNewsCheck. Retrieved from, http://www.tvnewscheck.com/articles/2009/10/01/daily.3/.

Koch, W. (2008 August 19). States want outdated TVs out of landfills. *USA Today*. Retrieved from, http://www.usatoday.com/printedition/news/20080819/ a_oldtvs19.art.htm.

Leichtman Research Group. (2009, November 30). Nearly half of U.S. households have an HDTV set (Press release). Retrieved from, http://www.leichtmanresearch.com/press/ 113009release.html.

Lifsher, M. & Chang, A. (2009, March 19). State mandates power-saving TVs. *The Los Angeles Times*. Retrieved from, http://articles.latimes.com/2009/nov/19/business/fi-big-screen-tvs19.

Martin, A. (2011, December 26). TV prices fall, squeezing most makers and sellers. New York Times. Retrieved from, http://www.nytimes.com/2011/12/27/business/tv-prices-fall-squeezing-most-makers-and-sellers.html?pagewanted=all.

Merli, J. (2011, April 6). Mobile DTV proponents all business at NAB. TV Technology. 29, 8. pp. 1, 26.

Middle Class Tax Relief and Job Creation Act of 2012. Pub. L. No. 112-96.

Negroponte, N. (1995). *Being Digital*. New York: Alfred A. Knopf.

Nielsen. (2011, May 3). Nielsen estimates number of U.S. television homes to be 114.7 million.

Nielsen Wire. Retrieved from, http://blog.nielsen.com/nielsenwire/media_entertainment/nielsen-estimates-number-of-u-s-television-homes-to-be-114-7-million/.

O'Neal, J. E. (2009, November 4). Mobile DTV standard approved. *TV Technology, 27*, 23.

OTA TV homes (2011). OTA TV homes include 46 million consumers (2011). *TV News Check*. Retrieved from, http://www.tvnewscheck.com/article/2011/06/06/51686/ota-tv-homes-include-46-million-consumers.

Richmond, S. (2012, February 12). Kodak to stop making digital cameras. *The Telegraph*.

Retrieved from, http://www.telegraph.co.uk/technology/news/9075217/Kodak-to-stop-making-digital-cameras.html.

Seel. P. B. (2010). Digital TV in 3D: A passing fad or the next step in the evolution of digital television. International Journal of Digital Television. 1, 3. 309-325.

Seel. P. B. (2011). Report from NAB 2011: Future DTV spectrum battles and new 3D, mobile, and IDTV technology. International Journal of Digital Television. 2, 3. 371-377.

Seel, P. B., & Dupagne, M. (2000). Advanced television. In A. E. Grant & J. H. Meadows (Eds.), *Communication Technology Update* (7th ed., pp. 75-88). Boston: Focal Press.

Seel, P. B., & Dupagne, M. (2010). Advanced television and video. In A. E. Grant & J. H. Meadows (Eds.), *Communication Technology Update* (12th ed., pp. 82-100). Boston: Focal Press.

Sharwood, S. (2012, January 10). Gadget of the week – smart televisions. *MyBusiness.com*. Retrieved from, http://www.mybusiness.com.au/technology/gadget-of-the-week-smart-televisions.

Shishikui, Y., Fujita, Y., & Kubota, K. (2009, January). Super Hi-Vision – The star of the show! *EBU Technical Review*, 1-13. Retrieved from, http://www.ebu.ch/en/technical/trev/trev_2009-Q0_SHV-NHK.pdf.

Spangler, T. (2011, December 14). How rosy does 3DTV look now? *Multichannel News*. Retrieved from, http://www.multichannel.com/blog/BIT_RATE/32958-How_Rosy_Does_3DTV_Look_Now_.php?rssid=20079.

Spangler, T. (2012, January 10). NBC to deliver 2012 Olympics in 3D with Panasonic. *Multichannel News*. Retrieved from, http://www.multichannel.com/article/478765-CES_NBC_To_Deliver_2012_Olympics_In_3D_With_Panasonic.php.

Starks, M. (2011). Editorial. *International Journal of Digital Television. 2*, 2. pp. 141-143.

Stelter, B. (2012, February 9), Youth are watching, but less often on TV. *New York Times*. pp. B1, B9.

Sugawara, M. (2008, Q2). Super Hi-Vision – Research on a future ultra-HDTV system. *EBU Technical Review*, 1-7. Retrieved from, http://www.ebu.ch/fr/technical/trev/trev_2008-Q2_nhk-ultra-hd.pdf.

Uranaka, T. (2010, February 16). Sony pulls plug on OLED TV in Japan. *Reuters.* Retrieved from, http://www.reuters.com/article/idUSTRE61F0ZO20100216.

Winslow, G. (2012, January 9). Tech you need to see. Broadcasting & Cable. 142, 2. p. 26.

YouTube Statistics. (2012). YouTube Inc. Retrieved from, http://www.youtube.com/t/press_statistics.

7

Multichannel Television Services

Jennifer H. Meadows, Ph.D.[*]

Why Study Multichannel Television Services

✦ 94.5 million households in the US subscribe to a multichannel television service (Frankel, 2012)

✦ 58 million households in the US subscribe to cable television alone (NCTA, 2012)

✦ Multichannel television services are making their programming available across multiple platforms such as mobile phones and tablets

✦ Multichannel television services have embraced many new communication technologies including, but not limited to, interactive television, smartphone apps, streaming, and 3-D.

Just several decades ago, people would sit down for an evening of television and have a choice of two to five channels. Nowadays, most people have so many channels to choose from that they have to use interactive program guides to help them decide which program to watch. Who would think there would be entire channels devoted to food, auto racing, and science fiction? Multichannel television services deliver this programming and more.

[*] Professor, Department of Communication Design, California State University, Chico (Chico, California).

Multichannel television services include cable television, direct broadcast satellite (DBS) services, and pay television services. (Internet protocol television services [IPTV] are also considered multichannel television services, but they will be discussed in Chapter 8.) With cable television services, television programming is delivered to the home via a coaxial cable or a hybrid system combining fiber optics and coaxial cable. The subscriber either uses a set-top box or connects the cable directly into the television. DBS customers receive programming using a small, pizza-sized satellite dish and a set-top receiver connected to a television.

Pay television services are available on both cable and DBS systems and include premium channels, pay-per-view (PPV), and video on demand (VOD). Premium channels are programming channels for which subscribers pay a monthly fee above the regular cable or DBS subscription fee. These channels usually contain a mix of movies, events, and original programming without commercials. HBO and Starz are examples of premium channels. Pay-per-view is a program such as a movie, concert, or boxing match that is ordered and then played at a specific time. Video on demand is programming that is available at any time. Users also have control over the program so the program can be paused, rewound, and fast-forwarded. VOD can be available for a one-time charge as well. For example, a movie can be ordered for a set fee. VOD can also be offered for a monthly fee. For example, subscription video on demand (SVOD) is a slate of programming offered on demand for a monthly charge. Many premium channels offer SVOD included in their monthly subscription rate. Finally, free VOD is available; its programming is varied, and offerings range from children's shows to fitness videos to broadcast network programming.

This chapter will discuss the origins of multichannel television services as well as recent developments such as interactive and online services, carriage contract battles, and new competition.

Background

The Early Years

Many people do not realize that cable television has been around since the beginning of television in the United States. Cable television grew out of a need to sell television sets. People were not going to purchase television sets if they had nothing to watch. It has not been established who was first, but communities in Oregon, Pennsylvania, and Arkansas have claimed to be the first to establish Community Antenna Television (CATV). These communities could not get over-the-air programming with regular television antennas because of geographical limitations. Antennas were erected on top of hills and mountains to receive signals from nearby cities, and then homes in the community were connected via coaxial cable. Appliance stores could sell televisions, and people who bought them had programming to watch (NCTA, n.d.). (See Figure 7.1)

Soon CATV operators began to offer customers distant channels, since their antennas could pick up other stations besides those in the local market. These new channels threatened local broadcast stations, and the FCC responded by limiting the importation of distant channels. Continuing into the early 1970s the FCC responded to concerns of broadcasters and the film industry by limiting cable's ability to offer any programming other than that offered by local broadcast channels (for example, sports and movies). There was not much growth in cable during this time.

Figure 7.1
Traditional Cable TV Network Tree & Branch Architecture

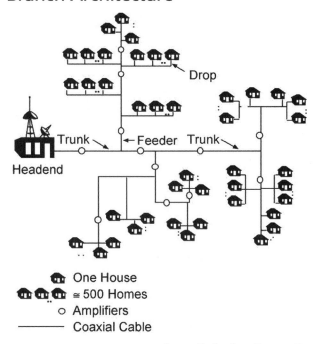

Source: Technology Futures, Inc.

The situation changed in 1972 when the FCC began to deregulate cable, and previous restrictions on cable programming were loosened. Also in the early 1970s, "the Open Skies" policy was established that allowed private companies into satellite communications (NCTA, n.d.). In 1972, HBO, the first premium channel, began as a local microwave service in Pennsylvania, and was offered to cable companies around the country via satellite. A few years later, Ted Turner put his small independent television station from Atlanta on the same satellite carrying the HBO service, giving cable companies another free channel and establishing the first "Superstation," WTBS. Use of satellites to deliver programming soon facilitated the creation of many cable networks that are still popular today including ESPN, A&E, CNN, and MTV.

This use of satellites was also key to the development of DBS services. Chances are, if you lived in a rural area in the 1970s, your community was not wired for cable television. With a television receive-only satellite dish (TVRO), people could receive television programming delivered via satellite.

In 1977, Taylor Howard, a professor at Stanford University, who worked with satellite technology, may have been the first to build a satellite dish to receive HBO programming at his home. This marked the beginning of TVRO satellites. The technology has limitations, though. First, it used the low-power C-band (3.7 GHz to 4.2 GHz) frequencies, which meant the dishes were large and unattractive. Some communities even banned the dishes because of their appearance. They were also expensive to install and complicated to operate. Finally, programming networks began to scramble their signals so TVRO users had to purchase decoding boxes and pay to unscramble the signals (Museum of Broadcast Communication, n.d.).

The Growth Years

Deregulation continued into the 1980s, allowing cable systems to accelerate their growth. The *Cable Communications Act of 1984* amended the *Communications Act of 1934* with regulations specific to cable. The most important change made by this act was that it removed the rights of a local franchising authority to regulate cable TV rates unless the area was served by fewer than three broadcast signals. When a cable company operates in a community, it has to have a franchising agreement with the community. This agreement covers issues such as public access requirements, subscriber service and renewal standards, and a franchise fee; it is negotiated between the franchising agency and the cable company. With the passage of the 1984 Act, cable companies were allowed to increase rates without government approval, and rates grew—and grew. At the same time, deregulation and rising rates allowed cable companies to raise capital to expand their services and upgrade their technology. However, cable customers found their cable rates rising significantly, with the average rate more than doubling from 1984 to 1992 as service standards dropped.

At the same time, new satellite television services and wireless cable companies were struggling to be established. Direct-to-home satellite service in the 1980s used the medium-power Ku-band (11.7 GHz to 12.2 GHz) and offered customers a limited amount of "cable" programming. The service was not successful for a number of reasons. First, the service only offered a limited number of channels. Second, the operators were unable to obtain the programming that customers wanted—popular cable programming networks. In addition, the service was expensive and performed poorly in bad weather (Carlin, 2006).

Another attempt at satellite television was made in 1983 when the International Telecommunications Union and the World Administrative Radio Conference established that the high power Ku-band (12.2 GHZ to 12.7 GHz) would be used for direct broadcast satellite service and assigned orbital positions and frequencies for each country. In the United States, the FCC established eight orbital positions and accepted eight applications for the slots. The applicants had to prove due diligence, which meant they had to begin constructing a satellite within a year and have the service operational within six years. All of those applicants failed. The FCC collected a new group of applicants in 1989, and those companies also failed to begin service by 1992. The services could not take off for two reasons. First, they could not transmit enough channels because there was no acceptable digital video compression standard. Without digital video compression, these satellite services could only broadcast a very limited number of channels, nowhere close to what cable systems were offering at the time. Digital video compression would allow several channels worth of programming to be squeezed into the space of one analog channel. Second, there needed to be a way for satellite services to get access to popular cable programming channels. Cable companies, at the time, were using their power to prevent any programming deals with the competition (DBS), leaving satellite providers with a small number of channels that few people wanted to watch.

These problems were solved in the early 1990s. First, the MPEG-1 digital video compression standard was approved in 1993, followed by the broadcast-quality MPEG-2 format in 1995. This standard allowed eight channels to be compressed into the space of one analog channel. Second, the *Cable Television Consumer Protection and Competition Act* (a.k.a. The Cable Act of 1992) forced cable programming companies to sell to other video distribution outlets for terms comparable to cable. Now, DBS had the channel capacity and the programming to adequately compete with cable. DirecTV (Hughes) and USSB (Hubbard) were the first to launch service in 1994. EchoStar launched their DISH service in 1996. Other DBS applicants failed to launch their services, and DirecTV and EchoStar obtained some of their channels. Rainbow DBS launched in 2003 and was used for the short-lived VOOM HD service.

Not to be outdone, the cable industry entered the satellite television service market with Primestar. This medium-power Ku-band service offered only a limited number of channels, so as not to compete with local cable systems. The consortium of cable systems involved in Primestar included Cox, Comcast, Newhouse, TCI, and Time Warner. Primestar eventually adopted digital video compression to offer more channels and directly compete with DirecTV. They highlighted the fact that subscribers did not have to buy the equipment; rather, they rented it just like a cable set-top box.

Primestar was eventually purchased, along with USSB, by DirecTV, making it the largest DBS service in the United States. EchoStar eventually took over the VOOM channels from Rainbow DBS and took over the orbital positions of DBS applicant MCI. Finally, one last DBS service was launched in 1999: Sky Angel, which offered religious programming. Due to satellite problems in 2006, the service moved to IPTV (Sky Angel, n.d.).

Consolidation within the satellite television market sparked a price war between DirecTV and DISH and between the DBS companies and cable. Subscribers no longer had to pay for equipment as DBS services began to offer free installation and hardware and even multiple room receivers. Cable still had a major advantage over DBS, because DBS subscribers could not get local broadcast stations through their satellite service. This was due to the *Satellite Broadcasting Act of 1988*, which prohibited the distribution of local broadcast stations over satellite to subscribers who lived in the coverage area of the station. This meant that DBS subscribers had to set up an antenna or subscribe to basic cable to get local channels. This problem was solved with

the *Satellite Home Viewer Improvement Act of 1999*, which allowed DBS companies to offer those local channels to their customers. The issue then was for DBS companies to have enough space on their satellites available to offer local channels in all markets in the United States.

Cable television at this time was reacting to its first real competition. After the boom years brought about, in part, by the deregulation of the *Cable Act of 1984*, the cable industry was perhaps a little complacent, raising prices and disregarding service. These complaints eventually led to the *1992 Cable Act* discussed earlier, which re-regulated basic cable rates. One of the most important provisions of the Act gave broadcasters negotiating power over cable companies. Broadcasters had for years been complaining about how cable operators were retransmitting their signals and collecting money for them, with none of the money coming back to broadcasters. The "must-carry" and "retransmission consent" provisions of the *1992 Act* let broadcasters decide if the cable system must carry their signal or an agreement had to be reached between the cable company and the broadcaster for retransmission consent. This consent could "cost" anything from money to time. The concept of "must-carry" would come back to haunt both cable operators and broadcasters as the digital television transition neared. As discussed in Chapter 6, broadcasters can transmit one HDTV and several SDTV channels. Broadcasters argue that, under must-carry, cable operators should be forced to carry all of those channels. Cable operators, on the other hand, say they should only have to carry the stations' primary signal. The Federal Communications Commission (FCC), thus far, has sided with the cable operators saying that multichannel must-carry would be an unnecessary burden to cable operators under the dual must-carry ruling.

While cable and DBS services were growing and developing quickly at this time, the same was not true for pay television services. Premium channels were popular, especially HBO and its main competitor, Showtime, but pay-per-view had failed to gain major success. The limitations of PPV are numerous and mostly outweigh the advantages. First, PPV programs had a very limited number of available start times. The programs could not be paused, rewound, or fast-forwarded. There was only a limited amount of programming available. Users needed to call the cable company to order the program and had to have a cable box to get them. By the time a movie was available in PPV, it had already been available for sale and rental at home video stores. Often times, as well, the price was higher for PPV than rental. The only real advantages of PPV were no late fees, you did not have to leave your house, and sometimes it was the only way to get certain special events such as championship boxing.

DBS solved some of these problems. Instead of having only a few channels devoted to PPV, DBS providers could have many channels of PPV and could offer programs at staggered start times so the viewer had more choice. While they often offer more channels of PPV than cable, DBS providers such as DirecTV also offer VOD services with a DVR receiver and a broadband connection. The program is ordered and delivered to the DVR over the Internet connection.

Digital Upgrades

As cable television systems upgraded their networks from analog to digital, new services and features began to roll out. For example, cable systems began to upgrade their networks from coax to hybrid fiber/coax (see Figure 7.2). This upgrade allowed cable systems to offer new services such as high-definition programming, DVR services, VOD, SVOD, broadband Internet access, and telephony. Video programming, broadband Internet access, and telephony make up the cable "triple play," which is one feature that the cable industry uses to differentiate its service from DBS. (For more on DVRs, see Chapter 17, and for more on cable Internet, see Chapter 23.)

The digital upgrades helped advance pay television services. First, the upgraded digital networks allowed cable systems to carry more channels of programming. Premium channels took advantage of this additional bandwidth by offering multiplexed versions of their services. So, for example, instead of just getting one HBO channel, a subscriber also gets different versions or "multiplexes"

of HBO including HBO2, HBO Signature, HBO family, etc. Most premium channels now offer a package of multiplexed channels to subscribers including Starz, Showtime, and Cinemax. Even "regular" cable programming channels are multiplexing. For instance, sports fans can now watch ESPN, ESPN2, ESPN Classic, ESPN U, and ESPN News. More advanced pay television services were also introduced, including subscription VOD. HBO was the first to offer HBO On Demand in 2001 that allows HBO subscribers with digital cable to access a selection of HBO programs on demand. These programs include original series, movies, and events. HBO even experimented with the service by making episodes of *The Wire* available first on demand before airing on HBO (Kaufman, 2007).

Figure 7.2
Hybrid Fiber/Coax Cable TV System

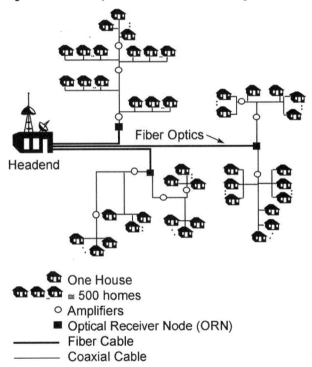

Source: Technology Futures, Inc.

Video on demand was the next service to be rolled out by cable companies. VOD has been tested for the last three decades, with the largest test being Time Warner's Full Service Network in Orlando (Florida) from 1994 to 1997. The Full Service Network eventually failed because of numerous factors including cost and technological limitations. The VOD feature of the service was popular with customers, though.

Video on demand is now offered to digital cable subscribers by the major cable multiple system operators (MSOs) including Comcast, Cox, Time Warner, and Cablevision. Subscribers have access to a variety of programming including new movies for a one-time charge. The fee usually entitles the viewer 24-hour access to the program. Free older movies are available as well as a selected number of television shows from broadcast and cable networks. Finally, special VOD only channels and programs have developed and are available by choosing from a menu of "channels" such as Comcast's Life and Home, News and Kids, and the Cutting Edge (On demand menu, n.d.).

High-Definition Programming

When it comes to high-definition programming, DBS services have been the most aggressive in developing and marketing the service. DirecTV started the battle when it announced that it would be offering 100 channels of HD content by 2008 (Berger, 2007). DISH also quickly added HD channels. As of mid-2012 Dish and DirecTV are still fighting over which service has the most HD channels. Both services use MPEG-4 AVC video compression for HD programming. The compression allows the companies to squeeze two channels of HD into the space formerly used by one. The biggest problem with the move to MPEG-4 AVC is that customers with older DirecTV and DISH MPEG-2 boxes had to upgrade to a new box to get the new HD channels (Patterson & Katzmaier, 2008).

Cable television companies are also bulking up their HD offerings, especially in response to competition from DBS. Not only do cable MSOs offer HD channels, but they are also able to offer HD VOD and HD SVOD. The local HD channels are a different issue. As discussed earlier, under the must-carry and retransmission consent rules of the *Cable Act of 1992*, broadcasters can decide if the cable company must carry their channel. With the digital transition, broadcasters can offer their primary signal in HD and several other digital multicast channels. Broadcasters want must-carry to apply to all of their digital channels, not just the primary channel. Then-FCC chairman, Kevin Martin, was a supporter of multicast must-carry, but the commission as a whole was not. Martin had to pull a vote on the subject in June 2006. The FCC voted that cable operators must carry the local broadcaster's signals in digital and analog form ("dual must-carry") for three years after the 2009 digital transition date. Cable systems are no longer required to carry analog signals as of 2012, and many MSOs such as Comcast are in the process of switching to digital only. This switch requires that subscribers with analog television sets get a set top box when they didn't have to previously (Pegoraro, 2012).

Regulation

A la carte. Arguing that cable customers are charged too much for channels that they do not even watch, then-FCC Chairman Martin (2005-2009) pushed for "a la carte." With a la carte, customers would choose what channels they wanted instead of purchasing programming in bundled tiers. Martin also argued that parents like a la carte because they could avoid channels that are not family-friendly. Cable responded to that concern with the establishment of family tiers. Spanish-speaking viewers, argued Martin, would also benefit by not having to pay for English language programming. The cable industry is vehemently against a la carte. They argue that a la carte would raise prices, limit diversity, and lower revenue for the development and expansion of new services. Under current regulations and as a result of court cases, the FCC cannot force the cable companies to break up their programming tiers.

Video Franchising Order. Cable companies are facing competition from telephone companies, which are rolling out IPTV (Internet protocol television) services using advanced fiber optic network technology with services including AT&T's U-Verse and Verizon's FiOS (discussed in more detail in Chapter 8). One of the difficulties of starting a new video service is the negotiation of franchising agreements, those agreements between the community and the video service provider. AT&T and Verizon argued that franchising agreements were hampering their efforts to roll out these new services and lobbied for national and statewide franchising agreements. Many states passed these. The FCC became involved when it ruled that local governments only have 90 days to negotiate a franchising agreement, and, if no agreement is reached, then the franchise would be granted. This procedure would allow the telephone company to avoid good faith negotiations and just wait until the deadline passed. Then, these companies could build out their systems as they please, perhaps avoiding lower income neighborhoods or rural areas (Bangeman, 2007). The same franchising rules are not applicable to cable.

Retransmission Consent and Carriage Contract Fights. *The Cable Act of 1992* requires that multichannel television providers negotiate with broadcasters to carry their channels. As discussed earlier in this chapter, broadcasters can choose to make cable systems carry their channel (must-carry) or negotiate some kind of payment (retransmission consent) (Peers, 2010; Ovide, 2010). In the 1990s, broadcasters were not successful at negotiating cash payments, but the tide has turned in favor of broadcasters in the past few years. Broadcasters are aware that cable companies pay as much at $4.00 per month per subscriber to carry specific channels. Because they are losing advertising revenue as more and more viewers turn to other sources of video, broadcasters want to have the same dual revenue stream that cable channels such as Discovery and ESPN have. These cable channels get revenue from advertising and carriage fees. In 2009 and 2010 there were several high profile standoffs between broadcasters and cable companies. Disney/ABC (which owns WABC in New York) and Cablevision settled at the last minute, with viewers only missing the opening of the 2010 *Oscars*.

3-D, Interactive & Online Begins

New 3-D television technology seemingly came out of nowhere in 2009. Although children's movies had been released in 3-D and were popular, it wasn't until *Avatar* was released that a wide cross section of Americans experienced 3-D without those annoying red and blue glasses. Many in the television industry believe that the next frontier for 3-D is the home. Companies including Panasonic and Samsung are selling flat screen 3-D televisions. But if people are going to buy these televisions there has to be something 3-D to watch. You can only watch *Cloudy with a Chance of Meatballs* so many times. Cable and DBS companies have begun to offer 3-D programming. Comcast is experimenting with 3-D sports along with CBS. The 2010 Masters golf tournament was broadcast in 3-D and made available to Comcast subscribers for free with 2 hours of 3-D coverage available each day (Dickson, 2010b). Cablevision offered a professional hockey game in 3-D to its subscribers in March 2010.

ESPN started ESPN 3D in June 2010. DirecTV was the first service to commit to carrying the channel and the DBS service launched three of its own 3-D channels including one called n3D that is sponsored by Panasonic. To watch the 3-D programming, subscribers will need both a 3-D television and 3-D glasses (Spangler, 2010c; Dickson, 2010a).

Multichannel television providers saw the writing on the wall when it came to Internet video. Cablevision launched a service called PC to TV Media Relay in June 2010 that allows subscribers to its broadband and television service to watch online content on their television on a dedicated channel (Worden, 2010). Other cable companies are using different strategies to keep their customers from switching to Internet only viewing. Comcast expanded its online service Fancast Xfinity TV. The service offers programming from 27 networks including HBO, CBS, Hallmark and the Travel Channel. The service is free to Comcast broadband and television subscribers (Spangler, 2009). Subscribers, though, only have access to networks they get through their cable service.

HBO is also reaching out to subscribers on the Internet. HBO GO was released in early 2010. The online service gives subscribers access to over 600 hours of programming. The service was first available to Verizon FiOS customers. Only regular HBO subscribers have access to HBO GO.

Mobile Services Roll Out

With the growing popularity of mobile devices such as smartphones, multichannel programming providers expanded their reach to include those devices. Mobile phone users can access this programming several ways. First they can access programs through their mobile phone provider. An example of this would be Verizon's V-Cast Mobile TV service. V-Cast users can watch "cable" channels including the Food Network, Comedy Central, and MTV. Other providers including AT&T and Sprint also offer these television services.

Downloading is another way users can get "cable" programming on mobile devices. Popular programming is available to download to mobile devices such as tablets and iPhones. So if a person missed last night's *South Park*, he or she could go to iTunes and buy the episode, and it could be watched on an iPod, iPhone, iPad, or a computer. Premium channels are using smartphone apps to gain new customers. For example, Showtime's free iPhone app has clips, games, and sneak previews. Of course, users can also order Showtime with the app.

Recent Developments

Since 2010 the way audiences watch television content has shifted. Increasingly audiences are using mobile devices and the Internet to connect to their television content, and multichannel television services are responding to this change with a myriad of services and technologies. In addition, carriage contract and retransmission consent fights continue to plague providers and increasingly, their subscribers. This section will review these and other recent developments in multichannel television services.

As the competition heats up among multichannel television services, they are rolling out advanced services to better compete with each other and with Internet video. For example, subscribers of many services can now get receivers or set top boxes with advanced DVRs. One such DVR is DISH's Hopper. The Hopper is a whole home DVR that allows up to six television sets to access the DVR at the same time. So one person could watch a live football game in the living room, another could watch a recorded television series and yet another could be recording a movie and watching an on demand movie with the Primetime Anytime service all at the same time (Hopper, 2012).

The concept of TV Everywhere has also hit multichannel television services. Audiences want to watch their content on all of their devices regardless of location. DISH offers TV Everywhere with the Sling Adapter. Users just have to hook up the Sling Adapter to their Dish receiver and download the Remote Access software to their mobile device and/or computer. Once set up, users can watch their DISH content, including material saved on their DVR anywhere regardless of location as long as they have a broadband Internet connection (TV Everywhere, 2012).

Other services offer streaming to subscribers. Comcast has offered their Xfinity Fancast service for years and now is rolling out Streampix, a service designed to compete with Netflix's streaming service. It offers full seasons of television series and movies on demand. Subscribers can access the service on computers, smartphones, tablets, and other mobile devices. Streampix is included with Comcast premium bundles, others can add it on for $4.99 per month (Streampix, 2012). Time Warner Cable has the TWC app allowing subscribers to watch their programming on smartphones and tablets, and it is free for subscribers. DirecTV launched DirecTV Everywhere service in May 2012. Subscribers can now access DirecTV content with computers and use the DirecTV app for access on smartphones, mobile devices and tablets (DirecTV Everywhere, 2012). DirecTV also launched an app for NFL Sunday Ticket giving subscribers access to that content on iPads and iPhones.

Premium channels are also using apps and streaming. HBO Go now has an app. Showtime has the Showtime Anytime App free for subscribers. Showtime also has apps for specific shows including *Dexter* and *House of Lies*. The Showtime Social app for the iPad allows users to participate in polls, games and conversations while watching the live broadcasts (Apps, 2012). While smartphone and mobile devices are quickly becoming popular ways to access programming, so too are gaming consoles. For example the Xbox 360 can be used to watch HBO Go and Comcast Xfinity (as long as users subscribe to these services) (Spangler, 2012).

While 3-D hasn't had the rapid growth expected, multichannel television providers are providing more and more content. This is important: after all, what is the incentive to purchase a 3-D television if there isn't any 3-D content to watch? DirecTV was the first to roll out 3-D services as discussed above and as of mid-2012 they offer 3 channels: n3D (sponsored by Panasonic), 3DNet (sponsored by Sony), and ESPN 3D. DirecTV Cinema offers 3-D movies on demand (Watch 3D, 2012). Cable systems are also offering limited 3-D programming. For example, Comcast has Xfinity 3D and ESPN 3D as well as On Demand 3-D movies from HBO and Starz (Comcast 3D Service, 2012).

While multichannel television providers are making their programming more accessible across platforms, sometimes the channels viewers want are the subject of some pretty contentious fights. The cable carriage fights discussed earlier have continued. The FCC has even become involved. The FCC issued an order in response to customer complaints over cable channels that disappear during contract disputes. The order clarified parts of the 1992 Cable Act to specify that multichannel television operators cannot drop channels while a contract is being disputed (Lieberman, 2011). Obviously, the providers were not happy losing this leverage tool. For example, in 2011 News Corp. and DirecTV were having difficulty negotiating a new deal over the carriage of several Fox-owned cable networks including FX and Fox Sports regional sports networks. The negotiations went down to the wire with DirecTV ready to let the contract expire. Fox responded by encouraging viewers to contact DirecTV. The producer of the popular FX show *Sons of Anarchy* even showed a short editorial warning fans they would miss important plot lines if they didn't contact DirecTV or switch to another provider (Flint, 2011). A similar fight occurred in New York when Time Warner Cable and the MSG Network couldn't reach an agreement. (Reynolds, 2011).

Retransmission consent continues to be a heated policy issue. For example, DirecTV filed an FCC complaint against Tribune Co. in 2012 after the company pulled 23 broadcast television stations in March 2012. At issue is a retransmission consent agreement that DirecTV claims was agreed upon by both parties but Tribune backed out of after its creditors disapproved. A deal was eventually reached after four days (Channick, 2012; Farrell, 2012). Retransmission consent is under fire in Washington as of mid-2012. The Next Generation Television Marketplace Act bill sponsored by Senator DeMint and Representative Scalise would eliminate must-carry and retransmission consent. Broadcasters are lobbying heavily against this bill, and thus far the FCC has stated it is "watching the marketplace" to see whether reform is needed (Donohue, 2012; Radia, 2012).

The FCC is also studying several other issues that impact multichannel television providers. Nothing is more annoying to a sports fan than to tune into a game only to find it blacked out because there wasn't a sellout; a perennial problem for teams like the Oakland Raiders. The FCC is reviewing the rules for cable and satellite providers although they would stay in place for local broadcasters (Schatz, 2012a). Another issue the FCC is studying is spectrum and the lack thereof. The agency is planning new rules for satellite airwaves that would allow licensees more flexibility to use that spectrum for other services (Schatz, 2012b). DISH wanted to begin offering wireless Internet service but the FCC asked them to hold off until the rules were studied (Ramachandran & Launder, 2012). DBS providers are seeking to bundle more services like cable and IPTV providers do. Cable operators are also seeking to expand their Internet services. For example, some companies are offering Wi-Fi networks to subscribers (Ramachandran, 2012).

Multichannel television operators may be forced by the marketplace to expand the variety of services they offer because more and more households are "cutting the cord." Fueled by the recession and increased availability of content online, many people are foregoing multichannel television services and turning to the Internet and the use of streaming devices. Devices such as Apple TV, Smart TVs, Boxee Box, Roku, and game consoles Xbox 360 and PlayStation 3 allow users to easily hook the Internet up to their television screen and enjoy content through sites including Hulu, Netflix, HBO Go, iTunes, Amazon, YouTube and other websites. And, with an antenna, high definition digital broadcast television is available for free (Sintumuang, 2012; Stewart, 2012).

Current Status

Figure 7.3 shows the change in market share from 2009 to 2011. Note that cable's share has decreased while both DBS and IPTV have increased. The top ten Multichannel Television Providers in the United States as of September 2011 are presented in Table 7.1. Cable still leads with the greatest share but over the years their market share has dropped significantly with greater competition from DBS and IPTV.

Figure 7.3
Multichannel TV Market Share

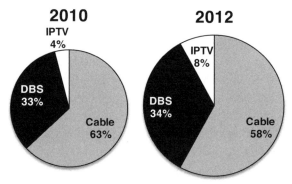

Source: NCTA (2012)

U.S. Cable

According to the NCTA, cable penetration as of December 2011 was 44.4% of total television households. That adds up to 58 million subscribers. As of December 2011, there were 46 million digital cable customers, 47.3 million cable Internet customers, and 25.3 million cable voice/phone customers (NCTA, 2012).

Comcast is the largest cable MSO in the United States with 22.6 million subscribers as of September 2011. Time Warner is second with 12.1 million subscribers, followed by Cox Communications with 4.8 million, and Charter Communications with 4.4 million subscribers (NCTA, 2012).

Table 7.1
Top 10 MVPDs as of September 2011

MSO	Subscribers
Comcast Cable Communications	22,630,000
DirecTV	19,760,000
Dish Network Corporation	13,945,000
Time Warner Cable, Inc.	12,109,000
Cox Communications, Inc.	4,789,000
Charter Communications, Inc.	4,371,000
Verizon Communications, Inc.	3,979,000
AT&T, Inc.	3,583,000
Cablevision Systems Corporation	2,264,000
Bright House Networks LLC	2,109,000

Source: NCTA (2012)

Table 7.2
Top 10 Programming Networks as of 2011

Network	Subscribers
TBS	102,800,000
Discovery	101,900,000
USA Network	101,800,000
TNT	101,700,000
The Weather Channel	101,700.000
Nickelodeon	101,600,000
Food Network	101,400,000
ESPN2	101,000,000
C-Span	101,000,000
CNN	101,000,000

Source: NCTA (2012)

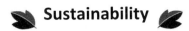

Sustainability

The biggest sustainability issue with multichannel television providers is the set top box. Older boxes and DVRs can consume almost as much power as a television set and often can't be turned off but can only be put into sleep mode. That sleep mode may not even be providing much energy savings. Providers are now encouraging and supplying customers with more efficient boxes (Ellis, 2012). CableLabs are testing new boxes with a "Light Sleep" mode that can cut energy use by as much as 20%. They note "Light sleep refers to a lower-power condition that allows essential activities within a set-top box to continue while energy consumption associated with other tasks, such as channel turning and video display, is discontinued" (Hiatt, 2012).

TBS has the greatest number of U.S. subscribers with an estimated 102.8 million. Table 7.2 shows the top 10 programming networks in 2011 (NCTA, 2012).

U.S. DBS

DISH Network had 13.9 million subscribers and DirecTV had 19.8 million subscribers in the United States as of September 2011. (NCTA, 2012) Subscriber growth is flat, which is why DBS providers are looking to offer new services like mobile Internet access.

U.S. Pay Television Services

HBO and Cinemax have the most premium channel subscribers with more than 41 million in the United States. HBO on Demand is the leading SVOD service (About HBO, 2012). Showtime is in second place with around 21.3 million subscribers (Carter, 2012), and is now aggressively pursuing HBO's core audience with original programming such as *Homeland*. Starz is third with 19.6 million subscribers. In the past, Starz differentiated itself from HBO and Showtime by focusing on movies rather than original series, but is now producing original series such as *Spartacus* (About Starz, n.d.).

PPV buy rates are down. UFC (mixed martial arts) events had been generating tremendous buy rates but only generated 6.8 million buys in 2011 compared to 9.2 in 2010 (Fox, 2012) Boxing events did fairly well in 2012 with the Pacquiao vs. Mosley fight bringing in 1.3 million buys (McKenna, 2012).

Factors to Watch

Multichannel television services are continuing to evolve. Changes will most likely occur in the way people get their services and the variety of services offered.

Broadband distribution and cross-platform services. Internet distribution will continue to thrive, and multichannel television services will expand their streaming services to capture their audiences and prevent cord-cutting.

Uncertainty over retransmission consent and carriage contracts. As a bill winds through Congress to eliminate retransmission consent and must-carry, look for increased broadcasting industry lobbying. What role the FCC will play in this battle remains to be seen.

Mobile Wireless Services. DBS providers are looking to better compete with cable companies by offering wireless Internet service. The FCC will determine if these companies will be allowed to use their satellite spectrum to deliver new services. Cable companies are experimenting with Wi-Fi networks as an add-on for their broadband customers.

Cutting the Cord. Even as multichannel television providers are rolling out streaming services and mobile apps, more and more users are deciding to cancel service and use already-available and lower-cost services like Netflix, Hulu, and YouTube and free over-the-air television. Many households cut their multichannel television service when the economy fell, but as it rises are these customers going to come back?

Bibliography

About HBO. (2012). HBO. Retrieved from http://www.hbo.com/#/about/index.html

About Starz (n.d.). Retrieved from http://starz.mediaroom.com/index.php?s=18.

Apps. (2012). Showtime. Retrieved from http://www.sho.com/sho/apps.

Bangeman, E. (2007). Telecoms get a break with new FCC franchise rules. *Ars Technica*. Retrieved from http://arstechnica.com/news.ars/post/20070306-telecoms-get-a-break-with-new-fcc-franchise-rules.html.

Berger, R. (2007). DirecTV's 100 channel promise. *TVtechnology.com*. Retrieved from http://www.tvtechnology.com/pages/s.0082/t.8585.html.

The Cable Communications Act of 1984. (1984). *Public Law* 98-549. Retrieved from http://www.publicaccess.org/cableact.html.

Carlin, T. (2006). Direct broadcast satellites. In A. Grant & J. Meadows (Eds.). *Communication technology update, 10th edition*. Boston, Focal Press.

Carter, B (2012). With "Homeland" Showtime makes gains on HBO. *The New York Times*. Retrieved from http://www.nytimes.com/2012/01/30/business/media/with-homeland-showtime-makes-gains-on-hbo.html

Channick, R. (2012). Tribune Co, DirecTV read deal over WSFL broadcasts. *SunSentinel*. Retrieved from http://www.sun-sentinel.com/business/ct-biz-0405-tribune-directtv-20120405-15,0,7649233.story

Comcast 3D Services (2012). Comcast. Retrieved from http://www.comcast.com/Corporate/Learn/DigitalCable/3D.html

Dickson, G. (2010a). ESPN declares 2D/3D production a success. Test may spur more cost-effective 3D techniques. *Broadcasting & Cable*. Retrieved from http://www.broadcastingcable.com/article/450008 ESPN_Declares_2D_3D_Production_a_Success.php

Dickson, G. (2010b, March 15). The Masters takes 3D leap. 3D coverage to be distributed by Comcast. *Broadcasting & Cable*. Retrieved from http://www.broadcastingcable.com/article/450259-The_Masters_Takes_3D_Leap.php

DirecTV Everywhere (2012). DirecTV. Retrieved http://support.directv.com/app/answers/detail/a_id/3666

Donohue, S. (2012). Genachowski: FCC watching marketplace to determine if transmission reform is warranted. *FierceCable*. Retrieved from http://www.fiercecable.com/story/genachowski-fcc-watching-marketplace-determine-if-retransmission-reform-war/2012-04-17

Ellis, L. (2012). A deeper dive on set-tops, power use. *Multichannel News*. Retrieved from http://www.multichannel.com/blog/Translation_Please/33218-A_Deeper_Dive_on_Set_Tops_Power_Use.php

Farrell, M. (2012). DirecTV files fcc complaint against tribune. *Multichannel News*. Retrieved from http://www.multichannel.com/article/482650-DirecTV_Files_FCC_Complaint_Against_Tribune.php

Flint, J. (2011). DirecTV and News Corp. reach new deal. Los Angeles Times. Retrieved from http://latimesblogs.latimes.com/entertainmentnewsbuzz/2011/10/directv-and-news-corp-reach-new-deal.html

Fox, J. (2012). 2011 Year in review: UFC PPV buyrates. *MMA Manifesto*. Retrieved from http://www.mma-manifesto.com/ufc-ppv-data/ppv-main/2011-year-in-review-ufc-ppv-buyrates.html

Frankel D. (2012) The good and bad news from the latest pay TV subscriber figures. Paidcontent.org. Retrieved from http://paidcontent.org/2012/03/20/419-the-good-and-bad-news-from-the-latest-pay-tv-subscriber-figures/

HBO GO about (n.d.). Retrieved from http://www.hbogo.com/#about/

Hiatt, K (2012). CableLabs-Energy Lab tests verify significant set-top power savings from "light sleep" mode. NCTA. Retrieved from http://www.ncta.com/ReleaseType/MediaRelease/CableLabs-Energy-Lab-Tests-Verify-Significant-Set-Top-Power-Savings-from-Light-Sleep-Mode.aspx

Hopper (2012). Dish. Retrieved from http://www.dish.com/technology/hopper/

Kaufman, D. (2007, July 22). HBO On Demand: "The Wire." *TV Week*. Retrieved from http://www.tvweek.com/news/2007/07/the_wire_hbo_on_demand.php.

McKenna, J. (2012), Pacquiao tops Mayweather in PPV buys for last three fights. *BoxingNews24*. Retrieved from http://www.boxingnews24.com/2012/01/pacquiao-tops-mayweather-in-ppv-buys-for-last-three-fights/

The Museum of Broadcast Communications. (n.d.). *Scrambled signals*. Retrieved from http://www.museum.tv/archives/etv/S/htmlS/scrambledsig/scrambledsig.htm.

Lieberman, D. (2011). FCC tells cable: Don't drop independent channels during contract fights. *Deadline New York*. Retrieved from http://www.deadline.com/2011/08/fcc-tells-cable-dont-drop-independent-channels-during-contract-fights/

National Cable and Telecommunications Association. (n.d.). *History of cable television*. Retrieved from http://www.ncta.com/About/About/HistoryofCableTelevision.aspx.

National Cable and Telecommunications Association. (2012). *Operating Metrics*. Retrieved from http://www.ncta.com/StatsGroup/operatingmetric.aspx.

On demand menu. (n.d.). *Comcast*. Retrieved from http://images.tvplanner.net/comcast_menuGuide.pdf.

Ovide, S. (2010, March 2). New York ABC station may go dark for cablevision customers. *The Wall Street Journal*. Retrieved from http://online.wsj.com/article/SB10001424052748704125804575096320101246524.html

Patterson, B. & Katzmaier, D. (2008). HDTV programming compared. *C/NET News*. Retrieved from http://www.cnet.com/4520-7874_1-5108854-3.html.

Peers, M. (2010, March 3). The ABC's of Cablevision's dispute over television fees. *The Wall Street Journal*. Retrieved from http://online.wsj.com/article/SB10001424052748704548604575097823903723394.html

Pegoraro, R. (2012). Do you need a box for digital cable. *USA Today*. Retrieved from http://www.usatoday.com/tech/products/story/2012-04-15/pegoraro-digital-cable/54262372/1

Radia, R. (2012). A free market defense of retransmission consent. *Openmarket.org*. Retrieved from http://www.openmarket.org/2012/04/11/a-free-market-defense-of-retransmission-consent/

Ramachandran, S. (2012) Cable firms warm to outdoor Wi-Fi. *The Wall Street Journal*. Retrieved from http://online.wsj.com/article/SB10001424052970203315804577211003213283714.html

Ramachandran, A. and Launder, W. (2012). At DISH Network, the wireless business beckons. *The Wall Street Journal*. Retrieved from http://online.wsj.com/article/SB10001424052970203918304577240843511338590.html

Reynolds, M. (2011). MSG Network, Time Warner Cable battle over carriage renewal. *Multichannel News*. Retrieved from http://www.multichannel.com/article/478058-MSG_Network_Time_Warner_Cable_Battle_Over_Carriage_Renewal.php

Schatz, A. (2012a). FCC to review sports blackout rules. *The Wall Street Journal*. Retrieved from http://online.wsj.com/article/SB10001424052970204409004577157200717279514.html

Schatz, A. (2012b). FCC plans new rules on satellite airwaves. *The Wall Street Journal*. Retrieved from http://online.wsj.com/article/SB10001424052702304724404577295580800235556.html

Sintumuang, K. (2012). Cutting the cord on cable. *The Wall Street Journal*. Retrieved from http://online.wsj.com/article/SB10001424052970203550304577138841278154700.html

Sky Angel History and Timeline (n.d). *Sky Angel*. Retrieved from http://www.skyangel.com/About/CompanyInfo/Timeline/

Spangler, T. (2009, December 15). Comcast keeps 'beta' tag on online TV service. Top cable operator hedging against kinks, ad models, windowing. *Multichannel News*. Retrieved from http://www.multichannel.com/article/440472-Comcast_Keeps_Beta_Tag_On_Online_TV_Service.php

Spangler, T. (2010c, March 29). DirecTV puts on ESPN's 3D glasses. Satellite operator to carry 3D telecasts of 25 World Cup matches and other events. *Multichannel News*. Retrieved from http://www.multichannel.com/article/450791-DirecTV_Puts_On_ESPN_s_3D_Glasses.php

Spangler, T. (2012). Xbox pipes in Comcast VOD, HBO Go And MLB.TV. *Multichannel News*. Retrieved from http://www.multichannel.com/article/482384-Xbox_Pipes_In_Comcast_VOD_HBO_Go_And_MLB_TV.php

Streampix (2012). Comcast. Retrieved from http://www.comcast.com/streampix

Stewart, C. (2012). Over-the-air TV catches second wind, aided by web. *The Wall Street Journal*. Retrieved from http://online.wsj.com/article/SB10001424052970204059804577229451364593094.html

TV Everywhere (2012). Dish. Retrieved from http://www.dish.com/technology/tv-everywhere/

Watch 3D Movies and TV with DirecTV (2012. DirecTV. Retrieved from http://www.directv.com/DTVAPP/content/technology/3d

Wilkerson, D. (2010, January 4). Dispute keeps Food Network, HGTV off Cablevision systems. Cable carrier, Scripps Interactive point fingers as signals go dark. *MarketWatch*. Retrieved from http://www.marketwatch.com/story/fee-spat-keeps-food-network-hgtv-off-cablevision-2010-01-04

Worden, N. (2010, February 25). Cablevision plans service to display web content on TV. *The Wall Street Journal*. Retrieved from http://online.wsj.com/article/SB10001424052748704240004575085041422759152.html

8

IPTV: Video over the Internet

Jeffrey S. Wilkinson, Ph.D.[*]

Why Study IPTV?

✦ Because IPTV is changing the business—and our perspective as consumers—of television and mobile video.

✦ Because IPTV is forcing advertisers to explore a variety of new approaches to reach people.

✦ Because IPTV is a global phenomenon that is rapidly being adopted by people all over the world.

We are firmly in the age of ubiquitous digital video which industry insiders are calling "TV Everywhere" (Dreier, 2012b,; Schaeffler, 2012). Broadband delivery of content and services to multiple devices in the home is blurring the lines between cable, telco, satellite, and broadcast businesses. Whether in five years we'll keep using OTT (over the top) boxes or rely only on our smart TVs remains to be seen. But IPTV service will include our mobile devices as well. Increasingly, we are relying on the Internet to deliver quality video news and entertainment programs and to enable us to upload our own content in a variety of digital forms. Perhaps the biggest question is whether we'll eventually get our TV from Web channels àla carte or through an aggregator such as Netflix or Hulu.

IPTV is defined by the International Telecommunications Union as "multimedia services such as television/video/audio/text/graphics/data delivered over IP-based networks managed to support the required level of quality of service (QoS)/quality of experience (QoE), security, interactivity, and reliability" (ITU-T Newslog, 2009). IPTV provides a more personalized interactive experience and the types of services are only limited by your imagination. IPTV systems around the world offer virtually all forms of content on demand.

Globally it can be more complicated than it seems because all the services and content involving digital video tend to use the term "IPTV." IPTV can involve streaming, satellite delivery of audio and video, wireline delivery of audio and video, and wireless delivery of audio and video. IPTV services are designed to seamlessly bring video to all screens all the time—televisions, computers, and mobile devices (such as mobile phones and tablets). It is difficult to find marketing material that does not use the term.

Media companies and service providers continually compete to bring digital services into the home. There is a lot of money at stake as consumers globally look for video on demand. Whether it is through a dish or fiber optic cable, a myriad of companies provide it through IPTV. In the United States, consumers can choose from satellite companies such as DirecTV or DISH, telco or cable companies such as SureWest or Comcast, and Web-based companies such as Google and Yahoo. What is a customer to do? This chapter hopes to sort out the confusion about IPTV and provide a glimpse as to where it's going.

---

[*] Professor, Houston Baptist University (Houston, Texas).

Background

Two basic and distinct forms of IPTV emerged (Light & Lancefield, 2007), centering around distribution via the PC (Web television) or through a set-top box (STB). The term "streaming" used to describe the former and IPTV the latter, but these lines have blurred further with high-powered mobile devices, hybrid broadcast-OTT boxes, and new "Smart TVs." IPTV is the digital standard for watching your favorite network program at home in surround-sound high definition or watching a sporting match live on your cellphone (or perhaps watching both while playing a videogame on your Wii). A third type of IPTV is "downloading," whereby a file with the media content is transferred over the Internet for storage on a computer or other networked device so that the user can access the content at any time.

Historically, streaming audio and video content over the Web began around 1995 when Progressive Networks launched RealAudio. At first Web audio and video were just an interesting add-on to computers (along with gaming, email, word processing, and simple surfing). After a brief partnership with Progressive Networks, Microsoft launched Windows Media Player, and shortly after that, Apple launched Quicktime, an MPEG-based architecture/codec. In 1999, Apple introduced QuickTime TV, using Akamai Technologies' streaming media delivery service. A few years later came Flash, DIVX, MPEG players, and others. As the technology improved and bandwidth increased, new applications sprang up. Sports highlights, news, and music clips became increasingly popular. Napster made (illegal) file-sharing a household phrase, and YouTube heralded the beginning of a new age, redefining what media professionals and audiences considered to be content.

Types of Streaming

Probably the most common distinctions are "live," "time-shifted," and "on demand." Among media companies and professional business applications, on-demand streamed video content is more common than live streamed content. Two leaders in on-demand streaming are Netflix and Hulu. To offer on-demand streaming, they have to have a streaming server with enough capacity to hold content that can be configured so the maximum number of simultaneous users can be accommodated (unlike broadcasting, the number of simultaneous users is limited to server capacity). For professional *live* streaming, you need all of the above and the addition of a dedicated computer (called a "broadcaster" or "encoder") to create the streams from the live inputs (such as a microphone or camera) by digitizing, compressing, and sending out the content to the streaming server. Most of the commercial Web video services offer content that is on-demand.

From a consumer perspective, true streaming is not downloading, but occurs when content takes a few seconds to buffer before playing. Nothing is actually stored on your hard drive. True streaming is enabled when the provider employs a special streaming server. According to Ellis (2012b), the most popular streaming servers are Microsoft's Smooth Streaming, Apple's HTTP Live Streaming (HLS), and Adobe's Dynamic Streaming.

The advantages of streaming are speed, (host) control, and flexibility. Streamed material is played back quickly—almost instantaneously. Control is maximized for the host, because the original content remains on the server, and access can be controlled using password, digital rights management (DRM), registration, or some other security feature. Finally, since streamed segments are placed individually on a host server and can be updated or changed as needed, there is tremendous flexibility. Increasingly, broadband connections enable delivery of high-definition content. Both Apple and Windows Media Video Websites offer HD clips that can be downloaded or streamed at resolutions of 720p and 1080p.

Consumer Streaming Platforms

There are several player-platforms for providing and playing streamed video. For over a decade, the main streaming players were Realplayer, Windows Media Player (WMP), and Apple Quicktime (until the launch of iTunes). The ubiquitous Flash plug-in used by YouTube is technically a browser plug-in, not a streaming player, because consumers cannot operate the player independently of the browser, save and manipulate files, or create playlists.

Table 8.1
Streaming Media Player Growth in Unique Users (in Thousands)

Month	iTunes	Apple QuickTime	iTunes+QuickTime	RealPlayer	Windows Media Player
Jan-04	1,118	15,458	16,576	28,593	51,056
Jan-05	5,370	13,136	18,506	28,182	60,782
Jan-06	18,568	12,817	31,385	28,687	71,112
Jan-07	27,396	13,934	41,330	31,309	72,510
Jan-08	35,269	12,531	47,800	25,800	75,810
Jan-09	44,764	13,832	58,596	20,709	81,795
Aug-10	43,257	16,157	59,414	10,609	70,025
Mar-11	44,650	14,404	59,054	8,823	68,324

Source: Nielsen Online cited in Website Optimization.com

According to Weboptimization.com, Nielsen Online has tracked the changes of the four most widely adopted players, Windows Media Player (Microsoft), Real (RealNetworks), QuickTime (Apple), and iTunes (Apple). Each has some technical differences, each has its merits, and all are regularly improved. Table 8.1 shows the number of unique users of the popular streaming players from January 2004 to March 2011. It's important to note that the combination of iTunes and QuickTime are expected to surpass Windows Media Player in 2012 (Apple iTunes Penetration, 2011).

Apple/QuickTime/iTunes. In 1999, Apple began offering a streaming application with the QuickTime 4 platform. QuickTime has been popular because it plays on both PC and Macintosh computers and delivers virtually any kind of file from your Web server. The QuickTime file format is an open standard and was adopted as part of the MPEG family of standards. Apple has a few types of servers (such as Xserve and Mac OSX server). To produce live events, Apple provides QuickTime Broadcaster. Most recently, Apple has been marketing and providing content and services to take advantage of the combined applications of iPhone, iTunes, iPod, and Apple TV.

Microsoft Windows. Windows Media Player has been the most-installed player in the world for several years (see Table 8.1). The latest version (WMP 12) has been positively reviewed and remains a standard for online video. In addition, Microsoft has

moved ahead with HTTP "smooth streaming" with Silverlight. Silverlight is a cross-browser, cross-platform plug-in for "creating rich media applications and business applications for the Web, desktop, and mobile devices" (What is Silverlight?, 2010). Silverlight is compatible across platforms because it is based on the commonly accepted MPEG-4 file format, while WMP continues to be the proprietary Microsoft format.

RealNetworks. Although the Realplayer continues to drop in popularity, Real must be credited for having been the first on the scene and having the foresight to give away players rather than sell them. Since 1995, several generations of improvements have been made in its products. But even though Real diversified to offer content such as music, movies, and gaming services, its popularity continues to wane.

Adobe/Adobe Media Player/Flash. In December 2005, Adobe acquired Macromedia and has since enjoyed great success with the Flash platform. In May 2008, Adobe announced the Open Screen Project. Supported by companies such as Cisco, Intel, Marvell, Motorola, Nokia, Samsung, Sony Ericsson, Toshiba, and Verizon Wireless, the project seeks to provide "rich Internet experiences across televisions, personal computers, mobile devices, and consumer electronics" (Adobe, 2008). Content providers such as BBC, MTV Networks, and NBC Universal are also involved. The Open Screen project employs the

Adobe Flash Player (and in the future, Adobe AIR) to allow developers and designers to publish content and applications across desktops. In so doing, Adobe surpassed Microsoft in the area of media support, particularly H.264/Advanced Audio Coding (AAC) audio and full HD video playback.

Podcasting and Music Streaming

We sometimes forget that streaming and downloading does not always mean video. A relative of video streaming, podcasting, remains an important aspect of IPTV. Podcasting refers to various types of online audio on-demand programs (Webster, 2009). Podcasts are common on the Web, and are typically programs such as a talk show, hosted music programs, or commentary. They are commonly pulled by the user as an automatic download via RSS (really simple syndication) through a service such as iTunes. According to Edison Media Research, in 2009 around 22% of Americans had ever listened to a podcast, and around 27 million had listened to a podcast in the past month (Webster, 2009). Music online also continues to be intricately involved with streaming. There are a number of pay services as well as radio stations that stream their audio programs to listeners, both live and on-demand. (For more on digital music, see Chapter 18).

Proprietary Platforms

The streaming platforms mentioned above are different from those provided by the so-called "traditional media" companies. As we are witnessing in the convergence of computers, television, and digital applications, content providers also seek to find their place in the new media environment. To stay relevant (and profitable), the race is on for distribution. It remains a question as to what companies will be able to use IPTV to supply all of a person's information, entertainment, and communication needs. Information now means not only news, but also banking, security, weather, and politics. Entertainment includes a variety of live and recorded experiences involving music, sports, and dramatic, comedic, and theatrical performances. Communication through technology can now involve all one-way or two-way interactions with family, friends, classmates, colleagues, and strangers.

The fight for who is chosen to deliver content and services is ongoing between modern media companies that have diversified from their traditional roots in either broadcast, entertainment, telephone, cable, satellite, or the Internet.

IPTV Providers

Gartner (2008) once defined IPTV as "the delivery of video programming (either broadcast or on-demand) over a carrier's managed broadband network to a customer's TV set. It does not include streaming media over the Internet to a PC." (p. 5). But as IPTV becomes "TV Anywhere" it will invariably come to include streaming media. IPTV is not a single service; it is a new carrier distribution platform over which several—if not all—communication and entertainment services are offered.

Therefore, IPTV includes regular television as well as HD, first-run films, older films, old TV shows, user-generated content, and an ever-increasing number of news, sports, and entertainment programming that includes features such as selecting camera angles, language, and real-time commentary. Still, most television watching remains relatively passive. Several of the added services sound good to consumers, but not everyone is ready to migrate to services such as surveillance and security (home, video, and banking). While it is important to bundle services, the foot in the door is still the home-TV experience. Many customers may still not care whether the provider is a telephone, cable, or satellite company. So, perhaps bundling HD content may still be the best means of differentiating services (Reedy, 2008).

While there are a number of IPTV providers in operation around the United States, the two biggest are AT&T's U-verse and Verizon FiOS.

AT&T. U-Verse TV offers up to 300 channels including HBO, Showtime, Cinemax, and Starz. Features include DVR, VOD, and HD. Packages range from $59 to $119 per month, and custom packages are also available. HD service costs an extra $10. U-verse can provide up to 10 Mb/s downstream and up to 1.5 Mb/s upstream.

Verizon. FiOS TV offers up to 200 channels including all the majors plus international channels. Features include VOD, HD, and Multi-Room DVR (control and watch DVR programs from multiple rooms). Pricing is generally $39.99 per month but varies depending on location. Some popular cable channels involve additional costs.

By the end of 2011 FiOS had roughly 4.2 million subscribers compared to U-verse with 3.8 million (AT&T, 2012; Shammo, 2012). AT&T's U-verse is slower but noticeably less expensive than Verizon FiOS and is projected to be the leading provider sometime in 2013 Both are projected to surpass 5 million subscribers earlier that year (O'Neill, 2012).

IPTV via P2P

While cable, telephony, and satellite are working to deliver the highest quality (and most expensive) programs and services into the home, the "other" delivery form of IPTV is also making inroads. So-called "P2P" or peer-to-peer networking became famous through Napster and associated with illegal file-sharing, so some prefer to call it "distributed streaming media" (Miller, 2007, p. 34). Either way, P2P is far less expensive than the STB approach. Some believe that delivery of high-definition video may need to use P2P in order to be cost-effective.

Well-known sources of content via P2P include BitTorrent and Vuze (formerly Azureus), and content owners such as Fox, Viacom, and Turner use P2P to publish and distribute content. The basic concept is that P2P moves digital content through several paths before reaching the user's (destination) computer. While OTT/STB systems need to purchase several servers to dedicate bandwidth and deliver programs, P2P becomes more efficient (and less expensive) as more clients join the distributed network. This is because the content can be drawn in pieces from multiple sources. This type of network tends to be less concerned with copyright and more about sharing popular files. Obscure or less common content will take longer to pull together because there will be fewer sources to draw from. In January 2012 the top five torrent sites were said to be Pirate Bay (around 2 billion page views per month), Torrentz, Kickass Torrents, Isohunt, and BTjunkie (Torrentfreak, 2012).

One of the factors influencing the STB-P2P debate is digital rights management. Controlling access to the content is a key element for STB providers, and they argue it is the only/best way to maintain appropriate (monetized) use. P2P sources such as BitTorrent and Abacast suggest that a more passive approach to DRM will win the heart and wallet of the consumer. In other words, they suggest marking the file so everyone knows where it came from, but then let it go.

Recent Developments

TV Program Creators Shift to the Web

There are increasing signs that Hollywood is following journalism to adopt a "Web-first" mentality. TV program creators are increasingly shifting to the "TV Everywhere" mentality. According to Coyle (2012), YouTube, Neflix and Hulu are rolling out increasing amounts of original programming and inevitably will appear more and more like traditional television. Schnitzer (2012) notes that program producers are increasingly pitching original programs specifically for the Web. This trend toward Web-only video programming will shift money from traditional television to online. One prediction is that the money for Web video will grow from a $2 billion marketplace in 2012 to $3 billion in 2013 and up to $7 billion by 2015 (Schnitzer, 2012).

Even Facebook debuted an original film in February 2012, entitled *Tomorrow when the War Began*. Published reports stated that Facebook would get 30% share of revenues from the movie's streaming (Arlen, 2012). This rise of so-called "f-commerce" (Facebook commerce) envisions increasing the use of social media and online platforms as a means of delivering quality original content to consumers (Arlen, 2012).

Successfully Streaming Sports

Sports continues to find its niche through streamed video. In addition to the estimated 111.3 million who watched the 2012 Super Bowl on television, NBC Sports reported a record number of identified streams (Stelter, 2012). Data from two measurement firms confirmed that 2.1 million unique users watched almost 4.6 million live video streams totaling around 78.6 million total minutes of streamed content from the football game (Winslow, 2012). In addition, over 1.8 million clips of the game and the game advertisements were also viewed online. During the regular season, the average number of unique users was around 300,000. NBC said these numbers show people have accepted the streamed content as a complement to the broadcast. The online stream had different camera angles and a live chat box. Meanwhile, ESPN partnered with Facebook for the 2012 NCAA basketball tournament, providing a redesigned SportsCenter page and new video player (Spangler, 2012d).

Finally, Universal Sports (a joint venture of NBC Sports Group and InterMedia Partners) announced a multiyear, multiplatform distribution deal with Dish Network. The deal would enable Dish customers to view extensive 2012 Olympic coverage and include access on customers' mobile devices and tablets (Reynolds, 2012).

On Demand Competition Heats Up

Netflix began 2011 as the pre-eminent movie rental successor to Blockbuster (which held the crown when people actually rented VHS tapes). But a series of missteps resulted in thousands of complaints and cancelled subscriptions. First, Netflix raised the price of its streaming service, which led many to drop their DVD-by-mail component. Then it said it would split off its DVD business as a new company called "Qwikster." After complaints, Netflix abandoned its Qwikster plans.

Netflix may have lost its strategic edge, and now it faces competition on a number of fronts. First, Hulu Plus and Amazon Prime are increasing in popularity. In early 2012, Comcast announced they were launching a direct competitor called Xfinity Streampix, a multiscreen subscription video service of movies and TV shows. Comcast said they had forged licensing agreements with a number of major firms that would enable customers to watch on multiple devices including TV's, computers, and mobile devices (Spangler, 2012b). At the same time, Verizon and Coinstar announced a joint venture combining Redbox's new release DVD rentals with video-on-demand streaming (Spangler, 2012a). The service (no

announced name at publication) was to launch in late 2012 and compete directly with Netflix.

Mobile Video Ads

Video is quickly becoming the norm rather than the exception for mobile ad campaigns. According to mobile video ad network *Rhythm New Media*, there was a 22% jump in the number of marketers using in-stream video in their mobile campaigns during the fourth quarter of 2011 (Whitney, 2012). Now, more than 9 out of 10 advertisers embraced video in their campaigns because the engagement rates are much higher with mobile devices. On average, 89% of mobile video ads are viewed to completion compared to 15-30% for computer-based viewing. The explanation given is that computer users are far more distracted when watching video in the home or office compared to mobile users (Whitney, 2012). The report also noted that in 2011 around 375 brands ran video campaigns on the Rhythm network, compared to 150 brands in 2010 and 29 in 2009.

Streaming Audio: Spotify

A digital music streaming service called Spotify landed in the U.S. from Europe in 2011 and generated excitement among music fans. Spotify allows music fans to listen to any song at any time. According to Dreier (2012b), this and other personalized music streaming services like Pandora and Slacker Radio continue to erode radio listenership (for more on radio, see chapter 10).

Current Status

The rise of IPTV is continuing at a steady pace, depending heavily on broadband. Globally, IPTV—providing video services over managed IP networks to consumers' televisions—has been rapidly rising since its commercial introduction in 2002. In 2011 it was reported that almost 10% of broadband-linked homes adopted IPTV, totaling over 50 million subscribers worldwide (IPTV News, 2011). The leader in this type of IPTV adoption is France, with over 11 million homes subscribed or roughly 50% of broadband-connected homes (IPTV News, 2011). China reported 10.5 million homes, and according to Nielsen (2012b), the United States had roughly 5.1

million homes with broadcast-only/broadband homes (compared to over 100 million U.S. homes with cable, telco, or satellite).

Online video use continues to grow in the U.S. According to data from comScore Video Metrix, 181 million U.S. Internet users watched nearly 40 billion videos of online content in January 2012 (comScore, 2012). These figures were up from two years earlier when it was estimated that there were over 140-million unique viewers (Lewin, 2010) watching an average of 3 hours of online video per month (comScore, 2010). The report noted that Google sites (mostly YouTube) reached almost 152 million of those users. The average viewer watched 22.6 hours of online video content during the month, with Google sites (7.5 hours) and Hulu (3.2 hours) showing the greatest viewer engagement.

Who is Watching Online

Not surprisingly, consuming video content online continues to correlate (negatively) with age. The largest audience group for online movies and television content continues to be young adults. According to Nielsen, the age groups 18-24 and 25-34 spent 6.5 to 7.5 hours per month watching video on the Internet, roughly twice the time reported by teens and seniors (Nielsen, 2012b). In terms of watching video on the Internet, there are noticeable differences in behaviors by ethnicity or race (see Table 8.2).

Online video viewing continues to be negatively related to age, but there should be some growth as early adopters get older. The same holds true for using a mobile phone to watch video. In terms of gender, men still tend to watch more online video than women, especially in the 18-49 category. Nielsen data showed men report spending around seven hours per month with online video and women report just under five hours per month. However, mobile phone video viewing for this group was identical at 4:20 per month for both men and women (Nielsen, 2011). In the 50+ age groups, men watched a bit more video online than women (2:44 versus 2:22), but women watch quite a bit more video using mobile phones (3:37 per month to 2:10 for men).

Who's Going Where for Video

By far the most popular source for online video is still YouTube. YouTube has been the change agent for cultures, countries, and the label used for an entire generation. The site has been credited for allowing other companies to test the waters and survive even as analysts have speculated how unprofitable YouTube itself has been for parent Google. But in the past couple of years Google has been able to monetize the video clips and increasing numbers of videos are advertising-supported (Lawler, 2011).

Table 8.2

Video Audience Composition—Monthly Time Spent (Hours:Minutes): Ethnicity & Race, Q3 2011

	White	African-American	Hispanic	Asian
Traditional TV	142:05	205:56	125:46	95:55
Watching Timeshifted TV (all TV homes)	11:52	8:25	6:50	8:14
DVR Playback (in Homes with DVRs)	25:16	21:36	22:01	21:24
Watching Video on Internet	3:52	6:11	6:29	9:28
Mobile Subscribers Watching Video on a Mobile Phone	3:37	5:30	4:20	5:47

Source: Nielsen (2012)

While YouTube and other sites are moving to offer so-called "premium content" (Schnitzer, 2012), full-length movies and TV shows are consistently among the most viewed content on the major video sharing sites (Lewin, 2010). Many movies and television shows are also widely available on peer-to-peer networks and BitTorrent sites.

For example, major television networks now provide more full-length episodes of primetime television shows for free online. ABC's *Lost* and *Desperate Housewives* were among the first free offerings, and many other shows from all networks soon followed. There are a number of ways to find and watch your favorite programs online, the most popular source by far is YouTube, followed by sites such as VEVO and Hulu (see Table 8.3). Table 8.4 lists the 'stickiest' online video sites. By far Netflix tops the list with viewers averaging over 10 hours, 7 minutes (Nielsen, 2012a).

Table 8.3

Top 10 Online Video Destinations Total Streams (Thousands)

Rank	Brand	Total Streams (000) Dec 2011
1	YouTube	13,782,781
2	Hulu	756,921
3	VEVO	435,411
4	AOL Media Network	358,784
5	Yahoo	338,700
6	Netflix	251,792
7	ESPN Digital Network	233,104
8	Comcast Digital Entertainment Websites	216,502
9	MSN/WindowsLive/Bing	205,260
10	Disney Online	167,892

Source: Nielsen Online (2012)

Table 8.4

Top Online Brands, Ranked by Time Spent Viewing per Viewer (500K Unique Viewer Minimum)

Video Brand	Dec 2011 Time per Viewer (hours:minutes)
Netflix	10:07
Hulu	3:08
YouTube	3:02
Justin.tv	2:28
Megavideo	2:10
Youkou	1:42
CWTV.com	1:32
CBS Entertainment Websites	1:05
Nickelodeon Family & Parents	1:04
ABC Television	1:03

Source: The Nielsen Company

Mobile Video

The integration of streaming services with home entertainment and mobile broadband has also helped drive up consumer adoption of smartphones. (For more on Mobile Telephones, see Chapter 20. For more on broadband networks, see Chapter 23.) The rise in smartphone sales is also changing what kind of video audiences have searched for in the past. In 2007, news was the top category, but in 2008, Nielsen reported that for mobile video, comedy was the solid number one (Covey, 2009). Music, films, news, weather, sports, and user-generated content represent other highest-viewed categories. Mobile video has become so common that it is no longer useful to divide by genre or category.

As more people adopt smartphones, overall use and influence of mobile video will rise. It may be that preference for short, entertaining video content simply reflects acceptance (and use) of mobile video content to pass short periods of inactivity. The brief periods when people are in transit or waiting for others, for example, are opportune times for a short burst of video entertainment.

Factors to Watch

Rise of the "Cord-Cutters"

Nielsen (2012b) notes that the number of homes that are "broadcast-only/broadband" rose over 20% the previous year. Although the numbers remain small compared to cable/telco/satellite homes that combine with broadband, the cost of keeping both may not prove to be sustainable for many households, especially when advances in other types of media technologies enable consumers to get "TV Everywhere." Some research notes that two out of three consumers report that mobile connectivity is more important than cable (Consumers say, 2012).

Previously, Graham (2009) suggested that the overall goal for consumers is ultimately to "personalize" their television experience and merge it with other communication and media devices both in and out of the home.

Graham posits the following conclusions for consumers and IPTV:

✦ Consumers want an environment that can be personalized similar to being able to customizing a car interior. Choices include volume, picture-in-picture, channel lineup/favorites, on-screen notification (such as for caller ID).

✦ Consumers want services to be independent of their location or device. People recognize that video quality is affected by bandwidth (mobile phone display demands are different from HDTV), but even recognizing this, they want any and all services available regardless whether they're at home or on the go.

✦ Consumers want their TV integrated with other services. ALL other services. Convergence includes the synchronization of Web, TV, telephone, security cameras, music playlists, etc.

✦ Consumers want "wide and deep" programming choices on demand. People want to be able to access any written, audio, or visual content ever produced, the so-called "long tail" of what's available via the Internet.

This somewhat utopian view is popular among industry insiders. We believe we know what people want, and what they want is every possible array of gadget and service we have to offer...for as much as we can charge ($100, $200, $300 per month?). But this view has to be balanced with the reality about technology. We have to remember that 20 years ago most people could not set the time on their VCRs. The IPTV multi-service multi-screen time-shifting global-interactive experience may simply overwhelm most consumers. In tough economic times, people may opt for watching old favorites for free on an increasing number of Web video sites.

Network Congestion and Pay-By-Volume Video

Video file sizes have always been an issue on the Web, and engineers have worked hard to reduce file size and maximize stream rates to balance Web traffic volume. The Web is not really built for all media and human communication. But the use of video continues to exponentially increase. Cisco is reporting that there will be more smartphones than humans by the end of 2012, consuming an average of 2.6 GB per month, and fully two-thirds of the traffic is video (Ellis, 2012b). As programmers and websites continue to upload higher-quality and lengthier content (movies, programs, webisodes, even YouTube clips), the danger of too much traffic slowing down the Web becomes more real.

Some countries are taking note. In Korea, Korea Telecom cut off access to consumers' smart TVs sold by Samsung. According to Ellis (2012b), the Maeil Business Newspaper wrote "KT insists smart TVs share the costs of quality maintenance of the Internet as they tend to hog the networks, while TV makers argue they have no obligation to do so." In the U.S., Time Warner has been experimenting with usage-based broadband billing in Texas (Spangler, 2012c). Despite some complaints, the carrier pitched "Essentials Broadband" as a way to tie usage with billing. Depending on the plan, customers could pay less for staying under the 5 GB/month ceiling. Using more, however, could result in additional charges. At least some Time Warner execs suggest this may be the future for how cable companies price and package products (Farrell, 2012).

Trans Border Content Flow

Globally, nations will have to think about the invisible border around our consuming audiences. Regarding HD, for example, the constraints are not physical, but regulatory. Since the Web is global, European or Asian content providers can compete with domestic companies for market share. In the United States, there are a number of ways for consumers to purchase services from content providers in other countries. The current does not always run both ways, however, and protectionism manifests itself in many forms. Many providers whose content (or advertising) is targeted at users in one country can be programmed to refuse to deliver streams to users in other countries, using the IP address of the user to identify the user's location.

For example, in early 2012 Mexican billionaire Carlos Slim announced the launch of an American Internet TV network channel called Ora.TV (Berrera, 2012). The English-language online news and entertainment channel is projected to feature a show hosted by former CNN talk show icon Larry King. Ora.TV would be free to users and rely on advertiser-support.

Regions of Growth

Projections for the future vary, but all are upbeat about IPTV. According to a report by Multimedia Research Group (MRG), the number of global IPTV subscribers have grown from 28 million in 2009 to 53 million in 2012 (O'Neil, 2012a). The same report estimated that the current growth curve would bring the numbers to over 105 million IPTV subscribers globally by 2015.

Furthermore, global IPTV market revenues are forecast to grow from US $12 billion to US $38 billion during that same period. This same study suggested that the greatest growth would be in Europe, followed by Asia (Smith, 2009).

European IPTV providers are generally telecommunications companies, and they don't face the degree of competition from cable TV as in the U.S. The incumbent operators there have direct broadband access to millions of subscribers. Top IPTV providers in Western Europe include Deutsche Telekom, Belgacom, France Telecom, Telecom Italia, British Telecom, Telefonica, and Swisscom (Focus Editors, 2010).

While most or all of these companies are firmly entrenched in their home country, services are also offered across borders in some cases. France Telecom offers service to Poland and Spain, and Telecom Italia also offers service to France, Germany, and the Netherlands.

In Asia, a number of industry watchers see China Telecom and China Unicom as having the largest potential. Japanese telecommunications company, NTT, as well as KT (Korea Telecomm) in Korea are seen as having large potential IPTV markets (Focus Editors, 2010).

Growth of Online Video Ads

The stability of video online enabled by broadband has resulted in huge growth in video advertising online over the past few years (Interactive Advertising Bureau, 2010). According to the Interactive Advertising Bureau, digital video Internet advertising revenues reached $7.9 billion in the third quarter of 2011, a 22 percent increase from the year before (Careless, 2012). Video ads work very well online because research findings indicate that people tend to finish online ads compared to TV commercials (Ellis, 2012b).

Projections are continuing to be positive for online video ads, as illustrated in Figure 8.5 (eMarketer, 2009). According to ad industry insiders, one trend driving this explosive growth is the increasing range of devices that access digital video, from web-connected TVs to iPads to smartphones. A second trend is the time-shifting and device-sharing capabilities that allow people to watch video out of the home. Since there is expanding variety in content types—from shorts to feature films—with a range of supported resolutions, the online ad market is also exploding in the type of spots that are becoming available (Careless, 2012).

Consumer-Generated Content

The joker in the deck regarding IPTV is the effect or influence of consumer-generated content. YouTube has changed the video landscape forever. From now on, Viacom and the BBC must compete with piano-playing pets and dancing ninjas for audience share. Human beings are resourceful, and we have not exhausted the possible genres or types of video content. How new forms of expression and creativity will influence future generations cannot be known, but media companies and providers of "professional" (paid-for) content will remain vigilant to adopt "the next big thing" in entertainment, information, or communication.

Program creators in the industry will continue to rely on standard program lengths (22 minutes for TV shows, for example) but probably experiment with other lengths and formats. User-generated content posted on YouTube does not have a standard length or narrative format, which is both a strength and a weakness from a marketing perspective. This unpredictability so far inhibits the revenue potential from sponsorship, product placement, or other means of generating revenue.

IPTV reflects the cacophony of the digital marketplace. With hundreds of channels, thousands of programs, and millions of clips and excerpts, it is easier than ever for individuals to create their own unique and personal media experiences.

The next stage may be mobile broadband high-definition video. No one really knows when or how it will pay for itself. Consumers may find it too inconvenient on a crowded bus or a noisy bar to warrant the cost. Or they may find it too dangerous in wind, rain, or snow to even sample the experience.

We can now vaguely see the time when we will be able to watch whatever we want, wherever we want, whenever we want, on any screen size. If we can afford it, our lives may simply be the spare moments we allow to happen between watching and being entertained.

Table 8.5

U.S. Online Advertising Spending, by Format, 2008–2014 (millions)

	2008	2009	2010	2011	2010	2013	2014
Search	$10,546	$10,782	$11,422	$12,172	$13,641	$14,694	$15,810
Banner ads	$4,877	$4,765	$4,923	$5,090	$5,411	$5,630	$5,800
Classifieds	$3,174	$2,215	$2,030	$1,915	$1,981	$2,077	$2,176
Lead Generation	$1,683	$1,521	$1,628	$1,739	$1,868	$1,984	$2,108
Rich Media	$1,642	$1,476	$1,558	$1,688	$1,868	$2,046	$2,142
Video	$734	$1,029	$1,440	$1,966	$2,858	$3,844	$5,202
Sponsorships	$387	$313	$316	$328	$351	$372	$388
E-mail	$405	$268	$283	$302	$323	$353	$374
Total	$23,448	$22,370	$23,600	$25,200	$28,300	$31,000	$34,000

Note: Numbers may not add up to total due to rounding

Source: eMarketer, December 2009

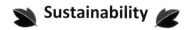

Sustainability

IPTV is considered to be one of the more sustainable technologies explored in this book. It will remain so for some time because the demand for content—high quality video that is interesting, entertaining, or both—is rapidly increasing rather than decreasing. Some aspects of this demand present implications that are worth noting, because they relate to how people use the technology and perceive it as having benefits and/or consequences.

With IPTV, once the initial setup is completed (involving computer and access to the Internet), the delivery of video content in electronic form to the consumer eliminates the need to use any additional paper, plastic, or fuel to move the content from the manufacturer to the user.

Computers do use electricity; however, computers also generate heat, which in the winter time can be useful, but in the summer months may require additional air conditioning.

According to Ellis (2012d), engineers and set-top box manufacturers are continually looking to make the boxes themselves more energy efficient. For example, the latest version (3.0) of the voluntary Energy Star requirements, proposed by the Environmental Protection Agency, asked for set-tops to use less (15%) power (or drop 3 watts, whichever is greater) while in "on" mode, and include a "deep sleep" mode to automatically kick in after awhile, just like computers. Three potential problems are (1) old boxes live a long time, (2) updates are usually sent at night when the box would be asleep, and (3) getting the wiring right is complex and could prove to be more of a hassle in the home if the box doesn't come back on as expected.

On the other hand, the availability of high-quality content that can be viewed in a home theater can reduce the need to use fuel to see a movie or experience other, similar content. This factor may be more important for adults, who increasingly may be concerned about travel time and competing with other viewers. This is not so much a factor for younger age groups, as movie going is more of a group socialization ritual and even "courting experience" for teens and young adults.

Conversely, the economics can shift very quickly. Content providers are always searching for ways to generate higher revenues and greater return from consumers. Whether consumers will shift to micropayments or pay-per-click models, or stay with traditional one-time rental charges, IPTV providers will find a way to go deeper into the wallet or purse of each consumer.

Bibliography

Adobe.com. (2008, May 1). *Adobe and industry leaders establish open screen project*. Retrieved from http://www.adobe.com/aboutadobe/pressroom/pressreleases/200804/050108AdobeOSP.html.

Apple iTunes penetration closing gap with Microsoft, April 2011 bandwidth report (2011, April 27). WebSiteOptimization.com. Retrieved from www.websiteoptimization.com/bw/1104/.

Arlen, G. (2012, February 20). Facebook's first movie debuts on February 24. *Multichannel News*. Retrieved from http://www.multichannel.com/blog/As_I_Was_Saying/33112-Facebook_s_First_Movie_Debuts_on_February_24.php.

AT&T Investor Update (2012, January 26). 4Q11 Earnings Conference Call. AT&T.com. Retrieved from http://www.att.com/Investor/Financial/Earning_Info/docs/4Q_11_slide_c.pdf

Barrera, C. (2012, March 13). Mexico's Slim aims for US Internet TV this year. *Reuters.com*. Retrieved from http://in.reuters.com/article/2012/03/12/slim-tv-idINDEE82B06520120312.

Careless, J. (2012, February 29). The state of online video advertising 2012. *Streamingmedia.com*. Retrieved from http://www.streamingmedia.com/Articles/Editorial/Featured-Articles/The-State-of-Online-Video-Advertising-2012-80985.aspx

comScore, Inc. (2010, March 8). comScore releases January 2010 U.S. online video rankings: Average YouTube viewer watched more than 93 videos in January, up 50 percent vs. year ago. comScore.com. Retrieved from http://www.comscore.com/layout/set/popup/Press_Events/Press_Releases/2010/3/comScore_Releases_January_2010_U.S._Online_Video_Rankings.

comScore, Inc. (2012, February 20). comScore releases January 2012 U.S. online video rankings: Long-form video content on the rise, reaching 6 minutes on average in January. *comScore.com* Retrieved from http://www.comscore.com/Press_Events/Press_Releases/2012/2/comScore_Releases_January_2012_U.S._Online_Video_Rankings

Consumers say cable TV more expendable than mobiles (2012, February 7). Marketing Charts. Retrieved from http://www.marketingcharts.com/television/consumers-say-cable-tv-more-expendable-than-mobiles-20986.

Covey, N. (2009, January). Tuned in … to your hand? Mobile video use in the U.S. *Nielsen.com/Consumer insight.* Retrieved from http://www.global-mediainsight.com/media/consumerinsight-mobilevideo.pdf.

Coyle, J. (2012, January 26). In original Internet shows, hints of coming change. *Yahoo News.* Retrieved from http://news.yahoo.com/original-internet-shows-hints-coming-change-231414999.html;_ylc=X3oDMTNrYmdzN3FqBF9TAzc2NjQ4MTEEYWN0A21haWxfY2IEY3QDYQRpbnRsA3VzBGxhbmcDZW4tVVMEcGtnAzQ3NzMxZmRiLThmMTYtMzIzZi1hZGVkLTFmZjNkYmFiMDIwMgRzZWMDbWl0X3NoYXJlBHNsawNtYWlsBHRlc3QD;_ylv=3.

Dreier, T. (2012, February 21). January video rankings: Overall viewing numbers continue decline. *Streamingmedia.com.* Retrieved from http://www.streamingmedia.com/Articles/News/Online-Video-News/January-Video-Ra nkings-Overall-Viewing-Numbers-Continue-Decline-80785.aspx.

Dreier, T. (2012, February 28). The state of media and entertainment video 2012. *Streamingmedia.com.* Retrieved from http://streamingmedia.com/Articles/Editorial/Featured-Articles/The-State-of-Media-and-Entertainment-Video-2012-80946.aspx.

Ellis, L. (2012a, February 6). Inside a Comcast 'AnyPlay' installation. Multichannel News. Retrieved from http://www.multichannel.com/blog/Translation_Please/33073-Inside_a_Comcast_AnyPlay_Installation.php

Ellis, L. (2012b, February 21). For the love of broadband. *Multichannel News.* Retrieved fromhttp://www.multichannel.com/blog/Translation_Please/33116-For_The_Love_of_Broadband.php.

Ellis, L. (2012c, February 27). On leaps and DASHes. *Multichannel News.* Retrieved fromhttp://www.multichannel.com/blog/Translation_Please/33127-On_Leaps_and_DASHes.php.

Ellis, L. (2012d, March 12). On making set-tops use less power. *Multichannel News.* Retrieved from http://www.multichannel.com/blog/Translation_Please/33165-On_Making_Set_Tops_Use_Less_Power.php

eMarketer.com (2009, December 11). US Online ad spend turn the corner. eMarketer.com. Retrieved from 2010 from http://www.emarketer.com/Article.aspx?R=1007415.

Farrell, M. (2012, March 1). Britt: Usage-based pricing inevitable. *Multichannel News.* Retrieved from http://www.multichannel.com/article/481271-Britt_Usage_Based_Pricing_Inevitable.php

Focus Editors (2010, March 18). Top IPTV providers. Focus.com. Retrieved from http://www.focus.com/fyi/top-iptv-providers/.

Gartner.com (2008, March 28). Gartner says worldwide IPTV subscribers will reach 48.8 million by 2010. Gartner.com. Retrieved from http://www.gartner.com/it/page.jsp?id=496291.

Graham, B. (2009, June). IPTV: Converged Television. White paper, Occam Networks. Retrieved from http://www.iptv-news.com/__data/assets/file/0007/145429/OCC_-_IPTV_White_Paper_6_09.pdf

Interactive Advertising Bureau (2010, April 7). Internet ad revenues reach record quarterly high of $6.3 billion in Q4 '09. IAB.com. Retrieved April 29, 2010 from http://www.iab.net/about_the_iab/recent_press_releases/press_release_archive/press_release/pr-040710

IPTV News (2011, September 27). Number of global IPTV subscribers passes 50mn. *IPTV News.* Retrieved from http://www.iptv-news.com/iptv_news/september_2011_2/number_of_global_iptv_subscribers_passes_50mn

ITU-T Newslog (2009, February 3). New IPTV standard supports global rollout. Retrieved from http://www.itu.int/ITU-T/newslog/CategoryView,category,QoS.aspx.

Lafayette, J. (2012, January 12). Hulu revenues rise 60% to 420M. Broadcasting & Cable.com. Retrieved from http://www.broadcastingcable.com/article/479050-Hulu_Revenues_Rise_60_to_420M.php.

Lawler, R. (2011, March 21). YouTube will be a $1.3B business in 2011: Report. *Gigaom.* Retrieved from http://gigaom.com/video/youtube-2011-revenues/

Lewin, J. (2010, March 13). Online video growth slows to 10.5%. *Podcasting news.* Retrieved from http://www.podcastingnews.com/2010/03/13/online-video-growth-slows-to-10-5/.

Light, C., and Lancefield, D. (2007). Strategies for success in IPTV. *IPTV-news.com.* Retrieved from http://www.iptv news.com/__data/assets/pdf_file/0011/51140/iptv_strategies_for_success_pwc_final.pdf.

Miller, R. (2007, June/July). Cookin' with P2P: Recipe for success or flash in the pan? *Streaming Media,* 32-38.

Nielsen Company (2011, August 1). American video habits by age, gender, ethnicity. *Nielsen Wire.* Retrieved from http://blog.nielsen.com/nielsenwire/online_mobile/american-video-habits-by-age-gender-and-ethnicity/.

Nielsen Company (2012a, January 25). December 2011: Top U.S. online video destinations. *Nielsen Wire.* Retrieved from http://blog.nielsen.com/nielsenwire/online_mobile/december-2011-top-u-s-online-video-destinations/.

Nielsen Company (2012b). Cross Platform Report Q3 2011. *Nielsen.com*. Retrieved from http://www.nielsen.com/us/en/insights/reports-downloads/2012/cross-platform-report-q3-2011.html?status=success

Nielsen Online cited in Website Optimization.com Source: http://www.websiteoptimization.com/bw/1104/

O'Neill, J. (2012a, March 6). IPTV growth strong, more likely as U.S. subscriber additions continue pace. *Fierce IPTV*. Retrieved from http://www.fierceiptv.com/story/iptv-growth-strong-more-likely-us-subscriber-additions-continue-apace/2012-03-06.

O'Neill J. (2012b, March 12). U-verse expected to pass FiOS subscriber numbers in 2013. *Fierce IPTV*. Retrieved from http://www.fierceiptv.com/story/u-verse-expected-pass-fios-subscriber-numbers-2013/2012-03-12

Reedy, S. (2008, March 17). The view from the living-room couch. *Telephony Online*. Retrieved from http://www.telephonyonline.com/iptv/news/telecom_view_livingroom_couch/index.html.

Reynolds, M. (2012, February 27). Universal Sports nets multiyear, multiplatform distribution deal with Dish. *Multichannel News*. Retrieved from http://www.multichannel.com/article/480991-Universal_Sports_Nets_Multiyear_Multiplatform_Distribution_Deal_with_Dish.php.

Schaeffler, J. (2012, February 20). Ubiquitous video: Everything to everyone, always. *Multichannel News*. Retrieved from http://www.multichannel.com/blog/mixed_signals/33113-Ubiquitous_Video_Everything_to_Everyone_Always.php.

Schnitzer, E. (2012, February 24). Ready or not, Web video gets an upfront. *Digiday*. Retrieved from http://www.digiday.com/video/deos-web-video-need-an-upfront/.

Shammo, F. (2012, January 24). 4th Quarter Earning Results. Verizon.com. Retrieved from http://www22.verizon.com/idc/groups/public/documents/adacct/4q_earnings_release_slides.pdf.

Smith, R. (2009, December 7). Global IPTV forecast exceeds 2009 prediction by 2M subscribers. Multimedia Research Group press release. Retrieved from http://www.mrgco.com/press_releases.html#gf1109.

Spangler, T. (2012a, February 6). Verizon, Coinstar tag team on Netflix rival: Telco will own 65% of joint enture with DVD vending machine operator. *Multichannel News*. Retrieved from http://www.multichannel.com/article/480151-Verizon_Coinstar_Tag_Team_On_Netflix_Rival.php.

Spangler, T. (2012b, February 21). Comcast takes aim at Netflix with "Streampix." *Multichannel News*. Retrieved from http://www.multichannel.com/article/480811-Comcast_Takes_Aim_At_Netflix_With_Streampix_.php.

Spangler, T. (2012c, February 27). Time Warner Cable revives usage-based Internet plan, but now it's optional. *Multichannel News*. Retrieved from http://www.multichannel.com/article/481059-Time_Warner_Cable_Revives_Usage_Based_Internet_Plan_But_Now_It_s_Optional.php

Spangler, T. (2012d, February 29). ESPN buddies up with Facebook. *Multichannel News*. Retrieved from http://www.multichannel.com/article/481199-ESPN_Buddies_Up_With_Facebook.php.

Stelter, B. (2012, February 7). 2.1 million streamed the Super Bowl, NBC says. *NYTimes.com*. Retrieved from http://www.mediadecoder.blogs.nytimes.com/2012/02/07/2-1-million-streamed-the-super-bowl-nbc-says/.

Torrentfreak.com (2012, January 7). Top 10 most popular Torrent sites of 2012. Retrieved from http://torrentfreak.com/top-10-most-popular-torrent-sites-of-2012-120107/.

Webster, T. (2009, April). The infinite dial 2009: Radios digital platforms. *Edison Media Research*. Retrieved from http://www.edisonresearch.com/home/archives/2007/03/ 2007_podcast_statistics_analysis.php.

What is Silverlight. (2010). Retrieved from http://www.microsfot.com/silverlight/what-is-silverlight/.

Whitney, D. (2012, March 8). Mobile video campaigns grow 22% quarter over quarter. *MediaPost.com*. Retrieved from http://www.mediapost.com/publications/article/169688/mobile-video-campaigns-grow-22-quarter-over-quart.html.

Winslow, G. (2012, February 7). Super Bowl XLVI most streamed game ever. *Broadcasting & Cable*. Retrieved from http://www.broadcastingcable.com/article/480240-Super_Bowl_XLVI_Most_Streamed_Game_Ever.php/.

9

Interactive Television

Cheryl D. Harris, Ph.D. *

Why Study Interactive Television?

◆ Interactive television fundamentally changes how we experience video content.

◆ Interactive television offers the opportunity to co-create media content.

◆ Interactive television and interactive advertising will impact multiple consumer electronic devices in daily use.

Television as an idea and experience has been facing obsolescence for several years, due to the proliferation of mobile and personal media delivery platforms. Replacing TV is a plethora of programming available either on-demand or at a scheduled time, and on a variety of electronic devices, allowing the viewer to interact with them by requesting more information, making a purchase, expressing an opinion, or contributing other content. The types of response permitted vary depending on the input device: available inputs on a mobile phone are likely different than those available on a large-screen home theater system complete with elaborate remotes and keyboards. Interactive inputs include handsets, touch screens, keyboards, mice, gesture recognition, and other feedback technologies. Nearly every news day reveals an innovative, new input option, as well as a new usage envisioned for interactive media. One can imagine interactive television (ITV) as a continuum where any content delivered "on demand" constitutes one

end of the spectrum, and runs all the way through applications that allow the viewer to fully shape the content to be delivered, as in interactive storytelling. Shopping applications, where the user responds to embedded tags or content to permit browsing and purchasing, falls somewhere in the middle of this continuum. Interestingly, the huge market for ITV shopping predicted in the past decade has cooled. Many experts have come to feel that ITV's potential is to realize pent-up audience desire to customize and socialize their viewing experience as much as possible, rather than being able to click and buy "Rachel's sweater" while watching it (the reference is to the character on the 1990's American sitcom, *Friends*, often mentioned as the touchstone of ITV shopping desires) (Baker, 2011).

Interactive television is a term used to describe the "convergence of television with digital media technologies such as computers, personal video recorders, game consoles, and mobile devices, enabling user interactivity. Increasingly, viewers are moving away from a 'lean back' model of viewing to a more active, 'lean forward' one" (Lu, 2005, p. 1). Interactive television is increasingly dependent on an Internet delivery system for advanced digital services (and in this case, also referred to as Internet protocol TV or IPTV). Another frequently used technical definition of a delivery system describes the process as slicing a signal into packets, "sending the packets out over a secure network..." and reassembling them at the endpoint (Pyle, 2007, p. 18). This process sounds similar to what is used to send e-mail across the network, but requires a highly layered and complex architecture to achieve it.

The potential of ITV has long been discussed and continues to enjoy its share of hyperbole:

---

* Chief Research Officer and CIO of the NYC research firm, Decisive Analytics.

"It will seem strange someday that I cannot chat with a friend on a show we're both watching…" or "that I can't get to my sports team with a few clicks of a button to see how the game is going currently" (Reedy, 2008).

"Imagine a television viewing experience so intuitive and interactive that a set-top box recognizes which viewer is watching and adapts to meet his or her entertainment needs" (Reedy, 2008). Many viewers are beginning to understand what video delivered over the Internet might provide, and their imaginations have already broken free of their living rooms. Multi-platform initiatives and mobile ITV have been added to the strategic planning of many key players in the ITV industry. In fact, many multichannel television operators, such as AT&T, Verizon, Comcast, and most of the largest cable TV companies, have begun to develop "app" stores such as that offered by Apple for its iPhone platform, in the hope that layering applications on top of programming will not only transform passive viewing into a "conversation" but also provide a launchpad for future targeted offers (Hansell, 2009). Video delivered to the mobile phone, although at present a frequently unsatisfying experience due to bandwidth limitations, small screen size, and other factors, is expected to increase both in offerings and in consumer demand. The unexpected explosion of tablet computing since 2010—particularly Apple's iPad—has revolutionized the interactive TV industry, and brought the concept of "TV Everywhere" much closer to reality (Baker, 2011).

Perhaps the most promising development in the ITV viewing experience is the marriage of programming with social media platforms that allow viewers to "co-view" and comment, even though not physically co-located (An Interactive Future, 2010, Vance, 2010). CNN has thoroughly integrated social media into its shows, frequently passing email and Twitter comments to its commentators, as does Al-Jazeera (a Qatar owned broadcaster). CNN encourages people to help create stories by uploading pictures and video to its iReport website, and even local newscasts are soliciting realtime viewer participation and interaction. Major investments are being made by media companies to

further "social TV", such as Yahoo's acquisition of IntoNow, which enables people to "check in" to content while watching. IntoNow has an iPhone app which "listens" to whatever show is being viewed, identifies it using SoundPrint technology, and shares that information with others that the viewer has specified (Yahoo acquires IntoNow, 2011.) The mobile phone and tablet app "Shazam" similarly identifies content and integrates it with social viewing and interactive opportunities. During the February 2012 Super Bowl advertisers Toyota, Best Buy, Pepsi, Bud Light, and FedEx made their ads "shazamable" using the company's mobile app that automatically recognizes audio. Considered the biggest interactive TV execution to date, it reached an audience of more than 100 million viewers. Shazam was also a partner for the 2012 Winter X Games, providing supplemental video, images, and information via mobile devices (Baysinger, 2012). Social viewing is now expected to be the ITV entry point for many new audiences in the near future (Bulekley, 2010.)

Industry opinion is that audiences are increasingly seeking shared, "clickable moments" in their interactions with media, and viewers are already spending millions of minutes (more than 70 million in 2010 alone) interacting with branded content (Broadcasting & Cable, 2010).

Researchers have indeed begun scrutinizing the characteristics and outcomes of "virtual co-viewing" in which millions of people may interactively watch programming together and share a variety of commentary, impressions, and critiques. One claim is that "the final goal of social interactive television is to provide the users an enriched shared experience" and that traditional non-interactive media forms will ultimately fall by the wayside (Cesar & Jensen, 2008). Young people between 16-24 years of age seem to be the "most avid adopters" of new forms of media consumption and the most likely to engage with media through a wider variety of devices than adults (Ursuet et. al., 2008; Obrist et al., 2008). Interestingly, "live TV" viewership without interactive components has dramatically eroded among audiences under age 25, and particularly so for children under the age of 11 (Steinberg, 2010).

Figure 9.1
Shazam and Winter X Games 2012

Caption: Viewers watching ESPN's 2012 Winter X Games could use the Shazam app to access additional, interactive content.

Source: C. Harris

The past several years have been a proving ground in Europe, Asia, and North America in terms of whether or not audiences will accept and demand ITV in the long run, once the novelty effect has worn off, and whether currently-understood ITV business models would be feasible (Corbelli, 2012; Porges, 2007; Burrows, 2007; Dickson, 2007; Harris, 1997). ITV vendors and developers have proliferated, with some major players rising and falling in short order, such as Canoe Ventures, shut down in early 2012. Even so, "the death of ITV has been greatly exaggerated" and, to the contrary, ITV finally is seen to have arrived in 2011-2012, if not in the form originally anticipated (Woerz, 2012).

For nearly 70 years, the notion of "watching television" has emphasized the centrality of the "television set" in the home as an important source of ad-supported news, information, and entertainment. Our ideas of what constitutes an "audience" and how to measure viewership have stuck rather closely to the iconographic status of that centralized, home-based television set. Many of those assumptions have been challenged as multi-set households, out-of-home viewing, and portable video/TV delivery devices have proliferated. Already, programming can be watched anywhere and on a multitude of devices such as tablets, mobile phones, iPods, seatback screens on an airplane, or mesmerizing big-screen monitors in home "entertainment centers." It has been widely reported that media delivery is tending to become more portable (untethered from a specific location) and personalized. Portability threatens the ability to adequately measure media exposure at the same time as it opens new opportunities for targeting. Personalization and customizability are perhaps more of a concern to the media industry because of the propensity for audiences who can customize media delivery to choose to strip out advertising messages and to shift programming out of the carefully constructed "programming schedules" so cherished by network executives.

Globally, television broadcasting is in the final stages of its transition to digital broadcasting. The move to digital television is taking place at the same time as the number of subscribers to broadband Internet access has reached 98 million U.S. households and 600 million worldwide by the end of 2011 (Corbelli, 2012), with 78% of U.S. households now subscribing to a broadband service. One obstacle to IPTV growth in the U.S.—as indeed in much of the world—is the unequal access to broadband services, which is concentrated in urban over rural areas, and tends to be associated with higher incomes. For example, in the U.S., 89% of households with annual incomes over $150,000 have broadband in the home, compared to just 29% with incomes of $15,000 or less. Minorities also tend to have less access to broadband (Tessler, 2010). The social and cultural implications of unequal access could be profound over time and require further study.

Wider availability of broadband service, coupled with digital program delivery, has long been considered a key condition in promoting interactive television in the United States. It should be noted, however, that U.S. broadband access is still considered to be costlier, less available, and offered at slower speeds than in several Asian countries, especially Japan (Brzeski, 2011; Berman, et al., 2006; McChesney & Podesta, 2006). At least in theory, search services and Internet browsing have put audiences in the habit of seeking interactivity, something the ITV platform can build on (Stump, 2005). Google, for example, may well prove to be a leader in combining its search, profiling, and advertising delivery services to provide highly customized ITV offerings. Google's highly-publicized acquisition of YouTube in 2006 for $1.65 billion, and the subsequent introduction of a nascent "video search" service that allows viewers to search video content by keywords, may eventually allow powerful data-mining of huge repositories of video content and the ability to proactively and intelligently match viewer interests with video materials (Google, 2006; Lenssen, 2007).

Background

The history of interactive television in the United States, to date, has been one of experimentation and, often, commercial failure. Conspicuous investments in various forms of interactive television ranged from the 1977 Qube TV service offered by Warner Amex in Columbus (Ohio), Dallas, and Pittsburgh to Time Warner's much-publicized FSN (Full Service Network) in Orlando in 1994-1997. An earlier, 1960s era effort called "Subscription TV (STV)," which debuted in Los Angeles and San Francisco and offered cultural events, sports, and even an interactive movie channel, fizzled out (Schwalb, 2003). Microsoft joined the fray with its purchase of WebTV in 1997, which, after three years, "topped out at about a million users before descending into marketing oblivion" (Kelly, 2002). Although MSN spent hundreds of millions of dollars to finance speculative programming (such as $100 million on the Web show *474 Madison*), it did not find an audience to support its programming.

Meanwhile, throughout 2006, a small, (then) anonymous crew using a cramped, makeshift room made to look like a teenager's bedroom, and an unknown volunteer actress, posted a series of videos on YouTube under the pseudonym "Lonely Girl15" and drew millions of obsessive viewers who posted streams of commentary, speculation, and blog postings throughout the Internet. Is this non-professional, user-generated content the future of the 500-million channel ITV universe (McNamara, 2006)?

Not surprisingly, the success of ventures such as YouTube, coupled with the apparent willingness of audiences to interact and contribute to these venues, have resulted in considerable investor interest. Nearly every week there is a new story in the press about the rise to "instant fame" of a YouTube contributor. Amateur Web videos are frequently shown on network news shows, and some YouTube creators have earned considerable income from ads placed alongside their video channels in the site. The number of online video viewers is expected grow by more than two-thirds to 941 million in 2013, up dramatically from 563 million viewers reported in 2008, and may reach 941 million viewers by 2013 (ABI Research, 2008).

While ITV efforts in the United States were having difficulty finding audiences in the last decade, European and U.K. ITV initiatives continued to be developed and, in some cases, flourished. As a result, American hardware and content providers have had the rare opportunity to watch and learn from several well-funded ITV applications abroad, such as BSkyB and the BBC's "Red Button" service (Warman, 2009). Interactive commercials are already commonplace in the United Kingdom; BSkyB, Britain's biggest satellite television service, "already plies 9 million customers with interactive ads" and that response in terms of clickthrough rates and conversions are much higher than Web-delivered ads (3-4% vs. .3%) (*The Economist*, 2009). Some European operators have found that gambling and gaming (not advertising) comprise a larger part of their revenue (Shepherd & Vinton, 2005).

Recent Developments

By 2005, EchoStar Communications' DISH Network and DirecTV had already rolled out ITV platforms in the United States, with a combined audience of about 25 million viewers (Morrissey, 2005). A majority of cable TV companies are currently offering video on demand (VOD) services or will in the near future, and, as previously mentioned, providers such as Verizon are beginning to layer applications such as Facebook, Twitter, etc. on top of their programming.

Access to digital television services worldwide jumped from just 16% in 2006 to 28% in 2009, and is predicted to reach 75% by 2014 (Baker, 2011; Global Digital Media, 2009). Parks Associates reported the number of telco/IPTV households worldwide grew by nearly 80% in 2008 to exceed 20 million. As illustrated in Figure 9.2, the number of global subscribers to ITV services was expected to reach 58 million by the end of 2012 (Global ITV forecast, 2011).

Figure 9.2
ITV Global Subscribers

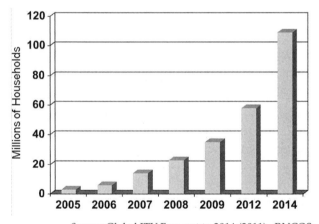

Sources:Global ITV Forecast to 2014 (2011). RNCOS; Digital Living Forecast Workbook, (2009). Parks Associates

What could hold up ITV's progress? The technology underlying ITV delivery is complex, and several key problems have yet to be solved, particularly those related to packet processing and security. The transport network supporting Internet services such as voice over IP (VoIP), video, and all the regular Internet traffic is described as "limited" in its ability to provide an adequate "quality of experience" from a user-perspective. Adding the heavy burden of almost unlimited video on demand to this infrastructure is proving worrisome to the engineers developing the means of managing all of these signal streams (Lafayette, 2010; Smart, 2010; Tomar, 2007). A positive development was the announcement in January 2008 by the International Telecommunications Union of the first set of global standards for IPTV, built with technical contributions from service providers and technology manufacturers as well as other stakeholders. This group committed to regular ongoing meetings so that these standards will continue to evolve (Standards for Internet Protocol TV, 2008). Canoe Ventures, though defunct by 2012, contributed the Enhanced Binary Interchange Format (EBIF) which positions interactive applications for broad roll-out by enabling the embedding of hotspots or clickable objects in an MPEG videostream. At one point, 25 million U.S. households were equipped with EBIF . However, linking tablets and other mobile devices to TV platforms may make EBIF and similar technology less necessary to the ITV experience (Lafayette, 2010).

Current Status
Media Buying/Planning

Confusion about how to buy or sell advertising on IPTV and ITV is rampant, even years after its introduction. Traditional television networks circulate content proposals to media buyers a year or more in advance, while newer video forms provide little lead time for buyers to make decisions. Viewers claim to be interested in interacting with advertising targeted to their interests: a surprising 66% said they were looking for an opportunity to do so. Although more than 40 major global advertisers are already including ITV in their ad-mix, agencies and advertisers still need to come to an agreement concerning how to treat the market for ITV products, both during the transitional period and when ITV is fully implemented. There is also concern that consumer-generated content (CGC)—content that individuals provide that include blogs (with/with-out RSS [really simple syndication]), podcasts, vblogs (blogs with video content), animations, newsletters, content "traces," and other information—will continue to compete for the same advertiser dollars as affiliated networks, but outside of the traditional media planning framework. More than $14 billion in revenue due to advanced ITV advertising is expected to be generated by 2015, according to a study by Bank of America Merrill Lynch, who also found that 73% of viewers said they would interact with ads for products in which they are interested. It's important to note that via the Google TV Ads platform alone, 1.5 billion impressions were being served each week by 2010 (Morabito, 2010). An encouraging sign for advertisers is that interactive advertising across delivery platforms is showing very high clickthrough rates—averaging 3-4%—compared to less than .3% for a typical web ad, so the future looks bright for ad revenue and advertiser ROI (*The Economist*, 2010).

Media Measurement

An upheaval in media measurement practices and accepted standards is currently underway, fueled in part by advertiser demand to better account for new technologies such as DVR, VOD, and portable media devices. The Nielsen Company continues to adhere to client demand to "follow the video" (Story, 2007; Whiting, 2006), but by early 2010 had introduced no comprehensive plan for doing so. Other media measurement players such as Integrated Media Measurement, Inc. (IMMI) proposed using cell phones adapted to measure consumer media exposure by sampling nearby sounds. The sound samples are then compared, and the database matches them to media content. This approach could potentially track exposure to compact discs, DVDs (digital videodiscs), video, movies seen in a theater, and videogames, among other types of media. No clear winner in the race to provide satisfactory media measurement has yet emerged. Established online ratings providers ComScore and NetRatings will also be well positioned to deliver ratings or measurement services to ITV.

However, there will be considerable pressure to produce an acceptable and highly accountable system for measuring media exposure and for determining ad effectiveness in the converged media environment. Some experts believe that the field of Web analytics, already relatively sophisticated after more a decade of development, may offer some solutions. In a converged media environment with Internet-delivered content as the primary focus, all exposure from all users could conceivably be tracked, without reliance on panel-based measurement schemes. Data mining models could then be used to profile and extract program and ad exposure information, as well as what audience members then did in response to exposure.

Lessons learned from this kind of data could eventually allow advertisers and content providers to apply powerful behavioral targeting techniques that would further customize media delivery.

Factors to Watch

Business Models

All the content delivery options now in play and expected to be available in the future create a number of questions for new business and revenue models that may support the content infrastructure. In competition for both viewers and advertising dollars will be contenders such as the download services (iTunes, Google, Yahoo), TV networks and producers, websites containing video offerings, and specialty programming targeted to devices such as cell phones. There is also the continuing threat from peer-to-peer or file-sharing networks that swap content, much of it illegally obtained, without anyone getting paid. Some believe that content providers, including television networks and movie studios, should put ads in their programming and give them away for free. Others believe the best value proposition is to emphasize the value of content over advertising and sell episodes or films directly, advertising-free, at a higher price than ad-supported media products. At the same time, numerous content providers can cite past failed experiments with a "pay wall" model in which users are expected to pay for content (which may have been previously offered for free), but refuse to do so. It is not clear if ITV/IPTV will manage to support itself through advertising revenue, bundled e-commerce, a micropayment or subscription system, or perhaps a combination of all of these (Deloitte Touche Tohmatsu, 2010).

Consultants are piling up with theories about how to win in the emerging marketplace. IBM recently released an influential report revealing their thinking about how ITV will stack up. First, analysts predict a "generational chasm" between baby boomers in early retirement or nearing retirement age who are accustomed to decades of passive media usage and the younger Generation X and Millennials. Described as in the "lean back" category, baby boomers may have splurged on a flat screen TV and DVR, but have not greatly modified their TV viewing habits in many years. Their children are likely to be much more media-evolved and more likely to be "multi-platform" media users, looking to smartphones, P2P (peer-to-peer) services, VOD—whatever improves convenience and access.

At a further remove, teenagers have been exposed to (and immersed in) high-bandwidth networks and services from very early ages and experiment unflinchingly with media and platforms. Mobile devices and multitasking behaviors are central to their lives. It is second nature for them to rip and share content and have different definitions of both privacy and piracy, ones perhaps unrecognizable to their parents. They expect—and have many of the tools to obtain—total control of media content (Steinberg, 2010; Berman, et al., 2006). At the same time, there is the potential for consumer backlash as it becomes clearer that an interactive, addressable media platform is one in which every consumer action is trackable (Chamberlain, 2010).

When programming tied to a schedule is no longer supported, pre-release content may command a premium price. It is not clear, however, what happens to any of the former television pricing models when the idea of a "fixed schedule" of programming is truly out the window. Some question remains as to whether or not *any* content needs to be offered live or "real-time" in the future. Sporting events, news, and even election results may have more value to viewers if under their control, but these types of live content may have even more

need for immediacy when viewers are getting instant updates from real-time, social networking applications including Twitter, Facebook, and even the ESPN Score Center App. These issues have yet to be put to the test. Interestingly, although Apple's business venture of offering individual recordings at an average of $.99 through its iTunes Store has been a huge success in its first few years (and has reportedly brought the traditional music business "to its knees"), its related video business over iTunes originally looked bleak, only to heat up significantly by 2010 (serving nearly a million videos per day by some estimates). iTunes video rental is expected to earn Apple more than $1 billion by 2015, according to Gleacher analyst Brian Marshall (Dalrymple, 2010).

New forms of content are also emerging, including efforts by companies interested in porting existing content to various alternative devices, and even those solely dedicated to developing new content for devices such as mobile phones. Ad formats that are in consideration for the support of content delivery include on-demand ads delivered to match stated interests:

✦ *Vertical ads* that link the viewer to topical information and related products.

✦ *Opt-in ads* accepted in exchange for free or discounted programming.

✦ *Hypertargeted ads* delivered with localization or profiled matching criteria.

✦ *Embedded advertising*, the digital equivalent of product placement.

✦ *Sponsored content*, longer-form programming sponsored by an advertiser, similar to the early sponsorship models of 1950s-era television (Kiley & Lowrey, 2005; Brightman, 2005).

Tomorrow's ITV will need to include robust deployment of several features and functions that so far are incomplete, such as (Smart, 2010):

✦ Voice Search and Command

✦ Collaborative Filtering and Rating Systems

✦ Micropayments

- ✦ Social Viewing: tight integration with social networks, realtime chat, etc.

- ✦ Realtime captioning

- ✦ Dynamic and personalized content discovery

Consumer-Generated Content

There is little doubt that the Internet has provided a powerful means of disintermediation (the process of businesses communicating or dealing directly with end users rather than through intermediaries). More than one observer has noted that the "blog" or Weblog has afforded everybody a printing press at little or no cost. Similarly, video programming can be created, distributed, and sold online without the assistance of the traditional media gatekeepers. Consumer-generated content is endemic online, ranging in quality from the primitive to the highly polished. Even seasoned television and film producers, as well as news correspondents, are said to be producing their own shows for online distribution and sale outside of the network and studio system (Hansell, 2009; 2006).

Few people are asking, however, whether or not there will really be an audience for all the available content in a future ITV environment. In the "50 million channel universe," how many of those channels will be able to survive and endure?

According to The Nielsen Company—and this finding is consistent over time—households receiving more than 60 channels tend to watch only about 15 of them on a regular basis (Webster, 2005). Will we see a similar concentration of interest once the novelty of ITV wears off? How will we effectively navigate such a vast universe of content?

Piracy and Digital Rights

Consumer-generated content, which is generally free of charge to those who wish to view it, is certainly a threat to established television business models, although a relatively small problem. However, the threat from file-sharing services such as BitTorrent or YouTube, which may facilitate the distribution of copyright-restricted content, is much greater. Such sites account for half the daily volume of data sent via the Internet by some estimates (Wray, 2008; Kiley & Lowrey, 2005), and may be even more since many file-sharing networks have effectively gone "underground" in the past few years. Industry analysts assume that billions of dollars are already lost each year to copyright theft and outright piracy (Brightman, 2005). In an all-digital content world, sharing content becomes much easier, and many file-sharing consumers do not see their actions as theft or piracy. Adding insult to injury, few encryption schemes hold up to the concerted—and sometimes well-coordinated—efforts of crackers (Tomar, 2007).

Media Delivery Options Proliferate

Devices through which media might be delivered are likely to proliferate in the coming years, assuming consumer demand for increased portability and personalized media delivery continues. Some of these devices might be entirely new in form, and others might be examples of converging functions in single devices. Gaming platforms as an entry point to ITV will continue to grow, as will the integration of tablet devices. The extent to which personalization might be taken as a result of consumer interest in customizing media experiences is still unclear. Early experiments in alternative interactive media suggest that there may be many ways of determining consumer interest and preferences, such as bioreactive devices, and consequently, our ideas of what constitutes interactive television or media today might not bear much resemblance to what might be considered "interactive" in a decade or less.

Bibliography

ABI Research. (2008, December 12.) As Online Video viewing shifts from PC to TV Screen, Viewers will Number Nearly One Billion by 2013. Retrieved from http://www.abiresearch.com/press/1327-As+Online+Video+Viewing+Shifts+From+PC+to+TV+Screen,+Viewers+Will+Number+Nearly+One+Billion+by+2013

An Interactive Future. (2010). *The Economist*, 395(8680), May 1, p. 15-16.

Baker, D. (2011). Lessons Learned. *Communications Technology*, April 15, 28(4).

Baysinger, T. (2012). Interactive TV: Alive and kicking. *Multichannel News*. March 5, p. 14.

Berman, S., Duffy, N. & Shipnuck, L. (2006). The end of TV as we know it. *IBM Institute for Business Value executive brief*. Retrieved from http://www-935.ibm.com/services/us/index.wss/ibvstudy/imc/a1023172?cntxt=a1000062.

Brightman, I. (2005). *Technology, media & telecommunications (TMT) trends: Predictions, 2005*. Retrieved from http://www.deloitte.com/dtt/section_node/0%2C1042%2Csid%25253D1012%2C00.html.

Broadcasting & Cable. (2010). Marketers push TV's engagement buttons. June 28, p. 5

Brzeski, P. (2011, Television connected. Campaign AsiaPacific, pp. 74-74

Bulekley, W. (2010). TR10: Social TV, Relying on relationships. Retrieved from www.technology review.com/communications/25084

Burrows, P. (2007, November 7). Microsoft IPTV: At long last, progress. *Business Week Online*.

Cesar, P. & Jensen, J. (2008). Social television and user interaction. *ACM Computers in Entertainment*, 6 (1), May, Article 4.

Chamberlain, D. (2010). Television Interfaces. *Journal of Popular Film & Television*, 38(2), pp. 84-88.

Corbelli, J. (2012). New TV behaviors contributing to advances in interactive TV. Retrieved from http://www.huffingtonpost.com/jacqueline-corbelli/new-tv-behaviors-contribu_b_1414915.html

Dalrymple, J. (2010). Hey Apple, go buy Netflix. CNET News, Retrieved from http://news.cnet.com/8301-13579_3-20026814-37.html

Deloitte Touche Tohmatsu. Media Predictions 2010.

Dickson, G. (2007, November 5). IPTV hits the heartland. *Broadcasting & Cable, 137* (44), 24.

Digital Living Forecast Workbook. (2009). Parks Associates

Global Digital Media (2009). Global Digital Media Trends and Statistics, Paul Budde Communication, PTY, Ltd.

Global ITV Forecast to 2014 (2011). RNCOS.

Google, (2006, October 9.) Google to acquire YouTube for $1.65 billion in stock. Google Press Release, Retrieved: http://www.google.com/intl/en/press/pressrel/google_youtube.html

Hansell, S. (2006, March 12). As Internet TV aims at niche audiences, the Slivercast is born. *New York Times*. Retrieved from http://www.nytimes.com/2006/03/12/business/ourmoney/12sliver.html.

Hansell, S. (2009, September 7). Getting people to do more than just sit and watch: Cable TV operators see iPhone as model for viewer interactivity. *The International Herald Tribune*.

Harris, C. (1997, November). Theorizing interactivity. *Marketing and Research Today, 25* (4), 267-271.

Kelly, J. (2002). Interactive television: Is it coming or not? *Television Quarterly, 32* (4), 18-22.

Kiley, D. & Lowrey, T. (2005, November 21). The end of TV (as you know it). *Business Week*, 40-44.

Lafayette, J. (2010). Interactive television is here, really. *Multichannel News*. October 25, p. 8.

Lenssen, P. (2007). Google Video now a Video Search Engine. Retrieved from: http://blogoscoped.com/archive/2007-06-14-n62.html

Lu, K. (2005). *Interaction design principles for interactive television*. Unpublished Master's Thesis, Georgia Institute of Technology.

McChesney, R. & Podesta, J. (2006, January/February). Let there be Wi-Fi: Broadband is the electricity of the 21st century, and much of America is being left in the dark. *Washington Monthly.* Retrieved from http://www.washingtonmonthly.com/features/2006/0601.podesta.html.

McNamara, M. (2006). LonelyGirl15: An online star is born. *CBS News Online*. Retrieved from http://www.cbsnews.com/stories/2006/09/11/blogophile/main1999184.shtml.

Midgley, N. (2008). Do you lean forward or lean back? August 14, *The Telegraph* (UK).

Morabito, Andrea (2010, February 21). Addressability's great, but interactivity is here now. *Multichannel News*, p. 6.

Morrissey, B. (2005, March 28). Can interactive TV revive the 30-second spot? *Adweek Online*. Retrieved from http://www.adweek.com/aw/esearch/article_display.jsp?vnu_content_id=1000855874.

Obrist, M. Bernhaupt, R., Tscheligi, M. (2008). Interactive TV for the Home: An ethnographic study on user's requirements and experiences. *International journal of Human-Computer Interaction.* 24(2), 174-196.

Parks Associates, (2010, March 23). Addressable, interactive TV revenue predicted to reach 133 million in 2010. Retrieved from: http://parksassociates.blogspot.com/2010/03/addressable-interactive-tv-advertising.html

Parks Associates. (2009, July 21). Telco/IPTV subscribers to total almost 40 million households worldwide in 2009. Retrieved from: http://newsroom.parksassociates.com/article_display.cfm?article_id=5170

Poggi, J. (2012). What is interactive TV, anyway? *Advertising Age*, February 27, 83(9), pp. 62-64.

Porges, S. (2007, December 4). The future of Web TV. *PC Magazine*, 19.

Pyle, K. (2007, November 5). What is IPTV? *Telephony, 247* (18).

Reedy, S. (2008, March 17). To IPTV and beyond. *Telephony, 248* (4). Retrieved from http://telephonyonline.com/iptv/news/telecom_iptv_beyond/.

Schwalb, E. (2003). *ITV handbook: Technologies and standards.* Saddle River, NJ: Prentice Hall.

Schuk, C. (2010, January 4.) Predictions for mobile TV in 2010. *Broadcast Engineering.*

Shepherd, I. & Vinton., M. (2005, May 27). ITV report: Views from the Bridge. *Campaign*, 4.

Smart, J. (2010). Tomorrow's interactive television: The iPad and its successors could revolutionize television, *The Futurist*, November-December, pp. 41-46.

Standards for Internet protocol TV. (2008, January 8). *Computer Weekly*, 151.

Steinberg, B. (2010). Does anyone under 30 watch live TV these days? *Advertising Age*, September 27, 81(34), p. 46.

Story, L. (2007, June 28). Nielsen adds to cell phone tracking. *New York Times*. Retrieved from http://www.nytimes.com/2007/06/28/business/media/28adco.html?_r=1&scp=2&sq=nielsen+june+28%2C+2007&st=nyt&oref=slogin.

Stump, M. (2005, October 31). Interactive TV unchained: How Web-created habits are stoking interest in participatory TV—finally. *Multichannel News*, 14.

Tessler, J. (2010, February 16). U.S. broadband figures show 40% lack broadband, *The Huffington Post*. Retrieved from: http://www.huffingtonpost.com/2010/02/16/us-broadband-figures-show_n_463849.html

The Economist (2009, October 10). Shop after you drop. *Interactive Television Advertising*. U.S. edition.

Tomar, N. (2007, December 10). IPTV redefines packet processing requirements at the edge. *Electronic Engineering Times*, 31.

Tong-Hyung, K. (2009, November 26). Mobile TV to become interactive. *Korea Times*.

Ursuet, M., Thomas, M., Kegel, I., Williams, D., Tuomola, M., Lindsted, I., Wright, T. (2008). Interactive TV narratives: Opportunities, progress, and challenges. ACM *Transactions on Multimedia Computing*, Communications and Applications, 4(4), Article 25.

Vance, A. (2010, January 4). Watching TV together, miles apart. *The New York Times*, B:1.

Warman, M. (2009, May 2.) Ten years of pressing red: Matt Warman celebrates a decade of interactive TV, and looks at the future of the BBC Service. *The Daily Telegraph.*

Webster, J. (2005). Beneath the veneer of fragmentation: Television audience polarization in a multichannel world. *Journal of Communication, 55* (2), 366–382.

Whiting, S. (2006, March 1). To our clients. In N. M. R. Clients (Ed.). New York: Nielsen Media Research.

Woerz, C. (2012). RIP Canoe. Long live ITV! *Multichannel News*. March 5, p. 31.

Wray, R. (2008, February 22). Filesharing law unworkable. *The Guardian*. Retrieved from http://www.guardian.co.uk/technology/2008/feb/22.

Yahoo acquires IntoNow for TV Checkins. (2011). Retrieved from http://www.forbes.com/sites/tomiogeron/2011/04/25/yahoo-acquires-intonow-for-tv-check-ins/

10

Radio Broadcasting

Gregory Pitts, Ph.D.[*]

(While) radio is valued, radio is also taken for granted. Because it is so pervasive, radio is sometimes overlooked, just like water or electricity
— National Association of Broadcasters (n.d.).

Radio is the last analog medium. To not face the digital evolution and join it, to ignore it and remain complacent, will put analog radio where the 45-RPM record and cassette tapes are today
— Kneller (2010).

Why Study Radio?

+ Broadcast radio remains important because it's free—there's no subscription or expensive receiver.

+ Around the world, there are *billions* of AM or FM receivers. In the U.S. alone, there are 800 million radios.

+ Radio technology plays a major communications role around the world for populations in political, economic, and social transition.

Radio experienced its golden age in the 1930s and 1940s. It was *the* medium for live entertainment and news broadcasts, but the enthusiastic embrace of television after World War II put radio on a technology path for the next 60 years that has been dominated by a music box role. But radio broadcasters have endeavored to remain relevant to consumers, as newer technologies have emerged. The most exotic innovation—beyond improvements in the radio tuner itself—was the arrival of FM stereo broadcasting in 1961. Today, audiences and media companies are redefining the term "radio." Satellite-delivered audio services from Sirius-XM, streaming audio options—such as Pandora, and audio downloads (both music and full-length programming) are allowing consumers to think anew about the meaning of the word *radio*. Radio is just as likely to refer to personal audio media—multiple selections and formats of audio content provided by a variety of sources—beyond FM and AM radio. Radio is becoming a generic term for audio entertainment supplied by terrestrial broadcast frequency, satellite, Internet streaming, mobile phones, and portable digital media players via podcasts, some of which come from traditional radio companies and still others that are the product of technology innovators (Green, et al., 2005). Arbitron and Edison Research describe today's media environment as "The Infinite Dial" where broadband or high speed Internet access is changing the media consumption experience (Arbitron, 2012a). The public reports listening to radio each week—broadcast radio reaches 93% of the U.S. population—but the growth in the number of portable digital devices, from smartphones to media players, is changing the access pattern. The next frontier for smartphones, tablets, and other audio devices is the automobile, as car manufacturers add external inputs to enable these devices to work with automobile audio systems. Some automobile manufacturers are even adding Internet connectivity (Arbitron, 2012b).

[*] Professor, Department of Communications, University of North Alabama (Florence, Alabama).

As you read about radio technology, it is important to remember that technology is dispersed and adopted around the world at different rates. Much of the discussion in this chapter will take a North American or Western European perspective. The economic, regulatory and political environments in the United States and other countries in these regions are different than in parts of the world with a different development agenda. In these places, radio likely occupies a more relevant position in society. Countries that are transitioning to market economies and fair elections are just now beginning to license commercial or community radio stations. These stations bring the traditional benefit of radio—free over-the-air programming with local productions costs—to a host of new listeners who have never experienced station choice.

An effort by the U.S. radio industry to add technological sizzle through digital over-the-air radio broadcasting (called HD Radio, HD2, and HD3) has largely fallen flat with only 8% of adults surveyed by the Pew project saying they'd ever listened to the service (Pew, 2012). The National Association of Broadcasters has not ignored radio innovation. NAB identifies five other initiatives that promote radio technology and program availability. These include:

✦ NAB's Flexible Advanced Services for Television and Radio On All Devices (FASTROAD), to help accelerate deployment of new technologies.

✦ Mobile phones with built-in FM radio tuners.

✦ The National Radio Systems Committee (NRSC), a jointly sponsored NAB and Consumer Electronics Association (CEA) committee to recommend technical standards for radio receivers.

✦ The Radio Data System (RDS) that allows analog FM stations to provide digital data services, such as song title and artist or traffic information.

✦ Radio Heard Here, the consumer promotional phase of the Radio 2020 campaign to remind consumers and the media industry of radio's value (NAB, n.d.).

Radio remains an important part of the daily lives of millions of people. Personality and promotion driven radio formats thrust themselves into the daily routines of listeners. Radio station ownership consolidation has led to greater emphasis on formats, format branding, and promotional efforts designed to appeal to listener groups and, at the same time, yield steady returns on investments for owners and shareholders through the sale of advertising time. But advertising loads and the availability of personal choice technology, such as portable digital media players and personalized online audio, are driving listeners to look for other options.

Critics have been quick to point to the malaise brought upon the radio industry by consolidated ownership and cost-cutting, but the previous ownership fragmentation may never have allowed today's radio to reach the point of offering HD radio as a competitor to satellite and streaming technologies. Through consolidation, the largest owner groups have focused their attention on new product development to position radio to respond to new technological competition. There have been technology stumbles in the past:

✦ *FM broadcasting*, which almost died because of lack of support from AM station owners and ultimately took more than 35 years to achieve 50% of all radio listening in 1978.

✦ *Quad-FM* (quadraphonic sound) never gained market momentum.

✦ *AM stereo*, touted in the early 1980s as a savior in AM's competitive battle with FM.

These technologies did not fail exclusively for want of station owner support, but it was an important part of their failure. Large ownership groups have an economic incentive to pursue new technology. HD radio best exemplifies the economy of scale needed to introduce a new radio technology but, HD radio hasn't been seen by consumers as technology worthy of adoption in a marketplace with digital downloads, streaming audio and satellite services.

This chapter examines the factors that have redirected the technological path of radio broadcasting. It also explores factors that will impact the future of radio.

Background

The history of radio is rooted in the earliest wired communications—the telegraph and the telephone—although no single person can be credited with inventing radio. Most of radio's "inventors" refined an idea put forth by someone else (Lewis, 1991). Although the technology may seem mundane today, until radio was invented, it was impossible to simultaneously transmit entertainment or information to millions of people. The radio experimenters of 1900 or 1910 were as enthused about their technology as are the employees of the latest tech startup. Today, the Internet allows us to travel around the world without leaving our seats. For the listener in the 1920s, 1930s, or 1940s, radio was the only way to hear live reports from around the world.

Probably the most widely known radio inventor/innovator was Italian Guglielmo Marconi, who recognized its commercial value and improved the operation of early wireless equipment. The one person who made the most lasting contributions to radio and electronics technology was Edwin Howard Armstrong. He discovered regeneration, the principle behind signal amplification, and invented the superheterodyne tuner that led to a high-performance receiver that could be sold at a moderate price, thus increasing home penetration of radios. In 1933, Armstrong was awarded five patents for frequency modulation (FM) technology (Albarran & Pitts, 2000). The two traditional radio transmission technologies are amplitude modulation and frequency modulation. AM varies (modulates) signal strength (amplitude), and FM varies the frequency of the signal. It's also worth noting that the patent fights today between the three biggest technology companies—Google, Apple and Microsoft—reflect similar struggles in the evolution of radio between 1900 and 1940.

The oldest commercial radio station began broadcasting in AM in 1920, with the technology advantage of being able to broadcast over a wide coverage area. AM signals are low fidelity and subject to electrical interference. FM, which provides superior sound, is of limited range. Commercial FM took nearly 20 years from the first Armstrong patents in the 1930s to begin significant service and did not reach listener parity with AM until 1978 when FM listenership finally exceeded AM listenership.

FM radio's technological add-on of stereo broadcasting, authorized by the Federal Communications Commission (FCC) in 1961, along with an end to program simulcasting (airing the same program on both AM and FM stations) in 1964, expanded FM listenership (Sterling & Kittross, 1990). Other attempts, such as Quad-FM (quadraphonic sound), ended with disappointing results. AM stereo, introduced in the early 1980s to help AM's competitive battle with FM, languished for lack of a technical standard because of the inability of station owners and the FCC to adopt an AM stereo system (FCC, n.d.-a; Huff, 1992). Ultimately, consumers expressed minimal interest in AM stereo.

Why have technological improvements in radio been slow in coming? One obvious answer is that the marketplace did not want the improvements. Station owners invested in modest technological changes; they shifted music programming from the AM to the FM band. AM attracted listeners by becoming the home of low-cost talk programming. Another barrier was the question of what would happen to AM and FM stations if a new radio service were created. Would existing stations automatically be given the first opportunity to occupy new digital space, as an automatic grant, eliminating the possibility that new competition would be created? What portion of the spectrum would a new digital service occupy? Were listeners ready to migrate to a new part of the spectrum? New radio services would mean more competitors for the limited pool of advertising revenue. Radio listeners expressed limited interest in new radio services at a time when personal music choice blossomed through the offering of 45-RPM records, followed by 8-track and then cassette tapes, and then CDs and portable digital media players. If radio owners were reluctant to embrace new technology offerings, consumers were not reluctant. Radio is important because it was free and familiar but new devices throughout the years and today's unlimited digital dial appear to have captured the attention of the public, policy makers and electronics manufacturers (Pew, 2012; Pew, 2011).

The Changing Radio Marketplace

The FCC elimination of ownership caps mandated by the *Telecommunications Act of 1996* set the stage for many of the changes that have taken place in radio broadcasting in the last decade. Before the ownership limits were eliminated, there were few incentives for broadcasters, equipment manufacturers, or consumer electronics manufacturers to upgrade the technology. Outside of the largest markets, radio stations were individual small businesses. (At one time, station owners were limited to seven stations of each service. Later, the limit was increased to 18 stations of each service, before deregulation eventually removed ownership limits.) Analog radio, within the technical limits of a system developed nearly 100 years ago, worked just fine. The fractured station ownership system ensured station owner opposition to FCC initiatives and manufacturer efforts to pursue technological innovation.

The compelling question today is whether anyone cares about the technological changes in terrestrial radio broadcasting. Or, are the newest changes in radio coming at a time when public attention has turned to other sources and forms of audio entertainment? The personal audio medium concept suggests that *local* personality radio may not be relevant when listeners can access both mega-talent personalities and local stars through satellite services, online, and with podcasting.

Recent Developments

There are four areas where technology is affecting radio broadcasting:

1) New technologies that offer substitutes for radio.

2) Delivery competition from satellite digital audio radio services (SDARS).

3) New voices for communities: low-power FM service.

4) New digital audio broadcasting transmission modes that are compatible with existing FM and AM radio.

New Competition—Internet Radio, Digital Audio Files, and Podcasts

Listening to portable audio devices and streaming audio are becoming mainstream practices. Online listening may include content originating from over-the-air stations, including HD Radio or FM stations, begging the question of which distribution venue will be more valuable to consumers in the future—broadband or over-the-air. Forty-four percent of all Americans age 12 and over own a smartphone—half of all mobile phone users. Six in ten (61%) own a digital device, including smartphones, digital media players or tablets (Arbitron, 2012b). The Pew Research Center's Project Excellence in Journalism asked survey respondents which technology or device had the greatest impact on their lives. Only one person in five (22%) indicated radio had a big impact on the user's life. Mobile phones and broadband Internet were described as big impact technologies by about half the respondents (Pew, 2011). About 40% of Americans listen to audio on digital devices each week; this number is expected to double by 2015 (Pew, 2012). As this number rises, the number of hours and minutes per day spent listening to radio will likely drop.

High-speed Internet connectivity—wired or wireless—and the accompanying smart devices, phones, netbooks, and tablets, are technological challengers for terrestrial radio. These sexier technologies offer more listener choice and they lure consumer dollars to the purchase of these technologies. (For more information on digital audio and Internet connectivity, see Chapters 18 and 21.) The opportunity to control music listening options and to catalog those options in digital form presents not just a technological threat to radio listening, but also a lifestyle threat of greater magnitude than listening to tapes or CDs. Listeners have thousands of songs that can be programmed for playback according to listener mood, and the playback will always be commercial-free and in high fidelity. As digital audio file playback technology migrates from portable players to automotive units, the threat to radio will increase. Radio stations are responding by offering streaming versions of their program content. The iHeartRadio application from Clear Channel Digital is one example of a radio station owner's response to alternative delivery. TuneIn Radio offers smartdevice access to local radio streams, plus national and international streams and online only services.

Consumers around the world use mobile phones to receive music files, video clips, and video games. Missing from most mobile phones is an FM or AM tuner, once again fostering an environment where consumers grow up without the choice of broadcast radio listening. Apple, after substantial lobbying by the broadcast industry, now offers a conventional FM tuner on the iPod nano model. The NAB has aggressively supported efforts to equip music players and mobile phones with radio tuners, through its *Radio Rocks My Phone* initiative (NAB, n.d.). Ostensibly including the FM tuner will give listeners greater access to local information but this will only be of value if local stations commit to hire personnel to program local information—something more compelling than just music—rather than rely on technology to reduce personnel costs.

Nearly three-fourths of radio listening takes place in cars. Arbitron, Edison Research and Scarborough Research report that more than half (55%) of 18-24 year olds use their iPod/digital media player to listen to audio in the car (Arbitron, 2012a). The sophisticated audio systems in newer cars allow for the integration of consumer smartphones and other devices, bringing a host of new capabilities to the car (Cheng, 2010). Included in the features is the ability to run mobile programs such as Internet audio programs from Pandora to other online audio service as well as providing consumers with seamless access to their own content from personal audio files.

Internet radios and mobile devices offer access to thousands more online audio/radio services than any FM tuner ever could (Taub, 2009). *Streamingradioguide.com* is a Web guide listing nearly 16,000 online U.S. stations—almost all of the commercial, non-commercial and low-power radio stations in the U.S. By comparison, local over-the-air reception usually provides access to fewer than 100 stations even in a major metropolitan area.

Competition from Satellite Radio

Subscriber-based satellite radio service, a form of out-of-band digital "radio," was launched in the United States in 2001 and 2002 by XM Satellite Radio and Sirius Satellite Radio. The competitors received regulatory approval to merge in July 2008 to become Sirius-XM. Satellite service was authorized by the FCC in 1995 and, strictly speaking, is not a radio service. Rather than delivering programming primarily through terrestrial (land-based) transmission systems, each service uses geosynchronous satellites to deliver its programming (see Figure 10.1). (Terrestrial signals do enhance reception in some fringe areas, such as tunnels.) Nearly 22 million people subscribe to the 135 music and news, sports, and talk channels. Sirius XM concluded 2011 with the addition of 1.7 million net subscribers (Sirius XM, 2012). Users pay a monthly subscription fee of between $8 and $18 and must have a proprietary receiver to decode the transmissions.

Figure 10.1
Satellite Radio

Source: J. Meadows & Technology Futures, Inc.

There is a willingness among consumers to pay for audio service but the cost for Sirius XM to attract and retain subscribers remains high; the typical conversion rate from trial subscriptions is about 45% (Radio Business Reports, 2010).

Helping the growth of satellite radio has been an array of savvy partnerships and investments, including alliances with various automobile manufacturers and content relationships with personalities and artists, including Howard Stern, Martha Stewart, Oprah Winfrey, Rosie O'Donnell, Jamie Foxx, Barbara Walters, and Opie & Anthony. Sirius-XM Radio is the "Official Satellite Radio Partner" of the NFL, Major League Baseball, NASCAR, NBA, NHL, PGA Tour, and major college sports.

New Voices for Communities: Low-Power FM Service

The FCC approved the creation of a controversial new classification of noncommercial FM station in January 2000 (Chen, 2000). LPFM, or low-power FM, service limits stations to a power level of either 100 watts or 10 watts (FCC, n.d.-b). The classification was controversial because existing full-power stations were afraid of signal interference. The service range of a 100-watt LPFM station is about a 3.5-mile radius. LPFM stations do not have the option of adopting HD Radio but they do provide free analog programming to supplement existing FM broadcasts. As of mid-2012, the number of licensed LPFM stations in the U.S. is 830 (FCC, 2012).

President Obama signed the Local Community Radio Act of 2010 into law on January 4, 2011. The LCRA seeks to expand the licensing opportunities for LPFM stations by eliminating the third adjacent channel separation requirement enacted by Congress at the behest of commercial broadcasters in 2000 when LPFM service was created (FCC, 2012). The change increases the likelihood of finding a frequency for an LPFM station. Under the old rules, a full power FM on 102.9 MHz would be protected from any LPFM closer than 102.1 or 103.7. This didn't just protect the full-power station, it decreased the likelihood of finding a frequency for a station operation. Now an LPFM could operate on 102.3 or 103.5. The FCC has further democratized

the inquiry process by creating a Low Power FM Channel Finder, available at: http://fcc.us/ICCZe9.

New Digital Audio Broadcasting Transmission Modes

Most free, over-the-air AM and FM radio stations broadcast in analog, but their on-air and production capabilities and the audio chain, from music and commercials to the final program signal delivered to the station's transmitter, is digitally processed and travels to a digital exciter in the station's transmitter where the audio is added to the carrier wave. The only part of the process that remains analog is the final transmission of the over-the-air FM or AM signal.

AM and FM radio made the critical step toward digital transmission in 2002, when the FCC approved the digital broadcasting system proposed by iBiquity Digital (marketed as HD radio). The FCC calls stations providing the new digital service hybrid broadcasters because they continue their analog broadcasts (FCC, 2004). iBiquity's identification of "HD" Radio is a marketing label, not a reference to an FCC station classification.

The HD Radio digital signal eliminates noise and multipath distortion, provides better audio quality, including surround sound, and provides digital information delivery, including traffic information, song tagging, and other forms of consumer information. This technology consists of an audio compression technology called perceptual audio coder (PAC) that allows the analog and digital content to be combined on existing radio bands, and digital broadcast technology that allows transmission of music and text while reducing the noise and static associated with current reception. The system does not require any new spectrum space, as stations continue to broadcast on the existing analog channel and use the new digital system to broadcast on the same frequency. As illustrated in Figure 10.2, this digital audio broadcasting (DAB) system uses a hybrid in-band, on-channel system (IBOC) that allows simultaneous broadcast of analog and digital signals by existing FM stations through the use of compression technology, without disrupting the existing analog coverage. The FM IBOC system is capable of delivering near-CD-quality audio and new data services including song titles and traffic/weather bulletins. The so-called killer application to attract consumers to HD radio is the ability to offer a second, third or fourth audio channel. For example, many affiliates of National Public Radio offer classical music or jazz on their main channel and talk or other programming on the side channels.

For broadcasters, HD radio will allow one-way wireless data transmission similar to the radio broadcast data system (RBDS or RDS) technology that allows analog FM stations to send traffic and weather information, programming, and promotional material from the station for delivery to smart receivers. HD radio utilizes multichannel broadcasting by scaling the digital portion of the hybrid FM broadcast. IBOC provides for a 96 Kb/s (kilobits per second) digital data rate, but this can be scaled to 84 Kb/s or 64 Kb/s to allow 12 Kb/s or 32 Kb/s for other services, including non-broadcast services such as subscription services.

Terrestrial digital audio broadcasting involves not only regulatory procedures but also marketing hurdles to convince radio station owners, broadcast equipment manufacturers, consumer and automotive electronics manufacturers and retailers, and most important, the public to support the technology. You can't listen to an HD signal unless you have a radio receiver equipped to decode HD signals. As with satellite radio's earliest efforts to attract subscribers, receiver availability has been a significant barrier to consumer acceptance. Between 2006 and 2010, the number of people interested in HD radio never rose above 8% and the number of stations broadcasting HD peaked in 2011 at 2,103 (Pew, 2012). Receiver choices remain limited; prices have declined but cost between $49 and $400 for portable, home, or automotive tuners. They are often difficult to tune in, sometimes requiring several seconds to lock on a frequency (Boehret, 2010). Listening to regular radio remains easy; the number of conventional (analog) FM receivers in the U.S. is estimated at 800 million (FCC, 2004).

There is no current plan to eliminate analog FM and AM broadcasts, and the HD radio transmissions will not return any spectrum to the FCC for new uses. Thus, there are questions as to whether consumers want the new service, given the expense of new receivers, the abundance of existing receivers, and the availability of other technologies including subscriber-based satellite-delivered audio services, digital media players with audio transfer and playback, and competition from digital devices. As was true with satellite radio, gaining the interest of the automotive industry to offer HD radio as an optional or standard audio feature is crucial. Unlike satellite radio, no automotive manufacturers are investors in iBiquity Digital, although 22 automobile brands have committed to adding the service (iBiquity, 2012).

Figure 10.2
Hybrid and All-Digital AM & FM IBOC Modes

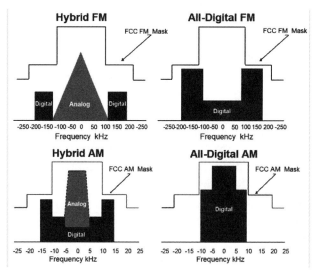

Source: iBiquity

iBiquity Digital's HD radio gives listeners, who are used to instant access, one odd technology quirk to get used to. Whenever an HD radio signal is detected, it takes the receiver approximately 8.5 seconds to lock onto the signal. The first four seconds are needed for the receiver to process the digitally compressed information; the next 4.5 seconds ensure robustness of the signal (iBiquity, 2003). The hybrid (analog and HD) operation allows receivers to switch between digital and analog signals, if the digital signal is lost. Receivers compensate for part of the lost signal by incorporating audio buffering technology into their electronics that can fill in the missing signal with analog audio. For this approach to be effective, iBiquity Digital recommends that analog station signals operate with a delay, rather than as a live signal. Effectively, the signal of an analog FM receiver, airing the same programming as an HD receiver, would be delayed at least 8.5 seconds. As a practical matter, iBiquity Digital notes, "Processing and buffer delay will produce off-air cueing challenges for remote broadcasts..." (iBiquity, 2003, p. 55).

A different form of DAB service is in operation in a number of countries. The Eureka 147 system broadcasts digital signals on the L-band (1452-1492 MHz) or a part of the spectrum known as Band III (around 221 MHz). The service is in operation in fourteen countries around the world, including in the UK, with 85% coverage and 14 million receiving devices in the market. Germany expects 99% population coverage by 2014. China operates stations reaching 8% of the country's population. China has the potential to establish DAB as a universal format. With a state-controlled economy and technology marketplace, the government of China could direct a country-wide rollout of the technology, creating a marketplace with 1.3 billion potential listeners. Eighteen additional countries are conducting experimental tests and 13 more have expressed interest in the system (World DAB, n.d.). Eureka technology is not designed to work with existing AM and FM frequencies. That is one reason why broadcasters in the United States rejected the Eureka 147 system in favor of the "backward and forward" compatible digital technology of iBiquity Digital's IBOC that allows listeners to receive analog signals without having to purchase a new receiver for the DAB system (FCC, 2004).

The World DAB Forum, an international, non-government organization to promote the Eureka 147 DAB system, reports that more than 500 million people around the world can receive the 1,400 different DAB/DAB+/DMB services (World DAB, n.d.). As with digital broadcasting in the United States, proponents of Eureka 147 cite the service's ability to deliver data as well as audio. Examples of data applications include weather maps or directional information that might be helpful to drivers or emergency personnel. As with the iBiquity

Digital projections, the Eureka numbers seem impressive until put into perspective: 500 million people can potentially receive the signal, but only if they have purchased one of the required receivers. Eureka 147 receivers have been on the market since 1998 and are compatible across Europe; about 320 models of commercial receivers are currently available and range in price from around $55 to more than $1,000 (World DAB, n.d.).

Two new services, DAB+ and digital multimedia broadcasting (DMB), offer the potential for DAB to leap beyond ordinary radio applications. DAB+ is based on the original DAB standard, but uses a more efficient audio codec. It provides the same functionality as the original DAB radio services including services following traffic announcements and PAD multimedia data (dynamic labels such as title artist information or news headlines, complementary graphics, and images) (World DAB, n.d.).

An early effort by iBiquity Digital and its broadcast equipment–manufacturing partners introduced HD Radio to other countries, particularly in Europe. While the technology attracted some attention, it does not appear to be gaining station or regulatory converts.

Current Status

Company ownership and investment in technology matter. A significant investment in technology can serve as a stimulus for future growth, development and expansion of radio. Unfortunately, the two largest group owners of radio stations, Clear Channel and Cumulus Broadcasting, do not appear to be interested in serving as a growth catalyst for radio.

The growth opportunities presented by the infinite dial versus the traditional radio dial are apparent to the largest radio group owner, CC Media Holdings, the parent of Clear Channel Communications. Clear Channel was founded in 1972 in San Antonio, Texas, as the owner of a single radio station. Today, the company is the largest owner of radio stations in the U.S, owning more than 850 radio stations in 150 cities in the U.S. that reach about 110 million listeners per week (Flint, 2012a). MTV co-founder and former CEO Bob Pittman was named CEO in 2011. Recent company moves included renaming the radio unit Clear Channel Media and Entertainment. Clear Channel holds $20 billion in debt from when it was taken private by Bain Capital and Thomas H. Lee Partners.

Broadcast radio remains an important revenue center for the company, but it appears to be a static source of revenue—not a growth area. Radio revenues are a source for debt repayment but not an area for future growth. The company's iHeartRadio streaming application is targeted to reach listeners through the infinite dial. Clear Channel recently committed to invest $300 million in multimedia investments in Ryan Seacrest Productions as part of its strategic shift towards streaming digital content instead of broadcast radio (Flint, 2010b).

Cumulus Broadcasting purchased rival Citadel Media, after Citadel emerged from bankruptcy, in 2011 for $2.4 billion. In April 2012, Cumulus announced a deal to sell about 50 stations in smaller markets but also to add stations in two larger markets (Sisario, 2012). Cumulus' strategy is business oriented, not technology oriented: the company is creating radio ownership clusters in larger cities but selling stations in smaller markets with lower advertising revenue. Building larger clusters gives the radio group owner clout to sell advertising by reducing the competition impact but it does little to ensure support for the technology.

Both companies have become high-stakes radio operators, but their debt loads push their focus towards maximizing revenue rather than investing in traditional radio programming or radio technology.

Terrestrial broadcast radio remains a big part of the lives of most people. Each week, more than 241 million people hear the nearly 15,859 FM, LPFM, and AM radio stations in the U.S. Advertisers spent $17.4 billion on radio advertising in 2011—a substantial amount, but still less than the industry's 21.3 billion in 2007. The decline resulted from the soft economy as well as advertising shifts to other media, including online sources (FCC, 2012; RAB, n.d.-a, U.S. Bureau of the Census, 2011). In fairness, ad expenditures for radio are trending up since

sinking to about $16 billion in 2009. Radio listening statistics are impressive, but a closer examination shows persistent radio industry declines, ranging from declining ad revenue to a daily drop in listeners.

The FCC estimates there are nearly 800 million radios in use in U.S. households, private and commercial vehicles, and commercial establishments (FCC, 2004). All of these radios will continue to receive analog signals from radio stations. Radio listening is steady at 93% reached each week, but Internet access at any location is now 85%, up from 72% in 2002. Time spent listening to radio was about 3 hours per day in 2003; it is 2 hours and 8 minutes in 2012 (RAB, 2003; RAB, n.d.-b). It's not that radio doesn't have something to offer, it's just that other services have more ways to offer content. Still, the radio content is free—except for the opportunity cost of listening to commercials—and some sort of signal is available nearly anywhere in the world you travel.

Radio programming is also shifting away from music and back to its roots as a program formatted medium. Soap operas and mysteries aren't returning, but talk programming, long popular on the AM band, now occupies many FM frequencies. In the largest markets, some of the programming may be local, but much of the programming is syndicated through a radio network, such as Clear Channel's Premiere Network. These programming changes result in fewer job opportunities in programming and on-air operation, though the pressure to increase revenue results in more efforts to hire sales personnel.

Factors to Watch

Radio stations have been in the business of delivering music and information to listeners for nearly a century. Public acceptance of radio, measured through listenership more than any particular technological aspect, has enabled radio to succeed. Stations have been able to sell advertising time based on the number and perceived value of their audience to advertising clients. Technology, when utilized by radio stations, focused on improving the sound of the existing AM or FM signal or reducing operating costs.

Digital radio technology has modest potential to return the radio industry to a more relevant status among consumers. The plethora of alternative delivery means suggests that radio may be entering the competitive arena too late to attract the attention of consumers. Chris Anderson (2006), writing in Wired, promotes the notion of The Long Tail, where consumers, bored with mainstream media offerings, regularly pursue the digital music road less traveled. As Business Week noted, "Listeners, increasingly bored by the homogeneous programming and ever-more-intrusive advertising on commercial airwaves, are simply tuning out and finding alternatives" (Green, et al., 2005).

Table 10.1

Radio in the United States at a Glance

Number of Radios

Households with radios	99%
Average number of radios per household	8
Number of radios in U.S. homes, autos, commercial vehicles and commercial establishments	800 million

Source: U.S. Bureau of the Census (2011) and FCC (2004)

Radio Station Totals

AM Stations	4,762
FM Commercial Stations	6,555
FM Educational Stations	3,712
Total 15,029	
FM Translators and Boosters	6,097
LPFM Stations	830

Source: FCC (2012)

Radio Audiences

Persons Age 12 and Older Reached by Radio:	
Each week:	92.8% (About 241.5 million people)
Each day:	69.8% (About 182 million people)
Persons Age 12 and Older Radio Reach by Daypart:	
6–10am	74.9%
10–3pm	82.3%
3–7pm	81.5%
7–12 Mid.	59.4%
12 Mid–6am	25.7%
Where Adults Age 18 and Older Listen to the Radio:	
At home:	17.8% of their listening time
In car:	60.4% of their listening time
At work or other places:	10.4% of their listening time
Daily Share of Time Spent With Various Media:	
Broadcast Radio	77%
TV/Cable	95%
Newspapers	35%
Internet/Web	64%
Magazines	27%

Source: Radio Advertising Bureau Marketing Guide (n.d.-b)

Satellite Subscribers

SIRIUS-XM Satellite Radio	21.9 million

Source: Sirius-XM Satellite Radio (2012)

As technology gets easier to interface with car audio systems, consumers will have greater ability to easily store and transfer digital audio files to and from a variety of small personal players that have a convenience advantage. The competitive nature of radio suggests that the battle for listeners will lead to fewer format options and more mass appeal formats, as stations attempt to pursue an ever-shrinking radio advertising stream.

Localism—the ability of stations to market not only near-CD-quality audio content but also valuable local news, weather, and sports information—has been cited as the touchstone for the terrestrial radio industry. In his farewell address in 2005, retiring NAB President Eddie Fritts presented this challenge: "Our future is in combining the domestic with the digital. Localism and public service are our franchises, and ours alone" (Fritts farewell, 2005, p. 44). But even radio localism is under attack by newspapers and television stations as these competitors attempt to offer micro-local content through Internet and smart device delivery. Why wait for the radio station to provide weather, traffic or sports scores when the content is available on your mobile phone as text, audio or video? But ease of access and use of radio technology that requires only a receiver and no downloading or monthly fees may keep radio relevant for a core group of listeners unwilling to pay for new services and new technologies.

Sustainability

Radio is often the leading communications medium in transitional countries in Africa and Asia for the same reasons that radio remains popular in the United States. Radio receivers are relatively cheap, they are easy to use, and in transitional countries, radio messages can overcome transportation logistical issues (no roads or poor roads that make newspaper delivery difficult), and country literacy problems. You don't have to know how to read to understand a speaker on the radio. Furthemore, the U.S. Agency for International Development (USAID) has promoted the distribution of wind-up and solar radio receivers that don't require economically disadvantaged listeners to buy batteries and thus produce the waste of discarded batteries. Similar wind-up radios are marketed in the U.S., though primarily as emergency radios. In the United States, there are some novel examples of radio stations using solar energy to power transmitters.

More than 200,000 wind-up or solar radios have been distributed in Sudan and South Sudan, giving people in a war-torn region access to a primary news source. Even the radio station transmitter and production equipment can be powered fully or partially through solar power, ensuring an uninterrupted source of programming. The full story of USAID's radio projects is available at http://1.usa.gov/z8flyq. (USAID, 2012).

Bibliography

Albarran, A. & Pitts, G. (2000). *The radio broadcasting industry*. Boston: Allyn and Bacon.

Anderson, C. (2006). *The long tail: Why the future of business is selling less of more*. New York: Hyperion.

Arbitron (2012a). The infinite dial 2012: Navigating digital platforms. Retrieved from http://www.arbitron.com/study/digital_radio_study.asp.

Arbitron (2012b). Weekly online radio audience jumps more than 30 percent in past year says new Arbitron/Edison research study. Retrieved from http://arbitron.mediaroom.com/index.php?s=43&item=813.

Boehret, K. (2010, January 27). Reaching for the height of radio. *The Wall Street Journal*, p. D8.

Borzo, J. (2002, March 5). Phone fun. *Wall Street Journal*, R8.

Chen, K. (2000, January 17). FCC is set to open airwaves to low-power radio. *Wall Street Journal*, B12.

Cheng, R. (2010, April 28). Car phones getting smarter. *The Wall Street Journal*, p. B5.

Federal Communications Commission. (n.d.-a). *AM stereo broadcasting*. Retrieved from http://www.fcc.gov/mb/audio/bickel/amstereo.html.

Federal Communications Commission. (n.d.-b). *Low-power FM broadcast radio stations*. Retrieved from http://www.fcc.gov/mb/audio/lpfm.

Federal Communications Commission. (2004). In the matter of digital audio broadcasting systems and their impact on the terrestrial radio broadcast services. *Notice of proposed rulemaking*. MM Docket No. 99-325. Retrieved from http://hraunfoss.fcc.gov/edocs_public/attachmatch/FCC-04-99A4.pdf.

Federal Communications Commission. (2004). In the matter of economic impact of low-power FM stations on Commercial FM radio: Report to Congress pursuant to section 8 of the Local Community Radio Act of 2010. Retrieved from http://www.fcc.gov/document/ex-parte-documents-received-12162011.

Federal Communications Commission. (2012, April 12)). *Broadcast station totals as of March 31, 2012*. Retrieved from http://www.fcc.gov/document/broadcast-station-totals-march-31-2012.

Flint, J. (2012a) Clear Channel hires executive to lead company beyond radio. *Los Angeles Times*. Retrieved from articles. Latimes/2012/Jan/17/business/la-fi-ct-clear-channel-20120117

Flint, J. (2012b), Ryan Seacrest and Clear Channel deepen business relationship. *Los Angeles Times*. Retrieved from articles. Latimes.com/2012/Feb/01/business/la-fi-ct-Seacrest-clearchannell-20120201

Fritts' farewell: Stay vigilant, stay local. (2005, April 25). *Broadcasting & Cable*, 44.

Green, H., Lowry, T. & Yang, C. (2005, March 3). The new radio revolution. *Business Week Online*. Retrieved from http://yahoo.businessweek.com/technology/content/mar2005/ tc2005033_0336_tc024.htm.

Huff, K. (1992). AM stereo in the marketplace: The solution still eludes. *Journal of Radio Studies, 1*, 15-30.

iBiquity Digital Corporation. (2003). *Broadcasters marketing guide, version 1.0*. Retrieved from http://www.ibiquity.com/hdradio/documents/BroadcastersMarketingGuide.pdf.

iBiquity Corporation. (2012, January 9). HDRadio receiver manufacturers and retailers poised for a big year. Retrieved from http://www.ibiquity.com/press_room/news_releases/2012/1550.

Kneller, H. (2010, January 18). Nautel responds to "HD Radio in Brazil" article. *Radio Business Reports*. Retrieved from http://www.rbr.com/radio/ENGINEERING/95/20134.html?print

Lewis, T. (1991). *Empire of the air: The men who made radio*. New York: Harper Collins.

National Association of Broadcasters. (n.d.). *Innovation in Radio*. Retrieved from http://www.nab.org/radio/innovation.asp.

Pew Research Center. (2012). The state of the news media 2012: An annual report on American journalism. Retrieved from http://stateofthemedia.org/.

Pew Research Center. (2011). The state of the news media 2011: An annual report on American journalism. Retrieved from http://pewresearch.org/pubs/1924/state-of-the-news-media-2011.

Radio Advertising Bureau. (n.d.-a). *Radio revenue trends*. Retrieved from http://www.rab.com/public/pr/yearly.cfm.

Radio Advertising Bureau. (n.d.-b). *Radio Marketing Guide*. Retrieved from http://www.rab.com/whyradio/RadioFacts.cfm..

Radio Advertising Bureau. (2003). Radio marketing guide and factbook for advertisers 2003-2004 edition. New York: Radio Advertising Bureau.

Radio Business Reports. (2010, April 20). Analysts expecting strong Q1 from Sirius XM. Retrieved from http://www.rbr.com/radio/23490.html.

Sirius XM Radio. (2012, January 4). SIRIUS XM Adds Approximately 1,700,000 New Subscribers in 2011. Retrieved April 25, 2012 from .http://investor.sirius.com/releasedetail.cfm?ReleaseID=637122.

Sterling, C. & Kittross, J. (1990). *Stay tuned: A concise history of American broadcasting*. Belmont, CA: Wadsworth Publishing.

Taub, E. A. (2009, December 30). Internet radio stations are the new wave. *The New York Times*. Retrieved May 2, 2010 from http://www.nytimes.com/2009/12/31/technology/personaltech/31basics.html?_r=1&scp=3&sq=internet%20radio%20receivers&st=Search

The Nielsen Company. (October 29, 2009) *How U.S. adults use radio and other forms of audio*. Retrieved from http://www.researchexcellence.com.

U.S. Bureau of the Census. (2011). *Statistical abstract of the United States*. Washington, DC: U.S. Government Printing Office.

USAID. (2012, January/February) Radio for a new nation, *Frontlines*. Retrieved from http://www.usaid.gov/press/frontlines/fl_jan12/FL_jan12_DRG_SUDAN_RADIO.html.

World DAB: The World Forum for Digital Audio Broadcasting. (n.d.). Country information. Retrieved April 22, 2012 from http://www.worlddab.org/country_information_

11

Digital Signage

Jeffrey S. Wilkinson, Ph.D. &
Janet Kolodzy, M.S.J.*

Most people have experienced digital signage without thinking twice. It can be as big as the Times Square digital billboards or as small as a digital photo frame in a reception area. Digital signage alerts passengers to the next train, informs students about a visiting speaker on campus, or provides cooking tips to a supermarket shopper. Digital signage can involve an LED or plasma screen, a touch screen kiosk, or a mobile phone screen. It is a fast-growing industry that is attracting audio-visual suppliers, electronic integrators, network developers, marketers, and others who see it as a new medium for any message. Digital signage proponents argue that anything a paper sign once did, a digital sign can do better, and in a timelier, more uniform, more efficient, and more available fashion (Little, 2010). Paper and digital signs are compared in Table 11.1.

The Digital Signage Association defines digital signage as "the use of electronic displays or screens (such as LCD, LED, plasma or projection) to deliver entertainment, information and/or advertising in public or private spaces, outside of home" (Digital Signage FAQs, 2010). But others involved in the industry indicate a more focused use for business communication "where a dynamic messaging device is used to take the place of, or supplement, other forms of messaging" (Yackey, 2009).

In the forward of Keith Kelsen's *Unleashing the Power of Digital Signage*, digital signage is referred to as an "experience medium, a place that engages people in the experience" (Kelsen, 2010). The future of digital signage is in its capacity to engage and connect with individuals on each person's terms, anywhere, anyhow, and any time. Kelsen maintains that broadband networks and mobile devices combined with screen displays create new layers of "connectedness" of media, messages, and audiences. Digital signage, like mobile devices, allows the audience to "opt in" where they want to opt in. Digital signage "is technology that meets viewers in their environment with potentially the right message at the right time" (Kelsen, 2010, p. xiii).

Retailers and marketers have adopted the use of digital signage in greater proportion than other industries, but its potential use in educational, health care, and internal business communication has led to consistent annual growth even amid tough economic times. Digital signage involves the marriage of certain hardware, software, and content for presenting text, video, and graphics. New developments providing easier, cheaper, and more energy-efficient offerings in each of these areas are enabling the overall growth of digital signage.

From the audience perspective, however, issues of distraction and intrusion continue to be of concern as digital signage expands beyond limited pockets of usage to national networked displays. Those in the digital signage industry are examining ways to develop a standard system of both measurement of digital signage impact and of operation or presentation. Digital signage providers are also developing an independent trade association.

---

* Jeffrey S. Wilkinson is Professor, Journalism and Mass Communication program, Houston Baptist University (Houston, Texas and Janet Kolodzy is Associate Professor, Department of Journalism, Emerson College (Boston, Massachusetts).

Table 11.1
Paper versus Digital Signage

Traditional/Paper Signs	Digital Signage
✦ Displays a single message over several weeks	✦ Displays multiple messages for desired time period
✦ No audience response available	✦ Allows audience interactivity
✦ Changing content requires new sign creation	✦ Content changed quickly and easily
✦ Two-dimensional presentation	✦ Mixed media = text, graphics, video, pictures
✦ Lower initial costs	✦ High upfront technology investment costs

Source: Janet Kolodzy

Background

Digital signage emerged from a variety of ancestors: Audio-visual equipment, outdoor advertising billboards, trade show displays, television and computer monitors, video recorders, and media players. Its precursors range from Turner Broadcasting's Checkout Channel, which aired news and information for those waiting in the checkout line, to the electronic displays on New York's Times Square. Yet, digital signage truly came to the fore over the past decade with the invention of flexible flat display screens and multimedia players with a variety of content files (documents, digital pictures, videos, animation, etc.) that can be controlled, updated, and enhanced via content management systems by users and not just by suppliers.

In fact, even the term "digital signage" has had dozens of variations and interpretations before it became a generally accepted term in the industry. Terms such as "Captive Audience Networks" and "Digital Signage Broadcasting" to "Dynamic or Digital Out-Of-Home (DOOH)" and "Digital Displays" are covered by the digital signage umbrella (Schaeffler, 2008). A digital signage resource directory lists integrators, installers, networks, content services, displays, media players, and control systems among businesses connected to the industry.

Lars-Ingemar Lundstrom, a Swedish digital signage manager and author of *Digital Signage Broadcasting* said "Digital signage is very different from most other kinds of media because it is really a combination of existing technologies" (Lundstrom, 2008, p. xii). In many ways, digital signage is a combination of Internet and broadcasting designed to present information. It can present images and information in real-time, live via broadcast, or from stored memory via the Internet. The technology can arrange that presentation in a variety of ways, with a screen devoted solely to one image or divided up into several segments using video, still images, and text (either moving continuously via a "crawl" or stationary in a graphic). "Digital signage systems allow automatic content storage at several locations en route to the viewer. The stored content may also be updated at any time" (Lundstrom, 2008, p. 5).

The development of durable and flexible displays, of software and content management systems, and now Internet and wireless networks to connect screens in multiple locations have all opened up a range of uses for digital signage. The rise of an Internet Protocol TV (IPTV) format (see Chapter 8 of this text) provides the basis for this new communication medium (Schaeffler, 2008).

Technology Needs: Hardware and Software.

As illustrated in Figure 11.1, typical digital signage involves a screen, a media player, content, and a content management system. A TV set connected to a VCR playing a videotape in a store was a raw form of digital signage. Add an antenna or connect it to cable, and that TV could be considered part of a network.

Today, the options and variations in digital signage in hardware, software, and networking are as vast as the types of display screens, media players, and digital images available in the consumer market.

Figure 11.1
Digital Signage System

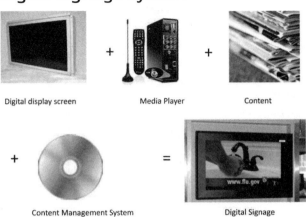

Digital display screen   Media Player   Content

Content Management System   Digital Signage

Source: Janet Kolodzy

Plasma screens, Liquid Crystal Display (LCD) monitors, Light Emitting Diode (LED) screens, and projection screens are part of the digital signage hardware display options. Environmental conditions such as rain, heat, dust, and even kitchen grease for digital signs in cafeterias have led to modifications in digital signage display screens that are different from the viewing screens sold in the consumer electronics market. Innovations in screen size, resolution, brightness, and image retention (also called "burn-in") appear first in digital signage. Alan C. Brawn, in *Digital Signage Magazine*, noted that displays are now available that are nearly four times brighter than a typical 40-inch LCD flat panel (Brawn, 2009). A plasma or LCD screen used for digital signage could cost 10 to 20 times as much as a typical consumer grade television or computer screen, but is designed to run for more hours, dissipate more heat and be more secure (Digital Signage FAQ, n.d.). An LED screen for a digital billboard can use up to 50,000 LED tubes but modifications are being made to make them burn brighter and longer and use less electricity.

When it comes to software and servers, digital signage software experts are split into two camps: 1) premise-based systems, which involve in-house servers and software or 2) Software as a Service (SaaS), which is like cloud computing, with off-site servers and applications accessed via the Web. The difference is the equivalent of the debate over whether Excel software on your own computer is better than using the Google Docs spreadsheet application.

Supporters of premise-based systems say they provide better security and greater flexibility in uploading and distributing real-time data, particularly if designed for in-house communication (Collard, 2009). For example, the Dallas Cowboys stadium uses a premise-based system by Cisco systems that connects its video, digital content, and interactive fan services and involves nearly 3,000 displays (Cisco, 2009).

SaaS systems are often the choice of businesses making an initial venture into digital signage. Rather than installing a server in-house, a software provider will host the server and/or the software for the digital signage system, eliminating the need for extensive in-house technical support. Computing uses the "cloud," similar to Google applications like Google Sites and Google Docs.

When it upgraded its internal communication system with digital signage at its campus, Boston's Brigham and Women's Hospital turned to Smithcurl Communications to set up a system using media players and a dedicated server. The hospital uses Carousel media players and a software application for creating, storing, and then displaying bulletins about hospital activities. The dedicated server is a part of the hospital's "server farm." The system's set-up has some elements of a premise-based system since its own servers are used, but is also a SaaS since software updates and servicing is provided by an off-site firm (personal interview). The media players used for digital signage and what they actually present to audiences also figure into the technology configuration. When digital signage first emerged, media players were often limited to one form of media presentation (video or DVD player, MP3 files, jpgs). Today, personal computers can present multiple forms of media simultaneously on different parts of the screen, and media players for digital signage can do the same. Memory cards and flash drives can store and present content on displays with minimal need for updating. Also, wireless networks allow material to be presented on different screens in either the same way or using different configurations.

Types of Digital Signage.

In *Unleashing the Power of Digital Signage*, Keith Kelsen called digital signage "the fifth screen" of communication. Chronologically, the movie screen was the first screen, television the second, the computer monitor the third, and the mobile phone screen the fourth (Kelsen, 2010). This fifth screen can be found in ever-increasing locations, ranging from a price display in a retail store to a large sports screen or outdoor billboard. Kelsen identifies three environments suited for this fifth screen: Point of wait (where people are in a waiting area or mode like a doctor's office or elevator), point of sale, and point of transit (where people are in transit like at an airport) (Kelsen, 2010).

Boston's Brigham and Women's Hospital is an example of how people at a point of wait benefit from digital signage. The hospital uses more than two dozen monitors in more than a half-dozen buildings comprising its main campus (illustrated in Figure 11.2). BWH's David Connolly said the initial impetus to adopt digital signage was to reduce clutter from posters and paper signage. Now, the digital signage network cycles through some 35 still-frame messages and video covering topics ranging from hand washing to weekly rounds to National Nutrition Month activities. About 50 hospital employees have been trained on the content management system to submit postings. The communications department publishes the submissions, updating the rotation daily. The submissions are saved as jpg files and are uploaded on the hospital's Intranet system.

More digital signage networks are being used at the hospital's clinics and sites in other parts of metropolitan Boston. Video presentations about key health issues, such as flu shots, are extending the use to more than a digital bulletin board. St. Joseph Hospital in Orange County, California uses digital signage to coordinate its operating facility, involving information on treatment rooms, pre-operative activities, and patient readiness (Collard, 2010).

Exponential growth has occurred with retail businesses using digital signage at points of sale. Many multiplex movie theater refreshment counters now use screens to display snack options and run ads for soft drinks. Restaurants and food stands use digital signage as menu boards, allowing chain restaurants to update and revise daily specials and offerings at multiple locations. Mall shoppers can view digital screens with items and brands being promoted or on sale. In supermarkets, digital screens can be found in certain sections, such as the deli, with recipe demonstrations and information for certain items such as hummus or dinner rolls that may be featured in the recipes. A Digital Signage Association survey found two-thirds of 1,200 respondents reported their business was using digital signage for brand messaging and marketing. Less than a fourth were simply running ads on their screens (Bickers, 2009).

Figure 11.2
Traditional & Digital Signs at Boston's Brigham & Women's Hospital

Main lobbies and waiting areas at Boston's Brigham and Women's Hospital are equipped with digital signage of hospital activities, replacing many poster board signs.

Source: Janet Kolodzy

At the point of transit, digital signage plays the key role of "wayfinding." Digital signs at transit hubs such as airports, train stations, and subway stops as well as displays in buses, subway cars, and taxicabs represent point-of-transit digital signage. Digital signs supplying transit information can be found at transit stops and most airports in the U.S., as well as in major international hubs, which feature digital signage for providing passengers with travel information. Digital signs provide navigational tools for people to find out where they need to go and how to get there.

Besides finding directions, digital signs also present advertising and entertainment. New York and Hong Kong taxi riders can watch ads as well as news updates on screens embedded in the backs of the taxi's front seat. During the 2008 Olympics, Beijing subway riders were offered public transit etiquette reminders, food ads, and Olympic highlights on screens built into the sides of the subway cars.

On a larger scale, digital billboards also represent point-of-transit digital signage. Some digital billboards are used to present timely news and information, such as national AMBER Alerts on missing children. But mostly they are still seen as a more modern version of roadside advertising. Local governments that have placed restrictions on traditional paper or vinyl billboards have done the same with digital versions. The U.S. government also has begun setting standards on brightness of the signs and acceptable content (such as restricting moving, flashing, intermittent, and other fast-moving visuals) (Schaeffler, 2008).

Some use digital signage as a form of community art. Boston's public television station WGBH, the producer of extensive PBS children's programming, has had a 30 foot by 45-foot LED display on its studios overseeing the Massachusetts Turnpike since 2006 (WGBH website, 2012). The digital mural was the first digital signage of its kind in the city (see Figure 11.3). Two governmental agencies, the Turnpike Authority and the Boston Redevelopment Authority, as well as community groups, all played a role in approving the display that WGBH personnel refer to as a "gift to the community" showcasing WGBH and community activities (Bruner, 2010). Although it has all the aspects of a digital billboard because of the size and placement of the display, WGBH's Vice President for Communication and Government Relations Jeanne Hopkins said the very restrictive use standards placed on the display has led to it being viewed "more like public art." She added, "our intention is to say this is WGBH and here are images of what we do and to connect with Boston" (personal communication, March 2010).

Figure 11.3
WGBH Digital Billboard

Only two or three images a day are rotated through like a slide show on the 30 by 45-foot LED digital mural on the WGBH public television station's Allston-Brighton headquarters.

Source: WGBH.

Unlike digital billboard advertising that may change video, animation, or information frequently, the WGBH mural displays at most three still images in sequence over a 30-second time frame. "We wanted the pace to be slow from the beginning," said Cynthia Bruner, the station's director of constituent community. The images do not contain wording or phone numbers to keep driving distractions minimal for the estimated half-million vehicles that pass it weekly. "Safety is our No. 1 prerequisite," she said, adding "We don't want anyone puzzling out what's displayed." Even the WGBH logo was not displayed on the mural for the first year. The images, which change daily, only run from 6:30 a.m. to 8 p.m. At night, a night sky image is displayed. Community activities and key events are displayed such as the Boston Marathon and the August 2009 death of Senator Ted Kennedy. Promotional art of WGBH's children's programming tends to be very popular and featured on weekends (Bruner, 2010).

Recent Developments

Interactivity, Engagement, Intrusion

The areas of greatest growth and discussion involve the development of networks and control of content. These two factors are pushing digital signage in new directions and raising the bar on how deeply to engage consumers. NEC Corporation and others have developed digital signage with sensors which try to tailor messages toward individuals who come within range of the signs. The NEC system, called the Next Generation Digital Signage Solution, uses cameras and software to assess the probable age and gender of someone nearby, then provide an ad suited to him or her. This technology mirrors the science-fiction advertising system portrayed in the 2002 film *Minority Report* with Tom Cruise (McGlaun, 2010). This signage uses interactive touch screens and so-called gesture technology to further engage individuals.

But consumers consistently object to the use of these technologies on privacy grounds, and in 2011 the Digital Signage Federation (DSF) agreed to adopt a set of guidelines limiting the intrusiveness of the techniques described above. In February, 2011, the Digital Signage Federation agreed to adopt a comprehensive set of digital signage privacy standards for its members. According to Geiger (2011), the privacy standards state that companies should obtain consumers' opt-in consent before collecting directly identifiable information through digital signage (such as facial recognition or behavioral tracking). Companies are prohibited from collecting information on minors under 13 (or as defined by state law) through digital signage. Companies should also provide notice of any ongoing data collection in the physical location in which digital signage units operate—like a sign at the entrance of a supermarket—even if the system collects only "anonymous" data.

While digital signage has great potential as a communication medium, thanks to technological advances which provide interactivity, greater attention is now being placed on the content on digital signage and what works and does not work. Industry experts have noted that broadcast or print-designed ads do not translate well to digital signage. A 15-second or 30-second television ad is often too long for digital billboards or retail signs.

Also, digital screens are being segmented for different messages to be projected to different audiences. One area might be devoted to a video display, while another might be just text of weather and time, while another part could be a still-image ad. Kelsen (personal interview, March 9, 2010) said content needs to be relevant to the consumer so they don't get confused with a "hodgepodge" of ads, indicating that there is a "symbiotic relationship" between digital signal technology and content.

The industry is paying attention. In early 2012, Inwindow Outdoor and Intel announced a pilot program to install so-called "Experience Stations" at five mall and hotel locations in the U.S. The experimental seven-foot tall, free-standing kiosks feature 70-inch high definition screens and immersive technologies such as "gesture interaction, multi-touch screens and the means to allow consumers with NFC-enabled phones to conduct transactions at the site" (Inwindow Outdoor and Intel, 2012). In conjunction with the kiosks, Intel offers the "Intel® Audience Impression Metrics Suite" (Intel AIM Suite) to measure and analyze the time a user spends interacting with an advertisement. The software determines the probable age bracket and gender of each user in order to customize content. For example, when a user approaches an Experiences Station, the left three-quarters of the 70" screen features an interactive advertisement common in these types of interactive campaigns. Each ad has a component involving either the touch screen or the 3-D gesture camera to encourage the user to participate further. Meanwhile, the right quarter of the screen features a menu of applications the user can access via hand movements. For the pilot program, apps will include a directory of the mall or hotel, weather information, a virtual photo booth, movie trailers and show times, and special sales or promotions at selected mall retailers. The Experience Stations can be seen at malls in Philadelphia, Atlanta, Dallas and New York as well as at The Hilton New York.

Similarly, Verizon and Stratacache also announced a means for retailers to interact more closely with customers through digital signage (Stratacache and Verizon, 2012). Stratacache's interactive digital-signage software combined with Verizon's 4G LTE network and infrastructure allows customers to browse product catalogs, download digital coupons, view product tutorials, give brand feedback, and use social media.

Not to be outdone, Dubai-based Advanced Interactive Media Solutions, a Scala Middle East partner and provider of digital signage solutions, deployed a digital signage and kiosk campaign to enhance brand awareness through interactive gaming functions (Dubai firm gamifies, 2012). The custom designed kiosks were installed at the Mall of Emirates, Deira City Centre and Mirdif City Centre. The kiosks used interactive digital content that integrated social media and interactive gaming features. The digital signage kiosks were deployed with back-to-back, 42-inch touchscreen displays inviting visitors to play a memory game and register for more features. The campaign also featured built-in camera functionalities and Facebook integration. When idle, the kiosk displayed brand ads while inviting the public to "Play Scratch, Match & Win Game and get a chance to win instant prizes." Once the user touched the screen, the interactive memory game is launched.

Signage and Religion

Not only malls and highways are subject to digital signage, but even houses of worship. Whether as a point of waiting or point of transit, places of worship have steady traffic and loyal, repeat customers. There are tens of thousands of buildings used by congregations in the U.S., and to capture market share, StrandVision Digital Signage announced an offer to provide qualified organizations a basic package for free for up to five years (StrandVision offers free software, 2012). The "House of Worship offer" is solely for churches, mosques, synagogues, temples and other public places of worship. The Basic Package offer includes 80 hours per week of digital signage playback time for one playback location, 50 fully customizable pages that can be used to display text, including

scrolling text and newsfeed crawls, graphics, photos and animated weather radar. It also includes page dwell time controls, advanced page scheduling, access to RSS feeds and five user-defined databases for membership, music, calendar, and other lists, as well as 10MB of data, image and sound storage. The system also can be configured to display prayer requests from members of the congregation. StrandVision uses a cloud-based digital signage console to select and design their pages. Organizations have to supply their own high-speed Internet connection, a standard television (such as a flat-screen LCD), and a personal computer to complete the system.

Signage as Journalism

Since March 2010, *New York Times* content has been delivered to some 850 digital screens in business district restaurants and cafes in five major U.S. cities: New York, Los Angeles, Boston, Chicago, and San Francisco (RMG, 2010). The set-up by RMG Networks displays *New York Times* content (short-form text, photos, and videos) every 30 seconds for updating, with different *Times*' sections (such as Health, Business, Technology, Movies, Travel, and Best Sellers) featured in informational loops that run in a seven-minute programming wheel (Boyer, 2010), illustrated in Figure 11.4.

Figure 11.4
New York Times Digital Cafe Delivery

The New York Times has teamed with RMG Networks to provide Times' text, pictures and video on 800 digital screens in cafes in five major US cities.

Source: RMG Networks.

Mobile users can download the *Times'* full story content, and shows where the digital signage industry expects expansion. Nearly 38% of the 1,200 respondents to the 2009 State of the Digital Signage Industry survey for the Digital Signage Association identified interaction with mobile phones as the technology that will impact digital signage the most in the next five years (Bickers, 2009).

Preliminary examination of download rates and consumer interaction from digital signage versus a computer find a higher percentage (3%) for mobile phones compared to less than 1% for computers (Kelsen, 2010). That rate jumps to 30% if mobile phones are set to a discoverable mode, enabling better haphazard recognition of messages transmitted from digital signage. According to Kelsen (2010), digital signage can use different media platforms to reach different audiences any time and place and with continuity. He said digital signage connections with mobile phones gives consumers a means to interact and engage without being physically present, for example, responding to contests or even buying a product via the mobile phone (Kelsen, 2010).

Current Status

The numbers are sometimes contradictory, but all the research suggests that digital signage is rapidly growing worldwide. A news release from Intel corporation predicts double-digit growth to continue with global digital signage to be 10 million media players and a corresponding 22 million digital signs by 2015 (Avalos, 2011). According to a research report from Global Industry Analysts Inc. (GIA), the global digital signage market should hit nearly $14 billion by 2017 (Global digital signage, 2011). The U.S. is said to be the largest market for digital signage, and the Asia-Pacific region to be the fastest-growing. A more conservative prediction by ABI research reports that in 2010 the global digital signage industry grew to $1.3 billion and will grow to $4.5 billion by 2016 (ABI research, 2011).

Industry figures indicate the majority of digital signage installations are IP-based, underscoring the evolution of digital signage away from static advertising; each media player requires connection to a remote content management server. Whether the connection is wired or wireless, in general all the content is more timely, more localized, and therefore, more relevant. As a result, the worldwide market is accelerating in terms of number of installed units and total revenues even as the cost of deployment is steadily declining (Pierson, 2011).

Digital billboards continue to undergo government scrutiny. In 2012 it was reported that a federal study of the distraction effects of these signs may have been "botched" in favor of the industry and remains "cloaked in secrecy" (Levin, 2012). While previous studies have estimated a risk of crashing if glance times run between 3/4 of a second to 2 seconds, the federal study reported that the average glance was only 1/10 of a second. Critics complained that this finding was practically impossible. The Outdoor Advertising Association of America has always aggressively pushed the signs despite voiced concerns by state and local government safety officials. Digital billboards change roughly every 6 to 8 seconds and are said to be more profitable than standard billboards, which number around 400,000 nationwide.

The growth of digital billboards in the U.S. has been fairly moderate, with a few hundred added each year. The number of displays has increased from around 400 in 2007 to around 2,000 in 2010 and estimated up to 3,200 in 2012 (Levin, 2012).

But there are widely-varying estimates about the size and predicted growth of the digital signage industry. According to an article posted on *Digital Signage Today,* the digital place-based advertising (DPA) or digital out-of-home (DOOH) market stood between $2 and $5 billion worldwide (Platt, 2012). Some of the variation stems from the relative immaturity of the industry, lack of measurement standards, and conflicting definitions about what exactly constitutes digital signage. An article in *the Economist* reported global spending on digital billboards and posters reached $2.6 billion in 2011, and was predicted to double by 2016 to $5.2 billion worldwide (Billboard boom, 2011). Meanwhile, MagnaGlobal estimated global DPA at $2.1 billion in 2010 while PQ Media estimated the figure to be $5.06 billion (Platt, 2012). Another research firm, Kinetic, reported global DOOH reached $3.3 billion in 2011. According to the Kinetic figures, China led the way with $1.8 billion spent, followed by the U.S. ($1.1 billion) and the United Kingdom ($157 million). In terms of industry growth, PQ Media placed U.S. DPA growth at 15% in 2010 and 16% in 2011 (Platt, 2012).

Factors to Watch

Globally the top three sectors of adoption continue to be retail, corporate and transportation. Other sectors such as healthcare and hospitality are also growing significantly. In countries such as China and India, ongoing work in building and road construction is facilitating adoption of digital signage as a means to reach consumers on the go as well as when they reach their destination. In the U.S. this was exemplified by the new headquarters opened by JetBlue Airways in 2012. The New York facility on Long Island features two three-story "Wing Walls." These 36-foot tall digital signage installations feature dynamic video and live streaming content. The display is said to create "a unique visual experience at the stairwell and central hub of the airline's new home" (JetBlue, 2012). The Wing Walls feature 14 stacked LCD screens which cover three floors of the building. The displays create an interesting space that crewmembers and visitors can enjoy. The software combines still images, high definition video and live data feeds to create a variety of user experiences.

Trends in "Wayfinding" through Digital Signage.

As noted earlier in this chapter, wayfinding is one of the defining functions of digital signage. Almost all organizations rely on digital signage to help users negotiate physical space and get to where they need to go. Universities, hotels, casinos, cruise ships, hospitals and many others are seeing the importance of improving the visitor experience using wayfinding technology. According to the President and CEO of Four Winds Interactive, David Levin, there are seven trends in wayfinding and digital signage (2012):

1) The integration between digital signs and smartphones will become closer as wayfinding systems enable users to get directions and then quickly send those directions through SMS, Tags and other methods. Users no longer have to remember or write down the information from the sign.

2) Walkable destinations like campuses or cruise ships are considering step-by-step walking directions to supplement the traditional visible path depicted on the map.

3) The sophistication of images is improving, including 3-D depictions of building layouts, more accurate renderings of floor plans, and more realistic depictions of hallways and route details.

4) Property asset details are available for deeper engagement via touch interactivity. For example, hotels and resorts can allow patrons to view hours, menus, and more regarding facilities and services available. Also, universities are providing drill down details, such as contact information for departments and professors.

5) More multitouch capability is in the mix for two-finger zooming on images, which has been popularized by iPad and iPhone interfaces.

6) In some industries, such as hospitality, more promotional content is augmenting basic wayfinding screens. When a user touches a map, the action triggers content in another part of the screen (perhaps a coupon code).

7) Some wayfinding system managers are experimenting with sending text messages to mobile phones, including special offers. Typically, a person engages with the interactive screen and activates their profile via an affinity card or login. For example, in

the gaming industry a player loyalty system can be integrated with the wayfinding system in a casino and throughout a resort in high-traffic areas. These systems can search specific offers available that match a user profile and potentially increase redemption (Levin, 2012).

Digital signage has the potential to become one of the most ubiquitous communication technologies. If so, the growth of this medium will create new markets for hardware and networking services, but the most important new opportunities may be for those who will create the messages that appear on digital signage. These messages will draw from existing media, but the ultimate form and content of ads may be as different from today's media as Internet websites are different from broadcast and print. According to Intel's Jose Avalos (2012),

> "With the convergence of mobile devices, social media and digital signage, interactivity is everywhere. Instead of looking at each platform and channel separately—traditional vs. online, online vs. mobile, in-home vs. out-of-home, broadcast vs. narrowcast—brands are able to take a holistic approach from the start. That's why in retail, you are seeing less discussion about being 'multichannel' (that's a given) and more focus on being 'omnichannel' —bringing together branding assets with the technology to engage and influence a very demanding, very elusive mass audience at different touch points."

Since digital signage claims to be a new media experience, able to engage the senses and interact with consumers, it may be useful to think about what it can become. For example, Caltron has adopted a live TV streaming option into their Digital Signage Players, so that users have added options for the networkable players. The MP-02V player allows users to stream live TV content such as the news or time-sensitive material. The player can operate as a basic standalone device as well as be able to loop images and videos continuously, or it can be updated remotely through the Internet or an intranet (Caltron adds zoning, 2012). The importance of this development is that in time the only difference between Interactive Television and Digital Signage may be the name.

Finally, it seems the biggest factor to watch regards the boundaries for digital signage. As retailers and institutions increasingly adopt digital signage, is there a point of simply "too much?" Along the road, at school, at work, at church, in the bank, visiting the doctor or our state representative or just buying groceries—will we find ourselves in some dystopian consumers' hell, under constant bombardment from ads and information, all tailored just for us?

As a public health issue there may be limits to what we can attend to, but from a mental health perspective, there may be limits to what we can stand. Few consumers are comfortable with signage that knows your gender, age, and buying behaviors because we know at some point another human being can use it to peek into our lives without our consent. Although the industry has adopted sensible guidelines respecting privacy, there is always the danger of one company trying to best the others by going a little too far.

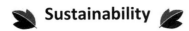

Sustainability

The impact of digital signage on the environment is complicated by its relationship with paper-based signs, which are eliminated by the use of such displays. A white paper by Samsung notes that the Clean Air Council reports Americans receive almost 4 million tons of junk mail each year and U.S. businesses use more than 21 million tons of paper, or about 175 pounds of paper for each person. Americans make nearly 400 billion photocopies each year, or about 750,000 copies every minute of every day (Slawsky, 2010). Electronic signs affect the environment, but could ease some of the problems caused by paper waste.

A 2009 study by MediaZest, a market media research firm, and co-sponsored by Cisco and Panasonic, looked at the carbon footprint of digital and conventional signage. It found the carbon consumption of a digital display is 7.5% lower than a traditional poster display over a period of three years (MediaZest Plc, 2009). The study compared all aspects of use from installation to shutdown, examining use of electricity, paper and ink.

With that in mind, the manufacturers of digital signage routinely announce improvements in energy consumption and eco-friendly parts for newer displays. Replacing old paper-based signage with an electronic display that can run 100,000 hours with hundreds or thousands of messages can help.

In early 2012, NEC announced an ultra-thin video wall display, the X463UN, made with environmental factors in mind. Not only does the model use less power and is made with mercury-free components, but it includes a "carbon footprint meter" which calculates and tracks carbon savings (NEC next-gen video wall, 2012). This professional-grade 46-inch large-screen panel is labeled "ENERGY STAR® 5.1", which meets energy efficiency guidelines set by the U.S. Environmental Protection Agency and the U.S. Department of Energy (NEC next-gen, 2012).

The development of Organic Light Emitting Diode (OLED) screens are touted by screen makers as a "greener" alternative to LCD and plasma screens. OLEDs are thin flexible plastic sheets that use less power because OLEDs do not require backlighting to brighten the image. Since the diodes are made from hydrogen and carbon, they are "organic." But those components also make OLEDs susceptible to deterioration. OLEDs have a lifespan 5 to 10 times shorter than some LCD displays. They have yet to be built in large formats, with sizes measured less than 20 inches, so they are now being tried out for use in mobile phones. Televisions with OLEDs are beginning to hit the consumer market. Another new technology, Laser Phosphor Display by Prysm, Inc. is designed for large-format displays and promises a small carbon footprint. A Prysm brochure states that its displays can consume fewer watts than a standard home light bulb, or about 100 watts per square meter of display (Prysm, Inc, 2010).

Bibliography

ABI research (2011, May 31). Digital signage revenue to approach $4.5 billion in 2016. ABI research. Retrieved from https://www.abiresearch.com/press/3687-Digital+Signage+Revenue+to+Approach+%244.5+Billion+in+2016.

Avalos, J. (2011, October 11). 22 million signs by 2015. Intel Cognovision. Retrieved fromf http://intel.cognovision.com/cognovision/news/64-22-million-digital-signs-by-2015.

Avalos, J. (2012, February 14). Digital signage and the interactive brand. Intel Cognovision. Retrieved from http://intel.cognovision.com/cognovision/news/89-digital-signage-and-the-interactive-brand.

Bickers, J. (2009). The State of the Digital Signage Industry Survey. Retrieved from http://www.digitalsignagetoday.com/white_paper.php?id=79

Billboard boom: The future of out-of-home advertising is rosy, and digital (April 20, 2011). *The Economist*. Retrieved from http://www.economist.com/node/18587305.

Boyer, D. (2010, March 11). VP and General Manager, NYTimes.com Today Network for RMG Networks. (S. a. Hughes, Interviewer)

Brawn, A. C. (2009, November). The World is Flat. Digital Signage, 5 (5), p. 17.

Bruner, C. a. (2010, March 5, 12). WGBH director of constituent communication. (J. Kolodzy, Interviewer)

Bunn, L. (2009, September). 1,000,000+ ads now playing on North America's Digital-Out-of-Home networks. Retrieved from http://lylebunn.com/PapersandArticles.aspx

Bunn, L. (2011, October 11). Triple-digit growth: Can the digital signage industry handle it? (Commentary). Digitalsignagetoday.com. Retrieved from http://www.digitalsignagetoday.com/article/185737/Triple-digit-growth-Can-the-digital-signage-industry-handle-it-Commentary

Caltron adds zoning, streaming to digital signage players (2012, April 2). *Digital Signage Weekly*. Retrieved from http://www.digitalsignageweekly.com/article/72670.aspx.

Cisco (2009, June 19). Retrieved from http://newsroom.cisco.com/dlls/2009/prod_061709.html

Collard, J. (2010, January 29). Aligning healthcare organizations and staff through digital signage. Retrieved from Digital Signage Today: http://digitalsignagetoday.com/article.php?id=23679

Collard, J. (2009, July/August). On-Premise, for robust data-mining solutions. *Digital Signage*, 5 (4), pp. 18-21.

Digital Signage Frequently Asked Questions. (n.d.). Retrieved from digitalsignageassociation.org: http://www.digitalsignageassociation.org/FAQs

Dubai firm 'gamifies' mall DOOH campaign (2012, April 6). Digitalsignagetoday. Retrieved from http://www.digitalsignagetoday.com/article/192757/Dubai-firm-gamifies-mall-DOOH-campaign.

Geiger, H. (2011, February 11). Digital signage federation adopts privacy standards. Center for Democracy & Technology. Retrieved from https://www.cdt.org/blogs/harley-geiger/digital-signage-federation-adopts-privacy-standards

Global digital signage market to close in on $14 billion by 2017 (2011, August 24). digitalsignageassociation. Retrieved from http://www.digitalsignagetoday.com/article/183779/Global-digital-signage-market-to-close-in-on-14-billion-by-2017.

Inwindow Outdoor and Intel experience stations (2012, January 17). *Digital Signage Weekly*. Retrieved from http://www.digitalsignageweekly.com/article/69436.aspx.

JetBlue HQ features digital signage (2012, April 5). AVTechnology online. Retrieved from http://avtechnologyonline.com/article/72962.aspx

Kelsen, K. (2010). *Unleashing the Power of Digital Signage*. Burlington, MA: Focal Press.

Levin, D. (2012, February 8). 7 ways wayfinding digital signage will evolve in 2012 (commentary). DigitalSignageToday.com. Retrieved from http://www.digitalsignagetoday.com/article/190165/7-ways-wayfinding-digital-signage-will-evolve-in-2012-Commentary.

Levin, M. (2012, February 14). Was study of digital billboard safety botched? Open Channel on MSNBC.com. Retrieved from http://openchannel.msnbc.msn.com/_news/2012/02/14/10400036-was-study-of-digital-billboard-safety-botched.

Little, D. (2010, Feb 11). DSA The Perspective. Retrieved from digitalsignageassociation.org/the-perspective: http://www.digitalsignageassociation.org/the-perspective

Lundstrom, L.-I. (2008). *Digital Signage Broadcasting; Broadcasting, Content Management and Distribution Techniques*. Burlington, MA : Focal Press.

McGlaun (2010, March 11). NC Develops 'Minority Report' Advertising System. dailytech.com. Retrieved from http://www.dailytech.com/NEC+Develops+Minority+Report+Advertising+System/article17876.htm

MediaZest Plc. (2009, April 14). Digital Signage: A Sustainable Advantage. mediazest.com. Retrieved from http://www.mediazest.com/cms/uploads/2bf2c3287731984c411c9abfd0ca1427/MediaZestGreenStudy.pdf

NEC next-gen video wall announced (2012, March 26). digitalsignageweekly. Retrieved from http://digitalsignageweekly.com/article/72392.aspx

Pierson, D. (2011, October 19). Digital signage Oh, the places you'll go. Digital Signage Today. Retrieved from http://www.digitalsignagetoday.com/blog/6692/Digital-signage-Oh-the-places-you-ll-go?rc_id=312

Platt, S.K. (2012, February 28). Just how big *is* the DOOH industry? (Commentary). Digitalsignagetoday.com. Retrieved from http://www.digitalsignagetoday.com/article/190863/Just-how-big-is-the-DOOH-industry-Commentary

Prysm, Inc. (2010,). Enable Immersive Experiences. Retrieved from prysm.com: http://www.prysm.com/Prysm_CompanyBrochure_011210_hr_opt.pdf

RMG Networks, The New York Times launch DOOH network. (2010, March 1). digitalsignagetoday.com. Retrieved from: http://digitalsignagetoday.com/article.php?id=23891

Schaeffler, J. (2008). *Digital signage: software, networks, advertising, and displays: A primer for understanding the business*. Focal Press.

Slawsky, R. (2010). Minimizing the environmental impact of digital signage. Whitepaper sponsored by Samsung. Retrieved from http://global.networldalliance.com/downloads/white_papers/Samsung_WP_Green-Technology_To-Launch.pdf

Stratacache and Verizon collaboration announced at NRF (2012, January 17). digitalsignageweekly. Retrieved from http://digitalsignageweekly.com/article/69442.aspx

StrandVision offers free software to houses of worship (2012, March 28). digitalsignageweekly. Retrieved from http://digitalsignageweekly.com/article/72494.aspx

Yackey, B. (2009, July 28). A beginner's guide to digital signage. digitalsignagetoday. Retrieved from digitalsignagetoday.com.

WGBH.com (2012, April 12). WGBH digital mural. WGBH.com. Retrieved from http://www.wgbh.org/about/mural.cfm.

12

Cinema Technologies

Michael R. Ogden, Ph.D. &
Maria Sanders, M.F.A.*

Why Study Cinema Technologies?

✦ A typical feature-length motion picture costs millions of dollars to make and requires the skills of hundreds of people.

✦ The global movie industry continues to see huge growth fuelled by "blockbuster" films, rising consumer income and technological innovations.

✦ New digital cinema and projection technologies are changing the workflow and distribution of movies

✦ In the U.S. alone, movie box office receipts topped $10 billion in 2011.

Storytelling is a universally human endeavor. With the advent of mass media—and, in particular, modern cinema—the role of storyteller in popular culture was subsumed by the "Culture Industry" (*c.f.* Horkheimer & Adorno, 1969; Adorno, 1975; Andrae 1979), an apparatus for the production of meanings and pleasures involving aesthetic strategies and psychological processes (Neale 1985) and bound by its own set of economic and political

* Michael R. Ogden is Professor & Director, Film & Video Studies Program and Maria Sanders is Assistant Professor of Film & Video Studies, Central Washington University (Ellensburg, Washington).

determinants and made possible by contemporary technical capabilities. In other words, cinema functions as a social institution providing a form of social contact desired by citizens immersed in a world of "mass culture." It also exists as a psychological institution whose purpose is to encourage the movie-going habit by providing the kind of entertainment desired by popular culture (Belton, 2013). Simultaneously, cinema evolved as a technological institution, it's existence premised upon the development of specific technologies, most of which originated during the course of industrialization in Europe and America in the late 19th and early 20th Centuries (*e.g.*, film, the camera, the projector and sound recording). The whole concept and practice of filmmaking evolved into an art form dependent upon the mechanical reproduction and mass distribution of "the story"—refracted through the aesthetics of framing, light and shade, color, texture, sounds, movement, the shot/counter-shot, and the *mise en scène* of cinema.

"Today, there is something remarkable going on in the way our culture now creates and consumes entertainment and media," observes Steven Poster, National President of the International Cinematographers Guild (2012, p. 6). The name most associated with film, Kodak, after 131 years in business as one of the largest producers of film stock in the world, filed for Chapter 11 bankruptcy (De La Merced, 2012). The company was hit hard by the recession and the advent of the RED cameras (One, Epic & Scarlet), the Arri Alexa and other high-end digital cinema cameras. In this world of "bits and bytes," Kodak became the latest giant to falter in the face of advancing technology—just as one year earlier, *Blockbuster* sold itself to Dish Network as its retail outlets lost ground to online competitors like *Netflix* (De La Merced, 2012).

Perhaps it was inevitable. The digitization of cinema began in the 1980s in the realm of special visual effects. By the early 1990s, digital sound was widely propagated in most theaters and digital nonlinear editing began to supplant linear editing systems for post-production. "By the end of the 1990s, filmmakers such as George Lucas had begun using digital cameras for original photography and, with the release of *Star Wars Episode I: The Phantom Menace* in 1999, Lucas spearheaded the advent of digital projection in motion picture theatres" (Belton, 2013, p. 417). As if lamenting the digital shift in cinematic storytelling, Poster states that, "...this technological overlay I'm talking about has made a century-old process (light meters, film dailies, lab color timing) that was once [invisible] to everyone but the camera team, visible and accessible to virtually anyone.... It is a loud wake-up call for the entire industry" (2012, p. 6).

As filmmakers grapple with the transition from film to digital image acquisition, another shift may also be in the works. Video capable digital single lens reflex (DSLR) cameras equipped with large image sensors, digital cinema cameras with increasing pixel depth and resolution, emerging systems of digital theater distribution, 3-D acquisition and projection technologies and faster frame-rates, all promise to provide moviegoers a more immersive cinema experience and hopefully re-energize moviegoers, lure them back into the movie theaters, and increase profits. As Mark Zoradi, President of Walt Disney Studios Motion Pictures Group stated, "The key to a good film has always been story, story, story; but in today's environment, it's story, story, story and blow me away" (cited in Kolesnikov-Jessop 2009).

Background

Cinema technology includes advances in image acquisition (*i.e.*, cinematography), the maturation of film and associated technologies that allow an image to be recorded, developments in the ability to transmit the moving image to an audience, the evolution of sound and color, the progression of widescreen capabilities, the generation of special effects, and the emergence (and eventual dominance) of digital technologies. However, until recently "no matter how often the face of the cinema...changed, the underlying structure of the cinematic experience...remained more or less the same" (Belton, 2013, p. 6). Yet, even that which is most closely associated with cinema's identity—sitting with others in a darkened theater watching "larger-than-life" images projected on a big screen—was not always the norm.

From Novelty to Narrative

The origins of cinema as an independent medium lie in the development of mass communication technologies evolved for other purposes (Cook, 2004). Specifically, photography (1826-1839), roll film (1880), the Kodak camera (1888), George Eastman's motion picture film (1889), the motion picture camera (1891-1893), and the motion picture projector (1895-1896) each had to be invented in succession for cinema to be born.

One important precursor to cinema's emergence was early experiments in series photography for capturing motion. In 1878, Eadweard Muybridge set up a battery of cameras triggered by a horse moving through a set of trip wires. Adapting a Zoëtrope (a parlor novelty of the era) for projecting the photographs, Muybridge arranged his photographs around the perimeter of a disc that was manually rotated while light from a "Magic Lantern" projector shown through each slide as it stopped momentarily in front of a lens. The image produced was then viewed on a large screen (Neale, 1985). If rotated rapidly enough, a phenomenon known as *persistence of vision* (an image appearing in front of the eye lingers a split second in the retina after removal of the image), allowed the viewer to experience smooth, realistic motion. Muybridge called his apparatus the Zoopraxiscope, which was used to project photographic images in motion for the first time to the San Francisco Art Association in 1880 (Neale, 1985). In 1882, French physiologist and specialist in animal locomotion, Étienne-Jules Marey, invented the Chronophotographic Gun in order to take series photographs of birds in flight (Cook, 2004). Shaped like a rifle, Marey's camera took twelve instantaneous photographs of movement per second, imprinting them on a rotating glass plate. A year later, Marey switched from glass plates to paper roll film. But like Muybridge, "Marey was not interested in cinematography.... In his view, he had invented a machine for dissection of motion similar to Muybridge's apparatus but more flexible, and he never intended to project his results" (Cook, 2004, p. 4).

In 1887, Hannibal Goodwin, an Episcopalian minister from New Jersey, first used celluloid roll film as a base for light-sensitive emulsions. George Eastman later appropriated Goodwin's idea and in 1889, began to mass-produce and market celluloid roll film on what would eventually become a global scale (Cook, 2004). Neither Goodwin nor Eastman was initially interested in motion pictures. However, it was the introduction of this durable and flexible celluloid film, coupled with the technical breakthroughs of Muybridge and Marey, that inspired Thomas Edison to attempt to produce recorded moving images to accompany the recorded sounds of his newly-invented phonograph (Neale, 1985). It is interesting to note that, according to Edison's own account (cited in Neale, 1985), the idea of making motion pictures was never divorced from the idea of recording sound. "The movies were intended to talk from their inception, so that in some sense the silent cinema represents a thirty-year aberration from the medium's natural tendency toward a total representation of reality" (Cook, 2004, p. 5).

Capitalizing on these innovations, W.K.L. Dickson, a research assistant at the Edison Laboratories, invented the first authentic motion picture camera, the Kinetograph—first constructed in 1890 with a patent granted in 1894. The basic technology of modern film cameras is still nearly identical to this early device. All film cameras, therefore, have the same five basic functions: a "light tight" body that holds the mechanism which advances the film and exposes it to light, a motor, a magazine containing the film, a lens that collects and focuses

light on to the film, and a viewfinder that allows the cinematographer to properly see and frame what he or she is photographing (Freeman, 1998).

Thus, using Eastman's new roll film, the Kinetograph advanced each frame at a precise rate through the camera thanks to sprocket holes that allowed metal teeth to grab the film, advance it, and hold the frame motionless in front of the camera's aperture at split-second intervals. A shutter opened, exposing the frame to light, then closed until the next frame was in place. The Kinetograph repeated this process 40 times per second. "For other cameras throughout the silent era, the speed was 16 frames per second and with the introduction of sound, the rate increased to 24 frames per second in order to produce better-quality voices and music" (Freeman, 1998, p. 405). When the processed film is projected at the same frame rate, realistic movement is presented to the viewer. However, for reasons of profitability alone, Edison was initially opposed to projecting films to groups of people. He reasoned (correctly, as it turned out) that if he made and sold projectors, exhibitors would purchase only one machine from him—a projector—instead of several Kinetoscopes (Belton, 2013) that allowed individual viewers to look at the films through a magnifying eyepiece. By 1894, Kinetographs were producing commercially viable films. Initially the first motion pictures (which cost between $10 and $15 each to make) were viewed individually through Edison's Kinetoscope "peepshows" for a nickel apiece in arcades (called, "Nickelodeons") modeled on the phonographic parlors that had proven so successful for Edison earlier (Belton, 2013).

It was after viewing the Kinetoscope in Paris that the Lumière brothers, Auguste and Louis, began thinking about the possibilities of projecting films on to a screen for an audience of paying customers. In 1894, they began working on their own apparatus, the Cinématograph that differed from Edison's machines by combining both photography and projection into one device and at a much lower (and thus, more economical) film rate of 16 frames per second. It was also much lighter and more portable (Neale, 1985). In 1895, the Lumière brothers demonstrated their Cinématograph to the

Société d'Encouragement pour l'Industries Nationale (Society for the Encouragement of National Industries) in Paris. The first film screened was a short actuality film of workers leaving the Lumière factory in Lyons (Cook, 2004). The actual engineering contributions of the Lumière brothers is quite modest when compared to that of W.K.L. Dickson—they merely synchronized the shutter movement of the camera with the movement of the photographic film strip. Their real contribution is in the establishment of cinema as an industry (Neale, 1985). As pointed out by Jaques Deslandes in his 1966 book, *Histoire Comparée du Cinéma* (Comparative History of Cinema), "This is what explains the birth of the cinema show in France, in England, in Germany, in the United States.... Moving pictures were no longer just a laboratory experiment, a scientific curiosity, from now on they could be considered a commercially viable public spectacle" (cited in Neale, 1985, p. 48).

Figure 12.1
The First Publicly Projected Film: Sortie des Usines Lumière à Lyon, 46 seconds, 1895

Source: Screen capture courtesy Lumière Institute

By the turn of the century, film producers were beginning to assume greater editorial control over the narrative, making multi-shot films and allowing for greater specificity in the story line (Cook, 2004). Such developments are most clearly apparent in the work of Georges Mèliés. A professional magician who owned and operated his own theater in Paris, Mèliés was one of the most important early filmmakers to establish the use of cinematic narrative: a created, cause-and-effect reality. Earlier films featured mostly recorded events—either live or staged—strung together without specific emphasis on storytelling to create meaning. Méliès created and employed a number of important narrative devices, such as the fade-in and fade-out, "lap" (overlapping) dissolve, and stop-motion photography (Cook, 2004). Though he didn't employ much editing within individual scenes, the scenes were connected in a way that supported a linear, narrative reality and by 1902, with the premiere of his one-reel film *Le Voyage Dans La Lune* (A Trip to the Moon), Méliès was fully committed to narrative filmmaking until the end of his career in 1913.

As middle-class American audiences, who grew up with complicated plots and fascinating characters from such authors such as Charles Dickens and Charlotte Brontë, began to demand more sophisticated film narratives, directors like Edwin S. Porter and D.W. Griffith began crafting innovative films in order to provide their more discerning audiences with the kinds of stories to which theatre and literature had made them accustomed (Belton, 2013). Influenced by Méliès, American filmmaker Edwin S. Porter is credited with developing the "invisible" technique of continuity editing, the illusion of continuous action maintained while cutting to different angles of a simultaneous event presenting the action in successive shots. Porter's Life of an American Fireman and The Great Train Robbery, both released in 1903, are the foremost examples of this new style of storytelling through crosscutting (or, inter-cutting) multiple shots depicting parallel action (Cook, 2004). Taking this a step further, D.W. Griffith, who was an actor in some of Porter's films, went on to become one of the most important filmmakers of all time, and truly the "father" of narrative form. Technologically and aesthetically, he advanced the art form in ways heretofore unimagined. He altered camera angles, employed close-ups, actively narrated events (and thus, shaped audience perceptions of them), he employed "parallel editing"—cutting back and forth from two or more simultaneous events taking place, in separate places thus creating suspense (Belton, 2013).

Even though Edison's Kinetograph camera had produced more than 5,000 films (Freeman, 1998), by 1910, other camera manufacturers such as Bell and Howell and Pathé (which acquired the Lumière patents in 1902) had invented simpler, lighter, more compact cameras that soon eclipsed the Kinetograph. In fact, "it has been estimated that, before 1918, 60% of all films were shot with a Pathé camera" (Cook, 2004, p. 42). Nearly all of the cameras of the silent era were hand-cranked. Yet, camera operators were amazingly accurate in maintaining proper film speed (16 fps) and could easily change speeds to suit the story. A cinematographer could crank a little faster (over-crank) to produce slow, lyrical motion, or they could crank a little slower (under-crank) to create the frenetic, sped-up motion that contributed to the silent slapstick comedies of the Keystone Film Company (Cook, 2004) when the films were projected back at normal speed. By the mid-1920s, the Mitchell Camera Corporation began manufacturing large, precision cameras that produced steadier images than had been possible previously. These cameras became the industry standard for almost 30 years until Panavision cameras eclipsed them in the 1950s (Freeman, 1998).

In the United States, the early years of commercial cinema were tumultuous as Edison sued many individuals and enterprises over patent disputes in an attempt to protect his monopoly and his profits (Neale, 1985). However, by 1908, the film industry was becoming more stabilized as the major film producers "banded together to form the Motion Picture Patents Company (MPPC) which sought to control all aspects of motion picture production, distribution and exhibition" (Belton, 2013, p. 12) through its control of basic motion picture patents. In an attempt to become more respectable, and to court middle-class customers, the MPPC began a campaign to improve the content of motion pictures—engaging in self-censorship to control any content that might prove offensive to middle-class tastes (Belton, 2013). The group also provided half-price matinees for women and children and improved the physical conditions of theaters. Distribution licenses were granted to 116 exchanges that could distribute films only to licensed exhibitors who paid a projection license of two dollars per week. Unlicensed producers and exchanges continued to be a problem, so in 1910 the MPPC created the General Film Company to distribute their films. This development proved to be highly profitable and "was...the first stage in the organized film industry where production, distribution and exhibition were all integrated, and in the hands of a few large companies" (Jowett, 1976, p. 34) presaging the emergence of the studio system ten years later.

The Studio System

For the first two decades of cinema, nearly all films were photographed outdoors. Many production facilities were like that of George Méliès who constructed a glass-enclosed studio on the grounds of his home in a Paris suburb (Cook, 2004), although Edison's Black Maria facility in New Jersey was probably the most famous site. However, as the industry out-grew these small, improvised facilities, it moved to California. Although the weather was conducive to outdoor productions, large soundstages were built to provide controlled staging for productions, necessitating more control over lighting.

By the second decade of the 20th Century, dozens of movie studios were operating in the U.S. and across the world; a highly-specialized industry grew in southern California that developed sophisticated techniques of cinematography, lighting, and editing. The Hollywood studios divided these activities into preproduction, production, and postproduction. During preproduction, a film was written and planned. The production phase was technology intensive, involving the choreography of actors, cameras and lighting equipment. Postproduction consisted of editing the films into coherent narratives and adding titles—in fact, film editing is the only art that is unique to cinema.

Figure 12.2
Cinema History Highlights

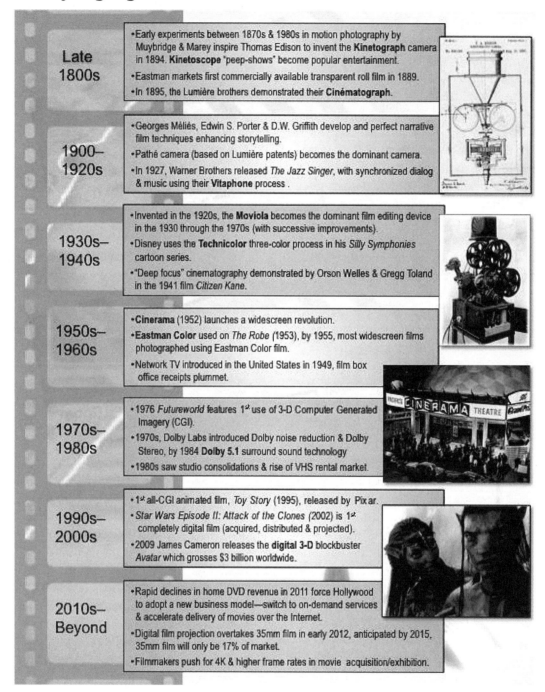

Late 1800s
- Early experiments between 1870s & 1980s in motion photography by Muybridge & Marey inspire Thomas Edison to invent the **Kinetograph** camera in 1894. **Kinetoscope** "peep-shows" become popular entertainment.
- Eastman markets first commercially available transparent roll film in 1889.
- In 1895, the Lumière brothers demonstrated their **Cinématograph**.

1900–1920s
- Georges Méliès, Edwin S. Porter & D.W. Griffith develop and perfect narrative film techniques enhancing storytelling.
- Pathé camera (based on Lumière patents) becomes the dominant camera.
- In 1927, Warner Brothers released *The Jazz Singer*, with synchronized dialog & music using their **Vitaphone** process .

1930s–1940s
- Invented in the 1920s, the **Moviola** becomes the dominant film editing device in the 1930 through the 1970s (with successive improvements).
- Disney uses the **Technicolor** three-color process in his *Silly Symphonies* cartoon series.
- "Deep focus" cinematography demonstrated by Orson Welles & Gregg Toland in the 1941 film *Citizen Kane*.

1950s–1960s
- **Cinerama** (1952) launches a widescreen revolution.
- **Eastman Color** used on *The Robe* (1953), by 1955, most widescreen films photographed using Eastman Color film.
- Network TV introduced in the United States in 1949, film box office receipts plummet.

1970s–1980s
- 1976 *Futureworld* features 1ˢᵗ use of 3-D Computer Generated Imagery (CGI).
- 1970s, Dolby Labs introduced Dolby noise reduction & Dolby Stereo, by 1984 **Dolby 5.1** surround sound technology
- 1980s saw studio consolidations & rise of VHS rental market.

1990s–2000s
- 1ˢᵗ all-CGI animated film, *Toy Story* (1995), released by Pixar.
- *Star Wars Episode II: Attack of the Clones* (2002) is 1ˢᵗ completely digital film (acquired, distributed & projected).
- 2009 James Cameron releases the **digital 3-D** blockbuster *Avatar* which grosses $3 billion worldwide.

2010s–Beyond
- Rapid declines in home DVD revenue in 2011 force Hollywood to adopt a new business model—switch to on-demand services & accelerate delivery of movies over the Internet.
- Digital film projection overtakes 35mm film in early 2012, anticipated by 2015, 35mm film will only be 17% of market.
- Filmmakers push for 4K & higher frame rates in movie acquisition/exhibition.

Source: M.R. Ogden

The heart of American cinema was now beating in Hollywood, and the institutional machinery of filmmaking that had evolved devised a three-phase business structure of production, distribution, and exhibition in getting their films from studios to theater audiences. Although the MPPC was formally dissolved in 1918 as a result of an antitrust suit initiated in 1912 (Cook, 2004), powerful new film companies, flush with capital, were emerging and with them, the advent of vertical integration. Through a series of mergers and acquisitions, formerly independent production, distribution and exhibition companies congealed into major studios; Paramount, Metro-Goldwin-Mayer (MGM), Warner Brothers, and Fox. "All of the major studios owned theater chains; the minors—Universal, Columbia, and United Artists—did not" (Belton, 2013, p. 68), but distributed their pictures by special arrangement to the theaters owned by the majors. The resulting economic system was quite efficient. "The major studios produced from forty to sixty pictures a year.... [But in 1945 only] owned 3,000 of the 18,000 theaters around the country.... [Yet] these theaters generated over 70% of all box-office receipts" (Belton, 2013, p. 69). As films and their stars increased in popularity, and movies became more expensive to produce, studios began to consolidate their power, seeking to control each phase of a film's life.

However, since the earliest days of the Nickelodeons, moralists and reformers had agitated against the corrupting nature of the movies and their effects on American youth (Cook, 2004). A series of scandals involving popular movie stars in the late 1910s and early 1920s resulted in ministers, priests, women's clubs and reform groups across the nation encouraging their membership to boycott the movies. In 1922, frightened Hollywood producers formed a self-regulatory trade organization—the Motion Picture Producers and Distributors of America (MPPDA). By 1930, the MPPDA adopted the rather draconian Hayes Production Code—a voluntary code that proved mandatory if the film was to be screened in America (Mondello, 2008)—intended to suppress immorality in film. Although the code aimed to establish high standards of performance for motion-picture producers, it "merely provided whitewash for overly enthusiastic manifestations of the 'new morality' and helped producers subvert the careers of stars whose personal lives might make them too controversial" (Cook, 2004, p. 186).

Sound, Color and Spectacle

Since the advent of cinema, filmmakers hoped for the chance to bring both pictures and sound to the screen. Although the period until the mid-1920s is considered the silent era, few films in major theaters actually were screened completely silent.

Pianists or organists—sometimes full orchestras—performed musical accompaniment to the projected images. At times, actors would speak the lines of the characters and machines and performers created sound effects. "What these performances lacked was fully synchronized sound contained within the soundtrack on the film itself" (Freeman, 1998, p. 408). By the late 1920s, experiments had demonstrated the viability of synchronizing sound with projected film. In 1927, Warner Brothers Studios released The *Jazz Singer*, with some synchronized dialog and music using their Vitaphone process; the first "talkie" was born. Vitaphone was a sound-on-disc process that issued the audio on a separate 16-inch phonographic disc that would be played on a turntable indirectly coupled to the projector motor while the film was being projected (Bradley, 2005). Other systems were also under development during this time, and Warner Brothers Vitaphone process had competition from Movietone, DeForest Phonofilm, and RCA's Photophone. Though audiences were excited by this new novelty, from an aesthetic standpoint, the advent of sound actually took the visual production value of films backward. Film cameras were loud and had to be housed in refrigerator-sized vaults to minimize the noise; and as a result, the mobility of the camera was suddenly limited. Microphones had to be placed very near the actors, resulting in restricted blocking and the odd phenomenon of actors leaning close to a bouquet of flowers as they recited their lines; the flowers, of course, hid the microphone. No question about it, though, sound was here to stay. Once sound made its appearance, the established major film companies acted cautiously, signing an agreement to only act together. After sound had proved a commercial success, the signatories adopted Movietone as the standard system—a sound-on-film method that recording sound as a variable-density optical track on the same strip of film that recorded the pictures (Neale, 1985). The advent of the "talkies" launched another round of mergers and expansions in the studio system. By the end of the 1920s, more than 40% of theaters were equipped for sound (Kindersley, 2006), and by 1931, "...virtually all films produced in the United States contained synchronized soundtracks" (Freeman, 1998, p. 408).

Movies were gradually moving closer to depicting "real life.". But life isn't black and white, and experiments with color filmmaking had been conducted since the dawn of the art form. Finally, in 1932, Technicolor introduced a practical color process that would slowly revolutionize moviemaking. Though aesthetically beautiful color processes were now available, they were extremely expensive and required strict oversight by the Technicolor Company, which insisted on a policy of strict secrecy during every phase of production. As a result, most movies were still produced in black and white well into the 1950s.

"In fact, the value of colour [sic] to the film industry fluctuated during the 1950s and 1960s as the relationship of the industry to television, and as the importance of colour [sic] within television, ...shifted and changed" (Neale, 1985, p. 143). It was only during the mid-1960s, when television had converted to color broadcasts and color television sets were in the majority of American homes, that the use of color in the cinema became universal.

The popularity of television and its competition with the movie industry helped drive more changes. The 4:3 aspect ratio (4 units wide by 3 units high, also represented as 1.33:1, said to be more aesthetically pleasing than a square box) set by Edison in the early years of film was the most common aspect ratio for most films until the 1960s (Freeman, 1998). The impetus for widescreen technology, and its adoption throughout the industry, was that films were losing money at the box office because of television. However, the studios response was characteristically cautious, initially choosing to release fewer but more expensive films (still in the standard Academy aspect ratio) hoping to lure audiences back to theaters with quality product (Belton, 2013). However, "[it] was not so much the Hollywood establishment...as the independent producers who engineered a technological revolution that would draw audiences back" (Belton, 2013, p. 327).

Because of their efforts, the 1950s and early 1960s saw the most pervasive technological innovations in Hollywood since the late 1920s. "A series of processes changed the size of the screen, the shape of the image, the dimensions of the films, and the recording and reproduction of sound" (Bordwell, Staiger & Thompson, 1985, p. 358). Cinerama (1952) launched a widescreen revolution that would permanently alter the shape of the motion picture screen. Cinerama was a widescreen process that required filming with a three-lens camera and projecting with synchronized projectors onto a deeply curved screen extending the full width of most movie theaters. This viewing (yielding a 146° by 55° angle of view) was meant to approximate that of human vision (160° by 60° angle of view) and fill a viewer's entire peripheral vision. Mostly used in travelogue-adventures, such as *This is Cinerama* (1952) and *Seven Wonders of the World* (1956), the first two Cinerama fiction films—*The Wonderful World of the Brothers Grimm* and *How the West Was Won*—were released in 1962, with much fanfare and critical acclaim.

However, three-camera and projector systems like Cinerama and CineMiracle (1957), were extremely expensive technologies and quickly fell into disuse. Single-camera and projector processes like MGM's Arnoldscope (1953) and Paramount Picture's VistaVision (1954) consisted of shooting—and, initially screening—the film on its horizontal axis (90° to the frame's normal orientation on the film strip) to give a wider and less grainy image (Bordwell, Staiger & Thompson, 1985) were unconventional and fared no better. Anamorphic processes that used special lenses to shoot or print squeezed images onto the film as a wide field of view that were unsqueezed in projection using the same lenses, produced an aspect ratio of 2.55:1—almost twice as wide as the Academy Standard aspect ratio (Freeman, 1998). When Twentieth Century-Fox released *The Robe* in 1953 using the CinemaScope anamorphic system, it was a spectacular success and just the boost Hollywood needed. Soon, other companies began producing widescreen films using similar anamorphic processes such as Panascope and Superscope and nearly all of these widescreen systems—including CinemaScope—incorporated stereophonic sound reproduction.

Figure 12.3
Film Aspect Ratios

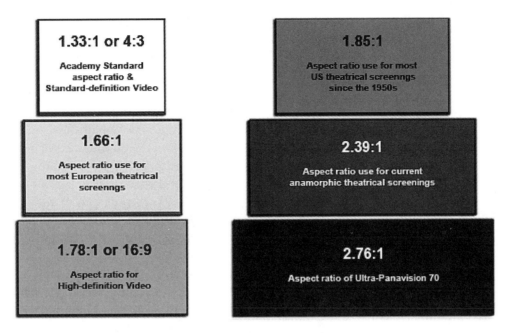

If widescreen films were meant to engulf audiences, pulling them into the action, "3-D assaulted audiences—hurling spears, shooting arrows, firing guns, and throwing knives at spectators sitting peacefully in their theatre seats" (Belton, 2013, p. 328). Stereoscopy and three-dimensional (3-D) cinematography, until recently, had been relatively unsuccessful at creating depth in an otherwise flat image (Freeman, 1998). The technology of 3-D is rooted in the basic principles of binocular vision and early attempts at reproducing monochromatic 3-D used an anaglyphic system—two strips of film, one tinted red, the other cyan and projected simultaneously for an audience wearing glasses with one red and one cyan filtered lens (Cook, 2004). When presented with slightly different angles of for each eye the brain processed the two images as a single 3-D image. The earliest 3-D film using the anaglyphic process was *The Power of Love* in 1922.

In the late 1930s, MGM released a series of anaglyphic shorts, but the development of polarized filters and lenses around the same time permitted the production of full-color 3-D images and experiments in anaglyphic films ceased in favor of the new method. In 1953, Milton Gunzberg released

Bwana Devil, a "dreadful" film shot using a polarized 3-D process called Natural Vision that drew in audiences and surprisingly broke box office records grossing over $5 million by the end of its run (Jowett, 1976). Natural Vision employed two interlocked cameras whose lenses were positioned to approximate the distance between the human eyes and recorded the scene on two separate negatives. In the theater, when projected simultaneously onto the screen, spectators wearing disposable glasses with polarized lenses perceived a single three-dimensional image (Cook, 2004). Warner Brothers released the second Natural Vision feature, *House of Wax* (1953), which featured six-track stereophonic sound and was a critical and popular success, returning $5.5 million on an investment of $680,000 (Cook, 2004). "Within a matter of months after the initial release of *Bwana Devil*, more than 4,900 theaters were converted to 3-D" (Belton, 2013, p. 329).

Although Hollywood produced 69 features in 3-D between 1953 and 1954, most were cheaply made exploitation films. By late 1953, the stereoscopic 3-D craze had peaked. Two large budget features shot in Natural Vision, MGM's *Kiss Me Kate* (1953) and Alfred Hitchcock's *Dial M for*

Murder (1954) were released "flat" because the popularity of 3-D had fallen dramatically. Although 3-D movies were still made decades later for special short films at Disney theme parks, 3-D was no longer part of the feature-film production process (Freeman, 1998).

One reason for 3-D's demise was that producers found it difficult to make serious narrative films in such a gimmicky process (Cook, 2004). Another problem was the fact that audiences disliked wearing the polarized glasses; many also complained of eyestrain, headaches and nausea. But, perhaps, the biggest single factor in 3-D's rapid fall from grace was cinematographers' and directors' alternative use of deep-focus widescreen photography—especially anamorphic processes that exploited depth through peripheral vision—and compositional techniques that contributed to the feeling of depth without relying on costly, artificial means. Attempts to revive 3-D, until most recently, have met with varying degrees of success seeing short runs of popularity in the 1980s with films like *Friday the 13th, Part III* and *Jaws 3-D* (both in 1983). Again, in 1995 with the release of the IMAX 3-D film, *Wings of Courage*—and later, *Space Station 3D* in 2002—the use of active display LCD glasses synchronized with the shutters of dual-filmstrip projectors using infrared signals presaged the eventual rise of digital 3-D films 10 years later.

Hollywood Becomes Independent

"The dismantling of the studio system began just before World War II when the U.S. Department of Justice's Antitrust Division filed suit against the eight major studios accusing them of monopolistic practices in their use of block booking, blind bidding, and runs, zones, and clearances" (Belton, 2013, p. 82). In 1948, the major studios were forced to divorce their operations from one another, separate production and distribution from exhibition, and divest themselves of their theater chains (Belton, 2013). Other factors also contributed to the demise of the studio system, most notably changes in leisure-time entertainment, competition with television and the rise of independent production (Cook, 2004).

Combined with the extreme form of censorship Hollywood studios imposed upon itself through the Hayes Production Codes—and "after World War II, with competition from TV on the family front, and from foreign films with nudity on the racy front" (Mondello, 2008)—movie studios were unable (or unwilling) to rein in independent filmmakers who chaffed under the antiquated Code. The U.S. Supreme Court ruled in 1952 (the "Miracle decision") that films constitute "a significant medium of communication of ideas" and were therefore protected by both the First and Fourteenth Amendments (Cook, 2004, p. 428). Further clarified in subsequent court rulings, by "the early 1960s films were guaranteed full freedom of expression" (Cook, 2004, p. 428). The influence of the Hayes Production Code, which had restricted certain morally ambiguous content in films, had all but disappeared by the end of the 1960s, replaced by the MPAA ratings system (MPAA, 2011) which was instituted in 1968 and revised in 1972 and again in 1984.

The major studios delayed the process of divesture as long as possible, but the studio system's previously rigid control over the assembly line of moviemaking was already disintegrating in the 1960s while up-and-coming independent production companies and the more "free-wheeling" counterculture were poised to influence popular cinema. Though the 1960s still featured big-budget, lavish movie spectacles, a parallel movement reflected the younger, more rebellious aesthetic of the "baby boomers." Actors and directors went into business for themselves, forming their own production companies and taking as payment, lump-sum percentages of the film's profits paid-out to their companies (Belton, 2013). The rise and success of independent filmmakers like Arthur Penn (*Bonnie and Clyde*, 1967), Stanley Kubrick (*2001: A Space Odyssey*, 1968), Sam Peckinpah (*The Wild Bunch*, 1969), Dennis Hopper (*Easy Rider*, 1969), and John Schlesinger (*Midnight Cowboy*, 1969), provided evidence that the studio system need not dominate popular filmmaking—and, outside of that system, filmmakers were freer to experiment with style and content.

In the early 1960s, an architectural innovation changed the way most people see movies—the move from single-screen theaters (and drive-ins) to multi-screen cineplexes. Although, the first multi-screen house with two theaters was built in the 1930s, it was not until the late 1960s, that film venues were built with four to six theaters. What these theaters lacked was the atmosphere that the early "movie palaces" had. While some put effort into the appearance of the lobby and concessions area, in most cases the "actual theater was merely functional" (Haines, 2003, p. 91). Continuing to grow the number of screens in one location, 1984 marked the opening of the first 18-plex theater in Toronto (Haines, 2003). The next step in this evolution was the addition of stadium seating—offering movie-goers a better experience by affording more comfortable seating with unobstructed views of the screen (EPS Geofoam, n.d.). Although the number of screens in a location seems to have reached the point of diminishing return, many theaters are now working on improving the atmosphere they create for their patrons. From bars and restaurants to luxury theaters with a reserved $29 movie ticket, many theater owners are once again working to make the movie-going experience something different from what you can get at home (Gelt and Verrier, 2009).

Rise of the Blockbusters

"Blockbuster" is a term traditionally used in Hollywood to designate any large-scale, big-budget production—*Intolerance* (1916) and *Gone With the Wind* (1939) would have both been called blockbusters in their day. The blockbuster "craze" actually started in order to exploit the spectacle and physical novelty of the big screen and "the film that demonstrated this most graphically was…[the] disastrous *Cleopatria* (1963—Todd-AO; 4 hours, 3 minutes), which took four years and $40 million to produce, nearly wrecking 20th Century–Fox. This film…did not break even until its sale to network television in 1966" (Cook, 2004, p. 401). Other early blockbuster films fared better, *The Sound of Music* (1965) and *Dr. Zhivago* (1965) were both big box-office successes (Cook, 2004).

By the 1970s, the average production budget for a single film increased by 178%—nearly four times the general rate of inflation (Cook, 2004). By 1975, it was not unusual for a single production company to have all of its capital tied up in five or six films annually, every one a potential blockbuster—compare this with MGM's average of 42 features per year during the 1930s (Cook, 2004). A Hollywood rule of thumb equates a film's break-even point with returning two-and-a-half times its negative cost (all costs required to produce the final cut of the master negative, excluding the costs associated with promotion, distribution and exhibition). A film is considered a success if it returns four times its negative cost. Big-budget blockbusters like *Jaws* (Steven Spielberg, 1975) and *Star Wars* (George Lucas, 1977) threw this conventional calculus out the window by returning as much as 200-times their initial investment (The Numbers, 2012a; 2012b). "The profits reaped by a success like *Jaws* or *Star Wars* could be immense, but a single big-budget flop could threaten the solvency of an entire studio. This condition clearly inhibited the creative freedom of people working within the industry…" (Cook, 2004, p. 858-859), more so now that production companies rely on sophisticated market segment analysis in order to discover what the public wants, and then to "pre-sell" it in order to raise the capitol to make the film (Epstein, 2005). But, even this model has proven untenable in an era of run-away production budgets.

Recent Developments

It's very difficult to find a blockbuster within the last decade that did not employ computer-generated imagery, or CGI. However, "[the] ability to create illusions on the screen has fascinated filmmakers since the 1890s when it was discovered that running film twice through a camera produced unusual double exposures" (Freeman, 1998, P. 409). Special effects—or, more commonly referred to now as "visual effects" (VFX)—are divided into mechanical, optical and CGI. "Mechanical effects include those devices used to make rain, wind, cobwebs, fog, snow, and explosions. Optical effects allow images to be combined…through creation of traveling mattes run through an optical printer" (Freeman, 1998, p. 409). The matte masks off an area of the film frame during original filming in the camera or optical printing and, in subsequent passes through the printer, imagery is inserted into the masked-out areas. Stanley Kubrick's *2001: A Space Odyssey* (1968) used sophisticated traveling mattes combined with miniatures of spacecraft and live-action to stunning effect (Cook, 2004).

Arguably the first movie ever to use computers to create a visual effect—a two-dimensional rotating structure on one level of the underground lab—was *The Andromeda Strain* in 1971, the work was considered extremely advanced for its time. Since the first use of 3-D CGI in American International Pictures' 1976 release of *Futureworld*—which featured a brief view of a computer-generated face and hand, the groundbreaking CGI effect was later awarded a Scientific and Engineering Academy Award in 1994—CGI technology has continued to progress rapidly. The first major production of George Lucas' visual effects company, Industrial Light & Magic (ILM), took a big step forward for CGI with the rendering of a 3-D wire-frame view of the Death Star trench depicted as a training aid for rebel pilots in *Star Wars IV: A New Hope* (1977). *Star Trek: The Wrath of Kahn* (1982) incorporated a one-minute sequence created by Pixar (a LucasFilm spin-off), that simulated the "Genesis Effect" (the birth and greening of a planet) and is cinema's first all-computer generated visual effects shot. It also introduced a fractal-generated landscape and a particle-rendering system to achieve a fiery effect (Dirks, 2009). *Tron* (1982) is the first live-action movie to use CGI for a noteworthy length of time (approximately 20 minutes in the famed Lightcycle sequence) in the most innovative sequence of its 3-D graphics world inside a video game. LucasFilm/Pixar created, arguably, the first fully photorealistic CGI character in a full-length feature with the sword-wielding medieval "stained-glass" knight composed of window pieces that came to life when he jumps out of a window frame in the film, *Young Sherlock Holmes* (1985). James Cameron's blockbuster action film, *Terminator 2: Judgment Day* (1991) also got a Best Visual Effects Oscar thanks to its depiction of Hollywood's first CGI main character, the villainous liquid metal T-1000 cyborg. *Toy Story* (1995), was the first successful

animated feature film from Pixar, and was also the first all-CGI animated film (Vreeswijk, 2012). In the *Lord of the Rings* trilogy (2001, 2002 and 2003), a combination of motion-capture performance and key-frame techniques brought to life the main digital character Gollum (Dirks, 2009) by using a motion capture suit (with sensors) and recording the movements of actor Andy Serkis. In the 2004 animated film, *The Polar Express*, the same motion capture technique is used for all its actors (Vreeswijk,2012). CGI use has grown exponentially and hand-in-hand with the increasing size of the film's budget it occupies. *Sky Captain and the World of Tomorrow* (2004) was the first big-budget feature to use only "virtual" CGI back lot sets. Actors Jude Law, Gwyneth Paltrow and Angelina Jolie were filmed in front of blue screens; everything else was added in post-production (Dirks, 2009).

More an "event" than a movie, James Cameron's *Avatar* (2009) ushered in a new era of CGI. Many believe that *Avatar*, a largely computer-generated, 3-D film—and the top-grossing movie in history, earning nearly $3 billion worldwide—has changed the movie-going experience (Muñoz, 2010). New technologies used in the film include CGI Performance Capture techniques for facial expressions, the Fusion Camera System for 3-D shooting, and the Simul-Cam for blending real-time shoots with CGI characters and environments (Jones, 2010). One of the greatest obstacles to CGI is effectively capturing facial expressions. In order to overcome this final hurdle, Cameron brought to life a technology he dreamed up in 1995, a tiny camera on the front of a helmet that was able to "track every facial movement, from darting eyes and twitching noses to furrowing eyebrows and the tricky interaction of jaw, lips, teeth and tongue" (Thompson, 2010).

Multichannel Sound

There's no mistaking the chest-rumbling crescendo associated with THX. It's nearly as recognizable as its patron's famous *Star Wars* theme. Developed by George Lucas' Lucasfilms, THX is not a cinema sound format, rather a standardization system that strives to "reproduce the acoustics and ambience of the movie studio, allowing audiences to enjoy a movie's sound effects, score, dialogue and visual presentation with the clarity and detail of the final mastering session" (THX, 2012). THX debuted in 1983 with Lucas' *Star Wars Episode VI: Return of the Jedi* and spread across the industry. Only movie theaters that meet clear specifications can be certified THX. The most recent self-reported company data states that there were close to 2,000 THX certified theaters worldwide (THX, 2012).

While THX sets the standards, Dolby Digital 5.1 Surround Sound is one of the leading audio delivery technologies in the cinema industry. In the 1970s, Dolby Laboratories introduced Dolby noise reduction (removing hiss from magnetic and optical tracks) and Dolby Stereo—a highly practical 35mm stereo optical release print format that fit the new multichannel soundtrack into the same space on the print occupied by the traditional mono track (Hull, 1999). Dolby's unique quadraphonic matrixed audio technique allows for the encoding of four channels of information (left, center, right and surround) on just two physical tracks on movie prints (Karagosian & Lochen, 2003). The Dolby stereo optical format proved so practical that today there are tens of thousands of cinemas worldwide equipped with Dolby processors, and over 25,000 movies have been released using the Dolby Stereo format (Hull, 1999).

By the late 1980s, Dolby 5.1 was introduced as the cinematic audio configuration documented by various film industry groups as best satisfying the requirements for theatrical film presentation (Hull, 1999). Dolby 5.1 uses "five discrete full-range channels—left, center, right, left surround, and right surround—plus a...low-frequency [effects] channel" (Dolby, 2010a). Because this low-frequency effects (LFE) channel is felt more than it is heard, and because it needs only one-tenth the bandwidth of the other five channels, it is refered to as a ".1" channel (Hull, 1999). Dolby also offers Dolby Digital Surround EX, a technology developed in partnership with Lucasfilm's THX that places a speaker behind the audience to allow for a "fuller, more realistic sound for increased dramatic effect in the theatre" (Dolby, 2010b). Dolby Surround 7.1 is the newest cinema audio format developed to provide more depth and realism to the cinema experience. By resurrecting the full range left extra, right extra speakers of the earlier Todd-AO 70mm magnetic format, but now calling them left center and right center, Dolby Surround 7.1 improves the spatial dimension of soundtracks and enhances audio definition thereby providing full-featured audio that better matches the visual impact on the screen. Movies released using Dolby Surround 7.1 include Academy nominated films such as *Toy Story 3* (2010), *Tron: Legacy* (2010), *Transformers: Dark of the Moon* (2011), *War Horse* (2011), the 3-D film *Hugo* (2011), as well as another 22 films slated for a 2012 release (Dolby, 2012).

Film's Slow Fade to Digital

With the rise of CGI intensive storylines and a desire to cut costs, celluloid film is quickly becoming an endangered medium for making movies as more filmmakers use digital cinema cameras capable of creating high-quality images without the time, expense, and chemicals required to shoot and process on film. "While the debate has raged over whether or not film is dead, ARRI, Panavision and Aaton quietly ceased production of film cameras in 2011 to focus exclusively on design and manufacture of digital cameras" (Kaufman, 2011). But, film is not dead yet, almost two-thirds of all narrative features nominated for Oscars in 2011 were shot on film—that is compelling evidence that film is alive and well among A-list filmmakers. "Of course, facts are funny things, and you could always turn that number around. Digital cinema has a very short history—*Star Wars Episode II: Attack of the Clones* (2002) was the first full-on 24p [high definition digital] release...and now [10-years later], more than one-third of the films [up for] the industry's highest honors were shot digitally" (Frazer, 2012).

Digital production also presents a significant savings for low-budget and independent filmmakers. Production costs using digital cameras and non-linear editing are a fraction of the costs of film production, sometimes as little as a few thousand dollars, and lower negative costs mean a faster track to profitability. Indeed, the 2009 horror film *Paranormal Activity* was shot for around $15,000 and generated close to $200 million worldwide (The Numbers, 2012d). Beyond the obvious attraction of such high-end digital cinema cameras as the

RED Epic or the Arri Alexa, smaller high definition digital still cameras (HDSLRs) with large sensors, interchangeable prime lenses and video recording capability are also making inroads in the specialty and independent film markets. Chuck Westfall, technical advisor for education at Canon USA notes that "Primetime is still very clearly a film dominated business but the use of the Canon EOS 5D Mark II on the season finale of *House* [in May 2010] and on series like *24* [during the 2009-2010 season] show that they are making their mark in primetime" (Winslow, 2010). The digital revolution, spurred by low-budget filmmaking, has pushed companies like RED to release smaller, cheaper, and lighter cameras, and Hollywood is re-purposing that practicality to film some of the most high-profile spectacle genre fare possible (Luzi, 2011).

While the question of film vs. digital has seen renewed urgency in 2012 because of a confluence of industry trends, digital acquisition continues to gain ground. Distributors are becoming more vocal about their reluctance to continue servicing exhibitors with 35mm prints (Frazer, 2012). What's more, alarms have been sounded by the Academy of Motion Picture Arts and Sciences itself. In 2007, the Academy turned its attention to the issues of digital motion picture data longevity in the major Hollywood studios. In their report, titled *The Digital Dilemma*, they concluded that, although digital technologies provide tremendous benefits, they do not guarantee long-term access to digital data compared to traditional filmmaking using motion picture film stock. Digital technologies make it easier to create motion pictures, but the resulting digital data is much harder to preserve (Science & Technology Council, 2007). The Academy's update to this initial examination of digital media archiving was published in 2012 as *The Digital Dilemma 2*, and focused on the new challenge of maintaining long-term archives of digitally originated features created by the burgeoning numbers of independent and documentary filmmakers. "Independent ('indie') filmmakers operating outside of the major Hollywood studios supply 75% of feature film titles screened in U.S. cinemas, despite facing substantial obstacles in doing so. As digital moviemaking technologies have lowered the barrier to entry for making films, competition among indie filmmakers seeking theatrical distribution has increased" (Science & Technology Council, 2012, p. 3-4). As new digital distribution platforms have emerged, making it easier for independent filmmakers to connect their films with target audiences (through video-on-demand and pay-per-view) and possible revenue streams, these platforms have not yet proven themselves when it comes to archiving and preservation (Science & Technology Council, 2012). "Unless and independent film is picked up by a major studio's distribution arm, its path to an audiovisual archive is uncertain. If a filmmaker's digital work doesn't make it to such a preservation environment, its lifespan will be limited—as will its revenue-generating potential and its ability to enjoy the full measure of U.S. copyright protection" (Science & Technology Council, 2012, p. 6). For now at least, the "digital dilemma" seems far from over.

As physical film in acquisition slowly yields to digital high-definition recording, so too has film editing made the digital shift. In 1989, Lightworks was introduced as the first and most advanced professional editing system on the market and it had competition right out of the gate when Avid Technology began taking orders the same year for their prototype Avid/1 digital non-linear, computer-based editor. By 1992, the National Association of Broadcasters (NAB) convention was rich with digital nonlinear editing systems—including a wide array of products from Avid Technology. Avid would continue to dominate the digital non-linear editing marked for both video and film—integrated as it was in the "digital intermediate" workflow as CGI and other VFX became an increasingly important part of cinematic storytelling. In 1999, Apple released Final Cut Pro 1.0 and "a new generation of desktop high-quality editing, specifically designed to take advantage both of the new DV formats and FireWire-fitted Macs" (Rubin, 2000, p. 72). Now that digital cinema cameras like the RED and Arri Alexa are coming into more common use, and the new non-linear editing systems have the capability of working with the digital footage at full resolution, it is now possible to shoot, edit and project a movie without ever having to leave the digital environment.

Digital 3-D

The first digital 3-D film released was Disney's *Chicken Little* shown on Disney Digital 3-D (PR Newswire, 2005). Dolby Laboratories outfitted about 100 theaters in the 25 top markets with Dolby Digital Cinema systems in order to screen the film.

The idea of actually shooting alive-action movies in digital 3-D did not become a reality until the creation of the Fusion Camera, a collaborative invention by director James Cameron and Vince Pace (*Hollywood Reporter*, 2005). The camera fuses two Sony HDC-F950 HD cameras "2½ inches apart to mimic the stereoscopic separation of human eyes" (Thompson, 2010). The camera was used to film 2008's *Journey to the Center of the Earth* and 2010's *Tron Legacy*.

Cameron used a modified version of the Fusion Camera to shoot 2009's blockbuster *Avatar*. The altered Fusion allows the "director to view actors within a computer-generated virtual environment, even as they are working on a 'performance-capture' set that may have little apparent relationship to what appears on the screen" (Cieply, 2010). Another breakthrough technology born from *Avatar* is the swing camera. For a largely animated world such as the one portrayed in the film, the actors must perform through a process called motion capture which records 360 degrees of a performance, but with the added disadvantage that the actors do not know where the camera will be (Thompson, 2010). Likewise, in the past, the director had to choose the shots desired once the filming was completed. Cameron tasked virtual-production supervisor Glenn Derry with creating the swing camera, which "has no lens at all, only an LCD screen and markers that record its position and orientation within the volume relative to the actors" (Thompson, 2010). An effects switcher feeds back low-resolution CG images of the virtual world to the swing camera allowing the director to move around shooting the actors photographically or even capturing other camera angles on the empty stage as the footage plays back (Thompson, 2010).

Of course shooting movies in 3-D is a fairly novel production method. Many films, such as Tim Burton's 2010 *Alice in Wonderland* are shot in 2-D and later converted. IMAX is the leader in 2-D to 3-D conversion but is facing some competition from smaller companies like Prime Focus Ltd. (Georgiades, 2010). The cost of 3-D conversion has decreased significantly from around $25-30 million to around $5 million per film (Georgiades, 2010). However, James Cameron may have helped kick off the 3-D craze with *Avatar* (2009), but he's also been the format's harshest critic, especially toward 3-D conversions. In particular, Cameron has slammed the habit of hastily converting films from 2-D in order to pad their grosses (Lang, 2012). "The conversion process is a creative process that uses technology. It is not a technological process, [Jon] Landau said. When you try to convert film in six weeks, it can only be a technological process" (Lang, 2012). So, when Cameron decided to convert *Titanic* (1997) to 3-D, he spent 60-weeks going over more than 260,000 frames of the movie to make sure the conversion looked "right" (Lang, 2012). When *Titanic 3-D* (2012) was released, to critical acclaim, it made more than $25 million over its first five days of release, more than the $18 million it cost to retrofit the film for 3-D screens, and it scored an A to A+ among a heavily female audience (Lang, 2012).

Figure 12.4

Vince Pace and James Cameron with Fusion 3-D Digital Cinema Camera

Source: CAMERON | PACE Group
Photo credit: Marissa Roth

The Digital Conversion

January 2012 marked the crossover point when digital projection technology surpassed 35mm. It is anticipated that, by the end of 2012, the share of 35mm will decline to 37% of global cinema screens, with digital accounting for the remaining 63% (Hancock, 2011). Demand for 35mm cinema film has declined from a peak level of 13 billion feet a year in 2008, to as little as 4 billion in 2012. Meanwhile, the cost of producing celluloid film is soaring due to rising prices for a key raw material, silver. This represents a dramatic decline for 35mm film, which was used in 68% of global cinema screens in 2010. It is projected that by 2015, 35mm will be used in just 17% of global movie screens, relegating it to a niche projection format (Hancock, 2011).

The conversion of movie theaters to digital projection allows studios and distributors to forgo the cost of making and transporting 35mm film in favor of hard drives, discs, and streaming. Digital Cinema Implementation Partners (DCIP) was formed in 2007 in cooperation with the exhibition companies AMC Entertainment Inc., Cinemark USA, Inc., and Regal Entertainment Group (Digital Cinema Implementation Partners, n.d.). Once formed, DCIP was charged with bring the major studios on-board to help provide incentives for exhibitors to take on the challenge—and massive cost—of converting their theaters from film to digital projection systems.

Early adopters of the digital systems numbered about 5,000 between 2005 and 2006 (Mead, 2008). But the largest exhibitors—instrumental in the formulation of the DCIP—were in the second wave. There are three mechanisms by which the digital conversion could be financed: distributors, exhibitors, or the government. The first model has been most prevalent in the U.S. with distributors paying a "virtual print fee" which is paid to a third party company that loans exhibitors the funds to finance the digital conversion over the course of 10–15 years (Screen Digest, 2006). In 2009, Paramount Pictures paid such a fee to some theaters that showed digital versions of their movies *Star Trek* and *Monsters vs. Aliens*. Others, such as AMC, Regal, and

Cinemark, have tried to lower costs by buying equipment in bulk from providers such as the DCIP. However, the recession had a chilling effect on upgrades and left many theater owners looking to upgrade having to finance their own transition (O'Connor, 2010). Digital conversion is estimated to cost about $70,000 per screen, which doesn't include the long-term maintenance and replacement costs that aren't associated with traditional film projectors. In April 2009, Sony Pictures joined Walt Disney, Viacom, Paramount Pictures, 20th Century Fox, Universal Pictures, and Lions Gate Entertainment to partner with the DCIP on a plan to convert 20,000 U.S. and Canadian cinema screens. The price tag for the conversion was estimated to be more than $1 billion. Analysts agree that it could take close to a decade to complete a full digital conversion. As of March 2010, there were 16,405 digital screens worldwide, about 14.8% of the modern cinemas, and 9,000 of those were equipped for digital 3-D projection (Screen Digest, 2010).

According to some sources, 3-D digital movies bring in from two times to four times the box office revenue of traditional 2-D movies, (Mead, 2008) and studios have been investing heavily in the format in hopes of increasing revenue. With the recent success of 3-D movies, theater owners must wrestle with the decision of upgrading to digital projection alone, or go for digital 3-D projection upgrades. While the transition to digital costs about $70,000 per screen, the upgrade to 3-D digital costs approximately $100,000 per screen (Screen Digest, 2010). Also, of the 7,600 digital movie screens in the country (as of mid-2010), 3,400 of those are digital 3-D capable. Even as the current economic climate shows signs of slow recovery, the major concern for theater owners is how to finance upgrades. Although many theater owners would like to upgrade to 3-D, some have not even upgraded to digital yet.

Current Status

In 2000, the average price of a movie ticket was $5.39 (and 1.39 billion were sold). The highest grossing film was *How the Grinch Stole Christmas* ($371 million, inflation adjusted). Walt Disney Pictures was the number one distributor with nearly

15% share and $1.1 billion in gross revenues. PG-13-rated films represented 42% of films released (R-rated films were at 34 percent). Comedy was the top genre and total box office gross receipts topped out at nearly $7.5 billion (The Numbers, 2012e). By 2011, the average price of a movie ticket had risen to $7.93 even as ticket sales dropped by 100 million. The highest grossing film was *Harry Potter and the Deathly Hallows: Part II* ($379 million, inflation adjusted). Paramount Pictures had displaced Disney (slipping to fourth) as the number one distributor with just over 19% share and nearly $2 billion in gross revenues. PG-13 films were 52% of films released (R-rated films dropped to just under 23 percent). Adventure and Action genres topped the charts and total box office gross receipts just barely broke $10 billion (The Numbers, 2012f). Box office revenues were relatively flat between 2000 and 2011 averaging $8.6 billion over the period, dropping slightly between 2004 and 2005 with a slow recovery beginning in 2006 that peaked at $10.6 billion in 2009 before dropping off again. The steady rise in the price of movie tickets—often greater than inflation—corresponds with big changes in the movie business. For Hollywood studios, the switch to mostly blockbuster tentpole movies has raised production costs and pushed up marketing expenses, which often reach as high as $70 million worldwide to publicize and distribute the biggest movies (Block, 2012). For exhibitors, the cost of building new multiplex theaters and, more recently, switching to digital projection and sound, has been a factor in the rising costs. The recent proliferation of 3-D movies also has led to higher ticket prices. Most theaters include a surcharge of about $3 per ticket to see a film in 3-D. In 2011, there were more 3-D releases than ever, but the average receipts for a 3-D movie was down from the previous year (Block, 2012).

PricewaterhouseCoopers (PwC), in its 2011-2015 *Global Entertainment and Media Outlook* report, projects that, after the economic down-turn in 2008-2009 and stagnation in 2010 that resulted in a drop in box office revenues, the world-wide film industry is on track to grow an average of 5.9% while the North American film industry can expect 5.2% growth through 2015 (PricewaterhouseCoopers, 2011, p. 59 & 68). Sales of Blu-ray and electronic-delivery (video on demand) are projected to make up for waning DVD sales and rentals while 3-D offerings will help boost box office revenues despite stagnant ticket sales. In North America, PwC estimates $12.2 billion in box office revenue and $27.9 billion in home video in 2012. Among other PwC predictions: The box office will grow to $15.5 billion because of rising prices for tickets and 3-D premiums while home video will rise to $33.9 billion. Every category of film, even the various home entertainment sub categories, will grow, including sell-through, courtesy of Blu-ray, in-store rentals, and kiosks such as Redbox (PricewaterhouseCoopers, 2011). The report notes that in 2010, seven 3-D titles accounted for 20% of the domestic box office: *Avatar, Toy Story 3, Alice in Wonderland, The Twilight Saga: Eclipse, Despicable Me, Shrek Forever After,* and *How to Train Your Dragon* (PricewaterhouseCoopers, 2011).

Despite the overall "bullishness" of the report, PwC warns that "the novelty effect of 3-D may be waning, and because of the higher price points for those releases, people may become more selective in choosing to go to a 3-D film. Nevertheless, we believe 3-D will have a long-term positive impact on admissions because it helps distinguish the theatrical experience from the home video and online experiences of watching a movie" (Bond, 2011).

Finally, electronic delivery of movies—thanks to a growing electronics market boosted by the proliferation of tablets, expanding broadband penetration, and faster broadband speeds and such media streaming services as Netflix, Apple's iTunes, Amazon.com, Hulu, and others—has had a profound impact on global film distribution practices and is expected to grow from $4.8 billion in 2012 to $7.6 billion in 2015. By comparison, that category generated just $1.2 billion in revenue in 2006 (PricewaterhouseCooper, 2011, p. 63). Asia-Pacific and Latin America are anticipated to be the fastest-growing regions for cinema entertainment. Bucking the trend in North America, new 3-D screens are generating explosive growth in the China, which is pacing the Asia-Pacific. Likewise, new 3-D screens are also boosting box office receipts in Latin America, China, and Russia.

Gone are the days when 3-D movie-goers were expected to don cheap paper glasses with blue and red lenses. RealD has been at the forefront of revolutionizing how 3-D movies are exhibited. In the past, 3-D movies were displayed using a different projector for each eye. RealD developed a new technology that uses "a liquid crystal adaptor that attaches to a single digital projector, synchronizing left and right eye images 144 times per second" (Verrier, 2009) projecting at 24fps and repeating each frame three times each (alternately) for left and right eye views. RealD also developed lightweight plastic glasses with gray lenses that look more like slightly oversized sunglasses. As of 2009, RealD's products account for approximately 90% of the U.S. 3-D exhibition market (Verrier, 2009). RealD premiered its new 3-D technology on 88 dig-ital 3-D screens with Disney's 2005 animated film *Chicken Little*. RealD has emerged as the market leader when it comes to outfitting movie theaters for 3-D exhibition. As of the end of 2009, RealD estimated that 100 million moviegoers had experienced their technology. This statistic is not surprising, given that RealD partners with 19 of the 20 top exhibitors in the world with "9,500 screens under contract, and 4,800 screens installed in 48 countries with 300 exhibition partners" (McClintock, 2009). Besides RealD, two other major suppliers of 3-D cinema technology include Dolby 3-D Digital Cinemas and IMAX Theaters. While the average 3-D ticket costs two to three dollars more than a regular ticket, some markets average higher and IMAX Theaters typically charge higher even ticket prices (McClintock, 2009).

 ## Sustainability

The production, distribution, and exhibition of a feature-length motion picture can have a substantial environmental impact. Transportation of people, equipment, and other materials produces carbon emissions; powering a studio or location shoot requires considerable electricity; and cast, crew, sets, and props generate tons of waste.

Creating industry-wide standards has been difficult. Films vary greatly in budget, necessary materials, locations, and energy usage. While the industry itself has been relatively slow to make extensive changes, the shift to digital rather than celluloid format does help reduce its overall carbon footprint. Shooting without celluloid film does away with the need for harmful chemicals used in the processing and storage of film. Distributing films digitally eliminates the cost and pollution generated by transporting large reels of film.

In 2009, a *Code of Best Practices for Sustainable Filmmaking* was published by American University, in conjunction with Filmmakers for Conservation and other groups. The code emphasizes calculating energy use, consuming less where possible, reducing travel, and compensating for consumption by using carbon offsets (Engel & Buchanan, 2009). It also provides a number of checklists for filmmakers to use in assessing and reducing environmental impact throughout each phase of production.

Independent filmmakers have also taken the impetus to make their productions as sustainable as possible. Seattle-based filmmaker Megan Griffiths earned the "SSF Tag" from the Sustainable Style Foundation for her 2011 film *The Off Hours*. Griffiths suggests five crucial tools for creating a sustainable set: buy local, use second-hand items, recycle and compost, and provide reusable containers like water bottles and dishes (The Off Hours, 2011).

The British film industry is leading the charge on a bigger scale. At the 2011 Cannes Film Festival, the UK Film Council and the British Standards Institution announced the establishment of a new industry standard, BS 8909, which outlines procedures for sustainability management. The new standard "encourages companies to address the environmental, social, and economic impacts of their work—from the initial concept for the film right through the process, even…merchandising and advertising" (BSI Group, 2011).

As fuel costs rise and the world economy fluctuates, it will become increasingly imperative for the entertainment industry to develop sustainable practices, particularly as public demand for "green" technology increases, and other highly-visible industries make significant changes.

Factors to Watch

At the National Association of Broadcaster's annual conventions in 2010 and 2011, the talk on the exhibit floor was all about 3-D acquisition. "It would be a lie to say that 3D technologies could be found at every booth on the show floor. But it was probably the case that there was 3D in at least every aisle. There was so much 3D that it tended to diminish all other news" (Schubin, 2010). To be sure, there were other technical innovations, LED studio lighting was nearly ubiquitous and there were innovations in removable-hard-drive storage, improvements in wireless distribution, and production switchers that could handle 22 inputs and switch up to 16 simultaneous shows. And then there was 3-D. At NAB 2011—as the major equipment manufacturers paraded out their latest 3-D camera rigs and projectors—James Cameron was the featured keynote speaker, and 3-D was definitely on his mind. Cameron, and his long-time technical collaborator, Vince Pace, "painted a very specific vision for the future of 3D broadcasting—a vision that differs from many earlier predictions. They see distinctions between 3D and 2D production fast disappearing, with directors and technicians simply putting 3D cameras where they put 2D cameras, shooting more or less the way they do now and grabbing one eye from the 3D cameras for 2D telecasts. That would eliminate the need for a separate 3D production and telecast. 'Otherwise the business model just doesn't make sense'" according to Cameron (Cohen, 2011). At NAB 2012, Cameron introduced what his company, the Cameron|Pace Group (CPG), calls a "5-D business model" (Giardina, 2012, April 16), meaning that a 2-D and a 3-D production are piggybacked on a single rig (thus, "5-D"). CPG offered this business and production model as promoting cost savings where the cost of separate 2-D and 3-D productions can equal that of 2-D alone (Giardina, 2012, April 16). However, Cameron offers this model primarily for live sports and event coverage and doesn't recommend the "5-D" model for movies or even episodic television. According to Cameron, "If I were producing an episodic series, I would produce it like *Avatar* with one 3D camera system.... I would encourage

people to go right to a native 3D and extract the 2D. I think episodic [television] will gravitate toward the feature model" (Giardina, 2012, April 16).

Although 3-D was definitely still on everyone's mind at NAB 2012, the buzz was about 4K-plus digital cinema cameras (Reeve, 2012) with faster frame rates and greater dynamic range (ratio of the brightest to the darkest portions in a frame measured in *f*-stops). That's great, but what is 4K? At the moment, there really is no "standard," but Digital Cinema Initiatives, LLC (DCI)—whose primary charge comes from the big studios that support it—seeks to establish and document voluntary specifications for a new generation of high-resolution digital cinema (DCI, 2011). As such, DCI defines 4K as having pixel dimensions of 4096x2160 at the top-end (the actual height being determined by the aspect ratio). RED's 4K camera is either 4096x2304 or 4096x2048, depending on aspect ratio. Other camera manufacturers are adopting the Quad-HD format—3840x2160—exactly twice the height and width of 1080p HD (thus, preserving the 16:9 aspect ratio). As of mid-2012, there is no single standard frame-size that can be called "the" 4K format. The first high-profile 4K cinema release was *Blade Runner: The Final Cut* (2007), a new cut and print of the 1982 Ridley Scott film. Unfortunately, at that time very few theaters were able to show it in its full resolution (Pendlebury, 2012). Still, camera manufacturers including Arri, and RED already deliver their version of a 4K camera, while Canon, JVC and Sony introduced prototype 4K cameras at NAB 2012—even Panasonic had a Vericam 4K "concept" camera on display; although, no details on specifications or availability.

While it may seem that a lot of 4K cameras were released—in reality—most were merely announced with shipping dates sometime in the future (Marine, 2012). Not to be out done, "RED Digital [intends] to upgrade its Epic camera from 5K to a 6K sensor within six months... [By the end of 2012] the RED Epic will be able to upgrade their 5K Mysterium-X sensor to the Red Dragon capable of 6K resolution at 85fps and 15 stops of dynamic range.... What's more RED has a 28K sensor in development" (*TVBEurope*, 2012). It's clear that 4K technology is coming—eventually—but it's not all here yet. "When HD finally arrived in a meaningful way there were two basic variations—1080i and 720p. Two frame-sizes each with a distinct scanning pattern (interlaced or progressive)—it was complicated by various frame-rates (23.976, 25, 29.97, 50, 59.94, etc.) but overall there was a standard" (Reeve, 2012). A production house could employ Sony cameras connected via SDI cable to a Grass Valley switcher that recorded to a Panasonic VTR and it would all work together. This is not yet the case for 4K. "There are no firm standards addressing how a 4K picture should be transmitted over a wire. Monitoring, off-board recorders, and projection, all rely on a handful of ad-hoc solutions wedged around existing formats and standards. HDMI is the closest we have to a usable standard for 4K video connectivity—and HDMI is not practical for most professional applications" (Reeve, 2012).

Interestingly, the camera that generated the most attention at the 2012 NAB show was not a 4K offering. The Blackmagic Design Cinema Camera surprised everyone. The Cinema Camera is a 2.5K resolution, 13-stop dynamic range, Thunderbolt-connected, built-in touch-screen LCD, SSD-recording camera that can shoot professional formats right out of the box and comes with the new version of Resolve 9 color correction software—all for $3,000 (MSRP). The only catch is a 15.6mm x 8.8mm (active) sensor size, which makes it equivalent to a Super-16 film camera, not a Super-35. Still, this is a "seriously disruptive camera" and one that targets the HDLSR filmmaker perfectly (Koo, 2012). Competition is good, and finally there is a professional camera at a low enough price point that will appeal to independent filmmakers. It will be exciting to see what they can do with the Cinema Camera going forward, and many expect to see a larger sensor in the next version of the camera.

Ever since the late 1920s and the introduction of synchronous sound in movies the standard frame rate has been 24 frames per second (fps). In the shift from the hand-cranked 16fps of the silent days to the new technical demands of the "talkies," a constant playback speed was necessary to keep the audio synchronized with the visuals. Of course, using more frames meant more costs for film and

processing, and the studios found 24fps was the cheapest, minimally acceptable frame rate they could use for showing these new "talking pictures" with relatively smooth motion. But, as Peter Jackson, director of the *Lord of the Rings* trilogy (2001, 2002 & 2003), pointed out while speaking at CinemaCon in 2012 (in a videotaped message), "with digital, there's 'no reason' to stay with 24[fps]…higher frame rates can result in smoother, more lifelike pictures while producing fewer motion artifacts" (Giardina, 2012, April 24). Jackson is set to release the first 3-D film shot at 48fps, *The Hobbit: An Unexpected Journey*, in late 2012 and screened a 10-minute clip of the film "in process" at the convention to mixed reviews. Speaking to the same group one year earlier, James Cameron emphasized that, although 3-D is now the "present" of cinema, the future of exhibition should not yet be concerned with pushing the resolution above and beyond 4K, but rather improving frame rates and light output (Billigton, 2011). Cameron further explained that, "if watching 3D in cinemas is like looking through a window—making the jump to 60fps was removing that window" (Billington, 2011).

Filmmakers like Cameron and Jackson who are advocating for higher frame rates (HFR) in pursuit of sharper, more realistic images on the screen, contend that films shot and delivered in 24fps have persistent visual problems. At 24fps, fast panning and sweeping camera movements are severely limited by visual artifacts and motion-blur that result from such movement. When a film is shot and shown in 3-D, the flaws of 24fps are even more obvious because of the technical challenges and the sheer volume of visual data being projected. According to Jackson, "shooting and projecting at 48fps does a lot to get rid of these issues. It looks much more lifelike, and it is much easier to watch, especially in 3-D" (Singer, 2011).

However, HFRs has its detractors who opine that 24fps films deliver a depth, grain and tone that is unique to the movie-going experience and not possible to recreate with digital video. They complain about the "Soap Opera Effect"—perceptions of a cool, sterile visual brought on by digital video—and that HFRs only make the images look too sharp and "glossy." Cameron's answer to the critics of HFRs is that the "filmic" style they so love comes from the angle of the shutter and lighting in the scene, not necessarily from the frame rate (Billington, 2011). However, even Roger Ebert agrees that "Hollywood needs a 'premium' experience that is obviously, dramatically better than anything at home, suitable for films aimed at all ages and worth a surcharge" (Ebert, 2010). Ebert's recommendation is MaxiVision48, a process that uses new film technology shot and projected at 48fps—doubling the image quality and providing a smoother projection that is absolutely jiggle-free (Ebert, 2010). HFRs may be coming sooner than later. Most digital cinemas are already using existing "Generation 2" projectors—those manufactured in 2010 or later—and all they would need is a software upgrade to be able to screen movies (2-D or 3-D) at 48fps or 60fps.

What is emerging now, and will have a profound impact on cinema's future, has the industry looking at "an entirely new kind of numbers game that has nothing to do with weekend grosses, '3-D,' '48fps' and '4K' could emerge as key players for Hollywood when it comes to crafting intensely credible fantasy worlds.… Moviegoers of the future might look back on today's finest films as quaint antiques, just as silent movies produced a century ago on the Metro Lot now occupied by Red Cinema seem laughably imperfect to 2012 viewers" (Hart, 2012). So, the drive is on to make theater operators fully ready for the HFR-driven movie experiences expected in late 2012 and beyond. For cinema businesses, the hope is that by adopting HFRs (like they have embraced 3-D and are gearing up for 4K) they will have more satisfied customers, more filled seats, and direct contributions to their respective bottom lines.

With the advent of cloud computing in the second decade of the 21st Century, the entertainment industry has taken advantage of solutions provided by working "in the cloud." Whereas the music industry has used cloud storage to record, produce and distribute millions of tracks, the film industry has been a little late in capitalizing on the benefits of cloud technology—but recent innovations are paving the way for future implementation. According to Steve Andujar, the CIO at Sony Pictures, cloud computing represents "[a] great opportunity to drive down costs and improve implementation of services" (Doperalski, 2012). While the cloud offers anytime-anywhere access to studio content, others caution that the potential of the cloud should be undertaken with caution. Paramount CIO Abe Wong stated that, "[you] have to look at possible vendor lock-in and what happens with your data once it is [on the cloud]" (Doperalski, 2012).

There are early signs of cloud computing finally beginning to find a niche in digital film production workflows. For example, a conglomerate of media organizations in Vancouver recently initiated a program called RenderCloud which will allow worldwide customers to save on travel and on-site costs—clients could work from wherever "home" is while still taking advantage of lenient digital tax laws available in British Columbia (Vlessing, 2012). According to the BC Film and Media president and CEO, Richard Brownsey, "[digital] media is changing the means by which content is created, distributed and consumed. RenderCloud will definitely contribute to our competitive position and to our success in international markets" (Desowits, 2012). Pixar is also staying on the cutting edge of the industry by developing technology it refers to as "cloudbursting" (Vlessing, 2012). Pixar partnered with GreenButton and Microsoft to deliver a new rendering service in the cloud. The basic idea is to make it a lot more affordable for film studios, advertising agencies or anybody else using Pixar's RenderMan software to access the compute resources needed to create animated films in 3-D. What the new Pixar service anticipates is the realization of significantly lower the costs in making these films, which, in turn, should make the technology more accessible (Vizard, 2012).

However, with Hollywood's understandable concerns over digital piracy and the protection of the incredible investment in intellectual property each film represents, the film industry wants some assurances from the cloud computing community. For years, pirated movies, television shows and music have been on the Internet. And for just as long, Hollywood and the entertainment business have been trying—and failing—to stop it (*The New*

York Times, 2012). If the results of a Google search for a film pops up a piracy site first (like The Pirate Bay or Megaupload), Hollywood is concerned (Doperalski, 2012). Recent disagreements between Hollywood and Silicon Valley over the now disgraced and indefinitely postponed House Bill "Stop Online Piracy Act" and its Senate companion "Protect IP Act" (SOPA/PIPA), have both Congress and the film studio execs licking their wounds from the backlash (Abrams, 2012). According to Jeff Chester, executive director for the Center for Digital Democracy, what Google and Facebook and their supporters "have delivered [is] a powerful blow to the Hollywood lobby. It's been framed as an Internet freedom issue, but at the end of the day it will be decided on the narrow interests of the old and new media companies" (Abrams, 2012). The big questions, of course, involve who should or shouldn't pay—or be paid—for Internet content.

Bibliography

Abrams, J. (2012, January 20). After protest, Congress puts off movie piracy bill. Yahoo News & Associated Press. Retrieved from http://news.yahoo.com/protest-congress-puts-off-movie-piracy-bill-202927971.html

Academy of Motion Picture Arts and Sciences (2012). *The digital dilemma 2: Perspectives from Independent Filmmakers, Documentarians and Nonprofit audiovisual archives*. Hollywood, CA. Retrieved from http://www.oscars.org/science-technology/council/projects/digitaldilemma2/

Adorno, T. (1975). Culture industry reconsidered. *New German Critique*, (6), Fall. Retrieved from http://libcom.org/library/culture-industry-reconsidered-theodor-adorno

American Widescreen Museum (2004). *Ultra-Panavision 70*. Retrieved from http://www.widescreenmuseum.com/widescreen/wingup1.htm

Andrae, T. (1979). Adorno on film and mass culture: The culture industry reconsidered. *Jump Cut: A Review of Contemporary Media*, (20), 34-37. Retrieved from http://www.ejumpcut.org/archive/onlinessays/JC20folder/AdornoMassCult.html

Belton, J. (2013). *American cinema/American culture* (4th Edition). New York: McGraw Hill.

Billington, A. (2011, April 4). CinemaCon: James Cameron demos the future of cinema at 60fps. FirstShowing.net. Retrieved from http://www.firstshowing.net/2011/cinemacon-james-cameron-demos-the-future-of-cinema-at-60-fps/

Block, A. (2012, February 9). Movie ticket prices hit all time high in 2011. *The Hollywood Reporter*. Retrieved from http://www.hollywoodreporter.com/news/movie-ticket-prices-increase-2011-288569

Bond, P. (2011, June 14). Film industry, led by electronic delivery, will grow in every category through 2015. *The Hollywood Reporter*. Retrieved from http://www.hollywoodreporter.com/news/film-industry-led-by-electronic-200881

Bordwell, D., Staiger, J. & Thompson, K. (1985). *The classical Hollywood cinema: Film style & mode of production to 1960*. New York: Columbia University Press.

Bradley, E.M. (2005). *The first Hollywood sound shorts, 1926-1931*. Jefferson, NC: McFarland & Company.

BSI Group. (2011). *UK film industry pioneers sustainability standard developed by BSI* [Press Release]. Retrieved from http://www.bsigroup.com/en/about-bsi/News-Room/BSI-News-Content/Disciplines/Sustainability/UK-film-industry-pioneers-sustainability-standard-developed-by-BSI/

Cieply, M. (2010, January 13). For all its success, will "Avatar" change the industry? *The New York Times* , C1.

Cohen, D. (2011, April 11). NAB: Cameron sets Pace on 3D future. *Variety*. Retrieved from http://www.variety.com/article/VR1118035268

Cook, D.A. (2004). *A history of narrative film* (4th ed.). New York, NY: W.W. Norton & Company.

DCI (2011). *Digital Cinema Initiatives: About DCI*. Retrieved from http://www.dcimovies.com/

De La Merced, M. (2012, January 19). Eastman Kodak files for bankruptcy. *The New York Times*. Retrieved from http://dealbook.nytimes.com/2012/01/19/eastman-kodak-files-for-bankruptcy/

Desowits, B. (2012, January 29). Vancouver taps a RenderCloud. *Immersed in Movies*. Retrieved from http://www.billdesowitz.com/?p=3937

Dirks, T. (2009, May 29). Movie history—CGI's evolution From *Westworld* to *The Matrix* to *Sky Captain and the World of Tomorrow*. AMC Film Critic. Retrieved from http://www.filmcritic.com/features/2009/05/cgi-movie-milestones/

Digital Cinema Implementation Partners. (n.d.). *About Us*. Retrieved from http://www.dcipllc.com/aboutus.xml

Dolby. (2012). *Dolby Surround 7.1 for Movies*. Dolby Laboratories. Retrieved from http://www.dolby.com/us/en/consumer/technology/movie/dolby-surround-7-1.html

Dolby. (2010a). *Dolby Digital Details*. Retrieved from http://www.dolby.com/consumer/understand/playback/dolby-digital-details.html

Dolby. (2010b). 5.1 Surround sound for home theaters, TV broadcasts, and cinemas. Retrieved from http://www.dolby.com/consumer/understand/playback/dolby-digital-details.html

Doperalski, D. (2012, March 2). Studios maneuver into cloud technology. *Variety*. Retrieved from http://www.variety.com/article/VR1118051006?refcatid=1009

Ebert, R. (2010, May 9). Why I hate 3-D (and you should too). *The Daily Beast*. Retrieved from http://www.thedailybeast.com/newsweek/2010/04/30/why-i-hate-3-d-and-you-should-too.html

Engel, L. & Buchanan, A. (2009). *Code of best practices for sustainable filmmaking*. Retrieved from http://www.centerforsocialmedia.org/fair-use/related-materials/codes/code-best-practices-sustainable-filmmaking

EPS geofoam raises stockton theater experience to new heights. (n.d.). Retrieved from http://www.falcongeofoam.com/Documents/Case_Study_Nontransportation.pdf

Epstein, E.J. (2005). How to finance a Hollywood blockbuster. *Slate*. Retrieved from http://www.slate.com/articles/arts/the_hollywood_economist/2005/04/how_to_finance_a_hollywood_blockbuster.html

Espejo, R. (2009), *The film industry* (pp. 181-183). Farmington Hills, MI: Greenhaven Press.

Frazer, B. (2012, February 24). Oscars favor film acquisition, but digital looms large. *Studio Daily*. Retrieved from http://www.studiodaily.com/2012/02/oscars-favor-film-acquisition-but-digital-looms-large/

Freeman, J.P. (1998). Motion picture technology. In M.A. Blanchard (Ed.), *History of the mass media in the United States: An encyclopedia*, (pp. 405-410), Chicago, IL: Fitzroy Dearborn.

Gelt, J. and Verrier, R. (2009, December 28) "Luxurious views: Theater chain provides upscale movie-going experience." *The Missoulian*. Retrieved from http://www.missoulian.com/busi ness/article_934c08a8-f3c3-11de-9629-001cc4c03286.html

Georgiades, A. (2010 March 1). Imax's status in 2D/3D conversion challenged by competitors. 3D CineCast. Retrieved April 1, 2012 http://3dcinecast.blogspot.com/2010/03/imaxs-status-in-2d3d-conversion.html

Giardina, C. (2012, April 16). NAB 2012: James Cameron and Vince Pace aiming for 3D profitability. *The Hollywood Reporter*. Retrieved from http://www.hollywoodreporter.com/news/james-cameron-nab-vince-pace-3d-312312

Giardina, C. (2012, April 24). CinemaCon 2012: Peter Jackson debuts 'The Hobbit' footage, touts 48 frame-per-second exhibition. *The Hollywood Reporter*. Retrieved from http://www.hollywoodreporter.com/news/cinemacon-2012-peter-jackson-hobbit-48-fps-exhibition-lord-of-rings-315685

Haines, R. W. (2003). *The Moviegoing Experience, 1968-2001*. North Carolina: McFarland & Company, Inc.

Hancock, D. (2011, November 15). The end of an era arrives as digital technology displaces 35mm film in cinema projection. *IHS Screen Digest Cinema Intelligence Service*. Retrieved from http://www.isuppli.com/Media-Research/News/Pages/The-End-of-an-Era-Arrives-as-Digital-Technology-Displaces-35-mm-Film-in-Cinema-Projection.aspx

Hart, H. (2012, April 25). Fast-frame Hobbit dangles prospect of superior cinema, but sill theaters bite? *Wired*. Retrieved from http://www.wired.com/underwire/2012/04/fast-frame-rate-movies/all/1

Hollywood Reporter. (2005, September 15). *Future of Entertainment*. Retrieved from http://www.hollywoodreporter.com/hr/search/article_display.jsp?vnu_content_id=1001096307

Horkheimer, M. & Adorno, T. (1969). *Dialectic of enlightenment*. New York: Herder & Herder.

Hull, J. (1999). *Surround sound: Past, present, and future*. Dolby Laboratories Inc. Retrieved from http://www.dolby.com/uploadedFiles/zz-_Shared_Assets/English_PDFs/Professional/2_Surround_Past.Present.pdf

IMAX.com - corporate - technology. (2010). Retrieved from http://www.IMAX.com/corporate/profile/technology/

Jones, B. (2012, May 30). New technology in AVATAR—Performance capture, fusion camera system, and simul-cam. AVATAR. Retrieved from http://avatarblog.typepad.com/avatar-blog/2010/05/new-technology-in-avatar-performance-capture-fusion-camera-system-and-simulcam.html

Jowett, G. (1976). *Film: The Democratic Art*. United States: Little, Brown & Company.

Karagosian, M. & Lochen, E. (2003). *Multichannel film sound*. MKPE Consulting, LLC. Retrieved from http://mkpe.com/publications/d-cinema/misc/multichannel.php

Kaufman, D. (2011). Film fading to black. *Creative Cow Magazine*. Retrieved from http://magazine.creativecow.net/article/film-fading-to-black

Kindersley, D. (2006). *Cinema Year by Year 1894-2006*. DK Publishing.

Kolesnikov-Jessop, S. (2009, January 9). Another dimension. *The Daily Beast*. Retrieved from http://www.thedailybeast.com/newsweek/2009/01/09/another-dimension.html

Koo, R. (2012, April 16). BlackMagic Design's Cinema Camera is a 2.5K RAW shooter with built-in monitor and recorder for $3K. *No Film School*. Retrieved from http://nofilmschool.com/2012/04/blackmagic-designs-cinema-camera-2-5k/

Lang, B. (2012, April 9). Titanic 3D: How James Cameron became a convert to 3D conversion. *The Wrap*. Retrieved from http://www.thewrap.com/movies/column-post/titanic-3d-team-dishes-re-release-everything-makes-conversion-difficult-was-there-36855

Luzi, E. (2011, January 5). Independent film and Hollywood: How technology is closing the gap on the great divide. *The Black and Blue*. Retrieved from http://www.theblackandblue.com/2011/01/05/independent-film-and-hollywood-how-technology-is-closing-the-gap-on-the-great-divide/

Marine, J. (2012, April 23). NAB 2012: Final recap—was this really the year of 4k? *No Film School*. Retrieved from http://nofilmschool.com/2012/04/nab-2012-final-recap-year-4k/

McClintock, P. (2009, December 14). 3D pays off at box office. *Variety*, Retrieved from http://www.variety.com/article/VR1118012750.html?categoryid=3762&cs=1&query=3D+cinema

Mead, B. (2008). The rollout rolls on: U.S. digital conversions nearing critical mass. *Film Journal International*, 40.

Mondello, B. (2008, August 12). Remembering Hollywood's Hays Code, 40 years on. *NPR*. Retrieved from http://www.npr.org/templates/story/story.php?storyId=93301189

Motion Picture Association of America (MPAA). (2011). *What each rating means*. Retrieved from http://www.mpaa.org/ratings/what-each-rating-means

Muñoz, L. (2010, August). James Cameron on the future of cinema. *Smithsonian Magazine*. Retrieved from http://www.smithsonianmag.com/specialsections/40th-anniversary/James-Cameron-on-the-Future-of-Cinema.html

Neal, S. (1985). *Cinema and technology: Image, sound, colour*. Bloomington, IN: Indiana University Press.

O'Connor, C. (2010, January 24). The future is now: digital and 3-D as 'Avatar' speeds up the revolution, northeast Ohio movie-theater owners wonder how to pay for the transition. *Plain Dealer*, E1.

Pendlebury, T. (2012, January 24). What is 4K? Next-generation resolution explained. *c|net*. Retrieved from http://reviews.cnet.com/8301-33199_7-57364224-221/what-is-4k-next-generation-resolution-explained/

Poster, S. (2012, March). President's letter. *ICG: International Cinematographers Guild Magazine*, 83(03), p. 6.

PR Newswire. (2005 , June 27). The Walt Disney Studios and Dolby Bring Disney Digital 3-D(TM) to Selected Theaters Nationwide With CHICKEN LITTLE. Retrieved from http://www.prnewswire.co.uk/cgi/news/release?id=149089

PricewaterhouseCooper (2011, June). *Global entertainment and media outlook 2011–2015: Industry overview*. Retrieved from http://boletines.prisadigital.com/PwCOutlook2011-Industry%20overview.pdf

Reeve, D. (2012, April 14). 4K and the future. *Edit Geek*. Retrieved from http://dylanreeve.com/videotv/2012/4k-and-the-future.html

Rubin, M. (2000). *Nonlinear* (4th Edition). Gainesville, FL: Triad Publishing Company.

Schubin, M. (2910, April 30). The elephant in the room: 3D at NAB 2010. *Schubin Cafe*. Retrieved from http://www.schubincafe.com/2010/04/30/the-elephant-in-the-room-3d-at-nab-2010/

Science & Technology Council (2007). *The Digital Dilemma*. Hollywood, CA: Academy of Motion Picture Arts & Sciences. Retrieved from http://www.oscars.org/science-technology/council/projects/digitaldilemma/index.html

Science & Technology Council (2012). *The Digital Dilemma 2*. Hollywood, CA: Academy of Motion Picture Arts & Sciences. Retrieved from http://www.oscars.org/science-technology/council/projects/digitaldilemma2/

Screen Digest. (2006). Digital cinema: rollout, business models and forecast to 2010. *Screen Digest*.

Screen Digest. (2009). US screen ad growth slowing in difficult market. *Screen Digest*, 252.

Screen Digest. (2010, March 3). Digital cinema building momentum as 3-D drives market. Retrieved from http://www.screendigest.com/press/releases/pdf/PR-DigitalCinemaand3D-03032010.pdf

Singer, M. (2011, April 12). Projecting the future of movies at 48 frames per second. *IFC*. Retrieved from http://www.ifc.com/fix/2011/04/will-the-future-of-movies-run

The New York Times (2012, February 8). Copyrights and Internet Piracy (SOPA and PIPA Legislation). *Times Topics*. Retrieved from http://topics.nytimes.com/top/reference/timestopics/subjects/c/copyrights/index.html

The Numbers (2012a). *Jaws*. Retrieved http://www.the-numbers.com/movies/1975/0JWS.php

The Numbers (2012b). *Star Wars Ep. IV: A New Hope*. Retrieved from http://www.the-numbers.com/movies/1977/0STRW.php

The Numbers (2012c). *The box office history for the Batman movies*. Retrieved from http://www.the-numbers.com/movies/series/Batman.php

The Numbers (2012d). *Box Office History for Paranormal Activity Movies*. Retrieved from http://www.the-numbers.com/movies/series/Paranormal-Activity.php

The Numbers (2012e). *US Movie Market Summary for 2000*. Retrieved from http://www.the-numbers.com/market/2000.php

The Numbers (2012f). *US Movie Market Summary for 2011*. Retrieved from http://www.the-numbers.com/market/2011.php

The Off Hours (2011). *Shooting sustainably*. Retrieved from http://www.theoffhoursfilm.com/p/shoot-it-green.html

Thompson, A. (2010, January). How James Cameron's innovative new 3D tech created Avatar. *Popular Mechanics* Retrieved from http://www.popularmechanics.com/technology/digital/visual-effects/4339455.

THX. (2012). *THX Certified Cinemas*. Retrieved from http://www.thx.com/professional/cinema-certification/thx-certified-cinemas/

TVBEurope (2012, April 19). NAB 2012: Red: Epic goes 6K and promises 28K device. Retrieved from http://www.tvbeurope.com/theworkflownews-content/full/nab-2012-red-epic-goes-6k-and-promises-28k-device

Verrier, R. (2009, March 26). 3-D technology firm reald has starring role at movie theater. *Los Angeles Times*

Vizard, M. (2012, January 27). Pixar animates cloud computing. *IT Business Edge*. Retrieved from http://www.itbusinessedge.com/cm/blogs/vizard/pixar-animates-cloud-computing/?cs=49627

Vlessing, E. (2012, January 27). Vancouver turns up cloud computing horsepower for Hollywood. *The Hollywood Reporter*. Retrieved from http://www.hollywoodreporter.com/news/vancouver-turns-up-cloud-computing-285279

Vreeswijk, S. (2012). A history of CGI in movies. *Stikkymedia.com*. Retrieved from http://www.stikkymedia.com/articles/a-history-of-cgi-in-movies

Winslow, G. (2010, October 11). Film fades to digital. *Broadcasting & Cable*. Retrieved from http://www.broadcastingcable.com/article/print/458279-Film_Fades_to_Digital.php

Young, S. M., Gong, J. J. & Van der Stede, W. (2010). The Business of making money with movies. *Strategic Finance*, 35–40.

Computers & Consumer Electronics

13

Personal Computers

Chris Roberts, Ph.D., and
Michael Andrews, M.A. [*]

Why Study Personal Computers?

✦ Computers are fundamental to, and have disrupted the development and economics of, every communications technology highlighted in this book.

✦ The dramatic improvements in size, power, and price of computers make their development techniques worthy of application to other fields.

✦ Computer adoption rates have risen greatly in developing-world nations during the past few years, with profound implications for education, communication, economics, and politics in those nations and worldwide.

Introduction

More than Neil Armstrong and Buzz Aldrin landed on the moon on July 20, 1969. A computer landed there, too. The Apollo Guidance System onboard the *Eagle* lunar module helped astronauts find their way to the surface and their way back home. Their 70-pound computer, running at 2.05 megahertz, had enough "brain memory" to hold 2,048 words, and enough "book" memory to store 36,864 words (Spicer, 2000).

If astronauts returned today, they might take an Apple iPad. The tablet computer weighs nearly 69 pounds less, runs 500 times faster, and holds thousands of times more information.

The computer industry's history continues to be one of smaller, faster, and smarter devices and programs. The 2010 Census showed that more than 40% of Americans were born since 1980, meaning America has 155 million "digital natives" (Palfrey and Gasser, 2008) who have never known a world without personal computers. During their lifetimes, computers have evolved from bulky desktops to increasingly smaller portable devices. Computers are so commonplace now as to be boring, whether desktop, laptop or hand held.

The industry has sold billions of machines since the first "personal computer" was sold in 1975. Computer makers sold nearly 300 computers per 1,000 U.S. residents in 2011, much more than the 1.4-per-1,000 rate of 1980 alone (Computer Industry Almanac, 2011).

The numbers show dramatic increases in the adoption and use of computers. Consider that:

✦ Computer makers shipped 353 million desktop, laptop, and tablet computers worldwide in 2011, up less than 1% from 2010 (Gartner, 2012). While a world recession and longer-lived computers contribute to flat sales of traditional PCs, the real answer lies in the boom of tablet computers, such as Apple's iPad. Apple will sell most of the 87 million tablets expected to sell globally in 2012, as the tablet market gobbles 21% of total computer sales (Computer Industry Almanac, 2012).

---

[*]Roberts is an assistant professor of journalism at the University of Alabama (Tuscaloosa, Ala.) Andrews is a doctoral student there.

✦ PC sales worldwide topped $325 billion worldwide in 2010, up just $8 billion since 2000 after adjusting for inflation. Even as sales and power rise, computer prices continue to fall (eTForecasts, 2012).

✦ The United States has 321 million computers in use—more computers than people. Worldwide, nearly 1.7 billion computers are in use, and, as shown in Table 13.1, the world is catching up to the United States, which leads in computer ownership and use (eTForecasts, 2012). America has 4% of the population but nearly 20% of the world's computers, even as most of those computers were built outside of the United States. There's at least one computer in use for every U.S. resident; the rate topped 100% since the previous edition of this book.

✦ 77% of American households owned a computer in 2010, up from 8% in 1984 and 62% in 2003 (U.S. Economics & Statistics Administration, 2011).

✦ Nearly 61% of PCs sold worldwide in 2011 were mobile units, triple the percentage of 2000 (Computer Industry Almanac, 2011). The price, speed, weight, and useful programs of portable devices have made them more common today than desktop machines.

✦ There's a wide geographic gap between people who use handheld computing devices and people who do not. While 89% of urban households have a handheld device (such as smartphones or tablets), the rate plunges to 10% in rural areas (U.S. Economics & Statistics Administration, 2011). The difference, of course, can be attributed to Internet access provided by telephone and cable companies.

✦ 68% of Americans have broadband Internet access, up from 4% in 2000 (U.S. Economics and Statistics Administration, 2011).

Table 13.1
Personal Computers in Use by Country

Notes: No. is millions of PCs in use. Share is percentage of all computers in use worldwide.
Note: 2011 data from http://www.c-i-a.com/pr02012012.htm

	1995		2005		2011	
	Number	Share	Number	Share	Number	Share
1. U.S.	108.2	35.5%	230.4	22.2%	310.6	19.4%
2. China	4.34	1.4%	63.72	7.0%	195.1	12.2%
3. Japan	23.3	7.6%	73.66	8.2%	98.1	6.1%
4. Germany	16.2	5.3%	50.42	5.6%	71.5	4.5%
5. India	2.12	0.7%	16.98	1.9%	57.0	3.6%
6. UK	14.5	4.8%	38.62	4.3%	54.5	3.4%
7. Russia	3.64	1.2%	22.76	2.5%	53.5	3.3%
8. France	11.7	3.9%	23.4	3.2%	53.5	3.3%
9. Brazil	3.15	1.0%	22.4	2.5%	48.1	3.0%
10. Italy	7.86	2.6%	25.96	2.9%	44.7	2.8%
9. South Korea	4.57	1.5%	28.38	3.1%	40.9	2.6%
Top 15 Total	**199.58**	**65.5%**	**668.6**	**74.0%**	**1,129**	**70.5%**
Worldwide Total	**305**	**100%**	**903.9**	**100%**	**1,601**	**1.0%**

Sources: Computer Industry Almanac Inc., eTForecasts

Figure 13.1
Percentage of U.S. Households with Computers, 2010

77 percent of U.S. households had computers in 2010. Utah was tops at 87 percent, and four Southern states last at 68 percent.

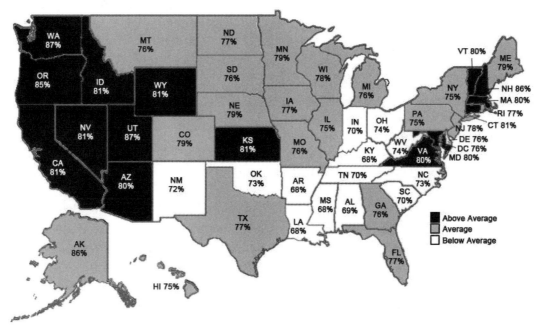

Source: Technology Futures, Inc.; *Data:* U.S. Department of Commerce (2012)

Table 13.2
U.S. Computer Ownership by Type

Percentage of American households who own:	
No computer	23%
Personal computer only (desktop, laptop, net/notebook)	58%
Handheld device and PC	17%
Handheld device only	2%

Source: U.S. Census Bureau, Current Population Survey School Enrollment and Internet Use Supplement, October 2010, and ESA calculations.

✦ The average American spent 35 hours on the Internet each month in 2010, second only to Canada's 43.5 hours a month. The average user worldwide was online 23 hours a month (El Akkad, 2011).

✦ We're creating and moving more information than ever. The Internet passed more than 21 exabytes per month during 2010, up from 5 exabytes per month in 2005. Networking company Cisco describes the increase as the jump from moving the equivalent of 1.4 billion DVDs of information online each month in 2005 to 12.8 billion DVDs in 2010 (Miller, 2010).

✦ While more households have computers, the "digital divides" of race and gender still exist in the United States. In 2001, 59% of white households had computers, compared to 38% of black households. In 2010, the rate rose to 80% of white households and 65% of black households. Similar increases occurred related to gender: In 2001, 61% of male households and 51% of female households had computers. In 2010, the rates rose to 79% for male and 74% for female households.

✦ Few consumer products have seen such dramatic increases in quality and declines in price. The IBM 5150, the original "personal computer" that hit the market in 1981, ran at 4.77 megahertz, had a monochrome monitor, no hard drive, and not quite enough memory to hold all the words in this chapter. It cost about $3,000, the equivalent of $7,423 after adjusting for inflation. Three decades later, that much money could buy a dozen computers that run hundreds of times faster and hold billions of times more data.

Background

A Brief History of Computers

As America boomed during the late 1800s, the U.S. Bureau of the Census needed a new way to meet its constitutional mandate to conduct a decennial headcount. It took seven years to compile 1880 data, too late for useful decision making. The agency hired employee Herman Hollerith, who built a mechanical counting device based on how railroad conductors punched tickets of travelers. The punched-card tabulation device helped the agency compile its 1890 results in about three months (Campbell-Kelly & Aspray, 1996) and was the first practical use of a "computer."

Hollerith, whose company later became a founding part of International Business Machines Corporation, owed a debt to 1800s British inventor Charles Babbage. While his "difference engine" was never built, Babbage's idea for a computer remains a constant regardless of the technology: Data is input into a computer's "memory," processed in a central unit, and the results delivered.

Early computers were first called "calculators," because "computers" were people who solved math equations. The early machines were built for a specific task—counting people, calculating artillery firing coordinates, or forecasting weather. The first general-purpose computers emerged at the end of World War II in the form of the 30-ton ENIAC, the "electronic numerical integrator and computer" that could count to 50 in a second (Aguilar, 1996). The next technological leap was Sperry-Rand's UNIVAC, or "UNIVersal Automatic Computer," which reached the market in 1950.

IBM controlled two-thirds of the computing market by 1975, when the introduction of the MITS Altair 8800 became the first practical PC on the market. It used an Intel chip and software designed by a new company called Microsoft (Freiberger & Swaine, 2000). An assembled box started at $600, or $2,500 in

current dollars. A year later, Apple demonstrated its first computer—which, unlike the Altair, came with a keyboard. The company's Apple II machine hit the market in 1977, and the company made half of the world's PC sales within three years. The early 1980s were marked by a Babel of personal computing formats, but a standard emerged after the August 1981 arrival of the IBM PC. The machine was powered by an Intel chip and MS-DOS (Microsoft-Disk Operating System), the programs that manage all other programs in a computer (Campbell-Kelly & Aspray, 1996).

The two powers behind the IBM PC took different paths. IBM's influence faded as competitors delivered machines with lower prices and higher performance. IBM controlled less than one-fourth of the computer market share in 1985 and in 2004 sold its PC business to Lenovo to focus on its server-based systems (Lohr, 2004). Microsoft, however, soon controlled the market for text-based operating systems and held off competitors (including IBM) in the transformation to operating systems with graphical user interfaces (GUI), which harness a computer's video capability to make the machine simpler to operate. In 1984 Apple debuted the Macintosh, which like its 1983 predecessor, the Lisa, was built upon a GUI that had an ease-of-use advantage over text-based systems and a premium price. Microsoft began selling a GUI operating system in late 1985, but its Windows software did not reach widespread adoption until its third version shipped in mid-1990. The mass acceptance of Windows gave Microsoft further dominance in the business of selling operating systems, and a Microsoft OS ran 90% of all PCs and 84% of all devices that accessed the Internet in January 2012 (Netmarketshare.com, 2012). See table 13.3.

The 1981 introduction of the Osbourne 1, a 24-pound machine with a 5-inch screen and $1,795 price tag (or $4,400 in current dollars), first brought the notion of a portable computer to the public (Oldcomputers.net, n.d.). In the past few years, laptops have overcome heat and weight issues to become at least as powerful as desktops. Mobile tablet computers—flat-screen devices with screens larger than a cellphone and touchscreens—were attempted in the 1990s and supported by a Windows operating system, but never reached wide acceptance. Apple's iPad introduction in 2010 led to much wider acceptance of these "post-PC" devices.

How Computers Work

Understanding the technology ecosystem of computers introduced in Chapter 1 requires differentiation of computer hardware, software, and messages. Hardware describes the physical components of a computer, such as the central processing unit, power controllers, memory, storage devices, input devices such as keyboards or touchscreens, and output devices such as printers and video monitors. Software is the term that describes the instructions regarding how hardware manipulates the information (data) (Spencer, 1992). The software, in turn manipulates the messages processed by the computer, from documents and spreadsheets to movies and music.

The most important piece of hardware is the central processing unit (CPU), or microprocessor, that is the brain of the computer and performs math and logic tasks. To do its work, the CPU's memory holds the data and software instructions. The memory is based upon a series of switches that, like a light switch in a house, are flipped on or off.

Original memory devices required vacuum tubes, which were expensive, bulky, fragile, and ran hot. The miniaturization of computers began in earnest after December 1947, when scientists perfected the first "transfer resistor," better known as a "transistor." Nearly a decade later, in September 1958, Texas Instruments engineers built the first "integrated circuit"—a collection of transistors and electrical circuits built on a single "crystal" or "chip." Thanks to miniaturization, CPUs once the size of buildings now can rest on a fingernail. Today, circuit boards hold the CPU and the electronic equipment needed to connect the CPU with other components. The "motherboard" is the main circuit board that holds the CPU, sockets for random access memory, expansion slots, and other devices. "Daughterboards" attach to the motherboard to provide additional components, such as extra memory or graphics cards.

The CPU needs two types of memory: random access memory (RAM) and storage memory. RAM chips hold the data and instruction set to be dealt with by the CPU. Before a CPU can do its job, data are quickly loaded into RAM—and wiped away from the RAM when the work is done. RAM, until a few years ago routinely measured in "megabytes" (the equivalent of typing a single letter of the alphabet one million times) is now stated in "gigabytes" (roughly one billion letters). Microsoft's Windows 7 operating system claims to function with as little as 1 gigabyte of RAM (Microsoft, 2009). Few PCs ship with less than 1 gigabyte of RAM; standard consumer-aimed computers ship with at least 2 gigabytes.

Think of RAM as "brain" memory, a quick-but-volatile memory that clears when a computer's power goes off or when a computer crashes. Think of storage memory as "book" memory—information that takes longer to access but is stored even after a computer's power is turned off. Storage memory devices use magnetic or optical media to hold information. Major types of storage memory for today's computers include:

✦ *Hard drives*, the rigid platters holding vast amounts of information. The platters spin at speeds of 5,400 to 15,000 revolutions per minute, and "read/write" heads scurry across the platters to move information into RAM or to put new data on the hard drive. The drives, which can move dozens of megabytes of information each second, are permanently sealed in metal cases to protect the sensitive platters. A drive's capacity is measured in gigabytes, and only the most basic desktop computers today ship with less than 250 gigabytes of hard-drive capacity. The drives almost always hold the operating system for a computer, as well as key software programs (PC World, 2007). Although nearly every computer has a built-in hard drive, external drives that plug into computers using universal serial bus (USB) or other ports are increasingly common. Many external drives are powered through the USB port, meaning the drive need not be plugged into a traditional electrical socket.

✦ *Solid-state drives (SSD)* use "flash" memory with no moving parts. These drives weigh less, load data into RAM much more quickly, are quieter, and use less energy than traditional hard drives. But SSDs generally have less storage capacity and cost more, limiting their sales to higher-priced machines.

✦ *Keydrives* (also called flashdrives or thumbdrives) are tiny storage devices that earned the name because they are the size of a thumb and can attach to a keychain. They use flash memory and plug into a computer using the USB port, which also powers the drive. Some larger-capacity keydrives hold 128 gigabytes of data. Prices have plunged, with 4 GB devices selling for less than $10 as of early 2012. Prices are higher for higher capacity and faster devices.

✦ *Other flash memory devices* can be connected to a computer. Most PCs ship with devices that can access the small memory cards used in digital cameras, music players, and other devices. Storage capacities and access speeds are also increasing.

✦ *Compact discs (CD)*, introduced in the early 1980s, are 12 centimeter wide, one millimeter thick discs hold nearly 700 megabytes of data, or more than an hour of music. They ship in three formats: CD-ROM (read-only memory) discs that come filled with data and can be read from but not copied to; CD-R discs that can be written to once; and CD-RW discs that can be written to multiple times. Most computers ship with CD drives capable of recording ("burning") CDs.

✦ *DVDs*, known as "digital versatile" or "digital video" discs, continue to replace CDs as the storage medium of choice. They look like CDs but hold much more information—typically 4.7 gigabytes of computer data, which is more than six times the capacity of a conventional CD. DVD players and burners are becoming standard equipment with new computers because DVD video has reached critical mass acceptance and because DVD players and burners are backward-compatible with CDs. DVD technology includes multiple formats, not all of which are

compatible with each other. The newest format is Blu-ray, which beat Toshiba's HD DVD format in 2008 and currently ships with a top double-layer capacity of 50 GB (Fackler, 2008). A growing number of devices can both read and write to Blu-ray discs.

Another key category of hardware is known as input and output devices. Input devices—which deliver information to the computer—include keyboards, mice, microphones, scanners, and touch-sensitive screens. Output devices that deliver information from the computer to users include monitors, printers, and speakers. Other devices, such as network cards or wireless systems, let computers communicate with the outside world by sending and receiving high-speed digital data signals through computer networks. Rarely seen on today's computers are modems, "modulator/demodulators" that translate the digital data of a computer into analog sounds that travel over telephone lines. Most computers and higher-powered portable devices come with Bluetooth, a protocol that uses short range wireless technology to connect computers to input and output devices.

Software

Computers need software—the written commands and programs that load in the computer's random access memory and are performed in its central processing unit. The most important software is the operating system, which coordinates with hardware and manages other software applications. The operating system controls a computer's "look-and-feel," stores and finds files, takes input data and formats output data, and interacts with RAM, the CPU, peripherals, and networks. Microsoft's Windows operating systems reigns supreme in sales against competing operating systems such as Apple's OS X, UNIX, and various versions of GNU/Linux. Tablet machines tend to run on other operating systems, such as Apple's iOS, Java, or Android. The iOS runs on roughly half of the world's mobile/tablet devices (Netmarketshare.com, 2012).

Operating systems provide the platform for applications—programs designed for a specific purpose for users. Programmers have created hundreds of thousands of applications that let users write, make calculations, browse the Web, create Web pages, send and receive e-mail, play games, edit images, download audio and video, and program other applications. Some of those applications are designed to be operated from a Web browser.

Recent Developments

Under the "Factors to Watch" section in the last edition of this book, we asked: "Will tablets take off?" The answer is a resounding "yes." Apple dominated a market niche that shipped 73 million tablets in 2011, and demand is expected to more than double in the next few years (DisplaySearch, 2012). While the computer industry sells millions of faster laptops and desktops, the rapid acceptance of tablets has led to dramatic changes in both hardware and software.

Hardware

The tablet has found a sweet spot between the too-tiny screens of smartphones and still-too-awkward laptops. Contributing to their success is near-ubiquitous Internet access provided by Wi-Fi networks and cellular companies, so users can easily move information and entertainment to and from their portable devices. Internet access is particularly vital for tablets, because most are closed systems with few or no physical connections to peripheral devices.

Apple dominates the market for general-use tablets against competitors such as Sony, Toshiba, and Samsung. Competitors are scrambling to provide comparable devices (or beat Apple's generally higher prices) to remain viable in the market—and general-use tablets compete with cheaper niche-driven devices marketed by booksellers, such as Amazon.com's Kindle Fire and the Barnes & Noble Nook in the United States. In other nations, the lower cost of tablets makes them an affordable alternative to PCs. In India, for example, Aakash is selling millions of tablets at $50, or $19 for students under a government subsidy (Tencer, 2012).

The tablet, along with fundamental changes in the world's economy, has led to more computer ownership in non-Western nations. PC sales in China reached nearly $12 billion in 2011, topping U.S. sales

for the first time to become the world's largest PC market (Kan, 2011).

Improvements in technology have led to the boom in smaller computing devices such as tablets and smartphones. The tablet has required new generations of computer chips designed exclusively for these low-powered devices, as well as heightened demand for flash storage that replace moving hard drives and touchscreens to replace external keyboards and other input devices. Most of these improvements are first introduced in traditional desktop and laptop PCs, which still dominate computer sales despite advances in tablets. Intel, which sells 80% of the world's computer processors, leads in PC processors with its line of "Sandy Bridge" processors (Volpe, 2011). They are better known under their i3, i5, and i7 designations and support Macintosh, Windows, and UNIX operating systems. Sales of the lines have been slower than anticipated, because of worldwide recession and higher sales of tablets and smartphones. The resulting backlog of processors has led Intel to delay introduction of its next line of processors, called "Ivy Bridge," until later in 2012 (Sumner, 2012).

The "Ivy Bridge" chips have 22-nanometer transistors, smaller than the 45-nanometer devices that shipped just two years ago. The reduction in size allows for greater storage and improvements when coupled with flash-storage devices. These chips will power "ultrabooks," an emerging category of slimmer laptops influenced by the Apple MacBook Air (Krause, 2011; forbes.com, 2012; Cross, 2011). A key improvement is their ability to power-up almost instantly, drastically reducing wait time.

The ultrabook, along with the boom in tablets, might spell the end of "netbooks," lower-powered and cheaper laptops that "took the market by storm" when introduced in 2007 (Bajarin, 2012). Their market share fell to 2% in 2011, down from 8% in 2010.

Laptops began outselling desktops in 2008 (Eddy, 2008), and one solution by desktop makers to hold market share has been to produce more all-in-one units. Computer companies in 2011 sold 14.5 million PCs that tuck the machine's innards behind the monitor, with Apple's iMac controlling a third of that market. DisplaySearch predicts that the industry will sell 23.3 million all-in-one units by 2014, a little less than 10% of all PCs sold, as all-in-one systems not sold by Apple become more common (Ricadela & Edwards, 2012).

These all-in-one units require fewer cords and cables—as does a new wireless monitor technology. Intel's WiDi (wireless display) debuted in 2010 to stream video from a computer (or other devices) without a complete physical connection to a monitor. The technology has not yet gained wide acceptance and is proprietary to Intel-made devices (Arar, 2011).

When devices plug into PCs, they may be using the new USB 3.0 standard. USB 3.0 moves data between devices at up to 5 gigabytes per second, 10 times faster than the 2.0 standard. The first 3.0-compliant devices shipped in 2009, but wider acceptance was not expected until later in 2012, after new Intel chips and Microsoft's new Windows 8 provides 3.0 support (EverythingUSB.com, 2012).

Much of the world's hard-drive production occurs in Thailand, where several plants were swamped by monsoons in the summer of 2011. The result has been a double-digit percentage shortage of conventional hard drives, with production cuts of 23 million computers in 2011 (Hillibish, 2012). The problems may be a boon for solid-state drives, which continue to sell at a premium price.

Software

Just as tablets have reshaped the computer hardware business during the past two years, they also have fundamentally changed the software business. Apple's iOS for its iPhone and iPad, which debuted in 2007 and introduced its fifth edition in late 2010, controls about 60% of tablet and phone market share. The Android operating system, controlled by Google, is eating into Apple's dominance at 40% and rising (Wauters, 2012).

Both iOS and Android are designed as the backbone for applications, or "apps," that serve specific functions on portable devices. Apple's rising sales of phones and tablets are directly related to the 550,000-and-growing number of available apps, available for free or sale at its iTunes store (Apple, 2012). A key change in software during the past few years has been public acceptance of Apple's requirement that all apps

must be acquired via iTunes, giving Apple both approval over third-party apps and a cut of revenues. Android's makers do not approve each of the 400,000-and-growing apps available for its platform. Both require that users download software, because neither offers physical sales of software, and PC software companies are also seeing more online sales.

The acceptance of these operating systems has led to changes in operating systems for desktop and laptop computers. Apple's OS X for Macintosh saw fundamental changes with its July 2011 "Lion" release, which among other things brought an iPad-like look and feel to some of its features. The newer "Mountain Lion" release, scheduled for summer 2012, is designed to offer more iOS integration in both look and operation. Like its sale of iOS apps, Apple's online store sells Mac software created by Apple and third parties; unlike the iOS, physical sales of software continue.

Apple's operating system controls less than 1 in 15 PCs worldwide, a testimony to the power of Microsoft and the flavors of Windows that control more than 90% of all PCs in use. The Windows 7 operating system debuted in October 2009 and runs more than one-third of the world's computers, because of its marketing prowess, the relatively short lifespan of a computer, and (to a lesser extent) Apple's decision to let users run Windows on a Macintosh. Microsoft, however, has stumbled in the market for tablet and phone operating systems. It is pinning its hope to regain market share on Windows 8, which will ship in 2012 with a look similar to tablets and versions aimed for touchscreens.

A third key category of PC operating systems are Linux-based, which are open-source and often free. Such systems hold a small market share, because they are rarely commercially advertised, perceived as difficult to install, and have a comparatively smaller catalog of software titles.

A fourth major operating system, Google's Chrome, debuted in June 2011. It runs "Chromebooks," lower-powered laptops that access applications and documents over the Internet. It has not gained wide acceptance, as critics cite "sluggish performance" of Chromebooks and public fascination with tablets (Parrish, 2012). But the concept of online storage of both applications and user files, known as storage in the "cloud," is taking off. Cloud storage can provide much greater capacity and efficiency for file storage, but keeping information in the cloud requires a fast Internet connection and extra attention to security.

Table 13.3
PC Operating Systems

Microsoft provides more than 90% of operating systems

Windows XP	47%
Windows 7	36%
Windows Vista	8%
Mac OS (multiple versions)	6%
Linux	2%

Source: Netmarketshare.com, January 2012

While operating systems need to be stored on a PC, the applications and data they produce do not. Instead of downloading and installing software on an individual hard drive, more users are creating and sharing documents online.

Microsoft's Office suite of software—with word processing, spreadsheet, and visual presentation programs—dominate the market and provide nearly half of the company's revenue. But in June 2011 Microsoft debuted its "Office 365" product that provides its Office suite in the cloud. This "software-as-a-service" is aimed at businesses at a price of $2 (email only) to $27 per subscriber per month (Perez, 2011). It competes against Google Docs, which debuted in 2007 with free and paid versions.

The shift to the cloud also has led to more services to store and deliver documents. Dropbox.com, Apple's iCloud, Microsoft's Skydrive and Google's Docs system are among competitors that let users store and share data. Proponents tout the safety of online storage compared to losing data when a single storage device crashes, as well as cheaper maintenance costs (Miller, 2009). Opponents of cloud systems worry about privacy violations and other issues (Robison, 2010).

Users cannot use the cloud without using Web browsing software. Microsoft's Internet Explorer controls a plurality of market share, but since its 2009

introduction Google's Chrome has come close to surpassing Firefox as the No. 2 browser as shown in Table 13.4.

Tablets and smartphones also have brought more attention to voice recognition software, which lets users speak commands to computers. Dragon Systems was among the first to bring the software to the market in 1985, and it has speech-to-text and vocal computer command applications for Windows, Mac, and tablet/phone operating systems (Zumalt, 2005). Apple and Android now bake voice-powered applications into their mobile systems.

Table 13.4
Web browser market share

Google's Chrome has gained nearly a great deal of market share since its 2009 debut.

Browser	Feb. 2010	Feb. 2012
Microsoft Internet Explorer	62.10%	52.9%
Firefox	24.40%	20.9%
Google Chrome	5.20%	18.9%
Apple Safari	4.50%	4.9%
Opera	2.30%	1.6%
Others	1.50%	0.8%

Source: NetMarketshare, February 2012

Current Status

The U.S. government reported total "final sales of domestic computers" of $219 billion in 2011, up from $96.2 billion in 2006 (U.S. Bureau of Economic Analysis, 2012).

Intel remains the leader in computer chip sales, snagging 83.7% of all CPU sales in 2011 while also expanding sales for phone and tablet markets. Its chief PC competitor is AMD, which has 10.2% of market share for PCs but has posted profits each year since 2009, after years of losses (McGriff, 2011).

Hewlett Packard continues to dominate in PC sales in the United States, topping Dell in 2005 and selling 17% of all PCs in 2011. Lenovo, which acquired IBM's computer manufacturing, remained second. Taiwan-based Acer ranked second in the past few years, but it fell to fourth in 2011 as netbook sales slowed and it made a transition into tablets (Gartner, 2012). See Table 13.5.

Microsoft remains the world's largest software seller. It reported profits of $23.5 billion on sales of $72 billion for the year ending December 2011, up from $16.3 billion in profits on $58.7 billion in sales for the year ending December 2009.

Apple is the largest general computing company, buoyed by sales of non-desktop and other products. It reported sales of $108 billion in the fiscal year ending in September 2011, and profits of $25.9 billion. The company sold 16.7 million Mac computers that year, plus another 72.3 million iPhones, 42.6 million iPods and 32.4 million iPads. The non-Mac side of Apple's business accounts for 80 percent of all of its revenue (Apple, Inc., 2011). The company's market capitalization topped $600 billion in April 2012, roughly the Gross Domestic Product of Thailand, home of the world's 25th largest economy.

Table 13.5
Personal Computer Market Share, 2011

Sales of desktops and laptops worldwide (not including the iPad) fell slightly in 2011.

Company	Shipments	Market share	Change from 2010
HP	60,554,726	17%	-4%
Lenovo	45,703,863	13%	20%
Dell	42,864,759	12%	2%
Acer	39,415,381	11%	-19%
ASUS	20,768,465	6%	10%
Others	143,499,792	41%	2%
Total	352,806,984	100%	1%

Source: Gartner Inc.

Factors to Watch

What happens with the world's top computer makers? As tablets take a substantial bite of overall computer sales, computer companies are struggling to match Apple in the tablet market. Meanwhile, Apple has introduced new versions of its iPad every year, with each new iteration having faster proces-

sors, higher resolution screens and cameras, and longer battery life.

Will tablet sales outlast the initial hype? Many believe so. Business Intelligence predicts that tablets will see a 50% compound growth through 2015 and soon outsell the 350 million PCs sold a year (Gorbry, 2012). Milanesi (2011) predicts that, up from 17 million tablet sales in 2010, more than 900 million will be sold worldwide within five years.

How will Windows 8 fare? Microsoft scored a hit with Windows 7 after its lackluster Vista OS, but Windows 7 sales are falling as PC sales decline. Some analysts see the 2012 introduction of Windows 8 as Microsoft's effort to capture tablet OS share while protecting its large lead in PC systems.

How will "ultrabooks" do in the market? New chips and manufacturing processes may mean the end of netbooks and a focus on "ultrabooks." Dell said it will focus on ultrabooks to the exclusion of netbooks (Murphy, 2012). Such a move might not be surprising as PC and notebook sales are expected to drop significantly in comparison to the ultrabook (forbes.com, 2012).

How will the Internet handle the traffic? The Internet is expected to move 486 exabytes of information in 2013, up from 60 exabytes in 2005, Cisco predicted (Miller, 2010). (An exabyte is 1,000 gigabytes.) The Internet's backbone must keep growing to move all that information. One solution has been the decision by the Internet Corporation for Assigned Names and Numbers (2012a) to increase the number of top-level domain names to handle new sites, including non-Latin languages. (Organizations would pay $185,000 per domain, so a company owning the "widgets.com" address could become "widgets") Another factor to watch is the concern from companies and others who fear that the expansion will mean higher costs and chances for fraud and confusion (Palmer, 2012).

How do we move all the traffic in the air? Tablets and smartphones are expected to be the dominant choice in accessing the Internet by 2015 (Bertolucci, 2011). As the number of people with wireless devices grows, wireless providers must find ways (and radio spectra) to move that data.

How does the Internet deal with a new address system? Internet Protocol (IP) addresses are sets of four numbers, separated by dots which connect computers and other devices to networks. (For example, FocalPress.com's IP address is 199.27.135.165.) ICANN (2012b) announced in February 2012 that the world had run out of IPv4 addresses, highlighting the need to move to a system called IPv6. With IPV4 IP addresses are 32 bit long, but with IPV6 IP addresses are 128 bit long allowing for 340 trillion, trillion IP addresses. The new system provides exponentially more addresses, but requires fundamental changes in network structure.

What's next for input? Touchscreen-focused tablets will continue to sell, even as more conventional PCs will ship with touchscreens and Windows 8 will provide improved touchscreen input for PCs. New input technology includes tablets with built-in cameras to detect hand motions to control devices (Graham-Rowe, 2011). Tactile display technology, will bring a sense of texture to touchscreens—simulated bumps, stickiness, and vibrations, for example, that could help with visually impaired users (Xu et al., 2011). Also, expect continued improvement in technology that responds to verbal commands.

Will Cloud make flash/jump drives unnecessary? Consumers buy millions of flashdrives to move and back up files (Britten, 2011), but continued acceptance of cloud computing might reduce sales of flashdrives.

What is the future of "jailbreak" software? Jailbreak software lets users install software not approved by Apple onto iPads and iPhones. (Stephens, 2012). Federal regulators have ruled jailbreak software is legal (Kravets, 2010), but Apple (n.d.) claims installation "disrupts services" and damages units, thereby voiding the warranties.

What happens in the anti-piracy battle? Hollywood and the computer industry say software piracy costs them billions of dollars per year. But public outcry in 2011 stopped Congressional votes on the Stop Online Piracy Act (SOPA) and the Protect Intellectual Property Act (PIPA), delaying a political solution to balance the need for protecting software creators and Internet freedom (MacKay, 2012).

What's next with chips? Chips for wireless devices outsold standard chips by nearly $5 billion in 2011 (Ogg, 2012), a trend expected to continue. Chipmakers are working on a 3-D transistor that promises to be more efficient than standard transistors (Venere, 2011a). Researchers in Switzerland have developed 3-D computer chips that can be stacked atop each other, instead of the traditional side-by-side configuration (HPCwire, 2012). And using ferroelectric materials may ease overheating problems, leading the way to instant-on and more powerful machines (Venere, 2011b).

Whither netbooks? Sales have plunged, but Acer is betting on a market for relatively cheap netbooks (Woyke, 2011). Acer considers its $250 netbook to be, feature-wise, comparable to more expensive notebooks. So it seems, at least as of May 2012, that the netbook may still be viable competition.

🖊 Sustainability 🖊

Want to compute while saving the planet? Recompute (2012) is marketing a "green" computer, built with cardboard and low-impact manufacturing processes, and an advance plan for disposal. The world's major computer makers haven't gone that far, but most of them continue to look for ways to build machines that run faster but use less energy and generate less heat. This has been done through new manufacturing techniques, hardware technologies, and software designed to cut a machine's energy use. An example is the arrival of liquid-crystal display monitors, which save more energy (and desktop space) than cathode-ray monitors. While improvements in cutting energy use and heat are occurring on all PC fronts, it is especially important on laptops, where heat and weight are particular nuisances.

But computers are objects with planned obsolescence, with expected lifespans of just a few years. Further complicating sustainability efforts are lead, solvents, and other materials than cannot easily be recycled. Nearly 30 million computers reached their end of life in 2009, and 38% were recycled (U.S. Environmental Protection Agency, 2011). That's an improvement over previous years—and a higher percentage than other electronic devices—but there's still a long way to go. (Electronics TakeBack Coalition, 2012).

Bibliography

Aguilar, R. (1996, February 14). ENIAC hits 50. Cnet. Retrieved from http://news.cnet.com/ENIAC-hits-50/2100-1023_3-204736.html.

Apple, Inc. (2011). *10-K Annual Report 2011*. Retrieved from http://investor.apple.com/sec.cfm#filings

Apple (2012, January 24). Retrieved from http://www.apple.com/pr/library/2012/01/24Apple-Reports-First-Quarter-Results.html

Apple (n.d.). Unauthorized modification of iOS has been a major source of instability, disruption of services, and other issues. Retrieved from http://support.apple.com/kb/HT3743.

Arar, Y. (2011, January 7). New WiDi adapters let notebooks wirelessly stream 1080p, Blu-ray content to HDTVs. PCWorld. Retrieved from www.pcworld.com/article/216023/new_widi_adapters_let_notebooks_wirelessly_stream_1080p_bluray_content_to_hdtvs.html.

Bajarin, T. (2012, January 30). Are netbooks finally dead? Retrieved from www.pcmag.com/article2/0,2817,2399496,00.asp.

Bertolucci, J. (2011, September 12). Tablets, phones to surpass PCs for Internet use in four years. Retrieved from http://www.pcworld.com/article/239870/tablets_phones_to_surpass_pcs_for_internet_use_in_four_years.html

Britten, S. (2011, September 19). Does "the cloud" make USB sticks obsolete? Retrieved from http://ezinearticles.com/?Does-The-Cloud-Make-USB-Sticks-Obsolete?&id=6570522.

Campbell-Kelly, M. & Aspray, W. (1996). *Computers: A history of the information machine*. New York: Basic Books.

Computer Industry Almanac, Inc. (2011, July 25). PC sales will top 370m units in 2011: Worldwide mobile PC sales to reach 227m units. Retrieved from www.c-i-a.com/pr072011.htm.

Computer Industry Almanac, Inc. (2012, January 4). Worldwide tablet sales will reach nearly 36% of total PC sales in 2015: U.S. tablet sales will top 43% of PC sales in 2015. Retrieved from www.c-i-a.com/pr012012.htm.

Cross, J. (2011, December 26). Ultrabooks: Laptops as light as air. *PCWorld*. Retrieved from www.pcworld.com/article/246691/ultrabooks_laptops_as_light_as_air.html.

DisplaySearch. (2012, January 4). Mobile PC outlooks shows growing influence of tablet PCs. Retrieved from www.displaysearch.com/cps/rde/xchg/displaysearch/hs.xsl/120104_mobile_pc_outlook_shows_growing_influence_of_tablet_pcs.asp.

Eddy, N. (2008, December 24). Notebook sales outpace desktop sales. *eWeek*. Retrieved from www.eweek.com/c/a/Midmarket/Notebook-Sales-Outpace-Desktop-Sales.

El Akkad, O. (2011, March 8). Canadians' Internet usage nearly double the worldwide average. *The Globe and Mail*. Retrieved from www.theglobeandmail.com/news/technology/canadians-internet-usage-nearly-double-the-worldwide-average/article1934508/

Electronics TakeBack Coalition (2012). State legislation. Retrieved from www.computertakeback.com/legislation/state_legislation.htm.

eTForecasts. (2012, February 1). PCs in-use worldwide reaches over 1.6b units in 2011: USA has nearly 311M PCs in-use. Retrieved from www.etforecasts.com/pr/pr020112.htm.

EverythingUSB.com (2011, November). SuperSpeed USB 3.0 FAQ. Retrieved from http://www.everythingusb.com/superspeed-usb.html.

Fackler, M. (2008, February 20.) Toshiba concedes defeat in the DVD battle. *New York Times*, C2.

Forbes.com (2012, January 13). Intel powering up ultrabooks as tablets take toll on PCs. *Forbes*. Retrieved from www.forbes.com/sites/greatspeculations/2012/01/13/intel-powering-up-ultrabooks-as-tablets-take-toll-on-pcs/2/

Freiberger, P. & Swaine, M. (2000). *Fire in the valley: The making of the personal computer*. New York: McGraw-Hill.

Gartner Inc. (2012, January 11). Gartner says worldwide PC shipments in fourth quarter of 2011 declined 1.4 percent; Year-end shipments increased 0.5 percent. Retrieved from www.gartner.com/it/page.jsp?id=1893523

Gorbry, Pascal-Emmanuel. (2012, February 14). Tablet sales will blow past PC sales to nearly 500 million units a year by 2015. *Business Insider*. Retrieved from http://articles.businessinsider.com/2012-02-14/tech/31057828_1_tablet-sales-post-pc-era-lower-prices.

Graham-Rowe, D. (2011,September 23). Taking touch beyond the touch screen. *Technology Review*. Retrieved from http://www.technologyreview.com/computing/38662/.

Hillibish, J. (2012, February 13). On computers: Hard-drive shortage helps to power solid-stage surge. *Canton (OH) Repository*. Retrieved from www.cantonrep.com/news/business/x574399521/On-Computers-Hard-drive-shortage-helps-to-power-solid-state-surge.

HPCwire (2012, January 26). Swiss scientists develop 3D computer chips. Retrieved from www.hpcwire.com/hpcwire/2012-01-26/swiss_scientists_develop_3d_computer_chips.html.

International Business Machines, Inc. (n.d.). The IBM PC's debut. Retrieved from www-03.ibm.com/ibm/history/exhibits/pc25/pc25_intro.html.

Internet Corporation for Assigned Names and Numbers (2012a, January). Generic top-level domains frequently asked questions. Retrieved from http://newgtlds.icann.org/en/applicants/customer-service/faqs/faqs-en.

Internet Corporation for Assigned Names and Numbers (2012b, February 3). Available pool of unallocated IPv4 Internet addresses now completely emptied. Retrieved from www.icann.org/en/news/releases/release-03feb11-en.pdf.

Kan, M. (2011, August 23). *PCWorld*. China overtakes US in PC sales earlier than expected. Retrieved from http://www.pcworld.com/businesscenter/article/238628/china_overtakes_us_in_pc_sales_earlier_than_expected.html

Kravets, David (2010, July 26). U.S. declares iPhone jailbreaking legal, over Apple's objections. Wired. Retrieved from http://www.wired.com/threatlevel/2010/07/feds-ok-iphone-jailbreaking/.

Krause, R. (2011, October 25). Intel hopes ultrabooks can fight off tablets. *Investors Business Daily*, 10/25/2011.

Lohr, S. (2004, December 8). Sale of IBM PC unit is a bridge between companies and cultures. *New York Times*, A1.

MacKay, A. (2012, January 26). Shelved anti-piracy act offers protection. *The Tennessean*. Retrieved from www.tennessean.com/article/20120126/OPINION03/301260025/Shelved-anti-piracy-act-offers-protection?odyssey=mod_sectionstories.

McGriff, D. (2011, December 29). Intel market share reach new high, may become monopoly. *Metro*. Retrieved from www.zimbabwemetro.com/32009/intel-market-share-reach-new-high-may-become-monopoly.

Microsoft. (2009, n.d.). Windows 7 system requirements. Retrieved from www.microsoft.com/windows/windows-7/get/system-requirements.aspx.

Milanesi, C. (2011, September 2). iPad and beyond: The future of the tablet market. Retrieved from http://www.gartner.com/DisplayDocument?doc_cd=217137&ref=g_noreg.

Miller, M. (2009, n.d.). Cloud computing: Web-based applications that change the way you work and collaborate online. Retrieved from http://ptgmedia.pearsoncmg.com/images/9780789738035/samplepages/0789738031_Sample.pdf.

Miller, M. (2010, March 25). Cisco: Internet moves 21 exabytes per month. *PCmag.com*. Retrieved from www.pcmag.com/article2/0,2817,2361820,00.asp.

Murphy, S. (2012, January 10). Delta unveils first-ever, ultra-sleek ultrabook. Mashable.com. Retrieved from http://mashable.com/2012/01/10/dell-ultrabook-xps-13/.

Netmarketshare.com (2012, January). Desktop operating system market share. Retrieved from www.netmarketshare.com/operating-system-market-share.aspx.

NetMarketshare, February 2012, http://marketshare.hitslink.com/browser-market-share.aspx?qprid=0

Ogg, E. (2012, February 1). Wireless shoves PCs aside in 2011 chip spending. Retrieved from http://gigaom.com/2012/02/01/wireless-shoves-pcs-aside-in-2011-chip-spending/.

Oldcomputers.net. (n.d.) Osbourne 1. Retrieved from http://oldcomputers.net/osborne.html.

Palfrey, J. and Gasser, U. (2008). *Born digital: Understanding the first generation of digital natives*. New York, NY: Basic Books.

Palmer, M. (2012, January 10). Icann to expand domain despite web of protest. *Financial Times*. Retrieved from http://www.ft.com/intl/cms/s/2/37cd6cf8-2745-11e1-864f-00144feabdc0.html.

Parrish, K. (2012, February 19). Google says faster Chromebooks on the way. Cnet. Retrieved from www.tomshardware.com/news/Chrome-OS-Chromebook-Sundar-Pichai-Google-Docs-Windows-8,14739.html.

PC World. (2007, July 23). How to buy a hard drive. *PC World*. Retrieved from www.pcworld.com/article/id,125778-page,3/article.html.

Perez, J. (2011, June 29). Microsoft Office 365 goes online: The cloud communications and collaboration suite is available in 40 markets globally. PCWorld. Retrieved from www.pcworld.idg.com.au/article/391754/microsoft_office_365_goes_live.

Recompute.com (2012, n.d.) Retrieved from www.recompute.com.

Ricadela, A. and Edwards, C. (2012, January 3). HP aims to stand out from mobile-device frenzy with desktop PCs. Bloomberg. Retrieved from www.bloomberg.com/news/2012-01-04/hp-aims-to-stand-out-from-mobile-device-frenzy-with-desktop-pcs.html.

Robison, W. (2010, n.d.). Free at what cost?: Cloud computing privacy under the Stored Communications Act. *The Georgetown Law Journal, 98* (4).

Spencer, D. (1992, n.d) *Webster's new world dictionary of computer terms, 4th ed*. New York: Prentice Hall.

Spicer, D. (2000, August 12). One giant leap: The Apollo guidance computer. Retrieved from http://drdobbs.com/184404139.

Stephens, J. (2012, January 23). Jailbreak iPhone 4S, iPad 2: "Absinthe" brings untethered jailbreak to Apple's A5 devices. *The Huffington Post.* Retrieved from www.huffingtonpost.com/2012/01/23/jailbreak-iphone-4s-ipad-2-absinthe_n_1224074.html.

Sumner, S. (2012, February 16). Intel delays Ivy Bridge processor. Retrieved from www.computing.co.uk/ctg/news/2152968/intel-delays-ivy-bridge-processor.

Tencer, D. (2012, January 4). Aakash, $47 tablet PC made by Canadian entrepreneurs, sells 1.4 million units in 2 weeks. *Huffington Post Canada.* Retrieved from www.huffingtonpost.ca/2012/01/04/aakash-tablet-pc-raja-suneet-singh-tuli_n_1183339.html.

U.S. Bureau of Economic Analysis. (2012, January 27). Final sales of domestic computers. Retrieved from www.bea.gov/national/xls/comp-gdp.xls.

U.S. Census Bureau, Current population survey school enrollment and internet use supplement, October 2010, and ESA calculations. http://www.esa.doc.gov/sites/default/files/reports/documents/exploringthedigitalnation-computerandinternetuseathome.pdf

U.S. Economics & Statistics Administration (2011, November 8). Exploring the digital nation: Computer and Internet use at home. Retrieved from www.esa.doc.gov/Reports/exploring-digital-nation-computer-and-internet-use-home.

U.S. Environmental Protection Agency (2011, n.d.). Statistics on the management of used and end-of-life electronics. Retrieved from http://www.epa.gov/epawaste/conserve/materials/ecycling/manage.htm

Volpe, J. (2011, August 2). AMD's market share tiptoes higher, Intel still ruler of the roost. Engadget. Retrieved from www.engadget.com/2011/08/02/amds-market-share-tiptoes-higher-intel-still-ruler-of-the-roos/

Venere, E. (2011b). New 3-D transistors promising future chips, lighter laptops. Retrieved from www.nanowerk.com/news/newsid=23653.php

Venere, E. (2011b). New 'FeTRAM' is promising computer memory technology. Retrieved from www.purdue.edu/newsroom/research/2011/110926AppenzellerMemory.html.

Wauters, R. (2012, January 26). Android reaches 39% tablet OS market share. Techcrunch. Retrieved from http://techcrunch.com/2012/01/26/android-reaches-39-tablet-os-market-share-standing-on-amazons-shoulders.

Woyke, E. (2011, May 4). Acer says death of netbooks is overstated. *Forbes.* Retrieved from www.forbes.com/sites/elizabethwoyke/2011/05/04/acer-says-death-of-netbooks-is-overstated.

Xu, C., Israr, A., Poupyrev, I., Bau, O. and Harrison, C. (2011, n.d.). Tactile display for the visually impaired using Tesla-Touch. Interactivity. Retrieved from http://delivery.acm.org/10.1145/1980000/1979705/p317-xu.pdf

Zumalt, J. (2005, December 4). Voice recognition technology: has it come of age? *Information Technology and Libraries, 24* (4).

14

Mobile Commerce

Why Study Mobile Commerce?

+ Mobile commerce use grew 86% from 2010 to 2011 (Butcher, 2011).

+ 41% of buyers have made a purchase on a mobile phone (Siwicki, 2011).

+ 66% of smartphone owners use their phone to aid in shopping (eMarketer, 2012).

+ Use of mobile wallet, mobile banking, and shopping apps is exploding.

Imagine running out of milk and making a quick stop and the supermarket to pick some up. At the checkout you realize that you forgot your wallet! So you pull out your smartphone, activate your mobile wallet app and tap the mobile payment terminal. Your payment is automatically deducted from your checking account, and you instantly receive a confirmation text message. At home you get a check in the mail. Take a snapshot of the check and you can then deposit it into your bank account with your bank's smartphone app. Now that you have money in your account, go ahead and use the Zappos app to buy that pair of shoes you have had your eye on. These transactions and much more are possible with mobile commerce technologies.

Mobile commerce is often viewed as the mobile extension of e-commerce. So, with mobile commerce, users use mobile devices such as tablets and smartphones to purchase goods and services. However, mobile commerce goes beyond this simple definition. The Mobile Marketing Association defines mobile commerce "the one or two-way exchange of value facilitated by a mobile consumer electronic device (e.g. mobile handset) which is enabled by wireless technologies and communication networks" (MMA, 2012). This involves the purchase of goods and services, perishable goods and services, and transfer of value or money.

The technologies used for mobile commerce include the mobile devices themselves (smartphones, tablets, laptops, digital media players), mobile networks such as Wi-Fi, cellular (3G, 4G), proximity communication technologies such as RFID and NFC, security and privacy technologies, mobile messaging (e.g. SMS) and mobile display (QR Codes, 2D barcodes)(MMA, 2012).

To give you an experience with mobile communications, we have posted the discussion of mobile commerce on the Communication Technology Update & Fundamentals website at http://www.tfi.com/ctu. You can download the chapter to almost any mobile device. And, unlike many mobile transactions, this one is free!

Bibliography

Butcher, D. (2011). Mobile commerce sees 86pc annual growth: study. *Mobile Commerce Daily*. Retrieved from
http://www.mobilecommercedaily.com/2011/01/25/mobile-commerce-fastest-growing-app-monetization-model-study

eMarketer (2012). Majority of US smartphone owners use devices to aid shopping. Retrieved from
http://www.emarketer.com/Article.aspx?R=1008971&ecid=a6506033675d47f881651943c21c5ed4

Mobile Marketing Association (2012). Mobile commerce. Retrieved from http://www.mmaglobal.com/wiki/mobile-commerce

Siwicki, B. (2011). IRCE 2011 Report: More mobile devices means more shopping, a survey finds. *Internet Retailer*. Retrieved from http://www.internetretailer.com/2011/06/15/irce-2011-report-more-mobile-devices-means-more-shopping

15

E-books

Ashley F. Miller, M. F. A. &
Larry Webster, B. A.[*]

Why Study The E-Book?

- Amazon sells more e-books than traditional titles (Amazon, 2011)

- More titles are released as e-books than in print (Bradley, Fulton, Helm & Pittner, 2011)

- Nearly half of Americans have read an e-book (Rainie, Zickuhr, Purcell, Madden, & Brenner, 2012)

Introduction

The e-book is a digitized version of a book, meant to be read on a computer, e-reader, or tablet. Many of the best-selling e-book titles are digital versions of popular print books without any significant structural changes from the print form, but some also introduce animation, video, hypertext, and social networking into the reading process. The goal of the e-book is to provide the ability to read books through an onscreen interface rather than on paper.

Using our communications ecosystem perspective to analyze e-books technology, it is clear that text and images are the content. Just as in printed books and periodicals, what is written is the message being communicated. What e-book technology brings us is a new way to distribute and consume the message.

An important co-development with the e-book is the e-reader, a lightweight, handheld device designed specifically for the reading of e-books and other digital text, such as newspapers and magazines. Unlike computers, many of which are stationary or heavy to carry, and some books, which can be bulky and heavy, e-readers can hold libraries of thousands of books and only weigh half a pound. E-readers also offer the ability to download new content at any time of the day and anywhere one can connect to a computer or the Internet.

Though an e-reader is not necessary to read an e-book, and many e-book users read on computer screens, e-readers have been key to the rising commercial success of the e-book (Rainie et al., 2012). Unlike a print book, which can be read without special devices, an e-book is entirely dependent upon the user owning a computer, tablet, mobile device, or a specialized e-reader to be able to access the content.

Background

The e-book pre-dates the e-reader by about 20 years. Michael Hart, widely considered to be the father of the e-book, began Project Gutenberg, a digital book library, in 1971, in an attempt to catalogue and make accessible all human knowledge ("Project Gutenberg," n.d.). For 20 years, the e-book continued being developed without any specialized reader and was something only used by the small number of people who had access to computers.

By the 1980s, an infrastructure of personal computers was in place that could enable a large number of individuals to read e-books using their personal computers, but the e-book did not become popular. The spread of e-books would be limited until a

---

[*] Miller is a doctoral student and Webster is a master's candidate in the School of Journalism and Mass Communications at the University of South Carolina, Columbia, South Carolina.

large-scale diffusion of personal computers, the Internet and online retailing created the right environment.

Figure 15.1
DATA Discman

Source: Peter Harris (Creative Commons Photo)

The first portable e-reader was introduced in the early 1990s. Sony's Data Discman used the compact disc as a method of storing data, which allowed for the reading of books without a bulky hard drive (Hoffelder, 2011). The Data Discman was similar to a portable gaming system—it accessed information from miniature CDs and displayed the information on a screen. Although primitive compared to current e-readers, it is easy to see the origins of current designs when looking at the first Data Discman. Sony continued to develop the Discman until the end of the decade, but it was never widely adopted (Hoffelder, 2011). From the creation of the first e-reader, it would take another 17 years before one was introduced to the public market that became popular.

One of the biggest technological advances in e-readers was the development of electronic ink (E Ink). A spin-off of MIT's Media Lab, E Ink Corporation combined chemistry, physics and electronics to create electronic ink which, when used in an e-reader or tablet, is so paper-like it can fool the readers eye. Electronic ink is really millions of small capsules, each containing black and white particles. A device such as an e-reader sends an electric charge to each capsule making it appear either black or white thus forming words or images on the screen (Electronic ink explained, n.d.)

Sony again led the market in 2006, when it offered the Sony Reader, the first e-reader to offer E Ink display. Unlike a normal backlit computer screen, E Ink screens behave more like normal paper and require external light to be read, making the experience much more like reading a paper book. Even with this advance, it was not until Amazon entered the scene the following year that the e-reader took off (Rainie et al., 2012).

Amazon, the online retailer that began as a book store and remains primarily invested in book sales, released the Kindle Reader in 2007, just in time for the holiday season. The release marked the first time that an e-reader was a popular success (Patel, 2007). The Kindle was not markedly different from the Sony Reader; the primary difference that allowed the Kindle to be successful was the existence of a company that already sold many books through online interactions. Though the public at large did not warm immediately to the e-reader, Amazon's customers had been primed for the e-book by purchasing books online and reading onscreen text for years. Amazon had a large enough reading customer base that, unlike Sony, they had a target audience that was easy to advertise to through their normal, day-to-day sales. Also, in 2008 Oprah claimed the Kindle as one of her "favorite things" sparking sales (Murph, 2008).

(Sony's failure and Amazon's success are an excellent example of the importance of the pre-diffusion theory discussed in Chapter 4. While Sony's focus and expertise was producing and distributing hardware, Amazon had expertise in distributing both hardware and software, making it much easier for the Kindle to achieve the diffusion threshold.)

With the Kindle came something new for e-books: specialized formatting for different devices. Before the Kindle, e-books were in universal formats such as PDF or plain text, but with the release of the Kindle, Amazon introduced a proprietary format that can only be read through the correct kind of device or software. Barnes & Noble's Nook followed in 2009 with a format that could not be read on the Kindle. Finally, setting the stage for the current e-reader marketplace, Apple released its iPad tablet in 2010. The iPad, like a computer, allows the reader to access both Kindle and Nook formats, but it also enables readers to download proprietary e-books from Apple's iBookstore that cannot be read on the other machines.

Recent Developments

E-readers

With Amazon.com, Barnes & Noble, and Apple all having significant online retail experience and the improvements in bandwidth making downloading e-books a simple and fast process, consumers have almost immediate access to any content they want. Early adopters of the e-reader had to download an e-book to their computer before they could transfer it to their e-reader, but e-readers now have Wi-Fi and 3G/4G broadband access, which allows consumers to search for, buy, download and read e-books no matter where they may be (Enderle, 2012).

As we look at the recent developments in the e-readers we have to look at two categories: dedicated e-readers and multifunctional tablets. After several false starts with Sony's Data Discman in the 1990s and early 2000s, dedicated e-readers finally hit their stride in 2007 when Amazon.com launched the Kindle (Kozlowski, 2010). Initially e-readers were limited to storing and displaying e-books, but that changed in 2010 with Apple's introduction of the iPad.

The iPad is a tablet computer that has many functions, only one of which is the ability to read e-books. In fact, the iPad is much more similar to a laptop than to an e-reader in every way except that it is much lighter than a laptop (Buchanan, 2010). The iPad lacks the E Ink display, so the reading experience is much more like reading on a computer (Reardon, 2011). Nevertheless, the iPad altered the landscape of the e-reader marketplace by introducing more functionality to a device that had almost all of the benefits of an e-reader.

Format

When Michael Hart began Project Gutenberg in 1971 his desire was to provide 99% of the public with access to free or very low-cost versions of books and documents that were already in the public domain. His goal was to select texts that would be of interest to the general public and make those texts accessible, readable and searchable on 99% of the hardware that anyone, anywhere might run (Hart, 1992). Selecting which texts to input to reach this 99% goal was a "best guess" process of selection by Hart and the volunteer staff working on the project. Making those texts available to the largest possible number of users was accomplished by selecting a ubiquitous format that ran on every computer and operating system, from DOS and Apple to UNIX and mainframe computers: plain ASCII text.

As e-books became a venture for publishers and booksellers, the formats for accessing the content became less universal. In addition to the various devices which are used for reading e-books, over the past several years, the various formats used have fragmented e-book consumers into groups that own a particular device and buy content from the supplier(s) which deliver content readable on that device.

To give an idea of the hodgepodge of formats, the four leaders in the e-book market provide e-readers capable of reading e-books in the formats shown in Table 15.1.

Table 15.1
Different E-reader Formats

e-reader	Format										
	DOC	EPUB	HTML	Kindle (AZW, TPZ)	MOBI,	Nook	PDB	PDF	PRC	RTF	TXT
Amazon (Kindle)	✦*		✦*	✦	✦			✦	✦		✦
Apple (iPad, iPod, iPhone):	✦	✦	✦	✦**		✦**		✦			
Barnes & Noble (Nook):		✦					✦	✦			
Sony Reader:	✦*	✦						✦		✦	✦

*Through conversion   **using Apps

Source: Technology Futures, Inc. Data: (BookFinder.com, n.d.)

All readers support PDF files, which might identify this as a possible universal format, but PDF does not offer many of the benefits of the e-reader, including resizing and searching the text; it just shows up as an image. Almost all of the platforms support the EPUB format, the closest to a universal format that is offered, but the largest of the suppliers, Amazon, does not support this standard. Although there have been some attempts and pressure to create a universal standard, none is forthcoming (Lee, Guttenberg & McCrary, 2002).

This forcing of formats onto users is a matter of convenience and cost (Schofield, 2010). It is convenient for a reader to stay with one supplier of content because switching to another supplier would mean switching to another e-reader and either converting original files to a format readable by the new device or in some cases having to repurchase entire libraries of books, which dramatically increases the cost beyond the initial reinvestment in new hardware. Even if a reader buys an e-reader or tablet, which has the capability of accessing content from the different suppliers through apps, there is the inconvenience of switching between apps to view desired e-book and an inability to easily search across entire an entire library of e-books.

Availability

Sales of e-books have grown enormously over the last several years (Rainie et al., 2012). This increase is primarily due to e-book retailers overcoming perhaps the biggest obstacles that kept e-books from taking off—content availability. Because of the low numbers of people with e-readers, retailers did not want to commit to large-scale availability of content until there were enough reading devices in circulation to warrant the expense of converting the content into electronic format; consumers did not want to invest in a reading device, which can cost upwards of $300, if there was limited content.

While there are many books that are not available through any individual bookseller, millions of titles are available on each. Furthermore, there is content that is available only in e-book format. In fact, there are far more books published in e-book form now than there are books published in print (Bradley et al., 2011).

Another major factor in availability was, and is, cost. In general, adopters of e-readers and e-books are wealthier than the average American (Rainie et al., 2012), but the cost of e-readers has dropped precipitously over time, and, as of mid-2012, the Kindle Touch costs only $80. It is still a major investment to people who can get books free from the library, borrow them from friends, or sell books after they've been read. With the capability to carry hundreds of books in a device smaller and lighter than one paperback book, e-textbooks seem like a natural choice for students not just in the U.S., but around the world. E-textbooks are not only lighter, but are far easier to update and keep current. However, using a textbook is different than reading a novel or newspaper. Students want to be able to highlight, take notes, and flip through pages easily. Current e-reader technology addresses these issues with some basic features. With improvement in these features, the market for e-textbooks should increase. There are also economic factors. Since they can't resell their used books as they can with printed textbooks, students need to be convinced that they will save money over time when considering the combined cost of the e-reader and the e-textbooks (Nelson & Hains, 2011). Once these issues are addressed, backpacks around the world will be a lot lighter.

Cost of content for e-readers is an important factor in the continued diffusion of e-reader technology. Realizing the importance of content to stimulate demand for e-readers, Amazon.com lowered the cost of its extensive catalog of titles to $9.99 or less in 2010. This made the content a loss-leader, which led to an increase in Kindle purchases. In 2010, when unveiling its iBookstore for the new iPad, Apple joined with five publishers to offer e-books on the "agency" model. This model of e-commerce, which Apple and other online retailers have used to sell a large variety of applications and product, allows the publisher to set the price with Apple being paid a percentage of each sale. Under pressure from publishers, Amazon.com agreed in 2010 to work under the agency model as well. But the agency model has been tied to an increase in the cost of books to the end user. After nearly two years under this model, the U.S. Department of Justice (DOJ) filed a suit against Apple and five publishers for colluding to keep the cost of e-books artificially high. The DOJ claims that this price fixing is harmful to consumers. As of mid-2012, three of the publishers have settled with the DOJ while Apple and two publishers want to have the case tried since they feel the agency model is a legitimate response to Amazon.com's earlier practice of selling products at a loss (Wharton, 2012). The outcome of this case will have a long-lasting impact on the future of e-readers and e-books.

Current Status

The 2011 holiday season was huge for the e-book and the tablet. In mid-December, 10% of Americans owned an e-reader; by mid-January 2012, that number had nearly doubled to 19%. Tablet ownership has increased at a similar rate. As of mid-2012, 29% of Americans own either a tablet or an e-reader, or both (Rainie et al., 2012).

Amazon and Barnes & Noble realized that they needed to keep pace with offering consumers a product that had at least some of the advanced capabilities of the iPad. The race for larger screens, e-mail and Web browsing began, and soon both companies had tablets (Kendrick, 2012). Before the holiday season of 2011, Amazon introduced the Kindle Fire, and Barnes & Noble introduced the Nook Tablet. Both of these devices offer capabilities similar to those of the iPad, despite coming from the lineage of their e-ink, book-reading based predecessors (Reardon, 2011).

Currently, e-readers and tablets have an equal share of the marketplace. See Figure 15.2. The Kindle dominates the e-reader market, at 62%, followed distantly by the Nook, at 22%. The tablet market is equally dominated by the iPad, at 61%, but Amazon has made a dent in this market as well because the Kindle Fire is second with 14%, a number that grew threefold between December 2011 and January 2012 (Rainie et al., 2012).

E-book sales continue to rise. In the first three days that it was available in March 2012, sales of the Harry Potter e-books broke $1.5 million (Hall, 2012), and the Association of American Publishers announced that e-book sales were up 73.2% in January 2012 over the sales in January 2011 (Souppouris, 2012). In the last week of 2011, for 42 of the 50 best-selling titles, their e-book sales were outpacing their print copies (Rainie et al., 2012).

Figure 15.2
E-reader Market Share

Percent of American adult e-reader owners age 18+ who own type of e-book reader

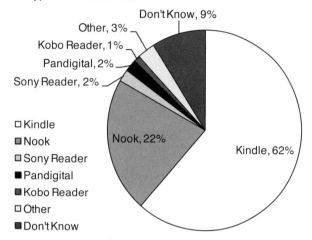

□ Kindle
▨ Nook
▨ Sony Reader
■ Pandigital
▨ Kobo Reader
□ Other
▨ Don't Know

Source: Pew Research Center (2012)

Beyond this, e-readers continue to evolve and try to meet user needs and requests. Many of the e-readers, including the Kindle, have been opened up to allow users to borrow books from their local libraries and to lend books they've bought electronically to friends who also have an e-reader. For the moment, these exchanges are limited to people who share the same kind of device—a Kindle can loan to a Kindle, but not to a Nook. For profiles of e-book users, see Table 15.2.

E-books are also far outpacing print books in the publishing world. In 2010, there were nearly 3 million books published non-traditionally, most of them online, and 300,000 that were published through traditional publishing houses (Bradley et al., 2011). Many of those traditionally published books were also released online. The ease of publishing and low cost of entry means that anyone can publish anything, even if the content has a small market. If the author publishes through Amazon, it automatically becomes part of their database and customers have the opportunity to stumble upon it.

Table 15.2
E-book Users

Portrait of e-book readers—29% of those who read books in the past 12 months.

All e-book users age 18 and older	9%
Gender	
Men	29
Women	28
Age	
18-29	34*
30-49	34*
50-64	23
65+	17
Race/Ethnicity	
White, non-Hispanic	29
Black, non-Hispanic	22
Hispanic (English and Spanish speaking)	23
Household Income	
Less than $30,000	20
$30,000-$49,999	25
$50,000-$74,999	35*
$75,000+	38*
Education level	
High school grad	19
Some college	34*
College graduate	35*

*indicates statistically significant difference between rows

Source: Pew Research Center (2012)

Factors to Watch

It is clear that further diffusion of e-book and e-reader technology would benefit from development of a standard format for the content, or the acceptance of an existing one. The interoperability achieved could help e-books reach the diffusion level predicted. However, the issue of digital rights management (DRM) still presents a drawback for the technology, introducing restrictions that make e-books less attractive than print books. We've all read a print book and passed it along to a friend. The ability to do so with an e-book is severely limited.

The huge growth in the number of titles published shows no signs of slowing, meaning that the availability of content is going to be overwhelming. Soon we will need better ways of sorting through all of the available content to be able to find what we are looking for. There has been a lot of progress in terms of matching content to consumer through sites such as Netflix and YouTube, which have always had an enormous amount of content, and undoubtedly the online system needs to get better at finding books for people.

It will also be interesting to watch the sales figures of traditional book titles and their relationship with e-book titles. Though e-book sales figures grew an incredible 72.3% in January 2012 over the previous year, traditional print titles also saw overall growth, though it was much smaller (Souppouris, 2012). The e-book seems to be expanding the number of books purchased overall, without necessarily taking market share away from traditional print books (Rainie et al., 2012), but prolonged expansion of both print books and e-books seems unsustainable. Clearly there is room for both in the marketplace, but evidence points to print books becoming more of a specialty item and e-books becoming the norm.

Finally, it will be important to monitor the legal arena as manufacturers, publishers, distributors, and consumers battle over the structure of the market and the revenues that will be produced. The DOJ's anti-trust suit against Apple and other publishers may be just an early skirmish in a battle to control consumer access to content.

 Sustainability

A book stored electronically is certainly more sustainable than one printed on paper, and if one reads it on a computer that would otherwise be running, the impact is minimal. However, the specialized e-readers produced specifically to read e-books are not particularly environmentally friendly, and fail in a one-to-one comparison with a printed book. The comparison is not one-to-one, though, because a reader can have any number of books on his or her e-reader. We need books in one form or another, so the question is not whether the e-readers are environmentally friendly but whether they are more or less environmentally friendly than printed books.

Both paperbacks and e-readers need resources and energy to be manufactured, and once manufactured, e-readers need additional energy to function. Of all the e-readers and tablets, only Apple releases information about the resources used in the creation of the device. Amazon, Barnes & Noble and Sony will not release information about his or her devices, but researchers like Cleantech (Kho, 2011) and Goleman & Norris (2010) have made estimates of the environmental and energy impact of these devices, based on composites from known information. They do not stand up well against a paperback.

Both paperbacks and hardbacks are much more environmentally friendly than an e-reader, but if a user reads enough books on the e-reader, a collection of printed books becomes more wasteful over time. Although e-readers require energy to run throughout their lives, they consume little energy, and the environmental impact of running an e-book after it has been created and delivered to a user is quite low. Depending on the estimates, if a user reads somewhere from 22.5-40 e-books on their e-reader, they will have a smaller carbon footprint than if they bought printed books (Goleman & Norris, 2010; Kho, 2011). Reading on an e-reader can even be more carbon-efficient than getting books from the library, if the user significantly cuts down on the number of car trips he or she makes to the library itself.

Currently, this analysis suggest that most e-readers are environmentally friendly, because the early adopters of the technology are heavier readers than the average consumer (Rainie et al., 2012). However, as the adoption of e-readers goes up, the trade-off becomes much closer. E-readers will need a reduced carbon footprint, along with elimination of some of the chemicals and minerals used in their creation to become an alternative that is clearly more sustainable than the traditional book.

Bibliography

Amazon. (2011, January 27). Amazon Media Room: Press Releases. *Amazon*. Retrieved from http://phx.corporate-ir.net/phoenix.zhtml?c=176060&p=irol-newsArticle&ID=1521090&highlight&ref=tsm_1_tw_kin_prearn_20110127

BookFinder.com. (n.d.). ebooks FAQ. *BookFinder.com*. Retrieved from http://www.bookfinder.com/books/ebooks_faq/

Bradley, J., Fulton, B., Helm, M. & Pittner, K. A. (2011). Non-traditional book publishing. *First Monday*, 16(8). Retrieved from http://ojphi.org/htbin/cgiwrap/bin/ojs/index.php/fm/article/viewArticle/3353

Buchanan, M. (2010, March 5). Official: iPad launching here April 3, Pre-Orders March 12. *Gizmodo*. Retrieved from http://gizmodo.com/5486444/official-ipad-launching-here-april-3-pre+orders-march-12

Electronic ink explained (n.d.) Retrieved from http://www.eink.com/technology.html

Enderle, R. (2012, April 3). Anticipating the 4th-gen iPad. *TG Daily*. Retrieved from http://www.tgdaily.com/opinion-features/62504-anticipating-the-4th-gen-ipad

Goleman, D. & Norris, G. (2010, April 4). E-Reader versus book: The Eco-Math. *danielgoleman*. Retrieved from http://danielgoleman.info/2010/e-reader-versus-book-the-eco-math/

Hall, J. (2012, April 6). Harry Potter ebook sales top 1m in three days. *Telegraph.co.uk*. Retrieved from http://www.telegraph.co.uk/culture/harry-potter/9188643/Harry-Potter-ebook-sales-top-1m-in-three-days.html

Hart, M. (1992, August). The history and philosophy of project Gutenberg. *Project Gutenberg*. Retrieved from http://www.gutenberg.org/

Hoffelder, N. (2011, October 9). Blast from the past: Sony Data Discman DD-S35. *The Digital Reader*. Retrieved from http://www.the-digital-reader.com/2011/10/09/blast-from-the-past-sony-data-discman-dd-s35/

Kendrick, J. (2012, March 14). Kindle Fire: Blurring the tablet and ereader markets. *ZDNet*. Retrieved from http://www.zdnet.com/blog/mobile-news/kindle-fire-blurring-the-tablet-and-ereader-markets/7148

Kho, N. D. (2011, December 4). E-readers or print books - which is greener? *San Francisco Chronicle*. Retrieved from http://www.sfgate.com/cgi-bin/article.cgi?f=/c/a/2011/12/01/HOCR1M0J6B.DTL

Kozlowski, M. (2010, May 17). A brief history of eBooks. *Good e-Reader*. Retrieved from http://goodereader.com/blog/electronic-readers/a-brief-history-of-ebooks/

Lee, K.-H., Guttenberg, N. & McCrary, V. (2002). Standardization aspects of eBook content formats. *Computer Standards & Interfaces*, 24(3), 227239. doi:10.1016/S0920-5489(02)00032-6

Murph, D. (2008). Oprah calls Kindle her "new favorite thing," gives everyone $50 off. *Engadget*. Retrieved from http://www.engadget.com/2008/10/25/oprah-calls-kindle-her-new-favorite-thing-gives-everyone-50/

Nelson, M. and Hains, E. (2011). E-books in higher education: Are we there yet? Educause center for Applied Research. Retrieved from: http://www.educause.edu/Resources/EBooksinHigherEducationAreWeTh/196653

Patel, N. (2007, October 21). Kindle sells out in 5.5 hours. *Engadget*. Retrieved from http://www.engadget.com/2007/11/21/kindle-sells-out-in-two-days/

Project Gutenberg. (n.d.).*Project Gutenberg*. Retrieved from http://www.gutenberg.org/wiki/Main_Page

Rainie, L., Zickuhr, K., Purcell, K., Madden, M. & Brenner, J. (2012, April 4). The rise of e-reading. *Pew Internet*. Retrieved April 9, 2012, from http://libraries.pewinternet.org/2012/04/04/the-rise-of-e-reading/?src=prc-headline

Reardon, M. (2011, December 6). An e-reader or tablet for Christmas? *CNET*. Retrieved from-http://news.cnet.com/8301-30686_3-57336098-266/an-e-reader-or-tablet-for-christmas/

Schofield, J. (2010, August 15). eBook DRM: Can't succeed with it, won't thrive without it. *Trusted Reviews*. Retrieved from http://www.trustedreviews.com/opinions/ebook-drm-can-t-succeed-with-it-won-t-thrive-without-it

Souppouris, A. (2012, March 30). Ebooks, young readers stimulate publishing industry growth. *The Verge*. Retrieved from http://www.theverge.com/2012/3/30/2913366/ebook-sales-by-demographic-january-2012-aap

Wharton (2012, April 27). E-book price-fixing: Finding the best model for publishers and readers. *Time Business*. Retreived from http://business.time.com/2012/04/27/e-book-price-fixing-finding-the-best-model-for-publishers-and-readers/

16

Video Games

Brant Guillory, M.M.C.[*]

Why Study Video Games?

- ✦ 72% of American households play computer and video games (ESA, 2012).

- ✦ 55% of gamers play on mobile phones and other mobile devices (ESA, 2012).

- ✦ Video game hardware and games generate billions in revenue each year.

- ✦ New gaming devices and games are pushing the boundaries of creativity and technology.

Video gaming is a multibillion dollar industry whose cultural penetration far belies its roots in entertaining mental exercises for overeager engineers. Video games include a variety of hardware and software, as well as multiple delivery and distribution models. Gamer culture has served as the subtext for successful media franchises, such as CBS's *The Big Bang Theory* and Disney's *Level Up*. Major video game conferences and events, such as E3 and PAX (Penny Arcade Expo) pull in tens of thousands of attendees.

In monetary terms, video games are easily competitive with the largest media. The opening day sales of *Call of Duty: Black Ops* exceeded $360 million worldwide, easily exceeding the largest-ever weekend movie gross through mid-2012 (*The Avengers*) and the first-day sales of the final *Harry Potter* book (TechWeb 2010; Thorsen, 2009). Additionally, videogame franchises are themselves becoming hot media properties, with such series as *Resident Evil, Bioshock, Fallout, HALO,* and *Mass Effect* spawning multiple sequels, websites, videos, downloadable games, and physical content ranging from action figures to comic books to coffee mugs.

"Video games" as a catch-all term includes games with a visual (and usually audio) stimulus, played through a digitally-mediated system (see Figure 16.1). Video games are available as software for other digital systems (home computers, mobile phones, tablets), standalone systems (arcade cabinets), or software for gaming-specific systems (platforms). There have also been tentative forays into games delivered through set-top boxes and digital integration with offline games.

A video game system will have some form of display, a microprocessor, the game software, and some form of input device. The microprocessor may be shared with other functions in the device. Input devices have also evolved in sophistication from simple one-button joysticks or keyboards to replicas of aircraft cockpits and race cars. Recent controllers have integrated haptic feedback (enabling users to "feel" aspects of a game), as well as accelerometers that detect the movements of the controllers themselves. Finally, new systems like Microsoft's Kinect enable games to be played using three-dimensional detection of the actions taken by a player's body. These systems include cameras used as input devices into the video game system.

---

[*] *Senior Consultant at Harnessed Electrons, and Editor-in-Chief of GrogNews.com, Raleigh, North Carolina*

Figure 16.1
Video Game Genres

Sports

Space

Military

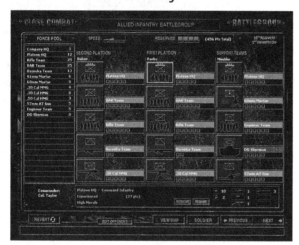

History

Source: Matrix Games *Background*

Video gaming has advanced hand-in-hand with the increases in computing power over the past 50 years. Some might even argue that video games have pushed the boundaries of computer processors in their quest for ever-sharper graphics and increased speed in gameplay. From their early creation on large mainframe computers, video games evolved through a variety of platforms, including standalone arcade-style machines, personal computers, and dedicated home gaming platforms.

As media properties, video games have shared characters, settings, and worlds with movies, novels, comic books, non-digital games, and television shows. In addition to a standalone form of entertainment, video games are often an expected facet of a marketing campaign for new major movie releases. Media licensing has become a two-way street, with video game characters and stories branching out into books and movies as well. As video gaming has spread throughout the world, the culture of video gaming has spawned over two dozen magazines and countless Web sites, as well as industry conventions, professional competitions, and a cottage industry in online "farming" of in-game items in massive multiplayer online role-playing games (MMORPGs).

Although some observers have divided the history of video games into seven, nine, or even 14 different phases, many of these can be collapsed into just a few broader eras, as illustrated in Figure

16.2, each containing a variety of significant milestones. Most histories of video games focus on the hardware requirements for the games, which frequently drove where and how the games were played. However, it is equally possible to divide the history of games by the advances in software (and changes in the style of gameplay), the diffusion of games among the population (and the changes in the playing audience), or the increases in economic power wielded by video games, measured by the other industries overtaken through the years. Regardless of the chosen path, as the history of video games developed, however, it became increasingly fragmented into specialty niches.

Most industry observers describe the current generation of home gaming consoles as the seventh generation since the release of the first-generation Magnavox Odyssey. Handheld consoles are often said to be on their fourth generation. No one has yet attempted to assign "generations" to computer gaming software, in large part because console "generations" are hardware-based and released in specific waves, while computer hardware is continually evolving, and major computer milestones

are the releases of new operating systems (Windows Vista, Mac OS X, etc).

The early years of video gaming were marked by small hobby programs, many developed on large university and corporate mainframes. Willy Higenbotham, a nuclear physicist with the Department of Energy, had experimented with a simple tennis game for which he had developed a rudimentary analog computer (Anderson, 1983). A team of designers under Ralph Baer developed a variety of video game projects for the Department of Defense in the mid-1960s, eventually resulting in a hockey game, which left their military sponsors nonplussed (Hart, 1996). Baer also led another team that developed *Chase*, the first video game credited with the ability to display on a standard television set. In the early 1960s, *SpaceWar* was also popular among the graduate students at MIT and inspired other work at the Pentagon. Although many different treatises have been written arguing over the invention of the video game, it is still unclear how much, if at all, any of the early video game pioneers even knew of each others' work; it is completely unknown if they drew any inspiration from each other.

Figure 16.2
Video Game Chronology

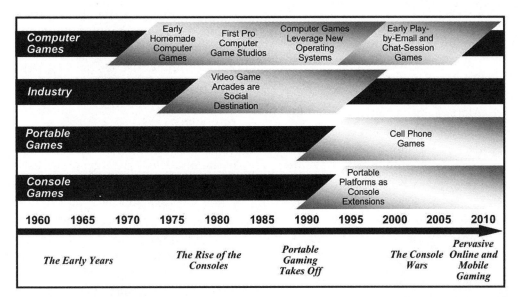

Source: Guillory (2008)

In the early 1970s, dedicated gaming consoles began to appear, starting with the Magnavox Odyssey in 1972. Built on switches, rather than a microprocessor, the Odyssey included a variety of "analog" components to be used in playing the video portions of the game, such as dice, play money, and plastic overlays for a common touchpad. The first home video game product built on a microprocessor was a home version of the popular coin-operated *Pong* game from Nolan Bushnell's Atari. Although it contained only one game, *Pong*, hard-coded into the set, it would be a popular product until the introduction of a console that could play multiple games by swapping out software (Hart, 1996).

The second generation of video gaming began approximately in 1977 with the rise of consoles. This generation was marked by the integration of home videogaming with other media licenses, whether tie-ins with popular movies such as *E.T. The Extra-Terrestrial* and *Raiders of the Lost Ark*, or 'ports' (adaptations) of popular arcade games, such as *Pac-Man*, *Defender*, or *Missile Command*. The Atari 2600 led the market for home video game sales, in which consumers would purchase a standard console and insert cartridges to play different games. While Colecovision and Intellivision (two other consoles) were popular in the market, nothing could compare with the market power wielded by Atari (which was eventually purchased by Warner Communications) from 1977 to 1982, during which an estimated $4 billion of Atari products were sold (Kent, 2001). Atari's success also led to the formation of Activision, a software company founded by disgruntled Atari game programmers. Activision became the first major game studio that designed their games exclusively for other companies' consoles, thus separating the games and consoles for the first time. However, during this time period, business deals began to evolve that tied certain media licenses to specific platforms, establishing several precedents in exclusivity among game 'families' and the console systems.

After a brief downturn in the market from 1981 to 1984, mostly as a result of business blunders by Atari, home video game consoles began a resurgence. Triggered by the launch of the Sega Master System in the mid-1980s and the Nintendo Entertainment System (NES) shortly thereafter, home video game sales continued to climb for both the games and the hardware needed to play them. The inclusion of 8-bit processors closed the gap between the performance of large standalone arcade machines and the smaller home consoles with multiple games and signaled the start of the decline of the video game arcade as a game-playing destination. By 1987, the NES was the best-selling toy in the United States (Smith, 1999). The NES also continued the platform-specific media tie-ins with their repeated use of the character "Mario"—first made popular in the *Donkey Kong* arcade game—and leveraged that character into a burgeoning empire that today spans over 50 titles.

During this time, video games also began to appear in popular culture not as mere accessories to the characters, but as central plots around which the stories were built. *Tron* (1982), *War Games* (1983), and *The Last Starfighter* (1984) all brought video gaming into a central role in their respective movie plots.

Computer games were also developing alongside video game consoles. Catering to a smaller market, computer games were seen as an add-on to hardware already in the home, rather than the primary reason for purchasing a home computer system. However, the ability to write programs for home computers enabled consumers to also become game designers and share their creations with other computer users. Thus, a generation of schoolkids grew up learning to program games on Commodore PET, Atari 800, and Apple II home computers.

The commercial success of the Commodore 64 in the mid-1980s gave game publishers a color system for their games, and the Apple Macintosh's point-and-click interface allowed designers to incorporate the standard system hardware into their game designs, without requiring add-on joysticks or other special controllers. Where console games were almost exclusively graphics-oriented, early computer games included a significant number of text-based adventure games, such as *Zork* and *Bard's Tale*, and a large number of military-themed board games converted for play on the computer by companies such as SSI (Falk, 2004). In 1988, the first of several TSR-licensed games for *Dungeons & Dragons* appeared, and SSI's profile continued to grow. Other prominent early computer game publishers included Sierra, Broderbund, and Infocom, among others. Nevertheless, home computer game sales continued to lag behind console game sales, in large part because of the comparatively high cost and limited penetration of the hardware. Additionally, video games were still seen as an 'add-on' to a primary media channel (television, computer, etc.) and had not yet developed their own market channel through which to distribute titles. Thus computer games tended to be sold where other computer software was sold, and consoles (and their supporting games) were typically found in home electronics stores, alongside television sets.

With video games ensconced in U.S. and Japanese households and expanding worldwide, it was only a matter of time before portable consoles began to rival the home siblings in quality and sophistication, and thus began the third phase in the history of video games.

Portable video games proliferated in the consumer marketplace beginning in the early 1980s. However, early handhelds were characterized by very rudimentary graphics used for one game in each handheld. In fact, "rudimentary" may even be generous in describing the graphics—the early Mattel handheld *Electronic Football* game starred several small red "blips" on a one-inch-by-three-inch screen in which the game player's avatar on the screen was distinguished only by the brightness of the blip.

Atari released the Lynx handheld game system in 1987. Despite its color graphics and relatively high-speed processor, tepid support from Atari and third-party developers resulted in its eventual demise. In 1989, Nintendo released Game Boy, a portable system whose controls mimicked the NES. With its low cost and stable of well-known titles ported from the main NES, the Game Boy became a major force in video game sales (Stahl, 2003). Although technically inferior to the Lynx—black-and-white graphics, dull display, and a slower

processor—the vast number of Nintendo titles for the Game Boy provided a major leg up on other handheld systems, as audiences were already familiar and comfortable with Nintendo as a game company. Sega's Gamegear followed within a year. Like the Lynx before it, superior graphics were not enough to overcome Nintendo's catalog of software titles or the head start in the market the Game Boy already had. By the mid-1990s, most families that owned a home game console also owned a handheld, often from the same company.

Although the portable revolution had not (yet) migrated to computer gaming, it was hardware limitations, rather than game design, that prevented the integration of computer games into portable systems. The release of the Palm series of handheld computers (Hormby, 2007) gave game designers a new platform on which they could develop that was not tied to any particular company. This early step toward handheld computing would include early steps toward handheld computer gaming.

The third and fourth generations of video game history begin to overlap as the console wars included the handheld products of various console manufacturers, coinciding with the release of Windows 95 for Intel-powered PC computers, which gave game designers a variety of stable platforms on which to program their games. The console wars of the late 1990s have continued to today, with independent game design studios developing their products across a variety of platforms.

As Nintendo began to force Sega out of the console market in the mid-1990s, another consumer electronics giant, Sony, was preparing to enter the market. With the launch of the PlayStation in 1995, Sony plunged into the video game platform market. Nintendo maintained a close hold on the titles it would approve for development on its system, attempting to position itself primarily as a "family" entertainment system. Sony developers, however, had the ability to pursue more mature content, and their stable of titles included several whose graphics, stories, and themes were clearly intended for the 30-year-old adults who began playing video games in 1980, rather than 13-year-old kids (Stahl, 2003). Sony and Nintendo (and to a lesser extent,

Sega) continued their game of one-upmanship with their improvements in hardware over the next several years.

As the graphical processing power of consoles increased, and games gained greater notoriety in the press as they pushed the edges of storytelling and explicit graphics, the Interactive Digital Software Association finally caved to public pressure and instituted a rating system for games, which sought to better inform consumers about the target ages for games, as well as the reasons for the ratings. The ISDA became the ESA in 2004 (ESRB, 2009), and the ratings for video games have become a standard feature of every game, both console and computer. More granular than movie ratings, video games ratings break down into more than a half-dozen age categories and more than twenty content descriptors. Controversies have (predictably) ensued; unlike movies, video games can easily incorporate alternate, hidden, or add-on content which might alter their ratings. Among the most famous ratings controversies was the "Hot Coffee" content in *Grand Theft Auto*, in which downloaded patches opened up sexually explicit and violent content (BBC, 2005).

By early 2001, Sega admitted defeat in the hardware arena and focused instead on software. The next salvo in the platform wars was about to be launched by Microsoft, which debuted the Xbox in late 2001. With built-in networking and a large hard drive, Microsoft's Xbox began to blur the lines between computer video gaming and platform-based video gaming. Additionally, building their console on an Intel processor eased the transition for games from PC to Xbox, and many popular computer titles were easily moved onto the Xbox. Around the same time, Sony entered the handheld arena to challenge Nintendo's Game Boy dominance with the PSP: PlayStation Portable. Capable of playing games as well as watching movies and (with an adapter) having online access, the PSP was intended to show the limitations of the Game Boy series with its greater number of features. Although the platform wars continue today, every one of them supports networked gaming, the cusp of the fifth generation of video gaming.

With high-speed data networks proliferating throughout North America, Japan, Korea, Western Europe, and (to a lesser extent) China and Southeast Asia, online gameplay has become a major attraction to many video gamers, especially through MMORPGs. These pervasive worlds host shared versions of a variety of different games, including sports, military, and sci-fi and fantasy games. MMORPGs are most commonly accessed through computer platforms rather than game consoles. Since its launch in 2004, *World of Warcraft* has grown to exceed 10 million simultaneous subscribers at any one time, though their rate of subscriber turnover continues to be high. MMORPGs have highly-developed in-game economies, and those economies have begun to spill over into the "real world." websites and online classified listings offer game-world items, money, and characters for sale to players seeking an edge in the game but are reluctant to sacrifice the time to earn the rewards themselves. Fans' reactions have not been universally positive to these developments, and some have started petitions to ban such behavior from the games (Burstein, 2008). MMORPGs were among the first widespread systems that allowed a distributed user base to share a single game, rather than forcing a physical co-location on the participants to play together.

Wireless networking has also extended the ability to participate in online-based games to handhelds, both dedicated to gaming (Nintendo DS) and consumer-oriented (personal digital assistants and cell phones). Moreover, many software-specific companies have designed their online game servers such that the players' platforms are irrelevant, and thus gamers playing on an Xbox might compete against other gamers online who are using PCs.

The 2006 release of Nintendo's Wii game console drew a new audience by attracting large numbers of older users to the motion-based games enabled by the Wii's motion-sensitive remote. Not long after its release, the Wii began to appear on the evening network news as a new activity in senior citizens homes and in stories about children and grandparents sharing the game (Potter, 2008). Although graphically inferior to the Xbox or PS3, the

Wii has developed an audience of players who had never tried video gaming before.

Recent Developments

By some estimates, video games may be in their seventh, tenth, or twelfth generation. Those generations have been collapsed into five for this chapter: the early years, the rise of the consoles and computer games, portable gaming, the console wars, and pervasive online gaming. Computer gaming roughly followed this same trajectory, although the introduction of portable computer gaming lags behind for hardware reasons. While the fourth generation described above is still ongoing, it seems as though the market has stabilized in that the three current major players in the console market (Nintendo, Microsoft, and Sony) appear likely to remain in the market for the long term. Similarly, with three major computer platforms (Windows, Macintosh, and UNIX/ Linux), computer gamers are expected to have a variety of choices for the foreseeable future as well.

The availability of broadband connections has resulted in many software companies selling games online directly to the consumer (especially for computer gaming), with manuals and other play aids available as printable files for those players who wish to do so. Steam, from Valve Corporation, is a download site that boasts over 25 million accounts (Steam, 2010) and delivers downloadable games directly to computer platforms. Most computer game manufacturers sell virtually every title as a download directly to their customers either directly or through online stores. These sales are *not* simply mail-orders of physical copies, but actual direct-to-PC downloads. This direct-to-consumer sales route has reduced the dependence on local computer software stores for computer games; these stores have reacted by stocking more console games.

Similarly, with the ability of consoles to hook into in-home data networks (either by Ethernet or wirelessly), direct-to-console downloads are also growing in popularity, as storefronts such as the Xbox Live Arcade sell digital-only copies of games that are stored directly on the console's hard drive. This low-overhead market channel has allowed low-cost games to proliferate, as they eschew any physical costs (packaging, disks, etc.), transportation costs (no shipping), or retail support costs (no markup by a brick-and-mortar middleman).

The networking of consoles has also started a migration of those consoles away from pure video gaming systems, and into more robust media hubs that can download (or stream) other non-game content. Netflix, a popular online movie rental business, is accessible on most consoles, enabling users to watch movies and television shows on-demand through their consoles. Additionally, consoles are now starting to ship with DVD and Blu-ray software built in, which allows one device to serve multiple purposes when connected to a user's television.

Social Gaming— Your Friends Help You Play

With the proliferation of social networking sites over the past decade, from MySpace to Facebook to Google+ and others, software companies and game designers have developed a new twist on video gaming that not only encourages social interaction, but very nearly *requires* it for the players to fully experience the games. Games such as *Farmville* and *Mafia Wars* on Facebook allow users to not only share their performance metrics online, they also allow users to invite their friends to join the game, and provide rewards to those recruiters. Additionally, players may help each other during the game by lending resources when online.

These sorts of persistent engagements have resulted in several effects. First, the lack of detailed commitment to learning rules, commands, or interfaces has resulted in very high rates of adoption of the games. Zynga Games, the largest of the social gaming developers/publishers, boasts over 65 million daily players. In comparison, *World of Warcraft* hovers at just over 10 million registered players at any one time, and Xbox Live has approximately 20 million users (Onlineschools.org, 2012). Second, many of the games have been designed with time-lapse effects that require the users to return to them after certain time intervals, resulting in continual engagement with the games.

Most importantly, though, is the business model through which many of these social games generate revenue. Players may play freely, but with time-lapse limitations, and certain in-game purchasing limits, attaining the highest-status rewards within the game (items for decorating a virtual restaurant, or virtual farm equipment, or just virtual cash for use with other online goods) can be extremely challenging. Social gaming companies offer these extensions within their games to players in exchange for real currency (Buckman, 2009). These monetary transactions have resulted in significant revenues for very small startups since 2005. Within the game design industry, however, there have been significant criticisms of social games as merely a time-lapse collection of clicks, and many videogame creators have come down starkly on either side of this debate (Tanz, 2012).

Another variation on the social gaming theme is the delivery of certain rules-light games through mobile platforms. Games such as *Words With Friends* include mobile clients accessible through smartphones that allow players to interact with other live players, in real time, from their phones. These smartphone games, sold through a mobile phone app infrastructure that has been created and diffused since 2006, are marked by incredibly high sales volumes, allowing even very inexpensive games (as low as 99¢) to gross tens of millions of dollars.

Regulatory Environment— Continuing Legislative Efforts to "Protect the Children"

The legislative landscape continues to be hostile to video games, continuing to treat them as a child-oriented medium as though the average videogame player was ten years old. However, prospective laws, once challenged in the courts, have continually been struck down. In 2009, the Ninth Circuit Court upheld a ruling that a California law was too restrictive and violated free speech rights (Walters, 2010). The law restricted the sale of violent videogames to minors. In 2011, the Supreme Court of the United States also upheld this ruling (Savage, 2011). Since that ruling, no new major challenges to videogame sales have arisen in the United States.

Console-Based Music Games— Better Than Karaoke!

Beginning with the release of *Guitar Hero* in 2005, console-based music games have skyrocketed from 'non-existent' to among the most popular games available. Based on a late-90s Japanese game called *GuitarFreaks*, *Guitar Hero* featured a guitar-shaped controller that was used to interact with an on-screen scroll of notes. Since the release of the original *Guitar Hero*, a competing franchise (*Rock Band*) has been introduced, as well as controllers for drums and keyboards and integration of vocals for both series of games. The musical videogame genre was also marked by the release of multiple versions branded with particular artists, such as The Beatles (*Rock Band*), Aerosmith (*Guitar Hero*), and Metallica (*Guitar Hero*). Support for the musical videogame genre also includes downloadable music tracks to add to the games. *Rock Band* downloads exceeded 2 million within the first 8 weeks of their availability (Bruno, 2008).

However, since early 2011, instrument-based games have fallen off significantly in popularity. Drops in sales, as well as higher hardware costs for manufacturing components, reduced the profitability of music-based games. This decline led, in turn, to massive layoffs across several companies with music-based games, and the announcement that Activision would be discontinuing the *Guitar Hero* franchise (Kaiser, 2011).

The drop-off in musical-imitation games did not kill the marketplace for music-interaction games, however. Numerous dance-oriented franchises have skyrocketed in popularity, with *Just Dance 2* and *3* both among the best-selling games of 2011 (see figure 16.3). Leveraging the variety of motion-based game controllers to register a user's "dance moves" these games have moved dance games beyond simple footpads registering steps.

Pervasive Mobile Gaming

With the increase in computing power available in handsets, mobile gaming has split along two lines. First, Nintendo and Sony both have handheld game platforms with wireless capability built in, allowing for head-to-head gameplay with other nearby systems, as well as shared gameplay through an Internet connection, where available. Platforms such as Nintendo's DS line and Sony's PSP machines are capable of establishing local networks for head-to-head gaming without any wireless service.

In addition, mobile phone handsets have sufficient computing power to allow for a variety of gaming. Nokia's N-Gage phone, while critically panned, showed that handheld multipurpose systems—such as a mobile smartphone—possessed sufficient memory and processor speed for true gaming (Carnoy, 2006). Apple's App Store, and the subsequent similar stores from Google (for the Android OS) and Microsoft (for the Windows Phone OS), have allowed the proliferation of huge numbers of "casual games" with simple, intuitive interfaces and playtimes measured in minutes rather than hours.

Additionally, the continued improvement of mobile phone hardware (larger screens, greater resolution, faster processors, accelerometers) has made the devices far more attractive to gamemakers. For consumers, the ability to have their games in-hand regardless of location, *without* an additional device, has proven quite popular. Sales of games for mobile phones have jumped dramatically over the past several years, with the loss of sales being felt primarily by the handheld "console" manufacturers—Sony and Nintendo (Farago, 2011).

Nintendo's latest addition to their mobile gaming family is the Nintendo 3DS. Building on the familiar two-screen platform of the DS, the 3DS incorporates a display that allows pixels to be 'aimed' at the player's eyes, in effect splitting the visual stimulus into two channels for the left and right eyes. This allows the game screen to project a 3-D–like image without requiring any special glasses or equipment for the player. Given the relatively short distances between handheld screens and the player's eyes (fewer than three feet), this sort of 'pixel aiming' can be used with single-player platforms. To date, no manufacturer has successfully developed a similar system for multi-player views, or larger displays like televisions.

In 2012 Sony introduced the PlayStation Vita. This handheld device incorporates a plethora of new technologies including 3G wireless and Wi-Fi (through AT&T), GPS, motion sensors, a front touch screen and rear touch pad, front and back cameras, and a stunning OLED display (PlayStation, 2012). It sounds like a fully equipped handheld gaming console, but these features could also describe a smartphone.

Broadband-Enabled Downloads for Consoles

In a manner similar to the Steam download service, console manufacturers have integrated online participation and downloadable content through their consoles. Not only can networks of players compete cooperatively or head-to-head around the world, but broadband networking has enabled the push of content through storefronts including the Xbox Live Marketplace and the Nintendo Wii Virtual Console.

Xbox Live Marketplace includes not only games, but movies from major studios. Nintendo's Virtual Console has seen competition from WiiWare (Chan, 2010) for the download market on the Wii consoles. Sony's PlayStation network is integrating connections to popular online destinations such as Facebook (Thorpe, 2009) and Netflix (Kennedy, 2009), further blurring the delivery lines between computers and other Internet-enabled devices.

Figure 16.3
TOP-SELLING VIDEO GAMES OF 2011

Title (Platforms)	Rank	Publisher
Call of Duty: Modern Warfare 3 (360, PS3, Wii, PC)	1	Activision Blizzard
Just Dance 3 (Wii, 360, PS3)	2	Ubisoft
Elder Scrolls V: Skyrim (360, PS3, PC)	3	Bethesda Softworks
Battlefield 3 (360, PS3, PC)	4	Electronic Arts
Madden NFL 12 (360, PS3, Wii, PSP, PS2)	5	Electronic Arts
Call of Duty: Black Ops (360, PS3, Wii, NDS, PC)	6	Activision Blizzard
Batman: Arkham City (360, PS3, PC)	7	Warner Bros. Interactive
Gears of War 3 (360)	8	Microsoft
Just Dance 2 (Wii)	9	Ubisoft
Assassin's Creed: Revelations (360, PS3, PC)	10	Ubisoft

Source: NPD Group

Current Status

No new platforms have been released since late 2006, although the three major platforms have all received upgrades to their current configurations. While some might argue that Microsoft's Kinect system is a new console, the ability to add the Kinect peripheral to existing Xbox hardware refutes this idea. In 2011, Nintendo announced a successor to the Wii called the Wii U, which is supposed to have a tablet-style controller (with touch screen) and a faster processor. The Wii U is not projected to hit the market until late 2012, and significant changes could occur before the release date.

Because consoles are primarily dependent on their software to maintain customer interest, constant hardware upgrades may not be as necessary, and in fact might be considered detrimental to sales if the consoles are not backward-compatible with older games in the same product family. Computer-based games are not as dependent on regular hardware updates, and software continues to appear daily for computer-based videogamers.

In 2011, US sales of video games totaled slightly more than $17 billion, of which approximately $5.5 billion were console sales (Matthews, 2012). Given the multi-function nature of desktop and laptop computers, counting the hardware for computer game sales makes little sense. While console sales have typically fueled a significant end-of-year uptick in sales during the holiday seasons, 2011 saw the opposite trend, as consumers had no significant new consoles to purchase, with the last major release of console having been over five years earlier.

"Gamer parents" will continue to be a phenomenon of interest, at least until sufficient numbers of the media and legislative leadership are themselves replaced by longtime gamers. Often used as a buttress against the argument that "video games are for kids," gamer parents are those game players that grew up with a game console in their households and are now raising their own children with consoles. The average game player is 37 years old and has been playing for over 12 years (ESA, 2012). Although legislative action has often been touted as a remedy for inhibiting access to video games that legislators feel is inappropriate, gamer parents have repeatedly noted that they are intimately familiar with video games and capable of making informed choices about their children's access to video games. In addition, gamer parents tend to take the lead in game purchases for their households, thus making them a valuable target for the corporate marketing machines. In fact, 91% of all game players under age 18 note that their parents are present when they purchase or rent their games (ESA, 2012). By way of comparison to the stereotype of teenaged videogamers, a 10-year-old child who started playing videogames at home on an Atari 2600 console in 1982 is today a 40-year-old gamer with 30 years of videogaming experience.

As noted above, legislative action against video games continues in multiple venues. Not every legislative action is opposed by industry trade groups, however. The Entertainment Software Association has consistently supported measures designed to prohibit access to sexually explicit games by minors, as well as supporting legislation that increases access to ratings information for consumers (Walters, 2008). However, laws intended to severely limit games access to a large segment of the population have yet to stand up to judicial scrutiny.

Factors to Watch

Industry-watchers have looked to Microsoft for almost half of a decade in anticipation of an expected foray into mobile, handheld gaming to compete with platforms from Nintendo (Game Boy / DS series) and Sony (PSP). An expected handheld product from 2006 turned out to be the Zune music player and, as of 2011, Microsoft has not yet announced a mobile gaming device, and no credible rumors seem to exist to the contrary. Even discussions with Microsoft insiders clearly leave the impression the Microsoft is focused on the Windows Phone mobile platform, eschewing any dedicated game-playing system.

While the industry was watching Microsoft in anticipation of a yet-to-appear handheld device, Apple's iPhone has stormed forward to snag a significant share of the mobile gaming marketplace. In fact while iOS and Android game sales have dominated over half of the mobile gaming market, Nintendo's DS has lost over half of its market share (Farago, 2011). Moreover, the introduction of the iPad has also contributed to the huge increase in iOS game sales, as the underlying OS, as well as the distribution channels, are shared with the iPhone. Tablet devices are now a significant factor in videogaming, especially for adaptations of popular

board games and social games played across networks.

Microsoft's Kinect for Xbox 360 has expanded on the motion-based gaming pioneered by Nintendo's Wii. Unlike the Wii and the PlayStation Move, which rely upon a remote control, Microsoft's Kinect relies on a camera that recognizes gestures, facial features, and body motion (Archibald, 2009). The ability to recognize motion will free game-players from at least part of the needed hardware for gameplay.

Nintendo has moved on beyond motion-sensitive controllers to incorporate new technologies into their handheld DS line, to varying degrees of success. While sales were flat for the DSi (with the digital camera), the 3DS that allowed viewing of 3-D images without any special glasses (Tabucki, 2010) was a qualified success. Nevertheless, it has not been enough to rescue Nintendo's plummeting market share.

The growth in the numbers of women playing video games is expected to continue to accelerate. 40% of the game-playing public are women, a 2% increase from 2008; adult women represent a greater share of the market (34%) than young males under 17 (18%) (ESA, 2012). The online titles favored by women are dependent not only on the continued diffusion of the software, but also on the continued diffusion of the high-speed Internet access needed to enable the online environment.

Government funding of new projects with video game developers will also continue as sponsors search for projects applicable to their specific fields. The U.S. Army's TCM-Gaming office, specifically designed to leverage video game technology for training purposes (Peck, 2007), has run into challenges with unifying the acquisition and development of game-based training tools across the Army enterprise. Nevertheless, government-focused events, such as the Interservice/Industry Training, Simulation and Education Conference (I/ITSEC) bring in over 20,000 attendees (IITSEC, 2012). With the continuing reduction in training budgets across the Department of Defense, military training organizations will continue to seek lower-cost alternatives to fielding large numbers of soldiers for maneuver exercises (Nichols, 2012). Many of these projects have also found commercial homes, such as *ARM-A*, the civilian version of the military simulator *VBS-2*. Additionally, some videogame projects have migrated in the opposite direction, with games such as *Close Combat* being adopted by the US Marine Corps. However, controversy continues to boil around military-themed games that depict events that seem too similar to current operations (Suellentrop, 2010).

Despite years of video game legislation being rejected by the courts, legislators will continue to react to media coverage of parental concern about video game content. Overwhelming demographic data shows that video gamers are typically adults, and 25% of them are over age 50. Nonetheless, many news outlets and legislators continue to view video games as toys for kids, and make no distinction in subject matter between mature-themed games and games clearly targeted at children. Legislative efforts are further complicated by legal precedents being established in cases about online

distribution of content, which is increasingly relevant as Internet-enabled consoles are connected to broadband networks.

All three major consoles and many computer games allow for collaborative online play. Expect to see two developments in this area. First, as game titles proliferate across platforms, expect to see more games capable of sharing an online game across those platforms, allowing a player on the Xbox to match up against an opponent on a PC system, as both players communicate through a common back-end server. Second, many of these online systems, such as the Xbox Live, already allow voice conversations during the game through a voice over Internet protocol system. (VoIP is discussed in more detail in Chapter 20.) As more digital cameras are incorporated into consoles, either as an integrated component or an aftermarket peripheral, expect these services to start offering some form of videoconferencing, especially for players involved in games such as chess, poker, or other "tabletop" games being played on a digital system.

 Sustainability

The video game industry seems to have a bi-polar approach to sustainability. On one hand, numerous games exist to promote sustainability, environmentalism, and Earth-friendly action. On the other hand, consoles and computers are full of dangerous metals, extracted in way profoundly unfriendly to the environment, and rarely recycled.

Columbite-tantalite, a rare mineral mined in conflicted areas of Africa (Vick, 2001), is used in the manufacture of many electronics components, including game consoles. Dubbed the "PlayStation War" by some media outlets (Peckham, 2008), Congo's conflict showed that the demand for electronic components had serious environmental ramifications.

Meanwhile, video games have been used by different organizations to capture the attention of younger game players in an attempt to instill environmental lessons in the audience. Sponsored by organizations including the UN and IBM, these games have gained some wide attention, with IBM's *PowerUp* being selected as the official game of the Earth Day Network in 2008 (Libby, 2009).

Finally, more attention is now being drawn to video game consoles and computers as "vampire devices" that continue to drain power even when not in use. Comparisons of the three most popular consoles show that the Wii uses dramatically less power than either the Xbox or PS3, but that all of them continue to draw power even in standby mode (Troast, 2009). Similarly, the rate of recycling of consoles and their related peripherals continues to lag compared to other industries, and is potentially more damaging to the environment than other household discards due to the high quantity of toxic metals used in the hardware. Greenpeace has ranked Nintendo and Microsoft as two of the worst manufacturers of electronic components (Greenpeace, 2010).

Sustainability in the video game industry remains elusive at best, and outright ignored at worst. Although there have been forays by individual game companies into environmentalism in the form of consciousness-raising games, the manufacturing processes and power consumption of video game consoles continue to pose significant environmental challenges.

Bibliography

Archibald, A. (2009). Project Natal 101. *Seattle Post-Intelligencer*. Retrieved from
http://blog.seattlepi.com/digitaljoystick/archives/169993.asp

Anderson, J. (1983). Who really invented the video game. *Creative Computing Video & Arcade Games 1* (1), 8. Retrieved
from http://www.atarimagazines.com/cva/v1n1/inventedgames.php.

BBC. (2005). Hidden sex scenes hit GTA rating. *BBC News*. Retrieved from
http://news.bbc.co.uk/2/hi/technology/4702737.stm

Bruno, A. (2008). *Rock Band, Guitar Hero* drive digital song sales. *Reuters*. Retrieved from
http://www.reuters.com/article/idUSN1934632220080120

Buckman, R. (2009). Zynga's Gaming Gamble. *Forbes*. 16 November 2009. Retrieved from
http://www.forbes.com/forbes/2009/1116/revolutionaries-technology-social-gaming-farmville-facebook-zynga.html

Burstein, J. (2008). Video game fan asks court to ban real sloth and greed from *World of Warcraft*. *Boston Herald*. Retrieved
from http://www.bostonherald.com/business/technology/general/view.bg?articleid= 1086549.

Carnoy, D. (2006). Nokia N-Gage QD. *C/NET News*. Retrieved from http://reviews.cnet.com/cell-phones/nokia-n-gage-qd/4505-6454_7-30841888.html.

Chan, T. (2010). WiiWare market grows to nearly $60M USD in 2009. *Nintendo Life*. Retrieved from
http://www.nintendolife.com/news/2010/02/wiiware_market_grows_to_nearly_usd60m_usd_in_2009

Entertainment Software Association. (2012). *Industry Facts*. Retrieved from http://www.theesa.com/facts/index.asp

Entertainment Software Rating Board. (2009). *Chronology of ESRB Events*. Retrieved from
http://www.esrb.org/about/chronology.jsp

Falk, H. (2004). *Gaming Obsession Throughout Computer History Association*. Retrieved from
http://gotcha.classicgaming.gamespy.com.

Greenpeace. (2010). How the companies line up. *Guide to Greener Electronics*. Retrieved from
http://www.greenpeace.org/international/en/campaigns/toxics/electronics/how-the-companies-line-up/

Farago, P. (2011). Is it game over for Nintendo DS and Sony PSP?. *Flurry Blog*. Retrieved from
http://blog.flurry.com/bid/77424/Is-it-Game-Over-for-Nintendo-DS-and-Sony-PSP

Hart, S. (1996). A brief history of home video games. *Geekcomix*. Retrieved from http://geekcomix.com/vgh/

Hormby, T. (2007). History of Handspring and the Treo (Part III). *Silicon User*. Retrieved from
http://siliconuser.com/?q=node/19.

IITSEC. (2012). I/ITSEC statistics. IITSEC.org. Retrieved from
http://www.iitsec.org/about/Pages/HighlightsFromLastIITSEC.aspx

Kaiser, T. (2011). Activision kills Guitar Hero, confirms company layoffs. *Daily Tech*. Retrieved from
http://www.dailytech.com/Activision+Kills+Guitar+Hero+Confirms+Company+Layoffs/article20879.htm

Kennedy, S. (2009). Netflix Officially Coming to PS3. *1up.com*. Retrieved from
http://www.1up.com/do/newsStory?cId=3176634

Kent, S. (2001). *The ultimate history of video games: From Pong to Pokemon—The story behind the craze that touched our lives and changed the world*. New York: Patterson Press.

Libby, B .(2009). Sustainability-themed computer games come to the classroom. *Edutopia*. Retrieved from
http://www.edutopia.org/environment-sustainability-computer-games

Linde, A. (2008). PC games 14% of 2007 retail games sales; World of Warcraft and Sims top PC sales charts. *ShackNews*. Retrieved from http://www.shacknews.com/onearticle.x/50939.

Matthews, M. (2012). NPD: Behind the numbers of 2011. *Gamasutra*. Retrieved from
http://gamasutra.com/view/news/39669/NPD_Behind_the_numbers_of_2011.php

Nichols, P. (2012). Personal communication with the author.

NPD Group / Riley, D. (2012). Annual 2011 Top 10 Games. Personal correspondence with author.

Onlineschools.org. (2012). The rise of social gaming. Retrieved from http://www.onlineschools.org/blog/social-gaming/.

Peck, M. (2007). Constructive progress. *TSJOnline.com*. Retrieved from http://www.tsjonline.com/ story.php?F=3115940.

Peckham, M. (2008). Did rare metallic ore fuel African "PlayStation War"? *PCWorld*. Retrieved from
http://blogs.pcworld.com/gameon/archives/007340.html

PlayStation (2012). PlayStation Vita system features. Retrieved from http://us.playstation.com/psvita/features/

Potter, N. (2008). Game on: A fourth of video game players are over 50. *ABC News*. Retrieved from http://abcnews.go.com/WN/Story?id=4132153.

Savage, D. (2011). Supreme Court strikes down California video game law. *Los Angeles Times*. Retrieved from http://articles.latimes.com/2011/jun/28/nation/la-na-0628-court-violent-video-20110628

Schramm, M. (2008). EA Mobile prez: iPhone is hurting mobile game development. *TUAW.com*. Retrieved from http://www.tuaw.com/2008/01/08/ea-mobile-prez-iphone-is-hurting-mobile-game-development/.

Smith, B. (1999). Read about the following companies: Nintendo, Sego, Sony. *University of Florida Interactive Media Lab*. Retrieved from http://iml.jou.ufl.edu/projects/Fall99/SmithBrian/aboutcompany.html.

Stahl, T. (2003). Chronology of the history of videogames. *The History of Computing Project*. Retrieved from http://www.thocp.net/software/games/games.htm.

Steam (2010). Steam realizes extraordinary growth in 2009. Press release retrieved from http://store.steampowered.com/news/3390/

Stohr (2010). Violent video game law gets top U.S. court hearing. *Bloomberg BusinessWeek*. Retrieved from http://www.businessweek.com/news/2010-04-26/violent-video-game-law-gets-top-u-s-court-hearing-update1-.html

Suellentrop, C. (2010). War games. *New York Times Magazine*. September 12, 2010. Pg 62.

Tabucki, H. (2010). Nintendo to make 3-D version of its DS handheld game. *New York Times*. March 23, 2010.

Tanz, J. (2012). The curse of cow clicker. *WIRED*. January 2012. Pg 98-101.

Techweb. (2010). COD Black Ops crosses $1 Billion Mark. *TECHWEB*. December 22, 2010. Retrieved from LexisNexis.

Thorpe, J. (2009). PlayStation 3 Firmware (v3.10) Update Preview. *Playstation.blog*. Retrieved from http://blog.eu.playstation.com/2009/11/17/playstation-3-firmware-v3-10-update-preview/

Thorsen, T (2009). Modern Warfare 2 Sells 4.7 million in 24 hours. *GameSpot*. Retrieved from http://www.gamespot.com/news/6239789.html

Troast, P. (2009). Vampire power check: Comparing the energy use of Xbox and Wii. *Energy Circle*. Retrieved from http://www.energycircle.com/blog/2009/12/29/vampire-power-check-comparing-energy-use-xbox-and-wii

Vick, K. (2001). Vital ore fuels Congo's war. *Washington Post*. March 19, 2001, Pg A01

Wai-Leng, L. (2007, November 16). MDA lifts ban on game with same-sex love scene. *The Straits Times*. Retrieved from http://www.straitstimes.com/Latest%2BNews/Singapore/STIStory_177468.html.

Walters, L. (2008). Another one bites the dust. *GameCensorship.com*. Retrieved from http://www.gamecensorship.com/okruling.html.

Walters, L. (2010). *GameCensorship.com*. Retrieved from http://www.gamecensorship.com/legislation.htm.

17

Home Video

Steven J. Dick, Ph.D.[*]

Why Study Home Video?

✦ Television has been in 98% of American homes since 1980.

✦ Home video revenues exceed network television revenues.

✦ Despite the national recession, Americans continue to spend on home video.

✦ 55% of American households purchased an HDTV between November 2007 and November 2011.

On June 12, 2009, full power television stations in the United States completed the transition to digital terrestrial broadcasting—the biggest change in television standards since the introduction of electronic television in 1945. While a substantial investment was required of both consumers and related industries, the change has produced viewing options unlike ever before.

Background

U.S. commercial television began in 1941 when the Federal Communications Commission (FCC) established a broadcasting standard. Over the years, different technologies have become more or less dominant in the delivery of home video. As this chapter considers each technology, issues of

[*] Media Industry Analyst, Modern Media Barn (Youngsville, Louisiana).The author wishes to gratefully acknowledge the support of the University of Louisiana at Lafayette and Cecil J. Picard Center for Child Development and Lifelong Learning.

compatibility, quality, and ease of use determine success or failure. As a means of organization, technologies will be divided into three general means of reception including: by air, by conduit, and by hand.

Reception by Air

Television stations licensed in 1941 were crude with low resolution pictures even compared to the 525-line, analog standard recently replaced. World War II stopped nearly all development, and only six stations were still broadcasting after the war. The FCC completely revised the transmission system after the war with the introduction of electronic encoding. Yet, post-war confusion led to more delays as the FCC was inundated with new applications, and it was clear that the original very high frequency (VHF) band would not provide enough space. After granting 107 licenses with 700 more to process, the FCC initiated a freeze on television applications in 1948 (Whitehouse, 1986). Initially, it was a short pause in processing, but the technical demands were daunting. Thus, from 1948 to 1952, there were only about 100 stations on the air nationally.

In 1952, the freeze was over, and the FCC formally accepted a plan to add ultra-high-frequency (UHF) television. Like VHF, UHF stations used 6 megahertz of bandwidth and encoded video using amplitude modulation (AM) and audio in frequency modulation (FM). However, UHF transmitted on a higher frequency requiring more electricity, existing television sets needed a second tuner for UHF, and new antennas were often needed. This put UHF stations in a second-class status that was almost impossible to overcome. It was not until 1965 that the FCC issued a *final* all-channel receiver law, forcing television manufacturers to include a second tuner for

UHF channels. Initially, television was broadcast in black-and-white. In 1953, color was added to the existing (luminance) signal. This meant that color television transmissions were still compatible with black-and-white televisions. This ability to be compatible with previous technology is called *reverse compatibility* and can be a major advantage in the adoption of a new technology.

Reception by Conduit

A combination of factors, including the public's interest in television, the FCC freeze on new stations, and the introduction of UHF television, created a market to augment television delivery. As discussed in **Chapter 7**, cable television's introduction in 1949 brought video into homes by wire conduit. At first, cable simply relayed over-the-air broadcast stations. In the 1970s, cable introduced a variety of new channels and expanded home video capability.

An analysis of FCC data reveals that a total of 105 national and regional programming networks started operation prior to 1992. The *Cable Consumer Protection and Competition Act of 1992* stimulated growth in multichannel services. By 2002, the number of program networks more than tripled to

344 with the biggest increase (111) between 1997 and 1999 (McDowell & Dick, 2003). From 1996 to 2005, the number of satellite-delivered programming networks increased from 145 to 565 (NCTA, 2007). Direct broadcast satelites (DBS) began to make serious inroads following the 1992 Cable Act. Then, the Telecommunications Act of 1996 also allowed telephone companies (telcos) to enter the market.

Today, fewer than 10% of U.S. households still receive television from traditional terrestrial broadcasting alone. Yet, traditional broadcast networks are still an essential part of the media landscape. The four top broadcast networks each still receive a weekly cumulative audience of 68% to 74% which is approximately double the top cable networks (Television Bureau of Adverting, 2011, See Figure 17.1).

For consumers, cable television introduced the separate set-top box. Initially, these allowed the cable companies to more efficiently transmit signals. However, they eliminated the need for external antenna and became one of the first external connections to the television. Today, cable companies can use the boxes to provide everything from video-on-demand to alarm services.

Figure 17.1

Weekly Cumulative Audience Reach For Top Broadcast and Cable Networks

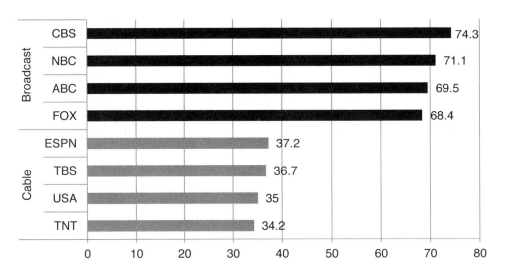

Source: TVB.org

Reception by Hand

At first, television had to be either live or on film. In 1956, Ampex developed videotape for the broadcast industry. These first machines were about the size of a double home refrigerator, used two inch wide videotape, and noisy vacuum systems held the tape in place. An hour long tape could weigh 30 pounds.

Sony introduced an open reel videotape recorder for the home in 1966. Open reel tape players were expensive and required the user to thread the tape through the mechanism. In 1969, Sony then developed the more user-friendly videocassette recorder (VCR), which eliminated the need to thread the tape through the machine. The first VCRs were expensive, had little to no content, and had a short recording time.

1977 saw the introduction of practical VCRs with two competing standards. Sony debuted the Betamax, and JVC the VHS. By 1982, a full-blown price and technology war existed between the two formats, and by 1986, 40% of U.S. homes had VCRs. Video distributers reluctantly distributed content in both formats until VHS eventually won the standard for the most homes and Betamax owners were left with incompatible machines.

VCRs gave consumers new power for on-demand programming through video rental stores or over-the-air recording. This record capability became the subject of a lawsuit (*Sony v. Universal Studios*, 1984, commonly known as the "Betamax" case), as a wary film industry attempted to protect its rights to control content. However, the U.S. Supreme Court determined that the record and playback capability in the home (time-shifting) was a justifiable use of the VCR and did not violate copyright. This decision (among others) legalized the VCR for home use and helped force the eventual legitimization of the video sales and rental industry. VCR penetration quickly grew from 10% in 1984 to 79% 10 years later. In 2006, the FCC estimated that 90% of television households had at least one VCR (FCC, 2006).

Despite the freedom VCRs gave consumers, they were susceptible to damage by dirt, overuse, magnets, and physical shock. In the 1980s, the first videodiscs challenged VCRs. Again, a format competition grew between videodisc formats offered by RCA and MCA/Phillips. RCA's "Selectavision" videodisc player used vinyl records with much smaller grooves to accommodate the larger signal. MCA and Philips introduced a more sophisticated "Discovision" format in 1984 that used a laser to read an optical disc. Selectavision sold a half million units in the first six months, and Discovision was sold to Pioneer and renamed "Laserdisc." Despite the higher quality signal, the discs were never accepted in the consumer market. RCA withdrew Selectavision rather quickly, and "Laserdisc" was marketed as a high-end video solution. Well over one million players were sold by Pioneer before the format was abandoned in the late 1990s in the face of the emerging DVD format.

Based on the compact audio disc (CD), the DVD (digital videodisc or digital versatile disc) was introduced in 1997 as a mass storage device for all digital content. Bits are recorded in optical format within the plastic disc. Unlike earlier attempts to record video on CDs (called VCDs), the DVD had more than enough capacity to store an entire motion picture in analog television quality plus multiple language tracks, and bonus content. DVDs were disadvantaged by the lack of a record capability. However, they were smaller, lighter, and more durable than VHS tapes.

The introduction of a high-definition DVD player resulted in yet another format battle. In 2001, the Blu-ray format, supported by Sony, Hitachi, Pioneer, and six others, competed against the HD-DVD format supported by Toshiba, NEC, and Microsoft (HDDVD.org, 2003). Unlike the Beta/VHS battle, Blu-ray could hold significantly more content (50 GB compared to 30 GB for HD-DVD and 9 GB for standard DVDs). The initial cost for the players was around $500, but fell dramatically into the $250 range as the format war continued (Ault, 2008). Both groups created exclusive deals with major film studios. Warner Brothers delivered a surprising blow at the 2008 Consumer Electronics Show by switching from HD-DVD to Sony's Blu-ray. Other studios, unhappy with multiple formats, soon followed suit. While Toshiba initially vowed to continue to fight, the company gave up within a month.

Display

The television set has become a fixture in American homes. By 1975, televisions were seen in 95% of homes, and 66% viewed them as a "necessity" (Taylor, 2010). The television "set" was appropriately named because it included *tuner(s)* to interpret the incoming signals and a *monitor* to display the picture. Tuners have changed over the years to accommodate the needs of consumers (e.g., UHF, VHF, cable-ready). Subprocessors later added interpreted signals for closed captioning, automatic color correction, and the V-chip (parental control).

The first type of television monitor was the cathode ray tube (CRT). The rectangular screen area of a CRT is covered with lines of phosphors that correspond to the picture elements (pixels) in the image. Color monitors use three streams of electrons, one for each color channel (red, blue, and green). The phosphors glow when struck by a stream of electrons sent from the back of the set. The greater the stream, the brighter the phosphor glows. The glowing phosphors combine to form an image.

The first United States color television standard was set by the National Television Standards Committee (NTSC), which called for 525 lines of video resolution with interlaced scanning. Interlacing means that the odd numbered video lines are transmitted first, and then the display transmits the even numbered lines. The whole process takes one-thirtieth of a second (30 frames of video per second). Interlaced lines ensured even brightness of the screen and a better feeling of motion (Hartwig, 2000).

Recent Developments

The most important recent development has been the transition to digital broadcasting (discussed in Chapter 6). While the 2009 economic downturn affected the media industry as much as any other industry, the transition, combined with the exciting new digital displays, created a perceived need to buy. The Consumer Electronics Association (CEA) reported an industry-wide 7.7% decrease in revenue in 2008 (CEA, 2009). But HD displays grew from below 20% penetration in mid-2007 to over 67% in late 2011 (Nielsen, 2011).

The transition to digital content caused consumers to make several changes in their home video environment. It is apparent that consumers chose to purchase a display to add rather than replace. The rush to meet the digital transition deadline corresponded with a growth in multi-set households. Multi-set homes increased from 75% in 2003 to 84% in 2011 (TVB, 2011). In 2011, 36% of U.S. households had four or more television sets (Nielsen, 2011).

There is also evidence of shifts in the way people consume programming. First, since 1998 adults have increased average daily viewership by about one hour (see Figure 17.2). Viewing among women increased from about 4.5 to 5.5 hours per day. Men's viewing followed, moving from four to five hours per day. Over the same years, children and teens consistently reported about 3.5 hours of viewership a day (TVB, 2011). A separate study through the U.S. Department of Education indicated a drop in viewership on school nights until 2004 (Dick et.al., 2011, See Figure 17.3). In 1984, 66% of nine year olds reported watching at least three hours of television on school nights. The percent dropped to 46% in 2004 but rose dramatically to 54% in 2008.

Figure 17.2

Daily Television Viewing for Adults

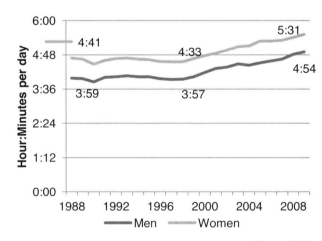

Source: TVB.org

Figure 17.3
Percent of Students Watching At Least Three Hours of Television on School Night

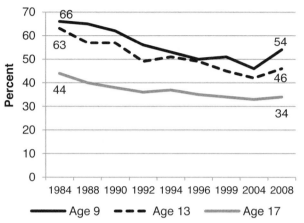

Source: http://nces.ed.gov/nationsreportcard/lttdata/

As consumers were faced with new equipment choices, companies had to actively compete for a place in the homes. Traditional cable television reached a penetration high of 71% in February 2001, and alternative multichannel services (mainly DBS) grew to 29.3% by November of 2009. Recently, the battle has shifted to high-profit, premium services. Mostly digitally delivered, premium services can include pay channels, and on-demand programming. Since 1995, traditional cable companies have given up a substantial percent of this market to other delivery systems (See Figure 17.4, U.S. Census, 2012).

Figure 17.4
Percent of Market for Premium TV Program Services

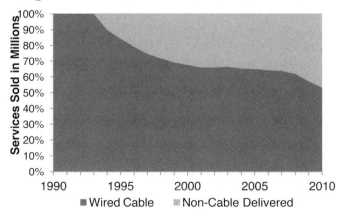

Source: U.S. Census

Digital video recorders (DVRs) have grown from having a fairly small but extremely loyal following to become an important supplemental service for satellite and cable television subscribers. Initial units were marketed under the names ReplayTV and TiVo. The heart of a DVR is a high-capacity hard drive capable of recording 40 or more hours of video. However, the real power of the DVR is the computer brain that controls it. The DVR is able to search out and automatically record favorite programs through a supplementary service that provides a program guide. Since it is a nonlinear medium, the DVR is able to record and playback at the same time. This ability gives the system the apparent ability to pause (even rewind) live television. Newer DVRs can provide on-demand programming and share content throughout the home.

Since 2003, consumers have shifted from VCR to digital formats (see Figure 17.5). Consumers have transitioned their playback systems as well. 2007 marked the transition year between the dominance of the VCR and the DVD. At the same time DVRs became much more popular, with DVR penetration growing between 2007 and 2011.

Figure 17.5
Technology Shifts in Home Video Penetration by Technology

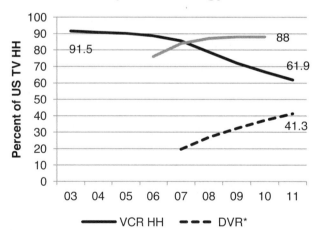

*Third Quarter Measure Used   *Source:* TVB.org

Figure 17.6
Choosing the Correct Size Television

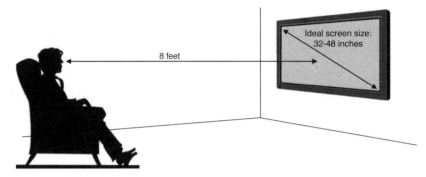

Selecting the right size set for a room is easy using this simple calculation: 1. Measure distance from TV to sitting position. 2. Divide by 2 and then by 3 to get ideal screen size range. The resulting numbers will be the ideal screen sizes. **Example:** Distance = 8 feet (or 96 inches), 96 / 2 = 48" set, 96 / 3 = 32" set, and Ideal set is 32" to 48".

Source: Technology Futures, Inc.

Current Status

As the digital market has grown, consumers have more choices than ever when they select a new television. While most digital sets will at least attempt to produce a picture for all incoming signals, some will be better able to do it than others. CEA suggests five steps in the decision process (CEA, 2007b):

1) Select the right size.

2) Choose an aspect ratio.

3) Select your image quality.

4) Pick a display style.

5) Get the right connection.

New sets are larger than ever, and it is easy to buy too large or small. Even with a high-definition set, if you sit too close, you see too much grain. If you sit too far away, you lose picture quality. The rule of thumb is to measure the distance from the picture to the seat. Divide that distance by three. The result is the smallest screen size for the room. Divide the distance by two and the result is the largest screen size for the room (see Figure 17.6).

Unlike analog, not all digital television signals are the same (See Chapter 6 for more on digital broadcast standards). The video monitor must be able to quickly interpret and display several incoming formats. Monitors display some video formats as transmitted—called native resolutions. All other signals are converted. If a monitor has only 720 lines of resolution, it cannot display 1,080 lines native, and the signal must be converted. The conversion process may reduce signal quality. The two aspects of format that should concern the buyer the most are lines of resolution and aspect ratio. CEA has established three quality levels for lines of resolution:

✦ *Standard definition* uses 480 lines interlaced. It is most like analog television (525 lines), but contains the circuitry to convert higher-quality images down to the lower-resolution screen.

✦ *Enhanced definition* sets use 480p or higher. The image more smoothly presents high-definition content because of the progressive scan; it meets the quality of standard DVDs.

✦ *High-definition* pictures are at resolutions of 720p up to 1080. They can display HD content and Blu-ray DVDs at full resolution.

Aspect ratio is the relationship of screen width to the height. Standard definition sets have an aspect ratio of 4:3 or four inches wide for every three inches tall. The new widescreen format is 16:9. Most televisions will attempt to fill the screen with the picture, but the wrong image for the screen distorts or produces a "letterbox" effect. In addition, picture size is a measure of the diagonal distance, and wider screens have proportionally longer diagonals. For example, a 55-inch diagonal set with a 4:3 aspect ratio has 1,452 square inches of picture space. The same 55-inch set with a 16:9 aspect ratio has only 1,296 square inches of picture space. Thus, it is misleading to compare the diagonal picture size on sets with different aspect ratios.

The major display styles are CRT, plasma, LCD, and projection. Although CRT screens tend to be smaller, for years they remained the most affordable choice for a bright picture and a wide viewing angle. LCD (liquid crystal display) and plasma are the new flat screen technologies. They take up less floor space and can be mounted like a picture on the wall. LCD displays tend to have a brighter image but a narrower viewing angle. Plasmas have a wider viewing angle but the shiny screens more easily reflect images from the room. Front or rear projection systems offer the best value for very wide images but use an expensive light bulb that must be replaced periodically. Projection systems are best in home theater installations.

Higher quality displays create video frames that bridge the motion between existing video frames. From an original 60 hertz frame rate, the system will create additional video frames to make the motion smoother and reduce perceived flicker. These sets are then marketed as 120 or 240 hertz sets. For presentation of motion pictures shot at 24 frames per second, the display can adapt to that frame rate or double it to 48 hertz—reducing flicker or a "video-like" image.

Finally, the right connections are essential to transmitting the highest quality image into the set. Analog video connecters will move an image to the monitor, but can severely limit quality. Depending on your video accessories, sets should ideally come with an HDMI input, or IEEE-1394 (Firewire) and/or component jacks. Many HD monitors also accept video from a computer. This means smaller screens can be used as a computer monitor and all can be used for internet video.

Factors to Watch

The future of home video will continue to highlight choices. The two areas to watch for the coming years are continued development of the monitor and more choices in delivery. The monitor market re-

mains extremely competitive and manufacturers are looking for an edge. Delivery systems are developing to reach the goal of anywhere, anytime, any-format video.

Monitor Development

3-D TV: The biggest advance in 3-D TV may be the move from active to passive glasses. Active glasses receive a signal from the monitor and shutter lenses so only one eye sees the picture at a time. Passive are similar to polarized lenses which allow specifically created images to be directed to each eye. Active lens glasses need to be powered by batteries. Thus, they are much more expensive (around $150), require recharging, and weigh more. The market must still answer the question of whether passive lenses produce a high quality image.

Organic Light Emitting Diodes: The new OLED monitors produce a bright, crisp image without the need for backlighting. As a result, they are more energy-efficient and thinner than other flat screen monitors.

Smart TVs: Some television receivers have added an array of interactive applications. Most allow the user to interact through the Internet with services such as Facebook and YouTube. For more information on Interactive television, see Chapter 9.

Delivery Systems

From May 2007 to the third quarter of 2011, consumers' use of time-shifted content nearly tripled (see Figure 17.7). In addition, Internet viewing doubled to more than four hours a month. The ultimate goal would be video content that follows its viewer from device to device and location to location. The most active users of online video are people ages 18-24 with an average of nearly 7.5 hours a month (Nielsen, 2011). While much of the online viewing is short form (e.g., YouTube, movie trailers), there is a growing consumption of program-length content. The term "catch up programming" has been attached to online consumption of program-length content. The term refers to people using the Internet to see old episodes of shows they missed.

Figure 17.7
Monthly Time Spent Viewing Time Shifted Programming*

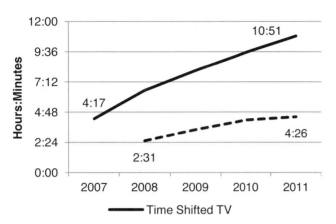

*Third Quarter Measure Used

Compiled From: Nielsen 2008, 2009, 2010, 2011

Time shifting content may be a symptom of larger changes in consumer behavior. In 2011 revenues of the valuable top 100 DVDs dropped to 37% of the 2007 sales (see Figure 17.8). Upheavals in the DVD market are causing some analysts to question the future of the format (McHugh, 2011). Content owners are continuing to tweak distribution windows to force extra revenue from the product. At the same time, lower-cost distributers such as Netflix and Redbox kiosk fight, sometimes in court, for the best content as early as possible (Mike, n.d.). Local video stores are proving to be too expensive as the most famous, Blockbuster, struggles to survive (Duncan, 2012).

Online distribution may quickly become the next frontier for content delivery. Companies such as Hulu, Google, Amazon and Apple have all stepped up efforts to distribute content online. Currently most of the sales are to computer and mobile devices. However, home video interfaces through devices supplied by Roku, gaming devices, and even some cable/satellite boxes will bring streaming to the big screen. In 2011, Netflix attempted to redefine itself as a home streaming company by dividing DVD distri-

bution and streaming services. Initially, the currently profitable DVD service was to be renamed Qwikster with the streaming service retaining the original brand name of Netflix. While changes were partially reversed, there is no doubt that companies plan to move streaming to the home video screen.

Figure 17.8
Top 100 DVDs Sales and Units Shipped

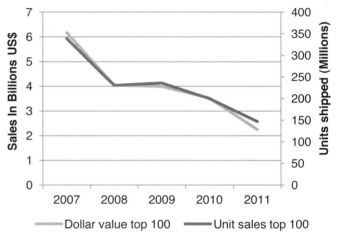

Source: http://www.the-numbers.com/dvd/charts/annual/2011.php

Conclusion

Options are just too enticing as a new generation of home video technologies comes of age. The industry is readying for an age of multiple platforms from the very large home theater to the small mobile device. Which devices and markets will become a success is up to consumers and producers alike. The consumer must accept the platform, and the producer must create a business model that will work for everyone.

Sustainability

In a study commissioned by the CEA, Roth and Williams (2011) calculated that consumer electronics in the U.S. consumed 193 TWh or 13.2% of residential electric consumption. The television accounted for 65 TWh, set-top boxes 26TWh, and DVD/Blu-ray 6.5. Newer technology has been generally designed to be more energy-efficient so flat panel televisions use less electricity than CRTs. Satellite and telco boxes are more energy-efficient than cable, and Blu-ray players use less electricity than standard DVDs. Finally, combined devices (i.e., combo set-top box and DVR) are more energy-efficient than individual units.

Given the spike in television sales, Pike Research considered the environmental costs of production (Boggio & Wheelock, 2011). CRTs' use of leaded glass and larger cabinets increases weight per unit but limits screen size to about 30 inches. The model predicts that each million dollars of LCD televisions produced requires 8.4 terra joules of energy and 10.5 million gallons of water. As large as these numbers seem, LCDs represent a 26% reduction in energy and 21% less water than the equivalent CRTs. Packaging is directly proportional to weight and volume, so similar savings are seen as smaller televisions hit the market. Not only are flat panel displays lighter than CRTs, they are getting lighter as time goes on. The average weight of a plasma TV in 2004 was 125 pounds—reduced to 59 pounds in 2010.

The annual energy cost for a single family home is approximately $2,200, and home electronics account for 4% of that cost (EnergyStar, n.d.). However, the growing use of personal electronic devices, battery chargers, power supplies, and instant-on capability is driving up electricity use. The transition to high definition has encouraged the adoption of larger flat screen televisions. As the diagonal dimension doubles, the powered space of the television grows by 4 (geometrically). Three factors determine the amount of electricity used: size, type, and setting (Katzmaer & Moskovciak, 2009).

- *Size:* While newer televisions are more efficient, larger screens requires more electricity. A 32 inch LCD screen uses about half the electricity of a 52 inch. However, the screen size nearly triples, so there it is not a proportional advantage for the smaller screen.

- *Type:* Plasmas use nearly twice as much electricity as LCDs. In tests by CNET.com (Katzmaer & Moskovciak, 2009), the average LCD uses 176 watts of power while the average plasma uses 338 watts. The projected annual energy costs of matched 52 inch sets are $27 for an LCD and $63 for a plasma. However, new technology is increasing the efficiency. Most LCDs use a florescent backlight (see section on technology). Some newer LCDs have adopted an array of more efficient light emitting diodes (LED). The LEDs not only use less power than the florescents, but LEDs can be turned down dynamically in dark scenes. The most advanced sets use "local dimming" to reduce light use in dark parts of the screens. Local dimming not only saves electricity, it improves reproduction of black and shadow detail (Norton, 2010).

- *Settings:* It is not surprising that the brighter the screen, the more the power. Thus, energy conservation can be achieved by controlling both the physical setting and picture setting. A darker room will allow the set to function at a lower light setting and saves power. At the very least, the set should be placed in a location that avoids direct exposure to either natural or artificial light. Beyond location, picture should be set to the lowest needed brightness and contrast. Other features such as dynamic lighting control (for room light or scene brightness), energy saver modes, and instant-on controls can save energy as well. However, all these changes used too aggressively can reduce image fidelity and convenience.

An Energy Star qualified set means that the television uses about 30% less electricity than standard sets of similar size. The smart buyer should keep aware of the Energy Star standard year because the standards are updated about every two years.

Bibliography

Ault, S. (2008, January 21). The format war cost home entertainment in 2007. *Video Business*. Retrieved from http://www.videobusiness.com.

Boggio, B. & Wheelock, C. (2011, July). Materials footprint reduction of televisions and computer monitors: 2004-2010. *Pike Research*. Retrieved from http://apps.ce.org/documents/PikeCEAFinal.pdf.

Consumer Electronics Association. (2007). *DTV—Consumer buying guide*. Retrieved from http://www.ce.org/Press/CEA_Pubs/1507.asp.

Consumer Electronics Association. (2009). Retrieved from http://www.ce.org/Research/Sales_Stats/default.asp.

Dick, S.J., Davie, W.R. & Miguez, B.B. (2011). "Adding depth to the relationship between reading skills and television viewing: an analysis of national assessment of educational progress (NAEP) Reading Scores" *Association for Education in Journalism and Mass Communication National Conference*, St Louis, MO

Duncan, G. (2012, January 13). Dish having trouble keeping Blockbuster stores open. *DigitalTrends.com.* Retrieved from http://www.digitaltrends.com/home-theater/dish-havingtrouble-keeping-blockbuster-stores-open/.

EnergyStar. (n.d.). Televisions for consumers. Retrieved from http://www.energystar.gov/index.cfm?fuseaction=find_a_product.showProductGroup&pgw_code=TV.

Federal Communications Commission. (2006). Annual assessment of the status of competition in the market for the delivery of video programming. Retrieved from http://www.fcc.gov/mb/csrptpg.html.

Hartwig, R. (2000). *Basic TV technology: Digital and Analog*, 3rd edition. Boston: Focal Press.

HDDVD.org. (2003). The different formats. Retrieved from http://www.hddvd.org/hddvd/ difformatsblueray.php.

International Telecommunications Union. (2006). Press release on digital terrestrial broadcasting. Retrieved http://www.itu.int/newsarchive/press_releases/2006/11.html.

Katzmaier, D & M. Moskovciak. (2009). The basics of TV power. *CNET Reviews*. Retrieved from http://reviews.cnet.com/green-tech/tv-power-efficiency/.

Katzmaier, D. (2010). Panasonic makes 3D HD official with VT25 plasma TV series. *CNET.com*. Retrieved from http://ces.cnet.com/8301-31045_1-10427983-269.html?tag=mncol.

Lee, S. (2007, November 16). Samsung leads in global LCD TV sales. *The Korea Herald*. Retrieved from LexisNexis.

McDowell, W & Dick, S (2003). Has Lead-in Lost its Punch? *The International Journal on Media Management, Vol. 5,* no. IV. pp. 285-293.

McHugh, B. (2011, March 8). The death of DVD. *DigitalTrends.com.* Retrieved from http://www.digitaltrends.com/computing/thedeath-of-dvd/.

Mike, S. (n.d). Blu-ray is the silver lining among dwindling DVD sales. *USA Today*, Retrieved from Academic Search Complete database 3/20/2010.

National Cable and Telecommunications Association. (2007). National video programming. Retrieved from http://www.ncta.org/Statistic/Statistic/NationalVideoProgramming.aspx

Nielsen. (2008). A2/M2 Three Screen Report: 3rd Quarter 2008. Retrieved from http://en-us.nielsen.com/sitelets/landing/a2m2/a2m2_h.html.

Nielsen. (2009). A2/M2 Three Screen Report: 3rd Quarter 2009. Retrieved from http://en-us.nielsen.com/sitelets/landing/a2m2/a2m2_h.html.

Nielsen. (2010). A2/M2 Three Screen Report: 1st Quarter 2010. Retrieved from http://en-us.nielsen.com/sitelets/landing/a2m2/a2m2_h.html

Nielsen (2011). State of the media: The cross platform report. Retrieved from http://www.nielsen.com/us/en/insights/reports-downloads/2011/cross-platform-report.html

Norton, T.J. (2010). Flat-panel HDTVs. home theater: 2010 Buyer's Guide. Pp 6-8.

Roth, K &Williams, R. (2011, December). Energy consumption of consumer electronics in US homes in 2010. Fraunhofer Center for Sustainable Energy Systems. Retrieved from http://www.ce.org/PDF/Energy-Consumption-of-CE-inUSHomes-2010.pdf.

Taylor, P. (2010, August 19). The fading glory of the television and telephone. *Pew Social and Demographic Trends*. Retrieved from http://www.pewsocialtrends.org/2010/08/19/the-fading-glory-of-the-television-and-telephone/.

Television Bureau of Adverting. (n.d.). Media trends track. Retrieved from http://tvb.org/nav/build_frameset.aspx.

Television Bureau of Adverting. (2011, December). TV basics. Retrieved from from http://www.tvb.org/media/file/TV_Basics.pdf.

United States Census (n.d.). Table 1142. Cable and premium TV—summary: 1975 to 2010. Retrieved from www.census.gov/compendia/statab/2012/tables/12s1142.xls.

Whitehouse, G. (1986). *Understanding the new technologies of mass media*. Englewood Cliffs, NJ: Prentice-Hall.

18

Digital Audio

Ted Carlin, Ph.D.*

Why Study Digital Audio?

◆ 3.6 billion digital audio downloads were purchased globally in 2011, an increase of 17 percent (combining singles and album downloads) over 2010.

◆ In the U.S., the world's largest music market, digital music has overtaken physical recording formats to become the primary source of revenues for record companies (32% globally). This compares with online revenue percentages of 5% for newspapers, 4% for books and 1% for films.

◆ The ability to store thousands of songs in a pocket-size device and select songs by title, artist or genre has been a game-changer. As a result, U.S. sales of portable digital audio products, consisting primarily of digital media players, exceeded home audio sales for the 7th consecutive year in 2011.

Producers, consumers and advertisers alike are gravitating to the digital domain, which offers ever-expanding media content options via a growing variety of devices. For example, Randall Roberts's *Los Angeles Times* review of Van Halen's latest album, *Different Kind of Truth*, effectively describes this digital evolution and the format choices today's music listeners have:

In the 28 years since Roth recorded a full album with Van Halen, the landscape has completely changed. When the band's original lineup last released a record, home taping was "killing" music and the question was whether to buy "1984" on LP or cassette, or borrow a friend's copy and tape over Foreigner "4."

Now the dilemma isn't just should you spend money on the CD ($14.99 list price) or a digital copy (also—frustratingly—$14.99). It's also, how much are you willing to commit to buying in? Will a few dropped bucks on a handful of the best individual tracks suffice? Or will "A Different Kind of Truth" be the perfect Spotify streaming album, not good enough to pay hard money for but worth a mouse-click when you've got a spare few minutes? Or should you just ask your computery friend to Sendspace you a pirated copy?

—Roberts, 2012

Just as in 1984, in the end, the consumer gets to make a choice—to buy, to rent, to steal—but today the choice is immediate and with fewer people in the way. Today's digital audio technology drives this choice by removing the traditional retail barriers between consumer and content, and enabling consumers to interact with content in new, direct, and personal ways. Through various software and hardware tools, consumers and content providers become intertwined in the discovery process, co-creating playlists, sharing recommendations, enabling file and information flow, and ultimately, facilitating an acquisition decision.

* Professor, Department of Communication/Journalism, Shippensburg University (Shippensburg, Pennsylvania).

Background

Analog Versus Digital

Analog means "similar" or "a copy." An analog audio signal is an electronic copy of an original audio signal as found in nature, with a continually varying signal. Analog copies of any original sound suffer some degree of signal degradation, called generational loss, and signal strength lessens and noise increases for each successive copy. However, in the digital domain, this noise and signal degradation can be eliminated (Watkinson, 2008).

Audio is digitized by sampling the amplitude (strength) of a waveform from a capturing device (typically a microphone) using an analog to digital converter (see Figure 18.1). Depending on the equipment used to make this digital copy, various samples of the original sound wave are taken at given intervals using a specified sampling rate (i.e., 32 kHz for broadcast digital audio; 44.1 kHz for CD and MP3; 192.4 kHz for Blu-ray) to create a discrete digital wave (Alten, 2010). These samples are then quantized as binary numbers at a specific bit level (16-bit, 32-bit, etc.); the higher the bit level, the higher the quality of the digital reproduction.

Figure 18.1
Analog Versus Digital Recording

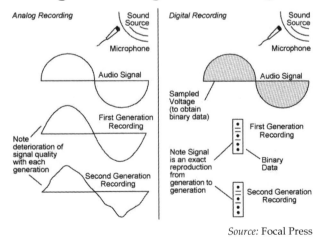

Source: Focal Press

File formats and codecs.

Once the signal is digitized, sampled, and quantized, the digital signal can be subjected to further processing—in the form of audio data compression—

to reduce the size of the digitized audio file even further. This is similar to "zipping" a text file to more easily send the digital file across the Internet and to store more digital files on devices.

Audio compression algorithms are typically referred to as *audio codecs*. As with other specific forms of digital data compression, there exist many "lossless" and "lossy" formulas to achieve the compression effect (Alten, 2010). Lossless compression works by encoding repetitive pieces of information with symbols and equations that take up less space, but provide all the information needed to reconstruct an exact copy of the original. Lossy compression works by discarding unnecessary and redundant information (sounds that most people cannot hear) and then applying lossless compression techniques for further size reduction. With lossy compression, there is always some loss of fidelity that becomes more noticeable as the compression ratio is increased.

Unfortunately for consumers, there is no one standard audio codec, and Table 18.1 provides a list of the major codecs in use in 2012. However, there is one codec that has emerged as the clear leader—MP3. Before MP3 came onto the digital audio scene in the 1990s, computer users were recording, downloading, and playing high-quality sound files using an uncompressed codec called .WAV. The trouble with .WAV files, however, is their enormous size. A two-minute song recorded in CD-quality sound uses about 20 MB of a hard drive in the .WAV format. That means a 10-song CD would take more than 200 MB of disk space.

The file-size problem for music downloads has changed thanks to the efforts of the Moving Picture Experts Group (MPEG), a consortium that develops open standards for digital audio and video compression. Since the development of MPEG, engineers have been refining the standard to squeeze high-quality audio into ever-smaller packages. MP3—short for MPEG 1 Audio Layer 3—can take music from a CD and shrink it by a factor of 12 (Digigram, 2010).

Digital Audio Technologies

Compact Disc

In the audio industry, nothing has revolutionized the way we listen to recorded music like the compact disc. Originally, engineers developed the CD solely for its improvement in sound quality over LPs and analog cassettes. After the introduction of the CD player, consumers became aware of the quick random-access characteristic of the optical disc system. In addition, the size of the 12-cm (about five-inch) disc was easy to handle compared with the LP. The longer lifetime of both the medium and the player strongly supported the acceptance of the CD format. The next target of development was the rewritable CD. Sony and Philips jointly developed this system and made it a technical reality in 1989. Two different recordable CD systems were established. One is the write-once CD named CD-R, and the other is the re-writable CD named CD-RW (Alten, 2010).

Digital Media Player

To play MP3s and other digital audio files, a computer-based or portable digital media player is needed. Hundreds of portable digital media players are available, from those with 512 MB flash drives to massive 160 GB hard drive-based models. They are sold by manufacturers such as Apple (iPod), Archos, Creative, LG, and Samsung. The amount of available disc space is most relative to the way a person uses the portable player, either as a song selector or song shuffler. Song selectors tend to store all of their music on players with larger drives and select individual songs or playlists as desired, whereas song shufflers are more likely to load a group of songs on a smaller drive and let the player shuffle through selections at random.

Table 18.1
Popular Audio Codecs

Codec	Developer	Date	Compression Type
AAC	MPEG	2002	lossy
AACplus or HE-ACC	MPEG	2003	lossy
AIFF	Electronic Arts/Apple	1985	uncompressed
ALAC	Apple	2004	lossless
AU	Sun	1992	uncompressed
FLAC	Xiph.org	2003	lossless
LAME	Cheng/Taylor	1998	Lossy
Monkey's Audio	M. Ashland	2002	lossless
MP3	Thomson/Fraunhofer	1992	lossy
MP3 Pro	Thomson/Fraunhofer	2001	lossy
MP3 Surround	Thomson/Fraunhofer	2004	lossy
Musepak	Buschmann/Klemm	1997	lossy
SDII (Sound Designer II)	Digidesign	1997	lossless
SHN (Shorten)	T.Robinson/W. Stielau	1993	lossless
Speex	Xiph.org	2003	lossy
Vorbis (Ogg Vorbis)	C. Montgomery/Xiph.org	2002	lossy
TTA (True Audio)	Alexander Djourik	2007	lossless
VoxWare MetaSound	A. Penry	2004	lossy
WavPack	D. Bryant	1998	lossless
WMA (Windows Media Audio)	Microsoft	2000	lossy
WMA Lossless	Microsoft	2003	lossless

Source: T. Carlin

Peer-to-Peer (P2P) File Sharing

In a P2P network, the "peers" are computer systems which are connected to each other via the Internet. Digital files can be shared directly between computers on the network without the need of a central server. In other words, each computer on a P2P network becomes a file server as well as a client.

The only requirements for a computer to join a P2P network are an Internet connection and P2P software such as Vuze or Limewire. These programs connect to a P2P network, for example BitTorrent, which allows the computer to access thousands of other computers on the network. Once connected to the network, the P2P client software allows you to search this computer "swarm" for torrent files located on other people's computers. The torrent files are "chunks" of the desired song or movie that are located and assembled on your computer to make one complete file.

So, rather than getting the whole file from one central server, the file is assembled, or "leeched," from pieces located on various clients within the swarm. Meanwhile, other users on the network can search for files on your computer, but typically only within a single folder that you have designated to share (Strufe, 2012). While P2P networking makes file sharing convenient and quick, is also has led to software piracy and illegal music downloads, as discussed below.

Podcasting

Podcasting is the distribution of audio or video files, such as radio programs or music videos, over the Internet using RSS (really simple syndication) for listening on mobile devices and personal computers (Podcast Alley, 2012). A podcast is basically a Web feed of audio or video files placed on the Internet for anyone to download or subscribe to. Podcasters' websites may also offer direct download of their files, but the subscription feed of automatically delivered new content is what distinguishes a podcast from a simple download or real-time streaming. A quick search of the Internet will uncover a myriad of content that is available—and accumulating daily.

Copyright Legislation, Cases & Actions

With this ever-increasing ability to create and distribute an indefinite number of exact copies of an original sound wave through digital reproduction comes the incumbent responsibility to prevent unauthorized copies of copyrighted audio productions and safeguard the earnings of performers and producers. Before taking a closer look at the various digital audio technologies in use, a brief examination of important legislative efforts and resulting industry initiatives involving this issue of digital audio reproduction is warranted.

Audio Home Recording Act of 1992

The *Audio Home Recording Act (AHRA) of 1992* exempts consumers from lawsuits for copyright violations when they record music for private, noncommercial use and eases access to advanced digital audio recording technologies. The law also provides for the payment of modest royalties to music creators and copyright owners, and mandates the inclusion of the Serial Copying Management Systems (SCMS) in all consumer digital audio recorders to limit multigenerational audio copying (i.e., making copies of copies). This legislation also applies to all future digital recording technologies, so Congress is not forced to revisit the issue as each new product becomes available (*AHRA*, 1992).

The Digital Performance Right in Sound Recordings Act of 1995

This law (*Digital Performance Right in Sound Recordings Act*, 1996) allows copyright owners of sound recordings to authorize certain digital transmissions of their works, including interactive digital audio transmissions, and to be compensated for others. This right covers, for example, interactive services, digital cable audio services, satellite music services, commercial online music providers, and future forms of electronic delivery.

No Electronic Theft Law (NET Act) of 1997

The *No Electronic Theft Law* states that sound recording infringements (including by digital means) can be criminally prosecuted even where no monetary profit or commercial gain is derived from the infringing activity. Punishment in such instances includes up to three years in prison and/or $250,000 in fines (*NET Act*, 1997).

Digital Millennium Copyright Act (DMCA) of 1998

The main goal of the DMCA was to make the necessary changes in U.S. copyright law to allow the United States to join two new World Intellectual Property Organization (WIPO) treaties that update international copyright standards for the Internet.

The DMCA amended copyright law to provide for the efficient licensing of sound recordings for Webcasters and digital subscription audio services via cable and satellite. In this regard, the DMCA:

✦ Made it a crime to circumvent anti-piracy measures [i.e., digital rights management (DRM) technology] built into most commercial software. DRM technology controls the trading and monitoring of a digital work. Apple's Fairplay and Blu-ray's Advanced Access Content System (AACS) are two prominent DRM technologies.

✦ Outlawed the manufacture, sale, or distribution of code-cracking devices used to illegally copy software.

✦ In general, limited Internet service providers from copyright infringement liability for simply transmitting information over the Internet. Service providers, however, are expected to remove material from users' websites that appear to constitute copyright infringement.

✦ Provided for a simplified licensing and compensation system for digital performances of sound recordings on the Internet, cable, and satellite systems. This licensing system is similar to ASCAP and BMI compulsory licensing for music used on radio and television stations (U.S. Copyright Office, 2012).

The U.S. Copyright Office designated a non-profit organization, SoundExchange, to administer the performance right royalties arising from digital distribution via subscription services. Once rates and terms are set, SoundExchange collects, administers, and distributes the performance right royalties due from the licensees to the record companies and artists (SoundExchange.com, 2012).

MGM Studios, Inc. v. Grokster, Ltd.

Although there has been a constant debate in all three of these copyright areas, it is the copyright protection pertaining to Internet music downloading that has led to the most contentious arguments. On June 27, 2005, the U.S. Supreme Court ruled unanimously against peer-to-peer (P2P) file-sharing service providers Grokster and Streamcast Networks. The landmark decision in *MGM Studios, Inc. v. Grokster, Ltd.* (545 U. S. 125 S. Ct. 2764, 2005) was a victory for the media industry and a blow to P2P companies. At the same time, the decision let stand the main substance of the Supreme Court's landmark "Betamax" ruling (*Sony Corp. of America v. Universal City Studios*, 1984), which preserved a technologist's ability to innovate without fear of legal action for copyright infringement, and which the media industry sought to overturn.

The Supreme Court found that technology providers should be held liable for infringement if they *actively promote* their wares as infringement tools. Writing for the court, Justice David Souter stated, "We hold that one who distributes a device with the object of promoting its use to infringe copyright, as shown by clear expression or other affirmative steps taken to foster infringement, is liable for the resulting acts of infringement by third parties" (*MGM Studios, Inc. v. Grokster, Ltd.*, 2005, p. 1).

The decision created a new theory of secondary infringement liability based on "intent to induce" infringement, which now extends the existing theory of contributory liability (knowingly aiding and abetting infringement). This inducement concept is derived from an analogous and established theory in patent law (Kalinsky & Sebald, 2005). Again, technology inventors must promote the illegal use of the product to be found liable:

...mere knowledge of infringing potential or of actual infringing uses would not be enough here to subject a [technology] distributor to liability.... The inducement rule, instead, premises liability on purposeful, culpable expression and conduct, and thus does nothing to compromise legitimate commerce or discourage innovation having a lawful promise.

—*MGM v. Grokster* (2005, p. 19)

Overall, this decision does not mean that P2P services have shut down altogether—as of mid-2012, the top 10 P2P services were uTorrent, Frostwire, BitComet, BitTorrent, Vuze, BitLord, SoMud, LimeRunner, Ares Galaxy and Shareaza (P2PON!, 2012). However, those P2P services that have been targeted by Recording Industry Association of America (RIAA) and the Department of Justice (DOJ) over the last decade, including Morpheus, LimeWire and Pirate Bay, have been shut down or forced to alter their practices.

DRM-Free Music

Although buying practices are rapidly changing, much of the music sold in the world is still sold on compact discs. CDs have no encryption. They are DRM-free and can play on any CD player, including computer drives. CDs also provide high-quality digital content that can easily be ripped to a digital file, copied, or shared (legal issues notwithstanding) at the discretion of the buyer.

Digital downloads, in contrast, are accessible online at any time, making their purchase convenient. Often sold as singles and not full albums, they are economical as well. That convenience comes at the cost of quality and, especially, portability. Smaller digital files appropriate for downloads mean that the purchaser gets the music with lesser sound quality. Because the major recording labels insisted (until 2007) that downloadable music be encrypted with DRM, and there was no universal, open-standard for that encryption, the music could only play on devices capable of decrypting the specific DRM encryption the music was encoded with (as opposed to universally on any digital media player).

One of the biggest developments in digital audio technologies was the 2008 announcement by the Big Four record companies, Amazon.com, Apple, and others to offer DRM-free music tracks over the Internet (Holahan, 2008). For years, DRM was simply a way to protect the rights of the artists and record labels whose music was being illegally distributed. Most in the music industry believed that the technology was a necessary evil that needed to be put in place for content creators to make sure that they were being fairly compensated for their work. However, as mentioned earlier in the chapter, DRM wraps music tracks in a copy-protection code that is not only restrictive but also confusing for many potential users. Very few consumers wanted to purchase music on one service using a specific DRM, only to find out later that they cannot play it on this digital media player, that computer, or this operating system.

However, DRM-free does not mean consumers are free from having to purchase the music. And, unlike the mid-2000s, where providers offered music tracks (or albums) for a single price, the 2010s have ushered in the era of variable pricing and limited-time discounts by many providers, including Amazon and iTunes. For example, rather than static track pricing of 99-cents each, services now offer tracks at $0.69, $0.99 or $1.29 depending on the age and popularity of the track. To further entice consumers, limited-time promotional offers—such as release date discounts or holiday specials—have become a standard marketing approach as well.

U.S. Department of Justice Operations & RIAA Lawsuits

The DOJ's Computer Crimes and Intellectual Property Section (CCIPS) is responsible for coordinating and investigating violations of the *U.S. Copyright Act*, the *Digital Millennium Copyright Act*, and other cyber laws discussed earlier in this chapter. The CCIPS, along with the Federal Bureau of Investigation's (FBI's) Cyber Division and numerous state Attorneys General, have been actively monitoring and investigating illegal operations associated with digital audio and copyright violations since 2004.

And, in an increased effort to implement the Obama administration's commitment to the importance of the Internet to U.S. innovation, prosperity, education and political and cultural life, the DOJ created a new Task Force on Intellectual Property to crack down on the growing number of domestic and international intellectual property crimes (DOJ, 2012a). The task force works closely with the President's Office of the Intellectual Property Enforcement Coordinator (IPEC) and the Commerce Department's newly created Internet Policy Task Force.

The RIAA and several of its member record companies provide assistance to the DOJ and FBI in their investigations. The legal issues surrounding digital audio are not limited to file sharing networks. The RIAA assists authorities in identifying music pirates and shutting down their operations.

Based on the *Digital Millennium Copyright Act*'s expedited subpoena provision, the RIAA sends out information subpoenas as part of an effort to track and shut down repeat offenders and to deter those hiding behind the perceived anonymity of the Internet. Information subpoenas require the Internet service provider (ISP) providing access to or hosting a particular site to provide contact information for the site operator. Once the site operator is identified, the RIAA takes steps to prevent repeat infringement. Such steps range from a warning e-mail to litigation against the site operator. The RIAA then uses that information to send notice to the operator that the site must be removed. Finally, the RIAA requires the individual to pay an amount designated to help defray the costs of the subpoena process (RIAA, 2012).

Recent Developments

Digital Audio Technologies

Wireless Digital Media

In addition to mobile smartphone users who can find many of the cloud, playlist and subscription services described below via downloaded apps or websites, the major wireless phone companies continue to offer music to data-equipped mobile phone subscribers.

AT&T eMusic Mobile. AT&T subscribers can download music, from about 2.5 million tracks, directly to their phone with eMusic Mobile. Users can purchase 5 songs for $7.49/month and receive a free MP3 copy online (AT&T, 2012).

Verizon Wireless Music. Subscribers can use either of Verizon's music management software options: Backup Assistant Plus or V CAST Music with Rhapsody. Both options allow users to purchase tracks from 69¢ to $1.29. V CAST users can opt in to a $9.99/month subscription that allows unlimited access to millions of available songs (Verizon Wireless, 2012).

Sprint Music Plus. Sprint Music Plus is powered by RealNetworks Inc., and allows users to create music playlists, search for music by artist, title or keyword, and organize full tracks/albums by artist, genre and custom playlists using the music library manager. Like V CAST, songs are available from 69¢ to $1.29 (Sprint, 2012).

Subscription-Based Services

With the evolution of track-based DRM-free Internet and wireless music options, astonishing growth has occurred in the subscription arena from 4 major services in 2010 (eMusic, Napster, Rhapsody and Zune) to close to 20 in mid-2012.

eMusic. eMusic started as the first online music store in 1998 and was the first to offer DRM-free tracks in 2007. It has licensing deals with all of the major record labels, but is known for its large number of contracts with independent labels and its diverse music catalog. eMusic is also one of the more expensive services, with the Basic plan of 24 downloads per month offered for $11.99/month (eMusic, 2012).

Rhapsody. Rhapsody, which purchased Napster from Best Buy in October 2011, offers two types of subscription services: Rhapsody Premier Plus and Rhapsody Premier. Premier, available for $9.99 per month, allows subscribers to listen to all available music (over 13 million tracks) online using a Windows PC, on a supported digital media player, on a supported home audio device, and on one mobile device. Rhapsody Premier Plus, available for $14.99 per month permits listening on up to three mobile devices (Rhapsody, 2012).

Zune Music Pass. From Microsoft, and for $14.99 per month, Zune Music Pass includes unlimited access to 4 playback devices synched to the Zune Marketplace online music store. The Zune devices come in five styles, all of which play music and videos, display pictures, and receive FM and HD radio broadcasts. They can share files wirelessly only with other Zunes and via USB (universal serial bus) with Microsoft's Xbox 360, and can sync wirelessly with Windows PCs. Microsoft, though, discontinued the Zune in 2011. The Zune software allows users to manage files on the player, rip audio CDs, and buy songs at the online store. The Zune Music Pass subscription allows subscribers to download as many songs as they like from Zune Marketplace and listen to them while their subscription is active (Zune, 2012).

Pandora. Built on the Music Genome Project, a patented mathematical algorithm that scans over 400 musical attributes of songs selected by users (like rhythm, tempo, syncopation, key tonality, vocal harmonies, etc.), Pandora creates customized "stations" based on similarly-matched artists, songs and styles to provide a free streaming playlist music service. Pandora also features a premium option: Pandora One, a $36 per year subscription that removes all visual and audio ads, increases bits-per-second to 192k, and removes the 12 skips per day limit (although you're still limited to six skips per station per hour).

Rdio. This online streaming service features three levels of subscription service, all without advertising: a free, but restricted-play-per-month Web-only service, an unlimited Web-only service ($4.99/month), and an unlimited web and mobile streaming service ($9.99/month). A family unlimited plan for two ($17.99/month) or three ($22.99/month) members can also be selected. Over 12 million songs are available from 12 different labels (rdio.com, 2012).

Spotify. Coming to the U.S. from Sweden, Spotify is a streaming music service similar to Pandora and Rdio. Spotify's free account is computer-based, advertiser supported, and does not allow playback on mobile devices. The Spotify Unlimited $4.99/month option removes the ads and has unlimited desktop streaming, while the $9.99 Premium option increases the bit-rate to 320k, removes ads, and enables mobile access.

Grooveshark. With over 35 million users, Grooveshark is the world's largest on-demand music streaming and playlist service. It is also being sued by the major record labels for copyright infringement (see below). Grooveshark is an ad-supported service that offers free music by enabling users to post their own tracks to the site and then share them with other users. In addition to its free tier, it has a $6-a-month advertising-free plan and a $9-a-month service that works on modified smartphones. Once a user finds a song or artist, a playlist can be started. Grooveshark will then recommend songs based on the selection, and the user can favorite songs, play the songs, add them to a queue or playlist, or embed them as a widget on a website. As with most playlist sites, users can also share Grooveshark musical selections with Twitter, Facebook, and Stumbleupon, or grab the RSS feeds of their activity to take with them (Grooveshark, 2012).

MOG. This service, with over 14 million songs streaming at a high-quality 320kbps, features three levels of service: Freeplay with advertising, Basic with no ads and unlimited music ($4.99/month) and Primo with unlimited music, no ads, mobile access and unlimited downloads ($9.99/month). MOG partnered with Rhapsody to allow Rhapsody subscribers to access all of Rhapsody's content through MOG. The MOG Music Network is a music blog network that aggregates original content (written by in-house editors) and syndicated content from over 1,300 affiliate blogs (MOG, 2012).

Sony Music Unlimited. This service offers two subscription plans, a Basic Plan ($3.99/month) and a Premium Plan ($9.99/month). The Basic Plan has two primary features—Pandora-like artist-based "radio" channels (My Channels) and iTunes-like music importing and synching of your already-purchased PC music library (Music Synch). The

Premium Plan includes these features and provides access to Sony's 10 million-song catalog on your PC, mobile devices, or Playstation (Sony Entertainment Network, 2012).

Free Playlist & Webcaster Services

Slacker Personal Radio. Slacker is an interesting playlist music service. On the one hand, the free version—like Pandora—lets users listen to pre-made stations or create stations based on artists, albums, or tracks they choose. When users create such a station, it is populated with tracks that are supposed to be harmonious with the original selection. If users purchase a Premium Radio subscription ($9.99 per month)—as with such subscription services as MoG, Rdio, Rhapsody, and Spotify—they additionally have the ability to play songs, albums, and single-artist stations on demand as well as cache albums and playlists on your portable devices (Slacker Personal Radio, 2012) .

last.fm. last.fm is a free global music playlist service that exposes its community of over 40 million users worldwide to new and relevant music through its proprietary "scrobbling" technology. Scrobbling allows the audience to track the music they play on last.fm, Radio.com and on more than 600 music applications. Last.fm then uses the collective intelligence to recommend the songs and artists that power its personalized radio stations. Related music will populate the station with the ability to love, ban, and skip tracks as appropriate. To play content on a mobile device, a $3/month subscription is required (last.fm, 2012).

Blip.fm. A blip is a combination of a song and a short message that accompanies it. Blip centers on the user as DJ and the individual songs that are blipped. The DJ would search for a track he wanted to blip, write a Twitter-style note about the selection, and blip it for listeners. Then, depending on user-selected settings, the blip could be broadcast to social sites such as Twitter, FriendFeed, or Tumblr, and even update a Last.fm scrobbler. DJs can reply to other DJs and can give out tokens of respect called "props." As a user starts to blip a bit more and add favorite friends as DJs, the blip-generated playlist starts to expand. Users can customize a few settings, but essentially every time DJs

blip, their songs will be populated in the user's mix for a potentially never-ending assortment of songs (Blip.fm, 2012).

Digster. Digster is a service that publishes playlists for use in Spotify and iTunes. Playlists are compiled by a team of Universal Music Group editors, can be imported into iTunes and Spotify, and can be listened to for free on Spotify Free, which is funded by ads. Ads can be disabled by paying a monthly fee. Every track and playlist on Digster is linked to a corresponding track on iTunes, so users can buy a playlist or a selection of tracks with just a few clicks (Digster, 2012).

SoundCloud. SoundCloud.com is a free basic service that allows sound creators, from home users to musical artists and composers, to instantly record audio on the site or via mobile applications and share them publicly or privately. The service operates much in the same way as Twitter, where registered users can follow other users and receive notification of new activity in their stream.

Listening to music via SoundCloud provides a different kind of visual experience. For example, each track is represented by a waveform with member comments layered on top. Comments are tied to specific points in the song, and will be displayed accordingly for future listeners to read as they listen to the song. SoundCloud offers additional features to users with paid subscriptions. Such users are given more hosting space and may distribute their tracks or recordings to more groups and users, create sets of recordings, and more thoroughly track the statistics for each of their tracks (SoundCloud, 2012).

turntable.fm. turntable.fm puts a different spin on digital music by giving users a free, social way to listen to Internet music. Users enter the site via Facebook or Twitter and choose between creating a music room or entering an existing one. A room, by default, can have 5 DJ's at once, and it is a turn based game. Each DJ has their turn to play a song after the DJ before them finishes theirs. It is almost like a competition between DJ's, whoever can get the most people bobbing to their song. Listeners start bobbing by clicking 'Awesome' when listening to a song they like. The DJs are represented by avatars sitting at a desk in the front of the room and the listeners by avatars standing in front of the desk. Listeners can chat and vote on each song—lame or awesome. Too many votes for lame and the song stops, but the DJ gets a point for each awesome vote.

The music can come from turntable.fm's library of over 11 million songs, powered by MediaNet, or users can upload music from their personal library. In addition, turntable.fm recently signed licensing agreements with all of the major record labels to operate as a streaming audio service with advertising (Sisario, 2012). An iPhone app is also available.

8tracks. This is a free non-interactive web radio service where users do the choosing of music. Members pick at least eight songs (hence the name) from their own collections, upload them and share them as handcrafted mixes that seem like a happy throwback from the cassette era. Users can find mixes created by Facebook friends or simply follow other members who share similar tastes (8tracks, 2012). And it's legal—8tracks takes advantage of a provision in the Digital Millennium Copyright Act, which gives webcasters a compulsory license to operate as a "non-interactive Webcaster." This means that 8tracks can stream any uploaded music as long as 8tracks operates, like it currently does, as a radio station and pays the Sound Exchange royalty fees.

Cloud Music Services

The three major cloud service providers offer similar products with a similar mission: Allow users to buy new music and access existing libraries from multiple devices, via streaming from the cloud.

Google Play with Google Music. Google Music is free to all users. This includes access on the web, desktop and mobile devices. Google does impose a library limit of 20,000 songs that a user may upload. However, purchased songs do not count against this cap. All music is streamed and does not require download to a device in order to listen. Google's mobile streaming product is available to both Android and iOS devices (Google, 2012).

iCloud with iTunes Match. This service is available from Apple for $24.99 a year. For that $24.99, users get the ability to upload 25,000 songs plus any iTunes purchases. Apple uses iTunes as its central music listening hub. Users can authorize up to ten devices for use with iTunes Match—five can be computers with iTunes—to stream or download songs. Apple's mobile solution is the most limited in terms of device access. Playlist syncing and file access is only available on an iOS device (Apple, 2012).

Amazon Cloud Drive with Cloud Player.

The service is free for up to 5GB of uploads. As with Google Music, Amazon.com MP3 purchases do not count against this cap. Unlimited space for all music, regardless of purchase location, is included with all paid storage plans of 20GB and up. Like Google Music, all music is streamed and does not require download to a device in order to listen. Amazon provides a mobile app for Android and an iPad-friendly web view of its library (Amazon, 2012).

Cyberlocker Services

The new "bad guy on the block" in illegal file sharing is the cyberlocker service (details in the next section). Cyberlockers are online data hosting services that provide remote storage space within a secure cloud-based storage system. They can be accessed globally over the Internet and are often called online storage or cloud storage services. Megaupload, RapidShare, Hotfile, 4Shared, and Mediafire are the most popular cyberlockers. The storage capacity provided by these cyberlockers varies depending on the price. Services normally offer some storage and downloading services for free, and then charge for premium accounts that include more storage capacity and faster file transfers (Wyman, 2012).

Because of the anonymity and restricted access they provide, cyberlockers are criticized for being used as a safe haven for piracy. Why? Cyberlocker users get an IP address (or URL), and then can share it with whom they choose. Unlike P2P programs such as BitTorrent clients, where the IP addresses of those sharing infringing files can easily be collected from the network using search crawlers, authorities are not able to track IP addresses of those who download infringing works through cyberlocker services. This makes it difficult to forward RIAA notices of infringement to such users. And, just as important, cyberlocker services, in order to stay within DMCA guidelines, do not provide search engines on their sites to allow users to search for what other users have uploaded there (Mullin, 2011). A number of third party search engines, like FilesTube, do provide this solution.

Copyright Legislation, Cases & Actions

Graduated Response. Beginning in July 2012, the RIAA is relying on new partnerships with major ISPs, including AT&T, Cablevision, Comcast, Time Warner Cable and Verizon, to track down pirated online content. In this new "graduated response" enforcement system, the RIAA alerts an ISP that a customer appears to be file sharing illegally. The ISP will then notify the person that he or she appears to be file sharing by sending a "copyright alert." If the behavior by the customer does not change, up to four more alerts are sent. If the customer ignores these, then the ISP may choose to use "mitigation measures" to limit, suspend or terminate the person's service. Monitoring will be via a third party company, which will watch BitTorrent networks and other public networks and gather IP addresses. Those who think that the ISP is in the wrong, can call for an independent review, at the cost of $35, before a mitigation measure is initiated (Center for Copyright Information, 2012).

The Pirate Bay. In February 2012, Sweden's Supreme Court refused to hear an appeal from the founders of The Pirate Bay P2P service, who were found guilty of copyright infringement and illegal file sharing in 2009. Previously, in November 2010, a Swedish appeals court upheld the convictions and increased the fines from $4.5 million to $6.5 million. As a result, The Pirate Bay switched its service from using torrent files to magnet links. The magnet links are a type of "trackerless" file that pre-calculates a torrent hash (the code helping leechers find peers with the file they seek) and places the hash within the link. Users looking for a file can then request it in a decentralized way,

rather than ask a centralized torrent server to connect the user with another peer. Ultimately, this prevents anti-piracy laws in any one country from shuttering the site at a moment's notice (Olanoff, 2012).

Megaupload. The DOJ describes cyberlocker Megaupload.com as a massive criminal operation in which the main website acted as a conduit to other sites where pirated content—including books, movies and music—was easily available. In carrying out the arrests, the DOJ worked with law enforcement agencies in at least eight other countries.

Seven individuals and two corporations were indicted by a Virginia grand jury with running an international organized criminal enterprise allegedly responsible for massive worldwide online piracy of numerous types of copyrighted works, through Megaupload.com and other related sites, generating more than $175 million in criminal proceeds and causing more than half a billion dollars in harm to copyright owners.

The DOJ describes this case as "among the largest criminal copyright cases ever brought by the United States and directly targets the misuse of a public content storage and distribution site to commit and facilitate intellectual property crime (DOJ, 2012b, p. 1). In addition, Megaupload allegedly offered financial incentives and a rewards program for users to upload popular copyrighted content and drive web traffic to the site via third party linking sites and search engines.

Grooveshark. Universal Music Group filed a lawsuit against Grooveshark.com on November 18, 2011 because, unlike similar online jukebox services Pandora and Spotify, the site did not obtain licenses to stream Universal content. Since January 2012, three other record labels (EMI, Sony and Warner Music) have joined the lawsuit. Ordinarily, websites are protected by the DMCA safe harbor provision which ensures that sites are not liable for copyright violations by their users. In order to preserve this legal shield, the site owners must respond to take-down notices provided by copyright owners. They must also ensure they are not directly controlling and profiting from the infringement. In Grooveshark's case, however, the facts provided by

Universal suggest the company may have forfeited the safe harbors (Peoples, 2012).

Current Status

CEA Sales Figures

Details on the current state of the digital audio marketplace from the *2011 Digital America* report included:

✦ Like video consumption, more than half (54%) of online U.S. adults listen to digital audio in the home.

✦ But unlike video, the preference for digital audio content skews toward downloaded audio (43%) versus streaming audio (37%).

✦ Those digital audio consumers spent an average of 2.6 hours per day listening to downloaded files versus two hours for streaming audio.

✦ One in four consumers expressed an interest in purchasing a home media connectivity system like those from Sonos or NuVo Technologies.

✦ Home audio equipment sales (wholesale) grew an estimated 6.2 percent in 2010 to $3.55 billion despite the weak economy. That followed two consecutive years of declines attributable, for the most part, to the recession. For 2011, CEA forecasts 6.4 percent growth for home audio sales.

✦ Portable audio equipment sales (wholesale) at an estimated $5.98 billion in 2010 were 160 percent higher than they were in 2004. That growth is attributed to the digital media player revolution (CEA, 2012a).

Nielsen SoundScan Data

Nielsen SoundScan, the sales source for the Billboard music charts, tracks sales of music and music video products throughout the United States and Canada. Sales data is collected weekly from over 14,000 outlets, including brick and mortar merchants, online retailers, and performance venues. SoundScan data from 2011 was compiled in the Nielsen Company Year-End Music Industry Report. Some of the report's most interesting findings:

✦ For the first time, digital music sales were larger than physical sales, accounting for 50.3% of all music purchases in 2011.

✦ Digital track sales set a new record with 1.27 billion sales in 2011—an increase of 100 million sales (8.4%) over 2010.

✦ Digital album sales exceeded 100 million for the first time with a new all-time high of 103.1 million sales (up from 86.3 million in 2010), an increase of nearly 20%.

✦ Digital album sales accounted for nearly 1 out of every 3 album purchases (31%) in 2011, compared to 26% in 2010, 20% in 2009, 15% in 2008, 10% in 2007 and 5.5% in 2006.

✦ For the last week of 2011 (week ending 1/1/2012), digital album sales set a new high with sales of 3.5 million.

✦ For the first time, more than 100 digital songs (112) exceeded the 1 million sales mark for the year.

✦ In 2011, eight different artists broke the 10 million digital track sales mark (BusinessWire, 2012).

IFPI Digital Music Report

The International Federation of the Phonographic Industry (IFPI) is the organization that represents the interests of the recording industry worldwide. IFPI is based in London and represents more than 1,400 record companies, large and small, in 75 different countries. IFPI produces an annual report on the state of international digital music, and the *Digital Music Report 2012* also provides some interesting information on the current state of the global digital music industry:

✦ The global number of paying subscribers for music services has grown by 65%, from an estimated 8.2 million in 2010 to more than 13.4 million in 2011.

✦ Digital music revenues to record companies grew by 8% globally in 2011 to an estimated $5.2 billion. This compares to growth of 5% in 2010 and represents the first time the year-on-year growth rate has increased since IFPI started measuring digital revenues in 2004.

✦ The top selling digital single of 2011 was Bruno Mars' *Just The Way You Are*, which sold more than 12.5 million copies. The combined sales of the top ten digital singles grew by 11% in 2011.

✦ Anti-piracy investigators used the latest automated technology to identify and remove infringing links worldwide. In 2011, it removed more than 15 million tracks, up from seven million in 2010, an increase of 115%.

✦ 28% of Internet users globally access unauthorized services on a monthly basis, according to IFPI. Around half of these are using peer-to-peer (P2P) networks. The other half is using other non-P2P unauthorized channels which are a fast-growing problem.

✦ The most heavily-used illegal music service in North America, LimeWire, was closed in October 2010 when a federal court in New York issued a permanent injunction against the company. The percentage of the U.S. Internet population using a P2P file-sharing service fell from 16% in the fourth quarter of 2007 to 9% in the fourth quarter of 2010, when Limewire ceased its file-sharing operations (IFPI, 2012).

Sustainability

One of the great features of digital audio is that it can be used to present, distribute and archive information on sustainability. There are a number of well-organized and potentially impactful websites for those interested in national and global sustainability efforts. Here are a few to consider:

Security & Sustainability Forum's website (http://securityandsustainabilityforum.org/archives/audio-interviews) provides sustainability information for industry, government, academics and others interested in the environmental impacts that threaten national security. Digital audio podcasts are available to the public on topics such as corporate sustainability, smart food decisions, sustainability and health impacts of climate change.

EcoTalk.com is a portal and guide to online audio programs, including presentations, presentation excerpts, panel discussions, documentary interviews, online interviews, talk radio guest appearances, broadcast radio news and feature stories, green performances, radio documentaries, and more. Their topical collections cover the full spectrum of environmental and sustainability-related issues.

SustainableCitiesCollective.com collects content and provides resources for all who work in or are interested in urban planning, sustainable development and urban economics. Looking at issues such as transportation, building practices, community planning and development, education, water, health and infrastructure, the group hopes to create a community where people can get involved and learn about the advances in how cities are becoming smarter and greener in the 21st century. Several presentations and conferences are available in their Audio Archive.

Via a series of podcasts, The **University of Oxford** archives an updated collection of meetings, lectures, and special presentations on sustainability issues such as population, transportation, city planning, and forest management. The collection is available to the public at http://podcasts.ox.ac.uk/keywords/sustainability.

And Duke University takes a different approach on its **Sustainable Duke** website (http://sustainability.duke.edu/about/index.html) by sharing audio interviews from students, staff and faculty in a series of "I believe" audio essays. The short pieces present their convictions about making Duke and the world around us more sustainable so that others "might connect with your own passion for making a difference."

Factors to Watch

By the end of 2012, the factors to watch in digital audio will be:

Subscription-based music streaming. As discussed, the explosion of cloud-based music streaming services has been rapid and diverse. This trend will continue as the current providers, as well as startups, vie for consumers in the always-dynamic mobile phone arena, where smartphones will be the driving force. ABI Research forecasts that by 2016 streaming cloud-based services will become a more important form of access to music than owning albums, songs or tracks. According to the ABI, this shift will primarily be driven by the growing use of mobile handsets, especially smartphones, as listening devices. ABI Research believes that number will exceed 161 million subscribers in 2016, a growth rate of nearly 95% per year (ABI Research, 2011).

HD Audio Streaming. Like the gradual proliferation of HD video in the market, there is growing interest in the development of high-fidelity HD audio streaming. The Guardian (Davenport & Arthur, 2012) reported that Apple is developing a new audio format that could allow the company to offer HD audio via iTunes. The format would also integrate an "adaptive streaming" process that would allow music being accessed from iCloud and iTunes Match by portable devices to be automatically adapted to fit bandwidth or storage constraints. Another company to watch in this area is MaxSound, whose Max Sound HD Audio process will be able to convert any audio file to high definition quality while significantly reducing the file size (Max Sound, 2012).

Illegal file sharing. The two factors to watch here are:

1) The impact of the Megaupload case on future lawsuits and interventions by government and copyright holders into cyberlocker activities.

2) The increased involvement of ISPs, as mentioned earlier, in the new graduated response initiative.

Expect to see continued innovation, marketing, and debate in the next few years. Which technologies and companies survive will largely depend on the evolving choices made by consumers, the courts, and the continued growth and experimentation with wireless mobile and Internet streaming technology. Chris Ely, CEA's manager of industry relations, sees a bright, but competitive future:

> Technology allows consumers to access almost any content they desire instantaneously on Internet-connected devices. The rise of mobile broadband has resulted in the emergence of connected devices that are able to stream content directly from the Internet, and services that allow consumers to store and access content without the need of a hard drive. Digital media consumption will continue to grow as the number of connected devices and services for accessing content improves and expands. Manufactures, content providers, aggregators and service providers must work together to ensure the content customers want is accessible through different devices
>
> —Consumer Electronics Association, 2012b

Bibliography

8tracks. (2012, March 16). About. Retrieved from http://8tracks.com/about.

ABI Research. (2011, March 17). Mobile cloud-based music streaming services will be mainstream by 2016. Retrieved from http://www.abiresearch.com/press/ 3640.

Alten, S. (2010). Audio in media, 9th edition. Belmont, CA: Wadsworth.

Amazon. (2012, March 16). Introducing Amazon Cloud Drive. Retrieved from https://www.amazon.com/clouddrive/learnmore.

Apple. (2012, March 16). iTunes in the cloud. Retrieved from http://www.apple.com/icloud/features/.

AT&T. (2012, March 16). eMusic Mobile. Retrieved from http://www.wireless.att.com/cell-phone-service/cell-phone-sales/promotion/eMusic.jsp.

Audio Home Recording Act of 1992, 17 U.S.C. §§ 1001–10 (1992).

Blip.fm (2012, March 15). FAQ. Retrieved from http://blog.blip.fm/faq/.

BusinessWire. (2012, January 5). *The Nielsen Company & Billboard's 2011 Music Industry Report*. Retrieved from http://www.businesswire.com/news/home/ 20120105005547/en/Nielsen-Company-Billboard%E2%80%99s-2011-Music-Industry-Report.

Center for Copyright Information. (2012, March 15). Frequently asked questions. Retrieved from http://www.copyrightinformation.org/faq.

Consumer Electronics Association. (2012). *Digital America 2011*: *Audio Overview*. Retrieved from http://www.ce.org/pdf/2011digitalamerica_abridged.pdf.

Consumer Electronics Association. (2012b, January 17). CEA study finds home media landscape shifting to digital content. Retrieved from http://www.ce.org/Press/CurrentNews/press_release_detail.asp?id=12286.

Davenport, T and Arthur, C. (2012, February 28). Apple developing new audio file format to offer 'adaptive streaming.' Retrieved from http://www.guardian.co.uk/technology/2012/feb/28/apple-audio-file-adaptive-streaming.

Department of Justice. (2012a, March 15). Intellectual Property Task Force. Retrieved from http://www.justice.gov/dag/iptaskforce/.

Department of Justice. (2012b, January 19). Justice Department charges leaders of Megaupload with widespread online copyright infringement. Retrieved from http://www.justice.gov/opa/pr/2012/January/12-crm-074.html.

Digital Performance Right in Sound Recordings Act, Pub. L. No. 104-39, 109 Stat. 336 (1996).

Digigram. (2010, March 11). About world standard ISO/MPEG audio. Retrieved from http://www.digigram.com/support/library.htm?o=getinfo&ref_key=282.

Digster. (2012, March 15). FAQ. Retrieved from http://digster.fm/support/faq/.

eMusic. (2012, March 16). Plans & Pricing. Retrieved from http://www.emusic.com/info/plans-pricing/.

Google. (2012, March 16). Google Play. Retrieved from https://play.google.com/about/features/.

Grooveshark.com. (2012, March 15). Background information. Retrieved from http://www.grooveshark.com/press.

Holahan, C. (2008, January 4). Sony BMG plans to drop DRM. *Business Week*. Retrieved from http://www.businessweek.com/technology/content/jan2008/tc2008013_398775.htm.

Home Recording Rights Coalition. (2000, April). HRRC's summary of the *Audio Home Recording Act*. Retrieved from http://www.hrrc.org/ahrasum.html.

IFPI. (2012, January 23). *IFPI digital music report 2012*. Retrieved from http://www.ifpi.org/content/library/DMR2012_key_facts_and_figures.pdf.

Kalinsky, R. & Sebald, G. (2005, August). Supreme Court's inducement theory in Grokster creates uncertainty. *IP Today*. Retrieved from http://www.iptoday.com/pdf_current/Kalinsky_Sebald_Final.pdf.

Last.fm. (2012, March 15, 2012). Subscribe to last.fm. Retrieved from http://www.last.fm/subscribe.

Max Sound. (2012, March 16). About Max Sound. Retrieved from http://experience.maxsound.com/.

MGM v. Grokster. (2003, April 25). Retrieved from http://www.cacd.uscourts.gov/CACD/ RecentPubOp.nsf/bb61c530eab0911c882567cf005ac6f9/b0f0403ea8d6075e88256d13005c0fdd? OpenDocument.

Metro-Goldwyn-Mayer Studios, Inc., et al. v. Grokster, Ltd., et al. (2005, June 27). 545 U. S. 125 S. Ct. 2764.

MOG. (2012, March 15). What is MOG? Retrieved from https://mog.com/#!what.

Mullin, J. (2011, January 19). How 'cyberlockers' became the biggest problem in piracy. Retrieved from http://m.paidcontent.org/article/419-how-cyberlockers-became-the-biggest-problem-in-piracy/.

No Electronic Theft (NET) Act, Pub. L. No. 105-147, 111 Stat. 2678 (1997).

Olanoff, D. (2012, February 28). The Pirate Bay makes official switch to magnet links. Retrieved from http://thenextweb.com/insider/2012/02/28/as-promised-the-pirate-bay-officially-drops-torrent-files-for-magnet-links/.

P2PON!. (2012, March 15). Top 10 most popular P2P file sharing clients of 2011. Retrieved from http://www.p2pon.com/top-10-most-popular-p2p-file-sharing-programs-in-2009-at-your-request/.

Peoples, G. (2012, March 1). Grooveshark files for dismissal of copyright-infringement case, blasts major labels' lawsuit. Retrieved from http://www.billboard.biz/bbbiz/industry/legal-and-management/grooveshark-files-for-dismissal-of-copyright-1006331352.story.

Podcast Alley. (2012). What is a podcast? Retrieved from http://www.podcastalley.com/what_is_a_podcast.php.

Rdio. (2012, March 15, 2012). Listen to music online. Retrieved from http://www.rdio.com/.

Recording Industry Association of America. (2012, March 15). About copyright notices. Retrieved from http://riaa.org/toolsforparents.php?content_ selector=resources-music-copyright-notices.

Rhapsody. (2012). Pricing & Plans. Retrieved from http://www.rhapsody.com/discover/pricing.html.

Roberts, R. (2012, February 4). Album Review: Van Halen's 'A Different Kind of Truth.' Retrieved from http://latimesblogs.latimes.com/music_blog/2012/02/ album-review-van-halens-a-different-kind-of-truth.html.

Sisario, B. (2012, March 18). *Digital notes: turntable.fm says it has reached deals with labels.* Retrieved from http://mediadecoder.blogs.nytimes.com/2012/03/13/ digital-notes-turntable-fm-says-it-has-reached-deals-with-labels/.

Slacker Personal Radio. (2012, March 16). About us. Retrieved from http://www.slacker.com/company/about/.

Sony Corp. of America v. Universal City Studios, Inc., 464 U.S. 417. (1984). Retrieved from http://caselaw.lp.findlaw.com/scripts/getcase.pl?navby=CASE&court=US&vol=464&page=417.

Sony Entertainment Network. (2012). Music Unlimited. Retrieved from http://www.sonyentertainmentnetwork.com/music-unlimited/.

SoundCloud. (2012, March 15, 2012). The tour. Retrieved from http://soundcloud.com/tour.

SoundExchange.com. (2012, March 15). FAQ. Retrieved from http://soundexchange.com/category/faq/.

Sprint. (2012, March 16). New Sprint Music Plus application provides access to full music tracks, ringtones, ringback tones. Retrieved from http://community.sprint.com/baw/community/sprintblogs/announcements/blog/2011/04/12/new-sprint-music-plus-application-provides-access-to-full-music-tracks-ringtones-ringback-tones.

Strufe, T, (2012, March 15). Peer-to-Peer Networks: Lecture. Retrieved from http://www.p2p.tu-darmstadt.de/teaching/winter-term-20112012/p2p-networks-lecture/.

U.S. Copyright Office. (2012). *The Digital Millennium Copyright Act of 1998: U.S. Copyright Office summary*. Retrieved from http://lcweb.loc.gov/copyright/legislation/dmca.pdf.

Verizon Wireless. (2012, March 15). Music overview. Retrieved from http://products.verizonwireless.com/index.aspx?id=fnd_music&lid=//global//entertainment%2Band%2Bapps//music.

Watkinson, J. (2008). *The art of digital audio, 4th edition.* London: Focal Press.

Wyman, B. (2012, January 20). So long, and thanks for all the pirated movies. Retrieved from http://www.slate.com/articles/business/technology/2012/01/megaupload_ shut-down_what_the_site_s_departure_means_for_other_traffic_hogging_cyberlockers_.html.

Zune. (2012). About Zune Music Pass. Retrieved from http://www.zune.net/en-US/support/zunepass/about/aboutzunepass.htm.

19

Digital Imaging & Photography

Michael Scott Sheerin, M.S.[*]

Why Study Digital Imaging & Photography?

- ✦ Digital photography is the most popular and ubiquitous visual medium in the world, and continues to grow.

- ✦ Digital photography offers a way to place our world in context, as well as a way to record our lives.

- ✦ New imaging software and photography apps make it easier to be creative and make it easier to share our creations with others.

> Big Brother is watching you.
> —from Orwell's 1984

George Orwell's classic novel *Nineteen Eighty-Four* deals with a loss of civil liberties, based on government's mass surveillance techniques. This practice was seen in a negative light by the people of Oceania (the mythical totalitarian state in the book). Flash forward to today. It's not just big brother watching you anymore. It's your big sister, your cousin, a spouse, friends and acquaintances. It's everyone around you, including yourself, watching through the prism of the lens, most often on a compact digital still camera (DSC) or mobile phone. Digital imagery of our lives and ourselves is captured and posted to social networks like Instagram (60 photos uploaded/second), Flickr (4.5 million photos uploaded/day), or Facebook (an estimated 100 billion photos posted by mid-2011) for everyone to see (Pingdom, 2012). And this is obviously something we like to do, not a "Big Brother" government powered scheme. This social surveillance via digital imaging is especially popular in Generation Y (18-32 year olds), as this generation takes 1.5 times more photos, uploads twice as many of these images, and emails 3% more photos than all other generations combined (PMA, 2012). And this surveillance takes place with complete compliance by the subject a vast majority of the time, as a typical Gen-Y'er probably poses for a picture more often in a month than a Baby Boomer does in a decade (purely anecdotal observation)! As Fred Ritchin, professor of Photography and Imaging at New York University's Tisch School of the Arts, points out, "we are obsessed with ourselves" (Brook, 2011).

This obsession with capturing our own image converges with other factors that have occurred in the digital imaging industry. The ubiquitous nature of the camera (83% of Gen Y own at least one camera phone) allows for the opportunity to record the image, while the "jump to screen" phenomenon has changed what happens to the image once recorded. An estimated 29.2 billion digital images will be taken (and saved) in 2012. However, of that 29.2 billion, an estimated 21.2 billion, or 73% of the digital images saved, will not be printed (see Figure

---

[*] Assistant Professor, School of Journalism and Mass Communications, Florida International University (Miami, Florida).

19.1) (PMA, 2012). The images instead will "jump to screen," as we view, transfer, manipulate, and post these images to be viewed on high-definition televisions (HDTV) and computer screens, Web pages, and social media sites. We will send them in e-mails, post them in collaborative virtual worlds, and take, transfer, and view them on smart phones, tablets, and other handheld devices, including DSCs. The digital image has allowed the photo industry to fully converge with the computer industry, thus changing the way we utilize and change these images "post shutter-release." These digital images are not the same as the photographs of yesteryear. Those analog photos were continuous tone images, while the digital image is made up of discrete pixels, ultimately malleable to a degree that becomes easier with each new version of photo-manipulating software. And unlike the discovery of photography, which happened when no one alive today was around, this sea of change in the industry has happened right in front of us; in fact, we are all participating in it—we are all "Big Brother." This chapter will look at some of the implications for society as digital images, both real and manipulated, with few reliable ways to differentiate between the two, enter into all our media.

Background

Digital images of any sort, from family photographs to medical X-rays to geo-satellite images, can be treated as data. This ability to take, scan, manipulate, disseminate, or store images in a digital format has spawned major changes in the communication technology industry. From the photojournalist in the newsroom to the magazine layout artist to the vacationing tourist posting to Facebook via Instagram, digital imaging has changed media and how we view images. The ability to manipulate digital images has grown exponentially with the addition of imaging software, and has become increasingly easy to do. Just broke up with your boyfriend? No more awkward crops needed to eliminate him from your profile picture, as Scalado software offers tools for your mobile device that allows removal of any moving object with a simple touch of the screen (Scalado, 2011)! Photoshop's CS6 promises to simplify this task even more, as the user only needs to identify the area that needs to be replaced and the Content-Aware algorithms will examine the nearby pixels and fill in the designated area, replacing the pixels as if no one was ever there in the first place (YouTube, 2012a).

Figure 19.1

Saved Digital Images—Printed vs. Not Printed (Billions of Images)

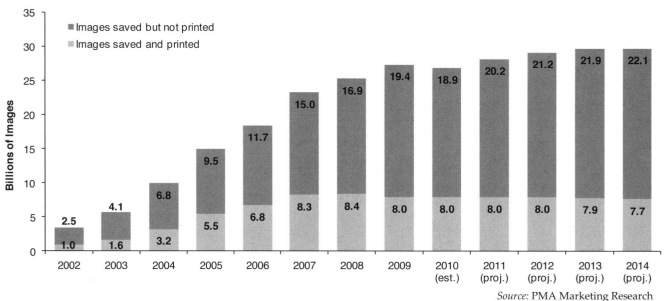

Source: PMA Marketing Research

Looking back, history tells us photo manipulation dates back to the film period. Images have been manipulated as far back as 1906, when a photograph taken of the San Francisco Earthquake was said to be altered as much as 30% according to forensic image analyst George Reid. A 1984 National Geographic cover photo of the Great Pyramids of Giza shows the two pyramids closer together than they actually are, as they were moved to fit the vertical layout of the magazine (Pictures that lie, 2012). In fact, repercussions stemming from the ease with which digital photographs can be manipulated caused the National Press Photographers Association (NPPA), in 1991, to update their code of ethics to encompass digital imaging factors (NPPA, 2012). Here is a brief look at how the captured, and now malleable, digital image got to this point.

The first photograph ever taken is credited to Joseph Niepce, and it turned out to be quite pedestrian in scope. Using a technique he derived from experimenting with the newly-invented lithograph process, Niepce was able to capture the view from outside his Saint-Loup-de-Varennes country house in 1826 in a camera obscura (Harry Ransom Center, University of Texas at Austin, 2012). The capture of this image involved an eight-hour exposure of sunlight onto bitumen of Judea, a type of asphalt. Niepce named this process heliography, which is Greek for sun writing (Lester, 2006).

The next 150 years included significant innovation in photography. Outdated image capture processes kept giving way to better ones, from the daguerreotype (sometimes considered the first photographic process) developed by Niepce's business associate Louis Daguerre, to the calotype (William Talbot), wet-collodion (Frederick Archer), gelatin-bromide dry plate (Dr. Richard Maddox), and the now slowly disappearing continuous-tone panchromatic black-and-white and autochromatic color negative films. Additionally, exposure time has gone from Niepce's eight-hour exposure to 1/500th of a second or less.

Cameras themselves did not change that much after the early 1900s until digital photography came along. Kodak was the first to produce a prototype digital camera in 1975. The camera had a resolution of .01 megapixels and was the size of a toaster (Kodak, 2012a). In 1981, Sony announced a still video camera called the MAVICA, which stands for magnetic video camera (Carter, 2012a). It was not until nine years later, in 1990, that the first DSC was introduced. Called the Dycam (manufactured by a company called Dycam), it captured images in monochromatic grayscale and had a resolution that was lower than most video cameras of the time. It sold for a little less than $1,000 and had the ability to hold 32 images in its internal memory chip (Aaland, 1992).

In 1994, Apple released the Quick Take 100, the first mass-market color DSC. The Quick Take had a resolution of 640 × 480, equivalent to a NTSC TV image, and sold for $749 (PCMAG.com, 2012). Complete with an internal flash and a fixed focus 50mm lens, the camera could store eight 640 × 480 color images on an internal memory chip and could transfer images to a computer via a serial cable. Other mass-market DSCs released around this time were the Kodak DC-40 in 1995 for $995 (Carter, 2012b) and the Sony Cyber-Shot DSC-F1 in 1996 for $500 (Carter, 2012c).

A DSC works in much the same way as a traditional still camera. The lens and the shutter allow light into the camera based on the aperture and exposure time, respectively. The difference is that the light reacts with an image sensor, usually a charge-coupled device (CCD) sensor, a complementary metal oxide semiconductor (CMOS) sensor, or the newer, live MOS sensor. When light hits the sensor, it causes an electrical charge. The size of this sensor and the number of picture elements (pixels) found on it determine the resolution, or quality, of the captured image. The number of thousands of pixels on any given sensor is referred to as the megapixels. The sensors themselves can be different sizes. A common size for a sensor is 18 × 13.5mm (a 4:3 ratio), now referred to as the Four Thirds System (Four Thirds, 2012). In this system, the sensor area is approximately 25% of the area of exposure found in a traditional 35mm camera.

The pixel, also known in digital photography as a photosite, can only record light in shades of gray, not color. In order to produce color images, each photosite is covered with a series of red, green, and blue filters, a technology derived from the broadcast industry. Each filter lets specific wavelengths of light pass through, according to the color of the filter, blocking the rest. Based on a process of mathematical interpolations, each pixel is then assigned a color. Because this is done for millions of pixels at one time, it requires a great deal of computer processing. The image processor in a DSC must "interpolate, preview, capture, compress, filter, store, transfer, and display the image" in a very short period of time (Curtin, 2012).

Recent Developments

As the digital imaging industry approaches the end of its third decade, most recent developments are happening on the post shutter-release side of the imaging process. However, camera hardware improvements continue to evolve, although some are taking a little longer than expected, according to Gordon Haff, who writes for CNET. The new Micro-Four Thirds cameras, or Interchangeable Lens Compacts (ILCs), show promise as a less bulky alternative to digital single lens reflex cameras (DSLRs), while maintaining a sensor that is about five times larger than those found on high-end DSCs. These cameras have electronic viewfinders (replacing the larger mirror-based systems found on DSLRs), but Haff writes that they are "a clunky $100ish add-on that has to be mounted on the camera's hot-shoe, an awkward arrangement" (Haff, 2011).

Digital image resolution continues to improve, not only on high-end DSLRs, but also for the DSCs. In their book *Converging Media*, Pavlik & McIntosh wrote, "Unlike the evolution of other types of media, the history of photography is one of declining quality" (Pavlik & McIntosh, 2004). Images shot with large format cameras in the 1880s were superior to the digital images of only a decade ago. But this statement is no longer accurate, as even most entry level DSC's now fall in the 12-15 Megapixels (MP) range (only 4% of recently purchased DSCs have a resolution less than 10 MP), and, as Roger N. Clark concludes in his study of digital still versus film resolution, the resolution obtained from an image sensor of 10 megapixels or more is equal to or greater than the resolution of 35mm film (Clark, 2012). Only camera phones still lag behind this resolution threshold, as a 2011 U.S. photo industry survey found that 68% of them were MP or less (PMA, 2012). And, according to market research firm IHS, the average resolution is only expected to be 5.7 MP megapixels by 2013 (IHS, 2010). This lack of quality in the majority of camera phones hasn't deterred their usage. The current "Instagram" trend to use filters that give an image a retro look, harking back to old analog film days, emphasizes the point that nostalgia trumps high-end digital resolution concerns for many. An Imaging Confluence study done by the NPD Group in 2011 finds that image taking with a smart phone increased 10% to 27% of the total number of images captured with all devices, while usage with other cameras dropped 8% (NPD Group, 2011). This trend seems likely to continue, as "photograph" resolution isn't as important to those sharing their images on mobile devices and social networking sites. And, as the number of camera phones used to shoot digital images continues to increase, improvements in the resolution and picture quality areas are imminent.

One such improvement is the iPhone SLR mount, which allows for a SLR lens to be used on an iPhone (Photojojo, 2012). However, this device doesn't increase the pixel resolution, only the zoom, focus, and depth of field quality of the smart phone. One product that promises to increase the pixel quality of the smart phone while allowing use of SLR lenses is the concept camera called the Camera Futura. In this design, the CMOS sensor will be incorporated within the mounted lenses body, and is slated to be 31.6 MP, bypassing the camera phone's sensor (Artefact, 2012). However, there currently is no future release date given for this camera.

One camera that just became available in February 2012 and is creating a buzz in the industry is the new Lytro (see Figure 19.2). The technology behind this camera is called light–field technology, which basically allows the user to take a picture without worrying about focus. After capturing what lead developer and CEO Ren Ng terms a "living picture," you can focus the image using proprietary software, and refocus as often as you desire (Lytro, 2012). Pre-release Lytros have been tested by various photographers, and their resulting images can be accessed and interacted with online on the Lytro site. A drawback, according to Joshua Goldman, senior editor at CNET, is the inability to perform simple editing tasks such as color or exposure adjustments. Additionally, there is no Wi-Fi capability or video capture available, and it currently has no Windows support, though Lytro promises to address that issue "sometime in 2012" (Goldman, 2012).

FIGURE 19.2
LYTRO CAMERA

Source (Lytro, 2012)

Turning to the new developments in terms of post shutter-release technologies, the last hardware trend to be covered involves memory cards. Sony's newly introduced XQD memory card promises to have write and read speeds up to 125 Mb/sec (Sony, 2012). The XQD card is a new format that utilizes PCI express data pathway technology and promises to be faster than the current Compact-Flash cards used in most DSLRs today. As of mid-2012, the XQD format is in development, backed by Canon and Nikon (available in the soon to be released Nikon D4 DSLR), and is projected to a storage capacity of 32 Gb (also available in 16 Gb) (Shankland, 2012). The memory card war doesn't stop there though, as Lexar introduced a new CompactFlash card that has a "minimum guaranteed sustained read transfer speed" of 150 Mb/sec and has 128 Gb of memory (Lexar, 2012). It should be noted that most DSLRs and probably all DSCs cannot reach the read/write speeds these cards currently offer. And for the amateur or professional who needs to upload their shots from a DSLR or DSC that is not pre-equipped with wireless functionality, Eye-Fi provides the ProX2

memory card. With 8Gb of storage, the ProX2 can "upload photos and videos from your camera through your Wi-Fi network" to your computer, smart phone or tablet (Eye-Fi, 2012).

Looking at trends on the software side, we see three categories emerge. The first one is the software and apps that allow for photo-manipulation, both professionally and on the consumer level, while the second and third categories deal with mobile devices and file formats, respectively.

1) PhaseOne, professional photographic workflow software, offers SDK apps that allow the user to add to the already robust features in Pro 6 and "build custom applications for image capturing and processing" (PhaseOne, 2012). Though PhaseOne offers the professional excellent photo editing capabilities among their other production functions, they do not match the pure photo-manipulation functions offered in Photoshop. With version CS6 set to be released in Spring 2012, some sneak peeks released via YouTube by Adobe reveal several new features, including upgrades in their Camera Raw 7 processor (currently available for free via Adobe's Lightroom) and the previously mentioned Content-Aware technology, as well as performance enhancers that allow for work to be done while saving, and less lag time (i.e. real time editing) in some of the memory intensive operations (YouTube, 2012b). Adobe's Creative Cloud offers the answer "to turn previously difficult, disparate workflows into one intuitive, natural experience, allowing you to create freely and deliver ideas on any desktop, tablet, or handheld device" (Adobe, 2012). It carries a $50/month service fee that gives you licenses to all their CS software (including all updates and new releases) and is set to be released before July of 2012.

2) From the mobile device category, Adobe's Photoshop Touch allows for touch screen capabilities for photo-manipulation on a tablet, and Revel promises to instantly

update and sync all your photos across your Mac and iOS devices (and promises a Windows version soon) (Paine, 2012). Similar apps can be found that have the same functionality as Revel. Apple offers iCloud for both Mac and PC users, and is free for those running iOS 5. According to Apple, "iCloud automatically and **securely** stores your content so it's always available to your iPhone, iPad, iPod touch, Mac, or PC" (Apple, 2012). Google+ social networking service also allows for instant photo uploading and syncing from a mobile device, with the added benefit of some basic editing and effect apps built in. It is free for PC and iOS users and offers unlimited photo storage for images with up to a 800X800 resolution (images larger than that count against a 1 Gb limit)(Freitas, 2011). The images that these platforms store and sync from mobile devices are also easy to manipulate right on the device. Photo-manipulation mobile apps such as Instagram (Apple's App of the Year in 2011), Snapseed, Scalado and CameraBag allow for professional type effects applications to be directly applied to a just captured image, which can then be posted to Facebook, Flickr, Picasso, or any other social networking site. One measure of the impact of these apps is Facebook's purchase of Instagram in April 2012 for $1 billion. Ritchin, in his essay "Of Other Times and Places" in *Aperture* magazine, predicts that these programs will take "advantage of this malleability and the pervasiveness of the photographic image on the Internet in powerful and potentially very exciting ways" (Ritchin, 2008).

3) The last category mentioned above deals with digital image file formats. Camera RAW is the "native" format of a digital image. A Camera RAW file is uncompressed and unprocessed. It includes all the information from each individual pixel plus metadata and obviously registers as a large file size. That, plus the fact that each manu-

facturer's RAW format is proprietary (and often even different among different camera models from the same manufacturer) and not supported across the board, is a problem the OpenRaw forum was established to address. To bypass this RAW compatibility/support problem, most users choose to save their images as JPEG files, but this format is a lossy one. To combat this issue, Adobe introduced the Digital Negative (DNG) file format back in 2004. Though it has been slow to gain acceptance, Adobe has made significant strides in improving the DNG format, including speed, in terms of faster data loads, "tiled" protocol that divides the file into parts that a processor can quickly read and process, and the option to use a lossy compression algorithm when saving (Shankland, 2012b). The aforementioned new Camera RAW 7 for Photoshop 6 has features that will only work on DNG files, thus encouraging use of this standardized file format. For images that will end up being web-based, Google introduced WebP in 2010, and continues to make improvements, with the goal to supplant both the popular JPEG and PNG formats. Claiming close to a 30% reduction in file size as compared to both formats (including support of an alpha channel), Google's goal with the WebP format is "to create smaller and richer images that can help make the Web faster" (Google, 2012).

On a sad, but somewhat inevitable note, Kodak filed for bankruptcy in early 2012. The company that started in 1880 and became the leader in film-based photography could not adapt to digital photography's arrival, even though it was the first to produce a prototype digital camera (Judkis, 2012). After a debtor-in-possession financing agreement was approved in February 2012 for $950 million, Kodak's immediate goals, according to Antonio M. Perez, Chairman and Chief Executive Officer, are to "bolster our liquidity in the U.S. and abroad, monetize our non-strategic intellectual property, fairly resolve legacy liabilities, and enable Kodak to focus on its most valuable business lines" (Kodak, 2012b).

Current Status

According to Consumer Electronics Association (CEA) 2011 research, DSCs are forecasted to reach 85% household penetration in 2012. Compare this to the 45% household penetration for smartphones, and you can see where the growth opportunity in the industry lies. Indeed, while DSCs were only projected to show a 1% increase in 2011 from the previous year (CEA, 2011), smartphones increased 8% in the first quarter of 2011 (NPD, 2011). Samsung holds the largest percentage of this growing smartphone market at 23%, followed by LG at 18% and Apple at 14% (NPD, 2011). Projected sales of DSCs units in 2011 were close to 37 million, 3 million of which were DSLRs, an increase of 27% from 2010 DSLR sales. Worldwide, 140 million DSCs were sold, with an 11% increase in total sales. All these DSCs and smart phones lead to a lot of image capturing, as over 400 billion images were taken in 2011, with 100 billion in the U.S. alone (CEA, 2011). Consider that PMA projects a much lower number, estimating that only 29.2 billion images were captured in the U.S., as previously noted (PMA, 2012).

The total size (in terms of dollars) of the U.S. market continues to decrease, though not as severely as it had from 2006 to 2009. One area responsible for the declining market value is the printing sector. The number of digital images printed is projected to be stable for the fifth straight year (approx. 14 billion), while the total number of images printed from all devices will fall for the ninth straight year (PMA, 2012). The real culprit is the steep decline of prints made from traditional sources (film). When DSC sales exceeded film camera sales in 2004, DSC usage followed suit, surpassing the number of images printed from film cameras in 2007. Prints made from film cameras have declined 84% since then. That year also represented the high water mark for the number of prints made from DSCs, even though DSC adoption continues to grow, as household penetration has increased by over 13% since 2007 (CEA, 2011). The economy is blamed in part for this decline, as economists state that 2007 was the start of the economic downturn, but another factor probably plays a more significant role. That is the aforementioned jump to screen phenomenon, as images are more often shared via the screen than via prints, illustrated by the fact that the number of images captured continues to increase, while the printing of them continues to decrease, in terms of percentage. The number of prints made has held at around 8 billion, though that figure is projected to start falling by 2013 (PMA, 2012).

Photobook Publishing & Image Sharing

The lone bright spot, as far as economic growth in the photo industry is concerned, is seen in the printing of custom products such as photobooks. This category has risen steadily since 2006, a 46% increase in growth over that time to over half a billion dollars more per year in 2011. It is projected to continue to grow, but at a slower rate, as estimates for 2014 indicate a 9% growth rate from 2011 (PMA, 2012). One of the main reasons for this continued growth is that the Gen Y'ers, the generation that takes 1.5 times more photos than all other generations combined, is, on average, 10% more likely to order products online or from a kiosk. Conversely, other generations are 10% more apt to use a home computer to make their digital prints. Additionally, 26% of Gen Y households own a digital photo frame, compared to only 13% of all others (PMA, 2012). The reason we take these images in the first place seems to be the same across all generations. In a 2009-2010 digital imaging survey conducted by PMA, it was found that over 90% of the time it is done to preserve memories. What we do after we capture the memory is where the Gen Y'ers separate themselves, as 56% of the time they will share these images on a social networking site, compared to only 30% sharing for all other groups (PMA, 2012).

Camera Phones

The Gen Y'ers are also setting the pace in camera phone ownership (83%, compared to 58% for all others), with 43% of them owning two devices (PMA, 2012). So it is a logical progression to state that more of the digital images taken by this generation come from camera phones as compared to the images taken by other generations. And since they are more apt to post these images to a social networking site, it can be deduced that there has been an increase in the number of images posted to social networks recently from smart phones. In 2009, according to research released by Ontela, Inc., only 11% of all images posted to Flickr came from a camera phone. Dan Shapiro, CEO of Ontela, said at the time, "The shortage of camera phone photos posted to the web presents a unique challenge for image hosting services. Obviously, people are finding the process of getting the photos posted to be too cumbersome" (Newton, 2012). New apps, such as the aforementioned Instagram and Google+, plus Pictage and Flickr's own mobile apps, have made this process seamless. If we look at Flickr's Camera Finder app, we see that in a typical month (February, 2012), the top camera used in the Flickr community was the Apple iPhone 4, ranked ahead of all DSCs. Flickr also states that due to the tagging process it uses to identify cameras, camera phones are under-represented in their data (Flickr, 2012). Perhaps a more accurate way to portray the increase in the number of photos taken with a camera phone is to look at Instagram's success. Since Instagram's launch in October, 2010, at least 400 million photos have been uploaded to the site (Litman, 2012)

Factors to Watch

✦ *Moore's Law remains in play*, as seen with the upcoming release of the Sony XQD memory card, as well as Lexar's new CompactFlash with a "minimum guaranteed sustained read transfer speed" of 150 Mb/sec and 128 Gb of memory. Newer cards will continue to offer more storage in years to come, as they increased in capacity from 64 GB to 128 GB between 2010 and 2012, with further increases to follow.

✦ *DSCs Vanishing Point (the option gap closure) becomes a reality.* This convergence continues to happen in two directions, as features once found only on high-end expensive DSLRs are now standard on compact, point-and-shoot DSCs, and image en-

hancement apps on camera phones help close the gap in image quality as compared to DSCs. The market for the Micro-Four Thirds cameras, the ILCs, is a perfect example of this technology convergence.

✦ *Faithful recordings of our past will blur with manipulated recordings.* How will we differentiate between faithful recordings and those images that have been manipulated to represent a "fantasy" world? How will this manipulation change the way we record our past, and how will it change the role of the digital image in society? As Frances Richard states in an article on the state of photography, "Media deliver data, and the opportunity to rewrite data, with instantaneous rapidity" (Richard, 2012).

✦ *Will hyper-photography give us an even better understanding of the image, and thus our lives?* Hyper-photography is Ritchin's name for interactive digital images that provide feedback about the subject matter from the subject themselves. "Whereas analog documentary photography shows what has already happened when it is often too late to help," writes Ritchin, "a proactive photography might show the future, according to expert predictions, as a way of trying to prevent it from happening" (Ritchin, 2012). Perhaps hyper-photography will shift the industry back to "faithful" recordings, or at least help us discern between reality and fantasy.

✦ *Privacy issues will remain, as the dissemination of digital photos on social networking sites increases.* In 2011, Facebook issued a policy change to allow users to un-tag themselves from photos posted by others, but is this enough? With the advent of the widespread use on social networking sites of facial recognition software, will our own role as "Big Brother" continue to help erode our privacy? As one commenter posted, "…the potential for corrupt governments to use it to punish civil disobedience is great" (Mello, 2012).

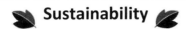

Sustainability

Consumer spending in the digital imaging industry, in all categories except custom products, continues to decrease. The lone exception is seen in the photobook market and offers some hope, as growth in this market is expected to continue to increase through 2014 (PMA, 2012). Other good news comes from the Gen Y demographic. This is a very active group in digital photography, spurring the continued increase in the taking and use of digital images. Monetizing that "use" category is the challenge, as the industry continues to reinvent itself to keep pace with the dynamic changes inherent with this technology. Consider start-up companies like Instagram that have seen phenomenal growth in a short period. Instagram has already been dubbed the "largest social mobile network" and it's less than two years old (Keath, 2011).

Economic sustainability is not the only way to look at the industry, as environmental sustainability is also important. This can be looked at in two ways. One is how digital imaging can help in our ability to monitor the environment. The other is how the industry works to make sure their policies and business practices are "green." A good example of the first factor comes from Rochester Institute of Technology (RIT). Led by John Schott, the Frederick and Anna B. Wiedman Professor in Imaging Science, RIT's Landstat project studies imagery data from satellites that "provides a wealth of historical information on environmental, land, and temperature changes that are greatly enhancing research in agriculture, climate change, and atmospheric science" (Gawlowicz, 2011). The second way that digital imaging is involved in environmental sustainability is illustrated by FujiFilm. Their sustainability efforts "are reflected in the inclusion of Fujifilm Holdings Corporation in the FTSE4Good Global Index, the Dow Jones Sustainability Index and the Morningstar Socially Responsible Investment Index (FujiFilm, 2012). Locally impacted by the earthquake and tsunami in Japan in 2011, FujiFilm both set up on-the-ground support sites and made monetary contributions (830 million yen) to aid the victims. Additionally, a photo rescue project was implemented, with the goal of restoring photos and photo albums that were damaged by water or mud (FujiFilm, 2011). And, in order to help raise awareness about issues of sustainability and conservation, FujiFilm sponsored the Rainforest Alliance's "Picture Sustainability" 2011 photography contest. "Powerful photography is not only visually impressive, but it can evoke emotional responses and stimulate a call to action," said Tensie Whelan, president of the Rainforest Alliance. "Winning photos will captivate a wide audience, connecting people to the concept of sustainability and illustrating the importance of the Rainforest Alliance's efforts to conserve the world's most fragile ecosystems" (Rainforest Alliance, 2011).

Bibliography

Aaland, M. (1992). *Digital photography*. Avalon Books, CA: Random House.

Adobe. (2012). Everything you need, everywhere you work. *Adobe Creative Cloud*. Retrieved from http://www.adobe.com/products/creativecloud.html.

Apple. (2012). What is iCloud? *iCloud*. Retrieved from http://www.apple.com/icloud/what-is.html.

Artefact. (2012). WVIL. Wireless Viewfinder Interchangeable Lens. *Artefact*. Retrieved from http://www.artefactgroup.com/wvil/.

Brandon, J. (2011). Phase One Capture One Pro 6; A top-level image handler. *Software & Computers*. Retrieved, fromhttp://www.shutterbug.com/content/phase-one-capture-one-pro-6-top-level-image-handler.

Brook, P. (2011). Raw meet: Fred Ritchin redefines digital photography. *Wired*. Retrieved from http://www.wired.com/rawfile/2011/09/fred-ritchin/all/1.

Carter, R. L. (2012a). *DigiCam History Dot Com*. Retrieved from http://www.digicamhistory.com/1980_1983.html.

Carter, R. L. (2012b). *DigiCam History Dot Com*. Retrieved from http://www.digicamhistory.com/1995%20D-Z.html.

Carter, R. L. (2012c). *DigiCam History Dot Com*. Retrieved from http://www.digicamhistory.com/1996%20S-Z.html.

Clark, R. N. (2012). Film versus digital information. *Clark Vision*. Retrieved from http://clarkvision.com/articles/how_many_megapixels/index.html.

Consumer Electronics Association. (2011). *Digital America 2011: U.S. consumer electronic industry today*. Retrieved from http://www.ce.org/pdf/2011digitalamerica_abridged.pdf

Curtin, D. (2012). *How a digital camera works*. Retrieved from http://www.shortcourses.com/guide/guide1-3.html

Eye-Fi. (2012). Overview. *Products*. Retrieved from http://www.eye.fi/products/prox2.

Flickr. (2012). Most popular cameras in the Flickr community. *Camera Finder*. Retrieved from http://www.flickr.com/cameras/.

Four Thirds. (2012). Overview. *Four Thirds: Standard.* Retrieved from http://www.four-thirds.org/en/fourthirds/whitepaper.html.

Freitas, D. (2011). Unlimited photo storage on Google Plus. *Google+Today.* Retrieved from http://www.googleplustoday.net/home/2011/9/22/unlimited-photo-storage-on-google-plus.html.

FujiFilm. (2011). Support activities by the FujiFilm Group. *Sustainability Report 2011.* Retrieved from http://www.fujifilm.com/sustainability/report/pdf/index/ff_sr_2011_all.pdf.

FujiFilm. (2012). Sustainability. *FujiFilm Global.* Retrieved from http://www.fujifilm.com/sustainability/activities/.

Gawlowicz, S. (2011). Imaging the earth. *Research at RIT.* Retrieved from http://www.rit.edu/research/imaging_story.php?id=63.

Google. (2012). WebP: A new image format for the Web *WebP.* Retrieved from http://code.google.com/speed/webp/.

Goldman, J. (2012). Lytro camera: 5 things to know before you buy *Crave.* Retrieved from http://news.cnet.com/8301-17938_105-20125910-1/lytro-camera-5-things-to-know-before-you-buy/.

Haff, G. (2011). Trends in digital photography: not so good. *CNET News.* Retrieved from http://news.cnet.com/8301-13556_3-20028327-61.html.

Harry Ransom Center - The University of Texas at Austin. (2012). The First Photograph. *Exhibitions.* Retrieved from http://www.hrc.utexas.edu/exhibitions/permanent/wfp/.

IHS. (2010). Cell phones pressure low-end digital still camera market. *Press Release.* Retrieved from http://www.isuppli.com/News/Pages/Cell-Phones-Pressure-Low-end-Digital-Still-Camera-Market.aspx.

Judkis, M. (2012). Kodak bankruptcy: Photographers mourn. The Style Blog. *Washington Post.* Retrieved from http://www.washingtonpost.com/blogs/arts-post/post/kodak-bankruptcy-photographers-mourn/2012/01/05/gIQAxiXjcP_blog.html

Keath, J. (2011). Instagram becomes the largest mobile social network. *SocialFresh.* Retrieved from http://socialfresh.com/instagram-largest-mobile-social-network/.

Kodak (2012a). Milestones-chronology: 1960-1975. *Our Company.* Retrieved from http://www.kodak.com/ek/US/en/Our_Company/History_of_Kodak/Milestones_-_chronology/1960-1979.htm

Kodak (2012b). Eastman Kodak company receives court approval of completed debtor-in-possession financing. *News and Media.* Retrieved from http://www.kodak.com/ek/US/en/Eastman_Kodak_Company_Receives_Court_Approval_of_Completed_Debtor-in-Possession_Financing.htm

Lester, P. (2006). *Visual communication: Images with messages.* Belmont, CA: Wadsworth.

Lexar. (2012). Lexar Professional 1000x CompactFlash Card, *Photo.* Retrieved from http://www.lexar.com/products/photo.

Litman, M. (2012). Social Media Digest. *Social Media Council Europe.* Retrieved from http://socialmediacouncil.eu/social-media-digest-6-feat-redbull-burberry-instagram-pinterest-and-boticca/.

Lytro. (2012). The Camera. *Lytro.* Retrieved from http://www.lytro.com/science_inside.

Mello, J. (2012). Google+ ties facial recognition to photo tagging, *Today @ PCWorld.* Retrieved from http://www.pcworld.com/article/245876/google_ties_facial_recognition_to_photo_tagging.html.

National Press Photographers Association. (2012). Digital manipulation code of ethics. *NPPA statement of principle.* Retrieved from http://www.nppa.org/professional_development/business_practices/digitalethics.html.

Newton, R. (2012). Camera phone pictures still suck. PR Web. from http://www.prweb.com/releases/2009/06/prweb2584154.htm

NPD Group. (2011). Consumers now take more than a quarter of all photos and videos on smartphones. *Press Releases.* Retrieved from https://www.npd.com/wps/portal/npd/us/news/pressreleases/pr_111222.

Paine S. (2012). The Inside View. *Adobe Revel.* Retrieved from http://www.photoshop.com/products/mobile/revel.

Pavlik, J. & McIntosh, S. (2004). Converging media: An introduction to mass communications. Pearson Education, MA: Allyn & Bacon.

PCMAG.com. (2012). 21 Great technologies that failed. features. Retrieved from http://www.pcmag.com/article2/0,2817,2325943,00.asp

PhaseOne. (2012). PhaseOne SDK. *Software.* Retrieved from http://www.phaseone.com/Phase%20One/Software/Phase-One-SDK/Features.aspx.

Photo Marketing Association Marketing Research Department (PMA). (2012). *Photo Industry 2011: Review and Forecast.* Jackson, MI: PMA.

Photojojo. (2012). The iPhone SLR Mount. *PhotoJoJo Store.* Retrieved from http://photojojo.com/store/awesomeness/iphone-slr-mount/.

Pictures that lie. (2012). *C/NET News*. Retrieved from http://news.cnet.com/2300-1026_3-6033210-20.html?tag=mncol.

Pingdom. (2012). Internet 2011 in numbers. *Royal Pingdom*. Retrieved from http://royal.pingdom.com/2012/01/17/internet-2011-in-numbers/.

Rainforest Alliance. (2011). Rainforest alliance launches third "Picture Sustainability" photo contest, Sponsored by FUJIFILM. *Press Release*. Retrieved from http://www.rainforest-alliance.com/newsroom/news/photo-contest-2011.

Richard, F. (2012). Photography's ghosts: the image and its artifice. *The Nation*. Retrieved from http://www.thenation.com/article/photographys-ghosts-image-and-its-artifice.

Ritchin, F. (2008). Of other times and places. *Aperture, 190,* 74-77.

Ritchin, F. (2012). Exposure time. *Essay—Change Observer*. from http://changeobserver.designobserver.com/entry.html?entry=11447#last.

Scalado. (2011). Don't let anything stand in your way. *Products*. Retrieved from http://www.scalado.com/display/en/Remove.

Shankland, S. (2012a). Sony launches first XQD cards. step aside, CompactFlash. *CNET News*. Retrieved from http://news.cnet.com/8301-30685_3-57353565-264/sony-launches-first-xqd-cards-step-aside-compactflash/.

Shankland, S. (2012b). Adobe offering new reasons to get DNG religion. *CNET News*. Retrieved from http://news.cnet.com/8301-30685_3-57371809-264/adobe-offering-new-reasons-to-get-dng-religion/?tag=mncol;txt.

Sony. (2012). Beyond Extreme. Sony XQD Memory Card. *Sony*. Retrieved from http://www.sony.net/Products/memorycard/en_us/xqd/index.html.

YouTube. (2012a). Sneak Peek #4, *Adobe Photoshop Channel*. Retrieved from http://www.youtube.com/user/Photoshop?feature=watch#p/c/3/UrlsnQ32YhY

YouTube. (2012b). Sneak Peek #2, *Adobe Photoshop Channel*, Retrieved from http://www.youtube.com/user/Photoshop?feature=watch#p/c/1C15DAB68A34A0D5/1/XLp1dR2sYkE.

IV

Networking Technologies

20

Telephony

William R. Davie, Ph.D.[*]

Why Study Telephony?

✦ The mobile phone era signals a global shift in telecommunications technology and social interaction.

✦ The ubiquity of mobile phone and smartphone penetration around the world commands economic attention.

✦ Mobile telephony's need for spectrum bandwidth threatens other electronic media.

Introduction

You may have heard the phrase, "there is an app for that!" Apple trademarked its tagline coined in one of its iPhone commercials (Gross, 2010). In 2009, Verizon produced a TV commercial spoofing the line while poking fun at its chief competitor, AT&T. "There's a Map for that," Verizon's spot gave its rival with a sideways glance with two comparative cellular maps. AT&T was not amused and filed suit for what it argued was a misleading advertisement (Bradley, 2009). Such commercial warfare indicates the intense competition in this fast growing branch of telephony, (ComScore, 2012).

Not everyone in the world has bought a mobile phone yet, but an increasing number have, and the number of subscribers in the United States alone outnumbers the population based on smartphone and "feature" mobile phone billing (CTIA, 2011).

This mobile lifestyle has the world's citizens pressing their mobile phones to achieve an amazing array of activities: to pay bills, check forecasts, read postings on Facebook, email, Tweet, text, go shopping ("m-commerce") hurl angry birds at green pigs, scan headlines from online news media, create personal soundtracks of music, and even make a phone call. Mobile is the way of the future, and in order to understand the technology, it is useful to consider the sum of its parts.

One way to explain mobile telephony is to think of it as a "stack" of four tiers (Grimmelmann, 2011). At the first level comes the app itself, which might be a video game for amusement, a calendar for appointments, an online newspaper for current events, a music store for favorite tunes, or virtually any square icon's program easily pressed into service. At the second tier, mobile apps rely on an operating system including Apple's iOS, Android, Symbian, or Mobile Windows among others. The third tier is the smartphone itself. Finally the fourth tier is cellular network that connects mobile devices to the rest of the world with acronyms like CDMA, GSM, EDGE, EVDO, and LTE, numbered by the generational technology (1G, 2G, 3G, 4G). AT&T and Verizon operate the largest cellular networks in the United States, but, globally, China Mobile serves the most subscribers.

What of those telephone landlines now; are they fast becoming just part of a bygone era? In a word, yes. The largest American telephone provider, AT&T, is looking forward to the time when it can replace landline phones using circuit-switched networks with the broadband model, and for good reason. (See Figure 20.1 for an explanation of the difference between circuit and packet-switched

[*] Professor, University of Louisiana, Lafayette

networks.) As the number of home customers relying on landline phone service drops in number, the cost of maintaining those networks grows. As a result, AT&T told the government its business model for landline phone services is in "a death spiral," and the Federal Communications Commission should find a way to make the transition to broadband telephone service more efficient through regulatory reform (AFP, 2011).

Figure 20.2

U.S. Mobile App Consumption, Time Spent per Category

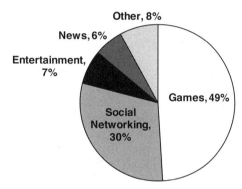

Source: Flurry Analytics, Dec. 2011

Background

The telephone, whether wired or wireless, mobile or tethered, is an essential part of life in the contemporary world. The evolution of this 19th century invention linked to Alexander Graham Bell's genius, along with other tinkerers, is emblematic of technological innovation, corporate oversight, federal intervention, and cultural migration. It seems apt that a Scottish inventor, who first migrated to Canada, and then chose Boston as his home, became telephone's patron saint for his "talking telegraph" that brought friends and families together for over 135 years. Alexander Graham Bell's desire to alleviate both his mother and future wife's hearing loss fueled his quest to invent a machine to amplify and transmit the voice over distances. Accounts of Bell's dramatic race to the U.S. patent office in 1876, arriving ahead of rival inventor Elisha Gray, his exhortation from the Smithsonian Institute's director to complete his invention, and a famous collision of spilled chemicals that produced an excited

telephone summons to Thomas A. Watson, his assisting electrical machine shop mechanic, are all part of Bell's legend (AT&T, 2010a).

In business terms, the Bell corporate legacy drew upon a trusteeship that collected the patents he developed with Watson, who was actually the one who built the first phone ringer, created the first phone switchboard, and designed crucial mechanisms necessary to transform Bell's experiments into a marketable product. Bell's future father-in-law, Gardiner Greene Hubbard, the father of one of Bell's deaf students, Thomas Sanders, and Bell himself formed the core of the company. Bell Telephone incorporated in 1877 with Hubbard serving as its first president. It later acquired a controlling interest in Western Electric Company, and Theodore N. Vail, general superintendent of the Railway Mail Service who impressed Hubbard with his eloquence at hearings in Washington, D.C., was chosen to lead the company.

American Telephone and Telegraph was born on March 3, 1885 (AT&T, 2010b), and Vail became its president twice: during its formation until 1888, and again from 1907-1919. It was Vail's philosophy and desire to build AT&T into a centralized monopoly, which he did through buying out smaller phone companies and creating a transcontinental phone line in 1915 (John, 1999). By the time he retired in 1919, AT&T was reputed to own every telephone pole, telephone switch, and telephone instrument in the country, and its status as a protected monopoly was secured by the creation of the Federal Communications Commission in 1934 (Thierer, 1994).

Vail's corporate monopoly exploited the technology to translate sound waves into electromagnetic signals, modulate them, and transmit them through wired lines. And it was Bell Telephone Laboratory, Inc. that offered an environment rich in experimentation, which became a model of American innovation. By the mid 20th century, Bell Lab schematics designed by engineers Claude Shannon and Warren Weaver, formed the communication model adopted by early social scientists (Shannon & Weaver, 1949). The electronic transmission of voice by telephony logically flows from a source to receiver, through a channel with feedback loops and intervening noise; interpersonal communication follows a similar pattern.

POTS—Plain Old Telephone Service

The backbone of Plain Old Telephone Service (POTS) is a telephone network to circulate human voices by wires and reach the exchange center where multiple calls can be rapidly switched to trunk and branch lines in order to reach their destination. This switching takes place over what is called the PSTN, Public-Switched Telephone Network (Livengood, Lin & Vaishnav, 2006). In order to direct telephony traffic with multiple calls arriving and leaving simultaneously, a seven-digit formula is used. The first three digits formed the prefix to reach the exchange code in a particular switching area, and the final four numbers gave the address to complete the call. This analog system of rotary dialing served a vast network of exchange areas circling the world, and to reach more distant networks more numbers were simply added to the address. In 1963, Bell began to replace rotary dial telephones with push button-touch tone models, and rotary dials had become something of a novelty by 1990 (AT&T, 2010b). The shift from analog to digital processing of telephony began in the 1990s, and at this juncture the FCC noted that "the transition away from the PSTN is already occurring, and is likely to accelerate" (FCC, 2011).

Digital Telephony

Telephony evolved through the conversion to digital processing and computer technology for voice mail, caller identification, voice-over Internet protocol (VoIP), and other innovations. The switching of telephone numbers through conversion to computer memory, Storage Program Control (SPC), made switching easier by means of centralized and distributed control systems where digital microprocessors routed vast numbers of phone calls through a block or series of exchanges (Viswanathan, 1992). In the late twentieth century, telephone engineers modified the system of digital transmission to offer data and video services along with the voice telephone circuitry familiar to the PSTN. New fiber optic glass strands replaced copper wires, and computer modems translated telephone calls into binary signals.

Pushing forward telephony even further was a set of digital technologies, beginning with the Integrated Services Digital Network (ISDN), which enabled voice and data information to use the PSTN's electronic circuitry. ISDN afforded access to packet switched networks in videoconferencing so remote callers could simultaneously share video, voice and text. Telephone's migration to broadband ISDN further accelerated the speed of traffic. Asynchronous Transfer Mode (ATM) allowed for the transport of synchronous (voice) and asynchronous (data) transmission. Computer Telephony Integration (CTI) enabled fax, Short Message Service (SMS), and directory services like caller identification (Database Systems Corp., 2012). Vocal telephony via the Internet through TCP/IP eventually gave rise to Voice-over Internet Protocol (VoIP), where transmitted packets of data bypass the PSTN altogether.

Voice Over Internet Protocol

Voice-over Internet Protocol (VoIP) is recommended by the Federal Communications Commission specifying as a "cheap and easy way to make international calls" services such as Fring, Truphone, and the most popular one of all, Skype (DeLaTorre, 2010). In addition, the phone services offered by most cable companies uses VoIP technology. Credit for pioneering VoIP goes to two electrical engineers, Alon Cohen and Lior Haramaty, co-founders of VocalTec Inc., an Israeli telecommunications firm holding patents for an "audio transceiver," a device capable of converting the packets of data to the sound waves for voice phone calls. VocalTec marketed in 1995 its digitizing telephone calls for Internet telecommunications (Marcial, 2000). A variety of standards and protocols make VoIP possible, including the mechanism of starting and terminating VoIP communications, SIP for Session Initiation Protocol. VoIP calls can come directly from a computer, a VoIP phone, or a phone adaptor to make the conversion from analog to digital Internet transmission. What these services have in common is the capacity to convert the human voice into a digital signal for Internet relay that eliminated the cost of PSTN phone calling.

Skype

Skype is a popular product of VoIP that was the brainchild of Swedish inventors Niklas Zennstrom and Janus Friis, who first became famous for a file sharing application called Kazaa. Skype's name suggests it technology (Sky peer-to-peer), where registered users of their proprietary software take and receive calls via computer and use local numbers to reach distant locales. Skype is offered in the United States, the United Kingdom, and select countries in Europe and Asia. Skype was purchased by Microsoft in 2011 and has been aggressive in marketing its VoIP applications for cellular phones, so the future for its services appears very bright (Thomann, 2006).

Birth of Mobile Phones

There is a romantic, sci-fi quality to the mobile phone's invention and its cellular networks. *Frequency hopping* keeps a cell phone's channel in sync while the phone moves to different locations across cells. The hopping principle owes some inspiration to a World War II patent registered by Heddy Lamar, famous film actress of the 1940s and her second husband, pianist and composer George Anthiel. They devised a system for radio control over torpedoes based on a patented design to synchronize frequency shifts in the U.S. Navy's radio control over torpedoes (Couey, 1997). While never adopted by the military, Frequency Hopping Spread Spectrum (FHSS) became part of the Code Division Multiple Access (FH-CDMA) format for early mobile phone transmissions.

The mobile phone itself came from an electrical engineer working on car phones for Motorola's research and development lab. Martin Cooper was inspired by the "communicator" used on the TV series *Star Trek* (*Time*, 2007) and began work on a completely portable phone independent of the automobile. In 1973, Cooper felt it time to summon reporters to view his original mobile phone in action, which he showed off on a city street by calling another engineer in Manhattan. Cooper's historic mobile phone call was placed to Joel S. Engel, head of research at Bell Labs, Motorola's competitor. This early mobile phone was bulkier than Captain Kirk's communicator and was dubbed "the brick" because it weighed almost two pounds (28 oz.), about five times the weight of today's mobile phone (*Economist*, 2009). Perfecting the mobile phone was one challenge but creating a transmitting network for relaying calls on the move was another matter.

The lack of cellular transmission centers needed to follow calls in transit challenged mobile's development, and AT&T was not particularly interested in encouraging entrepreneurs with their equipment. A Texas inventor, for example, built what he called the "Carterfone," which provoked the phone company enough to wage a battle to stop what it alleged was an illegal connecting device. Thomas Carter of Dallas designed his two-way radio attachment so that Texas ranchers and oil field workers could talk over distances using AT&T phones and lines. The homemade Carterfone sold about 3,500 units between 1955-66, and AT&T demanded that the FCC put a stop to it. The court decision that followed fell in favor of the Carterfone, and the precedent established is cited as allowing "any lawful device" to connect with phone company equipment (Lasar, 2008).

For more conventional mobile phones, AT&T needed a network of carefully spaced transmission centers, and Bell Telephone Labs was working on that solution. Joseph Engel along with Richard Frenkiel designed a cellular map that afforded growth in mobility links (Lemels, 2000). They caught the attention of the FCC's early mobile communications engineers, but it would take another generation before cellular phones and transmission networks were widely available to most Americans. Cooper's promotion of his first generation (1G) mobile phone with its brick size was a step forward in analog telecommunications, but besides a few business types like ones working on Wall Street, the DynaTAX 8000X was more a novelty than a market phenomenon. The rest of the world would have to catch up first (Oehmk, 2000).

2G Mobile Telephony

The arrival of second-generation (2G) mobile telephony in 1991 stimulated the world's interest in mobile due in large part to the standard known as Global System Mobile or GSM. This invention of the European Telecommunications Standards Institute (ETSI, 2012) defined GSM both by its search technology to locate network transmission centers and cellular frequencies providing the necessary channel for maintaining the mobile connection. In the United States, the telephone industry took a different approach and opened the market to competing 2G standards. Code Division Multiple Access (CDMA) was designed by Qualcomm and adopted by two American carriers, Sprint and Verizon, while AT&T and T-Mobile opted for GSM. One key difference is the use of the Subscriber Identity Module (SIM card), GSM phones are activated by a SIM card while CDMA phones are activated remotely using the mobile phone's serial number. Another 2G technology is Time Division Multiple Access or TDMA that increases the amount of data the cellular phone can transmit by dividing each cell channel into three time slots. CDMA multiplexes its transmissions across the allocated frequency range.

The mobile telephony channels range from ultra-high frequencies of 380 MHz to 2690 MHz around the world. In the United States most mobile phones are set at frequencies between 800–1900 MHz. Lower frequency channels penetrate building walls more easily, while higher frequencies encounter less interference from competing transmissions (AT&T, 2010b). Multi-band cell phones tend to travel well to different countries due to roaming features that tap different channels. The Finnish firm, Radiolinja began working closely with the phone company giant, Nokia in 1991 to develop mobile phones exploiting GSM capacity. They brought a lighter digital cell phone to the market, the Nokia 1011, which drew customers with its intriguing capacity for Short Message Services (SMS). The Nokia 1011 released on Nov. 10, 1991 attracted customers with its text messaging and international roaming features, plus encoding that was designed to prevent eavesdropping.

A few years later Motorola came closer to realizing Martin Cooper's future vision through the sale of Motorola StarTac, a mobile phone that flipped open easily in a clamshell design. It was the smallest mobile phone available at the time, weighing only 3.1 ounces. The StarTac phone afforded a longer battery life and could use a subtle vibration or ringtone to signal a call. Hollywood and television seem to admire the StarTac's look and feel, placing it prominently in action motion pictures and popular television series like HBO's *The Sopranos* (McCarthy, 2002).

Smartphone Evolution

Cellular transition to smartphone technology began in 1993 with the introduction of the IBM Simon, and it continued over the next two decades with additional features based on software applications. BellSouth sold the Simon with a touch screen design to open an address book, a calculator, and sketchpad, but it was not a market phenomenon—a digital harbinger instead. Nokia in 1996 moved next to the point position with its 9000 model combining mobile phone features with those of Hewlett-Packard's Personal Digital Assistant (PDA). Motorola's engineers advanced further the smartphone competition in 2003 when they introduced the MPx200. This joint venture with Microsoft came with a Windows-based operating system and a full package of AT&T wireless services such as email, instant messaging, and other apps. More Windows mobile-based smartphones followed in 2003 with the Tanager and Voyager models from the Taiwanese manufacturer HTC, and Samsung's SGH-i600. Strong competition entered the market in 2002 when Research in Motion (RIM), a Canadian firm, marketed its first smartphone, the BlackBerry.

BlackBerry to iPhone

The BlackBerry grew out of RIM's line of two-way pagers, and the popularity of its black keyboard design with the "QWERTY" top row of keys tailor made for "thumbing." In addition to its wireless email and mobile faxing features, BlackBerry attracted a corporate base of customers, and boasted 77 million users (Connors, 2012). On city streets, business types studying their mobiles, became known as a "BlackBerry jam," which became the name of the company's annual conference. President Barack Obama is one loyal BlackBerry user, who even refused to relinquish it when he entered the White House (LaVallee, 2009). Others remain loyal to the BlackBerry despite its sagging market share and newer competition that revolves around touchscreen technology.

Apple's tour de force, the multi-touch iPhone, went on sale in 2007 at a stunning price of $499. Rather than focus on sticker shock, it was clear that Apple's uncanny sense of its customers' native instincts proven by the popularity of the iPod meant the iPhone would be welcomed with open arms (Vogelstein, 2008). The iPhone's music download capacity, and other apps encased in its multi-touch screen interface invited customers to intuitively press, pinch, tap, or flick icon squares to meet their need for apps without hardware buttons or handheld styluses. iPhone's reliance on an operating system with a responsive Web browser made 2007 the year that millions decided to place what felt like a combination computer/mobile phone into their pocket or purse.

The following year, Apple came to market with a second-generation iPhone that was even more attractive than the first model at less than half the price, $199. Apple created a companion App Store to support its many uses with the genius stroke of creating free and paid applications for use on either the iPhone or iPod Touch. In 2011, Apple added an artificial intelligence assistant, Siri that gave the iPhone a robotic sound, which was viewed as ironic given that its rival was named Android.

The driving force behind Android's development was Google, Inc., the famous search engine company founded by two Stanford University students, Sergey Brin and Larry Page. Rumors circulated late in 2007 that a new "google phone" would challenge Apple's iPhone after a group calling itself the Open Handset Alliance announced its formation. Google was the leader of this alliance and had acquired the Android name with the aim of creating an open mobile operating system for multiple manufacturers and wireless carriers. Android would be "the first truly open and comprehensive platform for mobile devices," and would be used by T-Mobile, HTC, Qualcomm, and Motorola, among others (Open Handset Alliance, 2007). In 2008, T-Mobile released its "G1" using the Android operating system that some nicknamed "the Google phone," but Google instead in 2010 chose to introduce its own model, the Nexus One (Helft, 2010). Android uses a Linux-kernel based operating system and followed its open-source philosophy by inviting others to configure and modify its features based on the source code distributed freely under the GPL, General Public License.

Recent Developments

The market for smartphones continues to grow by leaps and bounds, and by all indications will continue to saturate the global market. In 2011, an estimated 472 million smartphones were placed in the hands of eager consumers around the world representing about 31% of all mobile sales (Gartner, 2012). Findings of another mobile research study in 2012 saw 42% of American mobile telephone subscribers using smartphones and about 44% of mobile users in leading European nations (France, Germany, Italy, Spain, and U.K.) making use of their smartphone apps. Facilitating the market penetration of smartphones were high-speed (4G) networks and Wi-Fi availability. In 2012, Google's Android and iPhone's operating systems dominated the market while Symbian struggled in European markets and Windows and BlackBerry operating systems found similar challenges in the United States.

In marketing terms, "Droid" refers to some hardware used in Android-based mobile phones, such as HTC's Droid Incredible or Motorola Mobility's Droid, and the Android name itself describes the operating system software used in more than 70 models of smartphones. Android's popularity surpassed Apple's iOS and was second only to RIM's BlackBerry until 2011, when Android took the lead in smartphone operating systems. The late Steve Jobs, Apple's co-founder, told his biographer that Android's operating system owed a great deal to the source code of iOS, which Jobs believed had been lifted illegally from Apple (Lee, 2012).

Nokia took aim at the smartphone market following its newfound partnership with Microsoft, and in 2012 released the Lumia 900 with a Windows-based operating system. Critics lauded its spectacular touch screen, larger capacity battery, but acknowledged the smaller number of apps available to the Windows OS left users longing for such popular apps as Pandora Radio, Instagram, and Words with Friends. While iPhone and Android smartphones boast close to half a million available apps, Windows had somewhere closer to 70,000. Adding to downbeat predictions for Lumia's success came reports of a data connection glitch just two days after its release. That unkind turn of events prompted Nokia to promise the owners of the Lumia 900 a new model with a $100 credit from AT&T (Bensinger, 2012).

Meanwhile, makers of the BlackBerry, Research in Motion (RIM), admitted a measure of defeat in the consumer smartphone competition against iPhone and Android models. RIM shipped only 11.1 million BlackBerrys in the first quarter of 2012, and following a shakeup in management that saw the exit of several key executives, the company promised that its future efforts would be directed toward the business market rather than ordinary consumers who were charmed by iPhones and Android-based smartphones (Ovide & Sheer, 2012).

The worldwide smartphone market grew in 2011 by more than 61% from the previous year's sales due in part to the launch of Apple's iPhone 4S. For the year, shipment volume exceeded 491 million units, up more than 186 million units from 2010. One of every three units shipped was a smartphone, and Samsung's Galaxy Nexus led the way, reported International Data Corporation (IDC, 2012). The soaring popularity of smartphones inspired other creative innovations, and one model in particular caught the gaming community's interest.

Recognizing the attractiveness of video gaming among younger demographics, Sony Ericcson launched a hybrid smartphone/game player called the Xperia Plus in May 2011, which some dubbed the PlayStation phone (Ackerman, 2011). Its Android-system smartphone made its debut at the Gaming Developer Conference in San Francisco. Verizon put the Xperia Plus on sale at a price of $200 along with a two-year contract. Gamers grew excited to find a smartphone equipped with a slide out panel using left and right shoulder buttons, two four-button wheels, and a four-way directional pad in the middle that worked like a joystick. Its critics noticed the 3G CDMA technology with slower upload speeds and network latency that curbed the glee over this hybrid smartphone/game player.

Current Status

As discussed in Chapter 3, diffusion of innovations provides a way of understanding how phases of adoption occur when a market embraces a new invention. Judging the adoption curve for mobile phones, the final phase of adoption is nearing given that the global number of subscriptions is roughly equivalent to 87% of the world's population. Mobile subscriptions were 4.7 billion worldwide in 2009, then jumped to 5.4 billion in 2010, and moved up again in 2011 to 6 billion. Two of the most populous countries, India and China, added 300 million mobile subscriptions in 2010, and today's combined total is 963 million Chinese subscribers and 884 million in India. Understandably, the top three cellular network providers in the world are China Mobile, China Unicom, and Bharti Airtel India (mobiThinking, 2012).

In terms of smartphone and mobile phone competition, the manufacturing brands leading the way are Nokia for its feature phone popularity and Samsung for its smartphones, which are substantially ahead of Apple sales. Samsung's popularity is due to its Galaxy line and the operating system by Android, which saw 329.4 million models shipped in 2011. Two thirds of the global market purchases are not smartphones, however, and a trusted mobile phone name is Nokia, which has shipped a total of 417.1 million mobile phones. By comparison, Apple shipped 93.2 million iPhones in 2011.

In the United States, the adoption curve for personal mobile phones has taken off over the last 17 years. The early adoption rate was a mere blip at 13% of the U.S. population in 1995, but by 2011 penetration passed 80% with many reporting multiple mobile phones per household (CTIA, 2011). In sheer numbers, 33 million Americans had a mobile phone in 1995 but subscriptions topped 300 million in 2011. Another way to look at the 17-year mobile phone adoption rate is to compare it with landline phones. It took 90 years for landlines to reach 100 million households and become integral to American life (CTIA, 2011a). In just 15 years, 47% of older teenagers felt that their mobile phone was a necessity of life and yet far fewer Americans felt their landline phone was that essential (Taylor & Wang, 2010).

Landline Use

A national survey in 2010 illustrates the U.S. trend toward mobile only with one of every four American households reporting they opted to cut the landline phone cord during the previous year. About 25% of all American households were managing to survive on cellular phone service only (Blumberg & Luke, 2010). Among those American households maintaining a landline phone in the home, about one in six (15.9%) said incoming calls were usually answered on mobile phones. The outward migration rate showed landline-only homes fell from about a third in 2005 to less than 13% in 2010 (Blumberg & Luke, 2010). Still landline phone customers have clear reasons for keeping the cord phone in the house. Cable companies meet that need for some home owners by serving an estimated 25.3 million U.S. customers with digital (VoIP) phone service over their fiber/coax lines that link to both the PSTN and the Internet (NCTA, 2012).

Landlines allow access to the whole family, so presumably voice mail reaches everyone sooner. The clearer reception without the "can you hear me now" phenomenon; freedom from re-charging cell batteries; and ease of access to 911 emergency service are among the reasons landline phone customers prefer a tethered option (Donahue, 2010). The criterion for mobile phone celibacy is not purely economic, but mobile subscriptions are advantageous for American adults living at or near poverty. In fact, the likelihood they are cellular only customers is roughly between 33 and 40%. Less than two percent of Americans are without phone service of any kind.

What the FCC has discovered in terms of total telephone revenue over the decade beginning in 2000, is a precipitous rise in mobile telephone revenues with a comparable decrease in toll service. Yet less noticeable is the steady decline of revenue for local service as Figure 20.1 illustrates.

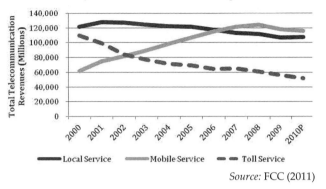

Figure 20.3
Total Telephone Revenue by Year

Source: FCC (2011)

Smartphone Penetration

In 2012, smartphone penetration continued to rise in the United States, and estimates reached between 42-48% of the population. Pew Center's figures in 2011 showed 83% of the American people owned a mobile phone, and about 35% of all American adults reported using a smartphone. For 25-34 year olds, the adoption rate reached nearly two-thirds of the population (66%). The curve continues to trend toward older, wealthier Americans. "When age and income are both taken into account, older subscribers with higher incomes are more likely to have a smartphone," the Pew Center reported (Smith, 2011). The projection based on current adoption rates is that at least half of all American adults will have a smartphone in the next two years.

American smartphone users are most often using one of two popular platforms—Android or iPhone—while Blackberry, Windows and Palm have fallen noticeably behind. Android is the current leader based on data compiled by three sources—Pew, Nielsen and Comscore—who agree that 36% of American smartphone owners use Android operating systems, 10% more than iOS users (26%), and Samsung's Galaxy line appears to be most popular for Android mobile phones. Nielsen's fourth quarter research saw an uptick in Apple's customer base in 2011 following the launch of the iPhone 4S (with Siri) in October. More than 44% reported an iPhone 4S preference, although not quite enough to overcome Android's 46.3% lead (Nielsen, 2012). Blackberry users totaled between 23-26% of the market followed by Windows and Palm platforms.

3G + 4G Networks

Some cellular networks employ 3G technology for mobile broadband use. 3G formats include Verizon and Sprint's EVDO (Evolution Data Optimized) and HSPA (High Speed Packet Access), the format used by AT&T and T-Mobile. Even though Verizon and Sprint opted for EVDO mobile broadband, HSPA proponents claim it excels in network efficiency and offers a greater capacity for handling peak data loads. HSPA is actually a fourth generation or 4G technology, which means it offers mobile communications virtually everywhere with the capacity for downloading music and videos at high speeds on secure networks. Such terms can become confusing. The rollout of 4G technologies such as Long Term Evolution (LTE) and Worldwide Interoperatiblity for Microwave Access (WiMAX) has moved EVDO and other 3G networks to the background given the priority of speed and access. WiMAX projects a radius for wireless reception that encompasses city boundaries as opposed to the confines of a coffee shop or neighborhood block. WiMAX speeds appear to be superior to cable and DSL although that can vary depending upon the locale and network involved. As of mid 2012, Sprint Nextel uses WiMAX for its 4G service.

Long Term Evolution or LTE is the standard bearer of 4G technology since its launch in 2009. What constitutes a 4G technology depends on standards set by the International Telecommunications Union (ITU), which lists peak speed requirements of 100 megabits per second for high-mobility communication and 1 gigabit per second for relatively stationary users (ITU, 2008).

In the United States, Verizon Wireless promoted its LTE network that was launched in 2010 as the leader in 4G technology using 700 MHz bandwidth of C-Block spectrum. Its public relations material promises that "4G LTE network will ultimately connect a full range of electronics devices," including automobiles, television, and home appliances. Sprint Nextel assured its customers that the roll out of 4G LTE services in 2012 across the Sunbelt cities of Atlanta, Dallas, Houston, and San Antonio would lead the way in services followed by Baltimore and Kansas City. The aim for Sprint Nextel is to give customers "better sig-nal strength, faster data speeds, expanded coverage, and better in-building performance" as part of the LTE experience (Sprint, 2012). What that means for Sprint's WiMAX services remains to be seen.

Corporate Merger Denied

AT&T proposed a merger with T-Mobile USA in 2011, announcing plans to combine its spectrum with T-Mobile's and reach 97% of the American people with 4G LTE wireless service. The company embarked on an advertising campaign aimed to convince the public that this merger would not cost American jobs or raise monthly bills but would improve wireless service instead. However, Sprint Nextel Corp. opposed the merger and filed a lawsuit to make its position known to the government. AT&T's counter arguments failed to persuade the U.S. Justice Department and AT&T called off the proposed merger.

Factors to Watch

In 2010, the White House announced plans to secure at least 500 MHz of additional spectrum for mobile- and fixed-wireless broadband use (Obama, 2010). Based on the President's initiative, the FCC began to identify broadcasters as "inefficient" users and tried to coax them to give up spectrum in exchange for a share of the proceeds from the auction of their bandwidth channel. Needless to say, this federal invitation to broadcasters to sacrifice spectrum for cellular media has not set well with the broadcasting industry. CBS Chief Executive Les Moonves said it plainly, "spectrum is our lifeblood" (Wyatt, 2011). CBS holds the licenses of 14 TV stations in large markets and the frequencies they occupy are just the sort of spectrum the FCC would like to repurpose for mobile.

From Washington's perspective, there is 120 megahertz of desirable bandwidth that would increase the number of wireless and cellular channels by as much as 22%. From the broadcaster's perspective, squeezing more TV channels into tighter spectrum spaces will cause interference, and their channels' technical value includes reception through buildings and obstacles. Until the government is more forthcoming about how it plans to share billions in auction fees, the broadcasters appear unlikely to volunteer to vacate their spectrum, even though fewer homes than ever watch television over the air, preferring the channels of cable, satellite and Internet instead. FCC Chair Julius Genachowski promised broadcasters the government will not force broadcasters to give up channels, but added that he will not undermine "the potential effectiveness of an auction by giving every broadcaster a new and unprecedented right to keep their exact channel location" (Wyatt, 2011). Consequently, if the FCC refuses to renew station licenses in order to repurpose their broadcast spectrum for auction, TV station managers vow to fight any confiscation in court.

There is a bandwidth jam in the United States, and chief executive officers for companies such as AT&T Mobility and Verizon stress their need for more spectrum with the launch of each new smartphone model. Popular uses of mobile apps for everything from commerce to health; from information to entertainment; drive consumers to smartphone adoption. It is estimated that one in five smartphone users now scan product barcodes, while one in eight employ mobiles to compare store prices. Social networking sites draw about half of smartphone owners to access their sites. Newer models have a greater need for bandwidth required to share customer photos, videos, and colorful graphics for word games. The iPhone 4S featuring Siri's responsive voice, for example, requires almost twice as much bandwidth as the iPhone 4, and three times as much as the iPhone 3G. Similar apps for Androids and other smartphones mean more sophisticated apps require more bandwidth to run them.

Even though Americans are fascinated by their smartphone's features—regularly downloading apps, texting friends and sharing videos—major carriers such as Sprint and Verizon are feeling the pinch of raising capital in order to build 4G networks and support more bandwidth. Smartphone manufacturers who invent new apps and design new models are gleaning profits without the same measure of investment. It's the cellular networks that support billions of mobile users, and that leaves these networks paying more for frequency bandwidth without commensurate income. Unless the business model changes, cellular providers predict

red ink for their financial statements will be needed between 2013-2015 (mobiThinking, 2012).

Cramming, Cellular Driving, and Security

Key factors to watch in terms of legal issues include intellectual property issues, mobile phone billing practices, and driving restrictions for mobile phone use. Crimes against both cellular and landline customers have caught the government's attention. Google has been addressing charges that its Android mobile software infringes on Oracle's Java technology, and reports say the outcome of the trial on that issue could spell damages of up to a billion dollars. The FCC moved to draft new rules to make the practice of "cramming" less attractive. Because all telephone bills, both landline and mobile phone are notoriously complex, fraud in the form of "cramming," when new cryptic charges appear on bills, are on the rise in mobile services (Gahran, 2011). The FCC estimated that 15-20 million American households received "mystery fees" on monthly landline phone bills, and only five percent of consumers are aware of the inexplicable charges for unauthorized products or services (FCC, 2011).

All of this fascination with mobile phones influences highway safety. Distracted driving is a leading cause of death according to the National Transportation Safety Board, which estimates than 3,000 fatalities in the United States each year can be attributed to either texting, mobile phone talking, or related distractions. As a result, as of mid-2012, ten states now prohibit all drivers from using handheld mobile phones, although hands-free mobile phones are still permitted. Thirty-seven states ban text messaging for all drivers (GHSA, 2011).

Security is becoming a larger concern for mobile phone users with the introduction of mobile viruses, worms and malware. Insidious efforts to compromise mobile apps through such hacking will have an estimated 277 million mobile devices employing some type of protection software to protect business data and other sensitive content stored on mobile phones. As the move to mobile-use over PCs or workstations continues to accelerate, Juniper research predicts the need for greater security software will grow into a multi-billion dollar industry (mobiThinking, 2012).

Sustainability

If "going green" is only a fad, then there is some cause for concern about the impact the mobile phone generation will have on the natural environment. E-waste best describes the estimated 100 million mobile phones discarded by Americans each year in the United States, although some just collect dust in drawers or have been left behind somewhere. Still mobile phones generally hold heavy metals in addition to certain flame retardants containing carcinogens, and so the health issues should not be ignored.

Once a mobile phone reaches a landfill, its elements of lead, nickel and cadmium can contribute to air and water pollution if the landfill has not been scientifically designed to prevent dangerous chemicals from seeping into our food and water supply. Of course not all mobile phones make it to the landfill, but the expenditure of energy resources needed for mining and manufacturing raw materials to replace the ones that do, adds to energy costs. The solution preferred by government agencies is recycling. The EPA estimates "if we recycled all of them we would save enough energy to power 18,500 U.S. homes for a year" (EPA, 2012).

How to recycle a mobile phone? One non-profit group, Recycling for Charities has set the goal of ridding the environment of e-waste, and then making donations to the charity of the mobile phone donor's choice (Recycling for Charities, 2012). Other organizations, such as mobile phone manufacturers, network carriers, and government solid waste programs offer recycling for unwanted mobile phones.

The EPA also reminds consumers to take certain precautions before donating their mobile phone to a recycling service to be sure to clear the phone's memory of stored information, and either use data erasing tools that are available on the Web, or find out how in the product manual to conduct a "factory hard reset." In some cases, mobile phone users also need to remove their SIM cards, and remember to terminate their mobile phone service.

Figure 20.4

Lifecycle of a Mobile Phone

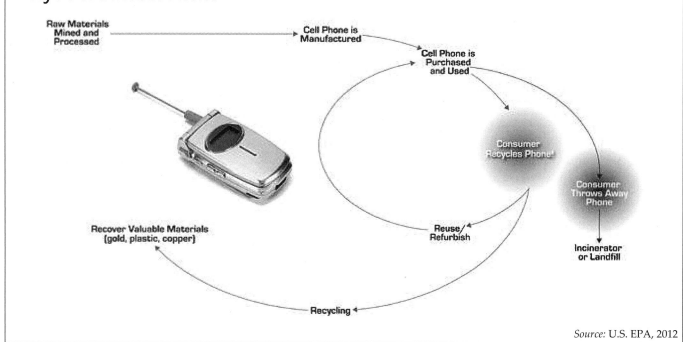

Source: U.S. EPA, 2012

Bibliography

ACA International. (2010). Wireless substitution: early release of estimates from the national health interview survey, January-June 2010, Department of Health and Human Services, National Center for Health Statistics, December 2010. ACA International *Wireless and Landline Phones Statistics on telephone subscribership in the U.S.* Retrieved from http://www.acainternational.org/products-wireless-and-landline-ones-6488.aspx

Ackerman, D. (2011). Gaming on the Sony Xperia Play phone (hands-on). cnet. . Retrieved from http://news.cnet.com/8301-17938_105-20037972-1.html

AFP. (2011, 30 Dec.). AT&T wants out of landline business. *Agence France-Presse*. Retrieved from http://www.google.com/hostednews/afp/article/ALeqM5hUZo87X2Kjw_tHbPPziSNwlraRog

AT&T. (2010a). Inventing the Telephone. *AT&T Corporate History.* Retrieved from http://www.corp.att.com/history/inventing.html

AT&T. (2010b). Milestones in AT&T History. *AT&T Corporate History.* Retrieved from http://www.corp.att.com/history/milestones.html

Bensinger, G. (2012, 11 April). Software glitch mars Nokia's U.S. re-entry. *Wall Street Journal Technology.* Retrieved from http://online.wsj.com/article/SB10001424052702304356604577338003061346114.html

Blumberg, S.J. & Luke J.V. (2010, 12 May). Wireless substitution: early release of estimates from national health interview survey, July-December 2009. *Centers for Disease Control.* Retrieved from http://www.cdc.gov/nchs/data/nhis/earlyrelease/wireless201005.pdf

Bradley, T. (2009). AT&T Sues Verizon Over "There's a map for that" Ads. *PCWorld BizFeed.* Retrieved from http://www.pcworld.com/businesscenter/article/181364/atandt_sues_verizon_over_theres_a_map_for_that_ads.html

Brooks, J. (1976). Telephone: the first hundred years. New York: Harper & Row Publishers.

ComScore. (2012). *2012 Mobile Future in Focus.* ComScore. Retrieved from http://www.comscore.com/Press_Events/Presentations_Whitepapers/2012/2012_Mobile_Future_in_Focus

Connors, W. (2012, March 29). Can CEO revive blackberry? *Wall Street Journal Marketplace*, B1, B4.

Couey, A. (1997). *Micro times — The birth of spread spectrum. How "the bad boy of music" and "the most beautiful girl in the world" catalyzed a wireless revolution — in 1941.* Retrieved from http://people.seas.harvard.edu/~jones/cscie129/nu_lectures/lecture7/hedy/lemarr.htm

CTIA. (2011). *Wireless Quick Facts.* CTIA — The Wireless Association. Retrieved from http://www.ctia.org/media/industry_info/index.cfm/AID/10323

Database Systems Corp. (2012). Computer telephony integration - Inbound/outbound CTI phone and software. Retrieved from http://www.databasesystemscorp.com/pscti.htm.

DeLaTorre, M. (2010). Can I make calls over the Internet from Wi-Fi hotspots? *Reboot.FCC.Gov. The Official Blog of the Federal Communications Commission.* Retrieved from http://reboot.fcc.gov/blog?entryId=524120

Donahue, W. (2010, 22 July). Landlines vs. cell phones - Is it time to cut the cord? *Tribune Newspapers.* Retrieved from http://articles.chicagotribune.com/2010-07-22/business/sc-cons-0722-save-landline-vs-cell-20100722_1_landline-cell-phones-outages

Economist. (2009). Brain Scan — Father of the cell phone. *The Economist* website. Retrieved from http://www.economist.com/node/13725793?story_id=13725793

EPA (2012). Recycle your cell phone. It's an easy call. U.S. Environmental Protection Agency. Retrieved at http://www.epa.gov/osw/partnerships/plugin/cellphone/pdf/cell-flyer.pdf

ETSI. (2012). *Cellular History.* ETSI website. Retrieved from http://www.etsi.org/website/technologies/cellularhistory.aspx

FCC. (2009). Comments — NBP Public Notice #25. Comments of AT&T Inc. on the transition from the legacy circuit-switched network to broadband. Retrieved from http://gigaom.files.wordpress.com/2009/12/1221attbb.pdf

FCC. (2011). *The Public Switched Telephone Network in Transition.* Retrieved from http://www.fcc.gov/events/public-switched-telephone-network-transition

Gahran, A. (2011, 20 June). FCC moves to fight mystery fees on your phone bill *Special to CNN, CNN Tech.* Retrieved from http://articles.cnn.com/2011-06-20/tech/phone.bill.cramming.gahran_1_phone-bills-cell-phone-mystery-fees?_s=PM:TECH

Gartner. (2012). Gartner Says Worldwide Smartphone Sales Soared in Fourth Quarter of 2011 With 47 Percent Growth. *Gartner newsroom. Press releases.* Retrieved from http://www.gartner.com/it/page.jsp?id=1924314

GHSA. (2011). Distracted driving what the research shows. *GHSA Governor's Highway Safety Association.* Retrieved from http://www.ghsa.org/html/stateinfo/laws/cellphone_laws.html; One text or call could wreck it all. Retrieved from http://www.distraction.gov/

Grimmelmann, J. (2011). Owning the stack: The legal war to control the smartphone platform. *Ars technical.* Retrieved from http://arstechnica.com/tech-policy/news/2011/09/owning-the-stack-the-legal-war-for-control-of-the-smartphone-platform.ars

Gross, D. (2010). Apple trademarks "There's an app for that". *CNNTech.* Retrieved from http://www.cnn.com/2010/TECH/mobile/10/12/app.for.that/index.html

Gurin, J. (2011, 12 July). Unauthorized fees: What's hiding in your phone bill? Consumer and Governmental Affairs Bureau Retrieved from http://www.fcc.gov/blog/unauthorized-fees-whats-hiding-your-phone-bill

Helft, M. (2010). Google introduces Nexus One, its rival to the iPhone. *New York Times—Internet.* Retrieved from http://www.nytimes.com/2010/01/06/technology/internet/06google.html

IDC. (2012). Smartphone maker hits all-time quarterly high due to seasonal strength and wider variety of offerings, according to IDC. *International Data Corporation. IDC Press Release.* Retrieved from http://www.idc.com/getdoc.jsp?containerId=prUS23299912

ITU. (2008, 27 March). International Telecommunications Union to Radiocommunication Bureau (Direct Fax N°. +41 22 730 57 85) Circular Letter 5/LCCE/27 March 2008 Administrations of Member States of the ITU and Radiocommunication Sector Members participating in the work of Working Parties 5A, 5B, 5C and 5D of Radiocommunication Study Group 5, IEEE L802.16-08/008

John, R. (1999). Theodore N. Vail and the civic origins of universal service. *Business and Economic History,* 28:2, 71-81.

LaVallee, A. (2009). Obama's Black-Ops BlackBerry. *WSJ Blogs—Digits.* Retrieved at http://blogs.wsj.com/digits/2009/01/23/obamas-black-ops-blackberry/?KEYWORDS=Obama%27s+BlackBerry

Lasar, M. (2008). *Any lawful device: 40 years after the Carterfone decision. Ars technical.* Retrieved from http://arstechnica.com/tech-policy/news/2008/06/carterfone-40-years.ars

Lee, T. (2012). Android is a "stolen product," then so was the iPhone. *Ars technica.* Retrieved from http://arstechnica.com/tech-policy/news/2012/02/if-android-is-a-stolen-product-then-so-was-the-iphone.ars

Lemels. (2000). LEMELS N-MIT *Inventor of the Week Archive—Cellular Technology.* Retrieved from http://web.mit.edu/invent/iow/freneng.html

Livengood, D., Lin, J. & Vaishnav, C. (2006, 16 May). Public Switched Telephone Networks: An Analysis of Emerging Networks. Engineering Systems Division, Massachusetts Institute of Technology. Retrieved from http://ocw.mit.edu/courses/engineering-systems-division/esd-342-advanced-system-architecture-spring-2006/projects/report_pstn.pdf

Marcial, G. (2000, 20 March). For a two-for-one deal, Dial VocalTec: This net telephony pioneer is that rare bird: A tech stock that's also a value play. *BusinessWeek.* Retrieved from http://www.businessweek.com/bwdaily/dnflash/mar2000/nf00321g.htm

McCarthy, M. (2002). HBO shows use real brands. *USA Today.* Retrieved http://www.usatoday.com/money/advertising/2002-12-02-sopranos_x.htm

mobiThinking, (2012). Global mobile statistics 2012: all quality mobile marketing research, mobile Web stats, subscribers, ad revenue, usage, trends... Retrieved from http://mobithinking.com/mobile-marketing-tools/latest-mobile-stats

NCTA (2012). Cable Phone Customers 1998-2011. National Cable & Telecommunications Association—NCTA (SNL Kagan). Retrieved from http://www.ncta.com/Stats/CablePhoneSubscribers.aspx

Nielsen. (2012). More US Consumers choosing smartphones as Apple closes the gap on Android. Retrieved from http://blog.nielsen.com/nielsenwire/consumer/more-us-consumers-choosing-smartphones-as-apple-closes-the-gap-on-android/

Nielsen. (2010). Survey: New U.S. smartphone growth by age and income
February 20, 2012 Retrieved from http://blog.nielsen.com/nielsenwire/online_mobile/survey-new-u-s-smartphone-growth-by-age-and-income/

Obama, B. (2010, 28 June). Presidential Memorandum: Unleashing the wireless broadband revolution. Memorandum for the heads of executive departments and agencies. Retrieved from http://www.whitehouse.gov/the-press-office/presidential-memorandum-unleashing-wireless-broadband-

Oehmk, T. (2000) Cell phones ruin the Opera? Meet the culprit. *New York Times - Technology.* Retrieved from http://www.nytimes.com/2000/01/06/technology/cell-phones-ruin-the-opera-meet-the-culprit.html

Open Handset Alliance. (2007). Industry leaders announce open platform for mobile devices. *Open Handset Alliance—Press Release*. Retrieved at http://www.openhandsetalliance.com/press_110507.html

Ovide, S. & Sheer I. (2012, 6 April) Microsoft banks on mobile apps. *Wall Street Journal Marketplace*. B1, B5.

Recycling for Charities (2012). Benefits of wireless recycling.
Retrieved at http://www.recyclingforcharities.com/blog/?p=9

Scocca, T. (2011). Associated Press Newstyles "Email" and "Cellphone". *Slate blogs*. Retrieved from http://www.slate.com/blogs/scocca/2011/03/18/associated_press_newstyles_email_and_cellphone.html

Shannon, C. & Weaver, W. (1949). *A Mathematical Theory of Communication*. Urbana, Ill: University of Illinois Press.

Smith, A. (2011). Thirty-five percent of American adults own a smartphone. *Smartphone Adoption and Usage*. Retrieved from http://pewinternet.org/Reports/2011/Smartphones.aspx

Sprint. (2012, 08 Feb.). Baltimore and Kansas City Sprint customers to benefit from 4G LTE and 3G enhancements in 2012 Sprint adds to the list of cities to benefit from new and improved network technology by mid-year. *Sprint. News Releases*. Retrieved from http://newsroom.sprint.com/article_display.cfm?article_id=2180

Taylor, P. & Wang, W. (2010). The fading glory of the television and telephone. *Pew Research Center*. Retrieved from http://pewresearch.org/pubs/1702/luxury-necessity-television-landline-cell-phone

Thierer, A.D. (1994). *Unnatural Monopoly: Critical Moments in the Development of the Bell System Monopoly*. The Cato Journal 14:2.

Thomann, A. (2006). *Skype—A Baltic Success Story. Corporate Communications*. Retrieved from https://infocus.creditsuisse.com/app/article/index.cfm?fuseaction=OpenArticle&aoid=163167&coid=7805&lang=EN

Time. (2007). Best Inventions of 2007. Best Inventors—Martin Cooper - 1926. *Time Specials*. Retrieved from http://www.time.com/time/specials/2007/article/0,28804,1677329_1677708_1677825,00.html

Viswanathan, T. (1992). *Telecommunication Switching Systems and Networks*. New Delhi: Prentice Hall of India. Retrieved from http://www.certified-easy.com/aa.php?isbn=ISBN:8120307135&name=Telecommunication_Switching_Systems_and_Networks

Vogelstein, F. (2008) The untold story: how the iPhone blew up the wireless industry. *Wired Magazine 16:02—Gadgets—Wireless*. Retrieved at http://www.wired.com/gadgets/wireless/magazine/16-02/ff_iphone?currentPage=1

Wyatt, E. (2011, 21 April). A clash over the airwaves. Business Day Media & Advertising. *The New York Times*. Retrieved at http://www.nytimes.com/2011/04/22/business/media/22spectrum.html?pagewanted=all

21

The Internet

Tim Brown, Ph.D. &
George Bagley, M.A. *

Why Study The Internet?

✦ The Internet has become more than just transferring information; we use it to make phone calls, video chat, and share pictures.

✦ More and more mobile devices are being sold every day, and mobile Internet usage continues to climb, making the Internet a part of our lives on the go as well as at work or home.

✦ We have come to expect our content to be on-demand; the Internet is providing us with ways to access music, movies, news and information in ways that we hadn't even thought of just five years ago.

It is arguable that as a technology, the Internet has single-handedly changed the way we do nearly everything. It is so pervasive in our lives that our use of the Internet and the World Wide Web prompted *Time* magazine to name "You"—the Internet using public—its "Person of the Year" in 2006, because of how much the public contributes to the world through this medium. It has come a long way from its beginnings as a military project 40 years ago. The Internet has gone beyond being just a useful tool in the workplace and the business world to become an integral interpersonal and mass communication medium.

Nearly 80% of Americans use the Internet (Zickuhr and Smith, 2012), and, as of mid-2010, China boasted the largest Internet-using population at 384 million people (Miniwatts Marketing Group, 2010). Our online activities both force and are enhanced by other technologies that keep growing and updating themselves to accommodate that use, such as Apple's iPad, the netbook, and smartphones. Many public places—airports, restaurants, even malls—now offer free Wi-Fi as a selling point.

What exactly is this technology that has taken over our lives? Martin Irvine of Georgetown University said that there are three components to the Internet. It is "a worldwide computing system using a common means of linking hardware and transmitting digital information, a community of people using a common communication technology, and a globally distributed system of information" (DeFleur & Dennis, 2002, p. 219). It is important to note, however, that the Internet does not act alone in providing us with seemingly endless information-seeking and communication opportunities. An integral part of this technology is the World Wide Web. While the Internet is a network of computers, the World Wide Web allows users to access that network in a user-friendly way. It provides an audio visual format and a graphical interface that is easier to use than remembering lines of computer code.

This chapter examines the quickly changing medium that is the Internet (and the World Wide Web) by reviewing its origins, the current state of Web 2.0, Internet mobility, security, and economics, and will introduce several topics that will be important areas of research in the future.

* Tim Brown, Ph.D. and George Bagley, M.A., are Associate Professors, Nicholson School of Communication, University of Central Florida (Orlando, Florida).

Background

Though it is now accessible to virtually anyone who has a compatible device, the Internet began as a military project. During the Cold War, the United States government wanted to maintain a communication system that would still function if the country was attacked by missiles and existing radio transmitters and telephone poles were disabled. The solution was to transmit information in small bits so that it could travel faster and be sent again more easily if its path were disrupted. This concept is known as packet-switching (illustrated in the previous chapter in Figure 20.1).

Many sources consider the birth of the Internet to have occurred in 1968 when the Advanced Research Projects Agency Network (ARPANET) was founded. Several universities, including UCLA and Stanford, were collaborating on military projects and needed a fast, easy way to send and receive information for those projects. Thus ARPANET became the first collection of networked computers to transfer information to and from remote locations using packet switching.

ARPANET users discovered that, in addition to sending information to each other for collaboration and research, they were also using the computer network for personal communication, so individual electronic mail, or e-mail, accounts were established. E-mail accounts allow users to have a personally identifiable user name, followed by the @ sign, followed by the name of the host computer system.

USENET was developed in 1976 to serve as a way for students at The University of North Carolina and Duke University to communicate through computer networks. It served as an electronic bulletin board that allowed users on the network to post thoughts on different topics through email. USENET then expanded to include other computers that were not allowed to use ARPANET.

In 1986, ARPANET was replaced by NSFNET (sponsored by the National Science Foundation) which featured upgraded high-speed, fiber-optic technology. This upgrade allowed for more bandwidth and faster network connections because the network was connected to supercomputers throughout the country. This technology is what we now refer to as the modern-day Internet. The general public could now access the Internet through Internet service providers (ISPs) such as America Online, CompuServe, and Prodigy. Every computer and server on the Internet was assigned a unique IP (Internet Protocol) address that consisted of a series of numbers (for example, 209.152.74.113).

The theory of Diffusion of Innovations (discussed in Chapter 3) points out that people look for low levels of complexity in an innovation to determine whether or not they want to adopt it; in other words, they want to know how easy the innovation is to use. That qualification presented a problem for the early versions of the Internet—much of it was still being run on "text-based" commands. Even though the public could now access the Internet, they needed a more user-friendly way to receive the information it contained and send information to others that didn't involve learning text based commands. In 1989, Tim Berners-Lee created a graphical interface for accessing the Internet and named his innovation the "World Wide Web." One of the key features of the World Wide Web was the concept of hyperlinks and common-language Web addresses known as "URLs" (uniform resource locators). This innovation allows a user to simply click on a certain word or picture and automatically retrieve the information that is tied to that link. The hyperlink sends a request to a special server known as a "domain name server," the server locates the IP address of the information, and sends that back to the original computer, which then sends a request for information to that IP address. The user's computer is then able to display text, video, images, and audio that has been requested. Today we know this as simple "point-and-click" access to information, but in 1989 it was revolutionary. Users were no longer forced to memorize codes or commands to get from one place to the next on the Internet—they could simply point to the content they wanted and access it.

It is worthwhile at this point to explain the IP address and domain name system in more detail. The domain name (e.g, google.com) is how we navigate the World Wide Web, but on the back end (which we don't see), the IP addresses—numbers—

are the actual addresses. The Internet Corporation for Assigned Names and Numbers, or ICANN, is responsible for assigning domain names and numbers to specific websites and servers. With 1.6 billion users on the Internet, that can be quite a task (ICANN, 2010). To try and keep things simple, ICANN maintains two different sets of "top level domain" names: generic TLD names (gTLD) such as .edu, .com, and .org, and country codes (ccTLD) such as .br for Brazil, .ca for Canada, and .ru for Russia. Table 21.1 lists the 21 gTLD names (there are 250 ccTLD names). This information will be discussed later in this chapter.

IP addresses used to consist of a set of four numbers (e.g., 209.152.74.113), in a system known as IPv4. With 256 values for each number, more than four billion addresses could be designated. The problem is that these addresses have been allocated, requiring a new address system. IPv6 is the designation for these new addresses, offering 340,282,366,920,938,000,000,000,000,000,000,000,000 separate addresses (Parr, 2011). Without getting too detailed, it is doubtful that these addresses will be used up any time soon.

Table 21.1
Top Level Domain Names

Top Level Domain	Definition
.aero	Air-transport industry sites
.arpa	Internet Infrastructure sites
.asia	Pan-Asia communication
.biz	Business sites
.cat	Catalan language and culture sites
.com	Commercial sites
.coop	Cooperative organization sites
.edu	Educational institution sites
.gov	Government sites
.info	General usage sites
.int	International sites
.jobs	Companies advertising jobs
.mil	Military sites
.mobi	Mobile devices
.museum	Museum sites
.name	Individuals' sites
.net	Networking and Internet-related sites
.org	Sites for organizations
.pro	Sites for professions
.travel	Travel related sites
.tel	Business and individuals to publish contact data

Source: Internet Corporation for Assigned Names and Numbers, 2010

The impact of the Internet upon business and commerce has been significant, creating new categories of each, e-business and e-commerce. Mesenbourg (1999) defines e-business as any procedure that a business organization conducts over a computer mediated network. E-business thus includes processes such as ordering new materials to aid in the production of goods, marketing to customers, or processing their orders, as well as automated employee services, such as training information housed on a company Intranet. E-commerce, on the other hand, is defined as any transaction over a computer mediated network that involves the transfer of ownership or rights to use goods or services. For example, when you purchase a song from iTunes or any other electronic music store on the Internet, you are engaging in e-commerce.

These definitions also point out the similarities between e-business and e-commerce. Certainly some of the processes involved in e-business could be classified as commerce—that is, the exchange of ownership rights. If a pharmacy electronically orders its drugs from pharmaceutical companies, that is an exchange of ownership rights of a good. Using the definitions above, such a transaction would be considered e-commerce, not e-business. However, the above scenario also involves the order of new materials to aid in the production of goods (e.g., filling prescriptions), which would fall under the definition of e-business. So, is there any real difference between the two?

Perhaps an easier way to define the difference might be to examine the recipient of the transaction. In the above example, one business is ordering goods from another business; that is, business to business or B2B. The pharmacy needs to purchase the raw materials (large quantities of medicine) in order to provide a finished product (filled prescriptions, packages of cold medicine) to the consumer. Therefore, the transaction between the two businesses (from one to the other) seems best to fall under the e-business category. However, the purchase of a song from iTunes is the transaction between the business (record company) and you (consumer), or business to consumer (B2C). Because so many transactions between businesses and consumers are retail based (a business selling a finished product to a consumer), it is perhaps best to view transactions to consumers as e-commerce.

Even with the clarification above, one can see that e-commerce can very easily be classified as a subset of e-business. The U.S. Federal Government defines both that way, and its figures offer support for those definitions. Revised figures from 20011 show that e-commerce accounted for 4.8% of all commerce that year, up from 3.4% in 2006 (Winters et al., 2012). E-commerce transactions in 2011 grew by 16% over the previous year, while total retail in the United States (both e-commerce and face-to-face) grew by only 8%. Basically, that means that electronic commerce growth is outpacing traditional commerce, although it is still a minor part of the economic equation.

Recent Developments

Web 2.0

The World Wide Web has come a long way since its invention. It is currently in a phase that has become known as "Web 2.0," which, according to The Pew Internet and American Life Project "is an umbrella term that is used to refer to a new era of Web-enabled applications that are built around user-generated or user-manipulated content, such as wikis, blogs, podcasts, and social networking sites" (*Web 2.0*, 2010). In other words, Web 2.0 is powered by the people who control the content.

Wikis are informational websites that are open for editing. Virtually anyone can edit a subject posting to include any sort of fact or opinion. This function can be troublesome, because not all information posted is factual. To test the credibility of one of the most popular wiki sites, Wikipedia, an instructor at the University of Central Florida modified the school's entry. The instructor claimed that he designed the school's Pegasus logo, when in fact, he did not. This entry remained on the website until he removed it several months later.

A blog is very similar to a wiki, except it is not generally open for anyone to edit. Typically it is run by one host, who can post anything including news, information, or simply his or her own opinion (De Zúñiga, Puig-I-Abril & Rojas , 2009). On demand video is another part of Web 2.0. Web sites such as YouTube allow users to watch, share, and publish videos, making the users active participants in media distribution (Hanson & Haridakis, 2008). Other video sites such as Hulu allow users to watch network television shows online at their convenience. Instant messaging was once one of the most popular uses of the Web, but its use has stagnated over the last few years.

Some of the most popular Web 2.0 applications are social networking sites. Social networking sites are generally defined as "a social utility that connects people, to keep up with friends, upload photos, share links and videos" (Top Sites, 2012). These sites are some of the most commonly visited websites in the country, and indeed the world. The number two most visited website in the world is Facebook, at least in the number of daily visitors (Google is first); if you're counting the number of daily *views*, then Facebook is by far the most popular site. Also, in the top 20 most visited websites are Twitter, Wikipedia and YouTube (Top Sites, 2012).

Facebook, in particular, has become a one-stop shop for practically any type of information. It is a portal to the rest of the Internet in one convenient location, much like AOL portals were in the early days of the World Wide Web. It is an interpersonal communication medium, in that you can send direct messages to friends, family members, and acquaintances. It has also become a mass communication medium. Businesses and corporations set up "fan pages," where Facebook users can "become a fan" of that company. This feature allows the companies to communicate or market to a large number of people with one simple wall posting or message. As of April 2012, Facebook reported that it had 901 million active users and more than three billion likes and comments per day (Ngak, C., 2012). (Social Networking is discussed in more detail in Chapter 22.)

Mobility

For a good portion of the Internet's history, desktop computing stations or stand-alone PC's were the only way to "get online." That was primarily because of the need for cables to connect the computer's modem to either a phone line or a broadband modem connection. But the growth of wireless technologies (Wi-Fi, Wi-Max, and cellular wireless broadband) has expanded both the types of devices

that can access the Internet and the type of content that is being generated and posted "online." Since 2010, the growth in broadband adoption in the home has slowed somewhat, with 62% of Americans using broadband in the home as of late 2011 (Zickuhr and Smith, 2012). However, the Pew Internet and American Life Project notes that more and more Americans, especially minorities and the economically disadvantaged, are accessing the Internet through mobile phones or other mobile devices. The study also notes that those who use their mobile devices to go online also do a wider range of things with their phones (email, maps, location-based services). That is also borne out by statistics from JiWire, a consumer Wi-Fi hotspot finder. The company points out that the total number of world-wide public Wi-Fi hotspots doubled between 2009 and 2011, with the vast majority in the U.S. free to users (*JiWire*, 2011). JiWire also notes that smartphone users are also buying tablet computers, with the vast majority (iPhone and Android) opting for the iPad. (Mobile telephony is discussed in more detail in Chapter 20).

Digital Diversity/Divide

The Internet access statistics among different socio-economic groups noted above is a promising sign that more people are gaining access to the Internet. There are two aspects of that concern—physical access and cognitive access. The difference can best be summed up by using the analogy of owning a car: just because you have a car doesn't necessarily mean you know how to drive it, and younger, novice drivers may not have the experience to know how to navigate the problems associated with driving on a crowded highway. Indeed, in the United States, physical (able to go online) and cognitive (knowing what to do online) access to the Internet seems to cross many economic and cultural barriers, although what people do online does tend to differ along those lines (Zickuhr and Smith, 2012).

Globally, availability of the Internet varies widely. Many developing countries still lack widespread Internet access, and the gap between the developed and developing worlds is still very wide (International Telecommunications Union, 2012). Although nearly 69% of the developed world has Internet access, only 20% of people living in the developing world can go online through fixed broadband connections (ITU, 2012). See Table 21.2. There are several projects underway to try and bridge that gap: some such as chip maker AMD's 50X15 project (50% of the world online by 2015) seem to have faltered, while others such as the One Laptop per Child program, which aims to provide low-cost ($100) computers to children in developing countries so they can learn to navigate both the computer itself (physical access) and the Internet (cognitive access), seem to be gaining momentum (50X15.org, 2012; One Laptop per Child, 2012). Critics, however, say that the time, effort, and money devoted to these projects would be better used if they focused on eliminating hunger, poverty, and drought in the developing world (Cohen, 2009; Dvorak, 2007). One note should be made about the digital divide statistics: the ITU reports that *mobile* Internet access is growing in developing countries, perhaps a sign that people in those countries are finding their own ways of accessing online content without programs such as those listed above (ITU, 2012). See Table 21.3.

Table 21.2
Internet Users by Level of Development

Year	Level	% (per 100 inhabitants)
2006	Overall	16
	Developing	9
	Developed	52
2007	Overall	19
	Developing	10
	Developed	55
2008	Overall	22
	Developing	14
	Developed	60
2009	Overall	26
	Developing	17.5
	Developed	64
2010	Overall	29.7
	Developing	21.1
	Developed	68.8

Source: International Telecommunications Union, 2012

Table 21.3
Mobile Cellular Subscriptions by Level of Development

Year	Level	% (per 100 inhabitants)
2006	Overall	37
	Developing	24
	Developed	95
2007	Overall	43
	Developing	30
	Developed	99
2008	Overall	58
	Developing	50
	Developed	103
2009	Overall	67
	Developing	56.8
	Developed	113.6
2010	Overall	78
	Developing	70.1
	Developed	114.2

Note: percentages over 100 reflect more than one cell phone per person

Source: International Telecommunications Union, 2010

Current Status

According to the Pew Internet and American Life Project, as of August 2011, 78% of American adults were online, with no significant gender difference. 94% of young people from ages 18-29 were online, 87% of people from ages 30-49 were online, 74% of people from ages 50-64 were online, and 41% of people over the age of 65 were online; all of these percentages have gone up since 2010. Internet usage also varies by ethnicity; whites are online the most, while English and Spanish speaking Hispanics have shown the most growth of any ethnic group. Pew also reports that the more education one has, the more likely one will be online, and the more income one makes, the more likely one will be online. 62% of Americans have home broadband access, which means that the Internet is not simply a novelty to be taken advantage of at work. 63% of Americans have accessed the Internet via a wireless connection, either using a laptop or mobile device (Zickuhr and Smith, 2012).

And what they're *doing* online is as interesting as how many are online. Americans still seem to be primarily content consumers, in that they search for information, check email, and shop or bank online. However, more and more Americans are starting to contribute content to their own blogs or content sites managed by others (Trend Data: Online activities 2012). Other content consumption comes from YouTube and Facebook, but more and more Americans are watching traditional television programs online. The Nielsen Company notes that those who are watching television online typically do so to "catch up" on their favorite show (Gibs, 2011). In early 2012, Barry Diller, formerly a network television executive, pushed Congress to allow online "television" services such as Aereo to operate freely (Friedman, 2012). Most online consumption of video and traditional broadcast television occurs either through sites such as Hulu.com or embedded video players in the network's own web portals.

Factors to Watch

Regulation

Attempts to regulate copyrighted content on the Internet personify the clash between old and new media. Prior to the digital information revolution introduced into our daily lives by the Internet, media companies exercised exclusivity over their content as a means to promulgate profitability. The idea was simple: we own the content, and if you want to view/use/engage it you must either pay for that access or have our permission. Such was the economic media model throughout most of the twentieth century.

The Internet, however, which is by its very structure a democratically shared and open-market environment, turned the tables on that reigning economic paradigm. Content heretofore preserved and carefully dispensed by media companies now began appearing on the World Wide Web in various guises such as Napster, YouTube and peer-to-peer networking. The result was a continuing series of shockwaves that reverberated throughout the world of traditional media as those companies witnessed the

music, TV programs and movies they previously vigorously controlled now freely shared and distributed online in the absence of any sense of governance by those companies.

In response, some of them, such as the Recording Industry Association of America, CBS and the Motion Picture Association of America, lobbied Congress to stop what they viewed as the illegal use of their copyrighted content. In response, the U.S. House of Representatives in 2012 crafted the bill now known as SOPA, or the Stop Online Piracy Act, while the U.S. Senate crafted its own version known as PIPA, or the Preventing Real Online Threats to Economic Creativity and Theft of Intellectual Property Act. The acts would have allowed copyright holders to seek a court order from the U.S. Dept. of Justice to bar websites determined guilty of infringing on federal criminal intellectual-property laws and would prohibit search engines from linking to these sites. Additionally, both acts would have required Internet service providers to block access to such sites.

The reaction to each (SOPA and PIPA) was overwhelming. In response to the bills, websites such as Wikipedia and Craigslist staged a global protest by blacking themselves out to users on January 18, 2012. Public support seemed solidly behind the protest, so much so that many co-sponsors of both bills withdrew their support. Speaker of the U.S. House of Representatives, John Boehner, even publicly conceded a lack of consensus for the SOPA. Neither bill made it to their respective floors for debate and subsequent vote.

Most recently, however, Congress has been considering another bill aimed at Internet content. The Cyber Intelligence Sharing and Protection Act (CISPA) was introduced in 2011 and passed by the U.S. House of Representatives in April 2012. It allows the U.S. government and agencies such as the military, along with private technology and manufacturing companies, to share information related to "cyber threats" to the United States. Originally the same protestors to SOPA and PIPA raised their alarm over CISPA as it contained language in reference to intellectual property. However, that language was removed in response to rising concern and the threat of SOPA-like protest. As of early 2012 it was unclear what the future of the legislation would be; what was clear, however, was that U.S. government officials seemed intent on having some kind of regulation over what most people consider a free and un-fettered communication tool.

Cloud Storage Services (Consumer and Industrial)

The growth of "the cloud" is a factor that has influenced Internet usage since 2010, but is poised to have an even bigger impact. Cloud computing can be defined as information, data, files and—in some cases—software applications that are stored on servers that are accessible on demand from anywhere (Mell and Grance, 2011). Large corporations and businesses have been using the cloud for some time, with companies such as Amazon providing much of the infrastructure. However, consumers have been able to access more and more cloud storage options, such as Dropbox, Box, Microsoft SkyDrive, Apple iCloud and Google Drive. Many of these options allow certain storage options for free, (e.g., 5GB of storage for free, with a yearly fee for more space) that allow users to keep important information available at a moment's notice. Some providers, such as Google, Apple and Amazon, also offer media content as part of their cloud services; unlike Internet music stations such as Pandora, these content providers store an individual's media content (music, movies, books, etc.) in the cloud and provide on-demand access to various devices.

Two things are worth watching with this growth: business integration and ownership/copyright. As more consumer models become widespread, companies are looking for ways to utilize these services for employees. However, not all of these services provide the enterprise security that some corporations require (King, 2012). Some experts believe that in order for these consumer grade options to thrive, they will need to look for ways to integrate into the enterprise world. But the concern over who owns the rights to the content on these cloud services continues to be an issue (Bott, 2012). While some sites such as Amazon and Apple's iCloud primarily store content that you've already purchased some rights to (but don't own outright), other sites such as Google have in the past claimed some usage rights to *your*

content that you provide, simply because you are using their services (Bott, 2012). These agreements often change, but the underlying concerns remain—once you put your content out there, who owns it?

Economics

Another concern is the viability of the Internet, and more specifically, the applications and products that many people use on the Internet. While Google may be among the more valuable media companies in the world, with a market capitalization of $200.05 billion as of April 27th, 2012, other companies have been popular and have brought in revenue, but have not found a way to generate profits the way that Google has (Ostrow, 2009). In addition, the content on the Internet, and how it's paid for, is also an economic concern. Earlier it was brought up that people are watching more television online. There is also some growth in the number of homes that are getting rid of cable or satellite television and relying on the Internet for their "extra programming" (Nielsen Reports, 2012). As more people decide to consume television online, there is the real concern that the advertising dollars will be harder to come by. Less advertising income usually means less money to pay for programming. The news industry has been on the front lines of this struggle. While television ad revenues have rebounded from the 2008 recession, newspaper advertising has been slow to recover, and news organizations are struggling to figure out how to effectively charge for their news product which they have previously given away online for free (Nakashima, 2012).

What seems clear from this chapter is that the Internet is, in many ways, an evolving entity. While packet switching and IP assignments don't change too much, the use of the Internet and the potential for it seem to grow and change with each person who logs on. What remains to be seen is how much things will continue to change. The growth of mobile access and the desire of many to have ubiquitous access to the Internet may lead us to realize that we really *do* need to be "on the grid" all the time. However, there are just as many critics who would argue the opposite—that too much of a good thing is, well, too much. Whatever the direction may be, it's clear that the uses of the Internet are as varied as the needs of the users who use it.

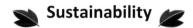 Sustainability

On the surface, the Internet would seem to be an ecologically friendly technology. By sending messages and transmitting information electronically rather than on paper, we're saving money and resources by not using paper for mail, books, and newspapers. In addition, converting existing documents and content to electronic formats allows more people to use that content without draining those natural resources. We don't have to build plants to produce paper, which means we don't have as much toxic waste polluting our air and water resources. So, it's a win-win, right?

Well, not exactly. Keep in mind that there is a trade off. Even though we are using fewer resources, we're also creating more of a need for power. Running the computers that make the Internet work takes energy, and the more electronic content we create, the more we need to use energy, usually electricity, to keep the content available. The more we need power, the more we need to produce it. In some ways, we're back to square one.

Enter the push for "Green IT" from numerous interests, including the U.S. Government (Green Information Technology Strategic Plan, 2009). The United States Department of Agriculture has developed a plan that not only promotes the use of other sustainable technologies (solar energy, water energy, and clean fuel automobiles), but also emphasizes the use of environmentally friendly information technology. Among the new policies for internal use, the USDA is pushing for more recycling of computer hardware and more proper disposal of the heavy metals that are often used in making computer hardware but can't be recycled. In addition, the Department is pushing for more collaboration technology (WiKis, open documents, etc.) that allows its employees to work together without circulating paper copies of documents. The goal is to reduce energy consumption in all areas, but particular in the use of technology and Internet-related activities in order to save money and resources.

But there is still a need for low energy-consuming hardware, and that's the second part of the Green IT push. Innovators are currently working on ways to reduce the power consumption of the hardware that we use (Gelsi, 2010). Indeed some manufacturers are using recyclable material when they make cell phones and computers (Green PC, 2010). And the push is getting help from other organizations such as Greenpeace holding big companies accountable for their energy emissions. What does the future hold? Only time will tell, but it appears that companies are beginning to realize that the energy savings can't stop with just transferring print to electronic files— it has to continue into saving the energy that keeps those computers running as well.

Bibliography:

50X15.org (2012). Retrieved from http://50x15.org/connected-global-population

Bott, E. (2012). Your data, your rights: How fair are online storage services? *ZDNet: The Ed Bott Report*. Retrieved from http://www.zdnet.com/blog/bott/your-data-your-rights-how-fair-are-online-storage-services/4877

Cohen, B. (2009) *The problems with One Laptop per Child*. (Blog) Retrieved, from http://scienceblogs.com/worldsfair/2009/01/the_problems_with_one_laptop_p.php

DeFleur, M. L. & Dennis, E. E. (2002). *Understanding mass communication: A liberal arts perspective.* Boston: Houghton-Mifflin

De Zúñiga, H. G., Puig-I-Abril, E. and Rojas, H. (2009). Weblogs, traditional sources online and political participation: an assessment of how the internet is changing the political environment. *New Media and Society, 11*(4), 553-574.

Dvorak, J.C. (2007) One laptop per child doesn't change the world. *PC Magazine* (2007, Dec. 4). Retrieved from http://www.pcmag.com/article2/0,2817,2227850,00.asp

Friedman, W. (2012) Barry Diller tells Senate: Online video same as trad TV. MediaDailyNews, www.mediapost.com. Retrieved from http://www.mediapost.com/publications/article/173190/barry-diller-tells-senate-online-video-same-as-tr.html

Gelsi, S. (2010) Green computing catches Silicon Valley's eye. *Marketwatch* (April 30, 2010). Retrieved from http://www.marketwatch.com/story/venture-capitalist-steve-jurvetson-eyes-green-it-2010-04-29?reflink=MW_news_stmp

Gibs, J. (2011, February). Do we watch the Web the same way we watch TV? Not really. *Nielsenwire*. Retrieved from: http://blog.nielsen.com/nielsenwire/consumer/do-we-watch-the-web-the-same-way-we-watch-tv-not-really/

Green Information Technology Strategic Plan (2009). United States Department of Agriculture (Report). Washington, D.C. Retrieved from http://www.educause.edu/Resources/TheGreenInformationTechnologyI/163740

Green PC made from recyclable materials (2010) *Ubergizmo.com.* Retrieved from http://www.ubergizmo.com/15/archives/2010/01/green_pc_made_from_recyclable_materials.html

Hanson, G. & Haridakis, P. (2008). YouTube users watching and sharing the news: A uses and gratifications approach. *The Journal of Electronic Publishing, 11*(3). Horrigan, J. (2009). *Wireless Internet Use.* Pew Internet and American Life Project. Pew Research Center, Washington D.C, Retrieved from http://www.pewinternet.org/Reports/2009/12-Wireless-Internet-Use.aspx

ICANN Internet Corporation for Assignment Names and Numbers (2010). Accessed from http://www.icann.org/

International Telecommunications Union (2012). *Measuring the Information Society* (Report). ITU, Geneva, Switzerland. Retrieved, from http://www.itu.int/ITU-D/ict/publications/idi/2011/index.html

JiWire Mobile Audience Insights Report (2012) JiWire Mobile Audience Media. Retrieved, from http://www.jiwire.com/downloads/pdf/JiWire_MobileAudienceInsightsReport_Q42011_2.pdf

King, R. (2012). Google Drive:What it could mean for the cloud storage market. *ZDNet: Between the lines.* Retrieved April 24, 2012 from http://www.zdnet.com/blog/btl/google-drive-what-it-could-mean-for-the-cloud-storage-market/74929

Mell, P and Grance, T.(2011). The NIST definition of cloud computing. Report from the National Institute of Standards and Technology, retrieved from http://csrc.nist.gov/publications/nistpubs/800-145/SP800-145.pdf

Mesenbourg, T. L. (1999). *Measuring electronic business: Definitions, underlying concepts, and measurement plans.* Retrieved from http://www.census.gov/epdc/www/ebusiness.htm.

Miniwatts Marketing Group (2010). China Internet usage stats and population report. Retrieved from: http://www.internetworldstats.com/asia/cn.htm

Nakashima, R. (2012) Nearly 300 newspapers now charging for access on websites, smartphones and tablets. Retrievedfrom http://articles.orlandosentinel.com/2012-04-03/news/sns-ap-us-newspaper-pay-walls_1_newspapers-rick-edmonds-print-subscriptions

Ngak, C. (2012) *Facebook grows to 901 million, Instagram in S-1Filing.* CBSNews.com, Tech Talk. Retrieved from: http://www.cbsnews.com/8301-501465_162-57419864-501465/facebook-grows-to-901-million-instagram-details-in-s-1-filing/

Nielsen Reports:How Americans are spending their media time... and money (2012) Nielson Wire. Retrieved from http://blog.nielsen.com/nielsenwire/online_mobile/report-how-americans-are-spending-their-media-time-and-money/

One Laptop per Child (2012) Retrieved from http://www.laptop.org/en/vision/index.shtml

Oppenheimer, A. (2012) *Region's one laptop per child plan has future.* "In My Opinion," The Miami Herald. Accessed from http://www.miamiherald.com/2012/04/21/2759975/regions-one-laptop-per-child-plan.html

Ostrow, A. (2009b) Facebook's 2010 revenue estimated at $710 million. Retrieved, from http://mashable.com/2009/12/07/facebook-2010-revenue/

Parr, B. (2011). IPv4 and IPv6: A short guide. Retrieved from http://mashable.com/2011/02/03/ipv4-ipv6-guide/

Top Sites. (2012). Alexa: A web information company. Retrieved from: http://www.alexa.com/topsites

Trend Data-Online activities, 2000-2009 (2012). Pew Internet and American Life Project (Report). Pew Research Center, Washington, D.C. Retrieved from: http://www.pewinternet.org/Static-Pages/Trend-Data/Online-Activities-20002009.aspx

Web 2.0 (2010). Pew Internet and American Life Project (Report). Pew Research Center, Washington, D.C. Retrieved from http://www.pewinternet.org/topics/Web-20.aspx

Winters, T. Davie, W. and Widenhamer, D. (2012) *Quarterly retail e-commerce sales: 4th Quarter 2011.* Retrieved from http://www.census.gov/retail/mrts/www/data/pdf/ec_current.pdf

Zickuhr, K. and Smith, A. (2012) *Digital Differences.* Retrieved, from http://www.pewinternet.org/reports/2012/digital-differenc es.aspx

22

Social Networking

Rachel A. Sauerbier, M.A. [*]

Why Study Social Networking?

+ Social networking sites account for more than 22% of all time spent online—over twice as much as the second most visited sites (online gaming sites).

+ Four out of five active Internet users visit social networking sites.

+ Social networking apps are the third most popular apps among smartphone users.

+ Facebook alone averages over 140 million unique visitors every month.

Introduction

Your dad is your Facebook friend. Grandma has over 500 followers on Twitter. Your thirteen-year-old cousin spends more time on Tumblr than on his homework. And it's very likely that as you get ready to graduate from college and join the professional ranks, you are wondering if you should create a LinkedIn profile. Needless to say, social networking and social media have become a global phenomenon. From its humble beginnings with SixDegrees.com, to Friendster, to Facebook, Twitter, LinkedIn and everything in between, the role of social networking websites has come to permeate almost every aspect of the online experience. Even with so much exposure, there is still some confusion as to what constitutes a social networking site (SNS), and which of the literally millions of Web pages on the Internet can be considered SNSs.

What is an SNS? According to boyd and Ellison (2008), there are three criteria that a website must meet to be considered an SNS. A website must allow users to "(1) construct a public or semi-public profile within a bounded system, (2) articulate a list of other users with whom they share a connection, and (3) view and traverse their list of connections and those made by others within the system" (boyd & Ellison, 2008, p. 211). These guidelines may seem to restrict what can be considered an SNS, as there are still literally hundreds of vastly diverse websites that are functioning as such.

Even as Facebook and Twitter continue to dominate the SNS world and MySpace continues to struggle for relevancy, there is one surprising site that is gaining momentum in the social media world: Tumblr. According to Nielsen (2011), Tumblr tripled their unique visitors from 4.2 million in May 2010 to 11.8 million in May 2011. Tumblr is one of several new social media websites that allow users more freedom of expression with their own "branding" than other SNSs like Twitter or Facebook. Rather than limiting their users to 140-character microblogs as Twitter does, or requiring their users to adopt the same standard layout as Facebook does, Tumblr allows its users to type as little or as much as they want, and they can add their own personality to their pages through the layout and design. Unlike blog sites such as WordPress, Tumblr is user-friendly so no matter if you are a novice or an expert Web designer, Tumblr is offering a social media experience unlike any other site. There are so many choices and different directions SNSs offer to Internet users.

[*] Doctoral Student Edward R. Murrow College of Communication, Washington State University, Pullman, WA

To understand this social media explosion, we must first understand how it began.

Background

SNSs have taken on many forms during their evolution. Social networking on the Internet can trace its roots back to listservs such as CompuServe, BBS, and AOL, where people would converge to share computer files and ideas (Nickson, 2009). CompuServe was started in 1969 by Jeff Wilkins, who wanted to help streamline his father-in-law's insurance business (Banks, 2007). During the 1960s, computers were still prohibitively expensive, so many small, private businesses could not afford a computer of their own. During that time, it was common practice to "timeshare" computers with other companies (Banks, 2007). Timesharing, in this sense, meant that there was one central computer that allowed several different companies to share access in order to remotely use it for general computing purposes. Wilkins saw the potential in this market, and with the help of two college friends, talked the board of directors at his father-in-law's insurance company into buying a computer for timesharing purposes. With this first computer, Wilkins and his two partners, Alexander Trevor and John Goltz, started up CompuServe Networks, Inc. By taking the basic concept of timesharing already in place and improving upon it, Wilkins, Trevor, and Goltz created the first centralized site for computer networking and sharing. In 1977, as home computers started to become popular, Wilkins started designing an application that would connect those home computers to the centralized CompuServe computer. The home computer owner could use the central computer for access, for storage or—most importantly—for "person-to-person communications—both public and private" (Banks, 2007).

Another two decades would go by before the first identifiable SNS would appear on the Internet. Throughout the 1980s and early 1990s, there were several different bulletin board systems (BBSs) and sites including America Online (AOL) that provided convergence points for people to meet and share online. In 1996, the first "identifiable" SNS was created—SixDegrees.com (boyd & Ellison, 2008). SixDegrees was originally based upon the concept that no two people are separated by more than six degrees of separation. The concept of the website was fairly simple—sign up, provide some personal background and supply the e-mail addresses of ten friends, family, or colleagues. Each person had his or her own profile, could search for friends, and for the friends of friends (Caslon Analytics, 2006). It was completely free and relatively easy to use. SixDegrees shut down in 2001 after the dot com bubble popped. What was left in its wake, however, was the beginning of SNSs as they are known today. There have been literally hundreds of different SNSs that have sprung from the footprints of SixDegrees. In the decade following the demise of SixDegrees, SNSs such as Friendster, MySpace, LinkedIn, Facebook, and Twitter have become Internet zeitgeists.

Friendster was created in 2002 by a former Netscape engineer, Jonathan Abrams (Milian, 2009). The website was designed for people to create profiles that included personal information—everything from gender to birth date to favorite foods—and the ability to connect with friends that they might not otherwise be able to connect to easily. The original design of Friendster was fresh and innovative, and personal privacy was an important consideration. In order to add someone as a Friendster contact, the friend requester needed to know either the last name or the e-mail address of the requested. It was Abrams' original intention to have a website that hosted pages for close friends and family to be able to connect, not as a virtual popularity contest to see who could get the most "Friendsters" (Milian, 2009).

Shortly after the debut of Friendster, a new SNS hit the Internet, MySpace. From its inception by Tom Anderson and Chris DeWolfe in 2003, MySpace was markedly different from Friendster. While Friendster focused on making and maintaining connections with people who already knew each other, MySpace was busy turning the online social networking phenomenon into a multimedia experience. It was the first SNS to allow members to customize their profiles using HyperText Markup Language (HTML). So, instead of having "cookie-cutter" profiles like Friendster offered, MySpace users could completely adapt their profiles to their own tastes, right down to the font of the page and music playing in the background. As Nickson (2009) stated, "it looked and felt hipper than the major competitor Friendster right from the start, and it conducted a campaign of sorts in the early days to show alienated Friendster users just what they were missing" (par. 15). This competition signaled trouble for Friendster, which was slow to adapt to this new form of social networking. A stroke of good fortune for MySpace also came in the form of rumors being spread that Friendster was going to start charging fees for its services. In 2005, with 22 million users, MySpace was sold to News Corp. for $580 million (BusinessWeek, 2005); News Corp. later sold it for only $35 million. MySpace, now with approximately 44 million users, has since been toppled as the number one SNS by Facebook, which has over 845 million users worldwide (Carlson, 2011; Facebook, 2012a).

From its humble roots as a way for Harvard students to stay connected to one another, Facebook has come a long way. Facebook was created in 2004 by Mark Zuckerberg with the help of Dustin Moskovitz, Chris Hughes and Eduardo Saverin (Facebook, 2012a). Originally, Facebook was only open to Harvard students, however, by the end of the year, it had expanded to Yale University, Columbia University, and Stanford University—the latter's hometown providing the new headquarters for the company in Palo Alto, CA. In 2005, the company started providing social networking services to anyone who had a valid e-mail address ending in .edu. By 2006, Facebook was offering its website to anyone over the age of 13 who had a valid e-mail address (Facebook, 2012b). What made Facebook unique, at the time, was that it was the first SNS to offer the "news feed" on a user's home page. In all other SNSs before Facebook, in order to see what friends were doing, the user would have to click to that friend's page. Facebook, instead, put a live feed of all changes users were posting—everything from relationship changes, to job changes, to updates of their status. In essence, Facebook made microblogging popular. This was a huge shift from MySpace, which had placed a tremendous amount of emphasis on traditional blogging, where people could type as much as they wanted to. Interestingly, up until July 2011, Facebook users were limited to 420 character status updates. As of November 2011, however, Facebook users have

a staggering 63,206 characters to say what's on their mind (Protalinski, 2011). The fact still remains, however, that Facebook's original limit on characters used in status updates changed the way people were using websites for social networking and paved the way for sites such as Twitter, with its limitation of 140-character "tweets" (Dsouza, 2010).

Twitter was formed in 2006 by three employees of podcasting company Odeo, Inc.: Jack Dorsey, Evan Williams, and Biz Stone (Beaumont, 2008). It was created out of a desire to be able to stay in touch with friends easier than allowed by Facebook, MySpace, and LinkedIn. Taking the concept of the 160 character limit text messaging imposed on users, Twitter shortened the message length down to 140 (to allow the extra 20 characters to be used for a user name) (Twitter, 2012). Twitter attributes a huge amount of its initial success to its usage at festivals like Austin, Texas' South by Southwest (SXSW). Twitter had already gone live a year before, but it was at the 2007 SXSW that the SNS exploded (Mayfield, 2007). Another helpful, if not totally unexpected, promotion of Twitter came from the unusually large number of celebrities who adopted the use of Twitter fairly early—so much so that websites including followfamous.com emerged to track which celebrities are using Twitter, even going so far as to have the tagline of their website as "find-follow-spy" (FollowFamous, 2009).

Not all SNSs have been used for social, personal, dating, or celebrity-stalking purposes. LinkedIn was created in 2003 by Reid Hoffman, Allen Blue, Jean-Luc Vaillant, Eric Ly, and Konstantin Guericke (LinkedIn, 2012). LinkedIn returned the concept of SNSs to its old CompuServe roots. According to Stross (2012), LinkedIn is unique because "among online networking sites, LinkedIn stands out as the specialized one—it's for professional connections only" (par. 1). So instead of helping the user find a long lost friend from high school, LinkedIn helps build professional connections, which in turn could lead to better job opportunities and more productivity. As of 2012, LinkedIn has over 135 million members worldwide and is leading the way in the unique section of SNSs that deals strictly with business relationships.

A relative newcomer to the world of SNSs is Google+ (aka, Google Plus). Created by the Internet giant, Google, Google+ is trying to capitalize on creating a more "realistic experience" of social interaction for its users. According to Google+ (n.d.), "Google+ makes connecting on the web more like connecting in the real world" (par. 1). Their unique approach to making the social experience online more closely match real world interactions comes from their use of social "circles," or as Google+ (n.d.) put it: "Circles make it easy to put your friends from Saturday night in one circle, your parents in another, and your boss in a circle by himself, just like real life" (par. 2). The concept of circles is to keep Google+ users from having the embarrassing experience of sharing inappropriate information about what they did Saturday night with their grandparents, alluding to the issues that have come up with "over share" mishaps that occur with relatively high frequency on Facebook and MySpace (Zukerman, 2011). Opened to the public in September 2011, Google+ had more than 90 million unique visitors as of February 2012 (Boulton, 2012). That number may be misleading, however. According to Gannes (2012a), "…if you registered for Google+ any time since it launched this summer, and you used any other Google product—say, search!—in the past day or week, while signed into your Google account, you got counted in those percentages" (par. 7). What is even more troubling about the misleading numbers is that even Google executives are not active on the site and even with "90 million" unique users, Google+ itself remains a veritable ghost town (Bercovici, 2011). It remains to be seen whether or not Google+ will become a heavyweight contender in the battle for SNS supremacy.

Recent Developments

SNSs have become the biggest, most relevant sites on the Internet today. Their impact is felt everywhere from Wall Street to all corners of the World Wide Web. The impact from SNSs has not always been positive, however. This section will explore the financial impact of SNSs on the world at large, how SNSs are integrating the Internet through application programming interface (API) "mashups," and how

SNSs are continuing to struggle with the privacy and safety of its members.

The biggest news story regarding SNSs in early 2012 was Facebook filing an initial public offering (IPO) to "go public" with the company. The social networking giant filed the IPO on February 1, 2012, and while it will not be available for public trading until the second quarter of 2012, there was immediate speculation that the company would be valued at over $100 billion when it does actually go public (Womack & Spears, 2012). To put this staggering number into perspective, if Facebook is actually valued between the speculative $75-100 billion when it opens for public trading, it will crush the now largest opening IPO for a company—Google's 2004 IPO, which was valued at $23 billion (Price, 2012). Facebook, Inc.'s announcement of the impending IPO came just months after it was announced that News Corp. had sold MySpace to advertising network Specific Media and Justin Timberlake for $35 million (Ehrlich, 2011), a fraction of the previously mentioned $580 million News Corp. paid for it in 2005. This drop in MySpace's valuation has knocked it out of economic competition with other SNS heavy hitters like LinkedIn (valued at $9 billion), Skype (valued at $8.5 billion) and Twitter (valued at $7.7 billion; Hendrick, 2012).

Figure 22.1
Valuation of Social Networking Companies

SNSs: 2005-2012 (in Billions)

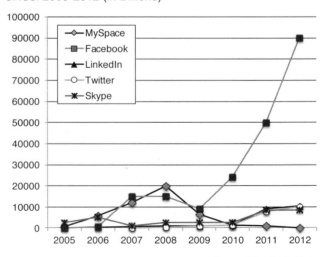

Source: Hendrick, Price

Probably one of the most telling developments for MySpace, beyond it selling for six percent of what it sold for in 2005, is the fact that it is now allowing its users to login with Facebook's API, Facebook Connect (Ostrow, 2010). Facebook Connect "allows websites, software, and even mobile devices to integrate with Facebook and send information both ways" (Parr, 2009). The Facebook API was originally developed in 2006; in 2007, Facebook announced their "Facebook Platform," an API that allowed third party developers to build applications within Facebook. Then in 2008, Facebook announced the release of Facebook Connect, a platform that "allows users to "connect" their Facebook identity, friends and privacy to any site" (Morin, 2008, par. 4). Even though Facebook Connect has been around since 2008, there has been a dramatic increase in its use since the beginning of 2011. By using Facebook Connect, sites ranging from Amazon.com to the Huffington Post to Mormon.org have created an enhanced browsing experience for their visitors, allowing visitors to share what they like and what they look at online with their Facebook friends.

The use of APIs on SNSs is not unique to Facebook. Most SNSs, including Twitter, Google+, Tumblr, StumbleUpon and Reddit have APIs that have added their site's own unique functionability to thousands of other websites across the Internet. Not only have SNSs added functionality to other websites, but there are a growing number of apps—like Seesmic Ping and SocialBlast—that allow users to post simultaneously to all of their different social media profiles. SNS integration is not just taking place across software, but also across multiple media platforms. According to Nielsen (2011), more than 40% of Americans access their SNS profiles via mobile Internet. This includes mobile phones, tablets, handheld gaming devices and portable digital media players. For the individuals who access their SNS through their mobile phone, it is the second most featured app on mobile phones (behind music player/downloader) and is the second most valued app on mobile phones behind GPS (Nielsen, 2011). This connectivity is allowing individuals to post to their SNS profiles anytime, anywhere. While "social networking on the go" has created a much more dynamic and synchronous user experience, it has also complicated the issue of privacy and safety on SNSs.

On December 27th, 2011, fifteen-year-old Amanda Cummings stepped in front of a bus in an attempt to take her own life. Six days after being struck by the bus in her hometown of Staten Island, NY, Cummings died from her injuries. According to the suicide note in her pocket, she could no longer tolerate the incessant bullying that targeted her both at school and on Facebook (Flegenheimer, 2012). Cummings' story is not unique. In 2010, cyberbullying researchers Sameer Hinduja and Justin Patchin conducted a random sample survey of 10-18 year old school children in the southern United States and found that over 14% of respondents had been bullied online in the past 30 days. When asked if they had ever been cyberbullied in their lifetime, this number jumped to over 20% (Hinduja & Patchin, 2010). Most industry experts urge parents to closely monitor the privacy settings and activities on their children's social media profiles (Collier & Magid, 2012). The threat to safety and privacy online is not something that only affects young people. As access to SNSs becomes easier through the use of third-party APIs and across multiple media platforms, the threat to one's personal safety and privacy continues to increase.

As more people create and maintain their SNS profiles, the need to protect their privacy online has increased. In February 2012, The Pew Internet and the American Life Project released a study on the privacy management practices on SNSs (Madden, 2012). According to Madden (2012), 58% of adults and 62% of teens have their social networking profile set to private (friends only). Even though over half of all people on SNSs have their profiles set to private, over 48% of all social media users found it difficult to maintain the privacy controls for their profiles (Madden, 2012). This comes as no surprise, as privacy has been an issue with SNSs since their infancy. In January 2012, Facebook came under fire again because of the debut of the timeline format (Purewal, 2012). Specifically, now Facebook users can search other profiles quickly and easily because Facebook has conveniently organized all updates, events, pictures and posts by year. What makes this even trickier for some Facebook users is that certain features (such as picture albums) that were once covered under a blanket security setting now have to be changed for every single picture in the album. This works great when there are specific pictures in an album that mom and grandma would not approve of, but overall, it has created a security nightmare when people find out that their previously private information is now public to all Facebook users.

Figure 22.2
Percent of Social Networking Site Users Who Have Taken These Steps on Their Profile

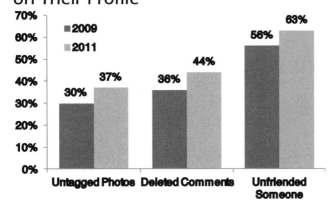

Source: Madden, 2012

It is not just Facebook that has come under fire for security issues. On September 9, 2011, NBC News' Twitter account was hacked, and a Tweet was released to its over 130,000 followers, stating that "ground zero" in New York City had been attacked again (Stelter & Preston, 2011). The Tweet was only live on the NBC News Twitter account for 40 seconds, but it gained national attention. During 2011 and 2012, the accounts of Lady Gaga, The Huffington Post, Barack Obama, and Fox News have all been hacked (Babbar, 2011; Santarelli, 2012; Veracode, n.d.). Overall, industry experts urge all social media users to be vigilant about the safety and security of their SNS profiles and to not indulge in oversharing. Not only does oversharing create the potential for profiles to be hacked, but it has also lead to individuals being mugged and homes being robbed (Kaye, 2010). As SNSs become more integrated into the day today lives of billions of people around the world, we are all going to have to adapt to these challenges and think about how and what we share on our profiles.

Figure 22.3
Demographic Breakdown of Social Media Users
Percent of Internet users within each group who use social networking sites

All Internet Users	65%
Gender	
Men	60
Women	69*
Age	
18-29	83***
30-49	70**
50-64	51*
65+	33
Race/Ethnicity	
White, non-Hispanic	63
Black, non-Hispanic	69
Hispanic (English and Spanish speaking)	66
Household Income	
Less than $30,000	68
$30,000-$49,999	70
$50,000-$74,999	63
$75,000+	68
Education level	
Less than high school	68
High school grad	61
Some college	65
College+	67
Geographic location	
Urban	67
Suburban	65
Rural	61

*indicates statistically significant difference between rows

Source: Pew Internet, 2011

Current Status

The popularity of SNS cannot be overstated. Over 65% of American adults had social media profiles as of 2011 (Madden & Zickuhr, 2011). According to the Pew Institute, 83% of Internet users between the ages of 18-29 have one or more social media profiles online (Madden & Zickuhr, 2011). This is a jump from five years earlier when only 67% of Internet users between the ages of 18-29 had social media profiles. Social media usage also increased among seniors, jumping from 7% of Internet users over the age of 65 having social media profiles in 2005 to 33% having social media profiles in 2011 (Madden & Zickuhr, 2011). See Figures 22.3 and 22.4.

Social networks and blogs are the most visited types of websites on the Internet. They accounted for 22.5% of total time spent online, more than twice the amount of time spent on the second most popular kind of websites: gaming sites (9%; Nielsen, 2011). Facebook continues to dominate social networking in the U.S., with Internet users spending more time on Facebook than on any other site (Nielsen, 2011).

Figure 22.4
Social Networking Site Use by Age Group, 2005-2011

The percentage of adult Internet users in each age group who use social networking sites.

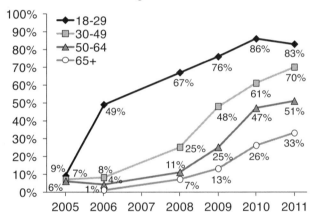

Note: Total n for Internet users age 65+ was <100, and so results for that group are not included.

Source: Pew Research, 2012

Globally, Facebook dominates social media with more than 140 million unique visitors every month. Twitter is in a distant second place with more than 50 million unique visitors every month (Nielsen, 2011). See Figures 22.5 and 22.6.

Social media has done more than connect us with our long-lost childhood friends. One of the more interesting new developments within the realm of social networking is how it is now being used by different businesses for advertising purposes. Nielsen (2011) reported that, on average, 53% of adult social networking users follow a specific brand on their SNS

profile. Carmichael (2011) reported that in an analysis done by social-media tracking company Infegy, in more than 40 million different posts and articles submitted to various SNSs, Apple has received more attention than any other company, with more than 12 million mentions in the past year. While SNS users are talking about all their favorite brands on their social media profiles, businesses are taking note and paying attention. According to Rao (2011) global advertising revenues from SNS worldwide reached more than $5.4 billion in 2011. She also predicts that the annual revenue generated by advertising on SNS will top $10 billion by 2013 (Rao, 2011). In total, 8.8% of all online advertising money went to SNS in 2011, up from 7.7% in 2010 (eMarketer, 2011). See Figure 22.7

Figure 22.5
Top U.S. Web Brands by Total Minutes, in Billions

Websites	Minutes on Website (in Billions)
Facebook	53.5
Yahoo!	17.2
Google	12.5
AOL Media Network	11.4
MSN/WindowsLive/Bing	9.5
YouTube	9.1
EBay	4.5

Source: Nielsen, 2011

Figure 22.6
Time Spent on the Internet

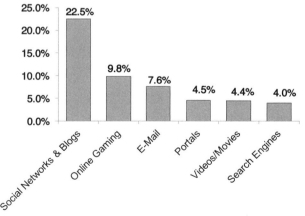

Source: Nielsen

Figure 22.7

Social Media Attention by Volume

Name	Volume	Reference Positivity	Article Positivity	Score
Apple	12,850,311	75%	71%	7,753,785
Amazon	11,173,839	79%	71%	7,101,823
LG	8,601,194	91%	88%	6,094,856
AT&T	7,913,587	71%	61%	2,056,554
E-Trade	6,341,774	69%	65%	3,001,556
Microsoft	6,013,165	83%	79%	4,285,016
HP	4,932,584	85%	86%	3,748,011
Sony	4,358,506	84%	86%	3,116,360
Fox	4,345,103	70%	61%	1,387,366
Ford	4,221,809	83%	77%	2,484,355

Source: Carmichael, 2011

Factors to Watch

Expect to see more third party app integration in Facebook. As part of the new rollout of the "timeline" format for Facebook, users are already able to use apps such as Angry Birds and Pinterest on their Facebook profiles. Expect to see more apps that became popular outside of Facebook get integrated into your profile. Also, the popularity of games on Facebook will continue to rise. Already, 50% of all logins to Facebook are specifically to play games (Digital Buzz, 2011). As the timeline format makes the access of games and apps easier and more attractive to users, there will be a continued growth of third party app use on Facebook.

Speaking of Pinterest, expect to see more apps and sites like it popping up over the next few years. Pinterest was developed by Ben Silbermann and Paul Sciarra and initially launched in March 2010. Pinterest allows users to organize and share their Internet discoveries with friends and other Pinterest users on virtual "pinboards" (Pinterest, n.d.). In fewer than two years since its initial lauch, Pinterest has created massive shockwaves throughout the Internet. Time Magazine named Pinterest one of the top 50 websites of 2011 (McCraken, 2011), and it became the tenth most trafficked SNS by the end of 2011 (Sloan, 2011), which is quite the accomplishment for a SNS

that is still "invite only." Pinterest has not only gained the attention of industry experts, but also the American public. Pinterest is the fastest-growing SNS in history, seeing over 16.1 million unique hits in January of 2012—over double the hits that the site saw just two months earlier in November (Gannes, 2012b).

As Pinterest gains the attention of the American public and venture capitalists like Andreesen Horowitz (Sloan, 2011), the website's parent company, Cold Brew Labs, has found itself in the middle of a burgeoning legal battle. As the company moves to monetize traffic on the site, it is also quickly trying to avoid the potential for a massive amount of copyright suits (Sherman, 2012). The issue stems from the often-copyrighted photos and content that Pinterest users post on their pinboards. To avoid the potential for lawsuits, Pinterest updated their terms and conditions for use on their website on April 6th, 2012, specifically asking users to only post content they have the right to post (Sherman, 2012). This move to clarify what should and should not be posted on Pinterest and placing the onus on the user does not completely clear Cold Brew Labs from being sued for copyright infringement, but it should hold the onslaught of impending lawsuits at bay for the time being.

As Facebook approaches one billion users, expect to see the rapidly-growing user base finally plateau. The reason for this will not be because there is a lack of interest in the social media giant, but rather because Facebook will hit a saturation point. As Dale (2012) stated: "There are only so many more people to add" (par. 6). As of January 2012, there are a little over 2.2 billion people in the world with access to the Internet (Internet World Stats, 2012). Unless the Chinese government finally allows Facebook to be openly used in their country, Mark Zuckerberg and company are going to be running out of people to add.

Expect to see more legislation in both North America and Europe regarding cyberbullying and online harassment. All 50 states in the United States already have some form of protection against cyberbullying (NCSL, 2011), but these statutes vary in their form of protection against cyberbullying, cyberharassment and cyberstalking. As all forms of cyberbullying become more prevalent, it will come as no surprise if there is a law against cyberbullying passed at the federal level.

Sustainability

The trend to "go green" has affected most large corporations, SNSs included. Each of the social media giants has released their own sustainability practices to the public. In November 2010, Facebook announced that it was "going green" by giving out environmentally-friendly tips and sharing green content (Kuo, 2010). The timing of this announcement was considered suspect, specifically because the environmental group Greenpeace was calling for a boycott of Facebook over their planned data center in Portland, OR which would run exclusively on coal energy (Kuo, 2010). Since the backlash from Greenpeace, Facebook has announced that it will re-think the plans for the new data center.

While Facebook is battling its own sustainability issues, the SNS itself is actually turning into a powerful tool for environmental advocates. In a slightly more than ironic twist of fate, in May of 2010, Greenpeace used Facebook to launch an aggressive campaign against the food conglomerate, Nestlé, for the former's policies regarding the use of palm oil and the destruction of rainforests (McCarthy, 2010). After the launch of the Facebook campaign against them, Nestlé agreed to partner with the Forest Group to establish more sustainable harvest practices. Twitter is another SNS that is being used by environmentalists to get their message out to a much larger audience. There are hundreds of different Twitterers on the Web that dedicate their Tweets to all things environmental. For a comprehensive list, websites such as tweetfind.com allow for easy searching. Both Twitter and Tumblr allow its users to "hashtag" what their posts concern, so it makes it easier for individuals to zero in on specific topics. For example, when searching for environmental topics, searching for #green and/or #environment will collate all recent posts that have been tagged with those search terms. While it is not revolutionary, it does help to bring people who want to help the environment closer together.

References

Babbar, S. (2011, December 27). Top 10 hacking scandals of 2011. *Hindustan Times*. Retrieved from http://www.hindustantimes.com/technology/SocialMedia-Updates/Top-10-hacking-scandals-of-2011/SP-Article1-787722.aspx

Banks, M.A. (2007, January 1). The Internet, ARPANet, and consumer online. *All Business*. Retrieved from http://www.allbusiness.com/media-telecommunications/Internet-www/10555321-1.html

Beaumont, C. (2008, November 25). The team behind Twitter: Jack Dorsey, Biz Stone and Evan Williams. *Telegraph*. Retrieved March 31, 2010 from http://www.telegraph.co.uk/technology/3520024/The-team-behind-Twitter-Jack-Dorsey-Biz-Stone-and-Evan-Williams.html

Bercovici, J. (2011, October 24). Why are so many tech titans ignoring Google Plus? *Forbes*. Retrieved from http://www.forbes.com/sites/jeffbercovici/2011/10/24/why-are-so-many-tech-titans-ignoring-google-plus/

Boulton, C. (2012, January 21). Google+ user engagement question amid Facebook rivalry. *eWeek.com*. Retrieved from http://www.eweek.com/c/a/Enterprise-Networking/Google-User-Engagement-Questioned-Amid-Facebook-Rivalry-332227/

boyd, d.m. & Ellison, N.B. (2008). Social networking sites: Definition, history, and scholarship. *Journal of Computer-Mediated Communication, 13*, 210-230.

BusinessWeek. (2005, July 29). MySpace: WhoseSpace?. *BusinessWeek*. Retrieved from
http://www.businessweek.com/technology/content/jul2005/tc20050729_0719_tc057.htm

Carlson, N. (2011). Twitter has less than 21 million "active" users. *Business Insider, SAI*. Retrieved from
http://www.businessinsider.com/twitter-has-less-than-21-million-active-users-2011-4

Carmichael, M. (2011, June 19). Top brand ad spending by category and social-media ranking. *Ad Age Blogs*. Retrieved from
http://adage.com/article/adagestat/top-brand-ad-spending-category-social-media-ranking/228101/

Caslon Analytics. (2006). Caslon Analytics social networking services. *Caslon Analytics*. Retrieved from
http://www.caslon.com.au/socialspacesprofile2.htm

Collier, A. & Magid, L. (2012, February 18). A parents' guide to Facebook. *Connectsafely.org*. Retrieved from
http://www.connectsafely.org/pdfs/fbparents.pdf

Dale, S. (2012, March 1). Future trends in social media & social networks. *Collabor8Now!* Retrieved from
http://collabor8now.com/2012/03/future

Digital Buzz. (2011, February 7). Facebook gaming: 10 Facebook gaming stats. *Digital Buzz*. Retrieved from
http://www.digitalbuzzblog.com/facebook-games-stats/

Dsouza, K. (2010, March 14). Facebook status update has 420 character limit too. *Techie Buzz*. Retrieved from http://techie-buzz.com/social-networking/facebook-has-a-420-character-status-update-limit-too.html

Ehrlich, B. (2011, June 29). MySpace sold to ad network for $35 million. *Mashable*. Retrieved from
http://mashable.com/2011/06/29/myspace-sold/

eMarketer. (2011, October 5). Social network revenues to reach $10 billion worldwide in 2013. *eMarketer*. Retrieved from
http://www.emarketer.com/Article.aspx?R=1008625

Facebook. (2012a). Newsroom fact sheet. *Facebook*. Retrieved from
http://newsroom.fb.com/content/default.aspx?NewsAreaId=22

Facebook. (2012b). Newsroom timeline. Retrieved from http://newsroom.fb.com/content/default.aspx?NewsAreaId=20

Flegenheimer, M. (2012, January 4). Accusations of bullying after death of teenager. *The New York Times*. Retrieved from
http://www.nytimes.com/2012/01/04/nyregion/accusations-of-bullying-after-death-of-staten-island-teen.html

FollowFamous. (2009). Find famous celebrities on Twitter. Follow Famous. Retrieved from http://www.followfamous.com/

Gannes, L. (2012a, January 19). About all those active Google+ users…. *All Things D.* Retrieved from
http://allthingsd.com/20120119/about-all-those-active-google-users/

Gannes, L. (2012b, March 13). Pinterest CEO Ben Silbermann's lesson for start-ups: Go your own way. *All Things D.* Retrieved from http://allthingsd.com/20120313/pinterest-ceo-ben-silbermanns-lesson-for-start-ups-go-your-own-way/

Google+. (n.d.). Overview. *Google+*. Retrieved from http://www.google.com/+/learnmore/

Hendrick, J. (2012). INFOGRAPHIC: Is there a tech bubble? *G+*. Retrieved from https://www.gplus.com/Internet-Bubble/insight/INFOGRAPHIC-Is-there-a-Tech-Bubble

Hinduja, S. & Patchin, J. W. (2010, February). Cyberbullying victimization. *Cyberbullying Research Center*. Retrieved from
http://www.cyberbullying.us/2010_charts/cyberbullying_victim_2010.jpg

Internet User Stats. (2012). Internet usage statistics: The Internet big picture. *Internet World Stats*. Retrieved from
http://www.internetworldstats.com/stats.htm

Kaye, R. (2010, August 5). Facebook friend or foe?. *CNN*. Retrieved from http://ac360.blogs.cnn.com/2010/08/05/facebook-friend-or-foe/

Kuo, I. (2010, November 4). Facebook friends the environment—or does it? *Venture Beat*. Retrieved from
http://venturebeat.com/2010/11/04/facebook-friends-the-environment-or-does-it/

LinkedIn. (2012). Company history. *LinkedIn*. Retrieved from http://press.linkedin.com/about

Madden, M. (2012, February 24). Privacy management on social media sites. *Pew Internet & American Life Project*. Retrieved from
http://pewinternet.org/~/media//Files/Reports/2012/PIP_Privacy_management_on_social_media_sites_022412.pdf

Madden, M. & Zickuhr, K. (2011, August 26). 65% of online adults use social networking sites. *Pew Internet and the American Life Project*. Retrieved from http://www.pewinternet.org/~/media//Files/Reports/2011/PIP-SNS-Update-2011.pdf

Mayfield, R. (2007, March 10). Twitter tips the tuna. *Ross Mayfield's Weblog*. Retrieved from
http://ross.typepad.com/blog/2007/03/twitter_tips_th.html

McCarthy, C. (2010, May 17). After Facebook backlash, Nestle steps up sustainability. *Cnet*. http://news.cnet.com/8301-13577_3-20005101-36.html

McCracken, H. (2011, August 16). The 50 best websites of 2011. *Time Magazine*. Retrieved from
http://www.time.com/time/specials/packages/article/0,28804,2087815_2088159_2088155,00.html

Milian, M. (2009, July 22) Friendster founder on social networking: I invented this stuff (updated). *The Los Angeles Times*. Retrieved from http://latimesblogs.latimes.com/technology/2009/07/friendster-jonathan-abrams.html

Morin, D. (2008, May 9). Announcing Facebook Connect. *Facebook Developers*. Retrieved from https://developers.facebook.com/blog/post/108/

NCSL. (2011, January 26). State cyberstalking, cyberharassment and cyberbullying laws. National Conference of State Legislatures. Retrieved from http://www.ncsl.org/issues-research/telecom/cyberstalking-cyberharassment-and-cyberbullying-l.aspx

Nickson, C. (2009, January 21). The history of social networking. *Digital Trends*. Retrieved from http://www.digitaltrends.com/features/the-history-of-social-networking/

Nielsen. (2011). State of the media: The social media report. *Nielsen*. Retrieved from http://blog.nielsen.com/nielsenwire/social/

Ostrow, A. (2010, November 18). You can now log in to MySpace with Facebook. *Mashable*. Retrieved from http://mashable.com/2010/11/18/you-can-now-login-to-myspace-with-facebook/

Parr, B. (2009, January 12). 10 great implementations of Facebook Connect. *Mashable*. Retrieved from http://mashable.com/2009/01/12/facebook-connect-implementations/

Pinterest. (n.d.). What is Pinterest? *Pinterest*. Retrieved from http://pinterest.com/about/

Price, S. (2012, February 2). Facebook sets historic IPO. *The Wall Street Journal*. Retrieved from http://online.wsj.com/article/SB10001424052970204879004577110780078310366.html

Protalinski, E. (2011, November 30). Facebook increases status update character limit to 63,206. *ZDNet*. Retrieved from http://www.zdnet.com/blog/facebook/facebook-increases-status-update-character-limit-to-63206/5754

Purewal, S. J. (2012, January 31). Facebook timeline privacy tips: Lock down your profile. *PC World*. Retrieved from http://www.pcworld.com/article/249019/facebook_timeline_privacy_tips_lock_down_your_profile.html

Rao, L. (2011, October 5). Global ad revenues from social networks to reach $5.4b in 2011; $10b in 2013. *TechCrunch*. Retrieved from http://techcrunch.com/2011/10/05/global-ad-revenues-from-social-networks-to-reach-5-4b-in-2011-10b-in-2013/

Santarelli, C. (2012, January 15). HuffPo Twitter hacked? Anti-gay and racist tweets come from the site's official accounts. The Blaze. Retrieved from http://www.theblaze.com/stories/huffpo-twitter-hacked-anti-gay-and-racist-tweets-come-from-sites-official-account/

Sherman, E. (2012, March 26). Pinterest tightens copyrights. *CBS Money Watch*.Retrieved from http://www.cbsnews.com/8301-500395_162-57404630/pinterest-tightens-copyright-rules/

Sloan, P. (2011, December 22). Pinterest: Crazy growth lands it as top 10 social site. CNET. Retrieved from http://news.cnet.com/8301-1023_3-57347187-93/pinterest-crazy-growth-lands-it-as-top-10-social-site/?tag=mncol;txt

Stelter, B. & Preston, J. (2011, September 9). Hackers take over NBC Twitter account. *The New York Times*. Retrieved from http://mediadecoder.blogs.nytimes.com/2011/09/09/hackers-take-over-nbc-twitter-account/

Stross, R. (2012, January 7). Sifting the professional from the personal. *The New York Times*. Retrieved from http://www.nytimes.com/2012/01/08/business/branchout-and-beknown-vie-for-linkedins-reach.html?_r=2

Twitter. (2012). About. *Twitter*. Retrieved from https://twitter.com/about

Veracode. (n.d.). Twitter hacks infographic. *Veracode*. http://www.veracode.com/resources/twitter-infographic

Womack, B. & Spears, L. (2012, February 24). Facebook insiders push $100 billion value. *Bloomberg*. Retrieved from http://www.bloomberg.com/news/2012-02-23/facebook-insiders-limit-ipo-by-pushing-100-billion-value-tech.html

Zukerman, E. (2011, December 16). Why Google+ will overtake Facebook in 2 years or less (opinion). Make Use Of. Retrieved from http://www.makeuseof.com/tag/google-overtake-facebook-2-years-opinion/

23

Broadband & Home Networks

John J. Lombardi, Ph.D.[*]

Why Study Broadband & Home Networks?

✦ Broadband technologies are becoming intrinsically linked to our communication, entertainment, and work needs.

✦ Broadband technologies are fast becoming the backbone to our national infrastructure. They are increasingly used to send, receive, and track distribution of our nation's energy needs.

✦ Broadband technologies are estimated to create hundreds of thousands of new jobs, shape of our educational system, and administer high quality healthcare.

Tim Berners-Lee, the man credited with developing the World Wide Web, has said "Anyone who has lost track of time when using a computer knows the propensity to dream, the urge to make dreams come true and the tendency to miss lunch" (FAQ, n.d.). The World Wide Web is just a bit more than two decades old. However, it is deeply engrained in the daily lives of millions of people worldwide. But the World Wide Web is just part of the growing Internet experience. The Internet is used in virtually all aspects of our

lives. In addition to surfing the Web, the Internet allows users to share information with one another. The Internet can be used to send and receive photos, music, videos, phone calls, or any other type of data.

At the beginning of the current decade there was more than one zettabyte of digital information in the world...a number that is expected to double every two years (ITU, 2012a). With benefits to healthcare, energy consumption, and an improved global economy, the importance of high speed Internet access around the globe will continue to grow.

The term "broadband" is generally used to describe high speed Internet. What constitutes "high speed," however, varies a bit from country to country. In the U.S., the FCC considers Tier 1 high speed Internet that which has speeds greater than or equal to 768 Kb/s, but less than 1.5 Mb/s (FCC, 2008). The Organisation for Economic Co-Operation and Development (OECD), an organization based in France that collects and distributes international economic and social data, considers broadband to be any connection with speeds of at least 256 Kb/s. Meanwhile the International Telecommunication Union considers broadband to be connection speeds of between 1.5 and 2.0 Mb/s (ITU, 2003).

While the FCC defines broadband as connections equal to or greater than 768 Kb/s, actual speeds in the U.S. are generally much faster, and they continue to rise. One source ranks the U.S. 31st

---

[*] .John Lombardi is Associate Professor, Department of Mass Communication, Frostburg State University (Frostburg, Maryland).

internationally with an average download speed of 12.75 Mb/s. South Korea is at the top of the international list at 32.58 Mb/s download speeds (Household download index, 2012).

The increasing connection speeds associated with broadband technology allow for users to engage in such bandwidth-intensive activities such as "voice-over-Internet-protocol" (VoIP), including video phone usage, "Internet protocol television" (IPTV), including increasingly complex video services such as Verizon's FiOS service, and interactive gaming. Additionally, the "always on" approach to broadband allows for consumers to easily create wireless home networks. A wireless home network can allow for multiple computers or other devices to connect to the Internet at one time. Such configurations can allow for wireless data-sharing between numerous networked devices within the home. Such setups allow information to easily flow from and between devices such as desktop computers, laptop computers, tablets, smart phones, and audio/video devices such as stereo systems, televisions, and DVD players. As an example, with a home wireless broadband network you could view videos on your television that are stored on your computer or listen to music that is stored on your computer through your stereo system. Additionally, movie rental firms such as Netflix allow subscribers to access certain remote content instantly. In this case subscribers could add movies to their "instant queue" and then access them directly through their television or mobile device. The key device in most home networks is a residential gateway, or router. Routers are devices that link all networked devices to one another and to the home broadband connection.

This chapter briefly reviews the development of broadband and home networks and residential gateways, discusses the types and uses of these technologies, and examines the current status and future developments of these exciting technologies.

Background

Broadband networks can use a number of different technologies to deliver service. The most common broadband technologies include digital subscriber line (DSL), cable modem, satellite, fiber optic networks, and wireless technologies. Thanks in part to the *Telecommunication Act of 1996* broadband providers include telephone companies, cable operators, public utilities, and private corporations.

DSL

Digital subscriber line (DSL) is a technology that supplies broadband Internet access over regular telephone lines with service being provided by various local carriers nationwide. There are several types of DSL available, but asymmetrical DSL (ADSL) is the most widely used for broadband Internet access. "Asymmetrical" refers to the fact that download speeds are faster than upload speeds. This is a common feature in most broadband Internet network technologies because the assumption is that people download more frequently than upload, and they download larger amounts of data. With DSL, the customer has a modem that connects to a phone jack. Data moves over the telephone network to the central office. At the central office, the telephone line is connected to a DSL access multiplexer (DSLAM). The DSLAM aggregates all of the data coming in from multiple lines and connects them to a high-bandwidth Internet connection.

A DSL connection from the home (or office) to the central office is not shared. As such, individual connection speeds are not affected by other users. However, ADSL is a distance-sensitive technology. This means that the farther your home is from the central office, the slower your connection speed will be. Also, this technology only works within 18,000 feet (about 3 ½ miles) of the central office (though "bridge taps" may be used to extend this range a bit). ASDL typically offers download speeds up to 1.5 Mb/s and upload speeds from 64 Kb/s to 640 Kb/s. Some areas have more advanced DSL services called ADSL2 and ADSL2+. These services offer higher bandwidth, up to 12 Mb/s with ADSL2 and 24 Mb/s with ADSL2+. Prices vary from a low of $19.95 per month for 3 Mb/s download to $50 per month for up to 24 Mb/s with AT&T's DSL service (AT&T, n.d.).

FTTN

Fiber-to-the-node is a hybrid form of DSL often times referred to as VDSL (very high bit-rate DSL). This service, used for services such as Verizon's FiOS, offers speeds up to 50 Mb/s downstream and 20 Mb/s upstream. This system employs a fiber optic cable that runs from the central office to a node in individual neighborhoods. A traditional copper wire then runs from the node (or VDSL gateway) to the home. The neighborhood node is a junction box in the neighborhood that contains a VDSL gateway that converts the digital signal on the fiber optic network to a signal that is carried on ordinary copper wires to the residence. Verizon's FiOS service offers speeds from 15 Mb/s downstream and 5 Mb/s upstream for $49.99 a month to 150 Mb/s downstream and 35 Mb/s upstream for $199.99 per month (Verizon, n.d.).

FTTH

Fiber-to-the-home employs fiber optic networks all the way to the home. Fiber optic cables have the advantage of being extremely fast (speeds up to 1 Gb/s) and are the backbone of both cable and telecommunications networks. Extending these networks to the home is still somewhat rare due to cost constraints. However, costs are coming down and Google announced in February 2012 that it is ready to begin wiring the twin cities of Kansas City, Kansas and Kansas City, Missouri with fiber optic cabling and networks cable of generating speeds up to 1 Gb/s (Kansas City is Fiber-Ready, 2012).

Cable Modem

Cable television providers offer Internet service. In this system a customer's Internet service can come into the home on the same cable that provides cable television service, and for some, telephone service. With the upgrade to hybrid fiber/coaxial cable networks, cable television operators began offering broadband Internet access. But how can the same cable that supplies your cable television signals also have enough bandwidth to also supply high speed Internet access? They can do this because it is possible to fit the download data (the data going from the Internet to the home) into the 6 MHz bandwidth space of a single television channel. The upload speed (the data going from the computer back to the Internet) requires only about 2 MHz of bandwidth space.

In the case of Internet through a cable service, the signal travels to the cable headend via the cable modem termination system (CMTS). The CMST acts like the DSLAM of a DSL service. From the cable headend, the signal travels to a cable node in a given neighborhood. A coaxial cable then runs from the neighborhood node to the home.

Cable modems use a standard called data over cable service interface specifications (DOCSIS). First-generation DOCSIS 1.0, which was used with first-generation hybrid fiber/coax networks, was capable of providing bandwidth between 320 Kb/s and 10 Mb/s. DOCSIS 2.0 raised that bandwidth to up to 30 Mb/s (DOCSIS, n.d.). DOCSIS 3.0 provides bandwidth well in excess of 100 Mb/s. In fact, some modem chipsets can bond up to eight downstream channels thus creating the possibility of delivering up to 320 Mb/s (Docsis 3.0, 2009). According to the Organisation for Economic Co-operation and Development (OECD), approximately 15% of U.S. residents receive their service from cable providers (see Table 23.2).

More and more cable Internet providers are moving toward FTTN systems (e.g. Verison's FiOS and Comcast's XFINITY). As such it is becoming increasingly difficult to accurately compare costs and speeds of traditional cable modem Internet access. However, Internet services provided by one of the nation's largest ISPs, Comcast, range in cost from about $40 per month for 1.5 Mb/s download speeds to up to $200 per month for 105 Mb/s service. Prices for cable broadband service are usually lower when bundled with other services (XFINITY Internet from Comcast, n.d.).

Although cable Internet provides fast speeds and, arguably, reasonable rates, this service is not without problems. Unlike DSL, cable Internet users share bandwidth. This means that the useable speed for individual subscribers varies depending upon the number of simultaneous users.

Satellite

For those people who live out of DSL's reach and in rural areas without cable, satellite broadband Internet access is an option. With this service, a modem is connected to a small satellite dish which then communicates with the service provider's satellite. That satellite, in turn, directs the data to a provider center that has a high-capacity connection to the Internet. Satellite Internet service cannot deliver the bandwidth of cable or DSL, but speeds are a great improvement over dial-up. For example, HughesNet offers home service with 1 Mb/s download and 200 Kb/s upload for $59.99 a month. Its highest-speed service for the residential market, Power 200, offers 2 Mb/s download and 300 Kb/s upload for $109.99 a month (HughesNet, 2012a). Higher speeds are available for home or small office networks, but the price goes up considerably. The fastest speed available is 5 Mb/s download and 1,024 Kb/s upload for $349.99 a month. These prices do not include the cost of installation or the purchase or leasing of equipment (Hughes Net, 2012b).

The two most popular satellite services in the U.S. are HughesNet and Wild Blue. HughesNet uses three DBS satellites on the high-power Ku band, while Wild Blue uses the Ka-band and 11 gateways located throughout the U.S. (Wild Blue, n.d).

Wireless

There are two different types of wireless broadband networks: mobile and fixed. Mobile broadband networks are offered by wireless telephony companies and employ 3G (and increasingly, 4G) networks (discussed in more detail in Chapter 20). Second generation (2G) mobile broadband networks generally use the Enhanced Data GSM Environment (EDGE) protocol (some refer to this as 2.75G because it is better than traditional 2G, but not quite at the level of true 3G networks). Third generation (3G) networks generally use Evolution, Data Optimized (EVDO), or High-Speed Uplink Packet Access (HSUPA).

In January 2012 the International Telecommunication Union agreed on specifications for "IMT-Advanced" mobile wireless technologies (this includes what is commonly referred to as LTE-Advanced in the U.S.). It is this technological standard that is employed in 4G mobile broadband networks and is touted as being "at least 100 times faster than today's 3G smart phones" (ITU, 2012b, para. 5).

Fixed broadband wireless networks use either WiFi or WiMAX. Wi-Fi uses a group of standards in the IEEE 802.11 group to provide short-range, wireless Internet access to a range of devices such as laptops, cell phones, and tablets. Wi-Fi "hotspots" can be found in many public and private locations. Some businesses and municipalities provide Wi-Fi access for free. Other places charge a fee.

WiMAX, which stands for worldwide interoperability for microwave access, is also known as IEEE 802.16. There are two versions: a fixed point-to-multipoint version and a mobile version. Unlike Wi-Fi which has a range of 100 to 300 feet, WiMAX can provide wireless access up to 30 miles for fixed stations and three to ten miles for mobile stations (What is wimax, n.d.). As of early 2012, Clear provides WiMAX service in selected locations throughout the United States, but service availability is still modest.

BPL

Broadband over power line (BPL) was, at one time, thought to be the wave of the future. Given that power lines went into every home, it was easy to understand how convenient it would be to use these cables to send broadband data into homes. The modem would actually be plugged into an electrical outlet in the subscriber's home as a means of obtaining the service. However, several factors have caused this technology to lose its appeal. BPL is quite susceptible to interference from radio frequencies, and other broadband services (listed above) provide a faster and more reliable connection. In late 2011 there were only 125 zip codes in the U.S. that had access to BPL, and many of them, according to one report, were initiated, but never deployed (Bode, 2011).

Home Networks

Computer networking was, at one time, only found in large organizations such as businesses, government offices, and schools. The complexity and cost of networking facilities was beyond the scope of most home computer owners. At one time a computer network required the use of an Ethernet network and expensive wiring called Cat (category) 5. Additionally, a server, hub, and router were needed. And all of this required someone in the household to have computer networking expertise, as network maintenance was regularly needed.

Several factors changed the environment to allow home networks to take off: broadband Internet access, multiple computer households, and new networked consumer devices and services. Because of these advances, a router (costing as little as $30) can be quickly installed. This router essentially splits the incoming Internet signal and sends it (either through a wired or wireless connection) to other equipment in the house. Computers, mobile phones, televisions, DVD players, stereo receivers, and other devices can be included within the home network. This setup allows for quick and easy file sharing. With a home network (the sending of signals through the house, once the signal reaches the house) users can, among other things, send video files from their computer to their television; they can send audio files from their computer to their stereo receiver; they can send a print job from their mobile phone to their printer; or with some additional equipment they could use their mobile phone to control home lighting and other electrical devices within the home.

There are two broad types of home networks:

✦ Wired networks (including Ethernet, phone lines, and power lines)

✦ Wireless networks (including Wi-Fi, Bluetooth, Zigbee, and Z-wave)

When discussing each type of home network, it is important to consider the transmission rate, or speed, of the network. Regular file sharing and low-bandwidth applications such as home control may require a speed of 1 Mb/s or less. The MPEG-2 and MPEG-4 digital video and audio from DBS services requires 3 Mb/s, DVD-quality video requires between 3 Mb/s and 8 Mb/s, and compressed high-definition television (HDTV) requires around 20 Mb/s.

Wired Networks

Traditional networks use Ethernet, which has a data transmission rate of 10 Mb/s to 100 Mb/s. There is also Gigabit Ethernet, used mostly in business, that has transmission speeds up to 1 Gb/s. Ethernet is the kind of networking commonly found in offices and universities. As discussed earlier, traditional Ethernet has not been popular for home networking because it is expensive to install and maintain and difficult to use. To direct the data, the network must have a server, hub, and router. Each device on the network must be connected, and many computers and devices require add-on devices to enable them to work with Ethernet. Thus, despite the speed of this kind of network, its expense and complicated nature make it somewhat unpopular in the home networking market, except among those who build and maintain these networks at the office.

Many new housing developments come with "structured wiring" that includes wiring for home networks, home theatre systems, and other digital data networking services such as utility management and security. One of the popular features of structured wiring is home automation, including the ability to unlock doors or adjust the temperature or lights. New homes represent a small fraction of the potential market for home networking services and equipment, so manufacturers have turned their attention to solutions for existing homes. These solutions almost always are based upon "no new wires" networking solutions that use existing phone lines or power lines, or they are wireless.

Phone lines are ideal for home networking. This technology uses the existing random tree wiring typically found in homes and runs over regular telephone wire—there is no need for Cat 5 wiring. The technology uses frequency division multiplexing (FDM) to allow data to travel through the phone line without interfering with regular telephone calls or DSL service. There is no interference because each service is assigned a different frequency. The Home Phone Line Networking Alliance (HomePNA) has presented several standards for phone line networking. HomePNA 1.0 boasted data transmission rates up to 1 Mb/s. It was replaced by HomePNA (HPNA) 2.0, which boasts data transmission rates up to 10 Mb/s and is backward-compatible with HPNA 1.0. HomePNA 3.1 provides data rates up to 320 Mb/s and operates over phone wires and coaxial cables, which makes it a solution to deliver video and data services (320 Mbps, n.d.). The home's power lines can also be used to distribute a signal around the house. In this scenario devices would be plugged in to outlets in various parts of the home to send and/or receive a signal. The main advantage to this approach is that it requires no new wires. Most homes have phone jacks in numerous rooms, but all rooms have electric lines. The primary downside to this approach is the speed. Data rates generally do not exceed 350 Mb/s. Homes with older wiring can experience slower rates if it works at all.

Wireless

The most popular type of home network is wireless. Currently, there are several types of wireless home networking technologies: Wi-Fi (otherwise known as IEEE 802.11a, 802.11b 802.11g, 802.11n, and 802.11ac), Bluetooth, and wireless mesh technologies such as ZigBee and Z-wave. Mesh technologies are those that do not require a central control unit. Wi-Fi , Bluetooth, and ZigBee are based on the same premise: low-frequency radio signals from the instrumentation, science, and medical (ISM) bands of spectrum are used to transmit and receive data. The ISM bands, around 2.4 GHz, not licensed by the FCC, are used mostly for microwave ovens and cordless telephones (except for 802.11a and 802.11ac, which operate at 5 GHz).

Wireless networks utilize a transceiver (combination transmitter and receiver) that is connected to a wired network or gateway (generally a router) at a fixed location. Much like cellular telephones, wireless networks use microcells to extend the connectivity range by overlapping to allow the user to roam without losing the connection (Wi-Fi Alliance, n.d.).

Wi-Fi is the most common type of wireless networking. It uses a series of similarly labeled transmission protocols (802.11a, 802.11b, 802.11g, 802.11n, and 802.11ac). Wi-Fi was originally the consumer-friendly label attached to IEEE 802.11b, the specification for wireless Ethernet. 802.11b was created in July 1999. It can transfer data up to 11 Mb/s and is supported by the Wi-Fi Alliance. A couple years later 802.11a was introduced, providing bandwidth up to 54 Mb/s. This was soon followed by the release of 802.11g, which combines the best of 802.11a and 802.11b, providing bandwidth up to 54 Mb/s. The 802.11n standard was released in 2007 and amended in 2009 and provides bandwidth over 100 Mb/s (Mitchell, n.d.). The newest standard, 802.11ac, is expected to roll out in 2012 and allow for speeds up to 1.3 Gb/s. However, because this new standard will operate only in the 5GHz frequencies, the transmission range of this Wi-Fi standard could be smaller than that of 802.11n Wi-Fi (Vaughan-Nichols, 2012).

Because wireless networks use so much of their available bandwidth for coordination among the devices on the network, it is difficult to compare the rated speeds of these networks with the rated speeds of wired networks. For example, 802.11b is rated at 11 Mb/s, but the actual throughput (the amount of data that can be effectively transmitted) is only about 6 Mb/s. Similarly, 802.11g's rated speed of 54 Mb/s yields a data throughput of only about 25 Mb/s. Tests of 802.11n have confirmed speeds from 100 Mb/s to 140 Mb/s (Haskin, 2007). Actual throughput of the 802.11ac protocol is expected to top out at about 800 Mb/s (Marshall, 2012).

Security is an issue with any network. Wi-Fi uses two types of encryption: WEP (Wired Equivalent Privacy) and WPA (Wi-Fi Protected Access). WEP has security flaws and is easily hacked. WPA fixes those flaws in WEP and uses a 128-bit encryption. There are two versions: WPA-Personal that uses a password and WPA-Enterprise that uses a server to verify network users (Wi-Fi Alliance, n.d.). WPA2 is an upgrade to WPA and is now required of all Wi-Fi Alliance-certified products (WPA2, n.d.).

While Wi-Fi can transmit data up to 140 Mb/s for up to 150 feet (depending upon the protocol), Bluetooth was developed for short-range communication at a data rate of up to 3 Mb/s and is geared primarily toward voice and data applications. Bluetooth technologies are good for transmitting data up to 10 meters. Bluetooth technology is built into devices such as laptop computers, music players (including car stereo systems), and mobile phones. Bluetooth-enhanced devices can communicate with each other and create an ad hoc network. The technology works with and enhances other networking technologies. Bluetooth 4.0 is the current standard and is slowly making its way into more and more consumer products. Bluetooth 4.0 is backwards compatible so there should be no communication issues between new and old devices. The main advantage of Bluetooth 4.0 is that it requires less power to run, thus making it useable in more and more (and smaller and smaller) devices (Lee, 2011).

ZigBee, also known as IEEE 802.15.4, is classified, along with Bluetooth, as a technology for wireless personal area networks (WPANs). Like Bluetooth 4.0, ZigBee's transmission standard uses little power. It uses the 2.4 GHz radio frequency to deliver data in numerous home and commercial devices (ZigBee, n.d.).

Usually, a home network will involve not just one of the technologies discussed above, but several. It is not unusual for a home network to be configured for HPNA, Wi-Fi , and even traditional Ethernet. Table 23.1 compares each of the home networking technologies discussed in this section.

Residential Gateways

The residential gateway, also known as the broadband router, is what makes the home network infinitely more useful. This is the device that allows users on a home network to share access to their broadband connection. As broadband connections become more common, the one "pipe" coming into the home will most likely carry numerous services such as the Internet, phone, and entertainment. A residential gateway seamlessly connects the home network to a broadband network, so all network devices in the home can be used at the same time.

The current definition of a residential gateway has its beginnings in a white paper developed by the RG Group, a consortium of companies and research groups interested in the residential gateway concept. The RG Group determined that the residential gateway is "a single, intelligent, standardized, and flexible network interface unit that receives communication signals from various external networks and delivers the signals to specific consumer devices through in-home networks" (Li, 1998). Residential gateways can be categorized as complete, home network only, and simple.

A complete residential gateway operates independent of a personal computer and contains a modem and networking software. This gateway can intelligently route incoming signals from the broadband connections to specific devices on the home network. Set-top box and broadband-centric are two categories of complete residential gateways. A broadband-centric residential gateway incorporates an independent digital modem such as a DSL modem with IP management and integrated wireless or HomePNA ports. Set-top box residential gateways use integrated IP management and routing with the processing power of the box. Complete residential gateways also include software to protect the home network, including a firewall, diagnostics, and security log.

Home network only residential gateways interface with existing DSL or cable modems in the home. These route incoming signals to specific devices on the home network, and typically contain the same types of software to protect the home network found in complete residential gateways.

Simple residential gateways are limited to routing and connectivity between properly-configured devices. Also known as "dumb" residential gateways, these have limited processing power and applications, and only limited security for the home network.

Table 23.1
Comparison of Home Networking Technologies

Protocol	How it Works	Standard(s)	Specifications
Ethernet	Uses Cat 5, 5e, 6, or 7 wiring with a server and hub to direct traffic	IEEE 802.3xx IEEE 802.3.1	10 Mb/s to 1 Gb/s*
HomePNA	Uses existing phone lines and OFDM	HPNA 1.0 HPNA 2.0 HPNA 3.0 HPNA 3.1	1.0, up to 1 Mb/s 2.0, 10 Mb/s 3.0, 128 Mb/s 3.1, 320 Mb/s
IEEE 802.11a Wi-Fi	Wireless. Uses electro-magnetic radio signals to transmit between access point and users.	IEEE 802.11a 5 GHz	Up to 54 Mb/s
IEEE 802.11b Wi-Fi	Wireless. Uses electro-magnetic radio signals to transmit between access point and users.	IEEE 802.11b 2.4 GHz	Up to 11 Mb/s
IEEE 802.11g Wi-Fi	Wireless. Uses electro-magnetic radio signals to transmit between access point and users.	IEEE 802.11g 2.4 GHz	Up to 54 Mb/s
IEEE 802.11n Wi-Fi	Wireless. Uses electro-magnetic radio signals to transmit between access point and users.	IEEE 802.11n 2.4 GHz	Up to 140 Mb/s
IEEE 802.11ac Wi-Fi	Wireless. Uses electro-magnetic radio signals to transmit between access point and users.	IEEE 802.11ac 5 GHz	Up to 1.3 Gb/s
Bluetooth	Wireless.	v. 1.0 (2.4 GHz) v. 2.0 + (EDR) v. 3.0 (802.11) v. 4.0 (802.11)	v. 1.0 (1 Mb/s) v. 2.0 (3 Mb/s) v. 3.0 (24 Mb/s) v. 4.0 (24 Mb/s + lower power)
Powerline	Uses existing power lines in home.	HomePlug v1.0 HomePlug AV HPCC HomePlug AV2	v. 1 (Up to 14 Mb/s) AV (Up to 200 Mb/s) AV2 (Up to 500 Mb/s)
ZigBee	Wireless. Uses Electro-magnet radio signals to transmit between access point and users	IEEE 802.15.4	250 Kb/s
Z-wave	Uses 908 MHz 2-way RF	Proprietary	9.6 Kbps

Source: J. Lombardi and J. Meadows

Working Together—The Home Network and Residential Gateway

A home network controlled by a residential gateway or central router allows multiple users to access a broadband connection at the same time. Household members do not have to compete for access to the Internet, printer, television content, music files, or movies. The home network allows for shared access of all controllable devices. Technological innovations have made it possible to access computer devices through a home network in the same way as you would access the Internet. Televisions and Blu-ray DVD players regularly come configured with hardware that allows for accessing streamed audio and video content without having to funnel it through a computer. Cell phone technology is more regularly being used to access home networks remotely. With this technology it is now possible to set your DVR to record a show or to turn lights on and off without being in the home. The residential gateway or router also allows multiple computers to access the Internet at the same time. This is accomplished by creating a "virtual" IP address for each computer. The residential gateway routes different signals to appropriate devices in the home.

Home networks and residential gateways are key to what industry pundits are calling the "smart home." Although having our washing machine tell us when our clothes are done may not be a top priority for many of us, utility management, security, and enhanced telephone services including VoIP are just a few of the potential applications for this technology. Before these applications can be implemented, however, two developments are necessary. First, appropriate devices for each application (appliance controls, security cameras, telephones, etc.) have to be configured to connect to one or more of the different home networking topologies (wireless, HPNA, or power line). Next, software, including user interfaces, control modules, etc., needs to be created and installed. It is easy to conceive of being able to go to a Web page for your home to adjust the air conditioner, turn on the lights, or monitor the security system, but these types of services will not be widely available until consumers have proven that they are willing to pay for them.

The National Broadband Plan

On March 16, 2010, the Federal Communications Commission unveiled its National Broadband Plan. The primary purpose of the nearly 376 page plan is to "create a high-performance America—a more productive, creative, efficient America in which affordable broadband is available everywhere, and everyone has the means and skills to use valuable broadband applications" (FCC, 2010a, p. 9). The plan was drafted after the U.S. Congress, in early 2009, directed the FCC to develop a plan to ensure every American has access to broadband capabilities (FCC, 2010a)

In a 2010 press release discussing the release of the National Broadband Plan, Blair Levin, Executive Director of the Omnibus Broadband Initiative, explains how significant this plan is. He stated, "In every era, America must confront the challenge of connecting the nation anew. Above all else, the plan is a call to action to meet that challenge for our era. If we meet it, we will have networks, devices, and applications that create new solutions to seemingly intractable problems" (FCC, 2010b, p. 1). FCC Chairman Julius Genachowski called the Plan

"a 21st century roadmap to spur economic growth and investment, create jobs, educate our children, protect our citizens, and engage in our democracy. It's an action plan, and action is necessary to meet the challenges of global competitiveness, and harness the power of broadband to help address so many vital national issues" (FCC, 2010b, p. 1).

The assumption, according to the report, is that the U.S. government can influence the broadband landscape in four general ways. First, the government can create policies that ensure robust competition among broadband players. The thought is that this competition will maximize consumer welfare, innovation, and investment. Second, the government can ensure efficient allocation and management of broadband assets. Third, the government can reform current service procedures that will support the launching of broadband in less affluent areas, and ensure that low-income Americans have physical and financial access to broadband technology. Fourth, the government can reform laws and policies to maximize broadband usage in areas traditionally overseen by the government such as public education, health care, and other government operations (FCC, 2010a).

In the National Broadband Plan, the FCC outlined six primary goals. They are:

✦ **Goal 1:** At least 100 million U.S. homes should have affordable access to actual download speeds of at least 100 megabits per second and actual upload speeds of at least 50 megabits per second.

✦ **Goal 2:** The United States should lead the world in mobile innovation, with the fastest and most extensive wireless networks of any nation.

✦ **Goal 3:** Every American should have affordable access to robust broadband service, and the means and skills to subscribe if they so choose.

✦ **Goal 4:** Every community should have affordable access to at least 1 Gb/s broadband service to anchor institutions such as schools, hospitals and government buildings.

✦ **Goal 5:** To ensure the safety of Americans, every first responder should have access to a nationwide public safety wireless network.

✦ **Goal 6:** To ensure that America leads in the clean energy economy, every American should be able to use broadband to track and manage their real-time energy consumption (FCC 2010a).

There are approximately 200 specific recommendations within the plan directed toward President Obama's administration, the U.S. Congress, or the commission itself. Nonetheless, each of these recommendations must be dealt with separately. As time goes by the FCC plans to issue dozens of notices of proposed rulemaking (NPRMs) (Gross, 2010).

Net Neutrality

The issue of "net neutrality" continues to circulate. Currently it is possible for Internet Service Providers to block or prioritize access to Web content. The Obama administration and the FCC, however, want to prevent this from happening. The proponents of net neutrality believe this is a free speech issue. They suggest that ISPs who block or prioritize access to certain Web content can easily direct users to certain sites and away from others. Supporters of the current system believe that new regulations would serve only to minimize investment (Bradley, 2009). FCC Chairman Julius Genachowski, in a 2009 statement said "it is vital that we safeguard the free and open Internet" (FCC, 2009).

The U.S. Court of Appeals for the District of Columbia disagrees. On April 6, 2010 the court ruled that the FCC has only limited power over Web traffic under current law. As such, the FCC cannot tell ISPs to provide equal access to all Web content. This ruling could, however, prompt Congress to enact legislation that would increase the authority of the FCC, giving it the authority to regulate Internet service. It is, nonetheless, uncertain whether Congress will be successful. It is also uncertain how, if at all, this ruling will impact the FCC's National Broadband Plan (Wyatt, 2010).

Regardless of the ruling, the FCC is still committed to promoting an open Internet. The FCC, in a statement released shortly after the court ruling said: "Today's court decision invalidated the prior Commission's approach to preserving an open Internet. But the Court in no way disagreed with the importance of preserving a free and open Internet; nor did it close the door to other methods for achieving this important end" (FCC, 2010c, p. 1).

Recent Developments

In order for the FCC to make meaningful inroads regarding the National Broadband Plan, significant funds will need to be raised and more spectrum space will need to be allocated (or, more likely, reallocated).

President Barrack Obama has continually pledged his support for the National Broadband Plan and has urged lawmakers to make this a priority. His 2011 State of the Union address called for a National Wireless Initiative to make high-speed wireless service available to 98 percent of Americans. The President believes that this is not only essential to enable business growth, to improve education, and to improve public safety, he also believes it will reduce the national deficit by approximately $10 billion (White House, 2011).

Additionally, the FCC has recently announced plans to reform the universal service and intercarrier compensation systems. The "universal service fund" is basically a surcharge placed on all phone and Internet services. Intercarrier compensation is basically a fee that one carrier pays another to originate, transport, or terminate various telephony-related signals. Jointly these fees generate about $4.5 billion annually. These fees will now go into a new "Connect America Fund" which is designed to expand high-speed Internet and voice service to approximately 7 million Americans in rural areas in a six-year period. Additionally, about 500,000 jobs and $50 billion in economic growth are expected (FCC, 2011a).

In terms of accessing additional spectrum space, there are two ways this can be done. The first way is to tap into the unused space that is located between allocated frequencies. This is referred to as "white space". In December 2011 the FCC announced that the Office of Engineering and Technology (OET) approved the use of a "white spaces database system". This is thought to be the first step toward using this available spectrum space. Expanding wireless services would be a primary use for this space (FCC, 2011b).

The second way, reclaiming space currently allocated to broadcasters, is a bit more challenging. Since the television transition from analog to digital transmissions in June 2009, there has been some unused spectrum space. Because digital television signals take up less spectrum space than analog signals, television broadcasters are generally using only part of the allocated spectrum space. However, as discussed in Chapter 6, very few broadcasters appear willing to give up their currently unused spectrum space, even if they would receive some financial compensation. Nonetheless, in February, 2012, Congress passed a bill that gives the FCC the ability to reclaim and auction spectrum space. Additionally, the legislation creates a second digital television (DTV) transition that will allow for current signals to be "repacked" (Eggerton, 2012).

Current Status

The statistics on broadband penetration vary widely. According to the OECD, which keeps track of worldwide broadband penetration, broadband subscribers in the U.S. have gradually increased over the last few years. As Table 23.2 illustrates, an estimated 27.3% of Americans had access to broadband service by mid-2011. This is more than a 400% increase since 2002. Despite this increase, the U.S.'s world standing for broadband access is considered low. (see Table 23.2).

The OECD currently ranks the United States 15th in the world for broadband penetration with 27.3 subscribers per 100 inhabitants (up from just

6.7 in 2002). The rankings are presented in Table 23.2. The United States has the largest number of broadband subscribers with 84.67 million. Fiber connections were most numerous in Korea (20.4) and Japan (16.4). The U.S. is above the OECD average penetration rates for overall broadband usage and for the usage of cable modems. However, the U.S. is below the OECD average for DSL and fiber penetration.

Approximately 309 million people worldwide subscribe to some type of broadband service (up from approximately 271 million in 2009). Worldwide DSL subscribers are the most abundant with nearly 176 million subscribers. Approximately 91 million people have cable Internet and over 40 million have fiber (see Figure 23.1). As mentioned above, Japan and Korea lead the way in terms of fiber usage. Figure 23.2 shows that in Japan, approximately 60% of all broadband subscribers utilize fiber networks. In Korea that number is about 56%. In the U.S., however, the number is 6%. The OECD global average is 13%.

Figure 23.1
Fixed (wired) broadband subscriptions by technology, June 2011

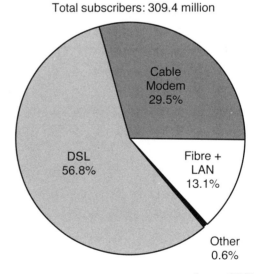

Total subscribers: 309.4 million

- Cable Modem 29.5%
- DSL 56.8%
- Fibre + LAN 13.1%
- Other 0.6%

Source: OECD, 2011

Table 23.2

Broadband Subscribers per 100 Inhabitants, by Technology, June 2011

	Rank	DSL	Cable	Fiber/LAN	Other	Total	Total Subs
Netherlands	1	21.2	16.0	1.3	0.0	35.5	6,392,000
Switzerland	2	27.2	10.6	0.2	0.3	38.3	2,983,281
Denmark	3	21.9	10.1	5.0	0.7	37.7	2,090,825
Korea	4	5.3	10.4	20.4	0.0	36.0	17,604,503
Norway	5	18.7	10.3	5.7	0.1	34.9	1,703,817
France	6	31.6	2.0	0.2	0.0	33.8	21,895,000
Iceland	7	29.3	0.0	4.4	0.0	33.6	106,896
U.K.	8	25.5	6.6	0.5	0.0	32.6	20,274,861
Germany	9	28.5	3.8	0.2	0.1	32.6	26,615,000
Sweden	10	16.5	6.3	9.0	0.1	31.9	2,995,000
Luxembourg	11	28.5	2.9	0.2	0.1	37.1	160,639
Belgium	12	16.9	14.6	0.0	0.1	31.6	3,3433,746
Canada	13	13.5	17.6	0.2	0.0	31.2	10,653,342
Finland	14	20.8	4.8	0.7	2.6	28.9	1,550,400
United States	15	10.2	15.0	1.8	0.3	27.3	84,672,000
Japan	16	6.0	4.5	16.4	0.0	27.0	34,360,672
New Zealand	17	24.4	1.5	0.1	0.0	26.0	1,138,830
Austria	18	16.9	7.6	0.1	0.0	24.7	2,068,623
Israel	19	14.3	10.0	0.0	0.0	24.2	1,847,000
Estonia	20	11.9	5.5	6.1	0.6	24.1	322,523
OECD	Average	14.3	7.4	3.3	0.2	25.1	

Source: OECD (2011)

Figure 23.2

U.S. Broadband Penetration

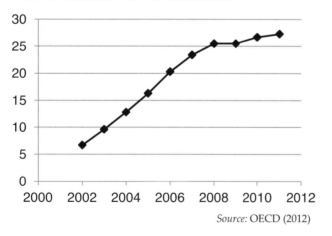

Source: OECD (2012)

Figure 23.3

Percentage of fiber connections in total broadband subscriptions

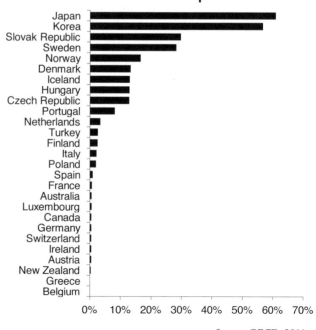

Source: OECD, 2011

Factors to Watch

Home networking offers countless global opportunities. In Korea, for instance, it is expected that the majority of homes will be connected to advanced home networking systems by 2015. This advanced system goes beyond what has been described above. The idea here is to network all home appliances as well as traditional electronic devices. Additionally, the advanced home networking system should support telemedicine and teletherapy processes. The development of home networking applications will continue to escalate if the overall market share continues to expand. The international home networking market is expected to top $150 billion in 2012 (Tae-gyu, 2010). In the U.S. the home networking market is on the rise. In 2010 this market grew 11% to $5.15, with a 46% growth spurt in 2009 (Infonetics Research, 2011).

Mobile broadband speeds will continue to increase. Currently, 4G LTE networks are becoming more and more prevalent. In theory 4G can reach speeds of 100 Mb/s down and 50 Mb/s up. More realistically, however, consumers can expect speeds of 5 to 12 Mb/s down and 2 to 5 Mb/s up (Smith, 2012). Regardless, this is a significant increase over 3G speeds (generally less than 1 Mb/s down) and there is already talk of 5G technology.

Aside from continued market growth and increased speeds, there are several topics that must be continually monitored. They include:

Spectrum Auctions

This issue is a long way from being resolved. While the FCC now has the authority to conduct auctions of unused spectrum space, they will have a difficult time finding anyone willing to give up space. At this point it seems unlikely that any large market (or network-owned) television stations will be willing to return any of their unused spectrum space. The resistance from broadcasters is that, while they may not be using the space now, they could very well use it in the future. Because digital transmissions take up considerably less spectrum space than analog transmissions, broadcasters can send out multiple channels of content using their spectrum space. Given that the analog-to-digital transition was only completed in the middle of 2009, there has been relatively little time for broadcasters to fully utilize their spectrum space.

Where the FCC may find some willing participants is with owners of small stations. In Los Angeles, for instance, there are numerous independent stations that cater to various ethnic groups. It's possible that such stations could join forces using one station's spectrum allocation for multiple channels of programming, thus freeing up spectrum originally assigned to another station (Flint, 2012).

Despite the apparent problems associated with acquiring large amounts of spectrum space, there is reason for optimism. Some industry leaders believe that relatively little additional spectrum space would be needed in order to address the nation's broadband needs (Flint, 2012).

Expanded Coverage Areas

With the recent FCC approval to begin creating "white space databases" we should begin to see wireless coverage areas expanding. LightSquared, a Virginia based company, had hoped to build the nation's first wholesale broadband network. Such an approach would allow companies who produce mobile devices, apps, games, etc. the opportunity to interface with a nationwide 4G LTE (long term evolution) network without having to build the infrastructure or having to contractually link (thus limiting potential reach) to an existing service provider such as AT&T, Verizon, etc.

LightSquared has run into a stumbling block, despite having purchased approximately $4 billion worth of spectrum. There is widespread concern that the spectrum LightSquared intends to use for its networks significantly interferes with GPS technologies. The FCC has stepped in to prevent LightSquared from operating (Needleman, 2012). The FCC contends that LightSquared has not dealt with the interference concerns in a manner that is likely to produce a realistic solution in a reasonable amount of time (FCC, 2012). Should they adequately address these concerns, however, they may once again be permitted to move forward.

Usage-Based Pricing

There continues to be mixed reaction to the idea of "usage-based pricing" for broadband service. Time-Warner, one of the nation's leading broadband providers, is beginning to offer some of its customers the option of paying less for their service if they will accept a 5 GB monthly cap (Ramachandran, 2012). This pricing system is common in the cellular phone world, but usage-based pricing on fixed-line broadband service is becoming hotly debated. Comcast, the nation's largest MSO, by contrast, will not move toward usage-based pricing (Farrell, 2012).

Health and Education

Part of the goal of the National Broadband Plan is to help improve health care and education in the U.S. Early in 2012 FCC Commissioner Mignon Clyburn spoke of the FCC's "Lifeline" program. The primary goal of this program is to increase the availability of broadband service to low-income Americans. Clyburn believes that broadband access is not a luxury, but a necessity. It is necessary to help ensure quality education and to help facilitate quality health care. She believes that the FCC must establish a "Broadband Adoption Pilot Program". This program would help determine how best to increase broadband access to low-income consumers (Clyburn, 2012).

 **Sustainability**

One may not immediately link issues of sustainability with improved broadband technologies. However, there are several ways in which broadband technologies can help with environmental sustainability. One way in which broadband technologies can help the environment is by making it easier for employees to telecommute, thereby saving fuel costs and reducing CO_2 emissions. But the possibilities go well beyond this one.

With increased access to broadband technologies, lower cost and easier access to education and business services would be possible. According to Fehrenbacher (2009) improved broadband services could lead to replacing physical goods with virtual goods. Books, CDs, and DVDs could be sent electronically, thereby eliminating the need to make physical copies of these products, greatly reducing energy consumption and CO_2 output. Products could also be made-to-order thus reducing the need to store large quantities of goods in warehouses requiring heating and cooling (Environmental sustainability, n.d.). According to Broadband for America, e-commerce can reduce air pollution by 36% and requires 16% less energy than conventional shopping (Environmental sustainability, n.d.).

Broadband technology can be used to improve home networks to allow for the control of home appliances, heating/cooling systems, sprinkler systems, and more. This allows for homeowners to continually and expeditiously monitor resource consumption. According to the FCC's National Broadband Plan, consumers who can easily monitor their own consumption are more likely to modify their usage, thus eliminating or at least reducing waste.

Smart grid technology, which relies on high-speed data transmissions, can significantly reduce energy usage. Most of the current electrical grids in the U.S. send power across many miles of power lines to various locations just in case a need for that electricity exists. A tremendous amount of electricity is wasted simply from its dissipating as it travels along power lines. Smart grid technology allows for electricity to travel only when needed and in the shortest distance possible, thus greatly reducing waste. Computer networks with high-speed broadband would be at the center of this technology. Additionally, smart grids can incorporate energy from a variety of sources (wind, solar, hydro-electric, etc.). Standard grids can only work with energy from one source at a time.

Bibliography

320 Mbps home networking specification released (n.d.). Retrieved,from HomePna website: http://www.homepna.org/products/specifications/.

AT&T. (n.d.). Retrieved from http://www.att.com/u-verse/shop/index.jsp?wtSlotClick=1-006ASL-0-1&shopFilterId=500001&ref_from=shop&addressId=&zip=22722#fbid=5CdOI9UJfIb

Bode, K. (20011, October 11). FCC clears up their powerline broadband rules. *DSLReports.com*. Retrieved from http://www.dslreports.com/shownews/FCC-Clears-Up-Their-Powerline-Broadband-Rules-116803

Bradley, T. (2009, September 22). Battle lines drawn in FCC net neutrality fight. *PC World*. Retrieved from http://www.pcworld.com/businesscenter/article/172391/battle_lines_drawn_in_fcc_net_neutrality_fight.html.

Clyburn, M. (2012, January 20). Why rural broadband adoption matters. *Communications Technology*. Retrieved from http://www.cable360.net/ct/news/ctreports/commentary/Why-Rural-Broadband-Adoption-Matters_50319.html.

DOCSIS: Data over cable service interface specifications. (n.d.). Retrieved from Javvin website: http://www.javvin.com/protocolDOCSIS.html.

Docsis 3.0. (2009, March 13). Retrieved from Light Reading website: http://www.lightreading.com/document.asp?doc_id=173525.

Eggerton, J. (2012, February 17). Congress approves spectrum incentive auction. *Broadcasting and Cable*. Retrieved from http://www.broadcastingcable.com/article/480721-Congress_Approves_Spectrum_Incentive_Auctions.php.

Environmental sustainability (n.d.). *Broadband for America*. Retrieved from http://www.broadbandforamerica.com/benefits/environmental.

FAQ (n.d.) w3.org. Retrieved from http://www.w3.org/People/Berners-Lee/FAQ.html

Farrell, M. (2012, February 28). Angelakis: No usage-based pricing for now. *Multichannel News*. Retrieved from http://www.multichannel.com/article/481109-Angelakis_No_Usage_Based_Pricing_For_Now.php.

Federal Communications Commission. (2008, June 12). Report and order and further notice of proposed rulemaking (WC Docket No. 07-38). Washington, DC: Federal Register.

Federal Communications Commission (2009, September 21). FCC chairman Julius Genachowski outlines actions to preserve the free and open internet [Press release]. Retrieved from http://hraunfoss.fcc.gov/edocs_public/attachmatch/DOC-293567A1.pdf.

Federal Communications Commission. (2010a). The national broadband plan. Retrieved from http://download.broadband.gov/plan/national-broadband-plan.pdf.

Federal Communications Commission (2010b, March 16). FCC Sends National Broadband Plan to Congress: Plan Details Actions for Connecting Consumers, Economy with 21st Century Networks. [Press release]. Retrieved from http://hraunfoss.fcc.gov/edocs_public/attachmatch/DOC-296880A1.pdf.

Federal Communications Commission (2010c, April 6). FCC Statement of Comcast v. FCC Decision. [Press release]. Retrieved from http://hraunfoss.fcc.gov/edocs_public/attachmatch/DOC-297355A1.pdf

Federal Communications Commission (2011a, November 18). FCC releases "connect America fund" order to help expand broadband, create jobs, benefit consumers. [Press Release]. Retrieved from http://www.fcc.gov/document/press-release-fcc-releases-connect-america-fund-order.

Federal Communications Commission (2011b, December 22). FCC chairman Genachowski announces approval of first television white space database and device. [Press Release]. Retrieved from http://www.fcc.gov/document/chairman-announces-approval-white-spaces-database-spectrum-bridge

Federal Communications Commission (2012). LightSquared request extention time to respond to PN (DA 12-230). Washington, DC: Government Printing Office.

Fehrenbacher, K. (2009, August 26). How high-speed broadband can fight climate change. *Benton Foundation*. Retrieved from http://www.benton.org/node/27386.

Flint, J. (2012, February 17). FCC can auction spectrum, but will broadcasters sell? LA Times. Retrieved from http://latimesblogs.latimes.com/entertainmentnewsbuzz/2012/02/broadcast-spectrum.html.

Gross, G. (2010, March 16). FCC officially releases national broadband plan. *PC World*. Retrieved from http://www.pcworld.com/businesscenter/article/191666/fcc_officially_releases_national_broadband_plan.html.

Haskin, D. (2007). FAQ: 802.11n wireless networking. *MacWorld*. Retrieved from http://www.macworld.com/article/57940/2007/05/80211nfaq.html.

Household download index (February 24, 2012) Retrieved from Net Index website: http://www.netindex.com/download/allcountries/

HughesNet, (2012a). Retrieved from http://www.hughesnet.com/residential-satellite-internet/plans.cfm.

HughesNet. (2012b). Retrieved from http://business.hughesnet.com/explore-our-services/business-internet/business-internet-high-speed/express-service-plans.

Infonetics Research (2011, April 7). Home network market up as new devices create "digital homes" and allow media sharing. [Press release]. Retrieved from http://www.infonetics.com/pr/2011/4Q10-Home-Networking-Devices-Market-Highlights.asp.

International Telecommunication Union (2012a). *Building our networked future based on broadband*. Retrieved from http://www.itu.int/en/broadband/Pages/overview.aspx.

International Telecommunication Union (2012b, January 18). IMT-Advanced standards announced for next-generation mobile technology. [Press Release]. Retrieved from http://www.itu.int/net/pressoffice/press_releases/2012/02.aspx

International Telecommunications Union. (2003). *Birth of broadband*. Retrieved from http://www.itu.int/osg/spu/publications/birthofbroadband/faq.html.

Kansas City is Fiber-Ready. (2012, February 6). Retrieved from http://googlefiberblog.blogspot.com/2012/02/weve-measured-utility-poles-weve.html

Lee, N. (2011, October 5). Bluetooth 4.0: What is it, and does it matter? Retrieved from http://reviews.cnet.com/8301-19512_7-20116316-233/bluetooth-4.0-what-is-it-and-does-it-matter/.

Li, H. (1998). Evolution of the residential-gateway concept and standards. *Parks Associates*. Retrieved from http://www.parksassociates.com/media/jhcable.htm.

Marshall, G. (2012, February 1). 802.11ac: what you need to know. Retrieved from http://www.techradar.com/news/networking/wi-fi/802-11ac-what-you-need-to-know-1059194.

Mitchell, B. (n.d.). Wireless standards- 802.11b 802.11a 802.11g and 802.11n: The 802.11 family explained. About.com. Retrieved from http://compnetworking.about.com/cs/wireless80211/a/aa80211standard.htm.

Needleman, R. (2012, February 17). Reporter's roundtable: LightSquared and the spectrum mess. *C/Net News*. Retrieved from http://www.cnet.com/8301-30976_1-57380506-10348864/reporters-roundtable-lightsquared-and-the-spectrum-mess/.

Ramachandran, S. (2012, February 29). Broadband pricing by usage: Time Warner offers consumption-based service, renewing a debat. *The Wall Street Journal*. Retrieved from http://online.wsj.com/article/SB10001424052970203833004577251761483000108.html

Smith, J. (2012, January 1). Ridiculous 4G LTE speeds hit Indianapolis for super bowl 46. *Gotta Be Mobile*. Retrieved from http://www.gottabemobile.com/2012/01/19/ridiculous-4g-lte-speeds-hit-indianapolis-for-super-bowl-46/.

Tae-gyu, K. (2010, February 7). Seamless home networking to debut in 2011. *Korea Times*. Retrieved from http://www.koreatimes.co.kr/www/news/biz/2010/02/123_60437.html.

Vaughan-Nichols, S.J. (2012, January 9). 802.11ac: Gigabit wi-fi devices will be shipping in 2012. ZDNet. Retrieved from http://www.zdnet.com/blog/networking/80211ac-gigabit-wi-fi-devices-will-be-shipping-in-2012/1867.

Verizon. (n.d.). *FiOS Internet*. Retrieved from http://www22.verizon.com/Residential/Bundles/Landing/fiosinternet_ultimate/fiosinternet_ultimate.htm

What is wimax (n.d.). Retrieved from http://www.wimax.com/general/what-is-wimax.

White House (2011, February 10). President Obama details plan to win the future through expanded wireless access. [Press Release]. Retrieved from http://www.whitehouse.gov/the-press-office/2011/02/10/president-obama-details-plan-win-future-through-expanded-wireless-access.

Wi-Fi Alliance. (n.d.). *Wi-Fi overview*. Retrieved from http://www.wi-fi.org/OpenSection/ why_Wi-Fi.asp?TID=2.

Wild Blue. (n.d.). *About Wild Blue*. Retrieved from http://www.wildblue.com/aboutwildblue/index.jsp.

WPA2. (n.d.). Retrieved from http://www.wi-fi.org/knowledge_center/wpa2/.

Wyatt, E. (2010, April 6). U.S. court of curbs F.C.C. authority on web traffic. *The New York Times*. Retrieved from http://www.nytimes.com/2010/04/07/technology/07net.html

XFINITY Internet from Comcast (n.d.). Retrieved from http://www.comcast.com/Corporate/Learn/highspeedinternet/highspeedinternet.html.

ZigBee. (n.d.). *ZigBee Alliance*. Retrieved from http://www.zigbee.org/About/AboutTechnology/ZigBeeTechnology.aspx.

Conclusions

24

Conclusions ...and the Future

August E. Grant, Ph.D.*

This book has introduced you to a range of ideas on how to study communication technologies, given you the history of communication technologies, and detailed the latest developments in about two dozen technologies. Along the way, the authors have told stories about successes and failures, legal battles and regulatory limitations, and changes in lifestyle for the end user.

In the process, we hope that you have a greater understanding of and appreciation for the technology ecosystem that supports all of the individual technologies discussed in this book. Understanding the interplay of technologies, organizations, social systems, and user factors will prepare you for a future in which technologies will become even more important to society, and perhaps, to your career.

So what can you do with this information? If you're entrepreneurial, you can use it to figure out how to get rich. If you're academically inclined, you can use it to inform research and analysis of the next generation of communication technology. If you're planning a career in the media industries, you can use it to help choose the organizations where you will work, or to find new opportunities for your employer or for yourself.

More importantly, whether you are in any of those groups or not, you are going to be surrounded by new media for the rest of your life. The cycle of innovation, introduction, and maturity of media almost always includes a cycle of decline as well. As new communication technologies are introduced and older ones disappear, your media use habits will change. What you've learned from this book should help you make decisions on when to adopt a new technology or drop an old one. Of course, those decisions depend upon your personal goals—which might be to be an innovator, to make the most efficient use of your personal resources (time and money), or to have the most relaxing life style.

This chapter explores a few of these issues, starting with comments regarding media that were not covered in this book, but which you should consider as part of the next generation of "new" communication technologies.

Other New Technologies

It is virtually impossible to discuss all of the technologies that may impact your life and career in a book such as this one. Some are so new that there is little written about them. Others have been in the "introduction" stage for so long that there is little "new" to discuss. And others we simply did not have the space to include. Here are a few to keep your eyes on:

* J. Rion McKissick Professor of Journalism, College of Mass Communications and Information Studies, University of South Carolina (Columbia, South Carolina).

✦ **The "cloud"** is a nebulous term that refers to computing power and storage that take place remotely from a computer or other device, somewhere on the Internet. Cloud computing promises to bring virtually unlimited computing power and storage capacity to any user by using capabilities of servers and other computers distributed across the Internet. Issues of privacy, security, and control of content remain, but any discussion of new technologies during the coming decade may have a cloud dimension. Cloud storage will impact every technology that requires storage of content in any form, from your personal text and music files to corporate data archives and video libraries. The most revolutionary aspect of cloud computing and storage may be the manner in which it will allow access and manipulation of content and data virtually anywhere, without dependence upon a specific access device.

✦ **Mobile Internet access** has a similar potential to revolutionize many aspects of our society, including commerce, education, law enforcement, and health care. This book has touched on a few of the emerging applications related to ubiquitous mobile Internet access, but these applications will likely pale in comparison with new applications that will apply the potential of anytime, anywhere connectivity. Among all of these applications, education may be affected the most, as students, teachers, workers, managers—virtually everyone— will have answers to almost any question available instantly from any location. One issue to watch is the degree to which consumers are willing to share information regarding where they are and what they doing. This information will be a boon to marketers, and it has an equal potential to revolutionize law enforcement and health care.

✦ **Health and medical applications** represent an enormous set of opportunities to apply the power of communication technologies. An aging population, new technologies for medical treatment and prevention, and increased coverage of previously uninsured people will lead to increased spending on health care over the next 20 years, and communication technologies have great potential to revolutionize health care delivery and preventive care.

✦ **Virtual reality** was promised as a cutting-edge entertainment technology, but has emerged as a key technology in a number of industries including architecture and education. In some ways, it is the antithesis of the Internet, conceived for entertainment but finding its role as a key technology in industry.

✦ **Facial and voice recognition technology** will usher in a new set of user interfaces that are more intuitive and personalized than traditional interfaces. Within a few short years, devices from telephones and microwave ovens to store kiosks and marketing systems will utilize facial and voice recognition, resulting in interfaces that more closely resemble a science fiction writer's dreams than today's keyboards and pushbuttons.

✦ **Near-field communication (NFC)** is an emerging standard for wireless communication that enables transmission of information over very short distances. As discussed in Chapter 14, NFC is an enabling technology for many forms of mobile commerce, including electronic wallets. But the applications of this powerful medium should allow developers the opportunity to create a new generation of portable devices capable of revolutionizing almost every area of communication.

These are just a few of the technologies that are just over the horizon as this book is being finalized in May 2012. By the time you read this, you will certainly know of others to add to the list. The key for you is to be able to apply the communication technology ecosystem, the lessons from the history of other technologies, and the theories discussed in

Chapter 3 to help you analyze those technologies and predict their place in your future.

Making Money from New Technologies

You have the potential to get rich from the next generation of technologies. Just conduct an analysis of a few emerging technologies using the tools in the "Fundamentals" section of the book; choose the one that has the best potential to meet an unmet demand (one that people will pay for); then create a business plan that demonstrates how your revenues will exceed your expenses from creating, producing, or distributing the technology. Sounds easy, right?

Conceptually, the process is deceptively easy. The difficult part is putting in the hours needed to plan for every contingency, solve problems as they crop up (or before they do), make the contacts you need in order to bring in all of the pieces to make your plan work, and then distribute the product or service to the end users. If the lessons in this book are any indication, two factors will be more important than all the others: the interpersonal relationships that lead to organizational connections—and a lot of luck!

Here are a few guidelines distilled from 20-plus years of working, studying, and consulting in the communication technology industries that might help you become an entrepreneur:

✦ **Ideas are not as important as execution.** If you have a good idea, chances are others will have the same idea. The ones who succeed are the ones who have the tools and vision to put the ideas into action.

✦ **Protect your ideas.** The time and effort needed to get a patent, copyright, or even a simple non-disclosure agreement will pay off handsomely if your ideas succeed.

✦ **There is no substitute for hard work.** Entrepreneurs don't work 40-hour weeks, and they always have a tool nearby to record ideas or keep track of contacts.

✦ **There is no substitute for time away from work.** Taking one day a week away from the job gives you perspective, letting you step back and see the big picture. Plus, some of the best ideas come from bringing in completely unrelated content, so make sure you are always scanning the world around you for developments in the arts, technology, business, regulation, and culture.

✦ **Who you know is more important than what you know.** You can't succeed as a solo act in the communication technology field. You have to a) find and partner with or hire people who are better than you in the skill sets you don't have, and b) make contacts with people in organizations that can help your business succeed.

✦ **Keep learning.** Study your field, but also study the world. The technologies that you will be working with have the potential to provide you access to more information than any entrepreneur in the past has had. Use the tools to continue growing.

✦ **Create a set of realistic goals.** Don't limit yourself to just one goal, but don't have too many. As you achieve your goals, take time to celebrate your success.

✦ **Give back.** You can't be a success without relying upon the efforts of those who came before you and those who helped you out along the way. The best way to pay it back is to pay it forward.

This list was created to help entrepreneurs, but they may be equally relevant to any type of career. Just as the communication technologies explored in this book have applications that permeate industries and institutions throughout society, the tools and techniques explored in this book can be equally useful regardless of where you are or where you are going.

Index

To continue your search for insight into the technologies explored
in this book, *Communication Technology Update and Fundamentals*,
please visit the companion website:

www.tfi.com/ctu